P9-DUJ-757

R

# America's Top Jobs™ for People Without College Degrees

## America's Top Jobs™ for People Without College Degrees

**Third Edition**

## J. Michael Farr

This newly revised ed

- 111 completely r
- Updated labor m
- Expanded section                                        dvice
- All new appendi                                        and industries
- An easy-to-use f

**America's Top Jobs™ for People Without College Degrees**
Good Jobs in Technical, Trade, Manufacturing, & Transportation Industries
**© 1997 by JIST Works, Inc.**

ude:

*ition*
*ok*
*tion Book*

---

**Other books in the *America's Top™ Jobs* series include:**

- *America's Top Jobs™ for College Graduates*
- *America's Top Medical, Education, & Human Services Jobs*
- *America's Top Office, Management, Sales, & Professional Jobs*
- *America's Top 300 Jobs* (Based on the Occupational Outlook Handbook)

- *America's Federal Jobs*
- *America's Military Careers*
- *America's Fastest Growing Jobs*
- *Career Guide to America's Top Industries*

These and other books from JIST can be ordered from your bookstore or distributor.

---

Published by JIST Works, Inc.
720 N. Park Avenue
Indianapolis, IN 46202-3431
Phone: 317-264-3720 Fax: 317-264-3709 E-mail: JISTWorks@AOL.com

Cover Design by Brad Luther

Printed in the United States of America

99  98  97  96        5  4  3  2  1

Library of Congress Cataloging-in-Publication Data
    Farr, J. Michael.
        America's top jobs for people without college degrees / J. Michael
    Farr.—3rd ed.
        p.    cm
        Rev. ed. of: America}s top technical and trade jobs. 2nd ed
    ©1994.
        ISBN 1-56370-282-7
        1.  Labor market—United States.   2.  Employment forecasting—United
    States.   3.  Occupations—United States.   4.  Vocational guidance—
    United States.   5.  Job hunting—United States.   I.  Farr, J.
    Michael.    America}s top technical and trade jobs.   II.  Title.
        HD5724.F27   1997
        331.7'02'0973—dc20                                           96-33111
                                                                       CIP

We have been careful to provide accurate information throughout this book, but it is possible that errors and omissions have been introduced. Please consider this in making any career plans or other important decisions. Trust your own judgment above all else and in all things.

ISBN 1-56370-282-7

# Preface

---

## Relax, you don't need to read this whole book.

While this is a big book, you really don't need to read it all. I've organized it into easy-to-use sections and you can use any number of them as you want.

The first section provides 111 thorough job descriptions. These descriptions cover all major jobs in the technical, trade, manufacturing, and transportation areas that do not require a four-year college degree. You can quickly identify jobs that interest you, then turn to those job descriptions. Other sections provide advice on career planning and job seeking, important labor market trends to consider, and a variety of other interesting information. Appendices provide information on all major jobs and industries as well as other information you may find useful.

Read and use just those sections that interest you. There is a lot of information in this revision, but I've tried to make it easier than ever to get to and use.

---

## Tips on Using This Book

On the average, those with more education or training earn more. But, as I point out several times in this book, averages and data can be misleading. I say this because how well you do in the labor market—or in life, for that matter—has little to do with averages. Good career planning is not about selecting a job that pays more or that is projected to have high rates of growth. Those may be issues for you, but good career planning has far more to do with finding work that you enjoy and are good at.

I hope this book helps. It provides lots of good information that can help you make better decisions about your career and additional education. The rest, of course, is up to you.

## Major Sections

I've made a number of changes in this edition besides the new and revised information throughout. You really don't need to "read" this book in a conventional, front-to-back sense. That should come as a great relief to you, since there is a lot of information contained in these pages. I've arranged it so you can quickly get to the information you need by organizing it into three easily accessible sections plus several useful appendices.

- **Section One: The Job Descriptions:** This section gives thorough descriptions of 111 jobs—many more than in the previous edition. These descriptions are easy to understand and packed with useful information, including working conditions, skills required, education or training needed, typical pay and benefits, and other details.

- **Section Two: An Introduction to Important Labor Market Trends:** Section Two presents updated information on trends in the labor market that you should consider in your career plans. For example, it reviews the earnings in different industries and at different levels of education and training.

- **Section Three: Career Planning and Job Search Advice:** This section contains a chart giving details on 250 jobs plus information and activities helpful for planning your career and for getting a good job in less time.

- **Section Four:** This section contains a number of excellent articles that provide insights to technical and trade occupations. All were researched and written by staff of the U.S. Department of Labor and are quite relevant to the present labor market.

- **Appendices:** The appendices provide additional information that will be useful in your career planning, including details on the 500 largest jobs in the United States.

## Who Can Use This Book

This is more than just a book of job descriptions. It has been compiled to be of great use for people in a variety of situations, including:

- **Those exploring career options:** The job descriptions in this book give a wealth of information on many of the most desirable jobs in the labor market.

- **Students and those considering more education or training:** The information in this book can help you avoid costly mistakes in choosing a career or in obtaining additional training or education—and increase your chances of planning a bright future.

- **Job seekers:** The information in this book will help you identify new job targets, prepare for interviews, and write targeted resumes. And the section providing job search advice has been proven to cut your job search time in half!

- **Counselors:** This is a valuable source of information on jobs and trends.

# Table of Contents

# Introduction

## How You Can Best Use This Book

Today's labor market is more competitive than ever and earning good pay is not as easy as it once was. More training is typically required to get better jobs now—and good career planning and job seeking skills are essential for long-term career success.

This book has been written to help. Most of the jobs it describes do not require a four-year college degree but do offer opportunities for growth and satisfaction. On the average, those with a four-year college degree do have higher earnings than those without. But individual earnings vary widely, and some workers without college degrees earn more than those who have degrees. Two out of five workers without a college degree earned more than the median for all workers, and one in six earned as much or more than the average for those with four-year college degrees!

It is clear that jobs that require training pay off. For example, high school graduates working in jobs that require at least some training make an average of $7,500 more a year than those working in jobs requiring no training. Additional details on earning at various levels of training are provided in Section Four.

I do not assume you will read this book cover to cover. Instead, you will most likely browse through it to find those sections that most interest you. I encourage you to do this, and have made changes in this revision that will make this easier. Here are some suggestions to help you browse effectively:

## Section One: The Job Descriptions

This is the main part of the book and the section most likely to interest you. In this edition, I have placed the descriptions up front, where they can be found quickly.

I considered several ways of organizing the jobs but settled on presenting them alphabetically. The list of job titles is included in the Table of Contents and at the beginning of the section.

If you are interested in medical jobs, for example, you can go through the list and quickly identify those you want to learn more about. You may also see other jobs that look interesting, and you should consider these as well. Page numbers are provided for locating each description.

### Information Included in the Descriptions

Each job description presents similar information and uses a standard format. Most require only one to two pages, and each is packed with information, including:

### Job Title

- Each description is headed by a job title in bold letters. This is the general title used most frequently to describe the job.

### Nature of the Work

- What workers do on the job, the equipment they use, and how closely they are supervised.
- How the duties of workers vary by industry, establishment, and size of firm.
- How the responsibilities of entry-level workers differ from those of experienced, supervisory, or self-employed workers.
- How technological innovations are changing what workers do and how they do it.
- Emerging specialties.

### Working Conditions

- Typical hours worked.
- The workplace environment.
- Susceptibility to injury, illness, and job-related stress.
- Necessary protective clothing and safety equipment.
- Physical activities required.
- Extent of travel required.

### Employment

- The number of jobs the occupation provides.
- Key industries employing workers in the occupation.
- Geographic distribution of jobs.
- The proportion of part-time (fewer than 35 hours a week) and self-employed workers in the occupation.

## Training, Other Qualifications, and Advancement

- Most significant sources of training, typical length of training, and training preferred by employers.
- Whether workers acquire skills through previous work experience, informal on-the-job training, formal training (including apprenticeships) offered by employers or unions, the Armed Forces, home study, or hobbies and other activities.
- Formal education requirements: high school, postsecondary vocational or technical training, college, or graduate or professional education.
- Desirable skills, aptitudes, and personal characteristics.
- Certification, examination, or licensing required for entry into the field, advancement, or independent practice.
- Continuing education or skill improvement requirements.
- Paths of advancement.

## Job Outlook

- Forces that will result in growth or decline in the number of jobs.
- Relative number of job openings the occupation provides. Occupations that are large and have high turnover rates generally provide the most job openings, reflecting the need to replace workers who transfer to other occupations or stop working.
- Degree of competition for jobs. Is there a surplus or a shortage of job seekers compared to the number of job openings available? Do opportunities vary by industry, size of firm, or geographic location? Job openings exist even in overcrowded fields, and good students or well-qualified individuals should not be deterred from undertaking training or seeking entry.

- Susceptibility to layoffs due to imports, slowdowns in economic activity, technological advancements, or budget cuts.

## Earnings

- Typical earnings of workers in the occupation.
- How earnings vary with experience, location, and tenure.
- Whether workers are compensated through annual salaries, hourly wages, commissions, piece rates, tips, or bonuses.
- Earnings of wage and salary workers compared to self-employed persons.
- Benefits, including health insurance, pensions, paid vacation and sick leave, and other benefits.

## Related Occupations

- Occupations that use similar aptitudes, interests, education, and training.

## Related D.O.T. Jobs

- The descriptions in this book are for major jobs that can be cross-referenced to more specialized jobs. The U.S. Department of Labor has done this work, and I have included these jobs and their titles. You can obtain brief descriptions for the jobs in the *Dictionary of Occupational Titles* as well as in the many other career information systems that are based on the *D.O.T.* coding system. Most large libraries will have a copy of the *D.O.T.* in the reference section.

## Sources of Additional Information

- Associations, government agencies, unions, and other organizations providing useful information.
- Free or inexpensive publications offering more information, some of which are available in libraries, school career centers, or guidance offices.

---

## *Key Phrases Used in the Descriptions*

Key phrases are used in each description to describe projected changes in employment or the relationship between the number of job openings and the number of job seekers. These phrases are described below.

*Changing employment through the year 2005*

| If the statement reads: | Employment is projected to: |
| --- | --- |
| Grow much faster than average | increase 36 percent or more |
| Grow faster than average | increase 21 to 35 percent |
| Grow about as fast as average | increase 10 to 20 percent |
| Grow more slowly than average, or little or no change | increase 0 to 9 percent |
| Decline | decrease 1 percent or more |

*Opportunities and Competition for Jobs*

| If the statement reads: | Job openings compared to jobseekers may be: |
| --- | --- |
| Excellent opportunities | Much more numerous |
| Very good opportunities | More numerous |
| Good or favorable opportunities | About the same |
| May face competition | Fewer |
| May face keen competition | Much fewer |

### *Consider Your Local and Personal Situation*

When reading the descriptions, keep in mind that the information they present is the average for the country. Conditions in your area may be quite different than the average. For example, average pay may be higher or lower, and the same job could be in great demand in one area but hard to obtain in another. People just entering a job will also typically earn considerably less than the average pay for more experienced workers.

## Section Two: Important Labor Market Trends Likely to Affect Your Future

Previous editions of this book began with information on labor market trends within major occupational groups and industries. I still believe this information is important for you to review, and I encourage you to read this section. It points out, for example, the importance of education and training in today's labor market and will give you other important information to consider in making long-term career plans.

## Section Three: Career Planning and Job Search Advice

For the past 20 years, I have been interested in helping people find better jobs in less time. If you have ever experienced unemployment, you know it is not a pleasant experience.

I know that most people who read this book do so because they want to improve themselves or need to get a job. That is why I have included this section. It is short, but it includes the basics that are most important in planning your career and in reducing the time it takes to get a job.

I know you will resist completing the activities in this section, but consider this: It is often not the best person who gets the job, it is the best job seeker. Those who do their homework often get jobs over those with better credentials. Those who have spent time planning their careers and who know how to conduct an effective job search have several distinct advantages over those who do not:

1. **They get more interviews,** including many that will never be advertised.

2. **They do better in interviews.** They present their skills more convincingly and are much better at answering problem questions. This can mean the difference between getting a job offer or sitting at home.

## Section Four: Articles of Interest

Because of my interest in helping people find better jobs, I try to stay current and informed about any trend that will ultimately affect the labor market. I have amassed quite a collection of reference materials including professional and trade journals not readily available to the average job seeker. I've selected the best articles from my collection to provide you with some insights regarding the future of occupations in the technical and trade industries. All the articles were researched and written by staff of the U.S. Department of Labor and published in various D.O.L. publications. The articles vary from what is considered a technical job to wage information for workers without college degrees to manufacturing in the industrial age. Though the material does not make for particularly exciting reading, it is current and relevant to today's current labor market.

## The Appendices

While the appendices do not make for exciting reading, they provide some useful information. For example, Appendix A allows you to explore a wide variety of jobs arranged by education or training levels. This is very helpful for exploring opportunities that become available as you obtain increasing levels of training or education. Appendix B reviews trends within major industries. I included this information because you can often use skills or training you already have in a variety of industries you may not have considered.

Appendix C provides growth projections on 500 jobs. It is not a fun read, I admit, but I included it to let you browse a list of jobs that cover about 90 percent of the labor force. This is a much bigger list of job titles than I could cover in this book, and reviewing it can help you identify possibilities you might not otherwise consider. Information on these jobs is available from various sources listed at the end of Section Two.

Keep in mind that this is simply a beginning in your search for information. What matters most is that you include elements of meaning and fun into your career and life plans. Otherwise, why bother?

## The Sources of Information Used in This Book

The best source of data on labor market trends is the U.S. Department of Labor. Their information is as reliable as it gets. The information on career planning and job search is mine, although it has been influenced by many people over the years.

One thing to note is that data in this book come from information collected and reported at different times. I have included some very recent data (for example, the job descriptions are based on a 1996 information source) while others may be based on information from 1992 that was published in 1994. In all cases, I have tried to find the most recent information available and have included previously published data because of its value.

## The Fastest Growing and Best Paying Jobs, Plus Other Interesting Details

I've collected a variety of interesting tidbits in this section from several governmental sources. Some of them are presented in greater detail in other sections of this book, but I present them here to give you an overview of things to think about.

## More Education = Higher Earnings

The newest data on lifetime earnings from the Bureau of the Census tell an old story: The more education you have, the more money you earn. In fact, the value of education has clearly increased during the past 20 years. The new estimate of annual earnings for those who are high school graduates is 2.5 times higher than the 1975 one ($7536 per year), which means earnings for this group rose about as fast as inflation. But the estimate for holders of bachelor's degrees is nearly three times higher than the 1975 average of $11,574.

| Earnings for people age 18 and over, by highest level of education, 1992 | | |
|---|---|---|
| **Education level** | **Mean annual earnings** | **Estimated earnings over work life (age 25-64)** |
| Professional degree | 74,560 | 3,013,000 |
| Doctorate degree | 54,904 | 2,142,000 |
| Master's degree | 40,368 | 1,619,000 |
| Bachelor's degree | 32,629 | 1,421,000 |
| Associate degree | 24,398 | 1,062,000 |
| Some college, no degree | 19,666 | 993,000 |
| High school only | 18,737 | 821,000 |
| Not a high school graduate | 12,809 | 609,000 |

## Earnings of Workers Without College Degrees

The average earnings for all workers, at all levels of education, is about $25,000 a year. The table that follows shows how much workers at various education levels earned compared with the average for all workers and the average for those with four-year college degrees. As you can see, many people without four-year degrees have relatively high earnings.

| **Education level** | **All workers** | **College grads** |
|---|---|---|
| Less than high school | 19.4% | 6.8% |
| High school | 37 | 14.5 |
| Some college, no degree | 48.4 | 23.1 |
| Associate degree | 55.6 | 27.8 |

| Occupational group | Percentage growth | Educational attainment | | | Median weekly earnings |
|---|---|---|---|---|---|
| | | **High school** | **1 to 3 years of college** | **4+ years of college** | |
| Executives, administrators and managers | 26 | 25 | 27 | 48 | 652 |
| Professional specialty | 37 | 9 | 19 | 72 | 596 |
| Technicians and related support | 32 | 26 | 45 | 29 | 489 |
| Marketing and sales | 21 | 46 | 32 | 22 | 346 |
| Administrative support and clerical | 13 | 50 | 37 | 13 | 341 |
| Service workers | 33 | 68 | 26 | 6 | 232 |
| Agriculture, forestry, fishing and related | 4 | 75 | 17 | 8 | 258 |
| Precision production, craft, and repair | 13 | 68 | 26 | 6 | 470 |
| Operators, fabricators, and laborers | 10 | 80 | 17 | 3 | 331 |
| **Averages** | **22** | **50** | **27** | **23** | **406** |

## Education and Earnings Within Occupational Groups

Obviously, some jobs pay better than others. The table above presents the percentage of people working in major occupational groups at various levels of education and their average earnings.

## High-Wage Jobs That Do Not Require a Degree

The table at right shows occupations paying an average of $36,000 a year and employing significant numbers of people without college degrees. New entrants into some of the listed jobs are required to have college degrees, but many employed in the field were hired before these requirements were standard.

| Number employed | Percentage not having a degree | (in thousands) |
|---|---|---|
| Accountants and auditors | 313 | 28 |
| Administrators and officials, public administration | 215 | 42 |
| Assemblers | 845 | 96 |
| Automobile mechanics | 480 | 96 |
| Bus, truck, and stationary engine mechanics | 274 | 98 |
| Carpenters | 606 | 93 |
| Computer operators | 367 | 82 |
| Computer programmers | 197 | 40 |
| Computer system analysts and scientists | 190 | 31 |
| Correctional institution officers | 261 | 91 |
| Designers | 154 | 53 |

| Number employed | Percentage not having a degree | (in thousands) |
|---|---|---|
| Electrical and electronic engineers | 121 | 26 |
| Electrical and electronic equipment repairers, except telephone | 271 | 87 |
| Electrical and electronic technicians | 212 | 83 |
| Electrical power installers and repairers | 101 | 96 |
| Electricians | 475 | 95 |
| Financial managers | 203 | 42 |
| Fire-fighting occupations | 155 | 90 |
| Health technologists and technicians | 808 | 79 |
| Industrial, mechanical, and all other engineers | 274 | 27 |
| Industrial machinery repairers | 487 | 96 |
| Insurance sales occupations | 200 | 55 |
| Investigators and adjusters, insurance and other | 673 | 75 |
| Machine operators and tenders, except precision | 3,667 | 96 |
| Machinists and precision metalworking occupations | 669 | 96 |
| Mail carriers and postal clerks | 513 | 89 |
| Managers, marketing, advertising, and public relations | 181 | 41 |
| Managers, properties and real estate | 201 | 65 |
| Managers, food service and lodging establishments | 469 | 78 |
| Managers and administrators not elsewhere classified | 2,065 | 57 |
| Other financial officers | 249 | 43 |
| Personnel, training, and labor relations specialists | 164 | 47 |
| Plumbers, pipefitters, and steamfitters | 287 | 96 |
| Police and detectives | 353 | 75 |
| Purchasing agents and buyers | 260 | 66 |
| Rail transportation occupations | 95 | 94 |
| Real estate sales occupations | 168 | 54 |
| Registered nurses | 656 | 51 |
| Sales occupations, other business services | 190 | 53 |
| Sales representatives, mining and manufacturing and wholesale | 635 | 56 |
| Science and engineering technicians | 287 | 75 |
| Secretaries | 2,326 | 90 |
| Stationary engineers and other plant and system operators | 230 | 91 |
| Supervisors, police and fire fighting | 92 | 71 |
| Supervisors, mechanics and repairers | 181 | 89 |
| Supervisors, construction occupations | 419 | 88 |
| Supervisors, production occupations | 1,010 | 87 |
| Supervisors, administrative support occupations | 519 | 73 |
| Supervisors and proprietors, sales occupations | 1,658 | 72 |
| Telephone and telephone line installers and repairers | 211 | 95 |
| Truck drivers | 2,000 | 96 |
| Welders and cutters | 438 | 98 |
| All other occupations | 26,021 | 70 |

# Fastest Growing Jobs Requiring a College Degree

Here is a list of the fastest growing jobs typically requiring a four-year college degree. These are all based on projections through the year 2005.

| Occupation | Percentage growth |
|---|---|
| Computer engineers and scientists | 112 |
| Systems analysts | 110 |
| Physical therapists | 88 |
| Teachers, special education | 74 |
| Operations research analysts | 61 |
| Occupational therapists | 60 |
| Teachers, preschool and kindergarten | 54 |
| Speech-language pathologists and audiologists | 48 |
| Psychologists | 48 |
| Construction managers | 47 |
| Management analysts | 43 |
| Recreational therapists | 40 |
| Social workers | 40 |
| Recreation workers | 38 |
| Podiatrists | 37 |
| Teachers, secondary schools | 37 |
| Teachers and instructors, vocational education and training | 36 |
| Instructors and coaches, sports and physical training | 36 |
| Personnel training and labor relations specialists | 36 |
| Marketing, advertising, and public relations managers | 36 |

# Fastest Growing Jobs Requiring Some Postsecondary Training

Here is a list of jobs that don't require a four-year college degree but do require formal training or education after high school or substantial on-the-job training. The projected increases are from 1992 through 2005. Some of these jobs can pay pretty well, so it's not entirely true that you have to have a four-year college degree to do well.

| Occupation | Percentage growth |
|---|---|
| Physical and corrective therapy assistants and aides | 93 |
| Paralegals | 86 |
| Occupation therapy assistants and aides | 78 |
| Medical assistants | 71 |
| Radiologic technologists and technicians | 63 |
| Medical records technicians | 61 |
| Legal secretaries | 57 |
| EEG technologists | 54 |
| Producers, directors, actors, and entertainers | 54 |
| Nuclear medicine technologists | 50 |

| Occupation | Percentage growth |
|---|---|
| Insurance adjusters, examiners, and investigators | 49 |
| Respiratory therapists | 48 |
| Cooks, restaurant | 46 |
| Data processing equipment repairers | 45 |
| Medical Secretaries | 45 |
| Food service and lodging managers | 44 |
| Dental hygienist | 43 |
| Surgical technologists | 42 |
| Pharmacy assistants | 42 |
| Licensed practical nurses | 40 |

## Fastest Growing Jobs Requiring High School Education or Less

Here is a list of the fastest growing jobs that don't require education beyond the high school level. As you can see, some have very high growth rates projected through 2005. A few of these jobs pay pretty well, although those, like detectives, often require substantial on-the-job experience. You should also realize (should you be pondering this list for good jobs you can get without going to school) that high school grads will often have to compete with those who have more education. For example, many detectives have college degrees, and those who do will often be given preference in hiring or promotion. I'm not saying you can't get ahead without an education, just that it is mighty competitive for some jobs if you don't have the best of credentials.

| Occupation | Percentage growth |
|---|---|
| Home health aides | 138 |
| Human service workers | 136 |
| Personal and home health care aides | 130 |
| Electronic pagination systems workers | 78 |
| Detectives, except public | 70 |
| Corrections officers | 70 |
| Child-care workers | 66 |
| Travel agents | 66 |
| Nursery workers | 62 |
| Subway and streetcar operators | 57 |
| Manicurists | 54 |
| Flight attendants | 51 |
| Guards | 51 |
| Paving, surfacing, and tamping equipment operators | 48 |
| Bakers, bread and pastry | 47 |
| Laundry and dry-cleaning machine operators and tenders except pressing | 46 |
| Amusement and recreation attendants | 46 |
| Baggage porters and bellhops | 46 |
| Nursing aides, orderlies, and attendants | 45 |
| Bicycle repairers | 45 |

## Manufacturing Remains an Important Source of Employment

Manufacturing accounts for 30 percent of the nation's total output of goods and services, only slightly less than its share three decades ago. One of every seven people in our workforce is employed in a manufacturing industry, and some industries are thriving. Even so, manufacturing employment lost 3 million workers between 1979 and 1992, and another 40,000 jobs are projected to be lost by 2005. While many jobs will remain in manufacturing, new openings tend to require more education and technical training than in the past.

### Manufacturing Industries with the Fastest Percentage Growth Rates

Here is a list of manufacturing industries that are projected to grow the fastest, in terms of the projected annual increases in the people they employ.

| Industry | Annual percentage change |
|---|---|
| Aircraft and missile parts and equipment | 3.2 |
| Miscellaneous publishing | 3 |
| Railroad equipment | 2.5 |
| Medical equipment and supplies | 2.4 |
| Truck and bus bodies, trailers, and motor homes | 2.4 |
| Miscellaneous plastic products | 2.4 |
| Millwork and structural wood members | 2.2 |
| Boat building and repairing | 2 |
| Books | 1.7 |
| Metal services | 1.7 |
| Miscellaneous chemical products | 1.5 |
| X-ray and other electromedical apparatus | 1.5 |
| Industrial machinery | 1.5 |
| Partitions and fixtures | 1.4 |
| Periodicals | 1.3 |

**Source:** BLS Occupational Outlook Quarterly, Vol. 38, #3

### Manufacturing Industries Projected to Generate the Most Job Growth

This list shows you the industries that are creating the most jobs in numerical terms.

| Industry | Thousands of jobs |
|---|---|
| Miscellaneous plastic products | 224 |
| Aircraft and missile parts and equipment | 85 |
| Medical instruments and supplies | 79 |
| Commercial printing and business forms | 78 |
| Metal products | 62 |
| Newspapers | 61 |
| Industrial machinery | 61 |

| Industry | Thousands of jobs |
|---|---|
| Millwork and structural wood members | 60 |
| Drugs | 41 |
| Miscellaneous publishing | 37 |
| Converted paper products, except containers | 37 |
| Metalworking machinery | 29 |
| Truck and bus bodies, trailers, and motor homes | 28 |
| Books | 28 |
| Metal services | 27 |

## Fastest Growing Jobs In Manufacturing

Here are the fastest growing manufacturing jobs, arranged in projected percentage of growth through 2005.

| Occupation | Percentage employment growth |
|---|---|
| All other printing workers, precision | 92.3 |
| Electronic pagination system workers | 77.9 |
| Systems analysts | 65.1 |
| All other printing press setters and set-up operators | 51.1 |
| Medical scientists | 47.5 |
| Computer engineers and scientists | 41.8 |
| Offset lithographic press operators | 40.3 |
| Cabinetmakers and bench carpenters | 37 |
| Screen printing machine setters and set-up operators | 36.7 |
| Advertising clerks | 34.3 |
| Meat, poultry, and fish cutters and trimmers | 32.9 |
| Biological scientists | 31 |
| All other printing, binding, and related workers | 30.3 |
| Wood machinists | 29.4 |
| All other professional workers | 29.2 |
| Operations research analysts | 28.4 |
| Reporters and correspondents | 26.9 |
| All other precision woodworkers | 26.7 |
| Paper goods machine setters and set-up operators | 26.3 |
| Personnel, training, and labor relations specialists | 26.3 |

# The Job Descriptions

## Introduction

This is the main part of the book and the section most likely to interest you. I considered several ways of organizing the jobs included but settled on presenting them alphabetically.

The introduction to the book provides additional information on what each description contains. If you are not the kind of person to read introductions, rest assured that the descriptions are easy to understand and well-written—so feel free to jump right in and begin reading those that interest you.

A good way to identify descriptions you want to explore is to use the Table of Contents as a checklist. Simply go through the list and quickly identify those jobs you want to learn more about.

Of course, there is more to selecting and learning about career options than reading job descriptions. For this reason, I suggest that you read Section Two, which provides advice on planning your career and on getting a good job. Other sections provide lots of useful information for helping you consider your options so you can make good decisions.

## Air Traffic Controllers

### Nature of the Work

The air traffic control system is a vast network of people and equipment that ensures the safe operation of commercial and private aircraft. Air traffic controllers coordinate the movement of air traffic to make certain that planes stay a safe distance apart. Their immediate concern is safety, but controllers also must direct planes efficiently to minimize delays. Some regulate airport traffic; others regulate flights between airports.

Although *airport tower or terminal controllers* watch over all planes traveling through the airport's airspace, their main responsibility is to organize the flow of aircraft in and out of the airport. Relying on radar and visual observation, they closely monitor each plane to ensure a safe distance between all aircraft and to guide pilots between the hangar or ramp and the end of the airport's airspace. In addition, controllers keep pilots informed about changes in weather conditions such as wind shear—a sudden change in the velocity or direction of the wind that can cause the pilot to lose control of the aircraft.

During arrival or departure, several controllers handle each plane. As a plane approaches an airport, the pilot radios ahead to inform the terminal of its presence. The controller in the radar room just beneath the control tower has a copy of the plane's flight plan and already has observed the plane on radar. If the way is clear, the controller directs the pilot to a runway; if the airport is busy, the plane is fitted into a traffic pattern with other aircraft waiting to land. As the plane nears the runway, the pilot is asked to contact the tower. There, another controller, who also is watching the plane on radar, monitors the aircraft the last mile or so to the runway, delaying any departures that would interfere with the plane's landing. Once the plane has landed, a ground controller in the tower directs it along the taxiways to its assigned gate. The ground controller usually works entirely by sight, but may use radar if visibility is very poor.

The procedure is reversed for departures. The ground controller directs the plane to the proper runway. The local controller then informs the pilot about conditions at the airport, such as the weather, speed and direction of wind, and visibility. The local controller also issues runway clearance for the pilot to take off. Once in the air, the plane is guided out of the airport's airspace by the departure controller.

After each plane departs, airport tower controllers notify *enroute controllers* who will next take charge. There are 22 enroute control centers located around the country, each employing 300 to 700 controllers, with more than 150 on duty during peak hours at the busier facilities. Airplanes generally fly along designated routes; each center is assigned a certain airspace containing many different routes. Enroute controllers work in teams of up to three members, depending on how heavy traffic is; each team is responsible for a section of the center's airspace. A team, for example, might be responsible for all planes that are between 30 to 100 miles north of an airport and flying at an altitude between 6,000 and 18,000 feet.

To prepare for planes about to enter the team's airspace, the radar associate controller organizes flight plans coming off a printer. If two planes are scheduled to enter the team's airspace at nearly the same time, location, and altitude, this controller may arrange with the preceding control unit for one plane to change its flight path. The previous unit may have been another team at the same or an adjacent center, or a departure controller at a neighboring terminal. As a plane approaches a team's airspace, the radar controller accepts responsibility for the plane from the previous controlling unit. The controller also delegates responsibility for the plane to the next controlling unit when the plane leaves the team's airspace.

The radar controller, who is the senior team member, observes the planes in the team's airspace on radar and communicates with the pilots when necessary. Radar controllers warn pilots about nearby planes, bad weather conditions, and other potential hazards. Two planes on a collision course will be directed around each other. If a pilot wants to change altitude in search of better flying conditions, the controller will check to determine that no other planes will be along the proposed path. As the flight progresses, the team responsible for the aircraft notifies the next team in charge. Through team coordination, the plane arrives safely at its destination.

Both airport tower and enroute controllers usually control several planes at a time and often have to make quick decisions about completely different activities. For example, a controller might direct a plane on its landing approach and at the same time provide pilots entering the airport's airspace with information about conditions at the airport. While instructing these pilots, the controller also would observe other planes in the vicinity, such as those in a holding pattern waiting for permission to land, to ensure that they remain well separated. Currently, the Federal Aviation Administration (FAA) is in the midst of developing and implementing a new automated air traffic control system. As a result, more powerful computers will help controllers deal with the demands of increased air traffic. Some traditional air traffic controller tasks—like determining how far apart planes should be kept—will be done by computer. Improved communication between computers on airplanes and those on the ground also is making the controller's job a little easier.

At present controllers sit at consoles with green-glowing screens that display radar images generated by a computer. In the future, controllers will work at a modern workstation computer that depicts air routes in full-color on a 20-by-20-inch screen. The controllers will select radio channels simply by touching on-screen buttons instead of turning dials or switching switches.

In addition to airport towers and enroute centers, air traffic controllers also work in flight service stations operated at more than 100 locations. These *flight service specialists* provide pilots with information on the station's particular area, including terrain, preflight and inflight weather information, suggested routes, and other information important to the safety of a flight. Flight service station specialists help pilots in emergency situations and participate in searches for missing or overdue aircraft. However, they are not involved in actively managing air traffic.

## Working Conditions

Controllers work a basic 40-hour week; however, they may work additional hours for which they receive overtime pay or equal time off. Because most control towers and centers operate 24 hours a day, seven days a week, controllers rotate night and weekend shifts.

During busy times, controllers must work rapidly and efficiently. This requires total concentration to keep track of several planes at the same time and make certain all pilots receive correct instructions. The mental stress of being responsible for the safety of several aircraft and their passengers can be exhausting for some persons.

## Employment

Air traffic controllers held about 23,000 jobs in 1994. They were employed by the federal government at airports—in towers and flight service stations—and in enroute traffic control centers. The overwhelming majority worked for the FAA. About 17,500 controllers were actively working controlling air traffic; 3,600 worked at flight service stations and another 750 worked in administrative staff positions. Some professional controllers conduct research at the FAA's national experimental center in Atlantic City, New Jersey. Others serve as instructors at the FAA Academy in Oklahoma City, Oklahoma. A small number of civilian controllers worked for the Department of Defense. In addition to controllers employed by the federal government, some worked for private air traffic control companies providing service to non-FAA towers.

## Training, Other Qualifications, and Advancement

Air traffic controller trainees are selected through the competitive Federal Civil Service system. Applicants must pass a written test that measures their ability to learn the controller's duties. Applicants with experience as a pilot, navigator, or military controller can improve their rating by scoring well on the occupational knowledge portion of the examination. Abstract reasoning and three-dimensional spatial visualization are among the aptitudes the exam measures. In addition, applicants generally must have three years of general work experience or four years of college, or a combination of both. Applicants also must survive a one-week screening at the FAA Academy in Oklahoma City which includes aptitude tests using computer simulator and physical and psychological examinations. Successful applicants receive drug screening tests. For airport tower and enroute center positions, applicants must be under 31 years old. Those 31 years old and over are eligible for positions at flight service stations.

Controllers must be articulate, because directions to pilots must be given quickly and clearly. Intelligence and a good memory also are important because controllers constantly receive information that they must immediately grasp, interpret, and remember. Decisiveness is also required because controllers often have to make quick decisions. The ability to concentrate is crucial because controllers must make these decisions in the midst of noise and other distractions.

Trainees learn their craft through a combination of formal and on-the-job training. They receive 7 months of intensive training at the FAA academy, where they learn the fundamentals of the airway system, FAA regulations, controller equipment, aircraft performance characteristics, as well as more specialized tasks. To receive a job offer, trainees must successfully complete the training and pass a series of examinations, including a controller skills test that measures speed and accuracy in recognizing and correctly solving air traffic control problems. Based on aptitude and test scores, trainees are selected to work at either an enroute center or a tower.

After graduation, it takes several years of progressively more responsible work experience, interspersed with considerable classroom instruction and independent study, to become a fully qualified controller. This training includes instruction in the operation of the new, more automated air traffic control system—including the automated Microwave Landing System that enables pilots to receive instructions over automated data links—that is being installed in control sites across the country.

Controllers who fail to complete either the academy or the on-the-job portion of the training are usually dismissed. Controllers must pass a physical examination each year and a job performance examination twice each year. Failure to become certified in any position at a facility within a specified time may also result in dismissal. Controllers also are subject to drug screening as a condition of continuing employment.

At airports, new controllers begin by supplying pilots with basic flight data and airport information. They then advance to ground controller, then local controller, departure controller, and finally, arrival controller. At an enroute traffic control center, new controllers first deliver printed flight plans to teams, gradually advancing to radar associate controller and then radar controller.

Controllers can transfer to jobs at different locations or advance to supervisory positions, including management or staff jobs in air traffic control and top administrative jobs in the FAA. However, there are only limited opportunities for a controller to switch from a position in an enroute center to a tower.

## Job Outlook

Competition for air traffic controller jobs is expected to remain extremely keen because the occupation attracts many more qualified applicants than the small number of job openings stemming from growth of the occupation and replacement needs. Turnover is very low; because of the relatively high pay and liberal retirement benefits, controllers have a very strong attachment to the occupation. Most of the current workforce was hired as a result of the controller's strike during the 1980s, so the average age of current controllers is fairly young. Most controllers will not be eligible to retire until 2005 or later.

Employment of air traffic controllers is expected to show little or no change through the year 2005. Employment growth is not expected to keep pace with growth in the number of aircraft flying because of the implementation of a new air traffic control system over the next 10 years. This computerized system will assist the controller by automatically making many of the routine decisions. Automation will allow controllers to handle more traffic, thus increasing their productivity.

Air traffic controllers who continue to meet the proficiency and medical requirements enjoy more job security than most workers. The demand for air travel and the workloads of air traffic controllers decline during recessions, but controllers seldom are laid off.

## Earnings

Air traffic controllers who started with the FAA in 1995 earned about $22,700 a year. Controllers at higher federal pay grade levels earned 5 percent more than other federal workers in an equivalent grade. A controller's pay is determined by both the worker's job responsibilities and the complexity of the particular facility. Earnings are higher at facilities where traffic patterns are more complex. In 1995, controllers averaged about $59,800 a year.

Depending on length of service, they receive 13 to 26 days of paid vacation and 13 days of paid sick leave each year, life insurance, and health benefits. In addition, controllers can retire at an earlier age and with fewer years of service than other federal employees. Air traffic controllers are eligible to retire at age 50 with 20 years of service as an active air traffic controller or after 25 years of active service at any age. There is a mandatory retirement age of 56 for controllers who manage air traffic.

## Related Occupations

Other occupations that involve the direction and control of traffic in air transportation are airline-radio operator and airplane dispatcher.

## Related *D.O.T.* Jobs

These job titles are related to or more specific than the more general description above. They will help you identify job options you may not otherwise discover. These descriptions are in the current edition of the *Dictionary of Occupational Titles* and classified by numerical order.

193.162-010 AIR-TRAFFIC COORDINATOR; 193.162-014 AIR-TRAFFIC-CONTROL SPECIALIST, STATION; 193.162-018 AIR-TRAFFIC-CONTROL SPECIALIST, TOWER; 193.167-010 CHIEF CONTROLLER

## Sources of Additional Information

A pamphlet providing general information about controllers and instructions for submitting an application is available from any U.S. Office of Personnel Management Job Information Center. Look under U.S. Government, Office of Personnel Management, in your telephone book to obtain a local Job Information Center telephone number, and call for a copy of the Air Traffic Controller Announcement. If there is no listing in your telephone book, dial the toll-free number 1-800-555-1212 and request the number of the Office of Personnel Management Job Information Center for your location.

# Aircraft Mechanics, Including Engine Specialists

## Nature of the Work

To keep aircraft in peak operating condition, aircraft mechanics and engine specialists perform scheduled maintenance, make repairs, and complete inspections required by the Federal Aviation Administration (FAA).

Many aircraft mechanics specialize in preventive maintenance. Following a schedule that is based on the number of hours the aircraft has flown, calendar days, cycles of operation, or a combination of these factors, mechanics inspect the engines, landing gear, instruments, pressurized sections, accessories—brakes, valves, pumps, and air-conditioning systems, for example—and other parts of the aircraft and do the necessary maintenance. They may examine an engine through specially designed openings while working from ladders or scaffolds, or use hoists or lifts to remove the entire engine from the craft. After taking the engine apart, mechanics may use precision instruments to measure parts for wear, and use x-ray and magnetic inspection equipment to check for invisible cracks. Worn or defective parts are repaired or replaced. They also may repair sheetmetal or composite surfaces, measure the tension of control cables, or check for corrosion, distortion, and cracks in the fuselage, wings, and tail. After completing all repairs, mechanics must test the equipment to ensure that it works properly.

Mechanics specializing in repair work rely on the pilot's description of a problem to find and fix faulty equipment. For example, during a preflight check, a pilot may discover that the aircraft's fuel gauge does not work. To solve the problem, mechanics may check the electrical connections, replace the gauge, or use electrical test equipment to make sure no wires are broken or shorted out. They work as fast as safety permits so that the aircraft can be put back into service quickly.

Mechanics may work on one or many different types of aircraft, such as jets, propeller-driven airplanes, and helicopters; or, for efficiency, they may specialize in one section of a particular type of aircraft, such as the engine, hydraulic, or electrical system. As a result of technological advances, mechanics spend an increasing amount of time repairing electronic systems such as computerized controls. They also may be required to analyze and develop solutions to complex electronic problems. In small, independent repair shops, mechanics usually inspect and repair many different types of aircraft.

## Working Conditions

Mechanics usually work in hangars or in other indoor areas, although they may work outdoors—sometimes in unpleasant weather—when the hangars are full or when repairs must be made quickly. This occurs most often to airline mechanics who work at airports because, to save time, minor repairs and preflight checks often are made at the terminal. Mechanics often work under time pressure to maintain flight schedules or, in general aviation, to keep from inconveniencing customers. At the same time, mechanics have a tremendous responsibility to maintain safety standards and this can cause the job to be stressful.

Frequently, mechanics must lift or pull objects weighing as much as 70 pounds. They often stand, lie, or kneel in awkward positions and occasionally must work in precarious positions on scaffolds or ladders. Noise and vibration are common when testing engines. Aircraft mechanics generally work 40 hours a week on 8-hour shifts around the clock. Overtime work is frequent.

## Employment

Aircraft mechanics held about 119,000 jobs in 1994. Over three-fifths of all salaried mechanics worked for airlines, nearly one-fifth for aircraft assembly firms, and nearly one-sixth for the federal government. Most of the rest were general aviation mechanics, the majority of whom worked for independent repair shops or companies that operate their own planes to transport executives and cargo. Very few mechanics were self-employed.

Most airline mechanics work at major airports near large cities. Civilian mechanics employed by the Armed Forces work at military installations. A large proportion of mechanics who work for aircraft assembly firms are located in California or Washington. Others work for the FAA, many at its facility in Oklahoma City. Mechanics for independent repair shops work at airports in every part of the country.

## Training, Other Qualifications, and Advancement

The majority of mechanics who work on civilian aircraft are certified by the FAA as "airframe mechanic," "powerplant mechanic," or "repairer." *Airframe mechanics* are authorized to work on any part of the aircraft except the instruments, power plants, and propellers. *Powerplant mechanics* are authorized to work on engines and to do limited work on propellers. Technicians called *repairers*—who are employed by FAA-certified repair stations and air carriers—work on instruments and on propellers. *Combination airframe-and-powerplant mechanics*—called A&P mechanics—can work on any part of the plane, and those with an inspector's authorization can certify inspection work completed by other mechanics. Uncertified mechanics are supervised by those with certificates.

The FAA requires at least 18 months of work experience for an airframe, powerplant, or repairer's certificate. For a combined A&P certificate, at least 30 months of experience working with both engines and airframes are required. To obtain an inspector's authorization, a mechanic must have held an A&P certificate for at least three years. Applicants for all certificates also must pass written and oral tests and demonstrate that they can do the work authorized by the certificate. Most airlines require that mechanics have a high school diploma and an A&P certificate.

Although a few people become mechanics through on-the-job training, most learn their job in one of about 192 trade schools certified by the FAA. Student enrollment in these schools varies greatly; some have as few as 50 students while at least one school has about 800 students. FAA standards established by law require that certified mechanic schools offer students a minimum of 1,900 actual class hours. Courses in these trade schools generally last from two years to 30 months and provide training with the tools and equipment used on the job. For an FAA certificate, attendance at such schools may substitute for work experience. However, these schools do not guarantee jobs or FAA certificates. Aircraft trade schools are placing more emphasis on newer technologies such as turbine engines, aviation electronics, and composite materials—including graphite, fiberglass, and boron—all of which are increasingly being used in the construction of new aircraft. Less emphasis is being placed on older technologies such as woodworking and welding. Employers prefer mechanics who can perform a wide variety of tasks. Mechanics learn many different skills in their training that can be applied to other jobs.

Some aircraft mechanics in the Armed Forces acquire enough general experience to satisfy the work experience requirements for the FAA certificate. With additional study, they may pass the certifying exam. Generally, however, jobs in the military services are too specialized to provide the broad experience required by the FAA. Most mechanics have to complete the entire training program at a trade school, although a few receive some credit for the material they learned in the service. In any case, military experience is a great advantage when seeking employment; employers consider trade school graduates who have this experience to be the most desirable applicants.

Courses in mathematics, physics, chemistry, electronics, computer science, and mechanical drawing are helpful because many of their principles are involved in the operation of an aircraft and knowledge of the principles often is necessary to make repairs. Courses that develop writing skills are also important because mechanics are often required to submit reports.

As new and more complex aircraft are designed, more employers are requiring mechanics to take ongoing training to update their skills. Recent technological advances in aircraft maintenance necessitate a strong background in electronics—both for acquiring and retaining jobs in this field. New FAA certification standards will make ongoing training mandatory. Every 24 months, mechanics will be required to take at least 16 hours of training to keep their certificate. Many mechanics take courses offered by manufacturers or employers, usually through outside contractors.

Aircraft mechanics must do careful and thorough work that requires a high degree of mechanical aptitude. Employers seek applicants who are self-motivated, hard-working, enthusiastic, and able to diagnose and solve complex mechanical problems. Agility is important for the reaching and climbing necessary for the job. Because they may work on the top of wings and fuselages on large jet planes, aircraft mechanics must not be afraid of heights.

As aircraft mechanics gain experience, they have the opportunity for advancement. Opportunities are best for those who have an aircraft inspector's authorization. A mechanic may advance to lead mechanic (or crew chief), inspector, lead inspector, and shop supervisor. In the airlines, where promotion is often determined by examination, supervisors may advance to executive positions. Those with broad experience in maintenance and overhaul have become inspectors with the FAA. With additional business and management training, some open their own aircraft maintenance facilities.

## Job Outlook

Job prospects for aircraft mechanics are expected to vary among types of employers. Opportunities are likely to be the best at the smaller commuter and regional airlines, FAA repair stations, and in general aviation. Because wages in these companies tend to be relatively low, there are fewer applicants for these jobs than for jobs with the major airlines. Also, some jobs will become available as experienced mechanics leave for higher paying jobs with airlines or transfer to another occupation. Mechanics will face more competition for airline jobs because the high wages and travel benefits attract more qualified applicants than there are openings. Prospects will be best for applicants with significant experience. Mechanics who keep abreast of technological advances in electronics, composite materials, and other areas will be in greatest demand. The number of job openings for aircraft mechanics in the federal government should decline as the size of the Armed Forces is reduced.

Employment of aircraft mechanics is expected to increase about as fast as the average for all occupations through the year 2005 and provide some jobs. A growing population and rising incomes are expected to stimulate the demand for airline transportation, and the number of aircraft is expected to grow. However, employment growth will be restricted somewhat by increases in productivity resulting from greater use of automated inventory control and modular systems that speed repairs and parts replacement.

Most job openings for aircraft mechanics through the year 2005 will stem from replacement needs. Each year, as mechanics transfer to other occupations or retire, several thousand job openings will arise. Aircraft mechanics have a comparatively strong attachment to the occupation, reflecting their significant investment in training. However, because aircraft mechanics' skills are transferable to other occupations, some mechanics leave for work in a related field.

Declines in air travel during recessions force airlines to curtail the number of flights, which results in less aircraft maintenance and, consequently, layoffs for aircraft mechanics.

## Earnings

In 1994, the median annual salary of aircraft mechanics was about $36,858. The middle 50 percent earned between $27,976 and $47,112. The top 10 percent of all aircraft mechanics earned over $53,872 a year and the bottom 10 percent earned less than $20,072. Mechanics who worked on jets generally earned more than those working on other aircraft. Airline mechanics and their immediate families receive reduced fare transportation on their own and most other airlines.

Earnings of airline mechanics generally are higher than mechanics working for other employers. Average hourly pay for beginning aircraft mechanics ranged from $8.70 at the smaller turbo-prop airlines to $13.56 at the major airlines in 1994, according to the Future Aviation Professionals of America. Earnings of experienced mechanics ranged from $14.48 to $21.12 an hour.

Almost one-half of all aircraft mechanics, including those employed by some major airlines, are covered by union agreements. The principal unions are the International Association of Machinists and Aerospace Workers and the Transport Workers Union of America. Some mechanics are represented by the International Brotherhood of Teamsters.

## Related Occupations

Workers in some other occupations that involve similar mechanical and electrical work are electricians, elevator repairers, and telephone maintenance mechanics.

## Related *D.O.T.* Jobs

These job titles are related to or more specific than the more general description above. They will help you identify job options you may not otherwise discover. These descriptions are in the current edition of the *Dictionary of Occupational Titles* and classified by numerical order.

621.261-022 EXPERIMENTAL AIRCRAFT MECHANIC; 621.281-014 AIRFRAME-AND-POWER-PLANT MECHANIC; 621.281-018 AIRFRAME-AND-POWER-PLANT-MECHANIC APPRENTICE; 621.684-014 RECLAMATION WORKER; 806.384-038 PRESSURE SEALER-AND-TESTER; 807.261-010 AIRCRAFT BODY REPAIRER; 807.381-014 BONDED STRUCTURES REPAIRER; 807.684-018 AIRCRAFT SKIN BURNISHER

## Sources of Additional Information

Information about jobs in a particular airline may be obtained by writing to the personnel manager of the company. For addresses of airline companies and information about job opportunities and salaries, contact:

❑ FAPA, 4959 Massachusetts Blvd., Atlanta, GA 30337. (This organization may be called toll free at 1-800-JET-JOBS, extension 190.)

For general information about aircraft mechanics, write to:

❏ Professional Aviation Maintenance Association, 500 Northwest Plaza, Suite 1016, St. Ann, MO 63074-2209.

For information on jobs in a particular area, contact employers at local airports or local offices of the state employment service.

# Aircraft Pilots

## Nature of the Work

Pilots are highly trained professionals who fly airplanes and helicopters to carry out a wide variety of tasks. Although most pilots transport passengers and cargo, others are involved in more unusual tasks, such as dusting crops, spreading seed for reforestation, testing aircraft, directing firefighting efforts, tracking criminals, monitoring traffic, and rescuing and evacuating injured persons.

Except on small aircraft, two pilots usually make up the cockpit crew. Generally, the most experienced pilot, the *captain*, is in command and supervises all other crew members. The *first officer* assists in communicating with air traffic controllers, monitoring the instruments, and flying the aircraft. Some large aircraft still have a third pilot in the cockpit—the *flight engineer*—who assists the other pilots by monitoring and operating many of the instruments and systems, making minor inflight repairs, and watching for other aircraft. New technology can perform many flight tasks, however, and virtually all new aircraft now fly with only two pilots, who rely more heavily on computerized controls. Flight engineer jobs could be completely eliminated in the future.

Before departure, pilots plan their flights carefully. They thoroughly check their aircraft to make sure that the engines, controls, instruments, and other systems are functioning properly. They also make sure that baggage or cargo has been loaded correctly. They confer with flight dispatchers and aviation weather forecasters to find out about weather conditions enroute and at their destination. Based on this information, they choose a route, altitude, and speed that should provide the fastest, safest, and smoothest flight. When flying under instrument flight rules—procedures governing the operation of the aircraft when there is poor visibility—the pilot in command, or the company dispatcher, normally files an instrument flight plan with air traffic control so that the flight can be coordinated with other air traffic.

Takeoff and landing are the most difficult parts of the flight and require close coordination between the pilot and first officer. For example, as the plane accelerates for takeoff, the pilot concentrates on the runway while the first officer scans the instrument panel. To calculate the speed they must attain to become airborne, pilots consider the altitude of the airport, outside temperature, weight of the plane, and the speed and direction of the wind. The moment the plane reaches takeoff speed, the first officer informs the pilot, who then pulls back on the controls to raise the nose of the plane.

Unless the weather is bad, the actual flight is relatively easy. Airplane pilots with the assistance of autopilot and the flight management computer, steer the plane along their planned route

and are monitored by the air traffic control stations they pass along the way. They regularly scan the instrument panel to check their fuel supply, the condition of their engines, and the air-conditioning, hydraulic, and other systems. Pilots may request a change in altitude or route if circumstances dictate. For example, if the ride is rougher than expected, they may ask air traffic control if pilots flying at other altitudes have reported better conditions. If so, they may request a change. This procedure also may be used to find a stronger tailwind or a weaker headwind to save fuel and increase speed.

In contrast, helicopters are used for short trips at relatively low altitude, so pilots must be constantly on the lookout for trees, bridges, power lines, transmission towers, and other dangerous obstacles. Regardless of the type of aircraft, all pilots must monitor warning devices designed to help detect sudden shifts in wind conditions that can cause crashes.

If visibility is poor, pilots must rely completely on their instruments. Using the altimeter readings, they know how high above ground they are and whether or not they can fly safely over mountains and other obstacles. Special navigation radios give pilots precise information which, with the help of special maps, tell them their exact position. Other very sophisticated equipment provides directions to a point just above the end of a runway and enables pilots to land completely "blind."

Once on the ground, pilots must complete records on their flight for their organization and the Federal Aviation Administration (FAA).

The number of nonflying duties that pilots have depends on the employment setting. Airline pilots have the services of large support staffs, and consequently, perform few nonflying duties. Pilots employed by other organizations such as charter operators or businesses have many other duties. They may load the aircraft, handle all passenger luggage to ensure a balanced load, and supervise refueling; other nonflying responsibilities include keeping records, scheduling flights, arranging for major maintenance, and performing minor aircraft maintenance and repair work.

Some pilots are instructors. They teach their students the principles of flight in ground-school classes and demonstrate how to operate aircraft in dual-controlled planes and helicopters. A few specially trained pilots are "examiners" or "check pilots." They periodically fly with other pilots or pilot's license applicants to make sure that they are proficient.

## Working Conditions

By law, airline pilots cannot fly more than 100 hours a month or more than 1,000 hours a year. Most airline pilots fly an average of 75 hours a month and work an additional 75 hours a month performing nonflying duties. Fifty percent of all pilots work more than 40 hours a week. The majority of flights involve overnight layovers. When pilots are away from home, the airlines provide hotel accommodations, transportation between the hotel and airport, and an allowance for expenses. Airlines operate flights at all hours of the day and night, so work schedules often are irregular. Flight assignments are based on seniority.

Those pilots not employed by the airlines often have irregular schedules as well; they may fly 30 hours one month and 90 hours the next. Because these pilots frequently have many nonflying responsibilities, they have much less free time than airline pilots. Except for business pilots, most do not remain away from home overnight. They may work odd hours. In addition, pilots working as instructors often give lessons at night or on weekends.

Airline pilots, especially those on international routes, often suffer jet lag—fatigue caused by many hours of flying through different time zones. The work of test pilots, who check the flight performance of new and experimental planes, may be dangerous. Pilots who are crop dusters may be exposed to toxic chemicals and seldom have the benefit of a regular landing strip. Helicopter pilots involved in police work may be subject to personal injury.

Although flying does not involve much physical effort, the mental stress of being responsible for a safe flight, no matter what the weather, can be tiring. Particularly during takeoff and landing, pilots must be alert and quick to react if something goes wrong.

## Employment

Civilian pilots held about 90,000 jobs in 1994. Three-fifths worked for airlines. Many others worked as flight instructors at local airports or for large businesses that fly company cargo and executives in their own airplanes or helicopters. Some pilots flew small planes for air taxi companies, usually to or from lightly traveled airports not served by the airlines. Others worked for a variety of businesses performing tasks such as crop dusting, inspecting pipelines, or conducting sightseeing trips. Federal, state, and local governments also employed pilots. Several thousand pilots were self-employed.

The employment of airplane pilots is not distributed like the population. Pilots are more concentrated in the states of California, Texas, Georgia, Washington, Nevada, Hawaii, and Alaska which have a higher amount of flying activity relative to their population.

## Training, Other Qualifications, and Advancement

All pilots who are paid to transport passengers or cargo must have a commercial pilot's license with an instrument rating issued by the FAA. Helicopter pilots must hold a commercial pilot's certificate with a helicopter rating. To qualify for these licenses, applicants must be at least 18 years old and have at least 250 hours of flight experience. The time can be reduced through participation in certain flight school curricula approved by the FAA. They also must pass a strict physical examination to make sure that they are in good health and have 20/20 vision with or without glasses, good hearing, and no physical handicaps that could impair their performance. Applicants must pass a written test that includes questions on the principles of safe flight, navigation techniques, and FAA regulations. They also must demonstrate their flying ability to FAA or designated examiners.

To fly in periods of low visibility, pilots must be rated by the FAA to fly by instruments. Pilots may qualify for this rating by having a total of 105 hours of flight experience, including 40 hours of experience in flying by instruments; they also must pass a written examination on procedures and FAA regulations covering instrument flying and demonstrate to an examiner their ability to fly by instruments.

Airline pilots must fulfill additional requirements. They must pass FAA written and flight examinations to earn a flight engineer's license. Captains and first officers also must have an airline transport pilot's license. Applicants for this license must be at least 23 years old and have a minimum of 1,500 hours of flying experience, including night and instrument flying. Because pilots must be able to make quick decisions and accurate judgments under pressure, many airline companies reject applicants who do not pass required psychological and aptitude tests.

All licenses are valid as long as a pilot can pass the periodic physical examinations and tests of flying skills required by government and company regulations.

The Armed Forces have always been an important source of trained pilots for civilian jobs. Military pilots gain valuable experience on jet aircraft and helicopters, and persons with this experience are generally preferred for civilian pilot jobs. This primarily reflects the extensive flying time military pilots receive. Persons without armed forces training also become pilots by attending flight schools. The FAA has certified about 600 civilian flying schools, including some colleges and universities that offer degree credit for pilot training. Over the projected period, federal budget reductions are expected to reduce military pilot training. As a result, FAA certified schools will train a larger share of pilots than in the past.

Although some small airlines will hire high school graduates, most airlines require at least two years of college and prefer to hire college graduates; almost ninety percent of all pilots have completed some college. In fact, most entrants to this occupation have a college degree. If the number of college educated applicants continues to increases, employers may make a college degree an educational requirement.

Depending on the type of aircraft in use, new airline pilots startas first officers or flight engineers. Although some airlines favor applicants who already have a flight engineer's license, they may provide flight engineer training for those who have only the commercial license. All new pilots receive several weeks of intensive training in simulators and classrooms before being assigned to a flight.

Organizations other than airlines generally require less flying experience. However, a commercial pilot's license is a minimum requirement, and employers prefer applicants who have experience in the type of craft they will be flying. New employees usually start as first officers, or fly less sophisticated equipment. Test pilots often are required to have an engineering degree.

Advancement for all pilots generally is limited to other flying jobs. Many pilots start as flight instructors, building up their flying hours while they earn money teaching. As they become more experienced, these pilots occasionally fly charter planes or perhaps get jobs with small air transportation firms, such as air taxi companies. Some advance to business flying jobs. A small number get flight engineer jobs with the airlines.

In the airlines, advancement usually depends on seniority provisions of union contracts. After 1 to 5 years, flight engineers advance according to seniority to first officer and, after 5 to 15 years, to captain. Seniority also determines which pilots get the more desirable routes. In a nonairline job, a first officer may advanceto pilot and, in large companies, to chief pilot or director ofaviation in charge of aircraft scheduling, maintenance, and flight procedures.

## Job Outlook

Pilots are expected to face considerable competition for jobs through the year 2005 because the number of applicants for new positions is expected to exceed the number of job openings. Competition will be especially keen early in the projection period due to a temporary increase in the pool of qualified pilots seeking jobs. Mergers and bankruptcies during the recent restructuring of the industry caused a large number of airline pilots to lose their jobs. Also, federal budget reductions resulted in many pilots leaving the Armed Forces. These and other qualified pilots seek jobs in this occupation because it offers very high earnings, glamour, prestige, and free or low cost travel benefits. As time passes, some pilots will fail to maintain their qualifications and the number of applicants competing for each opening should decline. Factors affecting demand, however, are not expected to ease that competition.

Relatively few jobs will be created from rising demand for pilots as employment is expected to increase more slowly than the average for all occupations through the year 2005. The expected growth in airline passenger and cargo traffic will create a need for more airliners, pilots, and flight instructors. However, computerized flight management systems on new aircraft will eliminate the need for flight engineers on those planes thus restricting pilot employment growth. In addition, the trend toward using larger planes in the airline industry will increase pilot productivity. Employment of business pilots is expected to grow more slowly than in the past as more businesses opt to fly with regional and smaller airlines serving their area rather than buy and operate their own aircraft. On the other hand, helicopter pilots are expected to grow more rapidly as the demand for the type of services they can offer expands.

Opportunities resulting from the need to replace pilots who leave the occupation also are expected to be limited. Aircraft pilots understandably have an extremely strong attachment to their occupation because it requires a substantial investment in specialized training that is not transferable to other fields and it generally offers very high earnings. Nevertheless, pilots who reach the mandatory retirement age will generate several thousand job openings each year.

Pilots who have logged the greatest number of flying hours in the more sophisticated equipment generally have the best prospects. This is the reason military pilots usually have an advantage over other applicants. Job seekers with the most FAA licenses will also have a competitive advantage. Opportunities for pilots in the regional commuter airlines and international service are expected to be more favorable as these segments are expected to grow faster than other segments of the industry.

Employment of pilots is sensitive to cyclical swings in the economy. During recessions, when a decline in the demand for air travel forces airlines to curtail the number of flights, airlines may temporarily furlough some pilots. Commercial and corporate flying, flight instruction, and testing of new aircraft also decline during recessions, adversely affecting pilots employed in those areas.

## Earnings

Earnings of airline pilots are among the highest in the nation. According to the Future Aviation Professionals of America (FAPA), the 1995 average starting salary for airline pilots ranged from about $13,000 at the smaller turboprop airlines to $27,900 at the larger major airlines. Average earnings for experienced pilots with six years of experience ranged from $37,500 at the turboprop airlines to almost $81,000 at the largest airlines. Some senior captains on the largest aircraft earned as much as $200,000 a year. Earnings depend on factors such as the type, size, and maximum speed of the plane, and the number of hours and miles flown. Extra pay may be given for night and international flights.

Generally, pilots working outside the airlines earn lower salaries. It was estimated that the median salary for chief pilots was $63,000 a year in 1994, for captains/pilots, $58,900 and for first officers, $42,800. Usually, pilots who fly jet aircraft earn higher salaries than nonjet pilots.

Data from the Future Aviation Professionals of America show that helicopter pilots averaged $29,200 a year. Average pay for helicopter pilots with five years of experience was about $45,600. Some helicopter pilots earn $65,000 to $75,00 a year.

Airline pilots generally are eligible for life and health insurance plans financed by the airlines. They also receive retirement benefits and if they fail the FAA physical examination at some point in their careers, they get disability payments. Some airlines provide allowances to pilots for purchasing and cleaning their uniforms. As an additional benefit, pilots and their immediate families usually are entitled to free or reduced fare transportation on their own and other airlines.

Most airline pilots are members of unions. Most airline pilots are members of the Airline Pilots Association, International, but those employed by one major airline are members of the Allied Pilots Association. Some flight engineers are members of the Flight Engineers' International Association.

## Related Occupations

Although they are not in the cockpit, air traffic controllers and dispatchers also play an important role in making sure flights are safe and on schedule, and participate in many of the decisions pilots must make.

## Related *D.O.T.* Jobs

These job titles are related to or more specific than the more general description above. They will help you identify job options you may not otherwise discover. These descriptions are in the current edition of the *Dictionary of Occupational Titles* and classified by numerical order.

196.167-101 CHIEF PILOT; 196.223-010 INSTRUCTOR, FLYING; 196.223-014 INSTRUCTOR, PILOT; 196.263-010 AIRLINE PILOT; 196.263-014 AIRLINE PILOT, COMMERCIAL; 196.263-018 AIRLINE PILOT, PHOTOGRAMMETRY; 196.263-022 CHECK PILOT; 196.263-026 CONTROLLER, REMOTELY PILOTED VEHICLE; 196.263-030 EXECUTIVE PILOT; 196.263-034 FACILITIES FLIGHT-CHECK PILOT; 196.263-038 HELICOPTER PILOT; 196.263-042 TEST PILOT; 621.261-018 FLIGHT ENGINNEER

## Sources of Additional Information

Information about job opportunities in a particular airline and the qualifications required may be obtained by writing to the personnel manager of the airline. For addresses of airline companies and information about job opportunities and salaries, contact:

❏ FAPA, 4959 Massachusetts Blvd., Atlanta, GA 30032. (This organization may be called toll free at 1-800-JET-JOBS, extension 190.)

For information on airline pilots, contact:

- ❏ Airline Pilots Association, 1625 Massachusetts Ave. NW, Washington, DC 20036.
- ❏ Air Transport Association of America, 1301 Pennsylvania Ave. NW, Suite 1110, Washington, DC 20006.

For information on helicopter pilots, contact:

- ❏ Helicopter Association International, 1619 Duke St., Alexandria, VA 22314.

For a copy of *List of Certificated Pilot Schools*, write to:

- ❏ Superintendent of Documents, U.S. Government Printing Office, Washington, DC 20402.

For information about job opportunities in companies other than airlines, consult the classified section of aviation trade magazines and apply to companies that operate aircraft at local airports.

# Animal Caretakers, Except Farm

## Nature of the Work

Most people like animals. But, as pet owners can attest, it is hard work taking care of them. Animal caretakers, sometimes called animal attendants or animal keepers, feed, water, groom, bathe, and exercise animals and clean and repair their cages. They also play with the animals, provide companionship, and observe behavioral changes that could indicate illness or injury.

Kennels, animal shelters, animal hospitals, pet stores, stables, veterinary facilities, laboratories, and zoological parks all house animals and employ caretakers. Job titles and duties vary by employment setting.

Kennel staff usually care for small companion animals like dogs and cats. Beginning attendants perform basic tasks, such as cleaning cages and dog runs. Experienced attendants may give basic treatment and first aid, bathe and groom animals, and clean their ears and teeth. Dog groomers specialize in maintaining the animals' appearance. Some groomers work in kennels and others operate their own grooming business. Caretakers also sell pet food and supplies, teach obedience classes, help with breeding, or prepare animals for shipping.

In addition to providing the basic needs of the animals, caretakers in animal shelters screen applicants for animal adoption, vaccinate newly admitted animals, and euthanize (put to death) seriously ill, severely injured, or unwanted animals.

Pet store caretakers provide basic care, sell pet supplies, and give advice to customers.

Workers in stables saddle and unsaddle horses, give them rubdowns, and walk them through a cool-off after a ride. They also feed and groom the horses, muck out stalls, polish saddles, clean andorganize the tack room, and store supplies and feed. Experienced staff may help train horses.

Animal caretakers in animal hospitals are like primary care nurses in human hospitals—they spend more time with the patients than anyone else. Busy veterinarians rely on caretakers to keep a constant eye on the condition of animals under their charge. Caretakers watch as animals recover from surgery, check whether dressings are still on correctly, observe the animals' overall attitude and notify a doctor if anything seems out of the ordinary. While among the animals, caretakers clean constantly to maintain sanitary conditions in the hospital.

In zoos, caretakers called keepers prepare the diets, clean the enclosures, monitor the behavior of exotic animals, and sometimes assist in research studies on their wards. Keepers also may answer questions from visitors about the natural habitat or eating habits of exhibited animals.

Keepers are generally assigned to work with a broad group of animals such as mammals, birds, or reptiles. In large zoological parks, keepers may work with a limited collection of animals such as primates, large cats, or dolphins.

## Working Conditions

People who love animals get satisfaction from working with and helping animals. However, some of the work may be physically demanding and unpleasant. Caretakers have to clean animal cages and lift heavy animals, or supplies like bales of hay. Also, the work setting is often noisy. Some duties—such as euthanizing a hopelessly injured or aged animal—may be emotionally stressful.

Animal caretakers can be exposed to bites, kicks, and disease from the animals they attend. Caretakers may work outdoors in all kinds of weather. Hours are irregular. Animals have to be fed every day, so caretakers rotate weekend shifts. In some animal hospitals and animal shelters an attendant is on duty 24 hours a day, which means night shifts. Most full-time caretakers work about 40 hours a week; some work 50 hours a week or more. Caretakers of show and sports animals travel to competitions.

## Employment

Animal caretakers held about 125,000 jobs in 1994. Most were employed in veterinary facilities and boarding kennels. Other employers were animal shelters, stables, pet stores, grooming shops, zoological parks, and local, state, and federal agencies. One out of every six caretakers is self-employed. More than a third work part-time.

## Training, Other Qualifications, and Advancement

Most animal caretakers working in kennels, pet stores, animal shelters, and stables are trained on the job. There are few formal training programs, but the American Boarding Kennel Association offers a home-study program for kennel technicians. Some states require certification of caretakers who euthanize animals. Training may be through a veterinarian or a state Humane Society. Otherwise, there are no formal training requirements in these settings; nonetheless, many employers look for people with some experience with animals. Caretakers start by cleaning cages and advance to giving medication and grooming. Most dog groomers learn their trade through on-the-job training, but a few grooming schools do exist.

Dog groomers may receive professional registration or certification from the National Dog Groomers Association of America. The American Boarding Kennels Association accredits kennels and offers a Certified Kennel Operator program, both of which show professional competency.

There are no formal education requirements for animal caretakers in veterinary facilities. They are trained on the job.

Large zoological parks may require their caretakers to have a bachelor's degree in biology, animal science, or a related field. They also require experience with animals, preferably as a volunteer in a zoo or as a paid keeper in a smaller zoo.

Advancement varies with employment setting. Kennel caretakers may be promoted to kennel supervisor, assistant manager, and manager. Caretakers with enough capital may open up their own kennels. Pet store caretakers may become store managers. Caretakers in animal shelters may become a humane agent, animal control officer, assistant shelter manager, or shelter director. The Humane Society of the United States offers seminars for animal shelter and control personnel. Zoo keepers may advance to senior keeper, assistant head keeper, head keeper, and assistant curator but few openings occur, especially for the higher level positions.

## Job Outlook

Employment opportunities for animal caretakers generally are expected to be good. Employment is expected to grow faster than the average for all occupations through the year 2005 as the population and economy expand and pet ownership grows. The number of dogs and cats has increased significantly over the last 10 years, and is expected to continue to increase in the future. More animals will require more caretakers to provide services.

Despite growth in demand for animal caretakers, the overwhelming majority of jobs will result from the need to replace workers leaving the field. Many animal caretaker jobs that require little or no training have work schedules which tend to be flexible; therefore, it is an ideal first job for people entering the labor force as well as for students and others looking for temporary or part-time work. Because turnover is quite high due to the hard physical labor and low pay, the overall availability of jobs should be very good. Much of the work of these animal caretakers is seasonal, particularly during vacation periods.

The outlook for caretakers in zoos, however, is not favorable. Job seekers will face keen competition because of expected slow growth in zoo capacity, low turnover, and the fact that the occupation attracts many candidates.

## Earnings

Animal caretakers who worked full-time earned a median weekly salary of $275 in 1994. The middle 50 percent earned between $211 and $368. The bottom 10 percent earned less than $182; the top 10 percent earned more than $536 a week. Generally, veterinary technicians, laboratory animal technologists, and zookeepers earn more than other animal caretakers.

## Related Occupation

Other occupations working with animals include agricultural and biological scientists, veterinarians, retail sales workers in pet stores, gamekeepers, game-farm helpers, poultry breeders, ranchers, and artificial-breeding technician.

## Related *D.O.T.* Jobs

These job titles are related to or more specific than the more general description above. They will help you identify job options you may not otherwise discover. These descriptions are in the current edition of the *Dictionary of Occupational Titles* and classified by numerical order.

410.674-010 ANIMAL CARETAKER; 410.674-022 STABLE ATTENDANT; 412.674-010 ANIMAL KEEPER; 412.674-014 ANIMAL-NURSERY WORKER; 418.381-101 HORSE SHOER; 418.674-010 DOG GROOMER; 418.677-010 DOG BATHER; 449.674-010 AQUARIST

## Sources of Additional Information

For more information on animal caretaking and the animal shelter and control personnel training program, write to:

❏ Animal Caretakers Information, The Humane Society of the United States, 2100 L St., NW, Washington, DC 20037.

To obtain a listing of grooming schools or the name of the nearest certified dog groomer in your area, send a stamped self-addressed envelope to:

❏ National Dog Groomers Association of America, Box 101, Clark, PA 16113.

For information on training and certification of kennel staff and owners, contact:

❏ American Boarding Kennel Association, 4575 Galley Rd., Suite 400-A, Colorado Springs, CO 80915.

# Automotive Body Repairers

## Nature of the Work

Thousands of motor vehicles are damaged in traffic accidents every day. Although some are sold for salvage or scrapped, most can be repaired to look and drive like new. Automotive body repairers straighten bent bodies, remove dents, and replace crumpled parts that are beyond repair. Usually, they can repair all types of vehicles, but most body repairers work on cars and small trucks. A few work on large trucks, buses, or tractor-trailers.

When a damaged vehicle is brought into the shop, body repairers generally receive instructions from their supervisors, who have determined which parts are to be restored or replaced and how much time the job should take.

Automotive body repairers use special machines to restore damaged metal frames and body sections to their original shape and location. They chain or clamp the frames and sections to alignment machines that usually use hydraulic pressure to align the damaged metal. "Unibody" designs, which are built without frames, must be returned to precise alignment, so repairers use bench systems to guide them and measure how much each section is out of alignment.

Body repairers remove badly damaged sections of body panels with a pneumatic metal-cutting gun or acetylene torch and weld in new sections to replace them. Repairers pull out less serious dents with a hydraulic jack or hand prying bar, or knock them out with handtools or pneumatic hammers. They smooth out small dents and creases in the metal by holding a small anvil against one side of the damaged area while hammering the opposite side. They remove very small pits and dimples with pick hammers and punches.

Body repairers also repair or replace the plastic body parts used increasingly on newer model vehicles. They remove the damaged panels and determine the type of plastic from which they are made. With most types, they can apply heat from a hot-air welding gun or by immersion in hot water, and press the softened panel back into its original shape by hand. They replace plastic parts which are badly damaged or more difficult to repair.

Body repairers use plastic or solder to fill small dents which cannot be worked out of the plastic or metal panel. On metal panels, they then file or grind the hardened filler to the original shape and sand it before painting. In many shops, automotive painters do the painting. In smaller shops, workers often do both body repairing and painting. A few body repairers specialize in repairing fiberglass car bodies.

In large shops, body repairers may specialize in one type of repair, such as frame straightening or door and fender repairing. Some body repairers also specialize in installing glass in automobiles and other vehicles. Glass installers remove broken, cracked, or pitted windshields and window glass. Curved windows sometimes must be cut from a sheet of safety glass. Glass installers apply a moisture-proofing compound along the edges of the glass, place it in the vehicle, and install rubber strips around the sides of the windshield or window to make it secure and weatherproof. Body repair work has variety and challenge—each damaged vehicle presents a different problem. Repairers must develop appropriate methods for each job, using their broad knowledge of automotive construction and repair techniques.

Body repairers usually work alone with only general directions from supervisors. In some shops, they may be assisted by helpers or apprentices.

## Working Conditions

The majority of automotive body repairers work a standard 40-hour week, but those who are self-employed may work 60 or more hours a week. They work indoors in body shops which are noisy because of the banging of hammers against metal and the whir of power tools. Most shops are well ventilated to partially disperse dust and paint fumes. Body repairers often work in awkward or cramped positions, and much of their work is strenuous and dirty. Hazards include cuts from sharp metal edges, burns from torches and heated metal, injuries from power tools, and fumes from paint.

## Employment

Automotive body repairers held about 209,000 jobs in 1994. Most worked for shops that specialized in body repairs and painting, and for automobile and truck dealers. Others worked for organizations that maintain their own motor vehicles, such as trucking companies and automobile rental companies. A few worked for motor vehicle manufacturers. About one automotive body repairer out of five was self-employed.

## Training, Other Qualifications, and Advancement

Most employers prefer to hire persons who have completed formal training programs in automotive body repair, but these programs are able to supply only a portion of employers' needs. Formal training is highly desirable because advances in technology in recent years have greatly changed the structure, the components, and even the materials used in automobiles. As a result, many new repair techniques have been created and many new skills are required. For example, the bodies of newer automobiles are increasingly made of a combination of materials—the traditional steel, plus aluminum and a growing variety of metal alloys and plastics—each requiring the use of somewhat different techniques to reshape and smooth out dents and small pits. Automotive body repair training programs are offered by high schools, vocational schools, private trade schools, and community colleges. Formal training in automotive body repair can enhance chances for employment and speed promotion to a journeyman position.

Employers also hire many persons without formal automotive body repair training. They learn the trade as helpers, picking up skills on the job from experienced body repairers. For helper jobs most employers prefer to hire high school graduates who know how to use handtools. Good reading and basic mathematics and computer skills are essential to becoming a fully skilled automotive body repairer. Restoring unibody automobiles to their original form requires such precision that body repairers often must follow instructions and diagrams in technical manuals and make very precise measurements of the position of one body section relative to another.

Helpers begin by assisting body repairers in tasks such as removing damaged parts and installing repaired parts. They learn to remove small dents and to make other minor repairs. They then progress to more difficult tasks such as straightening body parts and returning them to their correct alignment. Generally, to become skilled in all aspects of body repair requires three to four years of on-the-job training.

Certification by the National Institute for Automotive Service Excellence (ASE), which is voluntary, is recognized as a standard of achievement for automotive body repairers. To be certified, a body repairer must pass a written examination and must have at least two years of experience in the trade. Completion of a high school, vocational school, trade school, or community college program in automotive body repair may be substituted for one year of work experience. Automotive body repairers must retake the examination at least every five years to retain certification.

Automotive body repairers must buy their own handtools, but employers usually furnish power tools. Trainees generally accumulate tools as they gain experience, and many workers have thousands of dollars invested in tools.

Continuing education throughout a career in automotive body repair is becoming increasingly important. Automotive parts, body materials, and electronics continue to change and become more complex and technologically advanced. Gaining new skills, reading technical manuals, and attending seminars and classes is important for keeping up with these technological advances.

An experienced automotive body repairer with supervisory ability may advance to shop supervisor. Some workers open their own body repair shops. Others become automobile damage appraisers for insurance companies.

## Job Outlook

Employment of automotive body repairers is expected to increase about as fast as the average for all occupations through the year 2005. Opportunities should be best for persons with formal training in automotive body repair and mechanics.

Requirements for body repairers will increase because, as the number of motor vehicles in operation grows with the nation's population, the number damaged in accidents will increase as well. New automobile designs increasingly have body parts made of steel alloys, aluminum, and plastics—materials that are more difficult to work with than the traditional steel body parts. Also, new, lighter weight automotive designs are prone to greater collision damage than older, heavier designs and, consequently, are more time consuming to repair. Nevertheless, the need to replace experienced repairers who transfer to other occupations, retire, or stop working for other reasons will still account for the majority of job openings.

The automotive repair business is not very sensitive to changes in economic conditions, and experienced body repairers are rarely laid off. However, most employers hire fewer new workers during an economic slowdown. Although major body damage must be repaired if a vehicle is to be restored to safe operating condition, repair of minor dents and crumpled fenders can often be deferred.

## Earnings

Body repairers earned median weekly earnings of $456 in 1994. The middle 50 percent earned between $321 and $624 a week. The lowest-paid 10 percent earned less than $249 a week, while the highest-paid 10 percent earned over $790 a week. Helpers and trainees usually earn from 30 to 60 percent of the earnings of skilled workers.

The majority of body repairers employed by automotive dealers and repair shops are paid on an incentive basis. Under this method, body repairers are paid a predetermined amount for various tasks, and earnings depend on the amount of work assigned to the repairer and how fast it is completed. Employers frequently guarantee workers a minimum weekly salary. Helpers and trainees usually receive an hourly rate until they are skilled enough to be paid on an incentive basis. Body repairers who work for trucking companies, bus lines, and other organizations that maintain their own vehicles usually receive an hourly wage.

Many automotive body repairers are members of unions, including the International Association of Machinists and Aerospace Workers; the International Union, United Automobile, Aerospace and Agricultural Implement Workers of America; the Sheet Metal Workers' International Association; and the International Brotherhood of Teamsters. Most body repairers who are union members work for large automobile dealers, trucking companies, and bus lines.

## Related Occupations

Repairing damaged motor vehicles often involves working on their mechanical components as well as their bodies. Automotive body repairers often work closely with several related occupations including automotive and diesel mechanics, automotive repair service estimators, painters, and body customizers.

## Related *D.O.T.* Jobs

These job titles are related to or more specific than the more general description above. They will help you identify job options you may not otherwise discover. These descriptions are in the current edition of the *Dictionary of Occupational Titles* and classified by numerical order.

620.364-010 SQUEAK, RATTLE, AND LEAK REPAIRER; 620.684-034 USED-CAR RENOVATOR; 807.267-010 SHOP ESTIMATOR; 807.281-010 TRUCK-BODY BUILDER; 807.361-010 AUTOMOBILE-BODY CUSTOMIZER; 807.381-010 AUTOMOBILE-BODY REPAIRER; 807.381-018 FRAME REPAIRER; 807.381-022 SERVICE MECHANIC; 807.381-030 AUTO-BODY REPAIRER, FIBERGLASS; 807.484-010 FRAME STRAIGHTENER; 807.684-010 AUTOMOBILE-BUMPER STRAIGHTENER; 865.684-010 GLASS INSTALLER

## Sources of Additional Information

More details about work opportunities may be obtained from automotive body repair shops and motor vehicle dealers; locals of the unions previously mentioned; or local offices of the state employment service. The state employment service also is a source of information about training programs.

For general information about automotive body repairer careers, write to:

❏ Automotive Service Association, Inc., 1901 Airport Freeway, Bedford, TX 76021-5732.

❏ Automotive Service Industry Association, 25 Northwest Point, Elk Grove Village, IL 60007-1035.

For information on how to become a certified automotive body repairer, write to:

❏ ASE, 13505 Dulles Technology Dr., Herndon, VA 22071-3415.

For a directory of certified automotive body repairer programs, contact:

❏ National Automotive Technician Education Foundation, 13505 Dulles Technology Dr., Herndon, VA 22071.

For a directory of accredited private trade and technical schools that offer training programs in automotive body repair, write to:

❏ Accrediting Commission of Career Schools and Colleges of Technology, 2101 Wilson Blvd., Suite 302, Arlington, VA 22201.

For a list of public automotive mechanic training programs, contact:

❏ Vocational Industrial Clubs of America, P.O. Box 3000, 1401 James Monroe Highway, Leesburg, VA 22075.

# Automotive Mechanics

## Nature of the Work

Automotive mechanics, often called *automotive service technicians*, repair and service automobiles and occasionally light trucks, such as vans and pickups, with gasoline engines.

Anyone whose car or light truck has broken down knows the importance of the mechanic's job. The ability to diagnose the source of the problem quickly and accurately, one of the mechanic's most valuable skills, requires good reasoning ability and a thorough knowledge of automobiles. In fact, many mechanics consider diagnosing "hard to find" troubles one of their most challenging and satisfying duties.

When mechanical or electrical troubles occur, mechanics first get a description of the symptoms from the owner or, if they work in a dealership or large shop, the repair service estimator who wrote the repair order. The mechanic may have to test drive the vehicle or use a variety of testing equipment, such as engine analyzers, spark plug testers, or compression gauges to locate the problem. Once the cause of the problem is found, mechanics make adjustments or repairs. If a part is damaged or worn beyond repair, or cannot be fixed at a reasonable cost, it is replaced, usually after consultation with the vehicle owner.

During routine service, mechanics inspect, lubricate, and adjust engines and other components, repairing or replacing parts before they cause breakdowns. They usually follow a checklist to be sure they examine all important parts, such as belts, hoses, steering systems, spark plugs, brake and fuel systems, wheel bearings, and other potentially troublesome items.

Mechanics use a variety of tools in their work. They use power tools such as pneumatic wrenches to remove bolts quickly; machine tools such as lathes and grinding machines to rebuild brakes and other parts; welding and flame-cutting equipment to remove and repair exhaust systems and other parts; jacks and hoists to lift cars and engines; and a growing variety of electronic service equipment, such as infrared engine analyzers and computerized diagnostic devices. They also use many common handtools such as screwdrivers, pliers, and wrenches to work on small parts and get at hard-to-reach places.

Automotive mechanics in larger shops have increasingly become specialized. For example, *automatic transmission mechanics* work on gear trains, couplings, hydraulic pumps, and other parts of automatic transmissions. Because these are complex mechanisms and include electronic parts, their repair requires considerable experience and training, including a knowledge of hydraulics. *Tune-up mechanics* adjust the ignition timing and valves, and adjust or replace spark plugs and other parts to ensure efficient engine performance. They often use electronic test equipment to help them adjust and locate malfunctions in fuel, ignition, and emissions control systems. *Automotive air-conditioning mechanics* install and repair air-conditioners and service components such as compressors and condensers. *Front-end mechanics* align and balance wheels and repair steering mechanisms and suspension systems. They frequently use special alignment equipment and wheel-balancing machines. *Brake repairers* adjust brakes, replace brake linings and pads, repair hydraulic cylinders, turn discs and drums, and make other repairs on brake systems. Some mechanics specialize in both brake and front-end work.

*Automotive-radiator mechanics* clean radiators with caustic solutions, locate and solder leaks, and install new radiator cores or complete replacement radiators. They also may repair heaters and air-conditioners, and solder leaks in gasoline tanks.

## Working Conditions

Most automotive mechanics work a standard 40-hour week, but some self-employed mechanics work longer hours. Generally, mechanics work indoors. Most repair shops are well ventilated and lighted, but some are drafty and noisy. Mechanics frequently work with dirty and greasy parts, and in awkward positions. They often must lift heavy parts and tools. Minor cuts, burns, and bruises are common, but serious accidents are avoided when the shop is kept clean and orderly and safety practices are observed.

## Employment

Automotive mechanics held about 736,000 jobs in 1994. The majority worked for retail and wholesale automotive dealers, independent automotive repair shops, and gasoline service stations. Others were employed at automotive service facilities at department, automotive, and home supply stores, or maintained the automobile fleets of taxicab and automobile leasing companies, federal, state, and local governments, and other organizations. Motor vehicle manufacturers employed some mechanics to test, adjust, and repair cars at the end of assembly lines. Over 20 percent of automotive mechanics were self-employed.

## Training, Other Qualifications, and Advancement

Automotive technology is rapidly increasing in sophistication, and most training authorities strongly recommend that persons seeking trainee automotive mechanic jobs complete a formal training program after graduating from high school. However, some automotive mechanics still learn the trade solely by assisting and working with experienced mechanics.

Automotive mechanic training programs are offered in high schools, community colleges, and public and private vocational and technical schools, but postsecondary programs generally provide more thorough career preparation than high school programs. High school programs, while an asset, vary greatly in quality. Some offer only an introduction to automotive technology and service for the future consumer or hobbyist, while others aim to equip graduates with enough skills to get a job as a mechanic's helper or trainee mechanic after graduation.

Postsecondary automotive mechanic training programs vary greatly in format, but generally provide intensive career preparation through a combination of classroom instruction and hands-on practice. Some trade and technical school programs provide concentrated training for six months to a year, depending on how many hours the student must attend each week. Community college programs normally spread the training out over two years, supplement the automotive training with instruction in English, basic mathematics, computers, and other subjects, and award an associate degree.

The various automobile manufacturers and their participating dealers sponsor two-year associate degree programs at more than 100 community colleges across the nation. The manufacturers provide service equipment and late model cars on which students practice new skills, and insure that the programs teach the latest automotive technology. Curriculums are updated frequently to reflect changing technology and equipment. Students in these programs typically spend alternate 6- to 12-week periods attending classes full-time and working full-time in the service departments of sponsoring dealers. Because students spend time gaining valuable work experience, these programs may take as long as four years to complete, instead of the normal two years required to earn an associate degree in automotive service technology. However, they offer students the opportunity to earn money while going to school and promise a job upon graduation. Also, some sponsoring dealers provide students with financial assistance for tuition or the purchase of tools.

The National Automotive Technicians Education Foundation (NATEF), an affiliate of the National Institute for Automotive Service Excellence (ASE), certifies automobile mechanic training programs offered by high schools and postsecondary trade schools, technical institutes, and community colleges. While NATEF certification is voluntary, and many institutions have not sought it, certification does signify that the program meets uniform standards for instructional facilities, equipment, staff credentials, and curriculum. In early 1995, more than 850 high school and postsecondary automotive mechanic training programs had been certified by NATEF.

Knowledge of electronics is increasingly desirable for automotive mechanics because electronics is being used in a growing variety of automotive components. Engine controls and dashboard instruments were among the first components to use electronics, but now electronics are being used in brakes, transmissions, steering systems, and a variety of other components. In the past, problems involving electrical systems or electronics were usually handled by a specialist, but electronics are becoming so commonplace that most automotive mechanics must be familiar with at least the basic principles of electronics in order to recognize when an electronic malfunction may be responsible for a problem. In addition, automotive mechanics frequently must be able to test and replace electronic components.

For trainee mechanic jobs, employers look for people with good reading and basic mathematics and computer skills who can study technical manuals to keep abreast of new technology. People who have a desire to learn new service and repair procedures and specifications are excellent candidates for trainee mechanic jobs. Trainees also must possess mechanical aptitude and knowledge of how automobiles work. Most employers regard the successful completion of a vocational training program in automotive mechanics at a postsecondary institution as the best preparation for trainee positions. Experience working on motor vehicles in the Armed Forces or as a hobby is also valuable. Completion of high school is required by a growing number of employers. Courses in automotive repair, electronics, physics, chemistry, English, computers, and mathematics can provide a good basic educational background for a career as an automotive mechanic.

Beginners usually start as trainee mechanics, helpers, lubrication workers, or gasoline service station attendants and gradually acquire and practice their skills by working with experienced mechanics. Although a beginner can perform many routine service tasks and make simple repairs after a few months' experience, it usually takes one to two years of experience to acquire adequate proficiency to become a journey service mechanic and quickly perform the more difficult types of routine service and repairs. However, graduates of the better postsecondary mechanic training programs are often able to earn promotion to the journey level after only a few months on the job. An additional one to two years are usually required to become thoroughly experienced and familiar with all types of repairs. Difficult specialties, such as transmission repair, require another year or two of training and experience. In contrast, automotive radiator mechanics and brake specialists, who do not need an all-round knowledge of automotive repair, may learn their jobs in considerably less time.

In the past, many persons have become automotive mechanics through three- or four-year formal apprenticeship programs. However, as formal automotive training programs have increased in popularity, the number of employers willing to make such a long-term apprenticeship commitment has greatly declined.

Mechanics usually buy their handtools, and beginners are expected to accumulate tools as they gain experience. Many experienced mechanics have thousands of dollars invested in tools. Employers furnish power tools, engine analyzers, and other test equipment.

Employers increasingly send experienced automotive mechanics to manufacturer training centers to learn to repair new models or to receive special training in the repair of components such as electronic fuel injection or air-conditioners. Motor vehicle dealers may also send promising beginners to manufacturer sponsored mechanic training programs. Factory representatives come to many shops to conduct short training sessions.

Voluntary certification by ASE is widely recognized as a standard of achievement for automotive mechanics. Mechanics are certified in one or more of eight different service areas, such as electrical systems, engine repair, brake systems, suspension and steering, and heating and air conditioning. Master automotive mechanics are certified in all eight areas. For certification in each area, mechanics must have at least two years of experience and pass a written examination; completion of an automotive mechanic program in high school, vocational or trade school, or community or junior college may be substituted for one year of experience. Certified mechanics must retake the examination at least every five years.

Experienced mechanics who have leadership ability may advance to shop supervisor or service manager. Mechanics who work well with customers may become automotive repair service estimators. Some with sufficient funds open independent repair shops.

## Job Outlook

Job opportunities in this occupation are expected to be good for persons who complete automotive training programs in high school, vocational and technical schools, or community colleges. Persons whose training includes basic electronics skills should have the best opportunities. Persons without formal mechanic training are likely to face competition for entry-level jobs. Mechanic careers are attractive to many because extensive training is not required and they afford the opportunity for good pay and the satisfaction of skilled work with one's hands.

Employment of automotive mechanics is expected to increase about as fast as the average for all occupations through the year 2005. Growth in mechanic employment in automobile dealerships, independent automotive repair shops, specialty car care chains, and other establishments will be offset somewhat by declining employment in gasoline service stations, because fewer stations offer repair services.

Nevertheless, the number of mechanics is expected to increase because expansion of the driving age population will increase the number of motor vehicles on the road. The growing complexity of automotive technology, such as the use of electronic and emissions control equipment, increasingly necessitates that cars be serviced by skilled workers, contributing to growth in demand for highly trained mechanics. In addition, if the average age of automobiles in operation continues to be high, a significant proportion of consumers' vehicle operating expenditures will be spent on service and repairs, and less on purchasing vehicles. However, improvements in the reliability of automobiles, together with less frequent requirements for routine service, are expected to result in continued declines in the service and repair needs of cars.

More job openings are expected for automotive mechanics than for most other occupations because replacement needs, the main source of job openings, will be substantial, due in large part to the size of the occupation. Replacements will be needed as experienced workers transfer to other occupations or retire or stop working for other reasons.

Most persons who enter the occupation may expect steady work because changes in economic conditions have little effect on the automotive repair business. During a downturn, however, some employers may be more reluctant to hire inexperienced workers.

## Earnings

Median weekly earnings of automotive mechanics who were wage and salary workers were $439 in 1994. The middle 50 percent earned between $308 and $624 a week. The lowest paid 10 percent earned less than $228 a week, and the top 10 percent earned more than $792 a week.

Many experienced mechanics employed by automotive dealers and independent repair shops receive a commission related to the labor cost charged to the customer. Under this method, weekly earnings depend on the amount of work completed by the mechanic. Employers frequently guarantee commissioned mechanics a minimum weekly salary.

Some mechanics are members of labor unions. The unions include the International Association of Machinists and Aerospace Workers; the International Union, United Automobile, Aerospace and Agricultural Implement Workers of America; the Sheet Metal Workers' International Association; and the International Brotherhood of Teamsters.

## Related Occupations

Other workers who repair and service motor vehicles include diesel truck and bus mechanics, motorcycle mechanics, and automotive body repairers, painters, customizers, and repair service estimators.

## Related *D.O.T.* Jobs

These job titles are related to or more specific than the more general description above. They will help you identify job options you may not otherwise discover. These descriptions are in the current edition of the *Dictionary of Occupational Titles* and classified by numerical order.

620.261-010 AUTOMOBILE MECHANIC; 620.261-012 AUTOMOBILE-MECHANIC APPRENTICE; 620.261-030 AUTOMOBILE-SERVICE-STATION MECHANIC; 620.261-034 AUTOMOTIVE-COOLING-SYSTEM DIAGNOSTIC TECHNICIAN; 620.281-010 AIR-CONDITIONING MECHANIC; 620.281-026 BRAKE REPAIRER; 620.281-034 CARBURETOR MECHANIC; 620.281-038 FRONT-END MECHANIC; 620.281-062 TRANSMISSION MECHANIC; 620.281-066 TUNE-UP MECHANIC; 620.281-070 VEHICLE-FUEL-SYSTEMS CONVERTER; 620.381-010 AUTOMOBILE-RADIATOR MECHANIC; 620.381-022 REPAIRER, HEAVY; 620.682-010 BRAKE-DRUM-LATHE REPAIRER; 620.684-018 BRAKE ADJUSTER; 620.684-022 CLUTCH REBUILDER; 706.381-046 WHEELWRIGHT; 721.281-010 AUTOMOTIVE GENERATOR AND STARTER REPAIRER; 806.361-026 NEW-CAR GET-READY MECHANIC; 806.684-038 AUTOMOBILE-ACCESSORIES INSTALLER; 807.664-010 MUFFLER INSTALLER; 807.684-022 FLOOR SERVICE WORKER, SPRING; 825.381-014 AUTOMATIC-WINDOW-SEAT-AND-TOP-LIFT REPAIRER

## Sources of Additional Information

For more details about work opportunities, contact local automotive dealers and repair shops, or the local office of the state employment service. The state employment service also may have information about training programs.

A list of certified automotive mechanic training programs may be obtained from:

❑ National Automotive Technicians Education Foundation, 13505 Dulles Technology Dr., Herndon, VA 22071-3415.

Information on automobile manufacturer sponsored two-year associate degree programs in automotive service technology may be obtained from:

❑ ASSET Program, Training Department, Ford Parts and Service Division, Ford Motor Company, Room 109, 3000 Schaefer Rd., Dearborn, MI 48121.

❑ Chrysler Dealer Apprenticeship Program, National C.A.P. Coordinator, CIMS 423-21-06, 26001 Lawrence Ave., Center Line, MI 48015, or by calling 1-800-626-1523.

❑ General Motors Automotive Service Educational Program, National College Coordinator, General Motors Service Technology Group, 30501 Van Dyke Ave., Warren, MI 48090, or by calling 1-800-828-6860.

Information on how to become a certified automotive mechanic is available from:

❑ ASE, 13505 Dulles Technology Dr., Herndon, VA 22071-3415.

For general information about the work of automotive mechanics, write to:

❑ Automotive Service Association, Inc., 1901 Airport Freeway, Bedford, TX 76021-5732.

❑ Automotive Service Industry Association, 25 Northwest Point, Elk Grove Village, IL 60007-1035.

For a directory of accredited private trade and technical schools that offer programs in automotive technician training, write to:

❑ Accrediting Commission of Career Schools and Colleges of Technology, 2101 Wilson Blvd., Suite 302, Arlington, VA 22201.

For a list of public automotive mechanic training programs, contact:

❑ Vocational Industrial Clubs of America, P.O. Box 3000, 1401 James Monroe Highway, Leesburg, VA 22075.

# Barbers and Cosmetologists

## Nature of the Work

Looking your best has never been easy. It requires the perfect hairstyle, exquisite nails, a neatly trimmed beard, or the proper make-up to accent your coloring. More and more, it also requires the services of barbers and cosmetologists. As people increasingly demand styles that are better suited to their individual characteristics and have available to them a vast array of cosmetic products, they rely on these workers to help them make sense of the different options. Although tastes and fashions change from year to year, the basic job of barbers and cosmetologists remains the same—to help people look their best.

Barbers cut, trim, shampoo, and style hair. Many people still go to a barber for just a haircut, but an increasing number seek more personalized hairstyling services. Barbers trained in these areas work in barber shops and styling salons that serve both men and women. Today, it is common for a barber to color or perm a customer's hair. In addition, barbers may fit hairpieces, provide hair and scalp treatments, shave male customers, or give facial massages. In most states, barbers are licensed to perform all the duties of cosmetologists except skin care and nail treatment.

Cosmetologists primarily shampoo, cut, and style hair, but they also provide a number of other services. These workers, who are often called hairstylists, may advise patrons on how to care for their hair, straighten or permanent wave a customer's hair, or lighten or darken hair color. In addition, most cosmetologists are trained to give manicures, pedicures, and scalp and facial treatments; provide makeup analysis for women; and clean and style wigs and hairpieces. Other workers include electrologists—who remove hair from skin by electrolysis—and estheticians—who cleanse and beautify the skin. Cosmetologists generally are licensed to provide all of the services that barbers do except shaving men.

In addition to their work with customers, barbers and cosmetologists are expected to keep their work area clean and their hairdressing implements sanitized. They may make appointments and keep records of hair color and permanent wave formulas used by their regular patrons. A growing number also actively sell hair products and other cosmetic supplies. Barbers and cosmetologists who operate their own salons have managerial duties that include hiring, supervising, and firing workers, as well as keeping records and ordering supplies.

## Working Conditions

Barbers and cosmetologists generally work in clean, pleasant surroundings with good lighting and ventilation. Good health and stamina are important because these workers usually have to be on their feet for most of their shift. Prolonged exposure to some hair and nail chemicals may be hazardous and cause irritation, so special care must be taken when working with these chemicals.

Most full-time barbers and cosmetologists work 40 hours a week, but long hours are common in this occupation, especially among self-employed workers. This often includes evenings and weekends, when beauty and barber shops and salons are busiest. Although weekends and lunch periods are generally very busy, barbers and cosmetologists may have some time off during slack periods. One of every three barbers and cosmetologists works part-time. The abundance of part-time jobs attracts many persons who want to combine a job with family, school, or other responsibilities.

## Employment

Barbers and cosmetologists held about 709,000 jobs in 1994; 9 of every 10 were cosmetologists. Most worked in beauty salons, barber shops, or department stores, and a few were employed by hospitals, hotels, and prisons. Approximately four of every five barbers and half of all cosmetologists are self-employed.

Nearly every town has a barber shop or beauty salon, but employment in this occupation is concentrated in the most populous cities and states. Hairstylists usually work in cities and suburbs, where the greatest demand for their services exists. Stylists who set fashion trends with their hairstyles usually work in New York City, Los Angeles, and other centers of fashion and the performing arts.

## Training, Other Qualifications, and Advancement

Although all states require barbers and cosmetologists to be licensed, the qualifications necessary to obtain a license vary. Generally, a person must have graduated from a state-licensed barber or cosmetology school, pass a physical examination, and be at least 16 years old. Some states require graduation from high school while others require as little as an eighth-grade education. In a few states, completion of an apprenticeship can substitute for graduation from a school, but very few barbers or cosmetologists learn their skills in this way. Applicants for a license usually are required to pass a written test and demonstrate an ability to perform basic barbering or cosmetology services.

Some states have reciprocity agreements that allow licensed barbers and cosmetologists to practice in a different state without additional formal training. Other states do not recognize training or licenses obtained in another state; consequently, persons who wish to become a barber or a cosmetologist should review the laws of the state in which they want to work before entering a training program.

Public and private vocational schools offer daytime or evening classes in barbering and cosmetology. These programs usually last 6 to 12 months. An apprenticeship program can last from one to two years. Formal training programs include classroom study, demonstrations, and practical work. Students study the basic services—haircutting, shaving, facial massaging, and hair and scalp treatments—and, under supervision, practice on customers in school "clinics." Most schools also teach unisex hairstyling and chemical styling. Students attend lectures on barber services, the use and care of instruments, sanitation and hygiene, and recognition of certain skin ailments. Instruction also is given in selling and general business practices. There are also advanced courses for experienced barbers in hairstyling, coloring, and the sale and service of hairpieces. Most schools teach hairstyling of men's as well as women's hair.

After graduating from a training program, students can take the state licensing examination. The examination consists of a written test and, in some cases, a practical test of cosmetology skills. A few states include an oral examination in which the applicant is asked to explain the procedures he or she is following while taking the practical test. In many states, cosmetology training may be credited toward a barbering license, and vice versa. A few states have even combined the two licenses into one hair styling license. In most states, a separate examination is given for people who want only a manicurist, massage, or facial care license.

Persons who want to become barbers or cosmetologists must have finger dexterity and a sense of form and artistry. They should enjoy dealing with the public and be willing and able to follow patrons' instructions. Some cosmetology schools consider people skills to be so integral to the job that they require coursework in this area. Because hairstyles are constantly changing, barbers and cosmetologists must keep abreast of the latest fashions and beauty techniques. Business skills are important for those who plan to operate their own salons, and the ability to be an effective sales-person is becoming vital for nearly all barbers and cosmetologists.

Many schools help their graduates find jobs. During their first months on the job, new workers are given relatively simple tasks, such as giving shampoos, or are assigned the simpler hair-styling patterns. Once they have demonstrated their skills, they are gradually permitted to perform the more complicated tasks such as giving shaves, coloring hair, or applying a permanent.

Advancement usually is in the form of higher earnings as barbers and cosmetologists gain experience and build a steady clientele. Some barbers and cosmetologists manage large salons or open their own after several years of experience. Some teach in barber or cosmetology schools. Others become sales representatives for cosmetics firms, open businesses as beauty or fashion consultants, or work as examiners for state licensing boards.

### Job Outlook

Overall employment of barbers and cosmetologists is expected to grow about as fast as the average for all occupations through the year 2005. Population growth, rising incomes, and a growing demand for the services that they provide will stimulate the demand for these workers. Within this occupation, however, different employment trends are expected. Cosmetologists will account for virtually all of the employment growth, reflecting the continuing shifts in consumer preferences to more personalized services in unisex establishments. Demand for manicurists and for cosmetologists who are trained in nail care will be particularly strong. Employment of barbers is expected to decline slightly, but in spite of this decline, a couple of thousand job openings will arise annually for new barber licensees as older barbers retire.

Many job openings will become available in the cosmetology field due to the large size of the occupation and the expected employment growth. This is especially true for entry-level workers who are licensed to provide a broad range of cosmetology services. The level of competition for employment and customers may be greater at the higher-paying, prestigious salons, though, as applicants vie with a large pool of licensed and experienced cosmetologists. The number of part-time and self-employed, booth-renting cosmetologists should continue to grow, creating many opportunities for ambitious people to enter the field.

### Earnings

Barbers and cosmetologists receive income either from commissions or wages and tips. Their median annual income in 1994 was $14,800. A number of factors determine the total income for barbers and cosmetologists, including the size and location of the shop, the number of hours worked, customers' tipping habits, and the competition from other barber shops and salons. A cosmetologist's or barber's initiative and ability to attract and hold regular customers are also key factors, so these workers may play an important role in determining their earnings. In fact, 1 out of 10 barbers and cosmetologists earned over $26,800 in 1994. Earnings for entry-level workers are generally lower, ranging from the minimum wage to considerably more in prestigious or exceptionally busy salons.

A growing number of barbers and cosmetologists rent chairs or booths from salons on a daily or hourly basis. These workers are essentially self-employed, and their earnings are a function of their "book," or clientele list.

### Related Occupations

Other workers whose main activity consists of improving a patron's personal appearance include beauty consultants, make-up and wig specialists, and salon and health club managers. Other related workers are employed in the cosmetology industry as instructors and beauty supply distributors.

### Related *D.O.T.* Jobs

These job titles are related to or more specific than the more general description above. They will help you identify job options you may not otherwise discover. These descriptions are in the current edition of the *Dictionary of Occupational Titles* and classified by numerical order.

330.371-010 BARBER; 330.371-014 BARBER APPRENTICE; 331.674-010 MANICURIST; 331.674-014 FINGERNAIL FORMER; 332.271-010 COSMETOLOGIST; 332.271-014 COSMETOLOGIST APPRENTICE; 332.271-018 HAIR STYLIST; 332.361-010 WIG DRESSER; 333.071-010 MAKE-UP ARTIST; 333.271-010 BODY-MAKE-UP ARTIST; 339.361-010 MORTUARY BEAUTICIAN; 339.371-010 ELECTROLOGIST; 339.371-014 SCALP-TREATMENT OPERATOR

### Sources of Additional Information

A list of licensed training schools and licensing requirements for cosmetologists can be obtained from:

❑ National Accrediting Commission of Cosmetology Arts and Sciences, 901 North Stuart St., Suite 900, Arlington, VA 22203-1816.

Information about barber and cosmetology schools also is available from:

❑ American Association of Cosmetology Schools, 901 North Washington St., Suite 206, Alexandria, VA 22314.

❑ Accrediting Commission of Career Schools and Colleges of Technology, 2101 Wilson Blvd., Suite 302, Arlington, VA 22201.

For details on state licensing requirements and approved barber or cosmetology schools, contact the state board of barber examiners or the state board of cosmetology in your state capital.

## Bindery Workers

### Nature of the Work

The process of combining printed sheets into finished products such as books, magazines, catalogs, folders, or directories is known as "binding." Binding involves cutting, folding, gathering, gluing, stitching, trimming, sewing, wrapping, and other finishing operations. Bindery workers operate and maintain the machines performing these various tasks.

Job duties depend on the kind of material being bound. In firms that do *edition binding*, for example, workers bind books produced in large numbers or "runs." *Job binding* workers bind books produced in smaller quantities. In firms that specialize in *library binding*, workers repair books and provide other specialized binding services to libraries. *Pamphlet binding* workers produce leaflets and folders, and *manifold binding* workers bind business forms such as ledgers and books of sales receipts. *Blank book binding* workers bind blank pages to produce notebooks, checkbooks, address books, diaries, calendars, and note pads.

Some binding consists of only one step. Preparing leaflets or newspaper inserts, for example, requires only folding. Binding of books, on the other hand, requires the following steps.

Bookbinders assemble books from large, flat, printed sheets of paper. Many skilled bookbinders also bind magazines. Machines are used extensively throughout the process. Skilled bookbinders operate machines that first fold printed sheets into units known as "signatures," which are groups of pages arranged sequentially. Bookbinders then sew, stitch, or glue the assembled signatures together, shape the book bodies with presses and trimming machines, and reinforce them with glued fabric strips. Covers are created separately, and glued, pasted, or stitched onto the book bodies. The books then undergo a variety of finishing operations, often including wrapping in paper jackets.

A small number of bookbinders work in hand binderies. These highly skilled workers design original or special bindings for limited editions or restore and rebind rare books. The work requires creativity, knowledge of binding materials, and a thorough background in the history of binding. Hand bookbinding gives individuals the opportunity to work at the greatest variety of jobs.

Bindery workers in small shops may perform many binding tasks, while those in large shops are usually assigned only one or a few operations, such as operating complicated paper cutters or folding machines. Others specialize in adjusting and preparing equipment, and may when necessary perform minor repairs.

## Working Conditions

Binderies are often noisy and jobs can be fairly strenuous, requiring considerable lifting, standing, and carrying. They may also require stooping, kneeling, and crouching. Binding often resembles an assembly line, and workers should not mind performing repetitive tasks.

## Employment

In 1994, bindery workers held about 78,000 jobs, including more than 5,900 working as skilled bookbinders and nearly 72,000 working as lesser skilled bindery machine operators.

Although some bindery workers are employed by large libraries and book publishers, the majority of jobs are in commercial printing plants. Few publishers maintain their own manufacturing facilities, so most contract out the printing and assembly of books to commercial printing plants or bindery trade shops. Bindery trade shops, the second largest employer of bindery workers, specialize in binding for printers without binderies, or whose printing production exceeds their binding capabilities.

Bindery workers are employed in all parts of the country, but jobs are concentrated near large metropolitan areas such as New York, Chicago, Washington, D.C., Los Angeles, Philadelphia, and Dallas.

## Training, Other Qualifications, and Advancement

For bindery jobs, employers prefer high school graduates with basic mathematics and language skills. Accuracy, patience, neatness, and good eyesight are also important. Bindery work requires careful attention to detail, because mistakes at this stage in the printing process can cost a lot. Finger dexterity is essential to count, insert, paste, and fold, and mechanical aptitude is needed to operate the newer, more automated equipment. Artistic ability and imagination are necessary for hand bookbinding.

Most bindery workers learn the craft through on-the-job training. Inexperienced workers are usually assigned simple tasks such as moving paper from cutting machines to folding machines. They learn basic binding skills, including the characteristics of paper and how to cut large sheets of paper into different sizes with the least amount of waste. As workers gain experience, they advance to more difficult tasks and learn how to operate one or more pieces of equipment. Generally, it takes one to three months to learn how to operate the simpler machines well, but it can take up to one year to learn how to operate the more complex equipment, such as computerized binding machines.

Employers prefer to hire and train workers with some basic knowledge of binding operations. High school students interested in bindery careers can gain some exposure to the craft by taking shop courses or attending a vocational-technical high school. Occupational skill centers, usually operated by labor unions, also provide an introduction.

Formal apprenticeships are not as common as they used to be, but are still offered by some employers. They provide a more structured program that enables workers to acquire the high levels of specialization and skill needed for some bindery jobs. For example, a four-year apprenticeship usually is necessary to teach workers how to restore rare books and to produce valuable collectors' items.

Training in graphic arts is also an asset. Postsecondary programs in the graphic arts are offered by vocational-technical institutes, skill updating or retraining programs, and community and junior colleges. Some updating and retraining programs require students to have bindery experience; other programs are available through unions for members. Four-year colleges also offer programs, but their emphasis on preparing people for careers as graphic artists or managers in the graphic arts field. To keep pace with ever-changing technology, occasional retraining will become increasingly important for bindery workers.

Advancement opportunities in bindery work are limited. In large binderies, experienced bookbinders may advance to supervisory positions.

## Job Outlook

Employment of bindery workers is expected to grow more slowly than the average for all occupations through the year 2005 as demand for printed material grows but productivity in bindery operations increases. Most job openings for bindery workers will result from the need to replace experienced workers who change jobs or leave the labor force.

Growth of the printing industry will continue to spur demand for bindery workers by commercial printers. The volume of printed material should grow due to increased marketing of products through catalogs, newspaper inserts, and direct mail advertising. Book publishing is expected to continue to grow in response to rising school enrollments, and the expanding middle-aged and older population—age groups that do the most leisure reading.

Even though major technological changes are not anticipated, binding is becoming increasingly mechanized. New "in-line" equipment performs a number of operations in sequence, beginning with raw stock and ending with a complete finished product. Growth in requirements for bindery workers who assist skilled bookbinders will be slowed as binding machinery continues to become more efficient.

Opportunities for hand bookbinders are limited by the small number of establishments that do this highly specialized work. Experienced bindery workers will have the best opportunities.

## Earnings

Bindery workers in 1994 had median weekly earnings of about $396. The middle 50 percent earned about $283 to $539 a week. The lowest paid 10 percent earned less than $205 a week, while the highest paid 10 percent earned $673 a week or more. Workers covered by union contracts generally had higher earnings.

## Related Occupations

Other workers who set up and operate production machinery include papermaking machine operators, press operators, and various precision machine operators.

## Related *D.O.T.* Jobs

These job titles are related to or more specific than the more general description above. They will help you identify job options you may not otherwise discover. These descriptions are in the current edition of the *Dictionary of Occupational Titles* and classified by numerical order.

653.360-010 CASING-IN-LINE SETTER; 653.360-018 BINDERY-MACHINE SETTER; 653.382-010 FOLDING-MACHINE OPERATOR; 653.382-014 COLLATING-MACHINE OPERATOR; 653.662-010 STITCHING-MACHINE OPERATOR; 653.682-010 BOOK-SEWING-MACHINE OPERATOR II; 653.682-014 COVERING-MACHINE OPERATOR; 653-682-018 HEAD-BANDER-AND-LINER OPERATOR; 653.682-022 TINNING-MACHINE SET-UP OPERATOR; 653.685-010 BINDERY WORKER; 653.685-014 BOOK-SEWING-MACHINE OPERATOR I; 653.685-018 CASE-MAKING-MACHINE OPERATOR; 653.685-022 MAGAZINE REPAIRER; 653.685-026 ROUNDING-AND-BACKING-MACHINE OPERATOR; 653.685-030 SPIRAL BINDER; 692.685-146 SADDLE-AND-SIDE WIRE STITCHER; 794.687-026 FORWARDER; 977.381-010 BOOKBINDER; 977.381-014 BOOKBINDER APPRENTICE; 977.684-026 BENCH WORKER, BINDING

## Sources of Additional Information

Information about apprenticeships and other training opportunities may be obtained from local printing industry associations, local bookbinding shops, local offices of the Graphic Communications International Union, or local offices of the state employment service.

For general information on bindery occupations, write to:

❏ Graphic Communications International Union, 1900 L St. NW, Washington, DC 20036.

For information on careers and training programs in printing and the graphic arts, contact:

❏ Education Council of the Graphic Arts Industry, 1899 Preston White Dr., Reston, VA 22091-4326.

❏ PIA-PrintED Accreditation Program for the Graphic Arts, 100 Daingerfield Rd., Alexandria, VA 22314.

# Blue-Collar Worker Supervisors

## Nature of the Work

For the millions of workers who assemble manufactured goods, service electronics equipment, build office buildings, load trucks, or perform thousands of other activities, a blue-collar worker supervisor is the boss. These supervisors ensure that workers, equipment, and materials are used properly and efficiently to maximize productivity. They are often responsible for very expensive and complex equipment or systems. Supervisors make sure machinery is set up correctly and schedule or perform repairs and maintenance work. Supervisors create work schedules, keep production and employee records, monitor employees and ensure that work is done correctly and on time. They organize the workers' activities and make any necessary adjustments to ensure that work continues uninterrupted. Supervisors also train new workers and ensure the existence of a safe working environment.

Blue-collar worker supervisors may have other titles, such as first-line supervisor or foreman/forewoman. In the textile industry, they may be referred to as second hands; on ships they may be called boatswains. In the construction industry, they can be referred to as superintendents, crew chiefs, or foremen/forewomen, depending upon the type and size of their employer. Tool pushers or gang pushers are the common terms used to describe blue-collar supervisors in the oil drilling business.

Regardless of industry setting or job title, a supervisor's primary responsibility is to ensure that the work gets done. The way supervisors accomplish this task, however, is changing in some organizations. In companies that have restructured their operations for maximum efficiency, supervisors use computers to schedule work flow, monitor the quality of their workers' output, keep track of materials used, update their inventory control system, and perform other supervisory tasks. New management philosophies emphasize fewer levels of management and greater employee power and decision making. In the past, supervisors used their power and authority to direct the efforts of their subordinates; increasingly, supervisors are assuming the role of a facilitator for groups of workers, aiding in group decision making and conflict resolution.

Blue-collar worker supervisors have many interpersonal tasks related to their job as well. They inform workers about company plans and policies; recommend good performers for wage increases, awards, or promotions; and deal with poor performers by outlining expectations, counseling workers in proper methods, issuing warnings, or recommending disciplinary action. They also meet on a regular basis with their managers, reporting any problems and discussing possible solutions. Supervisors also meet among themselves to discuss goals, company operations, and performance. In companies with labor unions, supervisors must follow all provisions of labor-management contracts.

## Working Conditions

Many blue-collar worker supervisors work in a shop environment. They may be on their feet much of the time overseeing the work of subordinates and may work near loud and dangerous machinery. Other supervisors, such as those in construction and oil exploration and production, may work outdoors and are subject to all kinds of weather conditions.

Supervisors may be on the job before other workers arrive and stay after they leave. Some supervisors work in plants that operate around the clock and may work any one of three shifts as well as on weekends and holidays. In some cases, supervisors work all three shifts on a rotating basis; in others, shift assignments are made on the basis of seniority.

## Employment

Blue-collar worker supervisors held about 1.9 million jobs in 1994. Although salaried supervisors are found in almost all industries, 4 of every 10 worked in manufacturing—supervising the production of industrial machinery, motor vehicles, appliances, and thousands of other products. Other industries employing blue-collar worker supervisors included construction, wholesale and retail trade, public utilities, repair shops, transportation, and government. Employment is distributed in much the same way as the population, and jobs are located in all cities and towns.

## Training, Other Qualifications, and Advancement

When choosing supervisors, employers generally look for experience, job knowledge, organizational skills, and leadership qualities. Employers emphasize the ability to motivate employees, maintain high morale, and command respect. In addition, employers desire well rounded applicants who are able to deal with different situations and different types of people. Communication and interpersonal skills are extremely important attributes in this occupation.

Completion of high school is often the minimum educational requirement to become a blue-collar worker supervisor, but workers generally need training in human resources and management before they advance to these positions. Although many workers still rise through the ranks with high school diplomas, employers are increasingly hiring applicants with postsecondary technical degrees. In high-technology industries, such as aerospace and electronics, employers typically require a bachelor's degree or technical school training. Employers in the manufacturing sector generally prefer a background in engineering, mathematics, science, business administration, or industrial relations. Large companies usually offer better opportunities than smaller companies for promotion to blue-collar worker supervisor positions.

In most manufacturing companies, a degree in business or engineering combined with in-house training is needed to advance to department head or production manager. In the construction industry, supervisors increasingly need a degree in construction management or engineering, particularly if they expect to advance to project manager, operations manager, or general superintendent. Some use their skills and experience to start their own construction contracting firms. Supervisors in repair shops may open their own business.

## Job Outlook

No change is expected in the employment of blue-collar worker supervisors through the year 2005. Because the occupation is so large, however, many openings will arise from the need to replace workers who transfer to other occupations or leave the labor force.

Job prospects vary by industry. In manufacturing, employment of supervisors is expected to decline slightly as the trend continues for supervisors to oversee more workers. This reflects the increasing use of computers to meet supervisory responsibilities such as scheduling, the effects of worker empowerment programs that relieve supervisors of some of the more time-consuming tasks, and corporate downsizing. In construction and most other nonmanufacturing industries, employment of blue-collar worker supervisors is expected to rise along with the employment of the workers they supervise.

Because of their skill and seniority, blue-collar worker supervisors often are protected from layoffs during a recession. However, some in the highly cyclical construction industry may be laid off when construction activity declines.

## Earnings

Median weekly earnings for blue-collar worker supervisors were about $610 in 1994. The middle 50 percent earned between $450 and $810. The lowest 10 percent earned less than $360, while the highest 10 percent earned over $1,080. Most supervisors earn significantly more than their subordinates. While most blue-collar workers are paid by the hour, the majority of supervisors receive an annual salary. Some supervisors receive extra pay when they work overtime. Typical benefits for these workers include health and life insurance, pension plans, paid vacation, and sick leave.

## Related Occupations

Other workers with supervisory duties include those who supervise professional, technical, sales, clerical, and service workers. Some of these are retail store or department managers, sales managers, clerical supervisors, bank officers, head tellers, hotel managers, postmasters, head cooks, head nurses, and surveyors.

## Related *D.O.T.* Jobs

These job titles are related to or more specific than the more general description above. They will help you identify job options you may not otherwise discover. These descriptions are in the current edition of the *Dictionary of Occupational Titles* and classified by numerical order.

There are too many *D.O.T.* titles to list here. Most are variations related to a specific industry, and we have included a small number of representative *D.O.T.* titles as examples. Complete lists are available in various career software published by JIST or directly from the U.S. Department of Labor.

184.167-050 MAINTENANCE SUPERVISOR; 184.167-262 TRAIN DISPATCHER; 185.167-058 SERVICE MANAGER; 509.130-014 SUPERVISOR, POWER-REACTOR; 515.130-010 MILL SUPERVISOR; 519.131-010 FOUNDRY SUPERVISOR; 522.132-010 SUPERVISOR, MALT HOUSE; 526.131-010 BAKERY SUPERVISOR; 529.132-014 PLANT SUPERVISOR; 529.137-014 SANITARIAN; 529.137-074 SUPERVISOR, INSPECTION; 542.130-010 SUPERVISOR, NATURAL-GAS PLANT; 550.132-010 SUPERVISOR II; 559.132-010 ACID SUPERVISOR; 559.132-018 CATALYST OPERATOR, CHIEF; 559.134-010 QUALITY-CONTROL SUPERVISOR; 570.132-014 MILLING SUPERVISOR; 621.131-014 SUPERVISOR, AIRCRAFT MAINTENANCE; 939.137-010 CHIEF DISPATCHER

## Sources of Additional Information

For information on educational programs for blue-collar worker supervisors, contact:

❑ American Management Association, 135 West 50th St., New York, NY 10020.

❑ National Management Association, 2210 Arbor Blvd., Dayton, OH 45439.

❑ American Institute of Constructors, 466 94th Ave. North, St. Petersburg, FL 33702.

❑ Enterprises, 1429 Colonial Blvd., Suite 203, Fort Myers, FL 33907.

# Boilermakers

## Nature of the Work

Boilermakers and boilermaker mechanics make, install, and repair boilers, vats, and other large vessels that hold liquids and gases. Boilers supply steam to drive huge turbines in electric power plants and to provide heat or power in buildings, factories, and ships. Tanks and vats are used to process and store chemicals, oil, beer, and hundreds of other products.

Boilers and other high-pressure vessels are usually made in sections by casting each piece out of molten iron or steel. Manufacturers are increasingly automating this process to increase quality. The boiler sections are then welded together, often using automated orbital welding machines, which make more consistent welds than possible by hand. Small boilers may be assembled in the manufacturing plant; larger boilers are usually assembled on site.

Following blueprints, boilermakers locate and mark reference points on the boiler foundation for installing boilers and other vessels, using straightedges, squares, transits, and tape measures. They attach rigging and signal crane operators to lift heavy frame and plate sections and other parts into place. They align sections, using plumb bobs, levels, wedges, and turnbuckles; use hammers, files, grinders, and cutting torches to remove irregular edges so they fit properly; and bolt or weld them together. Boilermakers align and attach water tubes, stacks, valves, gauges, and other parts and test complete vessels for leaks or other defects. Usually they assemble large vessels temporarily in a fabrication shop to insure a proper fit and again on their permanent site.

Because boilers last for a long time—35 years or longer—boilermakers regularly maintain them and update components such as burners and boiler tubes to make them as efficient as possible. Boilermaker mechanics maintain and repair boilers and similar vessels. They clean or direct others to clean boilers and inspect tubes, fittings, valves, controls, and auxiliary machinery. They repair or replace defective parts, using hand and power tools, gas torches, and welding equipment, and may operate metalworking machinery to repair or make parts. They also dismantle leaky boilers, patch weak spots with metal stock, replace defective sections, or strengthen joints.

## Working Conditions

Boilermakers often use potentially dangerous equipment such as acetylene torches and power grinders, handle heavy parts, and work on ladders or on top of large vessels. Work may be done in cramped quarters inside boilers, vats, or tanks that often are damp and poorly ventilated. To reduce the chance of injuries, they may wear hard hats, harnesses, respirators, protective clothing, and safety glasses and shoes. Boilermakers usually work a 40-hour week but may experience extended periods of overtime when equipment is shut down for maintenance. Overtime work may also be required to meet construction or production deadlines.

## Employment

Boilermakers held about 20,000 jobs in 1994. About 44 percent worked in manufacturing, primarily in boiler manufacturing shops, iron and steel plants, petroleum refineries, chemical plants, and shipyards. One-third worked in the construction industry, assembling and erecting boilers and other vessels. Some also work for boiler repair firms, railroads, and in Navy shipyards and federal power facilities.

## Training, Other Qualifications, and Advancement

Most training authorities recommend a formal apprenticeship to learn this trade. Some people become boilermakers by working as helpers to experienced boilermakers, but generally lack the wide range of skills acquired through apprenticeship. Apprenticeship programs usually consist of four years of on-the-job training, supplemented by about 144 hours of classroom instruction each year in subjects such as set-up and assembly rigging, welding of all types, blueprint reading, and layout. Experienced boilermakers often attend apprenticeship classes to keep their knowledge current.

When an apprenticeship becomes available, the local union will publicize the opportunity by notifying local vocational schools and high school vocational programs. Qualified applicants take an aptitude test administered by the union specifically designed for boilermaking. The apprenticeship is awarded to the person scoring highest on this test.

When hiring helpers, employers prefer high school or vocational school graduates. Courses in shop, mathematics, blueprint reading, welding, and machine metalworking are useful. Mechanical aptitude and the manual dexterity needed to handle tools also are important.

Some boilermakers advance to supervisory positions; because of their broader training, apprentices generally have an advantage in promotion.

## Job Outlook

Persons who wish to become boilermakers may face some competition, due to the limited number of apprenticeships available and the relatively good wages a journey boilermaker earns. In addition, employment of boilermakers is expected to decline through the year 2005. However, a limited number of openings will arise from the need to replace experienced workers who leave the occupation.

Growth should be limited by several factors: The trend toward repairing and retrofitting rather than replacing existing boilers; the use of smaller boilers, which require less on-site assembly; automation of production technologies; and an increase in the use of imported boilers.

Most of the industries that purchase boilers are sensitive to economic conditions. Therefore, during economic downturns, construction boilermakers may be laid off. However, because boilers are maintained and repaired even during economic downturns, boilermaker mechanics generally have more stable employment.

## Earnings

According to the limited data available, boilermakers who usually worked full-time had median earnings of about $532 per week in 1994.

According to the International Brotherhood of Boilermakers, journey boilermakers earned $21.20 per hour in 1994. Apprentices started at 60 percent of journey wages, or about $12.70 hourly, with wages increasing gradually to the journey wage as progress is made in the apprenticeship. However, wages vary greatly around the country, with higher wages in Northeastern, Great Lakes, and Far Western cities than in other areas of the country.

Most boilermakers belong to labor unions. The principal union is the International Brotherhood of Boilermakers. Others are members of the International Association of Machinists, the United Automobile Workers, and the United Steelworkers of America.

## Related Occupations

Workers in a number of other occupations assemble, install, or repair metal equipment or machines. These include assemblers, blacksmiths, instrument makers, ironworkers, machinists, millwrights, patternmakers, plumbers, sheetmetal workers, tool and die makers, and welders.

## Related *D.O.T.* Jobs

These job titles are related to or more specific than the more general description above. They will help you identify job options you may not otherwise discover. These descriptions are in the current edition of the *Dictionary of Occupational Titles* and classified by numerical order.

805.261-010 BOILERMAKER APPRENTICE; 805.261-014 BOILERMAKER I; 805.361-010 BOILERHOUSE MECHANIC; 805.361-014 BOILERMAKER FITTER; 805.381-010 BOILERMAKER II

## Sources of Additional Information

For further information regarding boilermaking apprenticeships or other training opportunities, contact local offices of the unions previously mentioned, local construction companies and boiler manufacturers, or the local office of the state employment service.

For general information regarding boilermaking and opportunities in the boiler manufacturing industry, contact:

❏ American Boiler Manufacturing Association, 950 North Glebe Rd., Suite 160, Arlington, VA 22203-1824.

# Bricklayers and Stonemasons

## Nature of the Work

Bricklayers and stonemasons work in closely related trades that produce attractive, durable surfaces and structures. The work they perform varies in complexity, from laying a simple masonry walkway to installing the ornate exterior of a high-rise building. *Bricklayers* build walls, floors, partitions, fireplaces, chimneys, and other structures with brick, precast masonry panels, concrete block, and other masonry materials. Some specialize in installing firebrick linings in industrial furnaces. *Stonemasons* build stone walls as well as set stone exteriors and floors. They work with two types of stone—natural cut, such as marble, granite, and limestone, and artificial stone made from concrete, marble chips, or other masonry materials. Stonemasons usually work on structures such as houses of worship, hotels, and office buildings.

In putting up a wall, bricklayers build the corners of the structure first. Because of the necessary precision, these corner leads are very time consuming to erect and require the skills of the most experienced bricklayers on the job. After the corner leads are complete, less experienced bricklayers fill in the wall between the corners, using a line from corner to corner to guide each course or layer of brick. Because of the expense associated with building corner leads, an increasing number of bricklayers are using corner poles, also called masonry guides, that enable them to build the entire wall at the same time. They fasten the corner posts or poles in a plumb position to define the wall line and stretch a line between them. The line serves as a guide for each course of brick. Bricklayers then spread a bed of mortar (a cement, sand, and water mixture) with a trowel (a flat, bladed metal tool with a handle), place the brick on the mortar bed, and then press and tap it into place. As blueprints specify, they either cut brick with a hammer and chisel or saw them to fit around windows, doors, and other openings. Mortar joints are finished with jointing tools for a sealed, neat, and uniform appearance. Although bricklayers generally use steel supports or "lintels" at window and door openings, they sometimes build brick arches that support and enhance the beauty of the brickwork.

Bricklayers are assisted by hod carriers, or helpers, who bring brick and other materials, mix mortar, and set up and move the scaffolding.

Stonemasons often work from a set of drawings in which each stone has been numbered for identification. Helpers may locate and bring the prenumbered stones to the masons. A derrick operator using a hoist may be needed to lift large pieces into place.

When building a stone wall, masons set the first course of stones into a shallow bed of mortar. They align the stones with wedges, plumblines, and levels, and adjust them into position with a hard rubber mallet. Masons build the wall by alternating layers of mortar and courses of stone. As the work progresses, they remove the wedges and fill the joints between stones and use a pointed metal tool, called a "tuck pointer," to smooth the mortar to an attractive finish. To hold large stones in place, stonemasons attach brackets to the stone and weld or bolt them to anchors in the wall. Finally, masons wash the stone with a cleansing solution to remove stains and dry mortar.

When setting stone floors, which often consist of large and heavy pieces of stone, masons first trowel a layer of damp mortar over the surface to be covered. Using crowbars and hard rubber mallets for aligning and leveling, they then set the stone in the mortar bed. To finish, workers fill the joints and wash the stone slabs.

Masons use a special hammer and chisel to cut stone. They cut it along the grain to make various shapes and sizes. Valuable pieces often are cut with a saw that has a diamond blade. Some masons specialize in setting marble which, in many respects, is similar to setting large pieces of stone. Bricklayers and stonemasons also repair imperfections and cracks or replace broken or missing masonry units in walls and floors.

Most nonresidential buildings are now built with prefabricated panels made of concrete block, brick veneer, stone, granite, marble, tile, or glass. In the past, bricklayers did mostly interior work, such as block partition walls and elevator shafts. Now they must be more versatile and work with many materials. For example, bricklayers now install lighter-weight insulated panels used in new skyscraper construction.

*Refractory masons* are bricklayers who specialize in installing firebrick and refractory tile in high-temperature boilers, furnaces, cupolas, ladles, and soaking pits in industrial establishments. Most work in steel mills, where molten materials flow on refractory beds from furnaces to rolling machines.

## Working Conditions

Bricklayers and stonemasons usually work outdoors. They stand, kneel, and bend for long periods and often have to lift heavy materials. Common hazards include injuries from tools and falls from scaffolds, but these can be avoided when proper safety practices are followed.

## Employment

Bricklayers and stonemasons held about 147,000 jobs in 1994. The vast majority were bricklayers. Workers in these crafts are employed primarily by special trade, building, or general contractors. They work throughout the country but, like the general population, are concentrated in metropolitan areas. Nearly 3 of every 10 bricklayers and stonemasons are self-employed. Many of the self-employed specialize in contracting on small jobs such as patios, walks, and fireplaces.

## Training, Other Qualifications, and Advancement

Most bricklayers and stonemasons pick up their skills informally by observing and learning from experienced workers. Many get training in vocational education schools. The best way to learn these skills, however, is through an apprenticeship program, which generally provides the most thorough training.

Individuals who learn the trade on the job usually start as helpers, laborers, or mason tenders. They carry materials, move scaffolds, and mix mortar. When the opportunity arises, they are taught to spread mortar, lay brick and block, or set stone. As they gain experience, they make the transition to full-fledged craft workers. The learning period generally lasts much longer than an apprenticeship program, however.

Apprenticeships for bricklayers and stonemasons usually are sponsored by local contractors or by local union-management committees. The apprenticeship program requires three years of on-the-job training in addition to a minimum 144 hours of classroom instruction each year in subjects such as blueprint reading, mathematics, layout work, and sketching.

Apprentices often start by working with laborers, carrying materials, mixing mortar, and building scaffolds. This period generally lasts about a month and familiarizes them with job routines and materials. Next, they learn to lay, align, and join brick and block. Apprentices also learn to work with stone and concrete. This enables them to be certified to work with more than one masonry material.

Applicants for apprenticeships must be at least 17 years old and in good physical condition. A high school education is preferable, and courses in mathematics, mechanical drawing, and shop are helpful. The International Masonry Institute, a division of the International Union of Bricklayers and Allied Craftsmen,

operates training centers in several large cities that help job seekers develop the skills they will need to successfully complete the formal apprenticeship program.

Experienced workers can advance to supervisory positions or become estimators. They also can open contracting businesses of their own.

## Job Outlook

Job opportunities for skilled bricklayers and stonemasons are expected to be good as the growth in demand outpaces the supply of workers trained in this craft. Employment of bricklayers and stonemasons is expected to grow about as fast as the average for all occupations through the year 2005, and additional openings will result from the need to replace bricklayers and stonemasons who retire, transfer to other occupations, or leave the trades for other reasons. However, the pool of young workers available to enter training programs will also be increasing slowly and many in that group are reluctant to seek training for jobs that may be strenuous and have uncomfortable working conditions.

Population and business growth will create a need for new factories, schools, hospitals, offices, and other structures, increasing the demand for bricklayers and stonemasons. Also stimulating demand will be the need to restore a growing stock of old masonry buildings, as well as the increasing use of brick for decorative work on building fronts and in lobbies and foyers. Brick exteriors should continue to be very popular as the trend continues toward more durable exterior materials requiring less maintenance. Employment of bricklayers who specialize in refractory repair will decline, along with employment in other occupations in the primary metal industries.

Employment of bricklayers and stonemasons, like that of many other construction workers, is sensitive to changes in the economy. When the level of construction activity falls, workers in these trades can experience periods of unemployment.

## Earnings

Median weekly earnings for bricklayers and stonemasons were about $486 in 1994. The middle 50 percent earned between $338 and $648 weekly. The highest 10 percent earned more than $830 weekly; the lowest 10 percent, less than $261. Earnings for workers in these trades may be reduced on occasion because poor weather and downturns in construction activity limit the time they can work.

In each trade, apprentices or helpers usually start at about 50 percent of the wage rate paid to experienced workers. This increases as they gain experience.

Some bricklayers and stonemasons are members of the International Union of Bricklayers and Allied Craftsmen.

## Related Occupations

Bricklayers and stonemasons combine a thorough knowledge of brick, concrete block, stone, and marble with manual skill to erect very attractive yet highly durable structures. Workers in other occupations with similar skills include concrete masons, plasterers, terrazzo workers, and tilesetters.

## Related *D.O.T.* Jobs

These job titles are related to or more specific than the more general description above. They will help you identify job options you may not otherwise discover. These descriptions are in

the current edition of the *Dictionary of Occupational Titles* and classified by numerical order.

779.684-058 STONE REPAIRER; 861.361-010 COMPOSITION-STONE APPLICATOR; 861.361-014 MONUMENT SETTER; 861.381-010 ACID-TANK LINER; 861.381-014 BRICKLAYER; 861.381-018 BRICKLAYER; 861.381-022 BRICKLAYER APPRENTICE; 861.381-026 BRICKLAYER, FIREBRICK AND REFRACTORY TILE; 861.381-030 MARBLE SETTER; 861.381-038 STONEMASON; 861.381-042 STONEMASON APPRENTICE; 861.684-010 CUPOLA PATCHER; 861.684-014 PATCHER; 899.364-010 CHIMNEY REPAIRER

## Sources of Additional Information

For details about apprenticeships or other work opportunities in these trades, contact local bricklaying, stonemasonry, or marble setting contractors; a local of the union listed above; a local joint union-management apprenticeship committee; or the nearest office of the state employment service or state apprenticeship agency.

For general information about the work of either bricklayers or stonemasons, contact:

❏ International Union of Bricklayers and Allied Craftsmen, International Masonry Institute Apprenticeship and Training, 815 15th St. NW, Suite 1001, Washington, DC 20005.

Information about the work of bricklayers also may be obtained from:

❏ Associated General Contractors of America, Inc., 1957 E St. NW, Washington, DC 20006.

❏ Brick Institute of America, 11490 Commerce Park Dr., Reston, VA 22091-1525.

❏ Home Builders Institute, National Association of Home Builders, 1201 15th St. NW, Washington, DC 20005.

❏ National Concrete Masonry Association, 2302 Horse Pen Rd., Herndon, VA 22071.

# Broadcast Technicians

## Nature of the Work

Broadcast technicians install, test, repair, set up, and operate the electronic equipment used to record and transmit radio and television programs. They work with television cameras, microphones, tape recorders, light and sound effects, transmitters, antennas, and other equipment. Some broadcast technicians develop movie sound tracks in motion picture production studios.

In the control room of a radio or television broadcasting studio, these technicians operate equipment that regulates the signal strength, clarity, and range of sounds and colors of recording or broadcasts. They also operate control panels to select the source of the material. Technicians may switch from one camera or studio to another, from film to live programming, or from network to local programs. By means of hand signals and, in television, telephone headsets, they give technical directions to studio personnel.

Broadcast technicians in small stations perform a variety of duties. In large stations and at the networks, technicians are more specialized, although job assignments may change from day to day. The terms "operator," "engineer," and "technician" often are used interchangeably to describe these jobs. *Transmitter operators* monitor and log outgoing signals and operate transmitters. *Maintenance technicians* set up, adjust, service, and repair electronic broadcasting equipment. *Audio control engineers* regulate sound pickup, transmission, and switching of television pictures while *video control engineers* regulate their quality, brightness, and contrast. *Recording engineers* operate and maintain video and sound recording equipment. They may operate equipment designed to produce special effects, such as the illusions of a bolt of lightning or a police siren. *Field technicians* set up and operate broadcasting portable field transmission equipment outside the studio.

Television news coverage requires so much electronic equipment, and the technology is changing so fast, that many stations assign technicians exclusively to news. *Chief engineers, transmission engineers*, and *broadcast field supervisors* supervise the technicians who operate and maintain broadcasting equipment.

Technicians in the motion picture industry are called *sound mixers* or *rerecording mixers*. Mixers produce the sound track of a movie using a process called dubbing. They sit at sound consoles facing the screen and fade in and fade out each sound and regulate its volume. Each technician is responsible for certain sounds. Technicians follow a script that tells at precisely what moment, as the film runs through the projector, each of the sounds must be faded in and out. All the sounds for each shot are thus blended on a master sound track.

## Working Conditions

Broadcast technicians generally work indoors in pleasant surroundings. However, those who broadcast from disaster areas or crime scenes may work under less favorable conditions. Technicians doing maintenance may climb poles or antenna towers, while those setting up equipment do heavy lifting.

Technicians in large stations and the networks usually work a 40-hour week, but may occasionally work overtime under great pressure to meet broadcast deadlines. Technicians in small stations routinely work more than 40 hours a week. Evening, weekend, and holiday work is usual because most stations are on the air 18 to 24 hours a day, seven days a week. Those who work on motion pictures may be on a tight schedule to finish according to contract agreements.

## Employment

Broadcast technicians held about 42,000 jobs in 1994. About 7 out of 10 broadcast technicians were in radio and television broadcasting. Almost 2 in 10 worked in the motion picture industry. About 8 percent worked for cable and other pay television services. Some were self employed. Television stations employ, on average, many more technicians than radio stations. Some are employed in other industries, producing employee communications, sales, and training programs. Technician jobs in television are located in virtually all cities, while jobs in radio are also found in most smaller towns. The highest paying and most specialized jobs are concentrated in New York City, Los Angeles, Chicago, and Washington, D.C.—the originating centers for most of network programs. Motion picture production jobs are concentrated in Los Angeles and New York City.

## Training, Other Qualifications, and Advancement

The best way to prepare for a broadcast technician job in radio and television—particularly for those who hope to advance to supervisory positions or to jobs in large stations and at the networks—is to obtain technical school, community college, or college training in broadcast technology or in engineering or electronics. On the other hand, there is no formal training for jobs in the motion picture industry. People are hired as apprentice editorial assistants and work their way up to more skilled jobs. Reputation, determination, and luck are important in getting jobs.

Federal law requires a restricted radiotelephone operator permit for persons who operate and maintain broadcast transmitters in radio and television stations. No examination is required to obtain one. The Federal Communications Commission no longer requires persons working with microwave to have a general radiotelephone operator license; however, some states may require a license.

Beginners learn skills on the job from experienced technicians and supervisors. They generally begin their careers in small stations and, if qualified, move on to larger ones. Large stations generally only hire technicians with experience. Many employers pay tuition and expenses for courses or seminars to help technicians keep abreast of developments in the field.

Certification by the Society of Broadcast Engineers is a mark of competence and experience. The certificate is issued to experienced technicians who pass an examination.

Prospective technicians should take high school courses in math, physics, and electronics. Building electronic equipment from hobby kits and operating a "ham" or amateur radio are good experience, as is work in college radio and television stations.

Broadcast technicians must have an aptitude for working with electrical and mechanical systems and equipment and manual dexterity.

Experienced technicians may become supervisory technicians or chief engineers. A college degree in engineering is generally needed to become chief engineer at a large TV station.

## Job Outlook

People seeking beginning jobs as radio and television broadcast technicians are expected to face strong competition in major metropolitan areas, where the number of qualified job seekers greatly exceeds the number of openings. There, stations seek highly experienced personnel. Prospects for entry-level positions generally are better in small cities and towns for people with appropriate training.

Employment of broadcast technicians is expected to decline through the year 2005. Employment in radio and television broadcasting is expected to decline because of laborsaving technical advances such as computer-controlled programming and remote control of transmitters. This has shifted the emphasis from operations to maintenance work, which frequently is performed by commercial and industrial electronic equipment repairers employed by broadcasting equipment manufacturers.

Employment in the motion picture industry will grow about as fast as the average for all occupations. Job prospects are expected to remain competitive, however, because of the large number of people attracted to this relatively small field.

Virtually all job openings will result from the need to replace experienced technicians who leave the occupation. Turnover is relatively high for broadcast technicians. Many leave the occupation for electronic jobs in other areas such as computer technology or commercial and industrial repair because the number of jobs is limited in large cities where pay is high.

## Earnings

Television stations usually pay higher salaries than radio stations; commercial broadcasting usually pays more than educational broadcasting; and stations in large markets pay more than those in small ones.

According to a survey conducted by the National Association of Broadcasters and the Broadcast Cable Financial Management Association, the average earnings for technicians at radio stations were $23,569 a year in 1994. For chief engineer, average earnings were $43,500 and the range was $34,256 to $57,937. In television, the average earnings for operator technician were $24,260 a year, and salaries ranged from $16,422 in the smallest markets to $45,158 in the largest markets; for technical director, the average earnings were $25,962 and the range was $18,444 to $44,531; for maintenance technician, the average was $32,533 and the range was $24,210 to $50,235; and for chief engineer, the average was $53,655 and the salaries ranged from $38,178 in the smallest markets to $91,051 in the largest markets.

Earnings in the motion picture industry depend on skill and reputation, and, based on limited information, range from $20,000 to $100,000 a year.

## Related Occupations

Broadcast technicians need the electronics training and hand coordination necessary to operate technical equipment, and they generally complete specialized postsecondary programs. Others with similar jobs and training include drafters, engineering and science technicians, surveyors, air traffic controllers, radiologic technologists, respiratory therapy workers, cardiovascular technologists and technicians, electroneurodiagnostic technicians, and clinical laboratory technologists and technicians.

## Related *D.O.T.* Jobs

These job titles are related to or more specific than the more general description above. They will help you identify job options you may not otherwise discover. These descriptions are in the current edition of the *Dictionary of Occupational Titles* and classified by numerical order.

193.167-014 FIELD SUPERVISOR, BROADCAST; 193.262-018 FIELD ENGINEER; 193.262-038 TRANSMITTER OPERATOR; 194.062-010 TELEVISION TECHNICIAN; 194.122-010 ACCESS COORDINATOR, CABLE TELEVISION; 194.262-010 AUDIO OPERATOR; 194.262-014 SOUND CONTROLLER; 194.262-018 SOUND MIXER; 194.262-022 MASTER CONTROL OPERATOR; 194.282-010 VIDEO OPERATOR; 194.362-010 RECORDING ENGINEER; 194.362-014 RERECORDING MIXER; 194.362-018 TELECINE OPERATOR; 194.362-022 TECHNICIAN, NEWS GATHERING; 194.382-014 TAPE TRANSFEROR; 194.382-018 VIDEOTAPE OPERATOR; 962.167-010 MANAGER, SOUND EFFECTS; 962.382-010 RECORDIST

## Sources of Additional Information

For information about licensing, write to:

❏ Federal Communications Commission, Consumer Assistance Office, 1270 Fairfield Rd., Gettysburg, PA 17325-7245 or call 1 800 322-1117.

For information on careers for broadcast technicians, write to:

❑ National Association of Broadcasters Employment Clearinghouse, 1771 N St. NW, Washington, DC 20036.

For a list of schools that offer programs or courses in broadcasting, contact:

❑ Broadcast Education Association, National Association of Broadcasters, 1771 N St. NW, Washington, DC 20036.

For information on certification, contact:

❑ Society of Broadcast Engineers, 8445 Keystone Crossing, Suite 140, Indianapolis, IN 46240.

# Butchers and Meat, Poultry, and Fish Cutters

### Nature of the Work

Butchers and meat, poultry, and fish cutters carve animal carcasses into small pieces of meat suitable for sale to consumers. In meat-packing plants, *meatcutters* slaughter cattle, hogs, goats, and sheep and cut the carcasses into large wholesale cuts such as rounds, loins, ribs, and chucks to facilitate handling, distribution, and marketing. Meat trimmings are used to prepare sausages, luncheon meats, and other fabricated meat products. Meatcutters usually work on assembly lines, with each individual responsible for only a few of the many cuts needed to process a carcass. Depending on the type of cut, they may use knives, cleavers, meat saws, bandsaws, and other equipment.

In grocery stores, wholesale establishments that supply meat to restaurants, and institutional food service facilities, *butchers* separate the wholesale cuts of meat into retail cuts or individual size servings. They cut the meat into steaks and chops using knives and electric saws, shape and tie roasts, and grind beef for sale as chopped meat. Boneless cuts are prepared using knives, slicers, or power cutters, while bandsaws are required on bone-in pieces. Butchers in retail food stores also may weigh, wrap, and label the cuts and arrange them in refrigerated cases for display to customers. They also may prepare special cuts of meat ordered by customers.

*Poultry cutters* slaughter and cut up chickens, turkeys, and other types of poultry. The poultry processing industry is becoming increasingly automated, but many jobs such as trimming, packing, and deboning are still done manually.

*Fish cleaners* cut, scale, and dress fish in fish processing plants and wholesale and retail fish markets. They remove the head, scales, and other inedible portions and cut the fish into steaks or boneless fillets. In markets, they may wait on customers and clean fish to order.

Retail meat, poultry, and fish cutters also prepare ready-to-heat foods. This often entails filleting meat or fish or cutting it into bite-sized pieces, preparing and adding vegetables, or applying sauces or breading.

### Working Conditions

Working conditions vary by the type and size of establishment. In meat-packing plants and larger retail food establishments, butchers and meatcutters work in large meat-cutting rooms equipped with power machines and conveyors. In small retail markets, the butcher or fish cleaner may work in a space behind the meat counter. To avoid viral and bacterial infections, work areas must be clean and sanitary.

Butchers and meat, poultry, and fish cutters often work in cold, damp rooms. Cutting rooms are refrigerated to prevent meat from spoiling; they are damp because meat cutting generates large amounts of blood and fat. The low temperature, combined with the need to stand for long periods of time, makes the work tiring. Butchers and meat, poultry, and fish cutters are more susceptible to injury than other workers. In 1992, meat-packing plants had the highest incidence of work-related injury and illness of any industry. Cuts and even amputations, occur when knives, cleavers, and power tools are used improperly. The cool damp floors of meat processing areas increase the likelihood of slips and falls. Repetitive slicing and lifting often leads to cumulative trauma injuries, such as carpal tunnel syndrome. To reduce the incidence of cumulative trauma disorders, many employers have reduced work loads, redesigned jobs and tools, and increased awareness of early warning signs. Nevertheless, workers in this occupation still face a serious threat of a disabling injury.

### Employment

Butchers and meat, poultry, and fish cutters held about 351,043 jobs in 1994. Over four-fifths worked in meat-packing and poultry and fish processing plants and retail grocery stores, while others were employed by meat and fish markets, restaurants, hotels, and wholesale establishments. The majority of the 218,994 skilled butchers and meatcutters worked in retail grocery stores, while more than 9 out of 10 of the semiskilled meat, poultry, and fish cutters worked in meat-packing and poultry and fish processing plants. Skilled butchers and meatcutters are employed in almost every city and town in the nation, while semiskilled meat, poultry, and fish cutter jobs are concentrated in communities with food processing plants.

### Training, Other Qualifications, and Advancement

Most butchers and meat, poultry, and fish cutters acquire their skills informally on the job or through apprenticeship programs. A few learn their basic skills by attending trade and vocational schools. However, graduates of these schools may need additional on-the-job training and experience to work as butchers and meatcutters.

Generally, on-the-job trainees begin by doing less difficult jobs, such as removing bones. Under the guidance of experienced workers, they learn the proper use of tools and equipment and how to prepare various cuts of meat. After demonstrating skill with tools, they learn to divide quarters into wholesale cuts and wholesale cuts into retail and individual portions. Trainees may learn to roll and tie roasts, prepare sausage, and cure meat. Those employed in retail food establishments may learn marketing operations such as inventory control, meat buying, and record keeping.

Retail meatcutters and butchers who learn the trade through apprenticeship programs generally complete two years of supervised on-the-job training supplemented by classroom work. At the end of the training period, apprentices must pass a meat-cutting test. In some areas, apprentices may become meatcutters or butchers without completing the entire training program if they can pass the test.

Skills important in meat, poultry, and fish cutting are manual dexterity, good depth perception, color discrimination, and good eye-hand coordination. Also, physical strength is often needed to lift and move heavy pieces of meat. Butchers and fish cleaners who wait on customers must have a pleasant personality, a neat appearance, and the ability to communicate clearly. In some states a health certificate may be required for employment.

Butchers and meat, poultry, and fish cutters may progress to supervisory jobs, such as meat or seafood department managers in supermarkets. A few become meat or seafood buyers for wholesalers and supermarket chains. Some become grocery store managers or open their own meat or fish markets. In processing plants, butchers and meat, poultry, and fish cutters may move up to supervisory positions.

## Job Outlook

Overall employment of butchers and meat, poultry, and fish cutters is expected to grow more slowly than the average for all occupations through the year 2005 as more meat cutting and processing shifts from the retail store to the food processing plant. Nevertheless, job opportunities should be plentiful due to the need to replace experienced workers who transfer to other occupations or leave the labor force.

As the nation's population grows, the demand for meat, poultry, and seafood should continue to increase. Successful marketing by the poultry industry is likely to increase demand for rotisserie chicken and ready-to-heat products. Similarly, the development of lower fat and ready-to-heat products promises to stimulate the consumption of red meat. The demand for fish and seafood should reach record levels in the coming years.

Employment growth of semiskilled meat, poultry, and fish cutters who work primarily in meat-packing, poultry, and fish processing plants is expected to increase faster than the average for all occupations through the year 2005. Although much of the production of poultry and fabricated poultry products is performed by machines, the growing popularity of labor-intensive ready-to-heat goods promises to spur demand for poultry workers. Semiskilled meat and fish cutters also will be in demand as the task of preparing ready-to-heat meat and fish goods slowly shifts from the retail store to the processing plant. Although the supply of edible ocean fish is limited, advances in fish farming, or "aquaculture," are expected to reduce the gap between supply and demand, and produce ample opportunities for fish cutters.

Employment of skilled butchers and meatcutters, who work primarily in retail stores, is expected to decline gradually. Although meat is increasingly cut and processed at meat-packing plants, this transformation is proceeding slowly. At present, most red meat arrives at the grocery store partially cut up. The retail butcher performs the final processing—cutting wholesale meat cuts into steaks, chops, and roasts and packaging them for sale.

Eventually, as ready-to-heat goods become more popular, both fresh meat and prepared foods will be completely processed and packaged at the plant. Consumers and the retail stores are slowly adjusting to this trend, and the demand for retail meat, poultry, and fish cutters should decline.

## Earnings

Butchers and meatcutters had median weekly earnings of $329 in 1994. The middle 50 percent earned between $250 and $522 a week. The highest paid 10 percent earned over $702 a week. Meatcutters employed by retail grocery stores are generally among the highest paid workers.

Butchers and meat and fish cutters generally received paid vacations, sick leave, health insurance, and life insurance. Those who were union members and employed by grocery stores also had pension plans. However, poultry workers tended to rarely earn substantial benefits.

Many butchers and meat, poultry, and fish cutters are members of the United Food and Commercial Workers International Union. In 1992, nearly 30 percent of all butchers and meatcutters were union members or covered by a union contract.

## Related Occupations

Butchers and meat, poultry, and fish cutters must be skilled at both hand and machine work and must have some knowledge of processes and techniques involved in handling and preparing food. Other occupations in food preparation which require similar skills and knowledge include bakers, chefs and cooks, and food preparation workers.

## Related *D.O.T.* Jobs

These job titles are related to or more specific than the more general description above. They will help you identify job options you may not otherwise discover. These descriptions are in the current edition of the *Dictionary of Occupational Titles* and classified by numerical order.

316.681-010 BUTCHER, MEAT; 316.684-018 MEAT CUTTER; 316.684-022 MEAT-CUTTER APPRENTICE; 521.687-058 FISH CHOPPER, GANG KNIFE; 521.687-106 SAUSAGE-MEAT TRIMMER; 521.687-126 SKIN LIFTER, BACON; 525.361-010 SLAUGHTERER, RELIGIOUS RITUAL; 525.381-010 BUTCHER APPRENTICE; 525.381-014 BUTCHER, ALL-ROUND; 525.664-010 MEAT DRESSER; 525.684-010 BONER, MEAT; 525.684-014 BUTCHER, FISH; 525.684-018 CARCASS SPLITTER; 525.684-022 CRAB BUTCHER; 525.684-030 FISH CLEANER; 525.684-038 OFFAL SEPARATOR; 525.684-042 POULTRY KILLER; 525.684-046 SKINNER; 525.684-050 STICKER, ANIMAL; 525.684-054 TRIMMER, MEAT; 525.684-058 TURKEY-ROLL MAKER; 525.687-030 GAMBRELER; 525.687-066 POULTRY BONER; 525.687-074 POULTRY EVISCERATOR; 529.686-022 CUTLET MAKER, PORK

## Sources of Additional Information

Information about work opportunities can be obtained from local employers or local offices of the state employment service. For information on training and other aspects of the trade, contact:

❑ United Food and Commercial Workers International Union, 1775 K St. NW, Washington, DC 20006.

# Cardiovascular Technologists and Technicians

## Nature of the Work

Cardiovascular technologists and technicians assist physicians in diagnosing and treating cardiac (heart) and peripheral vascular (blood vessel) ailments.

Cardiovascular technicians who obtain electro(electrical)-cardio(heart)-grams(record), abbreviated EKGs or ECGs, which trace electrical impulses transmitted by the heart, are known as *electrocardiograph (ECG or EKG) technicians*. To take a "basic" EKG, technicians attach electrodes to the patient's chest, arms, and legs, then manipulate switches on a electrocardiograph machine to obtain the reading. The test is done before most kinds of surgery and as part of a routine physical examination, especially for persons who have reached middle age or have a history of cardiovascular problems.

More skilled EKG technicians perform Holter monitor and stress testing. For a Holter monitoring, technicians place electrodes on the patient's chest and attach a portable EKG monitor to the patient's belt. Following 24 to 48 hours of normal routine for the patient, the technician removes a cassette tape from the monitor and places it in a scanner. After checking the quality of the recorded impulses on an electronic screen, the technician prints the information from the tape so that it can be interpreted later. The printed output from the scanner is eventually used by a physician to diagnose heart ailments.

For a treadmill stress test, EKG technicians document the patient's medical history, explain the procedure, connect the patient to an EKG monitor, and obtain a baseline reading and resting blood pressure. Next, they monitor the heart's performance while the patient is walking on a treadmill, gradually increasing the treadmill's speed to observe the effect of increased exertion. Those cardiovascular technicians who perform EKG and stress tests are known as noninvasive technicians because the techniques they use do not require the insertion of probes or other instruments into the patient's body.

Cardiovascular technologists who specialize in cardiac catheterization procedures are called *cardiology technologists*. They assist physicians with invasive procedures in which a small tube, or catheter, is wound through a patient's blood vessel from a spot on the patient's leg into the heart to determine if a blockage exists or for other diagnostic purposes. In balloon angioplasty, a procedure used to treat blockages of blood vessels, technologists assist physicians who insert a catheter with a balloon on the end to the point of the obstruction. Technologists may prepare patients for these procedures by positioning them on an examining table, then shaving, cleaning, and administering anesthesia to the top of the patient's leg near the groin. During the procedures, they monitor patients' blood pressure and heart rate using EKG equipment and notify the physician if something appears wrong. Technologists may also prepare and monitor patients during open heart surgery and the implantation of pacemakers.

Cardiovascular technologists and technicians may also specialize in noninvasive peripheral vascular tests. They use ultrasound equipment that transmits sound waves, then collects the echoes to form an image on a screen. Individuals who focus on blood flows and circulation problems are known as *vascular technologists*, while those who use ultrasound on the heart are referred to as *echocardiographers*.

Some cardiovascular technologists and technicians schedule appointments, type doctor's interpretations, maintain patient's files, and care for equipment.

## Working Conditions

Technologists and technicians generally work five-day, 40-hour week, which may include Saturdays and Sundays. Those in catheterization labs tend to work longer hours and also may work evenings. They may also be on-call during the night and on weekends.

Cardiovascular technologists and technicians spend a lot of time walking and standing. Those who work in catheterization labs may face stressful working conditions, because they are in close contact with patients who have serious heart ailments. Some patients, for example, may encounter complications from time to time that have life or death implications.

## Employment

Cardiovascular technologists and technicians held about 30,000 jobs in 1994. Most worked in hospital cardiology departments, while some worked in cardiologists' offices, cardiac rehabilitation centers, or health maintenance organizations. About one-half were EKG technicians.

## Training, Other Qualifications, and Advancement

For basic EKGs, Holter monitoring, and stress testing, one-year certificate programs exist, although most EKG technicians are still trained on the job by an EKG supervisor or a cardiologist. On-the-job training usually lasts about 8 to 16 weeks. Applicants must be high school graduates. Most employers prefer to train people already in the health care field, nursing aides, for example. Some EKG technicians are students who are enrolled in two-year programs to become technologists, but work part-time to get experience and make contact with employers. Most vascular technologists are trained on the job although some have backgrounds in nursing and sonography.

Cardiology technologists need to complete a two-year junior or community college program. One year is dedicated to core courses followed by a year of specialized instruction in either invasive, noninvasive, or noninvasive peripheral cardiology. Those who are qualified in a related allied health profession only need to complete the year of specialized instruction.

Cardiovascular technologists must be reliable, have mechanical aptitude, and be able to follow detailed instructions. A pleasant, relaxed manner for putting patients at ease is an asset.

## Job Outlook

Employment of cardiovascular technologists and technicians is expected to grow more slowly than the average for all occupations through the year 2005, with technologists and technicians experiencing different patterns of employment change. Employment of cardiology technologists is expected to grow faster than average for all occupations. Growth will occur as the population ages, because older people have a higher incidence of heart problems. In contrast, employment of EKG technicians is expected to decline as hospitals train registered nurses and others to perform basic EKG procedures. Individuals trained in Holter monitoring and stress testing are expected to have more favorable job prospects than those who can only perform a basic EKG.

Most job openings for cardiovascular technologists and technicians should arise from replacement needs as individuals transfer to other jobs or leave the labor force. Relatively few job opportunities due to both growth and replacement needs are expected, however, because these occupations are small.

## Earnings

According to a University of Texas Medical Branch survey of hospitals and medical centers, the median annual salary of EKG technicians, based on a 40-hour week and excluding shift and area differentials, was $18,396 in October 1994. The average minimum salary was $15,793 and the average maximum was $22,985.

Based on limited information, the average salary for cardiovascular technologists was about $32,000 in 1994.

## Related Occupations

Cardiovascular technologists and technicians operate sophisticated equipment that helps physicians and other allied health practitioners diagnose and treat patients, so do nuclear medicine technologists, radiologic technologists, diagnostic medical sonographers, electroencephalographic technologists, perfusionists, and respiratory therapists.

## Related *D.O.T.* Jobs

These job titles are related to or more specific than the more general description above. They will help you identify job options you may not otherwise discover. These descriptions are in the current edition of the *Dictionary of Occupational Titles* and classified by numerical order.

078.264-010 HOLTER SCANNING TECHNICIAN; 078.362-018 ELECTROCARDIOGRAPH TECHNICIAN; 078.362-030 CARDIOPULMONARY TECHNOLOGIST; 078.362-050 SPECIAL PROCEDURES TECHNOLOGIST, CARDIAC CATHETERIZATION; 078.362-062 STRESS TEST TECHNICIAN; 078.364-014 ECHOCARDIOGRAPH TECHNICIAN; 078.367-010 CARDIAC MONITOR TECHNICIAN

## Sources of Additional Information

Local hospitals can supply information about employment opportunities.

For general information about a career in cardiovascular technology contact:

❑ American Society for Cardiovascular Professionals, 10500 Wakeman Dr., Fredericksburg, VA 22407.

For a list of accredited programs in cardiovascular technology, contact:

❑ Division of Allied Health Education and Accreditation, American Medical Association, 515 N. State St., Chicago, IL 60610.

For information on vascular technology, contact:

❑ The Society of Vascular Technology, 4601 Presidents Dr., Suite 260, Lanham, MD 20706-4365.

# Carpenters

## Nature of the Work

Carpenters are involved in many different kinds of construction activity. They cut, fit, and assemble wood and other materials in the construction of buildings, highways and bridges, docks, industrial plants, boats, and many other structures. Their duties vary by type of employer. A carpenter employed by a special trade contractor, for example, may specialize in one or two activities, such as setting forms for concrete construction or erecting scaffolding. However, a carpenter employed by a general building contractor may perform many tasks, such as framing walls and partitions, putting in doors and windows, hanging kitchen cabinets, and installing paneling and tile ceilings.

Local building codes often dictate where certain materials can be used, and carpenters have to know these requirements. Each carpentry task is somewhat different, but most tasks involve the same basic steps. Working from blueprints or instructions from supervisors, carpenters first do the layout—measuring, marking, and arranging materials. They then cut and shape wood, plastic, ceiling tile, fiberglass, or drywall using hand and power tools, such as chisels, planes, saws, drills, and sanders, and then join the materials with nails, screws, staples, or adhesives. In the final step, they check the accuracy of their work with levels, rules, plumb bobs, and framing squares and make any necessary adjustments. When working with prefabricated components, such as stairs or wall panels, the carpenter's task is somewhat simpler because it does not require as much layout work or the cutting and assembly of as many pieces. These components are designed for easy and fast installation and can generally be installed in a single operation.

Carpenters employed outside the construction industry do a variety of installation and maintenance work. They may replace panes of glass, ceiling tiles, and doors, as well as repair desks, cabinets, and other furniture. Depending on the employer, they may install partitions, doors, and windows; change locks; and repair broken furniture. In manufacturing firms, carpenters may assist in moving or installing machinery.

## Working Conditions

As in other building trades, carpentry work is sometimes strenuous. Prolonged standing, climbing, bending, and kneeling often are necessary. Carpenters risk injury from slips or falls, from working with sharp or rough materials, and from the use of sharp tools and power equipment. Many carpenters work outdoors.

Some carpenters change employers each time they finish a construction job. Others alternate between working for a contractor and working as contractors themselves on small jobs.

## Employment

Carpenters—the largest group of building trades workers—held about 992,000 jobs in 1994. Four of every 5 worked for contractors who build, remodel, or repair buildings and other structures. Most of the remainder worked for manufacturing firms, government agencies, wholesale and retail establishments, and schools. About 4 of every 10 were self-employed.

Carpenters are employed throughout the country in almost every community.

## Training, Other Qualifications, and Advancement

Carpenters learn their trade through on-the-job training and through formal training programs. Some pick up skills informally by working under the supervision of experienced workers. Many acquire skills through vocational education. Others participate in employer training programs or apprenticeships.

Most employers recommend an apprenticeship as the best way to learn carpentry. Because the number of apprenticeship programs is limited, however, only a small proportion of carpenters learn their trade through these programs. Apprenticeship programs are administered by local joint union-management committees of the United Brotherhood of Carpenters and Joiners of America and the Associated General Contractors, Inc. or the National Association of Home Builders. Training programs are administered by local chapters of the Associated Builders and Contractors and by local chapters of the Associated General Contractors, Inc. These programs combine on-the-job training with related classroom instruction. Apprenticeship applicants generally must be at least 17 years old and meet local requirements. For example, some union locals test an applicant's aptitude for carpentry. The length of the program, usually about three to four years, varies with the apprentice's skill.

On the job, apprentices learn elementary structural design and become familiar with common carpentry jobs such as layout, form building, rough framing, and outside and inside finishing. They also learn to use the tools, machines, equipment, and materials of the trade. Apprentices receive classroom instruction in safety, first aid, blueprint reading and freehand sketching, basic mathematics, and different carpentry techniques. Both in the classroom and on the job, they learn the relationship between carpentry and the other building trades.

Informal on-the-job training usually is less thorough than an apprenticeship. The degree of training and supervision often depends on the size of the employing firm. A small contractor who specializes in home-building may only provide training in rough framing. In contrast, a large general contractor may provide training in several carpentry skills. Although specialization is becoming increasingly common, it is important to try to acquire skills in all aspects of carpentry to have the flexibility to be able to do whatever kind of work may be available. Carpenters with a well-rounded background can switch from residential building to commercial construction to remodeling jobs, depending on demand.

A high school education is desirable, including courses in carpentry, shop, mechanical drawing, and general mathematics. Manual dexterity, eye-hand coordination, physical fitness, and a good sense of balance are important. The ability to solve arithmetic problems quickly and accurately also is helpful. Employers and apprenticeship committees generally view favorably training and work experience obtained in the Armed Services and the job corps.

Carpenters may advance to carpentry supervisors or general construction supervisors. Carpenters usually have greater opportunities than most other construction workers to become general construction supervisors because they are exposed to the entire construction process. Some carpenters become independent contractors. To advance, carpenters should be able to estimate the nature and quantity of materials needed to properly complete a job. They also must be able to estimate with accuracy how long a job should take to complete and its cost

## Job Outlook

Job opportunities for carpenters are expected to be plentiful through the year 2005, due primarily to extensive replacement needs. Well over 100,000 job openings will become available each year as carpenters transfer to other occupations or leave the labor force. The total number of job openings for carpenters each year usually is greater than for other craft occupations because the occupation is large and turnover is high. Since there are no strict training requirements for entry, many people with limited skills take jobs as carpenters but eventually leave the occupation because they find they dislike the work or cannot find steady employment.

Increased demand for carpenters will create additional job openings. Employment is expected to increase more slowly than the average for all occupations through the year 2005. Construction activity should increase slowly in response to demand for new housing and commercial and industrial plants and the need to renovate and modernize existing structures. Opportunities for frame carpenters will be particularly good. The demand for carpenters will be offset somewhat by expected productivity gains resulting from the increasing use of prefabricated components, such as prehung doors and windows and prefabricated wall panels and stairs, that can be installed much more quickly. Prefabricated walls, partitions, and stairs can be quickly lifted into place in one operation; beams, and in some cases entire roof assemblies, can be lifted into place using a crane. As prefabricated components become more standardized, their use will increase. In addition, stronger adhesives that reduce the time needed to join materials and lightweight cordless pneumatic and combustion tools such as nailers and drills, as well as sanders with electronic speed controls, will make carpenters more efficient as well as reduce fatigue.

Although employment of carpenters is expected to grow over the long run, people entering the occupation should expect to experience periods of unemployment. This results from the short-term nature of many construction projects and the cyclical nature of the construction industry. Building activity depends on many factors—interest rates, availability of mortgage funds, government spending, and business investment—that vary with the state of the economy. During economic downturns, the number of job openings for carpenters declines. The introduction of new and improved tools, equipment, techniques, and materials has vastly increased carpenters' versatility. Therefore, carpenters with all-round skills will have better opportunities than those who can only do relatively simple, routine tasks.

Job opportunities for carpenters also vary by geographic area. Construction activity parallels the movement of people and businesses and reflects differences in local economic conditions. Therefore, the number of job opportunities and apprenticeship opportunities in a given year may vary widely from area to area.

## Earnings

Median weekly earnings of carpenters, excluding the self-employed, were $424 in 1994. The middle 50 percent earned between $315 and $591 per week. Weekly earnings for the top 10 percent of all carpenters were more than $785; the lowest 10 percent earned less than $252.

Earnings may be reduced on occasion because carpenters lose work time in bad weather and during recessions when jobs are unavailable.

Many carpenters are members of the United Brotherhood of Carpenters and Joiners of America.

## Related Occupations

Carpenters are skilled construction workers. Workers in other skilled construction occupations include bricklayers, concrete masons, electricians, pipefitters, plasterers, plumbers, stonemasons, and terrazzo workers.

## Related *D.O.T.* Jobs

These job titles are related to or more specific than the more general description above. They will help you identify job options you may not otherwise discover. These descriptions are in the current edition of the *Dictionary of Occupational Titles* and classified by numerical order.

806.281-058 CARPENTER, PROTOTYPE; 860.281-010 CARPENTER, MAINTENANCE; 860.281-014 CARPENTER, SHIP; 860.361-010 BOAT BUILDER, WOOD; 860.361-014 BOAT BUILDER APPRENTICE, WOOD; 860.381-010 ACOUSTICAL CARPENTER; 860.381-022 CARPENTER; 860.381-026 CARPENTER APPRENTICE; 860.381-030 CARPENTER, BRIDGE; 860.381-034 CARPENTER, MOLD; 860.381-038 CARPENTER, RAILCAR; 860.381-042 CARPENTER, ROUGH; 860.381-046 FORM BUILDER; 860.381-050 JOINER; 860.381-054 JOINER APPRENTICE; 860.381-058 SHIPWRIGHT; 860.381-062 SHIPWRIGHT APPRENTICE; 860.381-066 TANK BUILDER AND ERECTOR; 860.381-070 TANK ERECTOR; 860.664-010 CARPENTER I; 863.684-010 COMPOSITION-WEATHERBOARD APPLIER; 869.361-018 SIGN ERECTOR-AND-REPAIRER; 869.381-010 HOUSE REPAIRER; 869.381-034 TIMBER FRAMER; 869.684-018 ASSEMBLER, SUBASSEMBLY; 869.684-034 LAY-OUT WORKER; 869.684-042 ROOF ASSEMBLER I; 869.684-058 STOPPING BUILDER; 962.281-010 PROP MAKER

## Sources of Additional Information

For information about carpentry apprenticeships or other work opportunities in this trade, contact local carpentry contractors, locals of the union mentioned above, local joint union-contractor apprenticeship committees, or the nearest office of the state employment service or state apprenticeship agency.

For general information about carpentry, contact:

❏ Associated Builders and Contractors, 1300 North 17th Street, Rosslyn, VA 22209.

❏ Associated General Contractors of America, Inc., 1957 E St. NW, Washington, DC 20006.

❏ Home Builders Institute, National Association of Home Builders, 1201 15th St. NW, Washington, DC 20005.

❏ United Brotherhood of Carpenters and Joiners of America, 101 Constitution Ave. NW, Washington, DC 20001.

# Carpet Installers

## Nature of the Work

Many buildings—including homes, offices, stores, and restaurants—have carpet that was installed by a carpet installer. Before installing the carpet, these craft workers first inspect the surface to be covered to determine its condition and, if necessary, correct any imperfections that could show through the carpet. They must measure the area to be carpeted and plan the layout, keeping in mind expected traffic patterns and placement of seams for best appearance and maximum wear.

When installing wall-to-wall carpet without tacks, installers first fasten a tackless strip to the floor, next to the wall. They then install the padded cushion or underlay. Next, they roll out, measure, mark, and cut the carpet, allowing for two to three inches of extra carpet for the final fitting. Using a knee kicker, they position the carpet, stretching it to fit evenly on the floor and snugly against each wall and door threshold. They then rough cut the excess. Finally, using a power stretcher, they stretch the carpet, hooking it to the tackless strip to hold it in place. The installer then finishes the edges using a wall trimmer.

Because most carpet comes in 12-foot widths, wall-to-wall installations require installers to tape or sew sections together for large rooms. They join the seams by sewing them with a large needle and special thread or by using heat-taped seams—a special plastic tape made to join seams when activated with heat.

On special upholstery work, such as stairs, carpet may be held in place with staples. Also, in commercial installations, carpet is often glued directly to the floor or to padding which has been glued to the floor.

Carpet installers use handtools such as hammers, drills, staple guns, carpet knives, and rubber mallets. They also may use carpet-laying tools, such as carpet shears, knee kickers, wall trimmers, loop pile cutters, heat irons, and power stretchers.

## Working Conditions

Carpet installers generally work regular daytime hours, but when recarpeting stores or offices, they may work evenings and weekends to avoid disturbing customers or employees. Installers usually work under better conditions than most other construction workers, although, the work is very labor intensive. Because carpets are installed in finished or nearly finished structures, work areas usually are clean, well-lighted, safe, and comfortable. Installers kneel, reach, bend, stretch, and frequently lift heavy rolls of carpet. They also may be required to move heavy furniture. Safety regulations may require that they wear knee pads or safety goggles when using certain tools.

## Employment

Carpet installers held about 66,000 jobs in 1994. Many worked for flooring contractors or floor covering retailers. About two-thirds of all carpet installers are self-employed.

Although installers are employed throughout the nation, they tend to be concentrated in urban areas where there are high levels of construction activity.

## Training, Other Qualifications, and Advancement

The vast majority of carpet installers learn their trade informally on the job as helpers to experienced installers. Others learn through formal apprenticeship programs, which include on-the-job training as well as related classroom instruction.

Informal training is often sponsored by individual contractors and generally lasts from about 1 1/2 to 2 years. Helpers begin with simple assignments, such as installing stripping and padding, or helping stretch newly installed carpet. With experience, helpers take on more difficult assignments, such as measuring, cutting, and fitting.

Apprenticeship programs and some contractor-sponsored programs provide comprehensive training in all phases of carpet laying. Most apprenticeship programs are union sponsored and consist of weekly classes and on-the-job training that usually last three to four years.

Persons who wish to begin a career in carpet installation as a helper or apprentice should be 18 years old and have good manual dexterity. Since carpet installers frequently deal directly with customers, they should be courteous and tactful. High school graduation is preferred, though not necessary: courses in general mathematics and shop are helpful. Some employers may require a driver's license and a criminal background check.

Carpet installers may advance to positions as supervisors or installation managers for large installation firms. Some installers become salespersons or estimators. Many installers who begin working for a large contractor or installation firm also eventually go into business for themselves as independent subcontractors.

### Job Outlook

Employment of carpet installers is expected to grow more slowly than the average for all occupations through the year 2005. Growth will be due primarily to the continued need to renovate and refurbish existing structures, which usually involves laying new carpet. Carpet as a floor covering continues to be popular and its usage is expected to grow in structures such as schools, offices, hospitals, and industrial plants.

Demand for carpet will also be stimulated by new, more durable fibers that are stain and crush resistant and which come in a wider variety of colors. More resilient carpet needs to be replaced less often, but these attractive new products may induce more people to replace their old carpeting, contributing further to the demand for carpet installers.

This occupation is less sensitive to changes in economic conditions than most other construction occupations. Because much of their work involves replacing carpet in existing buildings, renovation work usually allows employment of carpet installers to remain relatively stable even when new construction activity declines. In the many houses built with plywood, rather than hardwood floors, wall-to-wall carpeting is a necessity. Similarly, offices, hotels, and stores often cover concrete floors with wall-to-wall carpet, which must be periodically replaced.

### Earnings

Median weekly earnings of all full-time carpet installers were about $412 in 1994. The middle 50 percent earned between $272 and $613 per week. The top 10 percent earned more than $751 and the lowest 10 percent earned less than $195.

Carpet installers get paid either on an hourly basis or by the number of yards installed. The rates vary widely depending on the geographic location and whether the installer is affiliated with a union. Nonunion carpet installers are usually paid by the number of yards installed. In 1994, they received between $1.50 and $3.00 a yard. According to limited information available, union carpet installers earned between $16 and $25 an hour in 1994, including benefits. Benefits average about $3.50 to $4.00 an hour, most of which is for health insurance. Apprentices and other trainees usually start out earning about half of what an experienced worker earns, though their wage rate increases as they advance through the training program. Some installers belong to the United Brotherhood of Carpenters and Joiners of America or the International Brotherhood of Painters and Allied Trades.

### Related Occupations

Carpet installers measure, cut, and fit carpet materials. Workers in other occupations involving similar skills but using different materials include carpenters, cement masons, drywall installers, floor layers, lathers, painters and paperhangers, roofers, sheetmetal workers, terrazzo workers, and tilesetters.

### Related *D.O.T.* Jobs

These job titles are related to or more specific than the more general description above. They will help you identify job options you may not otherwise discover. These descriptions are in the current edition of the *Dictionary of Occupational Titles* and classified by numerical order.

864.381-010 CARPET LAYER

### Sources of Additional Information

For details about apprenticeships or work opportunities, contact local flooring contractors or retailers; locals of the unions previously mentioned; or the nearest office of the state apprenticeship agency or the state employment service.

For general information about the work of carpet installers, contact:

❑ Floor Covering Installation Contractors Association, P.O. Box 948, Dalton, GA 30722-0948.

For information concerning training contact:

❑ United Brotherhood of Carpenters and Joiners of America, 101 Constitution Ave. NW, Washington, DC 20001.

❑ International Brotherhood of Painters and Allied Trades, 1750 New York Ave. NW, Washington, DC 20006.

❑ New York City District Council of Carpenters Labor Technical College, 395 Hudson St., New York, NY 10014.

# Chefs, Cooks, and Other Kitchen Workers

### Nature of the Work

A reputation for serving good food is essential to any restaurant, whether it prides itself on hamburgers and French fries or exotic foreign cuisine. Chefs, cooks, and other kitchen workers are largely responsible for the reputation a restaurant acquires. Some restaurants offer a varied menu featuring meals that are time consuming and difficult to prepare, requiring a highly skilled cook or chef. Other restaurants emphasize fast service, offering hamburgers and sandwiches that can be prepared in advance or in a few minutes by a fast-food or short-order cook with only limited cooking skills.

*Chefs and cooks* are responsible for preparing meals that are pleasing to the palate and the eye. Chefs are the most highly skilled, trained, and experienced of all kitchen workers. Although the terms chef and cook are still used interchangeably, cooks are less skilled. Many chefs have earned fame for both themselves and the establishments where they work due to their skillful preparation of traditional dishes and refreshing twists in creating new ones.

*Institutional chefs and cooks* work in the kitchens of schools, industrial cafeterias, hospitals, and other institutions. For each meal, they prepare a small selection, but large quantity of entrees, vegetables, and desserts. *Restaurant chefs and cooks* generally prepare a wider selection of dishes for each meal, cooking most orders individually. Whether in institutions or restaurants, chefs and cooks measure, mix, and cook ingredients according to recipes. In the course of their work they use a variety of pots, pans, cutlery, and equipment, including ovens, broilers, grills, slicers, grinders, and blenders. They are often responsible for directing the work of other kitchen workers, estimating food requirements, and ordering food supplies. Some chefs and cooks also assist in planning meals and developing menus.

*Bread and pastry bakers*, called pastry chefs in some kitchens, produce baked goods for restaurants, institutions, and retail bakery shops. Unlike bakers who work in large, automated industrial bakeries, bread and pastry bakers need only to supply the customers who visit their establishment. They bake smaller quantities of breads, rolls, pastries, pies, and cakes, doing most of the work by hand. They measure and mix ingredients, shape and bake the dough, and apply fillings and decorations.

*Short-order cooks* prepare foods to order in restaurants and coffee shops that emphasize fast service. They grill and garnish hamburgers, prepare sandwiches, fry eggs, and cook French fried potatoes, often working on several orders at the same time. Prior to busy periods, they may slice meats and cheeses or prepare coleslaw or potato salad. During slow periods, they may clean the grill, food preparation surfaces, counters, and floors.

*Specialty fast-food cooks* prepare a limited selection of menu items in fast-food restaurants. They cook and package batches of food such as hamburgers and fried chicken, which are prepared to order or kept warm until sold.

Other kitchen workers, under the direction of chefs and cooks, perform tasks requiring less skill. They weigh and measure ingredients, fetch pots and pans, and stir and strain soups and sauces. They clean, peel, and slice potatoes, other vegetables, and fruits and make salads. They may cut and grind meats, poultry, and seafood in preparation for cooking. Their responsibilities also include cleaning work areas, equipment and utensils, and dishes and silverware.

The number and types of workers employed in kitchens depends on the type of establishment. For example, fast-food outlets offer only a few items, which are prepared by fast-food cooks. Smaller, full-service restaurants offering a casual dining atmosphere often feature a limited number of easy-to-prepare items, supplemented by short-order specialties and ready-made desserts. Typically, one cook prepares all of the food with the help of a short-order cook and one or two kitchen workers.

Large eating places tend to have varied menus and prepare more of the food they serve from start to finish. Kitchen staffs often include several chefs and cooks, sometimes called assistant or apprentice chefs or cooks, a bread and pastry baker, and many less skilled kitchen workers. Each chef or cook usually has a special assignment and often a special job title—vegetable, fry, or sauce cook, for example. Executive chefs coordinate the work of the kitchen staff and often direct the preparation of certain foods.

They decide the size of servings, sometimes plan menus, and buy food supplies.

## Working Conditions

Many restaurant and institutional kitchens have modern equipment, convenient work areas, and air-conditioning; but in older and smaller eating places, the kitchens often are not as well equipped. Working conditions depend on the type and quantity of food being prepared and the local laws governing food service operations. Workers generally must withstand the pressure and strain of working in close quarters, standing for hours at a time, lifting heavy pots and kettles, and working near hot ovens and grills. Job hazards include slips and falls, cuts, and burns, but injuries are seldom serious.

Work hours in restaurants may include late evenings, holidays, and weekends, while hours in factory, and school cafeterias may be more regular. Half of all short-order and fast-food cooks and other kitchen workers worked part-time; a third of all bakers and restaurant and institutional cooks worked part-time. Kitchen workers employed by public and private schools may work during the school year only, usually for 9 or 10 months. Similarly, establishments at vacation resorts generally only offer seasonal employment.

## Employment

Chefs, cooks, and other kitchen workers held more than 3.2 million jobs in 1994. Short-order and fast-food cooks held 760,000 of the jobs; restaurant cooks, 704,000; institutional cooks, 412,000; bread and pastry bakers, 170,000; and other kitchen workers, 1,190,000.

About three-fifths of all chefs, cooks, and other kitchen workers were employed in restaurants and other retail eating and drinking places. One-fifth worked in institutions such as schools, universities, hospitals, and nursing homes. The remainder were employed by grocery stores, hotels, and many other organizations.

## Training, Other Qualifications, and Advancement

Most kitchen workers start as fast-food or short-order cooks, or in one of the other less skilled kitchen positions. These positions require little education or training and most skills are learned on the job. After acquiring some basic food handling, preparation, and cooking skills, they may be able to advance to an assistant cook or short-order cook position. To achieve the level of skill required of an executive chef or cook in a fine restaurant, many years of training and experience are necessary. Even though a high school diploma is not required for beginning jobs, it is recommended for those planning a career as a cook or chef. High school or vocational school courses in business arithmetic and business administration are particularly helpful.

Many school districts, in cooperation with state departments of education, provide on-the-job training and sometimes summer workshops for cafeteria kitchen workers with aspirations of becoming cooks. Employees who have participated in these training programs are often selected for jobs as cooks.

An increasing number of chefs and cooks obtain their training through high school, post-high school vocational programs, and two- or four-year colleges. Chefs and cooks also may be trained in apprenticeship programs offered by professional culinary institutes, industry associations, and trade unions. An example is the three-year apprenticeship program administered by local chapters of the American Culinary Federation in cooperation with local employers and junior colleges or vocational education institutions. In addition, some large hotels and restaurants operate their own training programs for cooks and chefs.

People who have had courses in commercial food preparation may be able to start in a cook or chef job without having to spend time in a lower skilled kitchen job. Their education may give them an advantage when looking for jobs in better restaurants and hotels, where hiring standards often are high. Some vocational programs in high schools offer this kind of training, but usually these courses are given by trade schools, vocational centers, colleges, professional associations, and trade unions. Post secondary courses range from a few months to two years or more and are open in some cases only to high school graduates. The Armed Forces are also a good source of training and experience.

Although curricula may vary, students usually spend most of their time learning to prepare food through actual practice. They learn to bake, broil, and otherwise prepare food, and to use and care for kitchen equipment. Training programs often include courses in menu planning, determination of portion size, food cost control, purchasing food supplies in quantity, selection and storage of food, and use of leftover food to minimize waste. Students also learn hotel and restaurant sanitation and public health rules for handling food. Training in supervisory and management skills sometimes is emphasized in courses offered by private vocational schools, professional associations, and university programs.

Culinary courses are given by 550 schools across the nation. The American Culinary Federation accredited 70 of these programs in 1993. Accreditation is an indication that a culinary program meets recognized standards regarding course content, facilities, and quality of instruction. The American Culinary Federation has only been accrediting culinary programs for a relatively short time, and many programs have yet to seek accreditation.

Certification provides valuable formal recognition of the skills of a chef or cook. The American Culinary Federation certifies chefs and cooks at the levels of cook, working chef, executive chef, and master chef. It also certifies pastry professionals and culinary educators. Certification standards are based primarily on experience and formal training.

Important qualifications for chefs, cooks, and other kitchen workers include the ability to work as part of a team, possessing a keen sense of taste and smell, and personal cleanliness. Most states require health certificates indicating workers are free from communicable diseases.

Advancement opportunities for chefs and cooks are better than for most other food and beverage preparation and service occupations. Many acquire higher paying positions and new cooking skills by moving from one job to another. Besides culinary skills, advancement also depends on ability to supervise lesser skilled workers and limit food costs by minimizing waste and accurately anticipating the amount of perishable supplies needed. Some cooks and chefs gradually advance to executive chef positions or supervisory or management positions, particularly in hotels, clubs, or larger, more elegant restaurants. Some eventually go into business as caterers or restaurant owners, while oth-

ers become instructors in vocational programs in high schools, community colleges, and other academic institutions.

## Job Outlook

Job openings for chefs, cooks, and other kitchen workers are expected to be plentiful through the year 2005. Growth in demand for these workers will create many new positions, but most openings will arise from the need to replace the high proportion of workers who leave this occupation every year. There is substantial turnover in many of these jobs because of the minimal educational and training requirements. The occupation also offers many part-time positions, attractive to people seeking a short-term source of income rather than a career. Many of the workers who leave these jobs transfer to other occupations, while others stop working to assume household responsibilities or to attend school full-time.

Workers under the age of 25 have traditionally filled a significant proportion of the lesser skilled jobs in this occupation. The pool of young workers is expected to continue to shrink through the 1990s, but begin to expand after the year 2000. Many employers will be forced to offer higher wages, better benefits, and more training to attract and retain workers.

Employment of chefs, cooks, and other kitchen workers is expected to increase about as fast as the average for all occupations through the year 2005. Since a significant proportion of food and beverage sales by eating and drinking establishments is associated with the overall level of economic activity, sales and employment will increase with the growth of the economy. Other factors contributing to employment growth will be population growth, rising household incomes, and an increase in leisure time that will allow people to dine out and take vacations more often. As two income households are becoming more common, families may increasingly find dining out a convenience.

Employment in restaurants is expected to grow. As the average age of the population increases, demand will grow for restaurants that offer table service and more varied menus—which will require higher skilled cooks and chefs. The popularity of fresh baked breads and pastries in fine dining establishments should ensure continued rapid growth in the employment of bakers. However, employment of short-order and specialty fast-food cooks is expected to increase more slowly than other occupations in this group because most work in fast-food restaurants, which are expected to grow at a slower rate than in the past.

Employment of institutional and cafeteria chefs and cooks will grow more slowly than the average. Their employment is concentrated in the educational and health services sectors. Although employment in both sectors is expected to increase rapidly, growth of institutional and cafeteria cooks will not keep pace. Many high schools and hospitals are trying to make "institutional food" more attractive to students, staff, visitors, and patients. While some are employing more highly trained chefs and cooks to prepare more appealing meals, others are contracting out their food services. Many of the contracted companies emphasize fast-food and employ short-order and fast-food cooks instead of institutional and cafeteria cooks.

## Earnings

Wages of chefs, cooks, and other kitchen workers depend greatly on the part of the country and the type of establishment in which they are employed. Wages generally are highest in elegant restaurants and hotels, with many executive chefs earning over $40,000 annually. According to a survey conducted by the National Restaurant Association, median hourly earnings of cooks in 1994 were $6.85, with most earning between $6.00 and $8.00. Assistant cooks had median hourly earnings of $6.25, with most earning between $5.50 and $7.00.

The same survey indicated that short-order cooks had median hourly earnings of $6.50 in 1994; most earned between $5.50 and $7.25. Median hourly earnings of bread and pastry bakers were $6.50; most earned within the range of $6.00 to $7.68. Salad preparation workers generally earned less, with median hourly earnings of $5.50; most earned between $5.25 and $6.50.

Some employers provide employees with uniforms and free meals, but federal law permits employers to deduct from their employees' wages the cost or fair value of any meals or lodging provided, and some employers do so. Chefs, cooks, and other kitchen workers who work full-time often receive paid vacation and sick leave and health insurance, but part-time workers generally do not.

In some large hotels and restaurants, kitchen workers belong to unions. The principal unions are the Hotel Employees and Restaurant Employees International Union and the Service Employees International Union.

### Related Occupations

Workers who perform tasks similar to those of chefs, cooks, and other kitchen workers include butchers and meat cutters, cannery workers, and industrial bakers.

### Related *D.O.T.* Jobs

These job titles are related to or more specific than the more general description above. They will help you identify job options you may not otherwise discover. These descriptions are in the current edition of the *Dictionary of Occupational Titles* and classified by numerical order.

There are too many *D.O.T.* titles to list here. Most are variations related to a specific industry, and we have included a small number of representative *D.O.T.* titles as examples. Complete lists are available in various career software published by JIST or directly from the U.S. Department of Labor.

313.281-010 CHEF DE FROID; 313.361-014 COOK; 313.361-018 COOK APPRENTICE; 313.361-026 COOK, SPECIALTY; 313.361-030 COOK, SPECIALTY, FOREIGN FOOD; 313.361-038 PIE MAKER; 313.374-010 COOK, FAST FOOD; 313.374-014 COOK, SHORT ORDER; 313.381-010 BAKER; 313.381-014 BAKER, PIZZA; 313.381-018 COOK APPRENTICE, PASTRY; 313.381-026 COOK, PASTRY; 313.381-030 COOK, SCHOOL CAFETERIA; 313.381-034 ICE-CREAM CHEF; 313.687-010 COOK HELPER, PASTRY; 315.361-010 COOK; 315.361-022 COOK, STATION; 315.371-010 COOK, MESS; 315.381-010 COOK; 315.381-014 COOK, LARDER; 317.384-010 SALAD MAKER; 317.664-010 SANDWICH MAKER; 317.684-014 PANTRY GOODS MAKER; 317.687-010 COOK HELPER; 319.484-010 FOOD ASSEMBLER, KITCHEN

### Sources of Additional Information

Information about job opportunities may be obtained from local employers and local offices of the state employment service.

Career information about chefs, cooks, and other kitchen workers, as well as a directory of 2- and 4-year colleges that offer courses or programs that prepare persons for food service careers, is available from:

❑ The Educational Foundation of the National Restaurant Association, 250 South Wacker Dr., Suite 1400, Chicago, IL 60606.

For information on the American Culinary Federation's apprenticeship and certification programs for cooks, as well as a list of accredited culinary programs, write to:

❑ American Culinary Federation, P.O. Box 3466, St. Augustine, FL 32085.

For general information on hospitality careers, write to:

❑ Council on Hotel, Restaurant, and Institutional Education, 1200 17th St. NW, Washington, DC 20036-3097.

For general career information and a directory of accredited private career and technical schools offering programs in the culinary arts, write to:

❑ Accrediting Commission of Career Schools and Colleges of Technology, 2101 Wilson Blvd., Suite 302, Arlington, VA 22201.

# Clinical Laboratory Technologists and Technicians

### Nature of the Work

Clinical laboratory testing plays a crucial role in the detection, diagnosis, and treatment of disease. Clinical laboratory technologists and technicians, also known as medical technologists and technicians, perform most of these tests.

Clinical laboratory personnel examine and analyze body fluids, tissues, and cells. They look for bacteria, parasites, or other micro-organisms; analyze the chemical content of fluids; match blood for transfusions, and test for drug levels in the blood to show how a patient is responding to treatment. They also prepare specimens for examination, count cells, and look for abnormal cells. They use automated equipment and instruments that perform a number of tests simultaneously, as well as microscopes, cell counters, and other kinds of sophisticated laboratory equipment to perform tests. Then they analyze the results and relay them to physicians.

The complexity of tests performed, the level of judgment needed, and the amount of responsibility workers assume depend largely on the amount of education and experience they have.

*Medical technologists* generally have a bachelor's degree in medical technology or in one of the life sciences, or have a combination of formal training and work experience. They perform complex chemical, biological, hematological, immunologic, microscopic, and bacteriological tests. Technologists microscopically examine blood, tissue, and other body substances; make cultures of body fluid or tissue samples to determine the presence of bacteria, fungi, parasites, or other micro-organisms; analyze samples for chemical content or reaction; and determine blood glucose or cholesterol levels. They also type and cross-match blood samples for transfusions.

They may evaluate test results, develop and modify procedures, and establish and monitor programs to insure the accuracy of tests. Some medical technologists supervise medical laboratory technicians.

Technologists in small laboratories perform many types of tests, while those in large laboratories generally specialize. Technologists who prepare specimens and analyze the chemical and hormonal contents of body fluids are *clinical chemistry technologists*. Those who examine and identify bacteria and other microorganisms are *microbiology technologists*. *Blood bank technologists* collect, type, and prepare blood and its components for transfusions; *immunology technologists* examine elements and responses of the human immune system to foreign bodies. *Cytotechnologists*, prepare slides of body cells and microscopically examine these cells for abnormalities which may signal the beginning of a cancerous growth.

*Medical laboratory technicians* perform less complex tests and laboratory procedures than technologists. Technicians may prepare specimens and operate automatic analyzers, for example, or they may perform manual tests following detailed instructions. Like technologists, they may work in several areas of the clinical laboratory or specialize in just one. *Histology technicians* cut and stain tissue specimens for microscopic examination by pathologists, and *phlebotomists* draw and test blood. They usually work under the supervision of medical technologists or laboratory managers.

## Working Conditions

Hours and other working conditions vary according to the size and type of employment setting. In large hospitals or in independent laboratories that operate continuously, personnel usually work the day, evening, or night shift, and may work weekends and holidays. Laboratory personnel in small facilities may work on rotating shifts rather than on a regular shift. In some facilities, laboratory personnel are on-call, available in case of an emergency, several nights a week or on weekends.

Clinical laboratory personnel are trained to work with infectious specimens. When proper methods of infection control and sterilization are followed, few hazards exist.

Laboratories generally are well lighted and clean; however, specimens, solutions, and reagents used in the laboratory sometimes produce odors. Laboratory workers may spend a great deal of time on their feet.

## Employment

Clinical laboratory technologists and technicians held about 274,000 jobs in 1994. More than half worked in hospitals. Most others worked in medical laboratories and offices and clinics of physicians. Some worked in blood banks, research and testing laboratories, and in the federal government—at Department of Veterans Affairs hospitals and U.S. Public Health Service facilities. About one laboratory worker in six worked part-time.

## Training, Other Qualifications, and Advancement

The usual requirement for an entry-level position as a medical technologist is a bachelor's degree with a major in medical technology or in one of the life sciences. Universities and hospitals offer medical technology programs. It is also possible to qualify through a combination of on-the-job and specialized training.

Bachelor's degree programs in medical technology include courses in chemistry, biological sciences, microbiology, and mathematics, and specialized courses devoted to knowledge and skills used in the clinical laboratory. Many programs also offer or require courses in management, business, and computer applications.

Masters degrees in medical technology and related clinical laboratory sciences provide training for specialized areas of laboratory work or teaching, administration, or research.

After September 1, 1997, the Clinical Laboratory Improvement Act (CLIA) will require technologists who perform certain highly complex tests to have at least an associate degree. A grandfather clause will allow experienced workers to continue performing these tests.

Medical laboratory technicians generally have an associate degree from a community or junior college, or a certificate from a hospital, vocational or technical school, or from one of the Armed Forces. A few technicians learn on the job.

Nationally recognized accrediting agencies in the clinical laboratory science include the National Accrediting Agency for Clinical Laboratory Sciences, and the Accrediting Bureau of Health Education Schools (ABHES). National Accrediting Agency for Clinical Laboratory Sciences accredits over 391 programs that provide education for medical technologists, cytotechnologists, histologic technicians, specialists in blood bank technology, and medical laboratory technicians. ABHES accredits training programs for medical laboratory technicians.

Licensure and certification are methods of assuring the skill and competence of workers. Licensure refers to the process by which a government agency authorizes individuals to engage in a given occupation and use a particular job title. Some states require laboratory personnel to be licensed or registered. (Information on licensure is available from state departments of health, boards of occupational licensing, or occupational information coordinating committees.)

Certification is a voluntary process by which a nongovernmental organization such as a professional society or certifying agency grants recognition to an individual whose professional competence meets prescribed standards. Widely accepted by employers in the health industry, certification is a prerequisite for most jobs and often is necessary for advancement. Agencies that certify medical laboratory technologists and technicians include the Board of Registry of the American Society of Clinical Pathologists, the American Medical Technologists, the National Certification Agency for Medical Laboratory Personnel, and the Credentialing Commission of the International Society for Clinical Laboratory Technology. These agencies have different requirements for certification and different organizational sponsors.

Clinical laboratory personnel need analytical judgment and the ability to work under pressure. Close attention to detail is essential because small differences or changes in test substances or numerical readouts can be crucial for patient care. Manual dexterity and normal color vision are highly desirable. With the widespread use of automated laboratory equipment, computer skills are important. In addition, technologists in particular are expected to be good at problem solving.

Technologists may advance to supervisory positions in laboratory work or become chief medical technologists or laboratory managers in hospitals. Manufacturers of home diagnostic testing kits and laboratory equipment and supplies seek experienced technologists to work in product development, marketing, and sales. Graduate education in medical technology, one of the biological sciences, chemistry, management, or education usually speeds advancement. A doctorate is needed to become a laboratory director. Technicians can become technologists through additional education and experience.

## Job Outlook

Overall, employment of clinical laboratory workers is expected to grow about as fast as the average for all occupations through the year 2005. The rapidly growing older population will spur demand, since older people generally have more medical problems. Technological changes will have two opposite effects on employment. New, more powerful diagnostic tests will encourage more testing and spur employment. However, advances in laboratory automation and simpler tests, which make it possible for each worker to perform more tests, should slow growth. Research and development efforts are targeted at simplifying routine testing procedures so that nonlaboratory personnel—physicians and patients in particular—can perform tests now done in laboratories. Also, robots may prepare specimens, a job now done by technologists and technicians. Because the Clinical Laboratory Improvement Act regulations that are to take effect will impose academic standards for persons conducting some evaluations, job opportunities will be best for technologists who have at least an associate degree.

Fastest growth is expected in independent medical laboratories, as hospitals continue to send them a greater share of their testing. Rapid growth is also expected in offices and clinics of physicians. Slower growth is expected in hospitals. Although significant, growth will not be primary source of opportunities. As in most occupations, most will result from the need to replace workers who transfer to other occupations, retire, or stop working for some other reason.

## Earnings

Median annual earnings of full-time, salaried clinical laboratory technologists and technicians were $26,988 in 1994. Half earned between $19,240 and $35,204. The lowest 10 percent earned less than $14,820 and the top 10 percent more than $44,304.

Table 1 presents salary data for selected medical technology occupations from a University of Texas Medical Branch survey of hospitals and medical centers. The data are based on a 40-hour week and exclude shift and area differentials.

| Table 1: Median annual salary, medical technology occupations, 1994 | | | |
|---|---|---|---|
| Occupation | Minimum | Median | Maximum |
| Cytotechnologist | $29,772 | $37,107 | $43,477 |
| Histology technician | 21,975 | 26,624 | 32,337 |
| Medical laboratory technician | 20,443 | 24,461 | 30,414 |
| Medical technologist | 26,033 | 32,282 | 38,844 |
| Phlebotomist | 15,344 | 17,166 | 22,339 |

**Source:** National Survey of Hospitals and Medical Centers, University of Texas Medical Branch

## Related Occupations

Clinical laboratory technologists and technicians analyze body fluids, tissue, and other substances using a variety of tests. Similar or related procedures are performed by analytical, water purification, and other chemists; science technicians; crime laboratory analysts; food testers; and veterinary laboratory technicians.

## Related *D.O.T.* Jobs

These job titles are related to or more specific than the more general description above. They will help you identify job options you may not otherwise discover. These descriptions are in the current edition of the *Dictionary of Occupational Titles* and classified by numerical order.

078.121-010 MEDICAL TECHNOLOGIST, TEACHING SUPERVISOR; 078.261-010 BIOCHEMISTRY TECHNOLOGIST; 078.261-014 MICROBIOLOGY TECHNOLOGIST; 078.261-026 CYTOGENETIC TECHNOLOGIST; 078.261-030 HISTOTECHNOLOGIST; 078.261-038 MEDICAL TECHNOLOGIST; 078.281-010 CYTOTECHNOLOGIST; 078.381-014 MEDICAL-LABORATORY TECHNICIAN; 078.687-010 LABORATORY ASSISTANT, BLOOD AND PLASMA; 559.361-010 LABORATORY TECHNICIAN, PHARMACEUTICAL

## Sources of Additional Information

Career and certification information is available from:

❏ American Society of Clinical Pathologists, Board of Registry, P.O. Box 12277, Chicago, IL 60612.

❏ American Medical Technologists, 710 Higgins Rd., Park Ridge, IL 60068.

❏ American Society of Cytopathology 400 West 9th St., Suite 201, Wilmington, DE 19801.

❏ National Certification Agency for Medical Laboratory Personnel, 7910 Woodmont Ave., Suite 1301, Bethesda, MD 20814.

❏ International Society for Clinical Laboratory Technology, 818 Olive St., Suite 918, St. Louis, MO 63101.

For more career information, write to:

❏ American Association of Blood Banks, 8101 Glenbrook Rd., Bethesda, MD 20814-2749.

❏ Clinical Ligand Assay Society, 3139 S. Wayne Rd., Wayne, MI 48184.

For a list of educational programs accredited for clinical laboratory personnel, write to:

❏ National Accrediting Agency for Clinical Laboratory Sciences, 8410 W. Bryn Mawr Ave., Suite 670, Chicago, IL 60631.

For a list of training programs for medical laboratory technicians accredited by the Accrediting Bureau of Health Education Schools, write to:

❏ Secretary-ABHES, 29089 U.S. 20 West, Elkhart, IN 46514.

Information about employment opportunities in Department of Veterans Affairs medical centers is available from local medical centers and also from:

❏ Title 38 Employment Division (054D), Department of Veterans Affairs, 810 Vermont Ave. NW, Washington, DC 20420.

# Commercial and Industrial Electronic Equipment Repairers

## Nature of the Work

Commercial and industrial electronic equipment repairers, also called industrial electronics technicians, install and repair industrial controls, radar and missile control systems, medical diagnostic equipment, and communications equipment.

Those who work for the Defense Department install radar, missile control, and communication systems on aircraft, ships, and tanks, and in buildings and other structures. Some set up and service electronic equipment which controls machines and production processes in factories. They often coordinate their efforts with workers installing mechanical or electromechanical components.

## Working Conditions

Some electronic equipment repairers work shifts, including weekends and holidays, to service equipment in computer centers, manufacturing plants, hospitals, and telephone companies which operate round the clock. Shifts are generally assigned on the basis of seniority. Repairers may also be on call at any time to handle equipment failure.

Repairers generally work in clean, well-lighted, air-conditioned surroundings—an electronic repair shop or service center, hospital, military installation, or a telephone company's central office. However, commercial and industrial electronic equipment repairers may be exposed to heat, grease, and noise on factory floors. Some may have to work in cramped spaces.

The work involves lifting, reaching, stooping, crouching, and crawling. Adherence to safety precautions is essential to guard against work hazards such as minor burns and electrical shock.

## Employment

Commercial and industrial electronic equipment repairers held about 66,000 jobs in 1994. About one out of three repairers was employed by the federal government, almost all in the Department of Defense at military installations around the country. Repairers also were employed by electronic and transportation equipment manufacturers, machinery and equipment wholesalers, telephone companies, hospitals, electronic repair shops, and firms that provide maintenance under contract (called third-party maintenance firms).

## Training, Other Qualifications, and Advancement

Most employers prefer applicants with formal training in electronics. Electronic training is offered by public postsecondary vocational-technical schools, private vocational schools and technical institutes, junior and community colleges, and some high schools and correspondence schools. Programs take one to two years. The military services also offer formal training and work experience.

Training includes general courses in mathematics, physics, electricity, electronics, schematic reading, and troubleshooting.

A few repairers complete formal apprenticeship programs sponsored jointly by employers and locals of the International Brotherhood of Electrical Workers.

Applicants for entry-level jobs may have to pass tests that measure mechanical aptitude, knowledge of electricity or electronics, manual dexterity, and general intelligence. Newly hired repairers, even those with formal training, usually receive some training from their employer. They may study electronics and circuit theory and math. They also get hands-on experience with equipment, doing basic maintenance, and using diagnostic programs to locate malfunctions. Training may be in a classroom or it may be self-instruction, consisting of videotapes, programmed computer software, or workbooks that allow trainees to learn at their own pace.

Experienced technicians attend training sessions and read manuals to keep up with design changes and revised service procedures. Many technicians also take advanced training in a particular system or type of repair.

Good eyesight and color vision are needed to inspect and work on small, delicate parts and good hearing to detect malfunctions revealed by sound. Because field repairers usually handle jobs alone, they must be able to work without close supervision. For those who have frequent contact with customers, a pleasant personality, neat appearance, and good communications skills are important. Repairers must also be trustworthy because they may be exposed to money and other valuables in places like banks and securities offices, and some employers require that they be bonded. A security clearance may be required for technicians who repair equipment or service machines in areas where people are engaged in activities related to national security.

The International Society of Certified Electronics Technicians and the Electronics Technicians Association each administer a voluntary certification program. In both, an electronics repairer with four years of experience may become a Certified Electronics Technician. Certification, which is by examination, is offered in computer, radio-TV, industrial and commercial equipment, audio, avionics, wireless communications, video distribution, satellite, and radar systems repair. An Associate Level Test, covering basic electronics, is offered for students or repairers with less than four years of experience. Those who test and repair radio transmitting equipment, other than business and land mobile radios, need a General Operators License from the Federal Communications Commission.

Experienced repairers with advanced training may become specialists or troubleshooters who help other repairers diagnose difficult problems, or work with engineers in designing equipment and developing maintenance procedures.

Because of their familiarity with equipment, repairers are particularly well-qualified to become manufacturers' sales workers. Workers with leadership ability also may become maintenance supervisors or service managers. Some experienced workers open their own repair services or shops or become wholesalers or retailers of electronic equipment.

## Job Outlook

Overall employment of commercial and industrial electronic equipment repairers is expected to increase more slowly than the average for all occupations through the year 2005. Job prospects in private industry, however, should differ significantly from those within the federal government. Opportunities for employment outside of the federal government are expected to be good. Employment in nongovernment industries is expected to grow faster than the average for all occupations, as business and industrial firms install more electronic equipment to boost productivity and improve product quality. In addition, more electronic equipment will be used in energy conservation and pollution control. Because of cuts in the defense budget, however, employment in the federal government is expected to decline significantly.

### Earnings

In 1994, median weekly earnings of full-time electronic equipment repairers were $592. The middle 50 percent earned between $434 and $765. The bottom 10 percent earned less than $317, while the top 10 percent earned more than $947. Earnings vary widely by occupation and the type of equipment repaired, as shown in the following tabulation:

| | |
|---|---|
| Data processing equipment repairers: | $589 |
| Electronic repairers, communications and industrial equipment: | 542 |
| Office machine repairers: | 458 |

### Related Occupations

Workers in other occupations who repair and maintain the circuits and mechanical parts of electronic equipment include appliance and power tool repairers, automotive electricians, broadcast technicians, electronic organ technicians, and vending machine repairers. Electronics engineering technicians may also repair electronic equipment as part of their duties.

### Related *D.O.T.* Jobs

These job titles are related to or more specific than the more general description above. They will help you identify job options you may not otherwise discover. These descriptions are in the current edition of the *Dictionary of Occupational Titles* and classified by numerical order.

726.361-022 REPAIRER, PROBE TEST CARD, SEMICONDUCTOR WAFERS; 726.381-014 ELECTRONIC EQUIPMENT REPAIRER; 726.684-090 REWORKER, PRINTED CIRCUIT BOARD; 828.251-010 ELECTRONIC-SALES-AND-SERVICE TECHNICIAN; 828.261-014 FIELD SERVICE ENGINEER; 828.261-022 ELECTRONICS MECHANIC; 828.261-026 ELECTRONICS-MECHANIC APPRENTICE; 828.281-022 RADIOACTIVITY-INSTRUMENT MAINTENANCE TECHNICIAN

### Sources of Additional Information

For career, certification, and FCC licensing information, contact:

❏ The International Society of Certified Electronics Technicians, 2708 West Berry St., Fort Worth, TX 76109.

For certification, career, placement, and FCC licensing information, contact:

❏ Electronics Technicians Association, 604 North Jackson, Greencastle, IN 46135.

For a list of FCC licensing administrators, write to:

❏ Federal Communications Commission, Consumer Assistance Office, 1270 Fairfield Rd., Gettysburg, Pa 17325-7245 or call 1-800-322-1117.

For information on electronic equipment repairers in the telephone industry, write to:

❏ Communications Workers of America, 501 3rd St. NW, Washington, DC 20001.

## Communications Equipment Mechanics

### Nature of the Work

Installing, repairing, and maintaining complex and sophisticated telephone communications equipment are the responsibilities of communications equipment mechanics. Most communications equipment mechanics—sometimes referred to as telecommunication technicians—work either in telephone company central offices or on customers' premises installing and repairing telephone switching and transmission systems.

*Central office equipment installers*, or equipment installation technicians, set up, rearrange, and remove the switching and dialing equipment used in central offices. They install equipment in new central offices, add equipment in expanding offices, or replace outdated equipment. *Central office repairers*, often referred to as central office technicians or switching equipment technicians, test, repair, and maintain all types of local and toll switching equipment that automatically connects lines when customers dial numbers. When customers report trouble with their telephones, *trouble locators* working at special switchboards—sometimes called testboards—find the source of the problem. Trouble locators who work for cable television companies ensure that subscribers' television sets receive the proper signal. They may work with cable installers to track down the cause of the interference and make repairs.

Telephone companies have replaced trouble locators with *maintenance administrators*. Their jobs are largely automated; instead of using testboards and associated equipment to perform complex circuit tests, they enter instructions into a computer terminal and analyze the output. Maintenance administrators also update and maintain computerized files of trouble status reports.

*PBX installers*, also called systems technicians, install complex telephone equipment, often creating customized switching systems.

*PBX repairers*, with the assistance of maintenance administrators, locate the malfunction in customers' PBX or other telephone systems and make the necessary repairs. They also maintain associated equipment such as batteries, relays, and power supplies. Some PBX repairers maintain and repair equipment for mobile radiophones, microwave transmission equipment, switching equipment, and data processing equipment.

An increasing number of communications equipment repairers in the telephone industry are being trained to perform multiple tasks, ranging from splicing fiber optic cable, to programming switches, to installing telephones. As a result, the specific titles used above are becoming less common.

*Radio repairers and mechanics* install and repair stationary and mobile radio transmitting and receiving equipment. Some repair microwave and fiber optics installations. *Office electricians* handle submarine cable repeater and terminal circuits and related equipment. When trouble arises, they may rearrange cable connections to ensure that service is not interrupted. *Submarine cable equipment technicians* repair, adjust, and maintain the machines and equipment used in submarine cable offices or stations to control cable traffic.

Other communications equipment mechanics include *instrument repairers*, sometimes referred to as shop repairers or shop technicians, who repair, test, and modify a variety of communications equipment. *Data communications technicians* install and repair data communications lines and equipment for computer systems. They connect microcomputers or terminals to data communication lines.

## Working Conditions

Some electronic equipment repairers work shifts, including weekends and holidays, to service equipment in computer centers, manufacturing plants, hospitals, and telephone companies which operate round the clock. Shifts are generally assigned on the basis of seniority. Repairers may also be on call at any time to handle equipment failure.

Repairers generally work in clean, well-lighted, air-conditioned surroundings—an electronic repair shop or service center, hospital, military installation, or a telephone company's central office.

The work of most repairers involves lifting, reaching, stooping, crouching, and crawling. Adherence to safety precautions is essential to guard against work hazards such as minor burns and electrical shock.

## Employment

Communications equipment mechanics held about 118,000 jobs in 1994. Most worked for telephone companies. Others worked for electrical repair shops, cable television firms, railroads, air transportation, and the federal government.

## Training, Other Qualifications, and Advancement

Most employers prefer applicants with formal training in electronics. Electronic training is offered by public postsecondary vocational-technical schools, private vocational schools and technical institutes, junior and community colleges, and some high schools and correspondence schools. Programs take one to two years. The military services also offer formal training and work experience.

Training includes general courses in mathematics, physics, electricity, electronics, schematic reading, and troubleshooting. A few repairers complete formal apprenticeship programs sponsored jointly by employers and locals of the International Brotherhood of Electrical Workers.

Applicants for entry-level jobs may have to pass tests that measure mechanical aptitude, knowledge of electricity or electronics, manual dexterity, and general intelligence. Newly hired repairers, even those with formal training, usually receive some training from their employer. They may study electronics and circuit theory and math. They also get hands-on experience with equipment, doing basic maintenance, and using diagnostic programs to locate malfunctions. Training may be in a classroom or it may be self-instruction, consisting of videotapes, programmed computer software, or workbooks that allow trainees to learn at their own pace.

Experienced technicians attend training sessions and read manuals to keep up with design changes and revised service procedures. Many technicians also take advanced training in a particular system or type of repair.

Good eyesight and color vision are needed to inspect and work on small, delicate parts and good hearing to detect malfunctions revealed by sound. Because field repairers usually handle jobs alone, they must be able to work without close supervision. For those who have frequent contact with customers, a pleasant personality, neat appearance, and good communications skills are important. Repairers must also be trustworthy because they may be exposed to money and other valuables in places like banks and securities offices, and some employers require that they be bonded. A security clearance may be required for technicians who repair equipment or service machines in areas where people are engaged in activities related to national security.

The International Society of Certified Electronics Technicians and the Electronics Technicians Association each administer a voluntary certification program. In both, an electronics repairer with four years of experience may become a Certified Electronics Technician. Certification, which is by examination, is offered in computer, radio-TV, industrial and commercial equipment, audio, avionics, wireless communications, video distribution, satellite, and radar systems repair. An Associate Level Test, covering basic electronics, is offered for students or repairers with less than four years of experience. Those who test and repair radio transmitting equipment, other than business and land mobile radios, need a General Operators License from the Federal Communications Commission.

Experienced repairers with advanced training may become specialists or troubleshooters who help other repairers diagnose difficult problems, or work with engineers in designing equipment and developing maintenance procedures.

Because of their familiarity with equipment, repairers are particularly well qualified to become manufacturers' sales workers. Workers with leadership ability also may become maintenance supervisors or service managers. Some experienced workers open their own repair services or shops, or become wholesalers or retailers of electronic equipment.

## Job Outlook

Employment of communications equipment mechanics is expected to decline sharply through the year 2005. The telephone industry has almost completed a dramatic transformation from an electromechanical system to a completely electronic one. Digital systems, the most recent version of electronic switching, use computers and software to switch calls. Fewer workers are needed for maintenance and repair because the new systems are more reliable and compact and permit more efficient, centralized maintenance. In addition, the systems have self-diagnosing features which detect the source of problems and direct repairers to the defective part, which usually can simply be replaced. Once the transformation of the system has been completed, some time before 2005, the need for installers will drop sharply.

Decreased labor requirements due to improved technology have already caused some layoffs of communications equipment mechanics. Efficiencies resulting from consolidations and mergers of cable and telephone companies and pressure to reduce costs in the competitive environment following additional deregulation of the industry could cause further decreases in employment. Competition for available openings should intensify, making it much more difficult for other telephone workers to move into these positions without experience or formal training and virtually impossible for "outsiders" without the necessary skills to compete for jobs.

## Earnings

In 1994, median weekly earnings of full-time communications equipment repairers were $542.

According to a survey of workplaces in 160 metropolitan areas, beginning maintenance electronics technicians had median earnings of $10.75 an hour in 1993, with the middle half earning between $9.63 and $12.56 an hour. The most experienced repairers had median earnings of $18.40 an hour, with the middle half earning between $16.67 and $20.12 an hour.

## Related Occupations

Workers in other occupations who repair and maintain the circuits and mechanical parts of electronic equipment include appliance and power tool repairers, automotive electricians, broadcast technicians, electronic organ technicians, and vending machine repairers. Electronics engineering technicians may also repair electronic equipment as part of their duties.

## Related *D.O.T.* Jobs

These job titles are related to or more specific than the more general description above. They will help you identify job options you may not otherwise discover. These descriptions are in the current edition of the *Dictionary of Occupational Titles* and classified by numerical order.

722.281-010 INSTRUMENT REPAIRER; 726.381-014 INSTRUMENT INSPECTOR; 822.261-010 ELECTRICIAN, OFFICE; 822.281-010 AUTOMATIC-EQUIPMENT TECHNICIAN; 822.281-014 CENTRAL-OFFICE REPAIRER; 822.281-022 PRIVATE-BRANCH-EXCHANGE REPAIRER; 822.281-026 SIGNAL MAINTAINER; 822.281-030 TECHNICIAN, PLANT AND MAINTENANCE; 822.281-034 TECHNICIAN, SUBMARINE CABLE EQUIPMENT; 822.361-014 CENTRAL-OFFICE INSTALLER; 822.381-010 EQUIPMENT INSTALLER; 822.381-018 PRIVATE-BRANCH-EXCHANGE INSTALLER; 822.381-022 TELEGRAPH-PLANT MAINTAINER; 822.664-010 PROTECTIVE-SIGNAL-INSTALLER HELPER; 823.261-010 PUBLIC-ADDRESS SERVICER; 823.261-018 RADIO MECHANIC; 823.261-022 ANTENNA INSTALLER, SATELLITE COMMUNICATIONS; 823.261-030 DATA COMMUNICATIONS TECHNICIAN; 823.281-014 ELECTRICIAN, RADIO; 823.281-022 RIGGER; 825.261-010 ELECTRIC-TRACK-SWITCH MAINTAINER; 829.281-022 SOUND TECHNICIAN

## Sources of Additional Information

For career, certification, and FCC licensing information, contact:

❑ The International Society of Certified Electronics Technicians, 2708 West Berry St., Fort Worth, TX 76109.

For certification, career, placement, and FCC licensing information, contact:

❑ Electronics Technicians Association, 604 North Jackson, Greencastle, IN 46135.

For a list of FCC licensing administrators, write to:

❑ Federal Communications Commission, Consumer Assistance Office, 1270 Fairfield Rd., Gettysburg, Pa 17325-7245 or call 1-800-322-1117.

For information on electronic equipment repairers in the telephone industry, write to:

❑ Communications Workers of America, 501 3rd St. NW, Washington, DC 20001.

# Computer and Office Machine Repairers

## Nature of the Work

Computer and office machine repairers install equipment, do preventive maintenance, and correct problems. Computer repairers work on computers (mainframes, minis, and micros), peripheral equipment, and word processing systems, while office machine repairers work on photocopiers, cash registers, mail processing equipment, and typewriters. Some repairers service both computer and office equipment. They make cable and wiring connections when installing equipment, and work closely with electricians, who install the wiring.

Even with preventive maintenance, computers and other machines do break down. Repairers run diagnostic programs to locate malfunctions. Although some of the most modern and sophisticated computers have a self-diagnosing capacity that identifies problems, computer repairers must know enough about systems software to determine if the malfunction is in the hardware or in the software.

## Working Conditions

Some computer and office machine repairers work shifts, including weekends and holidays, to service equipment in computer centers, manufacturing plants, hospitals, and telephone companies which operate round the clock. Shifts are generally assigned on the basis of seniority. Repairers may also be on call at any time to handle equipment failure.

Repairers generally work in clean, well-lighted, air-conditioned surroundings—an electronic repair shop or service center, hospital, military installation, or a telephone company's central office.

The work of most repairers involves lifting, reaching, stooping, crouching, and crawling. Adherence to safety precautions is essential to guard against work hazards such as minor burns and electrical shock.

## Employment

Computer and office machine repairers held about 134,000 jobs in 1994. Approximately 75,000 worked mainly on computer equipment, and the other 59,000 repaired mainly office machines. Three of every five were employed by wholesalers of computers and other office equipment, including the wholesaling divisions of equipment manufacturers, and by firms that provide maintenance services for a fee. Others worked for retail establishments and some with organizations that serviced their own equipment.

Repairers work throughout the country, even in relatively small communities. Most repairers, however, work in large cities, where computer and office equipment is concentrated.

## Training, Other Qualifications, and Advancement

Most employers prefer applicants with formal training in electronics. Electronic training is offered by public postsecondary vocational-technical schools, private vocational schools and technical institutes, junior and community colleges, and some high schools and correspondence schools. Programs take one to two years. The military services also offer formal training and work experience.

Training includes general courses in computers, mathematics, physics, electricity, electronics, schematic reading, and troubleshooting. A few repairers complete formal apprenticeship programs sponsored jointly by employers and locals of the International Brotherhood of Electrical Workers.

Newly hired repairers, even those with formal training, usually receive some training from their employer. They may study electronics and circuit theory and math. They also get hands-on experience with equipment, doing basic maintenance, and using diagnostic programs to locate malfunctions. Training may be in a classroom or it may be self-instruction, consisting of videotapes, programmed computer software, or workbooks that allow trainees to learn at their own pace.

Experienced technicians attend training sessions and read manuals to keep up with design changes and revised service procedures. Many technicians also take advanced training in a particular system or type of repair.

Good eyesight and color vision are needed to inspect and work on small, delicate parts and good hearing to detect malfunctions revealed by sound. Because field repairers usually handle jobs alone, they must be able to work without close supervision. For those who have frequent contact with customers, a pleasant personality, neat appearance, and good communications skills are important. Repairers must also be trustworthy because they may be exposed to money and other valuables in places like banks and securities offices, and some employers require that they be bonded. A security clearance may be required for technicians who repair equipment or service machines in areas where people are engaged in activities related to national security.

The International Society of Certified Electronics Technicians and the Electronics Technicians Association each administer a voluntary certification program. In both, an electronics repairer with four years of experience may become a Certified Electronics Technician. Certification, which is by examination, is offered in computer, radio-TV, industrial and commercial equipment, audio, avionics, wireless communications, video distribution, satellite, and radar systems repair. An Associate Level Test, covering basic electronics, is offered for students or repairers with less than four years of experience. Those who test and repair radio transmitting equipment, other than business and land mobile radios, need a General Operators License from the Federal Communications Commission.

Experienced repairers with advanced training may become specialists or troubleshooters who help other repairers diagnose difficult problems, or work with engineers in designing equipment and developing maintenance procedures.

Because of their familiarity with equipment, repairers are particularly well qualified to become manufacturers' sales workers. Workers with leadership ability also may become maintenance supervisors or service managers. Some experienced workers open their own repair services or shops, or become wholesalers or retailers of electronic equipment.

## Job Outlook

Employment of computer and office machine repairers is expected to grow faster than the average for all occupations through the year 2005. However, employment of repairers will grow less rapidly than the anticipated increase in the amount of equipment because of the improved reliability of computer and office machines and ease of repair. Applicants for computer repairer positions will have the most favorable job prospects.

Employment of those who repair computers is expected to grow much faster than the average for all occupations. Demand for computer repairers will increase as the amount of computer equipment increases—organizations throughout the economy should continue to automate in search of greater productivity and improved service. The development of new computer applications and lower computer prices, will also spur demand. More repairers will be needed to install, maintain, and repair these machines.

Employment of those who repair office machines is expected to grow more slowly than the average for all occupations. Slow growth in the amount of non-computer-based office equipment will dampen the demand for these repairers.

## Earnings

In 1994, median weekly earnings of full-time electronic equipment repairers were $592. The middle 50 percent earned between $434 and $765. The bottom 10 percent earned less than $317, while the top 10 percent earned more than $947. Earnings vary widely by occupation and the type of equipment repaired, but median weekly earnings for office machine repairers were $458.

According to a survey of workplaces in 160 metropolitan areas, beginning maintenance electronics technicians had median earnings of $10.75 an hour in 1993, with the middle half earning between $9.63 and $12.56 an hour. The most experienced repairers had median earnings of $18.40 an hour, with the middle half earning between $16.67 and $20.12 an hour.

## Related Occupations

Workers in other occupations who repair and maintain the circuits and mechanical parts of electronic equipment include appliance and power tool repairers, automotive electricians, broadcast technicians, electronic organ technicians, and vending machine repairers. Electronics engineering technicians may also repair electronic equipment as part of their duties.

## Related *D.O.T.* Jobs

These job titles are related to or more specific than the more general description above. They will help you identify job options you may not otherwise discover. These descriptions are in the current edition of the *Dictionary of Occupational Titles* and classified by numerical order.

633.261-014 MAIL-PROCESSING-EQUIPMENT MECHANIC; 633.281-010 CASH-REGISTER SERVICER; 633.281-014 DICTATING-TRAN-

SCRIBING-MACHINE SERVICER; 633.281-018 OFFICE-MACHINE SERVICER; 633.281-022 OFFICE-MACHINE-SERVICER APPRENTICE; 633.281-026 SCALE MECHANIC; 633.281-030 STATISTICAL-MACHINE SERVICER; 706.381-010 ALIGNER, TYPEWRITER; 706.381-030 RE-PAIRER, TYPEWRITER

## Sources of Additional Information

For career, certification, and FCC licensing information, contact:

❏ The International Society of Certified Electronics Technicians, 2708 West Berry St., Fort Worth, TX 76109.

For certification, career, placement, and FCC licensing information, contact:

❏ Electronics Technicians Association, 604 North Jackson, Greencastle, IN 46135.

For a list of FCC licensing administrators, write to:

❏ Federal Communications Commission, Consumer Assistance Office, 1270 Fairfield Rd., Gettysburg, Pa 17325-7245 or call 1-800-322-1117.

# Computer and Peripheral Equipment Operators

## Nature of the Work

Computer and peripheral equipment operators oversee the operation of computer hardware systems, ensuring that these machines are used as efficiently as possible. This means that operators must anticipate problems before they occur and take preventive action as well as solve problems that do occur.

The duties of computer and peripheral equipment operators vary with the size of the installation, the type of equipment used, and the policies of the employer. Working from operating instructions prepared by programmers, users, or operations managers, computer operators set controls on the computer and on peripheral devices required to run a particular job. Computer operators or, in some large installations peripheral equipment operators, load the equipment with tapes, disks, and paper as needed. While the computer is running—which may be 24 hours a day for large computers—computer operators monitor the computer console and respond to operating and computer messages. Messages indicate the individual specifications of each job being run. If an error message occurs, operators must locate and solve the problem or terminate the program.

Traditionally, peripheral equipment operators have to prepare printouts and other output for distribution to computer users. Operators also maintain log books listing each job that is run and events such as machine malfunctions that occurred during their shift. In addition, computer operators may supervise and train peripheral equipment operators and computer operator trainees. They also may help programmers and systems analysts test and debug new programs.

As the trend toward networking computers accelerates, a growing number of these workers are operating personal computers (PCs) and minicomputers. More and more establishments are realizing the need to connect all their computers in order to

enhance productivity. In many offices, factories, and other work settings, PCs and minicomputers serve as the center of such networks, often referred to as local area networks or multi-user systems. While some of these computers are operated by users in the area, many require the services of full-time operators. The tasks performed are very similar to those performed on the larger computers.

As organizations continue to use computers in more areas of operation, they are also realizing opportunities to increase the productivity of computer operations. Automation, which traditionally has been the application of computer technology to other functional areas of an organization, is now reaching the computer room. Sophisticated software coupled with robotics now exist, enabling the computer to perform many routine tasks formerly done by computer and peripheral equipment operators. Scheduling, loading and downloading programs, mounting tapes, rerouting messages, and running periodic reports can be done without the intervention of an operator. These improvements will change what computer operators do in the future. However, in the computer centers that lack this level of automation, some computer operators still may be responsible for tasks traditionally done by peripheral equipment operators. As technology advances, many computer operators will essentially monitor an automated system. As the role of operators changes due to new technology, their responsibilities may shift to system security, troubleshooting, desk help, network problems, and maintaining large databases.

## Working Conditions

Computer operating personnel generally work in well-lighted, well-ventilated, comfortable rooms. Because many organizations use their computers 24 hours a day, seven days a week, computer and peripheral equipment operators may be required to work evening or night shifts and weekends. Shift assignments generally are made on the basis of seniority. Automated operations will lessen the need for shift work because many companies let the computer take over all operations during less desirable working hours. Because computer operators spend a lot of time in front of a computer monitor, as well as performing repetitive tasks such as loading and unloading printers, they may be susceptible to eyestrain, back discomfort, and hand and wrist problems.

## Employment

In 1994, computer operators and peripheral equipment operators held about 259,000 and 30,000 jobs, respectively. Although jobs for computer and peripheral equipment operators are found in almost every industry, most are in wholesale trade establishments; manufacturing companies; data processing service firms; financial institutions; and government agencies. These organizations have data processing needs that require large computer installations. A growing number are employed by firms in the computer and data processing services industry, as more companies contract out the operation of their data processing centers.

More than 1 out of 10 computer and peripheral equipment operators works part-time.

## Training, Other Qualifications, and Advancement

Previous work experience is the key to landing an operator job in many large establishments. Employers look for specific, hands-on experience in the type of equipment and related operating systems that they use. Additionally, computer-related formal training, perhaps through a junior college or technical school, is recommended. As computer technology changes and data processing centers become more automated, more employers will require candidates for the remaining operator jobs to have formal training as well as experience.

Workers usually receive on-the-job training in order to become acquainted with their employer's equipment and routines. The length of training varies with the job and the experience of the worker. Training is also offered by the Armed Forces and by some computer manufacturers.

Because computer technology changes so rapidly, operators must be adaptable and willing to learn. Greater analytical and technical expertise are also needed to deal with the unique or higher level problems that the computer is not programmed to handle, particularly by operators who work in automated data centers.

Computer and peripheral equipment operators must be able to communicate well in order to work effectively with programmers or users, as well as with other operators. Computer operators also must be able to work independently because they may have little or no supervision.

Peripheral equipment operators may advance to computer operator jobs. A few computer operators may advance to supervisory jobs. Through on-the-job experience and additional formal education, some computer and peripheral equipment operators may advance to jobs as programmers or analysts, although the move into these jobs is becoming more difficult as employers increasingly require candidates for more skilled computer professional jobs posses at least a bachelor's degree. Others may become specialists in areas such as network operations or support.

## Job Outlook

Employment of computer and peripheral equipment operators is expected to decline sharply through the year 2005. Many experienced operators are expected to compete for the small number of openings that will arise each year to replace workers who transfer to other occupations or leave the labor force.

Advances in technology have reduced both the size and the cost of computer equipment while increasing the capacity for data storage and processing. These improvements in technology have fueled an expansion in the use of computers in such areas as factory and office automation, telecommunications, medicine, and education.

The expanding use of software that automates computer operations gives companies the option of making systems user-friendly, greatly reducing the need for operators. Even if firms continue to employ operators in some capacity—which, for many, is extremely likely in the near future—these new technologies will require operators to monitor a greater number of operations at the same time and be capable of solving a broader range of problems that may arise. The result is that fewer and fewer operators will be needed to perform more highly skilled work.

Computer operators or peripheral equipment operators who are displaced by automation may be reassigned to support staffs that maintain personal computer networks or assist other members of the organization. Operators who keep up with changing technology, by updating their skills and enhancing their training, should have the best prospects of moving into other areas such as network administration. Others may be retrained to perform different job duties, such as supervising an entire operations center, maintaining automation packages, or analyzing computer operations to recommend ways to increase productivity. In the future, operators who wish to continue in the computer field will need to know more about programming, automation software, graphics interface, and open systems in order to take advantage of changing opportunities.

## Earnings

In 1994, full-time computer operators had median earnings of $21,300 a year. The middle 50 percent earned between $16,200 and $29,900. The lowest 10 percent earned less than $12,800 and the top 10 percent earned more than $39,500.

According to Robert Half International Inc., the average starting salaries for computer operator ranged from $20,000 to $31,500 in 1994. Salaries generally are higher in large organizations than in small ones.

In the federal government, computer operators with a high school diploma started at about $14,900 a year in 1995. Those with one year of college started at $16,700. Applicants with operations experience started at higher salaries. The average annual salary for all computer operators employed by the federal government in nonsupervisory, supervisory, and managerial positions was about $28,800 in 1994.

## Related Occupations

Other occupations involving work with computers include computer scientists and systems analysts, programmers, and computer service technicians. Other occupations in which workers operate electronic office equipment include data entry keyers, secretaries, typists and word processors, and typesetters and compositors.

## Related *D.O.T.* Jobs

These job titles are related to or more specific than the more general description above. They will help you identify job options you may not otherwise discover. These descriptions are in the current edition of the *Dictionary of Occupational Titles* and classified by numerical order.

213.362-010 COMPUTER OPERATOR; 213.382-010 COMPUTER PERIPHERAL EQUIPMENT OPERATOR; 213.582-010 DIGITIZER OPERATOR

## Sources of Additional Information

For information about work opportunities in computer operations, contact firms that use computers such as banks, manufacturing and insurance firms, colleges and universities, and data processing service organizations. The local office of the state employment service can supply information about employment and training opportunities.

# Computer Programmers

## Nature of the Work

Computer programmers write, and maintain the detailed

instructions—called "programs" or "software"—that list in a logical order the steps that computers must execute to perform their functions. In many large organizations, programmers follow descriptions prepared by systems analysts who have carefully studied the task that the computer system is going to perform. These descriptions list the input required, the steps the computer must follow to process data, and the desired arrangement of the output. Some organizations, particularly smaller ones, do not employ systems analysts. Instead, workers called *programmer-analysts* are responsible for both systems analysis and programming.

Regardless of setting, programmers write specific programs by breaking down each step into a logical series of instructions the computer can follow. They then code these instructions in a conventional programming language, such as C and FORTRAN, or one of the more advanced artificial intelligence or object oriented languages, such as LISP, Prolog, C++, or Ada.

The transition from a mainframe environment to primarily a PC-based environment has blurred the once rigid distinction between the programmer and the user. Increasingly adept users are taking over many of the tasks previously performed by programmers. For example, the growing use of packaged software, like spreadsheet and data base management software packages, allows users to write simple programs to access data and perform calculations.

Programmers in software development companies may work directly with experts from various fields to create software—either programs designed for specific clients or packaged software for general use—ranging from games and educational software to programs for desktop publishing, financial planning, and spreadsheets. Much of the programming being done today is the preparation of packaged software, one of the most rapidly growing segments of the computer industry.

Despite the prevalence of packaged software, many programmers are involved in updating, repairing, and modifying code for existing programs. When making changes to a section of code, called a "routine," programmers need to make other users aware of the task that the routine is to perform. They do this by inserting comments in the coded instructions so others can understand the program. Programmers using Computer-Aided Software Engineering (CASE) tools can concentrate on writing the unique parts of the program because the tools automate various pieces of the program being built. This also yields more reliable and consistent programs and increases programmers' productivity by eliminating some of the routine steps.

When a program is ready to be tested, programmers run it to ensure that the instructions are correct and will produce the desired information. They prepare sample data that test every part of the program and, after trial runs, review the results to see if any errors were made. If errors do occur, the programmer must make the appropriate change and recheck the program until it produces the correct results. This is called "debugging" the program.

Finally, programmers working in a mainframe environment prepare instructions for the computer operator who will run the program. They may also contribute to a user's manual for the program.

Programs vary depending upon the type of information to be accessed or generated. For example, the instructions involved in updating financial records are different from those required to duplicate conditions onboard an aircraft for pilots training in a flight simulator. Although simple programs can be written in a few hours, programs that use complex mathematical formulas or many data files may require more than a year of work. In most cases, several programmers may work together as a team under a senior programmer's supervision.

Programmers often are grouped into two broad types: Applications programmers and systems programmers.

*Applications programmers* usually are oriented toward business, engineering, or science. They write software to handle specific jobs, such as a program used in an inventory control system or one to guide a missile after it has been fired. They also may work alone to revise existing packaged software.

*Systems programmers*, on the other hand, maintain the software that controls the operation of an entire computer system. These workers make changes in the sets of instructions that determine how the central processing unit of the system handles the various jobs it has been given and communicates with peripheral equipment, such as terminals, printers, and disk drives. Because of their knowledge of the entire computer system, systems programmers often help applications programmers determine the source of problems that may occur with their programs.

## Working Conditions

Programmers generally work in offices in comfortable surroundings. Although they usually work about 40 hours a week, their hours are not always from 9 to 5. Programmers may work longer hours or weekends in order to meet deadlines or fix critical problems that occur during off hours.

Because programmers spend long periods of time in front of a computer monitor typing at a keyboard, they are susceptible to eyestrain, back discomfort, and hand and wrist problems.

## Employment

Computer programmers held about 537,000 jobs in 1994. Programmers are employed in most industries, but the largest concentrations are in data processing service organizations, including firms that write and sell software; firms that provide engineering and management services; manufacturers of computer and office equipment; financial institutions; insurance carriers; educational institutions; and government agencies. Applications programmers work for all types of firms, whereas systems programmers usually work for organizations with large computer centers or for firms that manufacture computers or develop software.

A growing number of programmers are employed on a temporary or contract basis. Rather than hiring programmers as permanent employees and then laying them off after a job is completed, employers increasingly are contracting with temporary help agencies, consulting firms, or directly with programmers themselves. A marketing firm, for example, may only require the services of several programmers to write and "debug" the software necessary to get a new database management system running. Such jobs may last from several months to a year or longer.

## Training, Other Qualifications, and Advancement

There are no universal training requirements for programmers because employers' needs are so varied. Computer applications have become so widespread that computer programming is taught at most public and private vocational schools, community and junior colleges, and universities. However, the level of education and quality of training that employers seek have been rising due to the growth in the number of qualified applicants and the increasing complexity of some programming tasks. Although some programmers obtain two-year degrees or certificates, bachelor's degrees are now commonly required. In the absence of a degree, substantial specialized experience or expertise may be needed.

The majority of programmers hold a four-year degree. Of these, some hold a B.A. or B.S. in computer science or information systems while others have taken special courses in computer programming to supplement their study in fields such as accounting, inventory control, or other business areas. College graduates who are interested in changing careers or developing an area of expertise may return to a junior college or technical school for more training.

Employers using computers for scientific or engineering applications prefer college graduates who have degrees in computer or information science, mathematics, engineering, or the physical sciences. Graduate degrees are required for some jobs. Employers who use computers for business applications prefer to hire people who have had college courses in management information systems (MIS) and business, and who possess strong programming skills. Knowledge of FORTRAN, COBOL, C, Fourth Generation Languages (4GL), CASE tools, systems programming, C++, Smalltalk, and other object oriented programming languages is highly desirable. General business skills and experience related to the operations of the firm are preferred by employers as well.

Most systems programmers hold a four-year degree in computer science. Extensive knowledge of a variety of operating systems is essential. This includes being able to configure the operating system to work with different types of hardware, and adapting the operating system to best meet the needs of the particular organization. They also must be able to work with database systems such as DB2, Oracle, or Sybase, for example.

The Institute for Certification of Computing Professionals confers the designation Certified Computing Professional (CCP) to those who have at least four years of experience or two years of experience and a college degree. To qualify, individuals must pass a core examination plus exams in two specialty areas, or an exam in one specialty area and two computing languages. Those with little or no experience may be tested for certification as an Associate Computer Professional (ACP). Certification is not mandatory, but it may give a job seeker a competitive advantage.

When hiring programmers, employers look for people with the necessary programming skills who can think logically and pay close attention to detail. The job calls for patience, persistence, and the ability to work on exacting analytical work, especially under pressure. Ingenuity and imagination are also particularly important when programmers design solutions and test their work for potential failures. Increasingly, interpersonal skills are important as programmers are expected to work in teams and interact directly with users. The ability to work with abstract concepts and do technical analysis is especially important for systems programmers because they work with the software that controls the computer's operation.

Beginning programmers may spend their first weeks on the job attending training classes since each business has its own development methodology, processes, and tools. After this initial instruction, they may work alone on simple assignments, or on a team with more experienced programmers. Either way, they generally must spend at least several months working under close supervision. Because of rapidly changing technology, programmers must continuously update their training by taking courses sponsored by their employer or software vendors.

For skilled workers, the prospects for advancement are good. In large organizations, they may be promoted to lead programmer and be given supervisory responsibilities. Some applications programmers may move into systems programming after they gain experience and take courses in systems software. With general business experience, both applications programmers and systems programmers may become systems analysts or be promoted to a managerial position. Other programmers, with specialized knowledge and experience with a language or operating system, may work in research and development areas such as multimedia or Internet technology. As employers increasingly contract out programming jobs, more opportunities should arise for experienced programmers with expertise in a specific area to work as consultants.

## Job Outlook

Employment of programmers is expected to grow about as fast as the average for all occupations through the year 2005. Employment is not expected to grow as rapidly as in the past as improved software and programming techniques continue to simplify programming tasks. In addition, greater use of packaged software—such as word processing and spreadsheet packages—should continue to moderate the growth in demand for applications programmers. As the level of technological innovation and sophistication increases, users will be able to design, write, and implement more of their own programs to meet their changing needs.

Although the proportion of programmers leaving the occupation each year is smaller than that of most occupations, most of the job openings for programmers will result from replacement needs. The majority of programmers who leave transfer to other occupations, such as manager or systems analyst. Jobs for both systems and applications programmers, however, should remain particularly plentiful in data processing service firms, software houses, and computer consulting businesses. These types of establishments remain part of one of the fastest growing industries—computer and data processing services. As companies look to control costs, those in need of programming services should look to this industry to meet these needs.

As computer usage expands, however, the demand for skilled programmers will increase as organizations seek new applications for computers and improvements to the software already in use. Employers are increasingly interested in programmers who can combine areas of technical expertise or who are adaptable and able to learn and incorporate new skills. One area of progress will be data communications. Networking computers so they can communicate with each other is necessary to achieve the greater efficiency that organizations require to remain competitive. Object-oriented languages will increasingly be used in the years ahead, further enhancing the productivity of programmers. Programmers will be creating and maintaining expert systems and embedding these technologies in more and more products.

The number and quality of applicants for programmer jobs have increased, so employers have become more selective. Graduates of two-year programs in data processing, and people with less than a two-year degree or its equivalent in work experience, are facing especially strong competition for programming jobs. Competition for entry-level positions even affects applicants with a bachelor's degree. Many observers expect opportunities for people without college degrees to diminish in coming years as programming tasks become more complex and more sophisticated skills and experience are demanded by employers. Prospects should be good for college graduates with knowledge of a variety of programming languages, particularly C++ and other object oriented languages, as well as newer languages that apply to computer networking, data base management, and artificial intelligence. In order to remain competitive, college graduates should keep up to date with the latest skills and technologies.

Many employers prefer to hire applicants with previous experience in the field. Firms also desire programmers who develop a technical specialization in areas such as client/server programming, multimedia technology, graphic user interface, or fourth- and fifth-generation programming tools. Therefore, people who want to become programmers can enhance their chances by combining work experience with the appropriate formal training. Students should try to gain experience by participating in a college work-study program, or undertaking an internship. Students also can greatly improve their employment prospects by taking courses such as accounting, management, engineering, or science—allied fields in which applications programmers are in demand. With the expansion of client/server environments, employers will continue to look for programmers with strong technical skills, as well as good interpersonal and business skills.

### Earnings

Median earnings of programmers who worked full-time in 1994 were about $38,400 a year. The middle 50 percent earned between about $30,000 and $49,200 a year. The lowest 10 percent earned less than $22,000, and the highest 10 percent, more than $60,600.

According to Robert Half International Inc., starting salaries in large establishments for 1994 ranged from $29,500 to $36,500 for programmers; $36,000 to $47,000 for programmer analysts; and $44,000 to $54,000 for systems programmers. Starting salaries in small establishments ranged from $25,000 to $34,000 for programmers and from $30,000 to $40,000 for programmer analysts.

Programmers working in the West and Northeast earned somewhat more than those working in the South and Midwest. On average, systems programmers earn more than applications programmers.

In the federal government, the entrance salary for programmers with a college degree or qualifying experience was about $18,700 a year in 1995; for those with a superior academic record, $23,200.

### Related Occupations

Programmers must pay great attention to detail as they write and "debug" programs. Other professional workers who must be detail-oriented include statisticians, engineers, financial analysts, accountants, auditors, actuaries, and operations research analysts.

### Related *D.O.T.* Jobs

These job titles are related to or more specific than the more general description above. They will help you identify job options you may not otherwise discover. These descriptions are in the current edition of the *Dictionary of Occupational Titles* and classified by numerical order.

030.162-010 COMPUTER PROGRAMMER; 030.162-018 PROGRAMMER, ENGINEERING AND SCIENTIFIC; 030.162-022 SYSTEMS PROGRAMMER; 030.167-010 CHIEF, COMPUTER PROGRAMMER

### Sources of Additional Information

State employment service offices can provide information about job openings for computer programmers. Also check with your city's chamber of commerce for information on the area's largest employers.

For information about certification as a computing professional, contact:

❏ Institute for the Certification of Computing Professionals, 2200 East Devon Ave., Suite 268, Des Plaines, IL 60018.

Further information about computer careers is available from:

❏ The Association for Computing Machinery, 1515 Broadway, New York, NY 10036.

# Concrete Masons and Terrazzo Workers

### Nature of the Work

Concrete—a mixture of Portland cement, sand, gravel, and water—is used for many types of construction projects. Whether small jobs, such as patios and floors, or huge dams or miles of roadway, *concrete masons* place and finish the concrete. They also may color concrete surfaces, expose aggregate (small stones) in walls and sidewalks, or fabricate concrete beams, columns, and panels.

*Terrazzo workers* create attractive walkways, floors, patios, and panels by exposing marble chips and other fine aggregates on the surface of finished concrete. Much of the preliminary work of terrazzo workers is similar to that of concrete masons.

In preparing a site for placing concrete, masons set the forms for holding the concrete to the desired pitch and depth and properly align them. They then direct the casting of the concrete and supervise laborers who use shovels or special tools to spread it. Masons then guide a straightedge back and forth across the top of the forms to "screed," or level, the freshly placed concrete. Immediately after leveling the concrete, masons carefully smooth the concrete surface with a "bull float," a long-handled tool about 8 by 48 inches that covers the coarser materials in the concrete and brings a rich mixture of fine cement paste to the surface.

After the concrete has been leveled and floated, finishers press an edger between the forms and the concrete and guide it along the edge and the surface. This produces slightly rounded edges and helps prevent chipping or cracking. They use a special tool called a "groover" to make joints or grooves at specific intervals that help control cracking. Next, finishers trowel the surface using either a powered or a hand trowel, a small, smooth, rectangular metal tool. Troweling removes most imperfections and brings the fine cement paste to the surface.

As the final step, masons retrowel the concrete surface back and forth with powered and hand trowels to create a smooth finish. For a coarse, nonskid finish, masons brush the surface with a broom or stiff-bristled brush. For a pebble finish, they embed small gravel chips into the surface. They then wash any excess cement from the exposed chips with a mild acid solution. For color, they use colored premixed concrete. On concrete surfaces that will remain exposed after forms are stripped, such as columns, ceilings, and wall panels, concrete masons cut away high spots and loose concrete with hammer and chisel, fill any large indentations with a Portland cement paste and smooth the surface with a rubbing carborundum stone. Finally, they coat the exposed area with a rich Portland cement mixture using either a special tool or a coarse cloth to rub the concrete to a uniform finish.

Attractive, marble-chip terrazzo requires three layers of materials. First, concrete masons or terrazzo workers build a solid, level concrete foundation that is 3 to 4 inches deep. After the forms are removed from the foundation, workers place a one-inch deep mixture of sandy concrete. Before this layer sets, terrazzo workers partially embed metal divider strips into the concrete wherever there is to be a joint or change of color in the terrazzo. These strips separate the different designs and colors of the terrazzo panels and help prevent cracks. For the final layer, terrazzo workers blend and place a fine marble chip mixture that may be color-pigmented into each of the panels, then hand trowel each panel until it is level with the tops of the ferrule strips. While the mixture is still wet, workers toss additional marble chips of various colors into each panel and roll a lightweight roller over the entire surface.

When the terrazzo is thoroughly dry, helpers grind it with a terrazzo grinder (somewhat like a floor polisher, only much heavier). Slight depressions left by the grinding are filled with a matching grout material and hand troweled for a smooth, uniform surface. Terrazzo workers then clean, polish, and seal the dry surface for a lustrous finish.

## Working Conditions

Concrete or terrazzo work is fast paced and strenuous. Since most finishing is done at floor level, workers must bend and kneel a lot. Many jobs are outdoors, but work is generally halted during rain or freezing weather. To avoid chemical burns from uncured concrete and sore knees from frequent kneeling, many workers wear kneepads. Workers usually wear water-repellent boots while working in wet concrete.

## Employment

Concrete masons and terrazzo workers held about 126,000 jobs in 1994; terrazzo workers accounted for a very small proportion of the total. Most concrete masons worked for concrete contractors or for general contractors on projects such as highways, bridges, shopping malls, or large buildings such as factories, schools, and hospitals. A small number were employed by firms that manufacture concrete products. Most terrazzo workers worked for special trade contractors who install decorative floors and wall panels.

Fewer than 1 out of 10 concrete masons and terrazzo workers was self-employed, a smaller proportion than in other building trades. Most self-employed masons specialized in small jobs, such as driveways, sidewalks, and patios.

## Training, Other Qualifications, and Advancement

Concrete masons and terrazzo workers learn their trades either through on-the-job training as helpers or through three-year apprenticeship programs. Many masons first gain experience as construction laborers.

When hiring helpers and apprentices, employers prefer high school graduates who are at least 18 years old, in good physical condition, and licensed to drive. The ability to get along with others also is important because concrete masons frequently work in teams. High school courses in shop mathematics and blueprint reading or mechanical drawing provide a helpful background.

On-the-job training programs consist of informal instruction from experienced workers in which helpers learn to use the tools, equipment, machines, and materials of the trade. They begin with tasks such as edging and jointing and using a straightedge on freshly placed concrete. As they progress, assignments become more complex, and trainees usually can do finishing work within a short time.

Three-year apprenticeship programs, usually jointly sponsored by local unions and contractors, provide on-the-job training in addition to a recommended minimum of 144 hours of classroom instruction each year. A written test and a physical exam may be required. In the classroom, apprentices learn applied mathematics, blueprint reading, and safety. Apprentices generally receive special instruction in layout work and cost estimating.

Experienced concrete masons or terrazzo workers may advance to become supervisors or contract estimators. Some open their own concrete contracting businesses.

## Job Outlook

Employment of concrete masons and terrazzo workers is expected to grow about as fast as the average for all occupations through the year 2005. In addition to job openings that will stem from the rising demand for the services of these workers, other jobs will become available as experienced workers transfer to other occupations or leave the labor force.

The demand for concrete masons and terrazzo workers will rise as the population and the economy grow. More masons will be needed to build highways, bridges, subways, factories, office buildings, hotels, shopping centers, schools, hospitals, and other structures. In addition, the increasing use of concrete as a building material—particularly in nonresidential construction—will add to the demand. More concrete masons also will be needed to repair and renovate existing highways, bridges, and other structures.

Employment growth of concrete masons and terrazzo workers, however, will not keep pace with the growth of these construction projects. Nevertheless, their productivity will increase as a result of the use of improved concrete pumping systems, continuous concrete mixers, quicker setting cement, troweling machines, prefabricated masonry systems, and other improved materials, equipment, and tools.

Employment of concrete masons and terrazzo workers, like that of many other workers, is sensitive to the ups and downs in the economy. Workers in these trades may experience periods of unemployment when the level of nonresidential construction falls. On the other hand, shortages of these workers may occur in some areas during peak periods of building activity.

## Earnings

Median weekly earnings of full-time concrete masons and terrazzo workers were about $407 in 1994. The middle 50 percent earned between $310 and $528 per week. The top 10 percent earned more than $701 and the lowest 10 percent earned less than $231.

According to the limited information available, average hourly earnings—including benefits—for concrete masons who belonged to a union and worked full-time ranged between $15.90 and $42.16 in 1994. Concrete masons in, New York, Boston, San Francisco, Chicago, Los Angeles, Philadelphia, and other large cities received the highest wages. Nonunion workers generally have lower wage rates than union workers. Apprentices usually start at 50 to 60 percent of the rate paid to experienced workers.

Concrete masons often work overtime, with premium pay, because once concrete has been placed, the job must be completed.

Annual earnings of concrete masons and terrazzo workers may be lower than the hourly rates suggest because bad weather and downturns in construction activity can limit the time they can work.

Many concrete masons and terrazzo workers belong to the Operative Plasterers' and Cement Masons' International Association of the United States and Canada, or to the International Union of Bricklayers and Allied Craftsmen. Some terrazzo workers belong to the United Brotherhood of Carpenters and Joiners of the United States.

## Related Occupations

Concrete masons and terrazzo workers combine skill with knowledge of building materials to construct buildings, highways, and other structures. Other occupations involving similar skills and knowledge include bricklayers, form builders, marble setters, plasterers, stonemasons, and tilesetters.

## Related *D.O.T.* Jobs

These job titles are related to or more specific than the more general description above. They will help you identify job options you may not otherwise discover. These descriptions are in the current edition of the *Dictionary of Occupational Titles* and classified by numerical order.

844.364-010 CEMENT MASON; 844.364-014 CEMENT-MASON APPRENTICE; 844.461-010 CONCRETE-STONE FINISHER; 844.684-010 CONCRETE RUBBER; 861.381-046 TERRAZZO WORKER; 861.381-050 TERRAZZO-WORKER APPRENTICE

## Sources of Additional Information

For information about apprenticeships and work opportu-nities, contact local concrete or terrazzo contractors; locals of unions previously mentioned; a local joint union-management apprenticeship committee; or the nearest office of the state employment service or apprenticeship agency.

For general information about concrete masons and terrazzo workers, contact:

- ❏ Associated General Contractors of America, Inc., 1957 E St. NW, Washington, DC 20006.
- ❏ International Union of Bricklayers and Allied Craftsmen, International Masonry Institute Apprenticeship and Training, 815 15th St. NW, Suite 1001, Washington, DC 20005.
- ❏ Operative Plasterers' and Cement Masons' International Association of the United States and Canada, 1125 17th St. NW, Washington, DC 20036.
- ❏ National Terrazzo and Mosaic Association, 3166 Des Plaines Ave., Suite 132, Des Plaines, IL 60018.
- ❏ Portland Cement Association, 5420 Old Orchard Rd., Skokie, IL 60077.
- ❏ United Brotherhood of Carpenters and Joiners of America, 101 Constitution Ave. NW, Washington, DC 20001.

# Construction and Building Inspectors

## Nature of the Work

Construction and building inspectors examine the construction, alteration, or repair of buildings, highways and streets, sewer and water systems, dams, bridges, and other structures to ensure compliance with building codes and ordinances, zoning regulations, and contract specifications. Inspectors generally specialize in one particular type of construction work or construction trade, such as electrical work or plumbing. They make an initial inspection during the first phase of construction, and follow-up inspections throughout the construction project to monitor compliance with regulations. In areas where severe natural disasters—such as earthquakes or hurricanes—are more common, inspectors monitor compliance with additional safety regulations.

*Building inspectors* inspect the structural quality and general safety of buildings. Some specialize—for example, in structural steel or reinforced concrete structures. Before construction begins, *plan examiners* determine whether the plans for the building or other structure comply with building code regulations and are suited to the engineering and environmental demands of the building site. Inspectors visit the work site before the foundation is poured to inspect the soil condition and positioning and depth of the footings. Later they return to the site to inspect the foundation after it has been completed. The size and type of structure and the rate of completion determine the number of other site visits they must make. Upon completion of the entire project, they make a final comprehensive inspection.

A primary concern of building inspectors is fire safety. They inspect structure's fire sprinklers, alarms, and smoke control systems, as well as fire doors and exits. In addition, inspectors may calculate fire insurance rates by assessing the type of constrution, building contents, adequacy of fire protection equipment, and risks posed by adjoining buildings.

*Electrical inspectors* inspect the installation of electrical systems and equipment to ensure that they function properly and comply with electrical codes and standards. They visit work sites to inspect new and existing wiring, lighting, sound and security systems, motors, and generating equipment. They also inspect the installation of the electrical wiring for heating and air-conditioning systems, appliances, and other components.

*Elevator inspectors* examine lifting and conveying devices such as elevators, escalators, moving sidewalks, lifts and hoists, inclined railways, ski lifts, and amusement rides.

*Mechanical inspectors* inspect the installation of the mechanical components of commercial kitchen appliances, heating and air-conditioning equipment, gasoline and butane tanks, gas and oil piping, and gas-fired and oil-fired appliances. Some specialize in inspecting boilers or ventilating equipment as well.

*Plumbing inspectors* examine plumbing systems, including private disposal systems, water supply and distribution systems, plumbing fixtures and traps, and drain, waste, and vent lines.

*Public works inspectors* ensure that federal, state, and local government construction of water and sewer systems, highways, streets, bridges, and dams conforms to detailed contract specifications. They inspect excavation and fill operations, the placement of forms for concrete, concrete mixing and pouring, asphalt paving, and grading operations. They record the work and materials used so that contract payments can be calculated. Public works inspectors may specialize in highways, structural steel, reinforced concrete, or ditches. Others specialize in dredging operations required for bridges and dams or for harbors.

*Home inspectors* conduct inspections of newly built homes to check that they meet all regulatory requirements. Home inspectors are also increasingly hired by prospective home buyers to inspect and report on the condition of a home's major systems, components, and structure. Typically, home inspectors are hired either immediately prior to a purchase offer on a home or as a contingency to a sales contract.

Construction and building inspectors increasingly use computers to help them monitor the status of construction inspection activities and keep track of permits issued. Details about construction projects, building and occupancy permits, and other documentation are now generally stored on computers so that they can easily be retrieved and kept accurate and up to date.

Although inspections are primarily visual, inspectors often use tape measures, survey instruments, metering devices, and test equipment such as concrete strength measurers. They keep a daily log of their work, take photographs, file reports, and, if necessary, act on their findings. For example, construction inspectors notify the construction contractor, superintendent, or supervisor when they discover a code or ordinance violation or something that does not comply with the contract specifications or approved plans. If the problem is not corrected within a reasonable or specified period of time, government inspectors have authority to issue a "stop-work" order.

Many inspectors also investigate construction or alterations being done without proper permits. Violators of permit laws are directed to obtain permits and submit to inspection.

## Working Conditions

Construction and building inspectors usually work alone. However, several may be assigned to large, complex projects, particularly because inspectors specialize in different areas of construction. Though they spend considerable time inspecting construction work sites, inspectors may spend much of their time in a field office reviewing blueprints, answering letters or telephone calls, writing reports, and scheduling inspections.

Inspection sites are dirty and may be cluttered with tools, materials, or debris. Inspectors may have to climb ladders or many flights of stairs, or may have to crawl around in tight spaces. Although their work is not considered hazardous, inspectors usually wear hard hats for safety.

Inspectors normally work regular hours. However, if an accident occurs at a construction site, inspectors must respond immediately and may work additional hours to complete their report.

## Employment

Construction and building inspectors held about 64,000 jobs in 1994. Over 50 percent worked for local governments, primarily municipal or county building departments. Employment of local government inspectors is concentrated in cities and in suburban areas undergoing rapid growth. Local governments employ large inspection staffs, including many plan examiners or inspectors who specialize in structural steel, reinforced concrete, boiler, electrical, and elevator inspection.

About 18 percent of all construction and building inspectors worked for engineering and architectural services firms, conducting inspections for a fee or on a contract basis. Most of the remaining inspectors were employed by the federal and state governments. Many construction inspectors employed by the federal government work for the U.S. Army Corps of Engineers or the General Services Administration. Other federal employers include the Tennessee Valley Authority and the Departments of Agriculture, Housing and Urban Development, and Interior.

## Training, Other Qualifications, and Advancement

Individuals who want to become construction and building inspectors should have a thorough knowledge of construction materials and practices in either a general area, like structural or heavy construction, or in a specialized area, such as electrical or plumbing systems, reinforced concrete, or structural steel. Construction or building inspectors need several years of experience as a manager, supervisor, or craft worker before becoming inspectors. Many inspectors have previously worked as carpenters, electricians, plumbers, or pipefitters.

Employers prefer to hire inspectors who have formal training as well as experience. Employers look for persons who have studied engineering or architecture, or who have a degree from a community or junior college, with courses in construction technology, blueprint reading, mathematics, and building inspection. Courses in drafting, algebra, geometry, and English are also useful. Most employers require inspectors to have a high school diploma or equivalent even when they qualify on the basis of experience.

Certification can enhance an inspector's opportunities for employment and advancement to more responsible positions. Most states and cities actually require some type of certification for employment. To become certified, inspectors with substantial experience and education must pass stringent examinations on code requirements, construction techniques, and materials. Many categories of certification are awarded for inspectors and plan examiners in a variety of disciplines, including the designation "CBO," Certified Building Official. (Organizations that administer certification programs are listed below in the section on Sources of Additional Information.)

Construction and building inspectors must be in good physical condition in order to walk and climb about construction sites. They also must have a driver's license. In addition, federal, state, and many local governments may require that inspectors pass a civil service examination.

Construction and building inspectors usually receive most of their training on the job. At first, working with an experienced inspector, they learn about inspection techniques; codes, ordinances, and regulations; contract specifications; and record keeping and reporting duties. They usually begin by inspecting less complex types of construction, such as residential buildings, and then progress to more difficult assignments. An engineering or architectural degree is often required for advancement to supervisory positions.

Because they advise builders and the general public on building codes, construction practices, and technical developments, construction and building inspectors must keep abreast of changes in these areas. Many employers provide formal training programs to broaden inspectors' knowledge of construction materials, practices, and techniques. Inspectors who work for small agencies or firms that do not conduct training programs can expand their knowledge and upgrade their skills by attending state-sponsored training programs, by taking college or correspondence courses, or by attending seminars sponsored by the organizations that certify inspectors.

## Job Outlook

Employment of construction and building inspectors is expected to grow faster than the average for all occupations through the year 2005. Growing concern for public safety and improvements in the quality of construction should continue to stimulate demand for construction and building inspectors. Despite the expected employment growth, most job openings will arise from the need to replace inspectors who transfer to other occupations or who leave the labor force. Replacement needs are relatively high because construction and building inspectors tend to be older, more experienced workers who have spent years working in other occupations.

Opportunities to become a construction and building inspector should be best for highly experienced supervisors and craft workers who have some college education, some engineering or architectural training, or who are certified as inspectors or plan examiners. Thorough knowledge of construction practices and skills in areas such as reading and evaluating blueprints and plans are essential. Governments—particularly federal and state—should continue to contract out inspection work to engineering, architectural and management services firms as their budgets remain tight. However, the volume of real estate transactions will increase as the population grows, and greater emphasis on home inspections should result in rapid growth in employment of home inspectors. Inspectors are involved in all phases of construction,

including maintenance and repair work, and are therefore less likely to lose jobs during recessionary periods when new construction slows.

## Earnings

The median annual salary of construction and building inspectors was $32,300 in 1994. The middle 50 percent earned between $25,200 and $43,800. The lowest 10 percent earned less than $19,400 and the highest 10 percent earned more than $57,500 a year. Generally, building inspectors, including plan examiners, earn the highest salaries. Salaries in large metropolitan areas are substantially higher than those in small local jurisdictions.

## Related Occupations

Construction and building inspectors combine a knowledge of construction principles and law with an ability to coordinate data, diagnose problems, and communicate with people. Workers in other occupations using a similar combination of skills include drafters, estimators, industrial engineering technicians, surveyors, architects, and construction contractors and managers.

## Related *D.O.T.* Jobs

These job titles are related to or more specific than the more general description above. They will help you identify job options you may not otherwise discover. These descriptions are in the current edition of the *Dictionary of Occupational Titles* and classified by numerical order.

168.167-030 INSPECTOR, BUILDING; 168.167-034 INSPECTOR, ELECTRICAL; 168.167-038 INSPECTOR, ELEVATORS; 168.167-046 INSPECTOR, HEATING AND REFRIGERATION; 168.167-050 INSPECTOR, PLUMBING; 168.267-010 BUILDING INSPECTOR; 168.267-102 PLAN CHECKER; 182.267-010 CONSTRUCTION INSPECTOR; 850.387-010 INSPECTOR OF DREDGING; 850.467-010 GRADE CHECKER

## Sources of Additional Information

Information about a career and certification as a construction or building inspector is available from the following model code organizations:

- ❏ International Conference of Building Officials, 5360 Workman Mill Rd., Whittier, CA 90601-2298.

- ❏ Building Officials and Code Administrators International, Inc., 4051 West Flossmoor Rd., Country Club Hills, IL 60478.

- ❏ Southern Building Code Congress International, Inc., 900 Montclair Rd., Birmingham, AL 35213.

Information about a career as a home inspector is available from:

- ❏ American Society of Home Inspectors, Inc., 85 West Algonquin Rd., Arlington Heights, IL 60005.

For information about a career as a state or local government construction or building inspector, contact your state or local employment service.

# Construction Managers

## Nature of the Work

Construction managers assume a wide variety of responsibilities and positions within construction firms. They are known by a range of job titles that are often used interchangeably—for example, *construction superintendent, general superintendent, project manager, general construction manager*, or *executive construction manager*. Construction managers may be owners or salaried employees of a construction management or contracting firm, or individuals working under contract or as salaried employees for the owner, developer, contractor, or management firm overseeing the construction project.

In the construction industry, managers and other professionals active in the industry—general managers, project engineers, cost estimators, and others—are increasingly referred to as *constructors*. The term constructor refers to a broad group of professionals in construction who, through education and experience, are capable of managing, coordinating, and supervising the construction process from conceptual development through final construction on a timely and economical basis. Given designs for buildings, roads, bridges, or other projects, constructors oversee the organization, scheduling, and implementation of the project to execute those designs. They are responsible for coordinating and managing people, materials, and equipment; budgets, schedules, and contracts; and the safety of employees and the general public.

In contrast with the *Occupational Outlook Handbook*, the term "construction manager" is used more narrowly within the construction industry to denote a firm, or an individual employed by the firm, involved in management oversight of a construction project. Under this narrower definition, construction managers generally act as agents or representatives of the owner or developer throughout the life of the project. Although they generally play no direct role in the actual construction of the building or other facility, they typically schedule and coordinate all design and construction processes. They develop and implement a management plan to complete the project according to the owner's goals that allows the design and construction processes to be carried out efficiently and effectively within budgetary and schedule constraints. In the *Occupational Outlook Handbook*, "construction manager" includes these workers as well as managers working directly for the contractors who actually perform the construction.

Generally, a *contractor* is the firm under contract to provide specialized construction services. On small projects such as remodeling a home, the construction contractor is usually a self-employed construction manager or skilled trades worker who directs and oversees employees. On larger projects, construction managers working for a *general contractor* have overall responsibility for completing the construction in accordance with the engineer or architect's drawings and specifications and prevailing building codes. They arrange for *subcontractors* to perform specialized craft work or other specified construction work.

Large construction projects, like an office building or industrial complex for example, are too complicated for one person to supervise. These projects are divided into many segments: Site preparation, including land clearing and earth moving; sewage systems; landscaping and road construction; building construction, including excavation and laying foundations, erection of structural framework, floors, walls, and roofs; and building systems, including fire protection, electrical, plumbing, air-conditioning, and heating. Construction managers may work as part of a team or may be in charge of one or more of these activities. They may have several subordinates, such as assistant project managers, superintendents, field engineers, or crew supervisors, reporting to them.

Construction managers plan, budget, and direct the construction project. They evaluate various construction methods and determine the most cost-effective plan and schedule. They determine the appropriate construction methods and schedule all required construction site activities into logical, specific steps, budgeting the time required to meet established deadlines. This may require sophisticated estimating and scheduling techniques, using computers with specialized software. Construction managers determine the labor requirements and, in some cases, supervise or monitor the hiring and dismissal of workers.

Managers direct and monitor the progress of field or site construction activities, at times through other construction supervisors. This includes the delivery and use of materials, tools, and equipment; the quality of construction, worker productivity, and safety. They are responsible for obtaining all necessary permits and licenses and, depending upon the contractual arrangements, direct or monitor compliance with building and safety codes and other regulations.

They regularly review engineering and architectural drawings and specifications to monitor progress and ensure compliance with plans and specifications. They track and control construction costs to avoid cost overruns. Based upon direct observation and reports by subordinate supervisors, managers may prepare daily reports of progress and requirements for labor, material, and machinery and equipment at the construction site. Construction managers meet regularly with owners, subcontractors, architects, and other design professionals to monitor and coordinate all phases of the construction project.

## Working Conditions

Construction managers work out of a main office from which the overall construction project is monitored or out of a field office at the construction site. Management decisions regarding daily construction activities are usually made at the job site. Managers usually travel when the construction site is in another state or when they are responsible for activities at two or more sites. Management of construction projects overseas usually entails temporary residence in another country.

Construction managers must be on call to deal with delays, bad weather, or emergencies at the site. Most work more than a standard 40-hour week since construction may proceed around-the-clock. This type of work schedule can go on for days, even weeks, to meet special project deadlines, especially if there have been unforeseen delays.

Although the work generally is not considered dangerous, construction managers must be careful while touring construction sites, especially when large machinery, heavy equipment, and vehicles are being operated. Managers must be able to establish priorities and assign duties. They need to observe job conditions and to be alert to changes and potential problems, particularly involving safety on the job site and adherence to regulations.

## Employment

Construction managers held about 197,000 jobs in 1994.

Over 85 percent were employed in the construction industry, primarily by specialty trade contractors—for example, plumbing, heating and air-conditioning, and electrical contractors—and general building contractors. Many also worked as self-employed independent contractors in the specialty trades. Others were employed by engineering, architectural, surveying, and construction management services firms, as well as local governments, educational institutions, and real estate developers.

## Training, Other Qualifications, and Advancement

Persons interested in becoming a construction manager need a solid background in building science and management, as well as related work experience within the construction industry. They need to be able to understand contracts, plans, and specifications, and be knowledgeable about construction methods, materials, and regulations. Familiarity with computers and software programs for job costing, scheduling, and estimating is increasingly important.

Traditionally, persons advanced to construction management positions after having substantial experience as construction craft workers—for example, as carpenters, masons, plumbers, or electricians—or after having worked as construction supervisors or as independent specialty contractors overseeing workers in one or more construction trades. However, more and more employers—particularly, large construction firms—seek to hire managers with industry work experience and formal postsecondary education in building science or construction management.

In 1994, over 100 colleges and universities offered 4-year degree programs in construction management or construction science. These programs include courses in project control and development, site planning, design, construction methods, construction materials, value analysis, cost estimating, scheduling, contract administration, accounting, business and financial management, building codes and standards, inspection procedures, engineering and architectural sciences, mathematics, statistics, and computer science. Graduates from four-year degree programs usually are hired as assistants to project managers, field engineers, schedulers, or cost estimators. An increasing number of graduates in related fields—engineering or architecture, for example—also enter construction management, often after having had substantial experience on construction projects.

Around 30 colleges and universities also offer a master's degree program in construction management or construction science, and at least two offer a Ph.D. in the field. Master's degree recipients, especially those with work experience in construction, typically become construction managers in very large construction or construction management companies. Often, individuals who hold a bachelor's degree in an unrelated field seek a master's degree in order to work in the construction industry. Doctoral degree recipients generally become college professors or work in an area of research.

Many individuals also attend training and educational programs sponsored by industry associations, often in collaboration with postsecondary institutions. A number of two-year colleges throughout the country offer construction management or construction technology programs.

Construction managers should be adaptable and be able to work effectively in a fast-paced environment. They should be decisive and able to work well under pressure, particularly when faced with unexpected occurrences or delays. The ability to coordinate several major activities at once, while being able to analyze and resolve specific problems is essential, as is the ability to understand engineering, architectural, and other construction drawings. Managers must be able to establish a good working relationship with many different people including owners, other managers, design professionals, supervisors, and craft workers.

Advancement opportunities for construction managers vary depending upon the size and type of company for which one works. Within large firms, managers may eventually become top-level managers or executives. Highly experienced individuals may become independent consultants; some serve as expert witnesses in court or as arbitrators in disputes. Those with the required capital may establish their own firms offering construction management services or their own general contracting firms overseeing construction projects from start to finish.

## Job Outlook

Employment of construction managers is expected to increase faster than the average for all occupations through the year 2005 as the level of construction activity and complexity of construction projects continues to grow. In addition, many job openings should result annually from the need to replace workers who transfer to other occupations or leave the labor force. Employers prefer applicants with previous construction work experience who can combine a strong background in building technology with proven supervisory or managerial skills. Prospects in construction management, engineering and architectural services, and construction contracting firms should be particularly favorable for persons with a bachelor's degree or higher in construction science, construction management, or construction engineering who have worked in construction.

Increased spending on the nation's infrastructure—highways, bridges, dams, water and sewage systems, and electric power generation and transmission facilities—will result in a greater demand for construction managers, as will the need to build more residential housing, commercial and office buildings, and factories. In addition, continuing maintenance and repair of all kinds of existing structures will also contribute to demand for these professionals.

The increasing complexity of construction projects also should lead to the creation of more manager jobs. Advances in building materials and construction methods and the growing number of multipurpose buildings, electronically operated "smart" buildings, and energy-efficient structures will require the expertise of more construction managers. In addition, the proliferation of laws setting standards for buildings and construction materials, worker safety, energy efficiency, and environmental pollution have further complicated the construction process and should increase demand for managers. As project owners and construction companies strive to keep costs in line and reduce the causes of disputes and litigation, they will continue to depend on the services and expertise of highly effective managers.

Employment of construction managers is sensitive to the short-term nature of many construction projects and cyclical fluctuations in construction activity. During periods of diminished construction activity—when many construction workers are laid off—many construction managers remain employed to plan, schedule, or estimate costs of future construction projects, as well as to manage maintenance, repair and renovation work which remains ongoing.

## Earnings

Earnings of salaried construction managers and incomes of self-employed independent construction contractors vary depending upon the size and nature of the construction project, its geographic location, and economic conditions. Based on limited information available, the average starting salary for construction managers in 1994 was around $30,000 annually. The average salary for experienced construction managers in 1994 ranged from around $40,000 to $100,000 annually. Many salaried construction managers receive benefits such as bonuses, use of company motor vehicles, paid vacations, and life and health insurance.

## Related Occupations

Construction managers participate in the conceptual development of a construction project and oversee its organization, scheduling, and implementation. Occupations that perform similar functions include architects, civil engineers, construction supervisors, cost engineers, cost estimators, developers, electrical engineers, industrial engineers, landscape architects, and mechanical engineers.

## Related *D.O.T.* Jobs

These job titles are related to or more specific than the more general description above. They will help you identify job options you may not otherwise discover. These descriptions are in the current edition of the *Dictionary of Occupational Titles* and classified by numerical order.

182.167-010 CONTRACTOR; 182.167-018 RAILROAD-CONSTRUCTION DIRECTOR; 182.167-026 SUPERINTENDENT, CONSTRUCTION; 182.167-030 SUPERINTENDENT, MAINTENANCE OF WAY; 182.167-034 SUPERVISOR, BRIDGES AND BUILDINGS

## Sources of Information

For information about a career as a construction manager contact:

❑ American Institute of Constructors, 466 94th Ave. North, St. Petersburg, FL 33702.

❑ Associated Builders and Contractors, 1300 North 17th St., Rosslyn, VA 22209.

❑ Associated General Contractors of America, 1957 E St. NW, Washington, DC 20006-5199.

❑ Construction Management Association of America, 7918 Jones Branch Dr., Suite 540, McLean, VA 22102.

Information on the accreditation requirements for construction science and management programs is available from:

❑ American Council for Construction Education, 1300 Hudson Lane, Suite 3, Monroe, LA 71201-6054.

# Correctional Officers

## Nature of the Work

Correctional officers are charged with overseeing individuals who have been arrested, are awaiting trial or other hearing, or who have been convicted of a crime and sentenced to serve time in a jail, reformatory, or penitentiary. They maintain security and observe inmate conduct and behavior to prevent disturbances and escapes. Many correctional officers work in small county and municipal jails or precinct station houses as deputy sheriffs or police officers with wide ranging responsibilities. Others are assigned to large state and federal prisons where job duties are more specialized. A relatively small number supervise aliens being held by the Immigration and Naturalization Service before being released or deported. Regardless of the setting, correctional officers maintain order within the institution, enforce rules and regulations, and may supplement whatever counseling inmates receive from psychologists, social workers, or other mental health professionals.

To make sure inmates are orderly and obey rules, correctional officers monitor inmates' activities, including working, exercising, eating, and bathing. They assign and supervise inmates' work assignments. Sometimes it is necessary to search inmates and their living quarters for weapons or drugs, to settle disputes between inmates, and to enforce discipline. Correctional officers cannot show favoritism and must report any inmate who violates the rules. A few officers hold staff security positions in towers, where they are equipped with high-powered rifles. Other, unarmed officers are responsible for direct supervision of inmates. They are locked in a cell-block alone, or with another officer, among the 50 to 100 inmates who reside there. The officers enforce regulations primarily through their communications skills and moral authority.

Other correctional officers periodically inspect the facilities. They may, for example, check cells and other areas of the institution for unsanitary conditions, weapons, drugs, fire hazards, and any evidence of infractions of rules. In addition, they routinely inspect locks, window bars, grille doors, and gates for signs of tampering.

Correctional officers report orally and in writing on inmate conduct and on the quality and quantity of work done by inmates. Officers also report disturbances, violations of rules, and any unusual occurrences. They usually keep a daily record of their activities. In the most modern facilities, correctional officers can monitor the activities of prisoners from a centralized control center with the aid of closed circuit television cameras and a computer tracking system. In such an environment, the inmates may not see anyone but officers for days or weeks at a time.

Depending on the offender's classification within the institution, correctional officers may escort inmates to and from cells and other areas and admit and accompany authorized visitors to see inmates. Officers may also escort prisoners between the institution and courtrooms, medical facilities, and other destinations. They inspect mail and visitors for contraband (prohibited items). Should the situation arise, they assist law enforcement authorities by investigating crimes committed within their institution and by helping search for escaped inmates.

Correctional officers may arrange a change in a daily schedule so that an inmate can visit the library, help inmates get news of their families, or help inmates in other ways. In a few institutions, officers receive specialized training, have a more formal counseling role, and may lead or participate in group counseling sessions.

Correctional sergeants directly supervise correctional officers. They usually are responsible for maintaining security and directing the activities of a group of inmates during an assigned watch or in an assigned area.

## Working Conditions

Correctional officers may work indoors or outdoors, depending on their specific duties. Some indoor areas of correctional institutions are well-lighted, heated, and ventilated, but others are overcrowded, hot, and noisy. Outdoors, weather conditions may be disagreeable, for example when standing watch on a guard tower in cold weather. Working in a correctional institution can be stressful and hazardous; correctional officers occasionally have been injured or killed by inmates.

Correctional officers usually work an eight-hour day, five days a week, on rotating shifts. Prison security must be provided around the clock, which often means that junior officers work weekends, holidays, and nights. In addition, officers may be required to work overtime.

## Employment

Correctional officers held about 310,000 jobs in 1994. Six of every 10 worked at state correctional institutions such as prisons, prison camps, and reformatories. Most of the remainder worked at city and county jails or other institutions run by local governments. About 9,000 correctional officers worked at federal correctional institutions, and about 4,000 worked in privately owned and managed prisons.

Most correctional officers work in relatively large institutions located in rural areas, although a significant number work in jails and other smaller facilities located in law enforcement agencies throughout the country.

## Training, Other Qualifications, and Advancement

Most institutions require that correctional officers be at least 18 or 21 years of age, have a high school education or its equivalent, have no felony convictions, and be a United States citizen. In addition, correctional institutions increasingly seek correctional officers with postsecondary education, particularly in psychology, criminal justice, police science, criminology, and related fields.

Correctional officers must be in good health. The federal system and many states require candidates to meet formal standards of physical fitness, eyesight, and hearing. Strength, good judgment, and the ability to think and act quickly are indispensable. Other common requirements include a driver's license, and work experience that demonstrates reliability. The federal system and some states screen applicants for drug abuse and require candidates to pass a written or oral examination, along with a background check.

Federal, state, and local departments of corrections provide training for correctional officers based on guidelines established by the American Correctional Association, the American Jail Association, and other professional organizations. Some states have special training academies. All states and local departments of correction provide informal on-the-job training at the conclusion of formal instruction. On-the-job trainees receive several weeks or months of training in an actual job setting under an experienced officer.

Academy trainees generally receive instruction on institutional policies, regulations, and operations; constitutional law and cultural awareness; crisis intervention, inmate behavior, and contraband control; custody and security procedures; fire and safety; inmate rules and legal rights; administrative responsibilities; written and oral communication, including preparation of reports; self-defense, including the use of firearms and physical force; first aid including cardiopulmonary resuscitation (CPR); and physical fitness training. New federal correctional officers must undergo 200 hours of formal training within the first year of employment. They must complete 120 hours of specialized correctional instruction at the Federal Bureau of Prisons residential training center at Glynco, Georgia, within the first 60 days after appointment. Experienced officers receive inservice training to keep abreast of new ideas and procedures.

Entry requirements and on-the-job training vary widely from agency to agency. For instance, correctional officers in North Dakota need two years of college with emphasis on criminal justice or behavioral science, or three years as a correctional, military police, or licensed peace officer. The department then provides 80 hours of training at the start, and follows up with 40 hours of training annually. On the other hand, Connecticut requires only that candidates be 18 years of age, have a high school diploma or GED Certificate, and pass a medical/physical examination, including drug screening. It then provides 520 hours of initial training, and follows up with 40 hours annually.

Correctional officers have the opportunity to join prison tactical response teams, which are trained to respond to riots, hostage situations, forced cell moves, and other potentially dangerous confrontations. Team members often receive monthly training and practice with weapons, chemical agents, forced entry methods, and other tactics.

With education, experience, and training, qualified officers may advance to correctional sergeant or other supervisory or administrative positions. Many correctional institutions require experience as a correctional officer for other corrections positions. Ambitious correctional officers can be promoted up to assistant warden. Officers sometimes transfer to related areas, such as probation and parole officer.

## Job Outlook

Job opportunities for correctional officers are expected to be plentiful through the year 2005. The need to replace correctional officers who transfer to other occupations or leave the labor force, coupled with rising employment demand, will generate many thousands of job openings each year. Some local and a few state correctional agencies have traditionally experienced difficulty in attracting qualified applicants, largely due to relatively low salaries and unattractive rural locations. This situation is expected to continue, ensuring highly favorable job prospects.

Employment of correctional officers is expected to increase much faster than the average for all occupations through the year 2005 as additional officers are hired to supervise and control a growing inmate population. Expansion and new construction of correctional facilities also are expected to create many new jobs for correctional officers, although state and local government budgetary constraints could affect the rate at which new facilities are built. Increasing public concern about the spread of crime and illegal drugs—resulting in more convictions—and the adoption of mandatory sentencing guidelines calling for longer sentences and reduced parole for inmates also will spur demand for correctional officers.

Layoffs of correctional officers are rare because security must be maintained in correctional institutions at all times.

## Earnings

According to a 1994 survey in *Corrections Compendium,* a national journal for corrections professionals, starting salaries of state correctional officers averaged about $19,100 a year, ranging from $13,700 in Kentucky to $29,700 in New Jersey. Professional correctional officers' salaries, overall, averaged about $22,900 and ranged from $17,000 in Wyoming to $34,100 in New York.

At the federal level, the starting salary was about $18,700 to $20,800 a year in 1995; supervisory correctional officers started at about $28,300 a year. Starting salaries were slightly higher in selected areas where prevailing local pay levels were higher. The 1995 average salary for all federal nonsupervisory correctional officers was about $31,460; for supervisors, about $57,100.

Correctional officers usually are provided uniforms or a clothing allowance to purchase their own uniforms. Most are provided or can participate in hospitalization or major medical insurance plans; many officers can get disability and life insurance at group rates. They also receive vacation and sick leave and pension benefits. Officers employed by the federal government and most state governments are covered by civil service systems or merit boards. Their retirement coverage entitles them to retire at age 50 after 20 years of service or at any age with 25 years of service. In the federal system and some states, correctional officers are represented by labor unions.

## Related Occupations

A number of related careers are open to high school graduates who are interested in protective services and the field of security. Bailiffs supervise offenders and maintain order in local and state courtrooms during legal proceedings. Bodyguards escort people and protect them from injury or invasion of privacy. House or store detectives patrol business establishments to protect against theft and vandalism and to enforce standards of good behavior. Security guards protect government, commercial, and industrial property against theft, vandalism, illegal entry, and fire. Police officers and deputy sheriffs maintain law and order, prevent crime, and arrest offenders.

Other corrections careers are open to persons interested in working with offenders. Probation and parole officers monitor and counsel offenders, process their release from correctional institutions, and evaluate their progress in becoming productive members of society. Recreation leaders organize and instruct offenders in sports, games, arts, and crafts.

## Related *D.O.T.* Jobs

These job titles are related to or more specific than the more general description above. They will help you identify job options you may not otherwise discover. These descriptions are in the current edition of the *Dictionary of Occupational Titles* and classified by numerical order.

372.367-014 JAILER; 372.567-014 GUARD, IMMIGRATION; 372.667-018 CORRECTION OFFICER; 372.677-010 PATROL CONDUCTOR; 375.367-010 POLICE OFFICER II

## Sources of Additional Information

Information about entrance requirements, training, and career opportunities for correctional officers on the state level may be obtained from state civil service commissions, state departments of corrections, or nearby correctional institutions and facilities.

Additional information on careers in corrections on the local level is available from:

❏ The American Jail Association, 2053 Day Road, Hagerstown, MD 21740-9795.

Information on entrance requirements, training, and career opportunities for correctional officers on the federal level may be obtained from:

❏ Federal Bureau of Prisons, National Recruitment Office, 320 First St. NW, Room 460, Washington, DC 20534.

❏ International Association of Correctional Officers, 1333 S. Wabash-Box 53, Chicago, IL 60605.

# Cost Estimators

## Nature of the Work

Accurately predicting the cost of future projects is vital to the survival of any business. Cost estimators develop cost information for owners or managers to use in making bids for contracts, in determining if a new product will be profitable, or in determining which of a firms' products are making a profit.

Regardless of the industry they work in, estimators compile and analyze data on all the factors that can influence costs—such as materials, labor, location, and special machinery requirements, including computer hardware and software. Job duties vary widely depending upon the type and size of the project. Estimators working in the construction industry and manufacturing businesses have different methods of and motivations for estimating costs.

On a large construction project, for example, the estimating process begins with the decision to submit a bid. After reviewing the architect's drawings and specifications, the estimator visits the site of the proposed project. The estimator needs to gather information on access to the site and availability of electricity, water, and other services, as well as surface topography and drainage. If the project is a remodeling or renovation job, the estimator might consider the need to control noise and dust and schedule work in order to accommodate occupants of the building. The information developed during the site visit generally is recorded in a signed report that is made part of the final project estimate.

After the site visit is completed, the estimator determines the quantity of materials and labor that the firm will have to furnish. This process, called the quantity survey or "takeoff," is completed by filling out standard estimating forms that provide spaces for the entry of dimensions, number of units, and other information. A cost estimator working for a general contractor, for example, will estimate the costs of all items the contractor must provide. Although subcontractors will estimate their costs as part of their own bidding process, the general contractor's cost estimator often analyzes bids made by subcontractors as well. Also during the takeoff process, the estimator must make decisions concerning equipment needs, sequence of operations, and crew size. Allowances for the waste of materials, inclement weather, shipping delays, and other factors that may increase costs are incorporated in the takeoff.

On completion of the quantity surveys, a total project cost summary is prepared by the chief estimator that includes the cost of labor, equipment, materials, subcontracts, overhead, taxes, insurance, markup, and any other costs that may affect the project. The chief estimator then prepares the bid proposal for submission to the developer.

Construction cost estimators also may be employed by the project's architect or owner to estimate costs or track actual costs relative to bid specifications as the project develops. In large construction companies that employ more than one estimator, it is common practice for them to specialize. For instance, one person may estimate only electrical work, whereas another may concentrate on excavation, concrete, and forms.

In manufacturing and other firms, cost estimators generally are assigned to the engineering or cost department. The estimators' goal in manufacturing is to accurately allocate the costs associated with making products. The job may begin when management requests an estimate of the costs associated with a major redesign of an existing product or the development of a new product or production process. When estimating the cost of developing a new product, for example, the estimator works with engineers, first reviewing blueprints or conceptual drawings to determine the machining operations, tools, gauges, and materials that would be required for the job. The estimator then prepares a parts list and determines whether it is more efficient to produce or to purchase the parts. To do this, the estimator must initiate inquiries for price information from potential suppliers. The next step is to determine the cost of manufacturing each component of the product. Some high technology products require a tremendous amount of computer programming during the design phase. The cost of software development is one of the fastest growing and most difficult activities to estimate. Some cost estimators now specialize in only estimating computer software development and related costs.

The cost estimator then prepares time-phase charts and learning curves. Time-phase charts indicate the time required for tool design and fabrication, tool "debugging"—finding and correcting all problems—manufacturing of parts, assembly, and testing. Learning curves graphically represent the rate at which performance improves with practice. These curves are commonly called "problem-elimination" curves because many problems—such as engineering changes, rework, parts shortages, and lack of operator skills—diminish as the number of parts produced increases, resulting in lower unit costs.

Using all of this information, the estimator then calculates the standard labor hours necessary to produce a predetermined number of units. Standard labor hours are then converted to dollar values, to which are added factors for waste, overhead, and profit to yield the unit cost in dollars. The estimator then compares the cost of purchasing parts with the firm's cost of manufacturing them to determine which is cheaper.

Computers are widely used because cost estimating may involve complex mathematical calculations and require advanced mathematical techniques. For example, to undertake a parametric analysis, a process used to estimate project costs on a per unit basis subject to the specific requirements of a project, cost estimators use a computer database containing information on costs and conditions of many other similar projects. Although computers cannot be used for the entire estimating process, they can relieve estimators of much of the drudgery associated with routine, repetitive, and time-consuming calculations. Computers also are used to produce all of the necessary documentation with the help of basic word-processing and spreadsheet software. This leaves estimators with more time to study and analyze projects and can lead to more accurate estimates. (More detailed information on various cost estimating techniques is available from the organizations listed under Sources of Additional Information below.)

## Working Conditions

Although estimators spend most of their time in an office, construction estimators must make frequent visits to work sites that are dirty and cluttered with debris. Likewise, estimators in manufacturing must spend time on the factory floor where it can be hot, noisy, and dirty. Cost estimators usually operate under pressure, especially when facing deadlines. Inaccurate estimating can cause a firm to lose out on a bid or lose money on a job that proves to be unprofitable. Although estimators normally work a 40-hour week, much overtime is often required. In some industries, frequent travel between a firm's headquarters and its subsidiaries or subcontractors also may be required.

## Employment

Cost estimators held about 179,000 jobs in 1994, primarily in construction industries. Others can be found primarily in manufacturing industries. Some cost estimators also worked for engineering and architectural services firms, business services firms, and throughout a wide range of other industries. Construction, operations research, production control, cost, and price analysts who work for government agencies also may do significant amounts of cost estimating in the course of their regular duties.

Cost estimators work throughout the country, usually in or near major industrial, commercial, and government centers, and in cities and suburban areas undergoing rapid change or development.

## Training, Other Qualifications, and Advancement

Entry requirements for cost estimators vary significantly by industry. In the construction industry, employers prefer applicants with a thorough knowledge of construction materials, costs, and procedures in areas ranging from heavy construction to electrical work, plumbing systems, or masonry work. Most construction estimators have considerable previous experience as a construction craft worker or manager. Individuals who combine this experience with some postsecondary training in construction estimating, or with a bachelor's or associate degree in civil engineering, architectural drafting, or building construction, have a competitive edge in landing jobs.

In manufacturing industries, employers prefer to hire individuals with a degree in engineering, science, operations research, mathematics, or statistics, or in accounting, finance, business, or a related subject. In high-technology industries, great emphasis is placed on experience involving quantitative techniques.

Cost estimators should have an aptitude for mathematics, be able to quickly analyze, compare, and interpret detailed and sometimes poorly defined information, and be able to make sound and accurate judgments based on this knowledge. Assertiveness and self-confidence in presenting and supporting their conclusions are important. Cost estimators should also be familiar with computers and their application to the estimating process, including word-processing and spreadsheet packages used to produce necessary documentation. In some instances, familiarity with special estimation software or programming skills may be useful.

Regardless of their background, estimators receive much training on the job. Working with an experienced estimator, they become familiar with each step in the process. Those with no experience reading construction specifications or blueprints first learn that aspect of the work. They then may accompany an experienced estimator to the construction site or shop floor where they observe the work being done, take measurements, or perform other routine tasks. As they become more knowledgeable, estimators learn how to tabulate quantities and dimensions from drawings and how to select the appropriate material prices.

Many colleges and universities include cost estimating as part of curriculums in civil engineering, industrial engineering, and construction management or construction engineering technology. Courses and programs in cost estimating techniques and procedures are offered by many technical schools, junior colleges, and universities. In addition, cost estimating is a significant part of master's degree programs in construction management offered by many colleges and universities. Organizations that represent cost estimators, such as American Association of Cost Engineers (AACE) International and the Society of Cost Estimating and Analysis, also sponsor educational programs. These programs help students, estimators-in-training, and experienced estimators stay abreast of changes affecting the profession.

Voluntary certification can be valuable to cost estimators because it provides professional recognition of the estimator's competence and experience. Both AACE International and the Society of Cost Estimating and Analysis administer certification programs. To become certified, estimators generally must have between three and seven years of estimating experience and must pass both a written and an oral examination. In addition, certification requirements may include publication of at least one article or paper in the field.

For most estimators, advancement takes the form of higher pay and prestige. Some move into management positions, such as project manager for a construction firm or manager of the industrial engineering department for a manufacturer. Others may go into business for themselves as consultants, providing estimating services for a fee to government or construction and manufacturing firms.

## Job Outlook

Overall employment of cost estimators is expected to grow about as fast as average for all occupations through the year 2005

as the levels of construction and manufacturing activity increase as the economy grows. However, even when construction and manufacturing activity decline, there should always remain a demand for cost estimators to accurately predict costs in all areas of business. Some job openings will also arise from the need to replace workers who transfer to other occupations or who leave the labor force altogether.

Growth of the construction industry, where over 60 percent of all cost estimators are employed, will be the driving force behind the rising demand for these workers. The fastest growing sectors of the construction industry are expected to be special trade contractors and those associated with heavy construction and spending on the nation's infrastructure. Construction and repair of highways and streets, bridges, and construction of more subway systems, airports, water and sewage systems, and electric power plants and transmission lines will stimulate demand for many more cost estimators. Job prospects in construction should be best for those workers with a degree in construction management, engineering, or architectural drafting, or who have substantial experience in various phases of construction or a specialty craft area.

Employment of cost estimators in manufacturing should remain relatively stable as firms continue to use their services to identify and control their operating costs. Experienced estimators with degrees in engineering, science, mathematics, business administration, or economics and who have computer expertise should have the best job prospects in manufacturing.

## Earnings

Salaries of cost estimators vary widely by experience, education, size of firm, and industry. According to limited data available, most starting salaries in the construction industry for cost estimators with limited training were between about $17,000 and $21,000 a year in 1994. College graduates with degrees in fields such as engineering or construction management that provide a strong background in cost estimating could start at about $30,000 annually or more. Highly experienced cost estimators earned $75,000 a year or more. Starting salaries and annual earnings in the manufacturing sector usually were somewhat higher.

## Related Occupations

Other workers who quantitatively analyze information in a similar capacity include appraisers, cost accountants, cost engineers, economists, evaluators, financial analysts, loan officers, operations research analysts, underwriters, and value engineers.

## Related *D.O.T.* Jobs

These job titles are related to or more specific than the more general description above. They will help you identify job options you may not otherwise discover. These descriptions are in the current edition of the *Dictionary of Occupational Titles* and classified by numerical order.

169.267-038 ESTIMATOR; 221.362-018 ESTIMATOR, PAPERBOARD BOXES; 221.367-014 ESTIMATOR, PRINTING

## Sources of Additional Information

Information about career opportunities, certification, and educational programs in cost estimating in the construction industry may be obtained from:

❏ AACE International, 209 Prairie Ave., Suite 100, Morgantown, WV 26505.

❏ Professional Construction Estimators Association of America, P.O. Box 11626, Charlotte, NC 28220-1626.

Similar information about cost estimating in government, manufacturing, and other industries is available from:

❏ Society of Cost Estimating and Analysis, 101 S. Whiting St., Suite 201, Alexandria, VA 22304.

# Dental Assistants

## Nature of the Work

Dental assistants perform a variety of patient care, office, and laboratory duties. They work at chair-side as dentists examine and treat patients. They make patients as comfortable as possible in the dental chair, prepare them for treatment, and obtain dental records. Assistants hand instruments and materials to dentists and keep patients' mouths dry and clear by using suction or other devices. Assistants also sterilize and disinfect instruments and equipment; prepare tray setups for dental procedures; provide postoperative instruction; and instruct patients in oral health care. Some dental assistants prepare materials for making impressions and restorations, expose radiographs, and process dental x-ray film as directed by a dentist. They may also remove sutures, apply anesthetics and cavity preventive agents to teeth and gums, remove excess cement used in the filling process, and place rubber dams on the teeth to isolate them for individual treatment.

Those with laboratory duties make casts of the teeth and mouth from impressions taken by dentists, clean and polish removable appliances, and make temporary crowns. Dental assistants with office duties schedule and confirm appointments, receive patients, keep treatment records, send bills, receive payments, and order dental supplies and materials.

Dental assistants should not be confused with dental hygienists, who are licensed to perform a wider variety of clinical tasks.

## Working Conditions

Dental assistants work in a well-lighted, clean environment. Their work area is usually near the dental chair, so that they can arrange instruments, materials, and medication, and hand them to the dentist when needed. Handling radiographic equipment poses dangers, but they can be minimized with safety procedures. Likewise, dental assistants wear gloves and masks to protect themselves from infectious diseases like hepatitis.

Most dental assistants have a 32- to 40-hour work week, which may include work on Saturday or evenings.

## Employment

Dental assistants held about 190,000 jobs in 1994. Almost one out of three worked part-time, sometimes in more than one dentist's office.

Almost all dental assistants work in private dental offices. Some work in dental schools, private and government hospitals, state and local public health departments, or in clinics.

## Training, Other Qualifications, and Advancement

Most assistants learn their skills on the job, though many are trained in dental assisting programs offered by community and junior colleges, trade schools, and technical institutes. Some assistants are trained in Armed Forces schools. Assistants must be a dentist's "third hand"; therefore, dentists look for people who are reliable, can work well with others, and have manual dexterity. High school students interested in careers as dental assistants should take courses in biology, chemistry, health, and office practices.

The American Dental Association's Commission on Dental Accreditation approved 235 training programs in 1995. Programs include classroom, laboratory, and preclinical instruction in dental assisting skills and related theory. In addition, students gain practical experience in dental schools, clinics, or dental offices. Most programs take one year or less to complete and lead to a certificate or diploma. Two-year programs offered in community and junior colleges lead to an associate degree. All programs require a high school diploma or its equivalent, and some require typing or a science course for admission. Some private vocational schools offer four- to six-month courses in dental assisting, but these are not accredited by the Commission on Dental Accreditation.

Certification is available through the Dental Assisting National Board. Certification is an acknowledgment of an assistant's qualifications and professional competence, but usually is not required for employment. In several states that have adopted standards for dental assistants who perform radiologic procedures, completion of the certification examination meets those standards. Candidates may qualify to take the certification examination by graduating from an accredited training program or by having two years of full-time experience as a dental assistant. In addition, applicants must have taken a course in cardiopulmonary resuscitation.

Without further education, advancement opportunities are limited. Some dental assistants working the front office become office managers. Others, working chair-side, go back to school to become dental hygienists.

## Job Outlook

Job prospects for dental assistants should be good. Employment is expected to grow much faster than the average for all occupations through the year 2005. Also, the proportion of workers leaving and who must be replaced is above average. Many opportunities are for entry-level positions that offer on-the-job training.

Population growth and greater retention of natural teeth by middle-aged and older people will fuel demand for dental services. Also, dentists are likely to employ more assistants, for several reasons. Older dentists, who are less likely to employ assistants, will leave and be replaced by recent graduates, who are more likely to use one, or even two. In addition, as dentists' workloads increase, they are expected to hire more assistants to perform routine tasks, so they may use their own time more profitably.

Most job openings for dental assistants will arise from the need to replace assistants who leave the occupation. For many, this entry-level occupation provides basic training and experience and serves as a stepping-stone to more highly skilled and higher paying jobs. Other assistants leave the job to take on family responsibilities, return to school, or for other reasons.

## Earnings

In 1993, median weekly earnings for dental assistants working full-time were about $329. The middle 50 percent earned between $255 and $391 a week. According to the American Dental Association, dental assistants who worked 32 hours a week or more averaged $370 a week in 1993; the average hourly earnings for all dental assistants were $10.20.

## Related Occupations

Workers in other occupations supporting health practitioners include medical assistants, physical therapy assistants, occupational therapy assistants, pharmacy assistants, and veterinary technicians.

## Related *D.O.T.* Jobs

These job titles are related to or more specific than the more general description above. They will help you identify job options you may not otherwise discover. These descriptions are in the current edition of the *Dictionary of Occupational Titles* and classified by numerical order.

079.361-018 DENTAL ASSISTANT

## Sources of Additional Information

Information about career opportunities, scholarships, accredited dental assistant programs, and requirements for certification is available from:

❑ American Dental Assistants Association, 203 N. Lasalle, Suite 1320, Chicago, IL 60601-1225.

❑ Commission on Dental Accreditation, American Dental Association, 211 E. Chicago Ave., Suite 1814, Chicago, IL 60611.

❑ Dental Assisting National Board, Inc., 216 E. Ontario St., Chicago, IL 60611.

# Dental Hygienists

## Nature of the Work

Dental hygienists clean teeth and provide other preventive dental care as well as teach patients how to practice good oral hygiene. Hygienists examine patients' teeth and gums, recording the presence of diseases or abnormalities. They remove calculus, stains, and plaque from teeth; apply cavity preventive agents such as fluorides and pit and fissure sealants; take and develop dental x-rays; place temporary fillings and periodontal dressings; remove sutures; and smooth and polish metal restorations. In some states, hygienists administer local anesthetics and anesthetic gas, and place and carve filling materials.

Dental hygienists also help patients develop and maintain good oral health. For example, they may explain the relationship between diet and oral health, inform patients how to select toothbrushes, and show patients how to brush and floss their teeth.

Dental hygienists use hand and rotary instruments to clean teeth, x-ray machines to take dental pictures, syringes with needles to administer local anesthetics, and models of teeth to explain oral hygiene.

## Working Conditions

Flexible scheduling is a distinctive feature of this job. Full-time, part-time, evening, and weekend work is widely available. Dentists frequently hire hygienists to work only two or three days a week, so hygienists may hold jobs in more than one dental office.

Dental hygienists work in clean, well-lighted offices. Important health safeguards include strict adherence to proper radiological procedures and use of appropriate protective devices when administering anesthetic gas. Dental hygienists also wear safety glasses, surgical masks and gloves to protect themselves from infectious diseases such as hepatitis. The occupation is one of several covered by the Consumer-Patient Radiation Health and Safety Act of 1981, which encourages the states to adopt uniform standards for the training and certification of individuals who perform medical and dental radiological procedures.

## Employment

Dental hygienists held about 127,000 jobs in 1994. Because multiple jobholding is common in this field, the number of jobs greatly exceeds the number of hygienists. About half of all dental hygienists usually worked part-time—less than 35 hours a week.

Almost all dental hygienists work in private dental offices. Some work in public health agencies, school systems, hospitals, and clinics.

## Training, Other Qualifications, and Advancement

Dental hygienists must be licensed by the state in which they practice. To qualify for licensure, a candidate must graduate from an accredited dental hygiene school and pass both a written and a clinical examination. The American Dental Association Joint Commission on National Dental Examinations administers the written examination that is accepted by all states and the District of Columbia. State or regional testing agencies administer the clinical examination. In addition, examinations on legal aspects of dental hygiene practice are required by most states. Alabama also allows candidates to take its examination if they have been trained through a state-regulated on-the-job program in a dentist's office.

In 1995, 212 programs in dental hygiene were accredited by the Commission on Dental Accreditation. Although some programs lead to a bachelor's degree, most grant an associate degree. Ten universities offer master's degree programs in dental hygiene.

An associate degree is sufficient for practice in a private dental office. A bachelor's or master's degree is usually required for research, teaching, or clinical practice in public or school health programs.

About half of the dental hygiene programs prefer applicants who have completed at least one year of college. Some of the bachelor's degree programs require applicants to have completed two years. However, requirements vary from school to school. These schools offer laboratory, clinical, and classroom instruction in subjects such as anatomy, physiology, chemistry, microbiology, pharmacology, nutrition, radiography, histology (the study of tissue structure), periodontology (the study of gum diseases), pathology, dental materials, clinical dental hygiene, and social and behavioral sciences.

Dental hygienists should work well with others and must have manual dexterity because they use dental instruments with little room for error within a patient's mouth. Recommended high school courses for aspiring dental hygienists include biology, chemistry, and mathematics.

## Job Outlook

Employment of dental hygienists is expected to grow much faster than the average for all occupations through the year 2005 in response to increasing demand for dental care and the greater substitution of hygienists for services previously performed by dentists. Job prospects are expected to remain very good unless the number of dental hygienist program graduates grows much faster than during the last decade and results in a much larger pool of qualified applicants.

Demand will be stimulated by population growth, and greater retention of natural teeth by the larger number of middle-aged and elderly people. Also, dentists are likely to employ more hygienists, for several reasons. Older dentists, who are less likely to employ dental hygienists, will leave and be replaced by recent graduates, who are more likely to do so. In addition, as dentists' workloads increase, they are expected to hire more hygienists to perform preventive dental care such as cleaning, so they may use their own time more profitably.

## Earnings

Earnings of dental hygienists are affected by geographic location, employment setting, and education and experience. Dental hygienists who work in private dental offices may be paid on an hourly, daily, salary, or commission basis.

According to the American Dental Association, dental hygienists who worked 32 hours a week or more averaged $675.50 a week in 1993; the average hourly earnings for all dental hygienists was $21.10.

Benefits vary substantially by practice setting, and may be contingent upon full-time employment. Dental hygienists who work for school systems, public health agencies, the federal government, or state agencies usually have substantial benefits.

## Related Occupations

Workers in other occupations supporting health practitioners in an office setting include dental assistants, ophthalmic medical assistants, podiatric assistants, office nurses, medical assistants, physician assistants, physical therapy assistants, and occupational therapy assistants.

## Related *D.O.T.* Jobs

These job titles are related to or more specific than the more general description above. They will help you identify job options you may not otherwise discover. These descriptions are in the current edition of the *Dictionary of Occupational Titles* and classified by numerical order.

078.361-010 DENTAL HYGIENIST

## Sources of Additional Information

For information on a career in dental hygiene and the educational requirements to enter this occupation, contact:

❏ Division of Professional Development, American Dental Hygienists' Association, 444 N. Michigan Ave., Suite 3400, Chicago, IL 60611.

❏ American Dental Association, Department of Career Guidance, 211 E. Chicago Ave., Suite 1804, Chicago, IL 60611.

For information about accredited programs and educational requirements, contact:

❏ Commission on Dental Accreditation, American Dental Association, 211 E. Chicago Ave., Suite 1814, Chicago, IL 60611.

The State Board of Dental Examiners in each state can supply information on licensing requirements.

# Dental Laboratory Technicians

## Nature of the Work

Dental laboratory technicians fill prescriptions from dentists for crowns, bridges, dentures, and other dental prosthetics. Dentists send a specification of the item to be fabricated along with an impression (mold) of the patient's mouth or teeth to the technicians. Then dental laboratory technicians, also called dental technicians, create a model of the patient's mouth by pouring plaster into the impression and allowing it to set. They place the model on an apparatus which mimics the bite and movement of the patient's jaw. The model serves as the basis of the prosthetic device. Technicians examine the model, noting the size and shape of the adjacent teeth or gaps within the gumline. Based upon these observations and the dentist's specifications, technicians build and shape a wax tooth or teeth using small hand instruments called wax spatulas and wax carvers. They use this wax model to cast the metal framework for the prosthetic device.

Once the wax tooth has been formed, dental technicians pour the cast and form the metal. Using small hand-held tools, they prepare the surface of the metal to allow the metal and porcelain to bond. They apply porcelain in layers to arrive at the precise shape and color of a tooth. Technicians place the tooth in a porcelain furnace to bake the porcelain onto the metal framework, then adjust the shape and color with subsequent grinding and addition of porcelain to achieve a sealed finish. The final product is an exact replica of the lost tooth or teeth.

In some laboratories, technicians perform all stages of the work, while in others, each does only a few. Dental laboratory technicians also may specialize in one of five areas: Orthodontic appliances, crown and bridge, complete dentures, partial dentures, or ceramics. Job titles may reflect specialization in these areas. For example, technicians who make porcelain and acrylic restorations are called *dental ceramists*.

## Working Conditions

Dental laboratory technicians generally work in clean, well-lighted, and well-ventilated areas. Technicians usually have their own workbenches, which may be equipped with Bunsen burners, grinding and polishing equipment, and hand instruments, such as wax spatulas and wax carvers.

The work is extremely delicate and quite time consuming.

Salaried technicians usually work 40 hours a week, but self-employed technicians frequently work longer hours.

## Employment

Dental laboratory technicians held about 49,000 jobs in 1994. Most jobs were in commercial dental laboratories, which usually are small, privately owned businesses with fewer than five employees. However, some laboratories are larger; a few employ over 50 technicians.

Some dental laboratory technicians worked in dentists' offices. Others worked for hospitals that provide dental services, including Department of Veterans Affairs hospitals. Some technicians work in dental laboratories in their homes, in addition to their regular job. Approximately one technician in seven is self-employed, a higher proportion than in most other occupations.

## Training, Other Qualifications, and Advancement

Most dental laboratory technicians learn their craft on the job. They begin with simple tasks, such as pouring plaster into an impression, and progress to more complex procedures, such as making porcelain crowns and bridges. Becoming a fully trained technician requires an average of three to four years depending upon the individual's aptitude and ambition, but it may take a few more years to become an accomplished technician.

Training in dental laboratory technology is also available through community and junior colleges, vocational-technical institutes, and the Armed Forces. Formal training programs vary greatly both in length and the level of skill they impart.

In 1995, 37 programs in dental laboratory technology were approved (accredited) by the Commission on Dental Accreditation in conjunction with the American Dental Association (ADA). These programs provide classroom instruction in dental materials science, oral anatomy, fabrication procedures, ethics, and related subjects. In addition, each student is given supervised practical experience in the school or an associated dental laboratory. Accredited programs generally take two years to complete and lead to an associate degree.

Graduates of two-year training programs need additional hands-on experience to become fully qualified. Each dental laboratory owner operates in a different way, and classroom instruction does not necessarily expose students to techniques and procedures favored by individual laboratory owners. Students who have taken enough courses to learn the basics of the craft generally are considered good candidates for training, regardless of whether they have completed the formal program. Many employers will train someone without any classroom experience.

Certification, which is voluntary, is offered by the National Board for Certification in five specialty areas: Crown and bridge, ceramics, partial dentures, complete dentures, and orthodontic appliances.

In larger dental laboratories, technicians may become supervisors or managers. Experienced technicians may teach or take jobs with dental suppliers in such areas as product development, marketing, or sales. Still, for most technicians, opening one's own laboratory is the way toward advancement and higher earnings.

A high degree of manual dexterity, good vision, and the ability to recognize very fine color shadings and variations in shape are necessary. An aptitude for detailed and precise work

also is important. Useful high school courses are art, metal and wood shop, drafting, and sciences. Courses in management and business may help those wishing to operate their own laboratories.

## Job Outlook

Job opportunities for dental laboratory technicians should be favorable despite the absence of growth in the occupation. Employers have difficulty filling trainee positions, probably because of relatively low entry-level salaries and lack of familiarity with the occupation. Also, experienced technicians who have built up a favorable reputation with dentists should have good opportunities for establishing laboratories of their own.

Although job opportunities are favorable, employment of dental laboratory technicians is expected to decline through the year 2005, due to changes in dental care. The fluoridation of drinking water, which has reduced the incidence of dental cavities, and greater emphasis on preventive dental care since the early-1960s have improved the overall dental health of the population. As a result, people are keeping their teeth longer. Instead of full or partial dentures, most people will need a bridge or crown.

Office-based, computer-aided equipment, designed to measure a patient's mouth and fabricate the required prosthetic device, is currently under development and is beginning to come into use in this country after years of testing in Europe. While not replacing the technicians completely, such equipment, when and if it comes into widespread use in this country, could reduce the amount of time required to produce dental prosthetics and, therefore, the demand for dental laboratory technicians.

## Earnings

The annual wage for all workers in dental laboratories was $22,269 in 1993. According to limited data, trainees in dental laboratories average only a little over minimum wage. However, earnings rise sharply with experience. In general, earnings of self-employed technicians exceed those of salaried workers. Technicians in large laboratories tend to specialize in a few procedures, and therefore tend to be paid a lower wage than those employed in small laboratories who perform a variety of tasks.

## Related Occupations

Dental laboratory technicians fabricate artificial teeth, crowns and bridges, and orthodontic appliances following the specifications and instructions provided by dentists. Other workers who make medical devices include arch-support technicians, orthotics technicians (braces and surgical supports), prosthetics technicians (artificial limbs and appliances), opticians, and ophthalmic laboratory technicians.

## Related D.O.T. Jobs

These job titles are related to or more specific than the more general description above. They will help you identify job options you may not otherwise discover. These descriptions are in the current edition of the *Dictionary of Occupational Titles* and classified by numerical order.

712.381-014 CONTOUR WIRE SPECIALIST, DENTURE; 712.381-018 DENTAL-LABORATORY TECHNICIAN; 712.381-022 DENTAL-LABORATORY-TECHNICIAN APPRENTICE; 712.381-026 ORTHODONTIC BAND MAKER; 712.381-030 ORTHODONTIC TECHNICIAN; 712.381-042 DENTAL CERAMIST; 712.381-046 DENTURE WAXER; 712.381-050 FINISHER, DENTURE; 712.664-010 DENTAL CERAMIST ASSISTANT

## Sources of Additional Information

For information about training and a list of approved schools, contact:

❏ Commission on Dental Accreditation, American Dental Association, 211 E. Chicago Ave., Chicago, IL 60611.

General information on grants and scholarships is available from dental technology schools.

For information on career opportunities in commercial laboratories, contact:

❏ National Association of Dental Laboratories, 3801 Mt. Vernon Ave., Alexandria, VA 22305.

For information on requirements for certification, contact:

❏ National Board for Certification in Dental Technology, 3801 Mt. Vernon Ave., Alexandria, VA 22305.

# Diesel Mechanics

## Nature of the Work

Diesel engines are more durable and heavier than gasoline engines. In addition, they are more fuel efficient than gasoline engines, in part because the higher compression ratios found in diesel engines help convert a higher percentage of the fuel into power. Because of their greater durability and efficiency, diesel engines are used to power most of the nation's heavy vehicles and equipment.

Diesel mechanics repair and maintain diesel engines that power transportation equipment, such as heavy trucks, buses, and locomotives; construction equipment such as bulldozers, cranes, and road graders; and farm equipment such as tractors and combines. A small number work on diesel-powered automobiles. Diesel mechanics also service a variety of other diesel-powered equipment, such as electric generators and compressors and pumps used in oil well drilling and irrigation systems.

Most diesel mechanics work on heavy trucks used in industries such as mining and construction to carry ore and building materials, and by private and commercial trucking lines for general freight hauling. Most light trucks are gasoline powered, and although some diesel mechanics may occasionally service gasoline engines, most work primarily on diesel engines.

Mechanics who work for organizations that maintain their own vehicles may spend much time doing preventive maintenance to assure safe operation, prevent wear and damage to parts, and reduce costly breakdowns. During a maintenance check on a truck, for example, they usually follow a regular checklist that includes the inspection of brake systems, steering mechanisms, wheel bearings, and other important parts. They usually repair or adjust a part that is not working properly. Parts that cannot be fixed are replaced.

In many shops, mechanics do all kinds of repairs, working on a vehicle's electrical system one day and doing major engine repairs the next. In some large shops, mechanics specialize in one or two types of work. For example, one mechanic may specialize in major engine repair, another in transmission work, another in electrical systems, and yet another in suspension or brake systems.

Diesel mechanics use a variety of tools in their work, including power tools such as pneumatic wrenches to remove bolts quickly; machine tools such as lathes and grinding machines to rebuild brakes and other parts; welding and flame-cutting equipment to remove and repair exhaust systems and other parts; common handtools such as screwdrivers, pliers, and wrenches to work on small parts and get at hard-to-reach places; and jacks and hoists to lift and move large parts. Diesel mechanics also use a variety of testing equipment, including ohmmeters, ammeters, and voltmeters when working on electrical systems and electronic components; and tachometers, dynamometers, and engine analyzers to locate engine malfunctions.

For heavy work, such as removing engines and transmissions, two mechanics may work as a team, or a mechanic may be assisted by an apprentice or helper. Mechanics generally get their assignments from shop supervisors or service managers, who may check the mechanics' work or assist in diagnosing problems.

## Working Conditions

Diesel mechanics usually work indoors, although they may occasionally make repairs on the road. They are subject to the usual shop hazards such as cuts and bruises. Mechanics handle greasy and dirty parts and may stand or lie in awkward or cramped positions to repair vehicles and equipment. Work areas usually are well-lighted, heated, and ventilated, and many employers provide locker rooms and shower facilities.

## Employment

Diesel mechanics held about 250,000 jobs in 1994. Nearly one-quarter serviced trucks and other diesel-powered equipment for customers of vehicle and equipment dealers, leasing companies, and independent automotive repair shops. Over one-fifth worked for local and long-distance trucking companies, and nearly one-seventh maintained the buses and trucks of bus lines, public transit companies, school systems, and federal, state, and local government. The remainder maintained the fleets of trucks and other equipment of manufacturing, construction, and other companies. A relatively small number were self-employed.

Diesel mechanics are employed in every section of the country, but most work in towns and cities where trucking companies, bus lines, and other fleet owners have large repair shops.

## Training, Other Qualifications, and Advancement

Although many persons are able to qualify for diesel mechanic jobs through years of on-the-job training in related, lesser skilled positions, training authorities recommend that persons seeking diesel mechanic jobs complete a formal diesel mechanic training program. Diesel technology is becoming more sophisticated and diesel engines increasingly use electronic components to control a growing variety of functions. Knowledge of basic electronics is becoming essential for diesel mechanics to diagnose whether a malfunction is caused by an electronic component or whether it can be traced to another source. Most employers prefer to hire graduates of formal training programs in diesel mechanics, and completion of such a program can speed advancement to the journey mechanic level. These one- to two-year programs, given by vocational and technical schools and community and junior colleges, lead to a certificate of completion or an associate degree. They provide a foundation in the basics of the latest diesel technology and electronics, and enable trainees to more quickly master the service and repair of the actual vehicles and equipment encountered on the job.

A formal four-year apprenticeship is another good way to learn diesel mechanics. However, apprenticeships are becoming less common because employers are reluctant to make such a long-term investment in training, especially when graduates of postsecondary diesel mechanic programs are increasing in number. Competition for the limited number of apprenticeship slots is often extremely keen. Typical apprenticeship programs for diesel truck and bus mechanics consist of approximately 8,000 hours of practical experience working on transmissions, engines, and other components and at least 576 hours of formal instruction to learn blueprint reading, mathematics, engine theory, and safety. Frequently, these programs include training in both diesel and gasoline engine repair.

Even though most employers prefer to hire graduates of formal post secondary training programs in diesel mechanics, the number of persons who complete such programs are too few to meet their needs. As a result, many diesel mechanics still learn their skills on the job. Unskilled beginners usually do tasks such as cleaning parts, fueling, lubricating, and driving vehicles in and out of the shop. As beginners gain experience and as vacancies become available, they usually are promoted to mechanics' helpers. In some shops, beginners—especially those having automobile service experience—start as mechanics' helpers.

Most helpers can perform routine service tasks and make minor repairs after a few months' experience. They advance to increasingly difficult jobs as they prove their ability. After they master the repair and service of diesel engines, they learn to work on related components such as brakes, transmissions, or electrical systems. Generally, at least three to four years of on-the-job experience is necessary to qualify as an all-round diesel truck or bus mechanic. Additional training on other components, such as hydraulic systems, may be necessary for mechanics who wish to specialize in other types of diesel equipment.

For unskilled entry-level jobs, employers generally look for applicants who have mechanical aptitude and are at least 18 years of age and in good physical condition. Completion of high school is required by a growing number of employers. Courses in automotive repair, electronics, English, mathematics, and physics provide a good basic educational background for a career as a diesel mechanic. Good reading and basic mathematics skills are needed to study technical manuals to keep abreast of new technology and learn new service and repair procedures and specifications. A state commercial driver's license is needed for test driving trucks or buses on public roads. Practical experience in automobile repair in a gasoline service station, in the Armed Forces, or as a hobby also is valuable.

Employers sometimes send experienced mechanics to special training classes conducted by truck, bus, diesel engine, parts, and equipment manufacturers where they learn the latest technology or receive special training in subjects such as diagnosing engine malfunctions. Mechanics also must read service and repair manuals to keep abreast of engineering changes.

Voluntary certification by the National Institute for Automotive Service Excellence (ASE) is recognized as a standard of achievement for diesel mechanics. Mechanics may be certified as Master Heavy-Duty Truck Technician or may be certified in one or more of six different areas of heavy-duty truck repair: brakes, gasoline engines, diesel engines, drive trains, electrical systems, and suspension and steering. For certification in each area, mechanics must pass a written examination and have at least two years of experience. High school, vocational or trade school, or community or junior college training in gasoline or diesel engine repair may substitute for up to one year of experience. To retain certification, mechanics must retake the tests at least every five years.

Most mechanics must buy their own handtools. Experienced mechanics often have thousands of dollars invested in tools.

Experienced mechanics who have leadership ability may advance to shop supervisors or service managers. Mechanics who have sales ability sometimes become sales representatives. A few mechanics open their own repair shops.

## Job Outlook

Employment of diesel mechanics is expected to increase about as fast as the average for all occupations through the year 2005. Because this is a large occupation, more job openings are expected for diesel mechanics than for most other occupations. Although employment growth will create many new jobs, most job openings will arise from the need to replace diesel mechanics who transfer to other fields of work or retire or stop working for other reasons.

Employment of diesel mechanics is expected to grow as freight transportation by truck increases. More trucks will be needed for both local and intercity hauling due to the increased production of goods. Additional diesel mechanics will be needed to repair and maintain growing numbers of buses and heavy construction graders, cranes, earthmovers, and other equipment. Due to the greater durability and economy of the diesel relative to the gasoline engine, buses and trucks of all sizes are expected to be increasingly powered by diesels, also creating new jobs for diesel mechanics.

Careers in diesel mechanics are attractive to many because wages are relatively high and skilled repair work is challenging and varied. Opportunities should be good for persons who complete formal training in diesel mechanics at community and junior colleges and vocational and technical schools, but others may face competition for entry-level jobs.

## Earnings

According to a survey of workplaces in over 160 metropolitan areas, diesel mechanics earned median earnings of $14.61 an hour in 1993. The middle 50 percent earned between $12.00 and $17.49 an hour. However, earnings may vary by industry and by geographic location.

Beginning apprentices usually earn from 50 to 75 percent of the rate of skilled workers and receive increases about every six months until they complete their apprenticeship and reach the rate of skilled mechanics.

The majority of mechanics work a standard 40-hour week, although many work as many as 70 hours per week, particularly if they are self employed. Those employed by truck and bus firms which provide service around the clock may work evenings, nights, and weekends. They usually receive a higher rate of pay for this work.

Many diesel mechanics are members of labor unions, including the International Association of Machinists and Aerospace Workers; the Amalgamated Transit Union; the International Union, United Automobile, Aerospace and Agricultural Implement Workers of America; the Transport Workers Union of America; the Sheet Metal Workers' International Association; and the International Brotherhood of Teamsters.

### Related Occupations

Diesel mechanics repair trucks, buses, and other diesel-powered equipment and keep them in good working order. Related mechanic occupations include aircraft mechanics, automotive mechanics, boat engine mechanics, farm equipment mechanics, mobile heavy equipment mechanics, and motorcycle mechanics and small-engine specialists.

### Related *D.O.T.* Jobs

These job titles are related to or more specific than the more general description above. They will help you identify job options you may not otherwise discover. These descriptions are in the current edition of the *Dictionary of Occupational Titles* and classified by numerical order.

620.281-046 MAINTENANCE MECHANIC; 620.281-050 MECHANIC, INDUSTRIAL TRUCK; 620.281-058 TRACTOR MECHANIC; 625.281-010 DIESEL MECHANIC; 625.281-014 DIESEL-MECHANIC APPRENTICE; 625.281-022 FUEL-INJECTION SERVICER; 625.361-010 DIESEL-ENGINE ERECTOR

### Sources of Additional Information

More details about work opportunities for diesel mechanics may be obtained from local employers such as trucking companies, truck dealers, or bus lines; locals of the unions previously mentioned; or the local office of the state employment service. Local state employment service offices also may have information about apprenticeships and other training programs.

For general information about careers as truck, bus, and diesel mechanics, write to:

❑ Automotive Service Industry Association, 25 Northwest Point, Elk Grove Village, IL 60007-1035.

❑ American Trucking Associations, Inc., Maintenance Council, 2200 Mill Rd., Alexandria, VA 22314-4677.

For a directory of accredited private trade and technical schools with training programs for diesel mechanics, contact:

❑ Accrediting Commission of Career Schools and Colleges of Technology, 2101 Wilson Blvd., Suite 302, Arlington, VA 22201.

❑ National Automotive Technicians Education Foundation, 13505 Dulles Technology Dr., Herndon, VA 22071-3415.

For a directory of public training programs for diesel mechanics, contact:

❑ Vocational Industry Clubs of America, P. O. Box 3000, 1401 James Monroe Highway, Leesburg, VA 22075.

Information on how to become a certified heavy-duty diesel mechanic is available from:

❑ ASE, 13505 Dulles Technology Dr., Herndon, VA 22071-3415.

## Dispensing Opticians

### Nature of Work

Dispensing opticians fit eyeglasses and contact lenses, following prescriptions written by ophthalmologists or optometrists.

Dispensing opticians help customers select appropriate frames, order the necessary ophthalmic laboratory work, and adjust the finished eyeglasses. In some states, they fit contact lenses under the supervision of an optometrist or ophthalmologist.

Dispensing opticians examine written prescriptions to determine lens specifications. They recommend eyeglass frames, lenses, and lens coatings after considering the prescription and the customer's occupation, habits, and facial features. Dispensing opticians measure clients' eyes, including the distance between the centers of the pupils and the distance between the eye surface and the lens. For customers without prescriptions, dispensing opticians may use a lensometer to record the present eyeglass prescription. They also may obtain a customer's previous record, or verify a prescription with the examining optometrist or ophthalmologist.

Dispensing opticians prepare work orders that give ophthalmic laboratory technicians information needed to grind and insert lenses into a frame. The work order includes lens prescriptions and information on lens size, material, color, and style. Some dispensing opticians grind and insert lenses themselves. After the glasses are made, dispensing opticians verify that the lenses have been ground to specifications. Then they may reshape or bend the frame, by hand or using pliers, so that the eyeglasses fit the customer properly and comfortably. Dispensing opticians also fix, adjust, and refit broken frames. They instruct clients about adapting to, wearing, or caring for eyeglasses.

Some dispensing opticians specialize in fitting contacts, artificial eyes, or cosmetic shells to cover blemished eyes. To fit contact lenses, dispensing opticians measure eye shape and size, select the type of contact lens material, and prepare work orders specifying the prescription and lens size. Fitting contact lenses requires considerable skill, care, and patience. Dispensing opticians observe customers' eyes, corneas, lids, and contact lenses with special instruments and microscopes. During several visits, opticians show customers how to insert, remove, and care for their contacts, and ensure the fit is correct.

Dispensing opticians keep records on customer prescriptions, work orders, and payments; track inventory and sales; and perform other administrative duties.

### Working Conditions

Dispensing opticians work indoors in attractive, well lighted, and well ventilated surroundings. They may work in medical offices or small stores where customers are served one at a time, or in large stores where several dispensing opticians serve a number of customers at once. Opticians spend a lot of time with customers, most of it on their feet. If they also prepare lenses, they need to take precautions against the hazards associated with glass cutting, chemicals, and machinery.

Most dispensing opticians work a 40-hour week, although some work longer hours. Those in retail stores may work evenings and weekends. Some work part-time.

## Employment

Dispensing opticians held about 63,000 jobs in 1994. About half work for ophthalmologists or optometrists who sell glasses directly to patients. Many also work in optical stores that offer one-stop shopping. Customers may have their eyes examined, choose frames, and have glasses made on the spot. Some work in optical departments of drug and department stores.

## Training, Other Qualifications, and Advancement

Employers generally hire individuals with no background in opticianry or those who have worked as ophthalmic laboratory technicians and then provide the required training. Training may be informal, on-the-job or formal apprenticeship. Some employers, however, seek people with postsecondary training in opticianry.

Knowledge of physics, basic anatomy, algebra, geometry, and mechanical drawing is particularly valuable because training usually includes instruction in optical mathematics, optical physics, and the use of precision measuring instruments and other machinery and tools. Because dispensing opticians deal directly with the public, they should be tactful and pleasant and communicate well.

Large employers generally offer structured apprenticeship programs, and small employers provide more informal on-the-job training. In the 21 states that license dispensing opticians, individuals without postsecondary training work from two to four years as apprentices. Apprenticeship or formal traineeship is offered in most of the other states as well.

Apprentices receive technical training and learn office management and sales. Under the supervision of an experienced optician, optometrist, or ophthalmologist, apprentices work directly with patients, fitting eyeglasses and contact lenses. In states requiring licensure, information about apprenticeships and licensing procedures is available from the state board of occupational licensing.

Formal opticianry training is offered in community colleges and a few colleges and universities. In 1995, there were about 40 programs. Of these, 24 were accredited by the Commission on Opticianry Accreditation and awarded two-year associate degrees in ophthalmic dispensing or optometric technology. There are also shorter programs, including some under one year. Some states that license dispensing opticians allow graduates to take the licensure exam immediately upon graduation; others require a few months to a year of experience.

Dispensing opticians may apply to the American Board of Opticianry and the National Contact Lens Examiners for certification of their skills. Certification must be renewed every three years through continuing education.

Many experienced dispensing opticians open their own optical stores. Others become managers of optical stores or sales representatives for wholesalers or manufacturers of eyeglasses or lenses.

## Job Outlook

Employment in this occupation is expected to increase faster than the average for all occupations through the year 2005 in response to rising demand for corrective lenses. The number of middle-aged and elderly persons is projected to increase rapidly. Middle age is a time when many people use corrective lenses for the first time, and elderly persons require more vision care, on the whole, than others.

Fashion, too, influences demand. Frames come in a growing variety of styles and colors—encouraging people to buy more than one pair. Finally, demand is expected to grow in response to products such as special lens treatments; photochromic lenses (glasses with lenses that become darker in sunlight), now available in plastic as well as glass; tinted lenses; and bifocal, extended wear, and disposable contact lenses.

Like other occupations in retail trade, a disproportionate number of openings will occur as young workers transfer to jobs in other occupations. Nevertheless, the need to replace those who leave the occupation and employment growth will result in relatively few job openings—because the occupation is small. This occupation is vulnerable to changes in the business cycle, with employment falling somewhat during downturns.

## Earnings

According to the Opticians Association of America, salaries for nonmanagerial dispensing opticians averaged about $26,700 in 1994, while managers averaged about $30,400. Apprentice opticians averaged about $19,400 a year. Those who run their own stores earned more than salaried workers. In addition to base salaries, many employers provide commissions, bonuses, and profit-sharing.

## Related Occupations

Other workers who deal with customers and perform delicate work include jewelers, locksmiths, ophthalmic laboratory technicians, orthodontic technicians, dental laboratory technicians, prosthetics technicians, camera repairers, and watch repairers.

## Related *D.O.T.* Jobs

These job titles are related to or more specific than the more general description above. They will help you identify job options you may not otherwise discover. These descriptions are in the current edition of the *Dictionary of Occupational Titles* and classified by numerical order.

299.361-010 OPTICIAN, DISPENSING; 299.361-014 OPTICIAN APPRENTICE, DISPENSING

## Sources of Additional Information

For general information about this occupation, contact:

❏ Opticians Association of America, 10341 Democracy Lane, Fairfax, VA 22030-2521.

For a list of accredited training programs, contact:

❏ Commission on Opticianry Accreditation, 10111 Martin Luther King, Jr. Hwy., Suite 100, Bowie, MD 20720-4299.

For general information on opticianry and a list of home-study programs, seminars, and review materials, contact:

❏ National Academy of Opticianry, 10111 Martin Luther King, Jr. Hwy., Suite 112, Bowie, MD 20720-4299.

# Drafters

## Nature of the Work

Drafters prepare technical drawings followed by production and construction workers to build everything from spacecraft or industrial machinery and other manufactured products to structures such as office buildings or oil and gas pipelines. Their drawings show the technical details of the products and structures from all sides, including exact dimensions, specific materials to be used, and procedures to be followed. Drafters fill in technical details, using drawings, rough sketches, specifications, codes, and calculations previously made by engineers, surveyors, architects, or scientists. For example, they use their knowledge of standardized building techniques to draw in the details of a structure. Some drafters employ a knowledge of engineering and manufacturing theory and standards to draw the parts of a machine in order to determine the number and kind of fasteners needed to assemble it. They may use technical handbooks, tables, calculators, and computers.

Traditionally, drafters sat at drawing boards and used compasses, dividers, protractors, triangles, and other drafting devices to prepare a drawing manually. Many drafters now use computer-aided drafting (CAD) systems to prepare drawings. These systems employ computer work stations to create a drawing on a video screen. They store it electronically so that revisions and/or duplications can be made easily. These systems also permit drafters to easily and quickly prepare variations of a design. A person who produces a technical drawing using CAD is still functioning as a drafter, and needs most of the knowledge of traditional drafters as well as CAD skills.

Because the cost of CAD systems is dropping rapidly, by the year 2005 it is likely that almost all drafters will use CAD systems regularly. However, manual drafting probably will still be used in certain applications, especially in specialty firms that produce many one-of-a-kind drawings with little repetition.

Many drafters specialize. *Architectural drafters* draw architectural and structural features of buildings and other structures. They may specialize by the type of structure, such as schools or office buildings, or by material used, such as reinforced concrete, masonry, steel, or timber.

*Aeronautical drafters* prepare engineering drawings used for the manufacture of aircraft and missiles.

*Electrical drafters* draw wiring and layout diagrams used by workers who erect, install, and repair electrical equipment and wiring in power plants, electrical distribution systems, and buildings.

*Electronic drafters* draw wiring diagrams, circuit board assembly diagrams, schematics, and layout drawings used in the manufacture, installation, and repair of electronic equipment.

*Civil drafters* prepare drawings and topographical and relief maps used in civil engineering projects such as highways, bridges, pipelines, flood control projects, and water and sewage systems.

*Mechanical drafters* draw detailed diagrams of machinery and mechanical devices, such as process piping systems, including dimensions, fastening methods, and other engineering information.

## Working Conditions

Drafters usually work in offices with lighting appropriate to their tasks. They often sit at drawing boards or computer terminals for long periods of time doing detailed work, which may cause eyestrain and back discomfort.

## Employment

Drafters held about 304,000 jobs in 1994. Over one-third of all drafters worked in engineering and architectural services, firms that design construction projects or do other engineering work on a contract basis for organizations in other parts of the economy; about one-third worked in durable goods manufacturing industries, such as machinery, electrical equipment, and fabricated metals; and the remainder were mostly employed in the construction, communications, utilities, and personnel supply services industries.

About 10,000 drafters worked in government in 1994, primarily at the state and local level.

## Training, Other Qualifications, and Advancement

Employers prefer applicants for drafting positions who have completed post-high school training in drafting, which is offered by technical institutes, junior and community colleges, and the extension divisions of colleges and universities. Employers are most interested in applicants who have well-developed drafting and mechanical drawing skills, a knowledge of standards and a solid background in computer-aided design techniques, and courses in mathematics, science, and engineering technology. In addition, communication and problem-solving skills are required.

Many types of publicly and privately operated schools provide some form of drafting training. The kind and quality of programs can vary considerably. Therefore, prospective students should be careful in selecting a program. They should contact prospective employers regarding their preferences and ask schools to provide information about the kinds of jobs obtained by graduates, type and condition of instructional facilities and equipment, and faculty qualifications.

*Technical institutes* offer intensive technical training but less theory and general education than junior and community colleges. Many offer two-year associate degree programs, which are similar to or part of the programs offered by community colleges or state university systems. Other technical institutes are run by private, often for-profit, organizations, sometimes called proprietary schools; their programs vary considerably in both length and type of courses offered.

*Junior and community colleges* offer curriculums similar to those in technical institutes but include more courses on theory and liberal arts. Often there is little or no difference between technical institute and community college programs. However, courses taken at junior or community colleges are more likely to be accepted for credit at four-year colleges than those at technical institutes. After completing a two-year program, many graduates obtain jobs as drafters while others continue their education in a related field at four-year colleges.

*Four-year colleges* usually do not offer drafting training, but college courses in engineering, architecture, and mathematics are useful for obtaining a job as a drafter.

*Area vocational-technical schools* are postsecondary public institutions that serve local students and emphasize training needed by local employers. Most require a high school diploma or its equivalent for admission. Many offer introductory drafting instruction.

*Other training* may be obtained in the Armed Forces in technical areas which can be applied in civilian drafting jobs. Some additional training may be needed, depending on the military specialty, but often this can be gained on the job.

Those planning careers in drafting should be able to draw freehand three-dimensional objects and do detailed work accurately and neatly. Artistic ability is helpful in some specialized fields, as is knowledge of manufacturing and construction methods. In addition, prospective drafters should have good communication skills because they work closely with engineers, surveyors, architects, and other professionals.

Both the American Design Drafting Association (ADDA) and the American Institute of Building Design (AIBD) have established certification programs for drafters. Although drafters are not generally required to be certified by employers, certification demonstrates that nationally recognized standards have been met. Individuals who wish to become certified must pass the Drafter Certification Test, which is administered periodically at ADDA-authorized test sites. Applicants are tested on their knowledge and understanding of basic drafting concepts such as geometric construction, working drawings, and architectural terms and standards.

Entry-level or junior drafters usually do routine work under close supervision. After gaining experience, they do more difficult work with less supervision and may advance to senior drafter, designer, or supervisor. Many employers pay for ongoing education, and with appropriate college degrees, drafters may become engineers or architects.

### Job Outlook

Employment of drafters is expected to change little through the year 2005. Industrial growth and increasingly complex design problems associated with new products and manufacturing increase the demand for drafting services. However, greater use of CAD equipment by architects and engineers, as well as drafters, may offset this growth in demand. Although productivity gains from CAD have been relatively modest since its use became widespread, the technology continues to advance. CAD is expected to become an increasingly powerful tool, simplifying many traditional drafting tasks and enabling some engineers and architects to do some drafting tasks themselves. Individuals who have at least two years of training in a technically strong drafting program and who have experience with CAD systems will have the best opportunities. Although few, if any, jobs will be generated by employment growth, many job openings are expected to arise as drafters move to other occupations, retire, or leave the labor force for other reasons.

Employment of drafters is highly concentrated in industries that are sensitive to cyclical swings in the economy, such as engineering and architectural services and durable goods manufacturing. During recessions, drafters may be laid off.

### Earnings

Median annual earnings of drafters who worked year round, full-time were about $28,500 in 1994; the middle 50 percent earned between $21,500 and $38,600 annually. The top 10 percent earned more than $50,200, while the bottom 10 percent earned less than $16,400.

According to a survey of workplaces in 160 metropolitan areas, the most experienced drafters had median earnings of about $38,600 a year in 1993, with the middle half earning between about $35,500 and $42,600 a year.

### Related Occupations

Other workers who prepare or analyze detailed drawings and make precise calculations and measurements include architects, landscape architects, engineers, engineering technicians, science technicians, cartographers, and surveyors.

### Related *D.O.T.* Jobs

These job titles are related to or more specific than the more general description above. They will help you identify job options you may not otherwise discover. These descriptions are in the current edition of the *Dictionary of Occupational Titles* and classified by numerical order.

There are too many *D.O.T.* titles to list here. Most are variations related to a specific industry, and we have included a small number of representative *D.O.T.* titles as examples. Complete lists are available in various career software published by JIST or directly from the U.S. Department of Labor.

001.261-010 DRAFTER, ARCHITECTURAL; 001.261-014 DRAFTER, LANDSCAPE; 002.261-010 DRAFTER, AERONAUTICAL; 002.261-014 RESEARCH MECHANIC; 003.261-014 CONTROLS DESIGNER; 003.281-014 DRAFTER, ELECTRONIC; 005.281-010 DRAFTER, CIVIL; 005.281-014 DRAFTER, STRUCTURAL; 007.161-010 DIE DESIGNER; 007.261-010 CHIEF DRAFTER; 007.261-022 DRAFTER, TOOL DESIGN; 007.281-010 DRAFTER, MECHANICAL; 010.281-014 DRAFTER, GEOLOGICAL; 017.261-026 DRAFTER, COMMERCIAL; 017.261-030 DRAFTER, DETAIL; 017.261-034 DRAFTER, HEATING AND VENTILATING; 017.261-038 DRAFTER, PLUMBING; 017.261-042 DRAFTER, AUTOMOTIVE DESIGN; 017.281-010 AUTO-DESIGN DETAILER; 017.281-026 DRAFTER, AUTOMOTIVE DESIGN LAYOUT; 017.281-034 TECHNICAL ILLUSTRATOR;

### Sources of Additional Information

Information on schools offering programs in drafting and other areas is available from:

❏ Accrediting Commission of Career Schools and Colleges of Technology, 2101 Wilson Blvd., Suite 302, Arlington, VA 22201.

# Drywall Workers and Lathers

### Nature of the Work

Drywall consists of a thin layer of gypsum sandwiched between two layers of heavy paper. It is used today for walls and ceilings in most buildings because it is both faster and cheaper to install than plaster.

There are two kinds of drywall workers: installers and finishers. *Installers*, also called *applicators*, fasten drywall panels to the inside framework of residential houses and other buildings. *Finishers*, or *tapers*, prepare these panels for painting by taping and finishing joints and imperfections.

Because drywall panels are manufactured in standard sizes—usually 4 feet by 8 or 12 feet—installers must measure, cut, and fit some pieces around doors and windows. They also saw or cut holes in panels for electrical outlets, air-conditioning units, and plumbing. After making these alterations, installers may glue, nail, or screw the wallboard panels to the wood or metal framework. Because drywall is heavy and cumbersome, a helper generally assists the installer in positioning and securing the panel. A lift is often used when placing ceiling panels.

After the drywall is installed, finishers fill joints between panels with a joint compound. Using the wide, flat tip of a special trowel, they spread the joint compound into and along each side of the joint with brushlike strokes. They immediately use the trowel to press a paper tape—used to reinforce the drywall and to hide imperfections—into the wet compound and to smooth away excess material. Nail and screw depressions also are covered with this compound, as are imperfections caused by the installation of air-conditioning vents and other fixtures. On large commercial projects, finishers may use automatic taping tools that apply the joint compound and tape in one step. Finishers apply second and third coats, sanding the treated areas after each coat to make them as smooth as the rest of the wall surface. This results in a very smooth and almost perfect surface. Some finishers apply textured surfaces to walls and ceilings with trowels, brushes, or spray guns.

*Lathers* apply metal or gypsum lath to walls, ceilings, or ornamental frameworks to form the support base for plaster coatings. Gypsum lath is similar to a drywall panel, but smaller. Metal lath is used where the plaster application will be exposed to weather or water, or for curved or irregular surfaces for which drywall is not a practical material. Lathers usually nail, screw, staple, or wire-tie the lath directly to the structural framework.

## Working Conditions

As in other construction trades, drywall and lathing work sometimes is strenuous. Applicators, tapers, finishers, and lathers spend most of the day on their feet, either standing, bending, or kneeling. Some finishers use stilts to tape and finish ceiling and angle joints. Installers have to lift and maneuver heavy panels. Hazards include falls from ladders and scaffolds, and injuries from power tools. Because sanding joint compound to a smooth finish creates a great deal of dust, some finishers wear masks for protection.

## Employment

Drywall workers and lathers held about 133,000 jobs in 1994. Most worked for contractors who specialize in drywall or lathing installation; others worked for contractors who do many kinds of construction. Nearly one-third were self employed independent contractors.

Most installers, finishers, and lathers are employed in urban areas. In other areas, where there may not be enough work to keep a drywall worker or lather employed full-time, the work is usually done by carpenters and painters.

## Training, Other Qualifications, and Advancement

Most drywall and lathing workers start as helpers and learn their skills on the job. Installer and lather helpers start by carrying materials, lifting and holding panels, and cleaning up debris. Within a few weeks, they learn to measure, cut, and install materials. Eventually, they become fully experienced workers. Finisher apprentices begin by taping joints and touching up nail holes,

scrapes, and other imperfections. They soon learn to install corner guards and to conceal openings around pipes. At the end of their training, they learn to estimate the cost of installing and finishing drywall and gypsum lath.

Some installers and lathers learn their trade in an apprenticeship program. The United Brotherhood of Carpenters and Joiners of America, in cooperation with local contractors, administers an apprenticeship program in carpentry that includes instruction in drywall and lath installation. In addition, local affiliates of the Associated Builders and Contractors and the National Association of Home Builders conduct training programs for nonunion workers. The International Brotherhood of Painters and Allied Trades conducts a two-year apprenticeship program for drywall finishers.

Employers prefer high school graduates who are in good physical condition, but they frequently hire applicants with less education. High school or vocational school courses in carpentry provide a helpful background for drywall work. Regardless of educational background, installers must be good at simple arithmetic.

Drywall workers and lathers with a few years' experience and leadership ability may become supervisors. Some workers start their own contracting businesses.

## Job Outlook

Replacement needs will account for almost all job openings for drywall workers and lathers through the year 2005. Tens of thousands of jobs will open up each year because of the need to replace workers who transfer to jobs in other occupations or leave the labor force. Turnover in this occupation is very high, reflecting the lack of formal training requirements and the ups and downs of the business cycle, to which the construction industry is very sensitive. Because of their relatively weak attachment to the occupation, many workers with limited skills leave the occupation when they find they dislike the work or because they can't find steady employment.

Additional job openings will be created by the rising demand for drywall work. Employment is expected to grow more slowly than the average for all occupations, reflecting the slow growth of new construction and renovation. In addition to traditional interior work, the growing acceptance of insulated exterior wall systems will provide additional jobs for drywall workers.

Despite the growing use of exterior panels, most drywall installation, finishing, and lathing are usually done indoors. Therefore, these workers lose less work time because of bad weather than some other construction workers. Nevertheless, they may be unemployed between construction projects and during downturns in construction activity.

## Earnings

Median weekly earnings for drywall workers and lathers were about $419 in 1994. The middle 50 percent earned between $311 and $596 weekly. The top 10 percent earned over $818 and the bottom 10 percent earned less than $257 a week. Trainees usually started at about half the rate paid to experienced workers and received wage increases as they became more highly skilled.

Some contractors pay these workers according to the number of panels they install or finish per day; others pay an hourly rate. A 40-hour week is standard, but sometimes the workweek may be longer. Those who are paid hourly rates receive premium pay for overtime.

## Related Occupations

Drywall workers and lathers combine strength and dexterity with precision and accuracy to make materials fit according to a plan. Other occupations that require similar abilities include carpenters, floor covering installers, form builders, insulation workers, and plasterers.

## Related D.O.T. Jobs

These job titles are related to or more specific than the more general description above. They will help you identify job options you may not otherwise discover. These descriptions are in the current edition of the *Dictionary of Occupational Titles* and classified by numerical order.

842.361-010 LATHER; 842.361-014 LATHER APPRENTICE; 842.361-030 DRY-WALL APPLICATOR; 842.664-010 TAPER; 842.684-014 DRY-WALL APPLICATOR; 869.684-050 SHEETROCK APPLICATOR

## Sources of Additional Information

For information about work opportunities in drywall application and finishing, contact local drywall installation contractors; a local of the unions previously mentioned; a local joint union-management apprenticeship committee; a state or local chapter of the Associated Builders and Contractors; or the nearest office of the state employment service or state apprenticeship agency.

For details about job qualifications and training programs in drywall application and finishing, write to:

❏ Associated Builders and Contractors, Inc., 1300 North 17th St., Rosslyn, VA 22209.

❏ International Brotherhood of Painters and Allied Trades, 1750 New York Ave. NW, Washington, DC 20006.

For information on training programs in drywall application and lathing, write to:

❏ United Brotherhood of Carpenters and Joiners of America, 101 Constitution Ave. NW, Washington, DC 20001.

❏ Home Builders Institute, National Association of Home Builders, 1201 15th St. NW, Washington, DC 20005.

# Electric Power Generating Plant Operators and Power Distributors and Dispatchers

## Nature of the Work

Although electricity is vital for most of our everyday activities, it only takes a downed power line for us to realize how much we take it and the people who help generate it for granted. Power plant operators control the machinery that generates electricity. Power distributors and dispatchers control the flow of electricity through substations and over a network of transmission and distribution lines to users.

Electric power generating plant operators who work in plants fueled by coal, oil, or natural gas regulate and monitor boilers, turbines, generators, auxiliary equipment, such as coal crushers, and switching gear. They operate switches to distribute power demands among generators, combine the current from several generators, and regulate the flow of electricity into power lines. When power requirements change, they start or stop generators and connect or disconnect them from circuits. Operators monitor instruments to see that electricity flows from the plant properly and that voltage is maintained. They also keep records of switching operations and loads on generators, lines, and transformers and prepare reports of unusual incidents or malfunctioning equipment during their shift.

Operators in newer plants with automated control systems work mainly in a central control room and usually are called control room operators and control room operator trainees or assistants. In older plants, the controls for the equipment are not centralized, and operators work throughout the plant, operating and monitoring valves, switches, and gauges. Job titles in older plants may be more varied than in newer plants. Auxiliary equipment operators work throughout the plant, while switchboard operators control the flow of electricity from a central point.

Operators of nuclear power plants are licensed by the Nuclear Regulatory Commission (NRC). NRC-licensed reactor operators are authorized to operate equipment that affects the power of the reactor in a nuclear power plant. In addition, an NRC-licensed senior reactor operator acts as the supervisor of the plant for each shift, and supervises operation of all controls in the control room.

Power distributors and dispatchers, also called load dispatchers or systems operators, control the flow of electricity through transmission lines to users. They operate current converters, voltage transformers, and circuit breakers. Dispatchers monitor equipment and record readings at a pilot board, which is a map of the transmission grid system showing the status of transmission circuits and connections with substations and large industrial users. Dispatchers anticipate power needs such as those caused by changes in the weather; they call control room operators to start or stop boilers and generators to bring production into balance with needs. They handle emergencies such as transformer or transmission line failures and route current around affected areas. They also operate and monitor equipment in substations, which step up or step down voltage, and operate switchboard levers to control the flow of electricity in and out of substations.

## Working Conditions

Because electricity is provided around the clock, operators, distributors, and dispatchers usually work one of three daily eight-hour shifts on a rotating basis. Workers usually rotate to a different daily shift schedule periodically so that duty on less desirable shifts is shared by all operators. Work on rotating shifts can be stressful and fatiguing because of the constant change in living and sleeping patterns. Operators, distributors, and dispatchers who work in control rooms generally sit or stand at a control station. This work is not physically strenuous, but requires constant attention. Operators who work outside the control room may be exposed to danger from electric shock, falls, and burns.

Nuclear power plant operators are subject to random drug and alcohol tests.

## Employment

Electric power generating plant operators and power distributors and dispatchers held about 43,000 jobs in 1994. Over 90 percent worked for electric utility companies and government agencies that produced electricity. Some worked for manufacturing establishments that produce electricity for their own use. Jobs are located throughout the country.

## Training, Other Qualifications, and Advancement

Employers seek high school graduates for entry-level operator, distributor, and dispatcher positions. Those with strong math and science skills are preferred. College level courses or prior experience in a mechanical or technical job may be helpful. Most entry-level positions are in helper or laborer jobs in power plants or in other areas of the utility such as power line construction. Workers may be assigned to train for any one of many utility positions in operations, maintenance, or other areas. Assignments depend on the results of aptitude tests, worker preferences, and availability of openings.

Workers selected for training as a power distributor or power plant operator at a conventionally fueled power plant undergo extensive on-the-job and classroom training provided by the employer. Several years of training and experience are required to become a fully qualified control room operator or power distributor. With further training and experience, workers may advance to shift supervisor. Because utilities generally promote from within, opportunities to advance by moving to another employer are limited.

Entrants to nuclear power plant operator trainee jobs must have strong math and science skills. Experience in other power plants or with Navy nuclear propulsion plants also is helpful. Extensive training and experience are necessary to pass the Nuclear Regulatory Commission's examinations for licensed reactor operator and senior reactor operator, including on-the-job and simulator training, classroom instruction, and individual study. Licensed reactor operators must pass an annual practical plant operation exam and a biennial written exam administered by their employer to maintain their license. With further training and experience, reactor operators may advance to senior reactor operators, who are qualified to be shift supervisors.

In addition to preliminary training as a power plant operator or power distributor or dispatcher, most workers are given periodic refresher training. Nuclear power plant operators are given frequent refresher training on a plant simulator.

## Job Outlook

People who want to become power plant operators and power distributors and dispatchers are expected to encounter keen competition for jobs. With relatively modest qualifications for employment, good wages, and low turnover in this moderately sized occupation, job opportunities are expected to be few compared to the number of eligible candidates.

Opportunities for those interested in working as power plant operators, distributors, and dispatchers will be affected by the pace of new plant construction and equipment upgrading. The pace of expansion in power generating capacity through the year 2005 is expected to be moderate because capacity was somewhat overbuilt in the past. The increasing use of automatic controls and more efficient equipment should further offset the need for new plant construction and operators. Also, few new nuclear power plants are likely to be operational before the year 2005.

A recent development in the utility industry is the Energy Policy Act of 1992. This legislation has increased competition in power generating utilities by allowing independent power producers, who generally have lower prices, to sell their power directly to industrial customers. As a result, utilities are restructuring their operations to reduce costs and compete effectively, resulting in fewer jobs at all levels and reducing job security.

Overall, employment of electric power generating plant operators, distributors, and dispatchers is expected to decline through the year 2005.

## Earnings

Earnings in the electric utility industry are relatively high. According to the limited information available, median weekly earnings for conventional power plant operators were about $857 in 1994. According to information from union contracts, wages for power plant operators ranged from $520 to $832 weekly. Nuclear power plant operators earned weekly wages of about $990 in 1994. Senior or chief operators in both nuclear and conventional power plants earned 10 to 15 percent more than operators.

## Related Occupations

Other workers who monitor and operate plant and systems equipment include stationary engineers, water and sewage treatment plant operators, waterworks pump station operators, chemical operators, and refinery operators.

## Related *D.O.T.* Jobs

These job titles are related to or more specific than the more general description above. They will help you identify job options you may not otherwise discover. These descriptions are in the current edition of the *Dictionary of Occupational Titles* and classified by numerical order.

820.662-010 MOTOR-ROOM CONTROLLER; 951.685-010 FIRER, HIGH PRESSURE; 952.167-014 LOAD DISPATCHER; 952.362-010 AUXILIARY-EQUIPMENT OPERATOR; 952.362-014 FEEDER-SWITCHBOARD OPERATOR; 952.362-018 HYDROELECTRIC-STATION OPERATOR; 952.362-022 POWER-REACTOR OPERATOR; 952.362-026 SUBSTATION OPERATOR; 952.362-030 SUBSTATION OPERATOR APPRENTICE; 952.362-034 SWITCHBOARD OPERATOR; 952.362-038 SWITCHBOARD OPERATOR; 952.362-042 TURBINE OPERATOR; 952.367-014 SWITCHBOARD OPERATOR ASSISTANT; 952.382-010 DIESEL-PLANT OPERATOR; 952.382-014 POWER OPERATOR; 952.382-018 POWER-PLANT OPERATOR

## Sources of Additional Information

For information about employment opportunities, contact local electric utility companies, locals of unions mentioned below, or an office of the state employment service.

For general information about power plant and nuclear reactor operators and power distributors and dispatchers, contact:

❏ International Brotherhood of Electrical Workers, 1125 15th St. NW, Washington, DC 20005.

❏ Utility Workers Union of America, 815 16th St. NW, Washington, DC 20006.

For a copy of Careers in Electric Power and a catalog of other guidance information, send $5 to:

❏ Edison Electric Institute, P.O. Box 2800, Kearneysville, WV 25430-2800.

# Electricians

## Nature of the Work

Electricity is essential for light, power, air-conditioning, and refrigeration. Electricians install, connect, test, and maintain electrical systems for a variety of purposes, including climate control, security, and communications. They also may install and maintain the electronic controls for machines in business and industry. Although most electricians specialize in either construction or maintenance, a growing number do both.

Electricians work with blueprints when they install electrical systems in factories, office buildings, homes, and other structures. Blueprints indicate the location of circuits, outlets, load centers, panel boards, and other equipment. Electricians must follow the National Electric Code and comply with state and local building codes when they install these systems. In factories and offices, they first place conduit (pipe or tubing) inside designated partitions, walls, or other concealed areas. They also fasten to the wall small metal or plastic boxes that will house electrical switches and outlets. They then pull insulated wires or cables through the conduit to complete circuits between these boxes. In lighter construction, such as residential, plastic-covered wire usually is used rather than conduit.

Regardless of the type of wire being used, electricians connect it to circuit breakers, transformers, or other components. Wires are joined by twisting ends together with pliers and covering the ends with special plastic connectors. When stronger connections are required, electricians may use an electric "soldering gun" to melt metal onto the twisted wires, which they then cover with durable electrical tape. When the wiring is finished, they test the circuits for proper connections.

In addition to wiring a building's electrical system, electricians may install coaxial or fiber optic cable for computers and other telecommunications equipment. A growing number of electricians install telephone and computer wiring and equipment. They also may connect motors to electrical power and install electronic controls for industrial equipment.

Maintenance work varies greatly, depending on where the electrician is employed. Electricians who specialize in residential work may rewire a home and replace an old fuse box with a new circuit breaker to accommodate additional appliances. Those who work in large factories may repair motors, transformers, generators, and electronic controllers on machine tools and industrial robots. Those in office buildings and small plants may repair all kinds of electrical equipment.

Maintenance electricians spend much of their time in preventive maintenance. They periodically inspect equipment and locate and correct problems before breakdowns occur. Electricians also may advise management whether continued operation of equipment could be hazardous. When needed, they install new electrical equipment. When breakdowns occur, they must make the necessary repairs as quickly as possible in order to minimize inconvenience. Electricians may replace items such as circuit breakers, fuses, switches, electrical and electronic components, or wire. When working with complex electronic devices, they may work with engineers, engineering technicians, or industrial machinery repairers.

Electricians use handtools such as screwdrivers, pliers, knives, and hacksaws. They also use power tools and testing equipment such as oscilloscopes, ammeters, and test lamps.

## Working Conditions

Electricians' work is sometimes strenuous. They may stand for long periods and frequently work on ladders and scaffolds. They often work in awkward or cramped positions. Electricians risk injury from electrical shock, falls, and cuts; to avoid injuries, they must follow strict safety procedures. Some electricians may have to travel to job sites, which may be up to 100 miles away.

Most electricians work a standard 40-hour week, although overtime may be required. Those in maintenance work may have to work nights, on weekends, and be on call. Companies that operate 24 hours a day may employ three shifts of electricians. Generally, the first shift is primarily responsible for routine maintenance, while the other shifts perform preventive maintenance.

## Employment

Electricians held about 528,000 jobs in 1994. More than half were employed in the construction industry. Others worked as maintenance electricians and were employed in virtually every industry. In addition, about 1 out of 10 electricians was self-employed.

Because of the widespread need for electrical services, jobs for electricians are found in all parts of the country.

## Training, Other Qualifications, and Advancement

The best way to learn the electrical trade is by completing a four- or five-year apprenticeship program. Apprenticeship gives trainees a thorough knowledge of all aspects of the trade and generally improves their ability to find a job. Although more electricians are trained through apprenticeship than workers in other construction trades, some still learn their skills informally on the job.

Large apprenticeship programs are usually sponsored by joint training committees made up of local unions of the International Brotherhood of Electrical Workers and local chapters of the National Electrical Contractors Association. Training may also be provided by company management committees of individual electrical contracting companies and by local chapters of the Associated Builders and Contractors and the Independent Electrical Contractors. Because of the comprehensive training received, those who complete apprenticeship programs qualify to do both maintenance and construction work.

The typical large apprenticeship program provides at least 144 hours of classroom instruction each year and 8,000 hours of on-the-job training over the course of the apprenticeship. In the classroom, apprentices learn blueprint reading, electrical theory, electronics, mathematics, electrical code requirements, and safety and first aid practices. They also receive specialized training in welding and communications and fire alarm systems. On the job, under the supervision of experienced electricians, apprentices must demonstrate mastery of the electrician's work. At first, they drill holes, set anchors, and set up conduit. Later, they measure, fabricate, and install conduit, as well as install, connect, and test wiring, outlets, and switches. They also learn to set up and draw diagrams for entire electrical systems.

Those who do not enter a formal apprenticeship program can begin to learn the trade informally by working as helpers for experienced electricians. While learning to install conduit, connect wires, and test circuits, helpers also are taught safety practices. Many helpers supplement this training with trade school or correspondence courses.

Regardless of how one learns the trade, previous training is very helpful. High school courses in mathematics, electricity, electronics, mechanical drawing, science, and shop provide a good background. Special training offered in the Armed Forces and by postsecondary technical schools also is beneficial. All applicants should be in good health and have at least average physical strength. Agility and dexterity also are important. Good color vision is needed because workers frequently must identify electrical wires by color.

Most apprenticeship sponsors require applicants for apprentice positions to be at least 18 years old and have a high school diploma or its equivalent. For those interested in becoming maintenance electricians, a background in electronics is increasingly important because of the growing use of complex electronic controls on manufacturing equipment.

Most localities require electricians to be licensed. Although licensing requirements vary from area to area, electricians generally must pass an examination that tests their knowledge of electrical theory, the National Electrical Code, and local electric and building codes.

Electricians periodically take courses offered by their employer or union to keep abreast of changes in the National Electrical Code, materials, or methods of installation.

Experienced electricians can become supervisors and then superintendents. Those with sufficient capital and management skills may start their own contracting business, although this may require an electrical contractor's license.

## Job Outlook

Job opportunities for skilled electricians are expected to be good as the growth in demand outpaces the supply of workers trained in this craft. There is expected to be a shortage of skilled workers during the next decade because of the anticipated smaller pool of young workers entering training programs.

Employment of electricians is expected to increase more slowly than the average for all occupations through the year 2005. As population and the economy grow, more electricians will be needed to install and maintain electrical devices and wiring in homes, factories, offices, and other structures. New technologies also are expected to continue to stimulate the demand for these workers. Increasingly, buildings will be prewired during construction to accommodate use of computers and telecommunications equipment. More and more factories will be using robots and automated manufacturing systems. Installation of this equipment, which is expected to increase, also should stimulate demand for electricians. Additional jobs will be created by rehabilitation and retrofitting of existing structures.

In addition to jobs created by increased demand for electri-

cal work, many openings will occur each year as electricians transfer to other occupations, retire, or leave the labor force for other reasons. Because of their lengthy training and relatively high earnings, a smaller proportion of electricians than other craft workers leave their occupation each year. The number of retirements is expected to rise, however, as more electricians reach retirement age.

Employment of construction electricians like that of many other construction workers, is sensitive to changes in the economy. This results from the limited duration of construction projects and the cyclical nature of the construction industry. During economic downturns, job openings for electricians are reduced as the level of construction declines. Apprenticeship opportunities also are less plentiful during these periods.

Although employment of maintenance electricians is steadier than that of construction electricians, those working in the automotive and other manufacturing industries that are sensitive to cyclical swings in the economy may be laid off during recessions. Also, efforts to reduce operating costs and increase productivity through the increased use of contracting out for electrical services may limit opportunities for maintenance electricians in many industries. However, this should be partially offset by increased demand by electrical contracting firms.

Job opportunities for electricians also vary by geographic area. Employment opportunities follow the movement of people and businesses among states and local areas and reflect differences in local economic conditions. The number of job opportunities in a given year may fluctuate widely from area to area. Some parts of the country may experience an oversupply of electricians, for example, while others may have a shortage.

## Earnings

Median weekly earnings for full-time electricians who were not self-employed were $574 in 1994. The middle 50 percent earned between $415 and $754 weekly. The lowest 10 percent earned less than $301, while the highest 10 percent earned more than $971 a week.

According to a survey of workplaces in 160 metropolitan areas, maintenance electricians had median hourly earnings of $17.45 in 1993. The middle half earned between $14.00 and $20.25 an hour. Annual earnings of electricians also tend to be higher than those of other building trades workers because electricians are less affected by the seasonal nature of construction.

Depending on experience, apprentices usually start at between 30 and 50 percent of the rate paid to experienced electricians. As they become more skilled, they receive periodic increases throughout the course of the apprenticeship program. Many employers also provide training opportunities for experienced electricians to improve their skills.

Many construction electricians are members of the International Brotherhood of Electrical Workers. Among unions organizing maintenance electricians are the International Brotherhood of Electrical Workers; the International Union of Electronic, Electrical, Salaried, Machine, and Furniture Workers; the International Association of Machinists and Aerospace Workers; the International Union, United Automobile, Aerospace and Agricultural Implement Workers of America; and the United Steelworkers of America.

## Related Occupations

To install and maintain electrical systems, electricians combine manual skill and a knowledge of electrical materials and concepts. Workers in other occupations involving similar skills include air-conditioning mechanics, cable installers and repairers, electronics mechanics, and elevator constructors.

## Related *D.O.T.* Jobs

These job titles are related to or more specific than the more general description above. They will help you identify job options you may not otherwise discover. These descriptions are in the current edition of the *Dictionary of Occupational Titles* and classified by numerical order.

729.381-018 STREET-LIGHT REPAIRER; 806.381-062 INSTALLER, ELECTRICAL, PLUMBING, MECHANICAL; 822.361-018 PROTECTIVE-SIGNAL INSTALLER; 822.361-022 PROTECTIVE-SIGNAL REPAIRER; 824.261-010 ELECTRICIAN; 824.261-014 ELECTRICIAN APPRENTICE; 824.281-010 AIRPORT ELECTRICIAN; 824.281-018 NEON-SIGN SERVICER; 824.381-010 STREET-LIGHT SERVICER; 824.681-010 ELECTRICIAN; 825.381-030 ELECTRICIAN; 825.381-034 ELECTRICIAN APPRENTICE; 829.261-018 ELECTRICIAN, MAINTENANCE; 952.364-010 TROUBLE SHOOTER I; 952.381-010 SWITCH INSPECTOR

## Sources of Additional Information

For details about apprenticeships or other work opportunities in this trade, contact offices of the state employment service, the state apprenticeship agency, local electrical contractors or firms that employ maintenance electricians, or local union-management electrician apprenticeship committees. This information may also be available from local chapters of the Independent Electrical Contractors, Inc.: the National Electrical Contractors Association; the Home Builders Institute; the Associated Builders and Contractors; and the International Brotherhood of Electrical Workers.

For general information about the work of electricians, contact:

❑ Independent Electrical Contractors, Inc., 507 Wythe St., Alexandria, VA 22314.

❑ National Electrical Contractors Association (NECA), 3 Metro Center, Suite 1100, Bethesda, MD 20814.

❑ International Brotherhood of Electrical Workers (IBEW), 1125 15th St. NW, Washington, DC 20005.

❑ Associated Builders and Contractors, 1300 North 17th St., Rosslyn, VA 22209.

❑ Homebuilders Institute, National Association of Home Builders, 1201 15th St. NW, Washington, DC 20005.

# Electroneurodiagnostic Technologists

## Nature of the Work

Electroneurodiagnostic technologists use an electroencephalograph (EEG) machine to record electrical impulses transmitted by the brain and the nervous system. They help physicians diagnose brain tumors, strokes, toxic/metabolic disorders, epilepsy and sleep disorders. They also measure the effects of infectious diseases on the brain, as well as determine whether individuals with mental or behavioral problems have an organic impairment such as Alzheimer's disease. Furthermore, they determine "cerebral" death, the absence of brain activity, and assess the probability of a recovery from a coma.

Electroneurodiagnostic technologists who specialize in basic or, "resting" EEGs are called EEG technologists. The range of tests performed by electroneurodiagnostic technologists is broader than, but includes, those conducted by EEG technologists. Because it provides a more accurate description of work typically performed in the field, the title electroneurodiagnostic technologists generally has replaced that of EEG technologist.

Electroneurodiagnostic technologists take patients' medical histories and help them relax, then apply electrodes to designated spots on the patient's head. They must choose the most appropriate combination of instrument controls and electrodes to correct for mechanical or electrical interference that come from somewhere other than the brain, such as eye movement or radiation from electrical sources.

Increasingly, technologists perform EEGs in the operating room, which requires that they understand anesthesia's effect on brain waves. For special procedure EEGs, technologists may secure electrodes to the chest, arm, leg, or spinal column to record activity from both the central and peripheral nervous systems.

In ambulatory monitoring, technologists monitor the brain, and sometimes the heart, while patients carry out normal activities over a 24-hour period. Then they remove the small recorder carried by the patients and obtain a readout. Technologists review the readouts, selecting sections for the physician to examine.

Using "evoked potential" testing, technologists measure sensory and physical responses to specific stimuli. After the electrodes have been attached, they set the instrument for the type and intensity of the stimulus, increase the intensity until the patient reacts, and note the sensation level. The tests may take from one to four hours.

For nerve conduction tests, used to diagnose muscle and nerve problems, technologists place electrodes on the patient's skin over a nerve and over the muscle. Then they stimulate the nerve with an electrical current and record how long it takes the nerve impulse to reach the muscle.

Technologists who specialize in and administer sleep disorder studies are called polysomnographic technologists. The sleep studies are conducted in a clinic called a "sleep center." During the procedure technologists monitor the patient's respiration and heart activity in addition to brain wave activity and must know the dynamics of the cardiopulmonary systems during each stage of sleep. They coordinate readings from several organ systems, separating them according to the stages of sleep, and relay them to the physician. For quantitative EEGs, technologists decide which sections of the EEG should be transformed into color-coded pictures of brain wave frequency and intensity, for interpretation by a physician. They may also write technical reports summarizing test results.

Technologists also look for changes in the patient's neurologic, cardiac, and respiratory status, which may indicate an emergency, such as a heart attack, and provide emergency care until help arrives.

Electroneurodiagnostic technologists may have supervisory or administrative responsibilities. They may manage an electroneurodiagnostic laboratory, arrange work schedules, keep records, schedule appointments, order supplies, provide instruction to less experienced technologists, and may also be responsible for the equipment's upkeep.

## Working Conditions

Electroneurodiagnostic technologists usually work in clean, well-lighted surroundings, and spend about half of their time on their feet. Bending and lifting are necessary because they may work with patients who are very ill and require assistance. Technologists who are employed in hospitals may do all their work in a single room, or may push equipment to a patient's bedside and obtain recordings there.

Most technologists work a standard workweek, although those in hospitals may be on-call evenings, weekends, and holidays. Those performing sleep studies usually work evenings and nights.

## Employment

Electroneurodiagnostic technologists held more than 6,000 jobs in 1994. Most worked in neurology laboratories of hospitals. Others worked in offices and clinics of neurologists and neurosurgeons, health maintenance organizations, and psychiatric facilities.

## Training, Other Qualifications, and Advancement

Although most electroneurodiagnostic technologists currently employed learned their skills on the job, employers are beginning to favor those who have completed formal training. Some hospitals require applicants for trainee positions to have postsecondary training while others only expect a high school diploma. Often, on-the-job trainees are transfers from another hospital job, such as a licensed practical nurse.

Formal postsecondary training is offered in hospitals and community colleges. In 1994, the Joint Review Committee on Education in Electroneurodiagnostic Technology had approved 14 formal programs. Programs usually last from one to two years and include laboratory experience as well as classroom instruction in human anatomy and physiology, neurology, neuroanatomy, neurophysiology, medical terminology, computer technology, electronics and instrumentation. Graduates receive associate degrees or certificates.

The American Board of Registration of Electroencephalographic and Evoked Potential Technologists awards the credential "Registered EEG Technologist" and "Registered Evoked Potential Technologist" to qualified applicants. The Association of Polysomnographic Technologists registers polysomnographic technologists. Applicants interested in taking the registration exam must have worked in a sleep center for at least one year. Although not generally required for staff level jobs, registration indicates professional competence, and usually is necessary for supervisory or teaching jobs.

Technologists should have manual dexterity, good vision, writing skills, an aptitude for working with electronic equipment, and the ability to work with patients as well as with other health personnel. High school courses in health, biology, and mathematics are useful.

Electroneurodiagnostic technologists who have significant experience can advance to chief or manager of a electroneurodiagnostic laboratory in a large hospital. Chief technologists generally are supervised by a physician—an electroencephalographer, neurologist, or neurosurgeon. Technologists may also teach or go into research.

## Job Outlook

Job prospects for qualified applicants are expected to be good. Employment of electroneurodiagnostic technologists is expected to grow faster than the average for all occupations through the year 2005, reflecting the increased numbers of neurodiagnostic tests performed. There will be more testing as new procedures are developed and as the size of the population grows. A very low number of openings each year are expected, however, because the occupation is very small. Most jobs will be found in hospitals but growth will be fastest in offices and clinics of neurologists.

## Earnings

According to a University of Texas Medical Branch survey of hospitals and medical centers, the median annual salary of EEG technologists, based on a 40-hour week and excluding shift or area differentials, was $24,710 in October 1994. The average minimum salary was $20,356 and the average maximum was $29,691.

## Related Occupations

Other health personnel who operate medical equipment include radiologic technologists, nuclear medicine technologists, sonographers, perfusionists, and cardiovascular technologists.

## Related *D.O.T.* Jobs

These job titles are related to or more specific than the more general description above. They will help you identify job options you may not otherwise discover. These descriptions are in the current edition of the *Dictionary of Occupational Titles* and classified by numerical order.

078.362-022 ELECTROENCEPHALOGRAPHIC TECHNOLOGIST; 078.362-042 POLYSOMNOGRAPHIC TECHNICIAN

## Sources of Additional Information

Local hospitals can supply information about employment opportunities.

For general information about a career in electroneurodiagnostics as well as a list of accredited training programs, contact:

❑ Executive Office, American Society of Electroneurodiagnostic Technologists, Inc., 204 W. 7th, Carroll, IA 51401.

For information on work in sleep studies, contact:

❑ Association of Polysomnographic Technology, P.O. Box 14861, Lenexa, KS 66285-4861.

Information about specific accredited training programs is also available from:

❑ Joint Review Committee on Electroneurodiagnostic Technology, Route 1, Box 63A, Genoa, WI 54632.

Information on becoming a registered Electroneuro-diagnostic technologist is available from:

❑ American Board of Registration of Electro-encephalographic and Evoked Potential Technologists, P.O. Box 916633, Longwood, FL 32791-6633.

# Electronic Equipment Repairers

## Nature of the Work

Electronic equipment repairers, also called service technicians or field service representatives, install, maintain, and repair electronic equipment used in offices, factories, homes, hospitals, aircraft, and other places. Equipment includes televisions, radar, industrial equipment controls, computers, telephone systems, and medical diagnosing equipment. Repairers have numerous job titles, which often refer to the kind of equipment they work with.

Electronic repairers install, test, repair, and calibrate equipment to ensure that it functions properly. They keep detailed records on each piece of equipment to provide a history of tests, performance problems, and repairs.

When equipment breaks down, repairers first examine work orders, which indicate problems, or talk to equipment operators. Then they check for common causes of trouble such as loose connections or obviously defective components. If routine checks do not locate the trouble, repairers may refer to schematics and manufacturers' specifications that show connections and provide instruction on how to locate problems. They use voltmeters, ohmmeters, signal generators, ammeters, and oscilloscopes and run diagnostic programs to pinpoint malfunctions. It may take several hours to locate a problem but only a few minutes to fix it. However, more equipment now has self-diagnosing features, which greatly simplifies the work. To fix equipment, repairers may replace defective components, circuit boards, or wiring, or adjust and calibrate equipment, using test equipment, small handtools such as pliers, screwdrivers, and soldering irons.

Field repairers visit worksites in their assigned area on a regular basis to do preventive maintenance according to manufacturers' recommended schedules, and whenever emergencies arise. During these calls, repairers may also advise customers on how to use equipment more efficiently and how to spot problems in their early stages. They also listen to customers' complaints and answer questions, promoting customer satisfaction and good will. Some field repairers work full-time at installations of clients with a lot of equipment.

Bench repairers work at repair facilities, in stores, factories, or service centers. They repair portable equipment—such as televisions and personal computers brought in by customers—or defective components and machines requiring extensive repairs that have been sent in by field repairers. They determine the source of a problem in the equipment, and may estimate whether it is wiser to buy a new part or machine or to fix the broken one.

## Working Conditions

Some electronic equipment repairers work shifts, including weekends and holidays, to service equipment in computer centers, manufacturing plants, hospitals, and telephone compa-nies which operate around the clock. Shifts are generally assigned on the basis of seniority. Repairers may also be on call at any time to handle equipment failure.

Repairers generally work in clean, well-lighted, air-conditioned surroundings—an electronic repair shop or service center, hospital, military installation, or a telephone company's central office. However, some, such as commercial and industrial electronic equipment repairers, may be exposed to heat, grease, and noise on factory floors. Some may have to work in cramped spaces. Telephone installers and repairers may work on rooftops, ladders, and telephone poles.

The work of most repairers involves lifting, reaching, stooping, crouching, and crawling. Adherence to safety precautions is essential to guard against work hazards such as minor burns and electrical shock.

## Employment

Electronic equipment repairers held about 389,000 jobs in 1994. Many worked for telephone companies. Others worked for electronic and transportation equipment manufacturers, machinery and equipment wholesalers, hospitals, electronic repair shops, and firms that provide maintenance under contract (called third-party maintenance firms). The distribution of employment in each occupation is presented in the following tabulation:

| | |
|---|---|
| Computer and office machine repairers | 134,000 |
| Communications equipment mechanics | 118,000 |
| Commercial and industrial electronic equipment repairers | 66,000 |
| Telephone installers and repairers | 37,000 |
| Electronic home entertainment equipment repairers | 34,000 |

## Training, Other Qualifications, and Advancement

Most employers prefer applicants with formal training in electronics. Electronic training is offered by public postsecondary vocational-technical schools, private vocational schools and technical institutes, junior and community colleges, and some high schools and correspondence schools. Programs take one to two years. The military services also offer formal training and work experience.

Training includes general courses in mathematics, physics, electricity, electronics, schematic reading, and troubleshooting. Students also choose courses which prepare them for a specialty, such as computers, commercial and industrial equipment, or home entertainment equipment. A few repairers complete formal apprenticeship programs sponsored jointly by employers and locals of the International Brotherhood of Electrical Workers.

Applicants for entry-level jobs may have to pass tests that measure mechanical aptitude, knowledge of electricity or electronics, manual dexterity, and general intelligence. Newly hired repairers, even those with formal training, usually receive some training from their employer. They may study electronics and circuit theory and math. They also get hands-on experience with equipment, doing basic maintenance, and using diagnostic programs to locate malfunctions. Training may be in a classroom or it may be self-instruction, consisting of videotapes, programmed computer software, or workbooks that allow trainees to learn at their own pace.

Experienced technicians attend training sessions and read manuals to keep up with design changes and revised service procedures. Many technicians also take advanced training in a particular system or type of repair.

Good eyesight and color vision are needed to inspect and work on small, delicate parts and good hearing to detect malfunctions revealed by sound. Because field repairers usually handle jobs alone, they must be able to work without close supervision. For those who have frequent contact with customers, a pleasant personality, neat appearance, and good communications skills are important. Repairers must also be trustworthy because they may be exposed to money and other valuables in places like banks and securities offices, and some employers require that they be bonded. A security clearance may be required for technicians who repair equipment or service machines in areas where people are engaged in activities related to national security.

The International Society of Certified Electronics Technicians and the Electronics Technicians Association each administer a voluntary certification program. In both, an electronics repairer with four years of experience may become a Certified Electronics Technician. Certification, which is by examination, is offered in computer, radio-TV, industrial and commercial equipment, audio, avionics, wireless communications, video distribution, satellite, and radar systems repair. An Associate Level Test, covering basic electronics, is offered for students or repairers with less than four years of experience. Those who test and repair radio transmitting equipment, other than business and land mobile radios, need a General Operators License from the Federal Communications Commission.

Experienced repairers with advanced training may become specialists or troubleshooters who help other repairers diagnose difficult problems, or work with engineers in designing equipment and developing maintenance procedures.

Because of their familiarity with equipment, repairers are particularly well qualified to become manufacturers' sales workers. Workers with leadership ability also may become maintenance supervisors or service managers. Some experienced workers open their own repair services or shops, or become wholesalers or retailers of electronic equipment.

## Job Outlook

Overall, employment of electronic equipment repairers is expected to decline through the year 2005. Although the amount of electronic equipment in use will grow very rapidly, improvements in product reliability and ease of service and lower equipment prices will cause a decline in the need for repairers. The following tabulation presents the expected job change in percent for the various electronic equipment repairer occupations:

| | |
|---|---|
| Computer and office machine repairers | 24 |
| Commercial and industrial electronic equipment repairers | 2 |
| Electronic home entertainment equipment repairers | -10 |
| Communications equipment mechanics | -35 |
| Telephone installers and repairers | -70 |

Employment of computer equipment repairers will grow much faster the than average for all occupations through the year 2005 as the number of computers in service increases rapidly. Employment of industrial equipment repairers outside the federal government will increase faster than the average as the amount of equipment grows. Mainly because of cuts in the defense budget, employment of repairers in the federal government will decline. Employment of those who repair electronic home entertainment equipment will decline modestly as equipment becomes more reliable and easier to service. Employment of repairers who handle telephone industry equipment—telephone installers and repairers and communication equipment mechanics—is expected to decline sharply because of improvements in equipment reliability, ease of maintenance, and low equipment replacement cost.

## Earnings

In 1994, median weekly earnings of full-time electronic equipment repairers were $592. The middle 50 percent earned between $434 and $765. The bottom 10 percent earned less than $317, while the top 10 percent earned more than $947. Earnings vary widely by occupation and the type of equipment repaired, as shown in the following tabulation:

| | |
|---|---|
| Telephone installers and repairers | $679 |
| Data processing equipment repairers | 589 |
| Electronic repairers, communications and industrial equipment | 542 |
| Office machine repairers | 458 |

Central office installers, central office technicians, PBX installers, and telephone installers and repairers employed by AT&T and the Bell Operating Companies and represented by the Communications Workers of America and the International Brotherhood of Electrical Workers earned between $469 and $1,063 a week in 1994.

According to a survey of workplaces in 160 metropolitan areas, beginning maintenance electronics technicians had median earnings of $10.75 an hour in 1993, with the middle half earning between $9.63 and $12.56 an hour. The most experienced repairers had median earnings of $18.40 an hour, with the middle half earning between $16.67 and $20.12 an hour.

## Related Occupations

Workers in other occupations who repair and maintain the circuits and mechanical parts of electronic equipment include appliance and power tool repairers, automotive electricians, broadcast technicians, electronic organ technicians, and vending machine repairers. Electronics engineering technicians may also repair electronic equipment as part of their duties.

## Related D.O.T. Jobs

726.381-014 ELECTRONIC EQUIPMENT REPAIRER

## Sources of Additional Information

For career, certification, and FCC licensing information, contact:

❏ The International Society of Certified Electronics Technicians, 2708 West Berry St., Fort Worth, TX 76109.

For certification, career, placement, and FCC licensing information, contact:

❏ Electronics Technicians Association, 604 North Jackson, Greencastle, IN 46135.

For a list of FCC licensing administrators, write to:

❏ Federal Communications Commission, Consumer Assistance Office, 1270 Fairfield Rd., Gettysburg, Pa 17325-7245 or call 1-800-322-1117.

For information on the telephone industry and career opportunities contact:

❏ United States Telephone Association, 1401 H St., Suite 600, Washington, DC 20005-2136.

For information on electronic equipment repairers in the telephone industry, write to:

❏ Communications Workers of America, 501 3rd St. NW, Washington, DC 20001.

# Electronic Home Entertainment Equipment Repairers

## Nature of the Work

Electronic home entertainment equipment repairers, also called service technicians, repair radios, televisions, stereos, recorders, public address systems, slide and motion picture projectors, video cameras, video games, home security systems, microwave ovens, and electronic organs. Some repairers specialize in one kind of equipment; others repair many types.

They replace faulty parts or make adjustments, such as focusing and converging the picture or correcting the color balance of a television set. They may also make recordings and listen to playbacks to detect problems. Some install and repair automobile radios.

## Working Conditions

Repairers generally work in clean, well-lighted, air-conditioned surroundings—an electronic repair shop or service center. However, some may have to work in cramped spaces.

The work of most repairers involves lifting, reaching, stooping, crouching, and crawling. Adherence to safety precautions is essential to guard against work hazards such as minor burns and electrical shock.

## Employment

Electronic home entertainment equipment repairers held about 34,000 jobs in 1994. Nearly one-third were self-employed, a larger proportion than in most other repairer occupations. Most repairers work in electronic repair shops and service centers or in stores that sell and service electronic home entertainment products. Employment is distributed in much the same way as the population.

## Training, Other Qualifications, and Advancement

Electronic training is offered by public postsecondary vocational-technical schools, private vocational schools and technical institutes, junior and community colleges, and some high schools and correspondence schools. Programs take one to two years. The military services also offer formal training and work experience.

Training includes general courses in mathematics, physics, electricity, electronics, schematic reading, and troubleshooting. A few repairers complete formal apprenticeship programs sponsored jointly by employers and locals of the International Brotherhood of Electrical Workers.

Applicants for entry-level jobs may have to pass tests that measure mechanical aptitude, knowledge of electricity or electronics, manual dexterity, and general intelligence. Newly hired repairers, even those with formal training, usually receive some training from their employer. They may study electronics and circuit theory and math. They also get hands-on experience with equipment, doing basic maintenance, and using diagnostic programs to locate malfunctions. Training may be in a classroom or it may be self-instruction, consisting of videotapes, programmed computer software, or workbooks that allow trainees to learn at their own pace.

Experienced technicians attend training sessions and read manuals to keep up with design changes and revised service procedures. Many technicians also take advanced training in a particular system or type of repair.

Good eyesight and color vision are needed to inspect and work on small, delicate parts and good hearing to detect malfunctions revealed by sound. Because field repairers usually handle jobs alone, they must be able to work without close supervision. For those who have frequent contact with customers, a pleasant personality, neat appearance, and good communications skills are important.

The International Society of Certified Electronics Technicians and the Electronics Technicians Association each administer a voluntary certification program. In both, an electronics repairer with four years of experience may become a Certified Electronics Technician. Certification, which is by examination, is offered in computer, radio-TV, industrial and commercial equipment, audio, avionics, wireless communications, video distribution, satellite, and radar systems repair. An Associate Level Test, covering basic electronics, is offered for students or repairers with less than four years of experience. Those who test and repair radio transmitting equipment, other than business and land mobile radios, need a General Operators License from the Federal Communications Commission.

Because of their familiarity with equipment, repairers are particularly well qualified to become manufacturers' sales workers. Some experienced workers open their own repair services or shops, or become wholesalers or retailers of electronic equipment.

## Job Outlook

Employment of electronic home entertainment equipment repairers is expected to decline through the year 2005. Improvements in reliability and ease of servicing should reduce service requirements even though the amount of equipment in use is expected to increase. Job opportunities should be good, nevertheless, due to the need to replace the many electronic home entertainment equipment repairers who transfer to higher paying occupations requiring a knowledge of electronics, such as computer and office machine repairer.

## Earnings

In 1994, median weekly earnings of full-time electronic equipment repairers were $592. The middle 50 percent earned between $434 and $765. The bottom 10 percent earned less than $317, while the top 10 percent earned more than $947. Earnings vary widely by occupation and the type of equipment repaired.

## Related Occupations

Workers in other occupations who repair and maintain the circuits and mechanical parts of electronic equipment include appliance and power tool repairers, automotive electricians, broadcast technicians, electronic organ technicians, and vending machine repairers. Electronics engineering technicians may also repair electronic equipment as part of their duties.

## Related *D.O.T.* Jobs

These job titles are related to or more specific than the more general description above. They will help you identify job options you may not otherwise discover. These descriptions are in the current edition of the *Dictionary of Occupational Titles* and classified by numerical order.

720.281-010 RADIO REPAIRER; 720.281-014 TAPE-RECORDER REPAIRER; 720.281-018 TELEVISION-AND-RADIO REPAIRER; 729.281-010 AUDIO-VIDEO REPAIRER; 730.281-018 ELECTRIC-ORGAN INSPECTOR AND REPAIRER; 823.361-010 TELEVISION INSTALLER; 828.261-010 ELECTRONIC-ORGAN TECHNICIAN

## Sources of Additional Information

For career, certification, and FCC licensing information, contact:

❏ The International Society of Certified Electronics Technicians, 2708 West Berry St., Fort Worth, TX 76109.

For certification, career, placement, and FCC licensing information, contact:

❏ Electronics Technicians Association, 604 North Jackson, Greencastle, IN 46135.

For a list of FCC licensing administrators, write to:

❏ Federal Communications Commission, Consumer Assistance Office, 1270 Fairfield Rd., Gettysburg, Pa 17325-7245 or call 1-800-322-1117.

# Elevator Installers and Repairers

## Nature of the Work

Elevator installers and repairers—also called *elevator constructors* or *elevator mechanics*—assemble, install, and replace elevators, escalators, dumbwaiters, moving walkways, and similar equipment in new and old buildings. Once the equipment is in service, they maintain and repair it. They are also responsible for modernizing older equipment.

In order to install, repair, and maintain modern elevators, which are almost all electronically controlled, elevator installers and repairers must have a thorough knowledge of electronics, electricity, and hydraulics. Many elevators today are installed with microprocessors, which are programmed to constantly analyze traffic conditions in order to dispatch elevators in the most efficient manner. With these computer controls, it is now possible to get the greatest amount of service with the least number of cars.

When installing a new elevator, elevator installers and repairers begin by studying blueprints in order to determine the equipment layout of the framework to install rails, machines, car enclosures, motors, pumps, cylinders, and plunger foundations. Once the layout analysis is completed, they begin equipment installation. Working on scaffolding or platforms, installers bolt or weld steel rails to the walls of the shaft to guide the elevator up and down.

Elevator installers put in electrical wires and controls by running tubing, called "conduit," along the shaft's walls from floor to floor. Once in place, mechanics pull plastic-covered electrical wires through the conduit. They then install electrical components and related devices required at each floor and at the main control panel in the machine room.

Installers bolt or weld together the steel frame of the elevator car at the bottom of the shaft, install the car's platform, walls, and doors, and attach guide shoes and rollers to minimize the lateral motion of the car as it travels through the shaft. They also install the outer doors and door frames at the elevator entrances on each floor.

For cabled elevators, these workers install geared or gearless machines with a traction drive sheave which moves heavy steel cables connected to the elevator car and counterweight. The counterweight moves in the opposite direction from the car and aids in its swift and smooth movement.

Elevator installers also install elevators in which a car sits on a hydraulic plunger that is driven by a pump. The plunger pushes the elevator car up from underneath, similar to a lift in an auto service station. They also install escalators. They put in place the steel framework, the electrically powered stairs, and the tracks, and install associated motors and electrical wiring. In addition to elevators and escalators, elevator installers also may install devices such as dumbwaiters and material lifts, which are similar to elevators in design, moving walkways, stair lifts, and wheelchair lifts.

The most highly skilled elevator installers and repairers, called "adjusters," specialize in fine-tuning all of the equipment after installation. Adjusters must make sure that the elevator is working according to specifications, such as stopping correctly at each floor within a specified time period. Once an elevator is operating properly, it must be maintained and serviced regularly to keep it in safe, working condition. Elevator maintenance mechanics generally do preventive maintenance—such as oiling and greasing moving parts, replacing worn parts, testing equipment with meters and gauges, and adjusting equipment for optimal performance. They also troubleshoot and may be called in to do emergency repairs.

A service crew usually handles major repairs—for example, replacing cables, elevator doors, or machine bearings. This may require cutting torches or rigging equipment—tools a maintenance mechanic would not normally carry. Service crews also do major modernization and alteration work, such as moving and replacing electrical motors, hydraulic pumps, and control panels.

Elevator installers and repairers usually specialize in installation, maintenance, or repair work. Maintenance and repair workers generally need more knowledge of electricity and electronics than installers because a large part of maintenance and repair work is troubleshooting. Similarly, construction adjusters need a thorough knowledge of electricity, electronics, and computers to ensure that newly installed elevators operate properly.

## Working Conditions

Most elevator installers and repairers work a 40-hour week. However, maintenance and service mechanics often work overtime when repairing essential elevator equipment. They are sometimes on 24-hour call. Maintenance mechanics, unlike most elevator installers, are on their own most of the day and typically service the same elevators periodically.

Elevator installers lift and carry heavy equipment and parts and may work in cramped spaces or awkward positions. Hazards include falls, electrical shock, muscle strains, and other injuries related to handling heavy equipment. Because most of their work is performed indoors in buildings under construction or in existing buildings, elevator installers and repairers lose less work time due to inclement weather than other building trades workers.

## Employment

Elevator installers and repairers held about 24,000 jobs in 1994. Most were employed by special trade contractors. Others were employed by field offices of elevator manufacturers; wholesale distributors; small, local elevator maintenance and repair contractors; or by government agencies or businesses that do their own elevator maintenance and repair.

## Training, Other Qualifications, and Advancement

Most elevator installers and repairers apply for their jobs through a local of the International Union of Elevator Constructors. Applicants for trainee positions must be at least 18 years old, have a high school diploma or equivalent, and pass an aptitude test. Good physical condition and mechanical aptitude also are important.

Elevator installers and repairers learn their trade in a program administered by local joint educational committees representing the employers and the union. These programs, through which the trainee learns everything from installation to repair, combine on-the-job training with classroom instruction in electrical and electronic theory, mathematics, applications of physics, and safety. Elevator installers and repairers in nonunion shops may complete training programs sponsored by independent contractors.

Generally, trainees or helpers must complete a six-month probationary period. After successful completion, they work toward becoming fully qualified mechanics within four to five years. In order to be classified a fully qualified mechanic, union trainees must pass a standard mechanics examination administered by the National Elevator Industry Educational Program. Most states and cities also require elevator constructors to pass a licensing examination.

Most trainees or helpers assist experienced elevator installers and repairers. Beginners carry materials and tools, bolt rails to walls, and assemble elevator cars. Eventually, they learn to do more difficult tasks, such as wiring, which requires a knowledge of local and national electrical codes.

High school courses in electricity, mathematics, and physics provide a useful background. As elevators become increasingly sophisticated, workers may find it necessary to acquire more advanced formal education—for example, in postsecondary technical school or junior college—with an emphasis on electronics. Workers with more formal education generally advance more quickly than their counterparts.

Many elevator installers and repairers also receive training from their employers or through manufacturers to become familiar with the company's particular equipment. Retraining is very important to keep abreast of technological developments in elevator repair. In fact, union elevator constructors typically receive continual training throughout their careers, either through correspondence courses, seminars, or formal classes. Although voluntary, this training greatly improves one's chances for promotion.

Some installers may receive further training in specialized areas and advance to mechanic-in-charge, adjuster, supervisor, or elevator inspector. Adjusters, for example, may actually be picked for the position because they possess particular skills or are seen to be more electronically inclined. Others workers may move into management, sales, or product design.

## Job Outlook

Employment of elevator installers and repairers is expected to increase about as fast as the average for all occupations through the year 2005, but relatively few new job opportunities will be generated because the occupation is small. Replacement needs, another source of jobs, also will be relatively low, in part, because a substantial amount of time is invested in specialized training that yields high earnings and workers tend to remain in this field. The job outlook for new workers is largely dependent on activity in the construction industry and opportunities may vary from year to year as conditions within the industry change. Job prospects should be best for those with postsecondary training in electronics or more advanced formal education.

Demand for elevator installers and repairers will increase as the stock of equipment needing repairs and the construction of new buildings with elevators and escalators increases. Growth also should be driven by the need to continually update and modernize older equipment, including improvements in appearance and the installation of more sophisticated equipment and computerized controls. Since equipment must always be kept in working condition, economic downturns will have less of an effect on employment of elevator maintenance and repair mechanics. The need for people to service elevators and escalators should increase as equipment becomes more intricate and complex.

## Earnings

Average weekly earnings for union elevator installers and repairers were about $820 in 1994, according to data from the International Union of Elevator Constructors. Rates vary with geographic location. Probationary helpers started at about 50 percent of the rate for experienced elevator mechanics, or about $410 a week. Nonprobationary helpers earned about 70 percent of this rate, or an average of about $574 a week. Mechanics-in-charge averaged $923 a week.

In addition to free continuing education, elevator installers and repairers receive basic benefits enjoyed by most other workers.

The proportion of elevator installers and repairers who are union members is higher than nearly any other occupation. Over

90 percent of elevator installers and repairers are members of the International Union of Elevator Constructors.

### Related Occupations

Elevator installers and repairers combine electrical and mechanical skills with construction skills such as welding, rigging, measuring, and blueprint reading. Other occupations that require many of these skills are boilermaker, electrician, industrial machinery repairer, millwright, sheetmetal worker, and structural ironworker.

### Related *D.O.T.* Jobs

These job titles are related to or more specific than the more general description above. They will help you identify job options you may not otherwise discover. These descriptions are in the current edition of the *Dictionary of Occupational Titles* and classified by numerical order.

825.261-014 ELEVATOR EXAMINER-AND-ADJUSTER; 825.281-030 ELEVATOR REPAIRER; 825.281-034 ELEVATOR-REPAIRER APPRENTICE; 825.361-010 ELEVATOR CONSTRUCTOR

### Sources of Additional Information

For further details about opportunities as an elevator installer and repairer, contact elevator manufacturers, elevator repair and maintenance contractors, a local of the International Union of Elevator Constructors, or the nearest local public employment service office.

# Emergency Medical Technicians

### Nature of the Work

Automobile accident injuries, heart attacks, near drownings, unscheduled childbirths, poisonings, and gunshot wounds all demand urgent medical attention. Emergency medical technicians (EMTs) give immediate care and then transport the sick or injured to medical facilities.

Following instructions from a dispatcher, EMTs—who usually work in teams of two—drive specially equipped vehicles to the scene of emergencies. If necessary, they request additional help from police or fire department personnel. They determine the nature and extent of the patient's injuries or illness while also trying to determine whether the patient has epilepsy, diabetes, or other preexisting medical conditions. EMTs then give appropriate emergency care following strict guidelines for which procedures they may perform. All EMTs, including those with basic skills, the EMT-Basic, may open airways, restore breathing, control bleeding, treat for shock, administer oxygen, immobilize fractures, bandage wounds, assist in childbirth, manage emotionally disturbed patients, treat and assist heart attack victims, give initial care to poison and burn victims, and treat patients with anti-shock trousers (which prevent a person's blood pressure from falling too low).

EMT-Intermediates, or EMT-Is, have more advanced training that allows them to administer intravenous fluids; use defibrillators to give lifesaving shocks to a stopped heart, as well as other intensive care procedures.

EMT-Paramedics, EMT-Ps, provide the most extensive prehospital care. In addition to the procedures already described, paramedics may administer drugs orally and intravenously, interpret electrocardiograms (EKGs), perform endotracheal intubations, and use monitors and other complex equipment.

When victims are trapped, as in the case of an automobile accident, cave-in, or building collapse, EMTs free them or provide emergency care while others free them. Some conditions are simple enough to be handled following general rules and guidelines. More complicated problems can only be carried out under the step-by-step direction of medical personnel by radio contact.

When transporting patients to a medical facility, EMTs may use special equipment such as backboards to immobilize them before placing them on stretchers and securing them in the ambulance. While one EMT drives, the other monitors the patient's vital signs and gives additional care as needed. Some EMTs work for hospital trauma centers or jurisdictions which use helicopters to transport critically ill or injured patients.

At a medical facility, EMTs transfer patients to the emergency department, report to the staff their observations and the care they provided, and help provide emergency treatment.

In rural areas, some EMT-Ps are trained to treat patients with minor injuries on the scene of an accident or at their home without transporting them to a medical facility.

After each run, EMTs replace used supplies and check equipment. If patients have had a contagious disease, EMTs decontaminate the interior of the ambulance and report cases to the proper authorities.

### Working Conditions

EMTs work both indoors and outdoors, in all kinds of weather. Much of their time is spent standing, kneeling, bending, and lifting. They may risk noise-induced hearing loss from ambulance sirens and back injuries from lifting patients. EMTs may be exposed to diseases such as Hepatitis-B and AIDS, as well as violence from drug overdose victims. The work is not only physically strenuous, but stressful—not surprising in a job that involves life-or-death situations. Nonetheless, many people find the work exciting and challenging.

EMTs employed by fire departments often have about a 50-hour workweek. Those employed by hospitals frequently work between 45 and 58 hours a week and those in private ambulance services between 48 and 51 hours. Some EMTs, especially those in police and fire departments, are on-call for extended periods. Because most emergency services function 24 hours a day, EMTs have irregular working hours that add to job stress.

### Employment

EMTs held about 138,000 jobs in 1994. Two-fifths were in private ambulance services, about a third were in municipal fire, police, or rescue squad departments, and a quarter were in hospitals. In addition, there are many volunteer EMTs. Most paid EMTs work in metropolitan areas. In many smaller cities, towns, and rural areas, there are no paid EMT jobs.

### Training, Other Qualifications, and Advancement

Formal training is needed to become an EMT. EMT-Basic training is 100 to 120 hours of classroom work plus 10 hours of internship in a hospital emergency room. Training is available in all 50 states and the District of Columbia, and is offered by police, fire, and health departments; in hospitals; and as a nondegree course in colleges and universities.

The EMT-Basic program provides instruction and practice in dealing with bleeding, fractures, airway obstruction, cardiac arrest, and emergency childbirth. Students learn to use and care for common emergency equipment, such as backboards, suction devices, splints, oxygen delivery systems, and stretchers.

EMT-Intermediate training varies from state to state, but includes 35 to 55 hours of additional instruction in patient assessment as well as the use of esophageal airways, intravenous fluids, and antishock garments. Training programs for EMT-Paramedics, of which there were about 85 in 1993, generally last between 750 and 2,000 hours. Refresher courses and continuing education are available for EMTs at all levels.

Applicants to an EMT training course generally must be at least 18 years old and have a high school diploma or the equivalent and a driver's license. Recommended high school subjects for prospective EMTs are driver education, health, and science. Training in the Armed Forces as a "medic" is also good preparation.

In addition to EMT training, EMTs in fire and police departments must be qualified as firefighters or police officers.

Graduates of approved EMT-Basic training programs who pass a written and practical examination administered by the state certifying agency or the National Registry of Emergency Medical Technicians earn the title of Registered EMT-Basic. Prerequisites for taking the EMT-Intermediate examination include registration as an EMT-Basic, required classroom work, and a specified amount of clinical experience and field internship. Registration for EMT-Paramedics by the National Registry of Emergency Medical Technicians or a state emergency medical services agency requires current registration or state certification as an EMT-Basic, completion of an EMT-Paramedic training program and required clinical and field internships as well as passing of a written and practical examination. Although not a general requirement for employment, registration acknowledges an EMTs qualifications and makes higher paying jobs easier to obtain.

All 50 states have some kind of certification procedure. In 31 states and the District of Columbia, registration with the National Registry is required at some or all levels of certification. Other states require their own certification examination or provide the option of taking the National Registry examination.

To maintain their certification, all EMTs must reregister, usually every two years. In order to reregister, an individual must be working as an EMT and meet a continuing education requirement.

EMTs should be emotionally stable, have good dexterity, agility, an physical coordination, and be able to lift and carry heavy loads. EMTs need good eyesight (corrective lenses may be used) with accurate color vision.

Advancement beyond the EMT-Paramedic level usually means leaving fieldwork. An EMT-Paramedic can become a supervisor, operations manager, administrative director, or executive director of emergency services. Some EMTs become EMT instructors, firefighters, dispatchers, or police officers, or others move into sales or marketing of emergency medical equipment. Finally, some become EMTs to assess their interest in health care and then decide to return to school and become registered nurses, physicians, or other health workers.

## Job Outlook

Competition for jobs will be keen in fire, police, and rescue squad departments because of attractive pay and benefits and good job security. Opportunities for EMTs are expected to be excellent in hospitals and private ambulance services, where pay and benefits usually are low.

Employment of EMTs is expected to grow much faster than average for all occupations through the year 2005. Driving the growth will be an expanding population. Also, the number of older people, who are more likely to need emergency services, is increasing rapidly. Additional job openings will occur as more states begin to allow EMT-Paramedics to perform primary care on the scene without transporting the patient to a medical facility.

Most job openings will occur because of this occupation's substantial replacement needs. Turnover is quite high, reflecting this occupation's stressful working conditions, limited advancement potential, and the modest pay and benefits in the private sector.

## Earnings

Earnings of EMTs depend on the employment setting and geographic location as well as the individual's training and experience. According to a survey conducted by the *Journal of Emergency Medical Services*, average starting salaries in 1995 were $19,919 for EMT-Ambulance or Basic, $21,818 for EMT-Intermediate, and $23,861 for EMT-Paramedic. EMTs working in fire departments command the highest salaries, as the accompanying table shows.

| Table 1: Average annual salaries of emergency medical technicians, by type of employer, 1995 | | | |
|---|---|---|---|
| | Employer | Paramedic | EMT-IEMT-Basic |
| All employers | $31,137 | $26,102 | $26,333 |
| Private ambulance services | 28,619 | 23,330 | 22,238 |
| Hospitals | 29,264 | 28,000 | 22,500 |
| Fire departments | 37,690 | 28,667 | 33,962 |

**Source:** Journal of Emergency Medical Services

Those in emergency medical services which are part of fire or police departments receive the same benefits as firefighters or police officers.

## Related Occupations

Other workers in occupations that require quick and level-headed reactions to life-or-death situations are police officers, firefighters, air traffic controllers, workers in other health occupations, and members of the Armed Forces.

## Related *D.O.T.* Jobs

These job titles are related to or more specific than the more general description above. They will help you identify job options you may not otherwise discover. These descriptions are in the current edition of the *Dictionary of Occupational Titles* and classified by numerical order.

079.364-026 PARAMEDIC; 079.374-010 EMERGENCY MEDICAL TECHNICIAN

## Sources of Additional Information

Information concerning training courses, registration, and job opportunities for EMTs can be obtained by writing to the State Emergency Medical Service Director.

General information about EMTs is available from:

❏ National Association of Emergency Medical Technicians, 102 W. Leake St., Clinton, MS 39056.

❏ National Registry of Emergency Medical Technicians, P.O. Box 29233, Columbus, OH 43229.

# Engineering Technicians

## Nature of the Work

Engineering technicians use the principles and theories of science, engineering, and mathematics to solve technical problems in research and development, manufacturing, sales, construction, and customer service. Their jobs are more limited in scope and more practically oriented than those of scientists and engineers. Many engineering technicians assist engineers and scientists, especially in research and development. Others work in production or inspection jobs.

Engineering technicians who work in research and development build or set up equipment, prepare and conduct experiments, calculate or record the results, and help engineers in other ways. Some make prototype versions of newly designed equipment. They also assist in routine design work, often using computer-aided design equipment.

Engineering technicians who work in manufacturing follow the general directions of engineers. They may prepare specifications for materials, devise and run tests to ensure product quality, or study ways to improve manufacturing efficiency. They may also supervise production workers to make sure they follow prescribed procedures.

*Civil engineering technicians* help civil engineers plan and build highways, buildings, bridges, dams, wastewater treatment systems, and other structures and perform related surveys and studies. Some inspect water and wastewater treatment systems to ensure that pollution control requirements are met. Others estimate construction costs and specify materials to be used.

*Electronics engineering technicians* use their knowledge of electronic circuits to help design, develop, and manufacture electronic equipment such as radios, radar, sonar, television, industrial and medical measuring or control devices, navigational equipment, and computers. They use measuring and diagnostic devices to test, adjust, and repair equipment. Workers who only repair electrical and electronic equipment are discussed in several other descriptions elsewhere in this book. Many of these repairers are often called electronics technicians.

*Industrial engineering technicians* study the efficient use of personnel, materials, and machines in factories, stores, repair shops, and offices. They prepare layouts of machinery and equipment, plan the flow of work, make statistical studies, and analyze production costs.

*Mechanical engineering technicians* help engineers design, develop, test, and manufacture machinery, industrial robotics, and other equipment. They may assist in the testing of a guided missile, or in the planning and design of an electric power generation plant. They make sketches and rough layouts, record data, make computations, analyze results, and write reports. When planning production, mechanical engineering technicians prepare layouts and drawings of the assembly process and of parts to be manufactured. They estimate labor costs, equipment life, and plant space. Some test and inspect machines and equipment in manufacturing departments or work with engineers to eliminate production problems.

*Chemical engineering technicians* are usually employed in industries producing pharmaceuticals, chemicals, and petroleum products, among others. They help design, install, and test or maintain process equipment or computer control instrumentation, monitor quality control in processing plants, and make needed adjustments.

## Working Conditions

Most engineering technicians work regular hours in laboratories, offices, electronics and industrial plants, or construction sites. Some may be exposed to hazards from equipment, chemicals, or toxic materials.

## Employment

Engineering technicians held about 685,000 jobs in 1994. About two-fifths worked in manufacturing, mainly in the electrical and electronic machinery and equipment, industrial machinery and equipment, instruments and related products, and transportation equipment industries. Nearly one-fourth worked in service industries, mostly in engineering or business services companies who do engineering work on contract for government, manufacturing, or other organizations.

In 1994, the federal government employed about 55,000 engineering technicians. The major employer was the Department of Defense, followed by the Departments of Transportation, Agriculture, and the Interior, the Tennessee Valley Authority, and the National Aeronautics and Space Administration. State governments employed about 36,000 and local governments about 27,000.

## Training, Other Qualifications, and Advancement

Although it is possible to qualify for some engineering technician jobs with no formal training, most employers prefer to hire someone who will require less on-the-job training and supervision. Training is available at technical institutes, junior and community colleges, extension divisions of colleges and universities, public and private vocational-technical schools, and through some technical training programs in the Armed Forces. Persons with college courses in science, engineering, and mathematics may also qualify for some positions but may need additional specialized training and experience.

Many types of publicly and privately operated schools provide technical training. The kind and quality of programs vary considerably. Therefore, prospective students should be careful in selecting a program. They should contact prospective employers regarding their preferences and ask schools to provide information about the kinds of jobs obtained by graduates, instructional facilities and equipment, and faculty qualifications. Graduates of programs accredited by the Accreditation Board for Engineering and Technology (ABET) are generally recognized to have achieved a minimum level of competence in the mathematics, science, and technical courses required for this occupation.

Technical institutes offer intensive technical training but less theory and general education than junior and community colleges. Many offer two-year associate degree programs, and are similar to or are part of a community college or state university system. Other technical institutes are run by private, often for-profit, organizations, sometimes called proprietary schools; their programs vary considerably in length and types of courses offered. Some are two-year associate degree programs.

Junior and community colleges offer curriculums similar to those in technical institutes but may include more theory and liberal arts. Often there may be little or no difference between technical institute and community college programs, as both offer associate degrees. After completing the two-year program, some graduates get jobs as engineering technicians, while others continue their education at four-year colleges. However, there is a difference between an associate degree in pre-engineering and one in engineering technology. Students who enroll in a two-year pre-engineering program may find it very difficult to find work as an engineering technician should they decide not to enter a four-year engineering program because pre-engineering programs usually focus less on hands-on applications and more on academic preparatory work. Conversely, graduates of two-year engineering technology programs may not receive credit for many of the courses they have taken if they choose to transfer to a four-year engineering program.

Four-year colleges usually do not offer engineering technician training, but college courses in science, engineering, and mathematics are useful for obtaining a job as an engineering technician. Many four-year colleges offer bachelor's degrees in engineering technology, but graduates of these programs are often hired to work as applied engineers, not technicians.

Area vocational-technical schools include postsecondary public institutions that serve local students and emphasize training needed by local employers. Most require a high school diploma or its equivalent for admission.

Other training in technical areas may be obtained in the Armed Forces. Many military technical training programs are highly regarded by employers. However, skills acquired in military programs often are narrowly focused, so they are not necessarily transferable to civilian industry, which often requires broader training. Therefore, some additional training may be needed, depending on the skills acquired and the kind of job.

Prospective engineering technicians should take as many high school science and math courses as possible to prepare for postsecondary programs in engineering technology. Most ABET-accredited two-year associate programs require, at a minimum, college algebra and trigonometry, and one or two basic science courses. More math or science may be required depending on the area of specialty. The type of technical courses required varies depending on the area of specialty, as well. For example, prospective mechanical engineering technicians may take courses in fluid mechanics, thermodynamics, and mechanical design; electrical engineering technicians may take classes in electric circuits, microprocessors, and digital electronics; and those preparing to work in environmental engineering technology need courses in environmental regulations and safe handling of hazardous materials. Because many engineering technicians may become involved

in design work, creativity is desirable. Good communication skills and the ability to work well with others is also important since they are often part of a team of engineers and other technicians.

Engineering technicians usually begin by performing routine duties under the close supervision of an experienced technician, engineer, or scientist. As they gain experience, they are given more difficult assignments with only general supervision. Some engineering technicians eventually become supervisors.

## Job Outlook

Employment of engineering technicians is expected to increase more slowly than the average for all occupations through the year 2005. The output of technical products will continue to grow, and competitive pressures will force companies to improve and update manufacturing facilities and product designs more rapidly than in the past. However, the growing availability and use of advanced technologies, such as computer-aided design and drafting and computer simulation, is expected to curtail employment growth of engineering technicians.

Like engineers, employment of engineering technicians is influenced by local and national economic conditions. The employment outlook also varies with the area of specialization and industry. Some types of engineering technicians, such as civil engineering and aeronautical engineering technicians, experience greater cyclical fluctuations than others. Technicians whose jobs are defense related may experience fewer opportunities because of defense cutbacks.

In addition to growth, nearly as many job openings will be to replace technicians who retire or leave the labor force for other reasons.

## Earnings

According to a survey of workplaces in 160 metropolitan areas, engineering technicians at the most junior level had median earnings of about $16,590 in 1993, with the middle half earning between $14,560 and $19,500 a year. Engineering technicians with more experience and the ability to work with little supervision had median earnings of about $34,530, and those in supervisory or senior level positions earned about $51,060.

In the federal government, engineering technicians could start at about $14,900, $16,700, or $18,700 in 1995, depending on their education and experience. Beginning salaries were slightly higher in selected areas of the country where the prevailing local pay level was higher. In 1995, the average annual salary for engineering technicians in supervisory, nonsupervisory, and management positions in the federal government was $38,850; for electronics technicians, $43,540; and for industrial engineering technicians, $41,080.

## Related Occupations

Engineering technicians apply scientific and engineering principles usually acquired in postsecondary programs below the baccalaureate level. Similar occupations include science technicians, drafters, surveyors, broadcast technicians, and health technologists and technicians.

## Related *D.O.T.* Jobs

These job titles are related to or more specific than the more general description above. They will help you identify job options you may not otherwise discover. These descriptions are in

the current edition of the *Dictionary of Occupational Titles* and classified by numerical order.

There are too many *D.O.T.* titles to list here. Most are variations related to a specific industry, and we have included a small number of representative *D.O.T.* titles as examples. Complete lists are available in various career software published by JIST or directly from the U.S. Department of Labor.

002.261-014 RESEARCH MECHANIC; 003.161-010 ELECTRICAL TECHNICIAN; 003.261-010 INSTRUMENTATION TECHNICIAN; 003.362-010 DESIGN TECHNICIAN, COMPUTER-AIDED; 005.261-014 CIVIL ENGINEERING TECHNICIAN; 007.161-026 MECHANICAL-ENGINEERING TECHNICIAN; 010.261-010 FIELD ENGINEER, SPECIALIST; 011.261-014 WELDING TECHNICIAN; 012.261-014 QUALITY CONTROL TECHNICIAN; 012.267-010 INDUSTRIAL ENGINEERING TECHNICIAN; 019.161-014 TEST TECHNICIAN; 019.261-018 FACILITIES PLANNER; 019.261-030 LABORATORY TECHNICIAN; 019.261-034 LASER TECHNICIAN; 019.267-010 SPECIFICATION WRITER; 019.281-010 CALIBRATION LABORATORY TECHNICIAN; 726.261-010 ELECTRONICS ASSEMBLER, DEVELOPMENTAL; 726.261-014 ELECTRICIAN, RESEARCH; 806.281-014 EXPERIMENTAL MECHANIC, ELECTRICAL

### Sources of Additional Information

A number of engineering technology-related organizations provide information on engineering technician and technology careers. The Junior Engineering Technical Society (JETS), at 1420 King St., Suite 405, Alexandria, VA 22314-2715, serves as a central distribution point for information from most of these organizations. Enclose a self-addressed, business-size envelope with four first class stamps to obtain a sampling of materials available.

# Farm Equipment Mechanics

### Nature of the Work

Today's farm is typically much larger than in the past, so few if any types of farming can be done economically without specialized machines. Farm equipment has grown in size, complexity, and variety. Many farms have several tractors equipped with from 40- to 400-horsepower diesel engines. Self-propelled combines, hay balers, swathers, crop dryers, planters, tillage equipment, grain augers, manure spreaders, and elevators are common, as well as spray and irrigation equipment.

As farm machinery has grown larger with more electronic and hydraulic controls, farmers have increasingly turned to farm equipment dealers for service and repair of the machines they sell. These dealers employ farm equipment mechanics, often called service technicians, to do this work and also to maintain and repair the smaller lawn and garden tractors many dealers sell to suburban homeowners.

Mechanics spend much of their time repairing and adjusting malfunctioning equipment that has been brought to the shop. But during planting and harvesting seasons, they may travel to farms to make emergency repairs on equipment so that important farming operations are not unduly delayed.

Mechanics also perform preventive maintenance. Periodically, they test, adjust, and clean parts and tune engines. In large shops, mechanics generally specialize in certain types of work, such as diesel engine overhaul, hydraulics, or clutch and transmission repair. Others specialize in repairing the air-conditioning units often included in the cabs of combines and large tractors,

or in repairing certain types of equipment such as hay balers. Some mechanics also repair milking, irrigation, and other equipment on farms. In addition, some mechanics who work for dealers and equipment wholesalers assemble new implements and machinery and sometimes do body work, repairing dented or torn sheet metal on tractors or other machinery.

Mechanics use many basic handtools, including wrenches, pliers, hammers, and screwdrivers. They also use precision equipment, such as micrometers and torque wrenches; engine testing equipment, such as dynamometers to measure engine performance; and engine analysis units and compression testers, to find worn piston rings or leaking cylinder valves. They use welding equipment or power tools to repair broken parts.

### Working Conditions

Generally, farm equipment mechanics work indoors. Modern farm equipment repair shops are well ventilated, lighted, and heated, but older shops may not offer these advantages. Farm equipment mechanics come in contact with grease, fuel and oil, hydraulic fluid, antifreeze, rust, and dirt, and there is danger of injury when they repair heavy parts supported on jacks or by hoists. Care must also be used to avoid burns from hot engine parts, cuts from sharp edges of machinery, and hazards associated with farm chemicals.

As with most agricultural occupations, the hours of work of farm equipment mechanics vary according to the season of the year. During the busy planting and harvesting seasons, mechanics often work six or seven days a week, 10 to 12 hours daily. In winter months, however, mechanics may work fewer than 40 hours a week, and some may be laid off.

### Employment

Farm equipment mechanics held about 41,000 jobs in 1994. Most worked in service departments of farm equipment dealers. Others worked in independent repair shops, and in shops on large farms. Most farm equipment mechanics worked in small repair shops. Nearly 1 out of 10 farm equipment mechanics was self-employed.

Because some type of farming is done in nearly every area of the United States, farm equipment mechanics are employed throughout the country. Employment is concentrated in small cities and towns, making this an attractive career choice for people who do not wish to live in a large city. However, many mechanics work in the rural fringes of metropolitan areas, so farm equipment mechanics who prefer the conveniences of city life need not live in rural areas.

### Training, Other Qualifications, and Advancement

Farm equipment mechanics must have an aptitude for mechanical work. With the development of more complex farm implements, technical training has become more important. A growing number of employers prefer to hire trainee farm equipment mechanics who have completed a one- or two-year training program in agricultural or diesel mechanics at a vocational or technical school or community or junior college. In general, employers seek persons with training or previous experience in diesel and gasoline engines, the maintenance and repair of hydraulics, and welding, all of which may be learned in many high schools and vocational schools. Mechanics also need a basic knowledge of electronics and must be able to read circuit diagrams and blueprints in order to make complex repairs to electrical and other systems.

Most farm equipment mechanics enter the occupation as trainees and become proficient in their trade by assisting experienced mechanics. The length of training varies with the helper's aptitude and prior experience. At least two years of on-the-job training usually are necessary before a mechanic can efficiently do the more routine types of repair work, and additional training and experience are required for highly specialized repair and overhaul jobs.

Many farm equipment mechanics enter this occupation from a related occupation. For example, they may have experience working as diesel mechanics, mobile heavy equipment mechanics, or automotive mechanics. A farm background is an advantage since working on a farm usually provides experience in basic farm equipment repairs. Persons who enter from related occupations also may start as trainees or helpers, but they may not require as long a period of on-the-job training.

A few farm equipment mechanics learn the trade by completing an apprenticeship program, which lasts from three to four years and includes on-the-job as well as classroom training in all phases of farm equipment repair and maintenance. Applicants for these programs usually are chosen from shop helpers.

Keeping abreast of changing farm equipment technology requires a great deal of careful study of service manuals and analysis of complex diagrams. Many farm equipment mechanics and trainees receive refresher training in short-term programs conducted by farm equipment manufacturers. These programs usually last several days. A company service representative explains the design and function of equipment and teaches maintenance and repair on new models of farm equipment. In addition, some dealers may send employees to local vocational schools that hold special week-long classes in subjects such as air-conditioning repair or hydraulics.

Persons considering a career in this field should have the manual dexterity needed to handle tools and equipment. Occasionally, strength is required to lift, move, or hold heavy parts in place. Difficult repair jobs require problem-solving abilities to diagnose the source of the machine's malfunction. Experienced mechanics should be able to work independently with minimum supervision.

Farm equipment mechanics usually must buy their own handtools, although employers furnish power tools and test equipment. Trainee mechanics are expected to accumulate their own tools as they gain experience. Experienced mechanics have thousands of dollars invested in tools.

Farm equipment mechanics may advance to shop supervisor, service manager, or manager of a farm equipment dealership. Some mechanics open their own repair shops. A few farm equipment mechanics advance to service representatives for farm equipment manufacturers.

## Job Outlook

Opportunities should be good for persons who have completed formal training in farm equipment repair or diesel mechanics; persons without such training are expected to encounter increasing difficulty entering mechanic jobs. Employment of farm equipment mechanics is expected to increase about as fast as the average for all occupations through the year 2005. The continued consolidation of farmland into fewer and larger farms and the use of new farming practices will cause farmers to invest in new, more efficient and specialized equipment, and the increasing complexity of equipment will force more farmers to rely on mechanics for service and repairs. Most job openings will arise from the need to replace experienced mechanics who retire.

The increasing sophistication of newer farm equipment is making it more difficult for farmers to do their own repairs, forcing them to rely more on skilled mechanics in the future. For example, many newer tractors have much larger, electronically controlled engines and air-conditioned cabs and feature advanced transmissions with many speeds. New planting equipment uses electronics to spread seeds more uniformly, and electronic controls help harvesters reduce waste. Although farm machinery is expensive and generally designed and manufactured to withstand many years of rugged use, it nevertheless requires periodic service and repairs. Increasingly this work will require a farm equipment mechanic.

Sales of smaller lawn and garden equipment constitute a growing share of the business of most farm equipment dealers. Most of the large manufacturers of farm equipment now offer a line of these smaller tractors and sell them through their established dealerships. Although relatively few mechanics are required to service this equipment, more will be needed as household demand for lawn and garden equipment increases as the nation's population grows.

The agricultural equipment industry experiences periodic declines—mostly in sales. Layoffs of mechanics, however, are uncommon because farmers often elect to repair old equipment rather than purchase new equipment.

## Earnings

Farm equipment mechanics had median weekly earnings of about $382 in 1994. The middle 50 percent earned between $294 and $528 a week. The lowest paid 10 percent earned less than $248 a week, and the top 10 percent earned over $696 a week. Most farm equipment mechanics also have the opportunity to work overtime during the planting and harvesting seasons, for which they generally are paid time and a half.

Very few farm equipment mechanics belong to labor unions, but those who do are members of the International Association of Machinists and Aerospace Workers; the International Union, United Automobile, Aerospace and Agricultural Implement Workers of America; and the International Brotherhood of Teamsters.

## Related Occupations

Other workers who repair large mobile machinery include aircraft mechanics, automotive mechanics, diesel mechanics, and mobile heavy equipment mechanics.

## Related *D.O.T.* Jobs

These job titles are related to or more specific than the more general description above. They will help you identify job options you may not otherwise discover. These descriptions are in the current edition of the *Dictionary of Occupational Titles* and classified by numerical order.

624.281-010 FARM-EQUIPMENT MECHANIC I; 624.281-014 FARM-EQUIPMENT-MECHANIC APPRENTICE; 624.361-014 SPRINKLER-

IRRIGATION-EQUIPMENT MECHANIC; 624.381-010 ASSEMBLY RE-PAIRER; 624.381-014 FARM-EQUIPMENT MECHANIC II; 624.381-018 FARM-MACHINERY SET-UP MECHANIC; 624.684-010 GREASER; 629.281-018 BAKERY-MACHINE MECHANIC

## Sources of Additional Information

Details about work opportunities may be obtained from local farm equipment dealers and local offices of the state employment service. For general information about the occupation, write to:

❑ North American Equipment Dealers Association, 10877 Watson Rd., St. Louis, MO 63127.

❑ Deere and Co., John Deere Rd., Moline, IL 61265.

# Firefighting Occupations

## Nature of the Work

Firefighters respond to a variety of emergency situations where life, property, or the environment are at risk. They frequently are the first emergency response team at the scene of an accident, fire, flood, earthquake, or act of terrorism. Every year, fires and other emergency conditions take thousands of lives and destroy property worth billions of dollars. Firefighters help protect the public against these dangers. This description provides information only about career firefighters; it does not cover volunteer firefighters, who perform the same duties, and who may comprise the majority of firefighters in your area.

Most calls that firefighters respond to involve medical emergencies, and many fire departments provide ambulance service for victims. Firefighters receive training in emergency medical procedures, and many fire departments require them to be certified as emergency medical technicians.

During duty hours, firefighters must be prepared to respond immediately to a fire or other emergency situation that arises. Each situation a firefighter encounters is unique. Because firefighting is dangerous and complex, it requires organization and teamwork. At every emergency scene, firefighters perform specific duties assigned by a superior officer. They may connect hose lines to hydrants, operate a pump, or position ladders. They may rescue victims and administer emergency medical aid, ventilate smoke-filled areas, operate equipment, and salvage the contents of buildings. Their duties may change several times while the company is in action. Sometimes they remain at the site of a disaster for several days or more, rescuing survivors and assisting with medical emergencies.

The job of firefighter has become more complicated in recent years due to the use of increasingly sophisticated equipment. In addition, many firefighters have assumed a wider range of responsibilities—for example, working with ambulance services that provide emergency medical treatment, assisting in the recovery from natural disasters such as earthquakes and tornadoes, and becoming involved with the control and cleanup of oil spills and other hazardous materials incidents.

Firefighters are primarily involved with protecting structures, but they also work at airports on crash and rescue crews, at chemical plants, by waterfronts, and in forests and wildland areas. In forests, air patrols locate fires and report their findings to headquarters by telephone or radio. Fire rangers patrol areas of the forest to locate and report fires and hazardous conditions and to ensure that travelers and campers are complying with fire regulations. When fires break out, firefighters use hand tools and water hoses to battle the blaze. Some specialized firefighters parachute from airplanes when necessary to reach inaccessible areas.

Most fire departments have a fire prevention division which is usually headed by a fire marshall. Fire inspectors are specially trained to conduct inspections of structures to prevent fires and to ensure fire code compliance. These firefighters may also check and approve plans for new buildings, working with developers and planners in that process. Fire prevention personnel often speak on these subjects before public assemblies and civic organizations. Some firefighters become fire investigators, who determine the origin and cause of fires. They collect evidence, interview witnesses, and prepare reports on fires where there may be arson or criminal negligence. Some investigators have police powers and may arrest suspects. They may also be called upon to testify in court.

Between alarms, firefighters have classroom training, clean and maintain equipment, conduct practice drills and fire inspections, and participate in physical fitness activities. They prepare written reports on fire incidents and review fire science literature to keep abreast of technological developments and administrative practices and policies.

## Working Conditions

Firefighters spend much of their time at fire stations, which usually have facilities for dining and sleeping. When an alarm comes in, firefighters must respond rapidly, regardless of the weather or hour. They may spend long periods on their feet, sometimes in adverse weather, tending to fires, medical emergencies, hazardous materials incidents, and other emergencies.

Firefighting is a very hazardous occupation. It involves risk of death or injury from sudden cave-ins of floors or toppling walls and from exposure to flames and smoke. Strong winds and falling trees and branches can make fighting forest fires particularly dangerous. Firefighters also may come in contact with poisonous, flammable, and explosive gases and chemicals, and radiation or other hazardous materials, that may have immediate or long-term effects on their health. For these reasons, they must wear all kinds of protective gear, which can be very heavy.

Work hours of firefighters are longer and vary more widely than hours of most other workers. Many work more than 50 hours a week; during some weeks, they may work significantly longer hours. In some cities, they are on duty for 24 hours, then off for 48 hours, and receive an extra day off at intervals. In other cities, they work a day shift of 10 hours for three or four days, a night shift of 14 hours for three or four nights, have three or four days off, and then repeat the cycle. In addition, firefighters often work extra hours at fires and other emergencies and are regularly assigned to work on holidays. Fire lieutenants and fire captains often work the same hours as the firefighters they supervise. Duty hours include time when firefighters study, train, and perform fire prevention duties.

## Employment

Firefighters held about 284,000 jobs in 1994. Nine of every 10 worked in municipal or county fire departments. Some very large cities have several thousand firefighters, while many small towns have only a few. Most of the remainder worked in fire departments on federal and state installations, including airports. Private firefighting companies employ a small number.

## Training, Other Qualifications, and Advancement

Applicants for municipal firefighting jobs may have to pass a written test; tests of strength, physical stamina, coordination, and agility; and a medical examination—including drug screening. Workers also may be monitored on a random basis for drug use after accepting employment. Examinations are open to persons who are at least 18 years old and have a high school education or the equivalent. Those who receive the highest scores have the best chances for appointment. The completion of community college courses in fire science may improve an applicant's chances for appointment. In fact, in recent years, an increasing proportion of entrants to this occupation have some postsecondary education.

As a rule, beginners in large fire departments are trained for several weeks at the department's training center. Through classroom instruction and practical training, the recruits study firefighting techniques, fire prevention, hazardous materials, local building codes, and emergency medical procedures, including first aid and cardiopulmonary resuscitation. Also, they learn how to use axes, saws, chemical extinguishers, ladders, and other firefighting and rescue equipment. After successfully completing this training, they are assigned to a fire company, where they undergo a period of probation.

A number of fire departments have accredited apprenticeship programs lasting three to four years. These programs combine formal, technical instruction with on-the-job training under the supervision of experienced firefighters. Technical instruction covers subjects such as firefighting techniques and equipment, chemical hazards associated with various combustible building materials, emergency medical procedures, and fire prevention and safety.

Most experienced firefighters continue studying to improve their job performance and prepare for promotion examinations. Today, firefighters need more training to operate increasingly sophisticated equipment and to deal safely with the greater hazards associated with fighting fires in larger, more elaborate structures. To progress to higher level positions, they must acquire expertise in the most advanced firefighting equipment and techniques and in building construction, emergency medical procedures, writing, public speaking, management and budgeting procedures, and labor relations. Fire departments frequently conduct training programs, and some firefighters attend training sessions sponsored by the National Fire Academy. These training sessions cover various topics, including executive development, anti-arson techniques, and public fire safety and education. Some states also have extensive firefighter training programs.

Many colleges and universities offer courses leading to two- or four-year degrees in fire engineering or fire science. Many fire departments offer firefighters incentives such as tuition reimbursement or higher pay for completing advanced training.

Among the personal qualities firefighters need are mental alertness, courage, mechanical aptitude, endurance, strength, and a sense of public service. Initiative and good judgment are ex-

tremely important because firefighters often must make quick decisions in emergencies. Because members of a crew eat, sleep, and work closely together under conditions of stress and danger, they should be dependable and able to get along well with others in a group. Leadership qualities are necessary for officers, who must establish and maintain discipline and efficiency as well as direct the activities of firefighters in their companies.

Opportunities for promotion are good in most fire departments. As firefighters gain experience, they may advance to a higher rank. The line of promotion usually is to engineer, lieutenant, captain, battalion chief, assistant chief, deputy chief, and finally to chief. Advancement generally depends upon scores on a written examination, job performance, and seniority. Increasingly, fire departments are using assessment centers—which simulate a variety of actual job performance tasks—to screen for the best candidates for promotion. Many fire departments now require a bachelor's degree, preferably in public administration or a related field, for promotion to positions higher than battalion chief. Some departments now require a master's degree for the chief and for executive fire officer certification from the National Fire Academy, or for a state chief officer certification.

## Job Outlook

Firefighters are expected to face considerable competition for available job openings. Firefighting attracts many people because a high school education usually is sufficient, earnings are relatively high, and a pension is guaranteed upon retirement. In addition, the work is frequently exciting and challenging and affords an opportunity to perform a valuable public service. Consequently, the number of qualified applicants in most areas generally exceeds the number of job openings, even though the written examination and physical requirements eliminate many applicants. This situation is expected to persist through the year 2005.

Employment of firefighters is expected to increase about as fast as the average for all occupations through the year 2005 as a result of the increase in the nation's population and fire protection needs. In addition, the number of paid firefighter positions is expected to increase as a percentage of all firefighter jobs. The increased level of specialized training required in this occupation makes it more difficult for volunteer firefighters to remain qualified for duty. Much of the expected job growth will occur in smaller communities with expanding populations that augment volunteers with career firefighters to better meet growing, increasingly complex fire protection needs. However, little growth is expected in large, urban fire departments. A small number of local governments are expected to contract for firefighting services with private companies.

In response to the expanding role of firefighters, some municipalities have combined fire prevention, public fire education, safety, and emergency medical services into a single organization commonly referred to as a public safety organization. Some local and regional fire departments are being consolidated into county-wide establishments in order to cut overhead, take advantage of economies of scale, reduce administrative staffs, and establish consistent training standards and work procedures.

Turnover of firefighter jobs is unusually low, particularly for an occupation that requires a relatively limited investment in formal education. Nevertheless, most job openings are expected to result from the need to replace those who retire or stop working for other reasons, or who transfer to other occupations.

Layoffs of firefighters are not common. Fire protection is an essential service, and citizens are likely to exert considerable pressure on city officials to expand or at least preserve the level of fire-protection coverage. Even when budget cuts do occur, local fire departments usually cut expenses by postponing equipment purchases or not hiring new firefighters, rather than by laying off staff.

## Earnings

Median weekly earnings for firefighting occupations were around $630 in 1994. The middle 50 percent earned between $490 and $775 weekly. The lowest 10 percent earned less than $380, while the highest 10 percent earned more than $975. The average annual salary for all firefighters in the federal government in nonsupervisory, supervisory, and managerial positions was about $27,100 in 1995. Fire lieutenants and fire captains may earn considerably more.

The law requires that overtime be paid to those firefighters who average 53 or more hours a week during their work period—which ranges from 7 to 28 days. Firefighters often earn overtime for working extra shifts to maintain minimum staffing levels or for special emergencies.

Firefighters receive benefits that usually include medical and liability insurance, vacation and sick leave, and some paid holidays. Practically all fire departments provide protective clothing (helmets, boots, and coats) and breathing apparatus, and many also provide dress uniforms. Firefighters generally are covered by pension plans that often provide retirement at half pay at age 50 after 25 years of service or at any age if disabled in the line of duty.

Many career firefighters are unionized, and belong to the International Association of Firefighters. Many company officers and chief officers belong to the International Association of Fire Chiefs.

## Related Occupations

A related fire protection occupation is the fire-protection engineer, who identifies fire hazards in homes and workplaces and designs prevention programs and automatic fire detection and extinguishing systems. Other occupations in which workers respond to emergencies include police officers and emergency medical technicians.

## Related D.O.T. Jobs

These job titles are related to or more specific than the more general description above. They will help you identify job options you may not otherwise discover. These descriptions are in the current edition of the *Dictionary of Occupational Titles* and classified by numerical order.

373.134-010 FIRE CAPTAIN; 373.167-010 BATTALION CHIEF; 373.167-014 CAPTAIN, FIRE-PREVENTION BUREAU; 373.167-018 FIRE MARSHAL; 373.267-010 FIRE INSPECTOR; 373.267-014 FIRE MARSHAL; 373.267-018 FIRE-INVESTIGATION LIEUTENANT; 373.363-010 FIRE CHIEF'S AIDE; 373.364-010 FIRE INSPECTOR; 373.663-010 FIRE FIGHTER, CRASH, FIRE, AND RESCUE; 379.687-010 FIRE-EXTINGUISHER-SPRINKLER INSPECTOR; 452.134-010 SMOKE JUMPER SUPERVISOR; 452.167-010 FIRE WARDEN; 452.364-014 SMOKE JUMPER; 452.367-010 FIRE LOOKOUT; 452.367-014 FIRE RANGER; 452.687-014 FOREST-FIRE FIGHTER

## Sources of Additional Information

Information about a career as a firefighter may be obtained from local fire departments and:

❏ International Association of Fire Chiefs, 4025 Fair Ridge Dr., Fairfax, VA 22033-2868.

❏ International Association of Firefighters, 1750 New York Ave. NW, Washington, DC 20006.

❏ Fire Administration, 16825 South Seaton Ave., Emittsburg, MD 21727.

Information about firefighter professional qualifications and a list of colleges and universities that offer two- or four-year degree programs in fire science or fire prevention may be obtained from:

❏ National Fire Protection Association, Batterymarch Park, Quincy, MA 02269.

# Flight Attendants

## Nature of the Work

It is the job of the flight attendants to see that all their passengers have a safe, comfortable, and enjoyable airplane flight.

At least one hour before each flight, attendants are briefed by the captain, the pilot in command, on such things as expected weather conditions and special passenger problems. The attendants check that the passenger cabin is in order, that supplies of food, beverages, blankets, and reading material are adequate, and that first aid kits and other emergency equipment are aboard and in working order. As passengers board the plane, attendants greet them, check their tickets, and assist them if necessary in storing coats and carry-on luggage.

Before the plane takes off, attendants instruct passengers in the use of emergency equipment and check to see that all passengers have their seat belts fastened and seat backs forward. In the air, they answer questions about the flight; distribute reading material, pillows, and blankets; and help small children, elderly or disabled persons, and any others needing assistance. They may administer first aid to passengers who become ill. Attendants also serve cocktails and other refreshments and, on many flights, heat and distribute precooked meals. After the plane has landed, flight avtendants assist passengers as they leave the plane. They then prepare reports on medications given to passengers, lost and found articles and cabin equipment conditions. Some flight attendants straighten up the plane's cabin.

Helping passengers in the event of an emergency is the most important responsibility of the flight attendant. This may range from reassuring passengers during occasional encounters with strong turbulence to directing passengers in evacuating a plane following an emergency landing.

Lead or first flight attendants aboard planes oversee the work of the other attendants while performing most of the same duties.

## Working Conditions

Since airlines operate around the clock year round, attendants may work at night and on holidays and weekends. They usually fly 75 to 85 hours a month. In addition, they generally spend about 75 to 85 hours a month on the ground preparing planes for flights, writing reports following completed flights, and waiting for planes that arrive late. Because of variations in scheduling and limitations on flying time, many attendants have 11 or more days off each month. Attendants may be away from their home base at least one-third of the time. During this period, the airlines provide hotel accommodations and an allowance for meal expenses.

The combination of free time and discount air fares provides flight attendants the opportunity to travel and see new places. However, the work can be strenuous and trying. Short flights require speedy service if meals are served. A rough flight can make serving drinks and meals difficult. Attendants stand during much of the flight and must remain pleasant and efficient regardless of how tired they are or how demanding passengers may be. Flight attendants are susceptible to injury because of the job demands in a moving aircraft.

## Employment

Flight attendants held about 105,000 jobs in 1994. Commercial airlines employed the vast majority of all flight attendants, most of whom were stationed in major cities at the airlines' home bases. A small number of flight attendants worked for large companies that operate their own aircraft for business purposes.

## Training, Other Qualifications, and Advancement

The airlines prefer to hire poised, tactful, and resourceful people who can deal comfortably with strangers. Applicants usually must be at least 19 to 21 years old. Flight attendants must have excellent health, good vision, and the ability to speak clearly.

Applicants must be high school graduates. Those having several years of college or experience in dealing with the public are preferred. More and more attendants being hired are college graduates. Flight attendants for international airlines generally must speak an appropriate foreign language fluently. Some of the major airlines prefer candidates who can speak two major foreign languages for their international flights.

Most large airlines require that newly hired flight attendants complete four to six weeks of intensive training in their own flight training centers. The airlines that do not operate training centers generally send new employees to the center of another airline. Transportation to the training centers and an allowance for board, room, and school supplies may be provided. Trainees learn emergency procedures such as evacuating an airplane, operating an oxygen system, and giving first aid. Attendants also are taught flight regulations and duties, and company operations and policies. Trainees receive instruction on personal grooming and weight control. Trainees for the international routes get additional instruction in passport and customs regulations and dealing with terrorism. Toward the end of their training, students go on practice flights. Attendants must receive 12 to 14 hours of training in emergency procedures and passenger relations annually.

After completing initial training, flight attendants are assigned to one of their airline's bases. New attendants are placed in "reserve status" and are called on either to staff extra flights or fill in for attendants who are sick or on vacation. Reserve attendants on duty must be available on short notice. Attendants usually remain on reserve for at least one year; at some cities, it may take five years or longer to advance from reserve status. Advancement takes longer today than in the past because experienced attendants are remaining in this career for more years than they used to. Attendants who no longer are on reserve bid for regular assignments. Because these assignments are based on seniority, usually only the most experienced attendants get their choice of base and flights.

Some attendants transfer within the company to flight service instructor, customer service director, recruiting representative, or various other administrative positions.

## Job Outlook

Opportunities should be favorable for persons seeking flight attendant jobs as the number of applicants is expected to be roughly in balance with the number of job openings. Those with at least two years of college and experience in dealing with the public should have the best chance of being hired.

As more career-minded people have entered this occupation, turnover—which traditionally has been very high—has declined somewhat. Still, most job openings through the year 2005 should flow from replacement needs. Many flight attendants are attracted to the occupation by the glamour of the airline industry and the opportunity to travel, but many eventually leave in search of jobs that offer higher earnings and require fewer nights be spent away from their families. Thousands of job openings will arise each year to replace flight attendants who transfer to another occupation or who leave the labor force.

Employment of flight attendants is expected to grow faster than the average for all occupations through the year 2005. Growth in population and income is expected to increase the number of airline passengers. Airlines enlarge their capacity by increasing the number and size of planes in operation. Since Federal Aviation Administration safety rules require one attendant for every 50 seats, more flight attendants will be needed.

Employment of flight attendants is sensitive to cyclical swings in the economy. During recessions, when the demand for air travel declines, many flight attendants are put on part-time status or laid off. Until demand increases, few new attendants are hired.

## Earnings

Beginning flight attendants had median earnings of about $12,700 a year in 1994, according to data from the Association of Flight Attendants. Flight attendants with six years of flying experience had median annual earnings of about $18,700, while some senior flight attendants earned as much as $40,000 a year. Flight attendants receive extra compensation for overtime and for night and international flights. In addition, flight attendants and their immediate families are entitled to reduced fares on their own and most other airlines.

Many flight attendants belong to the Association of Flight Attendants. Others are members of the Transport Workers Union of America, The International Brotherhood of Teamsters, or other unions.

Flight attendants are required to buy uniforms and wear them while on duty. Uniform replacement items are usually paid for by the company. The airlines generally provide a small allowance to cover cleaning and upkeep of the uniforms.

## Related Occupations

Other jobs that involve helping people as a safety professional and require the ability to be pleasant even under trying circumstances include emergency medical technician, firefighter, maritime crew and camp counselor.

## Related *D.O.T.* Jobs

These job titles are related to or more specific than the more general description above. They will help you identify job options you may not otherwise discover. These descriptions are in the current edition of the *Dictionary of Occupational Titles* and classified by numerical order.

352.367-010 AIRPLANE FLIGHT ATTENDANT

## Sources of Additional Information

Information about job opportunities in a particular airline and the qualifications required may be obtained by writing to the personnel manager of the company. For addresses of airline companies and information about job opportunities and salaries, contact:

❏ FAPA, 4959 Massachusetts Blvd., Atlanta, GA 30337. (This organization may be called toll free at 1-800-Jet-Jobs, extension 190.)

# Gardeners and Groundskeepers

## Nature of the Work

Attractively designed, healthy, and well-maintained lawns, gardens, trees, and shrubbery create a positive first impression, establish a peaceful mood, and increase property values. A growing number of individuals and organizations rely on the services of gardeners and groundskeepers to care for their landscaping.

Some landscape gardeners work on large properties, such as office buildings and shopping malls. Following plans drawn up by a landscape architect, gardeners plant trees, hedges, flowering plants, and turf areas and apply mulch for protection. For residential customers, these workers install lawns, terrace hillsides, build retaining walls, and install patios, as well as plant flowers, trees and shrubs.

Gardeners working for homeowners, estates, and public gardens feed, water, and prune the flowering plants and trees, and mow and water the lawn. Some landscape gardeners, called lawn service workers, specialize in maintaining lawns and shrubs for a fee. A growing number of residential and commercial clients, such as managers of office buildings, shopping malls, multi-unit residential buildings, and hotels and motels favor this full-service landscape maintenance. These workers perform a full range of duties, including mowing, edging, trimming, fertilizing, dethatching, and mulching. Those working for chemical lawn service firms are more specialized. They inspect lawns for problems and apply fertilizers, herbicides, pesticides, and other chemicals, as well as practice integrated pest management techniques.

Groundskeepers, often classified as either grounds managers or grounds maintenance personnel, maintain a variety of facilities including athletic fields, golf courses, cemeteries, university campuses, and parks. Grounds managers usually participate in many of the same tasks as maintenance personnel but typically have more extensive knowledge in horticulture, landscape design and construction, pest management, irrigation, and erosion control. In addition, managers usually have supervisory responsibilities.

Groundskeepers who care for athletic fields keep natural and artificial turf fields in top condition and mark out boundaries and paint turf with team logos and names before events. Groundskeepers must make sure the underlying soil on natural turf fields has the proper composition to allow proper drainage and support the appropriate grasses used on the field. They regularly mow, water, fertilize, and aerate the fields. In addition, groundskeepers apply chemicals and fungicides to control weeds, kill pests, and prevent diseases. Groundskeepers also vacuum and disinfect synthetic turf after use in order to prevent growth of harmful bacteria. They periodically remove the turf and replace the cushioning pad.

Workers who maintain golf courses are called greenskeepers. They do many of the same things other groundskeepers do. In addition, greenskeepers periodically relocate the holes on putting greens to eliminate uneven wear of the turf and add interest and challenge to the game. Greenskeepers also keep canopies, benches, ball washers, and tee markers repaired and freshly painted.

Cemetery workers prepare graves and maintain cemetery grounds. They dig graves to specified depth, generally using a back-hoe. They may place concrete slabs on the bottom and around the sides of the grave to line it for greater support. When readying a site for the burial ceremony, they position the casket-lowering device over the grave, cover the immediate area with an artificial grass carpet, erect a canopy, and arrange folding chairs to accommodate mourners. They regularly mow grass, apply fertilizers and other chemicals, prune shrubs and trees, plant flowers, and remove debris from graves. They also must periodically build the ground up around new grave sites to compensate for settling.

Groundskeepers in parks and recreation facilities care for lawns, trees, and shrubs, maintain athletic fields and playgrounds, clean buildings, and keep parking lots, picnic areas, and other public spaces free of litter. They may also remove snow and ice from roads and walkways, erect and dismantle snow fences, and maintain swimming pools. These workers inspect buildings and equipment, make needed repairs, and keep everything freshly painted.

Gardeners and groundskeepers use handtools such as shovels, rakes, pruning saws, saws, hedge and brush trimmers, and axes, as well as power lawnmowers, chain saws, snow blowers, and electric clippers. Some use equipment such as tractors and twin-axle vehicles. Park, school, cemetery, and golf course groundskeepers may use sod cutters to harvest sod that will be replanted elsewhere. Athletic turf groundskeepers use vacuums and other devices to remove water from athletic fields. In addition, some workers in large operations use spraying and dusting equipment.

In winter months, especially in the North, gardeners and groundskeepers may work removing snow from driveways, roadways, and parking lots.

## Working Conditions

Many of the jobs for gardeners and groundskeepers are seasonal, mainly in the spring and summer, when cleanup, planting, and mowing and trimming take place. Gardeners and groundskeepers work outdoors in all kinds of weather. They frequently are under pressure to get the job completed, especially when they are preparing for scheduled events, such as athletic competitions or burials.

They work with pesticides, fertilizers, and other chemicals, and must exercise safety precautions to prevent exposure. They also work with dangerous equipment and tools such as power lawnmowers, chain saws, and power clippers.

## Employment

Gardeners and groundskeepers held about 707,000 jobs in 1994. About 40 percent worked for lawn and garden service companies. More than 10 percent each worked for firms operating and building real estate and amusement and recreation facilities such as golf courses and race tracks. Others were employed by government, including parks departments, schools, hospitals, cemeteries, hotels, retail nurseries, and garden stores.

Almost one of every four gardeners and groundskeepers was self-employed, providing landscape maintenance directly to customers on a contract basis. One of every three worked part-time, most likely students working their way through school. Others working part-time were older workers who might have been cutting back their hours as they approached retirement.

## Training, Other Qualifications, and Advancement

There usually are no minimum educational requirements for entry-level jobs as gardeners and groundskeepers. Four in 10 workers do not have a high school diploma, although a high school diploma is necessary for some jobs. Experience can be obtained through home gardening or working in a nursery, a lawn care business, or a tree service. High school students may gain experience in the Future Farmers of America and other associations.

There are no national standards for gardeners and groundskeepers, but most states require certification for workers who apply pesticides. Certification requirements vary, but usually include passing a test on the safe use and disposal of insecticides, herbicides, and fungicides.

Employers prefer applicants with a good driving record and some experience driving a truck. Workers who deal directly with customers must get along well with people. Employers also look for responsible, self-motivated individuals, since many gardeners and groundskeepers work with little supervision.

Courses in agronomy, horticulture, and botany are helpful for advancement. There are many two- and four-year programs in landscape management, turf grass management, interiorscape, and ornamental horticulture. Courses include equipment use and care, landscape design, plant biology, and irrigation. There are cooperative education programs in which students work alternate semesters or quarters for a lawn care or landscape contractor.

Generally, a gardener or groundskeeper can advance to supervisor after several years of progressively responsible experience, including the demonstrated ability to deal effectively with both coworkers and customers. Supervisors can advance to grounds manager or superintendent for a golf course or other athletic facility, a cemetery, a campus, a school system, or manager of a lawn maintenance firm. Many gardeners and groundskeepers become landscape contractors.

The Professional Grounds Management Society offers certification to those managers who have a combination of eight years of experience and formal education beyond high school.

## Job Outlook

Those wishing to become gardeners and groundskeepers should find excellent job opportunities in the future. Because of high turnover in this occupation, a large number of job openings are expected to result from the need to replace workers who transfer to other occupations or leave the labor force. This occupation attracts many people who are trying to make money but who are not committed to the occupation. Some take gardening or groundskeeping jobs to earn money for school, others only take these jobs until a better paying job is found. Because wages for beginners are low and the work is physically demanding, many employers have difficulty attracting enough workers to fill all openings.

Employment of gardeners and groundskeepers is expected to grow about as fast as the average for all occupations through the year 2005 in response to increasing demand for gardening and landscaping services. Expected growth in the construction of commercial and industrial buildings, shopping malls, homes, highways, and parks and recreational facilities should stimulate demand for these workers. Developers are increasingly using landscaping services, both interior and exterior, to attract prospective buyers and tenants. In addition, owners of many existing buildings and facilities are upgrading their landscaping. Also, a growing number of homeowners are using lawn maintenance and landscaping services to enhance the beauty and value of their property and to conserve their leisure time. Growth in the number of parks, athletic fields, golf courses, cemeteries, and similar facilities also can be expected to add to the demand for these workers.

Employment opportunities in landscaping are tied to local economic conditions. During economic downturns, many individuals turn to landscaping as a second source of income or a new career. At the same time, demand for landscaping services often slows as corporations, governments, and homeowners reduce spending on all nonessential expenditures, increasing the level of competition for available jobs.

## Earnings

Median weekly earnings of gardeners and groundskeepers were about $287 in 1994; the middle 50 percent earned between $222 and $379. The lowest 10 percent earned less than $184, and the top 10 percent earned more than $508 a week.

## Related Occupations

Gardeners and groundskeepers perform most of their work outdoors. Others whose jobs may be performed outdoors or are otherwise related are botanist, construction workers, landscape architects, nursery workers, farmers, horticultural workers, tree surgeon helpers, and forest conservation workers.

## Related *D.O.T.* Jobs

These job titles are related to or more specific than the more general description above. They will help you identify job options you may not otherwise discover. These descriptions are in

the current edition of the *Dictionary of Occupational Titles* and classified by numerical order.

182.167-014 LANDSCAPE CONTRACTOR; 406.381-010 GARDENER, SPECIAL EFFECTS AND INSTRUCTION MODELS; 406.683-010 GREENSKEEPER II; 406.684-010 CEMETERY WORKER; 406.684-014 GROUNDSKEEPER, INDUSTRIAL-COMMERCIAL; 406.684-018 GARDEN WORKER; 406.687-010 LANDSCAPE SPECIALIST; 408.161-010 LANDSCAPE GARDENER; 408.662-010 HYDRO-SPRAYER OPERATOR; 408.684-010 LAWN-SERVICE WORKER; 408.684-014 SPRAYER, HAND; 408.684-018 TREE PRUNER; 408.687-014 LABORER, LANDSCAPE

## Sources of Additional Information

For career information, contact:

❏ Associated Landscape Contractors of America, Inc., 12200 Sunrise Valley Dr., Suite 150, Reston, VA 22091.

❏ Professional Lawn Care Association of America, 1000 Johnson Ferry Rd. NE, C-135, Marietta, GA 30068.

For career and certification information, contact:

❏ Professional Grounds Management Society, 120 Cockeysville Rd., Suite 104, Hunt Valley, MD 21031.

# General Maintenance Mechanics

## Nature of the Work

Most craft workers specialize in one kind of work such as plumbing or carpentry. General maintenance mechanics have skills in many different crafts. They repair and maintain machines, mechanical equipment, and buildings, and work on plumbing, electrical, and air-conditioning and heating systems. They build partitions, make plaster or drywall repairs, and fix or paint roofs, windows, doors, floors, woodwork, and other parts of building structures. They also maintain and repair specialized equipment and machinery found in cafeterias, laundries, hospitals, stores, offices, and factories. Typical duties include troubleshooting and fixing faulty electrical switches, repairing air-conditioning motors, and unclogging drains.

Those in small establishments, where they are often the only maintenance worker, do all repairs except for very large or difficult jobs. In larger establishments, their duties may be limited to the general maintenance of everything in a workshop or a particular area.

General maintenance mechanics inspect and diagnose problems and determine the best way to correct them, often checking blueprints, repair manuals, and parts catalogs. They obtain supplies and repair parts from distributors or storerooms. They use common hand and power tools such as screwdrivers, saws, drills, wrenches, and hammers as well as specialized equipment and electronic test devices. They replace or fix worn or broken parts, where necessary, or make adjustments.

These mechanics also do routine preventive maintenance and ensure that machines continue to run smoothly, building systems operate efficiently, and that the physical condition of buildings does not deteriorate. Following a check list, they may inspect drives, motors, and belts, check fluid levels, replace filters, and so forth. Maintenance mechanics keep records of maintenance and repair work.

## Working Conditions

General maintenance mechanics often do a variety of tasks in a single day, generally at a number of different locations in a building, or in several buildings. They may have to stand for long periods, lift heavy objects, and work in uncomfortably hot or cold environments and in awkward and cramped positions or on ladders. They are subject to electrical shock, burns, falls, and cuts and bruises. Most general maintenance workers work a 40-hour week. Some work evening, night, or weekend shifts, or are on call for emergency repairs.

Those employed in small establishments, where they may be the only maintenance worker, often operate with only limited supervision. Those working in larger establishments often work under the direct supervision of an experienced craft worker.

## Employment

General maintenance mechanics held about 1,273,000 jobs in 1994. They worked in almost every industry. More than one-third worked in service industries; most of these worked for elementary and secondary schools, colleges and universities, hotels, and hospitals and nursing homes. About 16 percent worked in manufacturing industries. Others worked for real estate firms that operate office and apartment buildings, wholesale and retail firms, or government agencies.

## Training, Other Qualifications, and Advancement

Most general maintenance mechanics learn their skills informally on the job. They start as helpers, watching and learning from skilled maintenance workers. Helpers begin by doing simple jobs such as fixing leaky faucets and replacing light bulbs and progress to more difficult tasks such as overhauling machinery or building walls.

Others learn their skills by working as helpers to other repair or construction workers such as carpenters, electricians, or machinery repairers. Necessary skills can also be learned in high school shop classes and postsecondary trade or vocational schools. It generally takes from one to four years of on-the-job training or school, or a combination of both, to become fully qualified, depending on the skill level required.

Graduation from high school is preferred for entry into this occupation. High school courses in mechanical drawing, electricity, woodworking, blueprint reading, science, and mathematics are useful. Mechanical aptitude, ability to use shop math, and manual dexterity are important. Good health is necessary because the job involves much walking, standing, reaching, and heavy lifting. Difficult jobs require problem-solving ability, and many positions require the ability to work without direct supervision. A growing proportion of new buildings rely on computers to control building systems, so familiarity with computers is helpful.

Many general maintenance mechanics in large organizations advance to maintenance supervisor or to one of the crafts such as electrician, heating/air-conditioning mechanic, or plumber. In small organizations, promotion opportunities are limited.

## Job Outlook

Job opportunities for people who want to be general maintenance mechanics should be plentiful through the year 2005. Employment is related to the number of buildings and amount of equipment needing maintenance and repair. Employment growth—expected to be about as fast as the average for all occupations through the year 2005—will occur as the number of office and apartment buildings, stores, schools, hospitals, hotels, and factories increases. Although the pace of construction of these facilities is expected to be slower than in the past, many opportunities arise because this is a large occupation with significant turnover, and many replacements are needed for those who leave the occupation.

General maintenance mechanics who work in manufacturing industries may be laid off during recessions.

## Earnings

Earnings vary widely by industry, geographic area, and skill level. According to a survey of workplaces in 160 metropolitan areas, general maintenance mechanics had median earnings of about $9.40 an hour in 1993, with the middle half earning between $7.90 and $11.05 an hour. Median earnings were about $9.40 an hour in service businesses and about $10.20 an hour in manufacturing businesses. On average, workers in the Midwest and Northeast earned more than those in the West and South. Mechanics earn overtime pay for work in excess of 40 hours per week.

Some general maintenance mechanics are members of unions, including the American Federation of State, County and Municipal Employees and the United Automobile Workers.

## Related Occupations

Some of the work of general maintenance mechanics is similar to that of carpenters, plumbers, industrial machinery mechanics, electricians, and air-conditioning, refrigeration, and heating mechanics.

## Related *D.O.T.* Jobs

These job titles are related to or more specific than the more general description above. They will help you identify job options you may not otherwise discover. These descriptions are in the current edition of the *Dictionary of Occupational Titles* and classified by numerical order.

899.261-014 MAINTENANCE REPAIRER, INDUSTRIAL; 899.381-010 MAINTENANCE REPAIRER, BUILDING

## Sources of Additional Information

Information about job opportunities may be obtained from local employers and local offices of the Job Service.

# Glaziers

## Nature of the Work

Glass serves many uses in modern buildings. Insulated and specially treated glass keeps in warmed or cooled air and provides good condensation and sound control qualities; tempered and laminated glass makes doors and windows more secure. In large commercial buildings, glass panels give skyscrapers a distinctive look while reducing the need for artificial lighting. The creative use of large windows, glass doors, skylights, and sun room additions make homes bright, airy, and inviting.

Glaziers generally work on four types of projects. Residential glazing involves work such as replacing glass in home windows, installing glass mirrors, shower doors and bathtub enclosures, and glass for table tops and display cases. On commercial interior projects, glaziers install items such as heavy, often etched, decorative room dividers and windows with speak holes and security glazing. Glazing projects may also involve replacement of storefront windows for establishments such as stores, supermarkets, auto dealerships, and banks. In construction of large commercial buildings, glaziers build metal framework extrusions and install glass panels or curtain walls.

Glaziers select, cut, install, and remove all types of glass as well as plastics, granite, marble, and similar materials used as glass substitutes. They may mount steel and aluminum sashes or frames and attach locks and hinges to glass doors. For most jobs, the glass is precut and mounted in frames at a factory or a contractor's shop. It arrives at the job site ready for glaziers to position and secure it in place. They may use a crane or hoist with suction cups to lift large, heavy pieces of glass. They then gently guide the glass into position by hand.

Once glaziers have the glass in place, they secure it with mastic, putty, or other pastelike cement, or with bolts, rubber gaskets, glazing compound, metal clips, or metal or wood molding. When they secure glass using a rubber gasket—a thick, molded rubber half-tube with a split running its length—they first secure the gasket around the perimeter within the opening, then set the glass into the split side of the gasket, causing it to clamp to the edges and hold the glass firmly in place.

When they use metal clips and wood molding, glaziers first secure the molding to the opening, place the glass in the molding, and then force spring-like metal clips between the glass and the molding. The clips exert pressure and keep the glass firmly in place.

When a glazing compound is used, glaziers first spread it neatly against and around the edges of the molding on the inside of the opening. Next, they install the glass. Pressing it against the compound on the inside molding, workers screw or nail outside molding that loosely holds the glass in place. To hold it firmly, they pack the space between the molding and the glass with glazing compound and then trim any excess material with a glazing knife.

For some jobs, the glazier must cut the glass manually at the job site. To prepare the glass for cutting, glaziers rest it either on edge on a rack or "A-frame" or flat against a cutting table. They then measure and mark the glass for the cut.

Glaziers cut glass with a special tool that has a very hard metal wheel about one-sixth of an inch in diameter. Using a straightedge as a guide, the glazier presses the cutter's wheel firmly on the glass, guiding and rolling it carefully to make a score just below the surface. To help the cutting tool move smoothly across the glass, workers brush a thin layer of oil along the line of the intended cut or dip the cutting tool in oil. Immediately after cutting, the glazier presses on the shorter end of the glass to break it cleanly along the cut.

In addition to handtools such as glass cutters, suction cups, and glazing knives, glaziers use power tools such as saws, drills, cutters, and grinders. An increasing number of glaziers use computers in the shop or at the job site to improve their layout work and reduce the amount of glass that is wasted.

## Working Conditions

Glaziers often work outdoors, sometimes in inclement weather. At times they work on scaffolds at great heights. They do a considerable amount of bending, kneeling, lifting, and standing. Glaziers may be injured by broken glass or cutting tools, falls from scaffolds, or from improperly lifting heavy glass panels.

## Employment

Glaziers held about 34,000 jobs in 1994. Most worked for glazing contractors engaged in new construction, alteration, and repair. Others worked for retail glass shops that install or replace glass and for wholesale distributors of products containing glass. Glaziers work throughout the country, but jobs are concentrated in metropolitan areas.

## Training, Other Qualifications, and Advancement

Many glaziers learn the trade informally on the job. They usually start as helpers, carrying glass and cleaning up debris in glass shops. They often practice cutting on discarded glass. After a while they are given an opportunity to cut glass for a job. Eventually, helpers assist experienced workers on simple installation jobs. By working with experienced glaziers, they eventually acquire the skills of a fully qualified glazier.

Employers recommend that glaziers learn the trade through a formal apprenticeship program that lasts three to four years. Apprenticeship programs, which are administered by the National Glass Association and local union-management committees or local contractors' associations, consist of on-the-job training, as well as 144 hours of classroom instruction or home study each year. On the job, apprentices learn to use the tools and equipment of the trade; handle, measure, cut, and install glass and metal framing; cut and fit moldings; and install and balance glass doors. In the classroom, they are taught basic mathematics, blueprint reading and sketching, general construction techniques, safety practices, and first aid. Learning the trade through an apprenticeship program usually takes less time and provides more complete training than acquiring skills informally on the job, but opportunities for apprenticeships are declining.

Local apprenticeship administrators determine how apprentices are recruited and selected. In general, applicants for apprenticeships and for helper positions must be in good physical condition and at least 17 years old. High school or vocational school graduates are preferred. In some areas, applicants must take mechanical aptitude tests. Courses in general mathematics, blueprint reading or mechanical drawing, general construction, and shop provide a good background.

Standards for acceptance into apprenticeship programs are rising to reflect changing requirements associated with new products and equipment. Glaziers need a basic understanding of electricity and electronics in order to be able to install electrochromatic glass and electronically controlled glass doors. In addition, the growing use of computers in glass layout requires more and more that glaziers be familiar with personal computers.

Because many glaziers do not learn the trade through a formal apprenticeship program, the National Glass Association (NGA) offers a series of written examinations which certify an individual's competency to perform glazier work at three progressively more difficult levels of proficiency. These levels include Level I, Glazier; Level II, Commercial Interior/Residential Glazier or Storefront/Curtainwall Glazier; and Level III, Master Glazier.

Advancement generally consists of increases in pay for most glaziers; some advance to supervisory jobs or become contractors or estimators.

## Job Outlook

Employment of glaziers is expected to increase more slowly than the average for all occupations through the year 2005 as a result of anticipated slow growth in residential and non-residential construction. Demand for glaziers will be spurred by the continuing need to modernize and repair existing structures and the popularity of glass in bathroom and kitchen design. Improved glass performance in insulation, privacy, safety, condensation control, and noise reduction are also expected to contribute to the demand for glaziers. In addition, job openings for glaziers will occur each year due to the need to replace experienced workers who retire or leave the occupation for other reasons.

People wishing to become construction glaziers should expect to experience periods of unemployment. These result from the limited duration of construction projects and the cyclical nature of the construction industry. During bad economic times, job openings for glaziers are reduced as the level of construction declines. Because construction activity varies from area to area, job openings—as well as apprenticeship opportunities—fluctuate with local economic conditions. Consequently, some parts of the country may experience an oversupply of these workers while others may have a shortage. Employment and apprenticeship opportunities should be greatest in metropolitan areas, where most glazing contractors and glass shops are located.

## Earnings

The median weekly earnings of glaziers were about $420 a week in 1994. The middle 50 percent earned between $330 and $530 a week. The lowest paid 10 percent earned less than $240 a week, while 10 percent with the highest pay earned $660 or more a week.

According to the *Engineering News Record*, union glaziers received an average hourly wage of $26.05 in 1994, including benefits. Wages ranged from a low of $15.80 in Dallas to a high of $40.27 in New York City. Glaziers covered by union contracts generally earn more than their non-union counterparts. Apprentice wage rates usually start at 50 to 60 percent of the rate paid to experienced glaziers and increase every six months. Because glaziers can lose time due to weather conditions and fluctuations in construction activity, their overall earnings may be lower than their hourly wages suggest.

Many glaziers employed in construction are members of the International Brotherhood of Painters and Allied Trades.

## Related Occupations

Glaziers use their knowledge of construction materials and techniques to install glass. Other construction workers whose jobs also involve skilled, custom work are bricklayers, carpenters, floor layers, paperhangers, terrazzo workers, and tilesetters.

## Related D.O.T. Jobs

These job titles are related to or more specific than the more general description above. They will help you identify job options you may not otherwise discover. These descriptions are in the current edition of the *Dictionary of Occupational Titles* and classified by numerical order.

865.361-010 MIRROR INSTALLER; 865.381-010 GLAZIER; 865.381-014 GLAZIER APPRENTICE

## Sources of Additional Information

For more information about glazier apprenticeships or work opportunities, contact local glazing or general contractors; a local of the International Brotherhood of Painters and Allied Trades; a local joint union-management apprenticeship agency; or the nearest office of the state employment service or state apprenticeship agency.

For general information about the work of glaziers, contact:

❑ International Brotherhood of Painters and Allied Trades, 1750 New York Ave. NW, Washington, DC 20006.

For information concerning training for glaziers contact:

❑ National Glass Association, Education and Training Department, 8200 Greensboro Dr., 3rd Floor, McLean, VA 22102.

❑ Glass Association of North America, White Lakes Professional Building, 3310 Southwest Harrison St., Topeka, KS 66611-2279.

# Guards

## Nature of the Work

Guards, also called security officers, patrol and inspect property to protect against fire, theft, vandalism, and illegal entry. Their duties vary with the size, type, and location of their employer.

In office buildings, banks, hospitals, and department stores, guards protect records, merchandise, money, and equipment. In department stores, they often work with undercover detectives to watch for theft by customers or store employees. Some guards patrol the outside of these buildings.

At ports, airports, and railroads, guards protect merchandise being shipped as well as property and equipment. They screen passengers and visitors for weapons, explosives, and other contraband. They ensure that nothing is stolen while being loaded or unloaded, and watch for fires, prowlers, and trouble among work crews. Sometimes they direct traffic.

Guards who work in public buildings, such as museums or art galleries, protect paintings and exhibits by inspecting people and packages entering the building. They also answer routine questions from visitors and sometimes guide tours.

In factories, laboratories, government buildings, data processing centers, and military bases where valuable property or information—such as information on new products, computer codes, or defense secrets—must be protected, guards check the credentials of persons and vehicles entering and leaving the premises. University, park, or recreation guards perform similar duties and also may issue parking permits and direct traffic. Golf course patrollers prevent unauthorized persons from using the facility and help keep play running smoothly.

At social affairs, sports events, conventions, and other public gatherings, guards provide information, assist in crowd control, and watch for persons who may cause trouble. Some guards patrol places of entertainment such as nightclubs to preserve order among customers and to protect property.

Armored car guards protect money and valuables during transit. Bodyguards protect individuals from bodily injury, kidnapping, or invasion of privacy.

In a large organization, a security officer often is in charge of the guard force; in a small organization, a single worker may be responsible for all security measures. Patrolling usually is done on foot, but if the property is large, guards may make their rounds by car or motor scooter. As more businesses purchase advanced electronic security systems to protect their property, more guards are being assigned to stations where they monitor perimeter security, environmental functions, communications, and other systems. In many cases, these guards maintain radio contact with other guards patrolling on foot or in motor vehicles. Some guards use computers to store information on matters relevant to security—for example, visitors or suspicious occurrences—during their hours on duty.

As they make their rounds, guards check all doors and windows, see that no unauthorized persons remain after working hours, and ensure that fire extinguishers, alarms, sprinkler systems, furnaces, and various electrical and plumbing systems are working properly. They sometimes set thermostats or turn on lights for janitorial workers.

Although some guards carry weapons, the trend is toward less use of armed guards. Guards may carry a flashlight, whistle, two-way radio, and a watch clock—a device that indicates the time at which they reach various checkpoints.

## Working Conditions

Most guards spend considerable time on their feet patrolling buildings, industrial plants, and grounds. Indoors, they may be stationed at a guard desk to monitor electronic security and surveillance devices or to check the credentials of persons entering or leaving the premises. They also may be stationed at gate shelters or may patrol grounds in all weather.

Because guards often work alone, there may be no one nearby to help if an accident or injury occurs. Some large firms use a reporting service that enables guards to be in constant contact with a central station outside the plant. If they fail to transmit an expected signal, the central station investigates. Guard work is usually routine, but guards must be constantly alert for threats to themselves and to the property that they are protecting. Guards who work during the day may have a great deal of contact with other employees and members of the public.

Many guards work alone at night; the usual shift lasts eight hours. Some employers have three shifts, and guards rotate to divide daytime, weekend, and holiday work equally. Guards usually eat on the job instead of taking a regular break away from the site.

## Employment

Guards held about 867,000 jobs in 1994. Industrial security firms and guard agencies employed 55 percent of all guards.

These organizations provide security services on contract, assigning their guards to buildings and other sites as needed. The remainder were in-house guards, employed in many settings including banks, building management companies, hotels, hospitals, retail stores, restaurants and bars, schools, and government.

Although guard jobs are found throughout the country, most are located in metropolitan areas.

## Training, Other Qualifications, and Advancement

Most states require that guards be licensed. To be licensed as a guard, individuals generally must be 18 years old, have no convictions for perjury or acts of violence, pass a background examination, and complete classroom training in such subjects as property rights, emergency procedures, and seizure of suspected criminals.

Most employers prefer guards who are high school graduates. Some jobs require a driver's license. Employers also seek people who have had experience in the military police or in state and local police departments. Most persons entering guard jobs have prior work experience, although it is usually unrelated. Because of limited formal training requirements and flexible hours, this occupation attracts some persons seeking a second job. For some entrants—for example, those retired from military careers or other protective services—guard employment is a second career.

Applicants are expected to have good character references, no police record, good health—especially in hearing and vision—and good personal habits such as neatness and dependability. They should be mentally alert, emotionally stable, and physically fit in order to cope with emergencies. Guards who have frequent contact with the public should be friendly and personable. Some employers require applicants to take a polygraph examination or a written test of honesty, attitudes, and other personal qualities. Many employers require applicants and experienced workers to submit to drug screening tests as a condition of employment.

Candidates for guard jobs in the federal government must have some experience as a guard and pass a written examination. Armed Forces experience also is an asset. For most federal guard positions, applicants must qualify in the use of firearms.

The amount of training guards receive varies. Training requirements generally are increasing as modern, highly sophisticated security systems become more commonplace. Many employers give newly hired guards instruction before they start the job and also provide several weeks of on-the-job training. More and more states are making ongoing training a legal requirement. For example, New York now requires guards to complete 40 hours of training after starting work. Illinois requires 20 hours for unarmed guards, plus an additional 20 hours for armed guards. Guards receive training in protection, public relations, report writing, crisis deterrence, first aid, drug control, and specialized training relevant to their particular assignment. Guards employed at establishments that place a heavy emphasis on security usually receive extensive formal training. For example, guards at nuclear power plants may undergo several months of training before being placed on duty under close supervision. Guards may be taught to use firearms, administer first aid, operate alarm systems and electronic security equipment, and spot and deal with security problems. Guards who are authorized to carry firearms may be periodically tested in their use according to state or local laws. Some guards are periodically tested for strength and endurance.

Although guards in small companies receive periodic salary increases, advancement is likely to be limited. However, most large organizations use a military type of ranking that offers advancement in position and salary. Higher level guard experience may enable persons to transfer to police jobs that offer higher pay and greater opportunities for advancement. Guards with some college education may advance to jobs that involve administrative and management duties. A few guards with management skills open their own contract security guard agencies.

## Job Outlook

Job openings for persons seeking work as guards are expected to be plentiful through the year 2005. High turnover and this occupation's large size ranks it among those providing the greatest number of job openings in the entire economy. Many opportunities are expected for persons seeking full-time employment, as well as for those seeking part-time or second jobs at night or on weekends. However, some competition is expected for the higher paying in-house guard positions. Compared to contract security guards, in-house guards enjoy higher earnings and benefits, greater job security, and more advancement potential, and are usually given more training and responsibility.

Employment of guards is expected to grow much faster than the average for all occupations through the year 2005. Increased concern about crime, vandalism, and terrorism will heighten the need for security in and around plants, stores, offices, and recreation areas. The level of business investment in increasingly expensive plant and equipment, including sophisticated computer systems, is expected to rise, resulting in growth in the number of guard jobs. Demand for guards will also grow as private security firms increasingly perform duties—such as monitoring crowds at airports and providing security in courts—formerly handled by government police officers and marshals. Because engaging the services of a security guard firm is easier and less costly than assuming direct responsibility for hiring, training, and managing a security guard force, job growth is expected to be concentrated among contract security guard agencies.

Guards employed by industrial security and guard agencies occasionally are laid off when the firm at which they work does not renew its contract with their agency. Most are able to find employment with other agencies, however. Guards employed directly by the firm at which they work are seldom laid off because a plant or factory must still be protected even when economic conditions force it to close temporarily.

## Earnings

According to a survey of workplaces in 160 metropolitan areas, guards with the least responsibilty and training had median hourly earnings of $6.00 in 1993. The middle half earned between $5.00 and $7.35 an hour. Guards with more specialized training and experience had median hourly earnings of $11.20.

Unionized in-house guards tend to earn more than the average. Many guards are represented by the United Plant Guard Workers Of America. Other guards belong to the International Guards Union of America or the International Union Of Security Officers.

Depending on their experience, newly hired guards in the federal government earned $14,900 or $16,700 a year in 1995. Beginning salaries were slightly higher in selected areas where the prevailing local pay level was higher. Guards employed by the federal government averaged about $23,300 a year in 1995. These workers usually receive overtime pay as well as a wage differential for the second and third shifts.

## Related Occupations

Guards protect property, maintain security, and enforce regulations for entry and conduct in the establishments at which they work. Related security and protective service occupations include bailiffs, border guards, correction officers, deputy sheriffs, fish and game wardens, house or store detectives, police officers, and private investigators.

## Related *D.O.T.* Jobs

These job titles are related to or more specific than the more general description above. They will help you identify job options you may not otherwise discover. These descriptions are in the current edition of the *Dictionary of Occupational Titles* and classified by numerical order.

372.563-010 ARMORED-CAR GUARD AND DRIVER; 372.567-010 ARMORED-CAR GUARD; 372.667-010 AIRLINE SECURITY REPRESENTATIVE; 372.667-014 BODYGUARD; 372.667-030 GATE GUARD; 372.667-034 GUARD, SECURITY; 372.667-038 MERCHANT PATROLLER; 376.667-010 BOUNCER; 379.667-010 GOLF-COURSE RANGER

## Sources of Additional Information

Further information about work opportunities for guards is available from local detective and guard firms and the nearest state employment service office.

Information about licensing requirements for guards may be obtained from the state licensing commission or the state police department. In states where local jurisdictions establish licensing requirements, contact a local government authority such as the sheriff, county executive, or city manager.

# Heating, Air-Conditioning, and Refrigeration Technicians

## Nature of the Work

What would those living in Chicago do without heating, those in Miami do without air-conditioning, or blood banks in all parts of the country do without refrigeration? Heating and air-conditioning systems control the temperature, humidity, and the total air quality in residential, commercial, industrial, and other buildings. Refrigeration systems make it possible to store and transport food, medicine, and other perishable items. Heating, air-conditioning, and refrigeration technicians install, maintain, and repair such systems.

Heating, air-conditioning, and refrigeration systems consist of many mechanical, electrical, and electronic components, including motors, compressors, pumps, fans, ducts, pipes, thermostats, and switches. In central heating systems, for example, a furnace heats air that is distributed throughout the building via a system of metal or fiberglass ducts. Technicians must be able to maintain, diagnose, and correct problems throughout the entire system. To do this, they may adjust system controls to recommended settings and test the performance of the entire system using special tools and test equipment.

Although they are trained to do both, technicians generally specialize in either installation or maintenance and repair. Some further specialize in one type of equipment—for example, oil burners, solar panels, or commercial refrigerators. Technicians may work for large or small contracting companies or directly for a manufacturer or wholesaler. Those working for smaller operations tend to do both installation and servicing, and work with heating, cooling, and refrigeration equipment.

*Furnace installers*, also called *heating equipment technicians*, follow blueprints or other specifications to install oil, gas, electric, solid-fuel, and multiple-fuel heating systems. After putting the equipment in place, they install fuel and water supply lines, air ducts and vents, pumps, and other components. They may connect electrical wiring and controls and check the unit for proper operation. To ensure the proper functioning of the system, furnace installers often use combustion test equipment such as carbon dioxide and oxygen testers.

After a furnace has been installed, technicians often perform routine maintenance and repair work in order to keep the system operating efficiently. During the fall and winter, for example, when the system is used most, they service and adjust burners and blowers. If the system is not operating properly, they check the thermostat, burner nozzles, controls, or other parts in order to diagnose and then correct the problem. During the summer, when the heating system is not being used, technicians do maintenance work, such as replacing filters and vacuum-cleaning vents, ducts, and other parts of the system that may accumulate dust and impurities during the operating season.

*Air-conditioning* and *refrigeration technicians* install and service central air-conditioning systems and a variety of refrigeration equipment. Technicians follow blueprints, design specifications, and manufacturers' instructions to install motors, compressors, condensing units, evaporators, piping, and other components. They connect this equipment to the duct work, refrigerant lines, and electrical power source. After making the connections, they charge the system with refrigerant, check it for proper operation, and program control systems.

When air-conditioning and refrigeration equipment breaks down, technicians diagnose the problem and make repairs. To do this, they may test parts such as compressors, relays, and thermostats. During the winter, air-conditioning technicians inspect the systems and do required maintenance, such as overhauling compressors.

When servicing equipment, heating, air-conditioning, and refrigeration technicians must use care to conserve, recover, and recycle chlorofluorocarbon (CFC) and hydrochlorofluorocarbon (HCFC) refrigerants used in air-conditioning and refrigeration systems. The release of CFCs and HCFCs contributes to the depletion of the stratospheric ozone layer, which protects plant and animal life from ultraviolet radiation. Technicians conserve the refrigerant by making sure that there are no leaks in the system; they recover it by venting the refrigerant into proper cylinders; and they recycle it for reuse with special filter-dryers.

Heating, air-conditioning, and refrigeration technicians use a variety of tools, including hammers, wrenches, metal snips, electric drills, pipe cutters and benders, measurement gauges, and acetylene torches, to work with refrigerant lines and air ducts. They use voltmeters, thermometers, pressure gauges, manometers, and other testing devices to check air flow, refrigerant pressure, electrical circuits, burners, and other components.

Cooling and heating systems sometimes are installed or repaired by other craft workers. For example, on a large air-conditioning installation job, especially where workers are covered by union contracts, duct work might be done by sheetmetal workers; electrical work by electricians; and installation of piping, condensers, and other components by plumbers and pipefitters. Room air-conditioners and household refrigerators usually are serviced by home appliance repairers.

## Working Conditions

Heating, air-conditioning, and refrigeration technicians work in homes, supermarkets, hospitals, office buildings, factories—anywhere there is climate control equipment. They may be assigned to specific job sites at the beginning of each day, or if they are making service calls, they may be dispatched to jobs by radio or telephone.

Technicians may work outside in cold or hot weather or in buildings that are uncomfortable because the air-conditioning or heating equipment is broken. In addition, technicians often work in awkward or cramped positions and sometimes are required to work in high places. Hazards include electrical shock, burns, muscle strains, and other injuries from handling heavy equipment. Appropriate safety equipment is necessary when handling refrigerants since contact can cause skin damage, frostbite, or blindness. Inhalation of refrigerants when working in confined spaces is also a possible hazard, and may cause asphyxiation.

Technicians usually work a 40-hour week, but during peak seasons they often work overtime or irregular hours. Maintenance workers, including those who provide maintenance services under contract, often work evening or weekend shifts, and are on call. Most employers try to provide a full workweek the year round by doing both installation and maintenance work and many manufacturers and contractors now provide or even require service contracts. In most shops that service both heating and air-conditioning equipment, employment is very stable throughout the year.

## Employment

Heating, air-conditioning, and refrigeration technicians held about 233,000 jobs in 1994. More than one-half of these worked for cooling and heating contractors. The remainder were employed in a wide variety of industries throughout the country, reflecting a widespread dependence on climate control systems. Some worked for fuel oil dealers, refrigeration and air-conditioning service and repair shops, and schools. Others were employed by the federal government, hospitals, office buildings, and other organizations that operate large air-conditioning, refrigeration, or heating systems. Approximately one of every eight technicians was self-employed.

## Training, Other Qualifications, and Advancement

Because of the increasing sophistication of heating, air-conditioning, and refrigeration systems, employers prefer to hire those with technical school or apprenticeship training. A sizable number of technicians, however, still learn the trade informally on the job.

Many secondary and postsecondary technical and trade schools, junior and community colleges, and the Armed Forces offer six-month to two-year programs in heating, air-conditioning, and refrigeration. Students study theory, design, and equipment construction, as well as electronics. They also learn the basics of installation, maintenance, and repair.

Apprenticeship programs are frequently run by joint committees representing local chapters of the Air-Conditioning Contractors of America, the Mechanical Contractors Association of America, the National Association of Plumbing-Heating-Cooling Contractors, and locals of the Sheet Metal Workers' International Association or the United Association of Journeymen and Apprentices of the Plumbing and Pipefitting Industry of the United States and Canada. Other apprenticeship programs are sponsored by local chapters of the Associated Builders and Contractors and the National Association of Home Builders. Formal apprenticeship programs generally last three or four years and combine on-the-job training with classroom instruction. Classes include subjects such as the use and care of tools, safety practices, blueprint reading, and air-conditioning theory. Applicants for these programs must have a high school diploma or equivalent.

Those who acquire their skills on the job usually begin by assisting experienced technicians. They may begin performing simple tasks such as carrying materials, insulating refrigerant lines, or cleaning furnaces. In time, they move on to more difficult tasks, such as cutting and soldering pipes and sheet metal and checking electrical and electronic circuits.

Courses in shop math, mechanical drawing, applied physics and chemistry, electronics, blueprint reading, and computer applications provide a good background for those interested in entering this occupation. Some knowledge of plumbing or electrical work is also helpful. A basic understanding of microelectronics is becoming more important because of the increasing use of this technology in solid-state equipment controls. Because technicians frequently deal directly with the public, they should be courteous and tactful, especially when dealing with an aggravated customer. They also should be in good physical condition because they sometimes have to lift and move heavy equipment.

All technicians who purchase or work with refrigerants must be certified so that they know how to handle them properly. To become certified to purchase and handle refrigerants, a technician must pass a written examination specific to the type of work in which they specialize. The three possible areas of certification are: Type I—servicing small appliances, Type II—high pressure refrigerants, and Type III—low pressure refrigerants. Exams are administered by organizations approved by the Environmental Protection Agency, such as trade schools, unions, contractor associations, or building groups.

Though no formal training is required for certification, training programs designed to prepare workers for the certification examination, as well as for general skills improvement training, are provided by heating and air-conditioning equipment manufacturers; the Refrigeration Service Engineers Society (RSES); the Air Conditioning Contractors of America (ACCA); the Mechanical Service Contractors of America; local chapters of the National Association of Plumbing-Heating-Cooling Contractors; and the United Association of Plumbers and Pipefitters. RSES, along with some other organizations, also offer basic self-study courses for individuals with limited experience. In addition to understanding how systems work, technicians must be knowledgeable about refrigerant products, and legislation and regulation that govern their use.

Advancement usually takes the form of higher wages. Some technicians, however, may advance to positions as supervisor or service manager. Others may move into areas such as sales and marketing. Those with sufficient money and managerial skill can open their own contracting business.

### Job Outlook

Job prospects for highly skilled air-conditioning, heating, and refrigeration technicians are expected to be very good, particularly those with technical school or formal apprenticeship training to install, remodel, and service new and existing systems. In addition to job openings created by rapid employment growth, thousands of openings will result from the need to replace workers who transfer to other occupations or leave the labor force.

Employment of heating, air-conditioning, and refrigeration technicians is expected to increase faster than the average for all occupations through the year 2005. As the population and economy grow, so does the demand for new residential, commercial, and industrial climate control systems. Technicians who specialize in installation work may experience periods of unemployment when the level of new construction activity declines, but maintenance and repair work usually remains relatively stable. People and businesses depend on their climate control systems and must keep them in good working order, regardless of economic conditions.

Concern for the environment and energy conservation should continue to prompt the development of new energy-saving heating and air-conditioning systems. An emphasis on better energy management should lead to the replacement of older systems and the installation of newer, more efficient systems in existing homes and buildings. Also, demand for maintenance and service work should increase as businesses and home owners strive to keep systems operating at peak efficiency. Regulations prohibiting the discharge of CFC and HCFC refrigerants and banning CFC production by the year 2000 also should result in demand for technicians to replace many existing systems, or modify them to use new environmentally safe refrigerants. In addition, the continuing focus on improving indoor air quality should contribute to the growth of jobs for heating, air-conditioning, and refrigeration technicians.

### Earnings

Median weekly earnings of air-conditioning, heating, and refrigeration technicians who worked full-time were $494 in 1994. The middle 50 percent earned between $363 and $670. The lowest 10 percent earned less than $287 a week, and the top 10 percent earned more than $817 a week.

Apprentices usually begin at about 50 percent of the wage rate paid to experienced workers. As they gain experience and improve their skills, they receive periodic increases until they reach the wage rate of experienced workers.

Heating, air-conditioning, and refrigeration technicians enjoy a variety of employer-sponsored benefits. In addition to typical benefits like health insurance and pension plans, some employers pay for work-related training and provide uniforms, company vans, and tools.

Nearly one out of every five heating, air-conditioning, and refrigeration technicians is a member of a union. The unions to which the greatest numbers of technicians belong are the Sheet Metal Workers' International Association and the United Association of Journeymen and Apprentices of the Plumbing and Pipefitting Industry of the United States and Canada.

### Related Occupations

Heating, air-conditioning, and refrigeration technicians work with sheet metal and piping, and repair machinery, such as electrical motors, compressors, and burners. Other workers who have similar skills are boilermakers, electrical appliance servicers, electricians, plumbers and pipefitters, sheetmetal workers, and duct installers.

### Related *D.O.T.* Jobs

These job titles are related to or more specific than the more general description above. They will help you identify job options you may not otherwise discover. These descriptions are in the current edition of the *Dictionary of Occupational Titles* and classified by numerical order.

637.261-014 HEATING-AND-AIR-CONDITIONING INSTALLER-SERVICER; 637.261-026 REFRIGERATION MECHANIC; 637.261-030 SOLAR-ENERGY-SYSTEM INSTALLER; 637.261-034 AIR AND HYDRONIC BALANCING TECHNICIAN; 637.381-010 EVAPORATIVE-COOLER INSTALLER; 637.381-014 REFRIGERATION UNIT REPAIRER; 827.361-014 REFRIGERATION MECHANIC; 862.281-018 OIL-BURNER-SERVICER-AND-INSTALLER; 862.361-010 FURNACE INSTALLER; 869.281-010 FURNACE INSTALLER-AND-REPAIRER, HOT AIR

### Sources of Additional Information

For more information about employment and training opportunities in this trade, contact local vocational and technical schools; local heating, air-conditioning, and refrigeration contractors; a local of the unions previously mentioned; a local joint union-management apprenticeship committee; a local chapter of the Associated Builders and Contractors; or the nearest office of the state employment service or state apprenticeship agency.

For information on career opportunities and training, write to:

❑ Associated Builders and Contractors, 1300 North 17th St., Rosslyn, VA 22209.

❑ Refrigeration Service Engineers Society, 1666 Rand Rd., Des Plaines, IL 60016-3552.

❑ Home Builders Institute, National Association of Home Builders, 1201 15th St. NW, Washington, DC 20005.

❑ National Association of Plumbing-Heating-Cooling Contractors, 180 S. Washington St., P.O. Box 6808, Falls Church, VA 22046.

❑ New England Fuel Institute, P.O. Box 9137, Watertown, MA 02272.

❑ Mechanical Service Contractors of America, 1385 Piccard Dr., Rockville, MD 20850-4329.

❑ Air Conditioning and Refrigeration Institute, 4301 North Fairfax Dr., Suite 425, Arlington, VA 22203.

❏ Air Conditioning Contractors of America, 1712 New Hampshire Ave., NW, Washington, DC 20009.

# Home Appliance and Power Tool Repairers

## Nature of the Work

Appliance and power tool repairers, often called service technicians, repair home appliances such as ovens, washers, dryers, refrigerators, window air-conditioners, and vacuum cleaners, as well as power tools such as saws and drills. Some repairers only service small appliances such as microwaves and vacuum cleaners; others specialize in major appliances such as refrigerators, dishwashers, washers, and dryers; and others only handle power tools or gas appliances.

To determine why an appliance or power tool fails to operate properly, repairers visually inspect it and run it to check for unusual noises, excessive vibration, fluid leaks, or loose parts. They may have to consult service manuals and troubleshooting guides to diagnose particularly difficult problems. They may disassemble the appliance or tool to examine its internal parts for signs of wear or corrosion. To check electrical systems for shorts and faulty connections, repairers follow wiring diagrams and use testing devices, such as ammeters, voltmeters, and wattmeters.

After identifying problems, they replace or repair defective belts, motors, heating elements, switches, gears, or other items. They tighten, align, clean, and lubricate parts as necessary. Repairers use common handtools, including screwdrivers, wrenches, files, and pliers, as well as soldering guns and special tools designed for particular appliances. When servicing appliances with electronic parts, they may replace circuit boards or other electronic components.

When servicing refrigerators, repairers must use care to conserve, recover, and recycle chlorofluorocarbon (CFC) and hydrochlorofluorocarbon (HCFC) refrigerants used in their cooling systems. The release of CFCs and HCFCs contributes to the depletion of the stratospheric ozone layer, which protects plant and animal life from ultraviolet radiation. Repairers conserve the refrigerant by making sure that there are no leaks in the system; they recover it by venting the refrigerant into proper cylinders; and they recycle it for reuse with special filter-dryers.

Repairers servicing gas appliances may check the heating unit and replace pipes, thermocouples, thermostats, valves, and indicator spindles. They also answer emergency calls for gas leaks. To install gas appliances, they may have to install pipes in customers' homes to connect the appliances to the gas line. They measure, lay out, cut, and thread pipe and connect it to a feeder line and to the appliance. They may have to saw holes in walls or floors and hang steel supports from beams or joists to hold gas pipes in place. Once the gas line is in place, they turn on the gas and check for leaks.

Repairers also answer customers' questions about the care and use of appliances. For example, they demonstrate how to load automatic washing machines, arrange dishes in dishwashers, or sharpen chain saws.

Repairers write up estimates of the cost of repairs for customers, keep records of parts used and hours worked, prepare bills, and collect payment.

## Working Conditions

Home appliance and power tool repairers who handle portable appliances usually work in repair shops which generally are quiet, well lighted, and adequately ventilated. Those who repair major appliances usually make service calls to customers' homes. They carry their tools and a number of commonly used parts with them in a truck or van and may spend several hours a day driving. They may work in clean comfortable rooms such as kitchens, but sometimes the appliance is in an area of the home that is damp, dirty, or dusty. Repairers sometimes work in cramped and uncomfortable positions when replacing parts in hard-to-reach areas of appliances.

Repairer jobs generally are not hazardous, but they must exercise care and follow safety precautions to avoid electrical shocks and injuries when lifting and moving large appliances. When servicing gas appliances and microwave ovens, they must be aware of the dangers of gas and radiation leaks.

Many home appliance and power tool repairers work a standard 40-hour week. Some work early mornings, evenings, and Saturdays. During hot weather, repairers of air-conditioners and refrigerators are in high demand by consumers and many work overtime. Repairers of power tools such as saws and drills may also have to work overtime during spring and summer months when use of such tools increases and breakdowns are more frequent.

Home appliance and power tool repairers usually work with little or no direct supervision, a feature of the job that appeals to many people.

## Employment

Home appliance and power tool repairers held about 70,000 jobs in 1994. More than 1 out of 10 was self-employed. Almost 2 out of 3 salaried repairers worked in retail establishments such as department stores, household appliance stores, and fuel dealers. Others worked for gas and electric utility companies, electrical repair shops, and wholesalers.

Appliance and power tool repairers are employed in almost every community, but jobs are concentrated in the more highly populated areas.

## Training, Other Qualifications, and Advancement

Employers generally require a high school diploma for home appliance and power tool repairer jobs. Many repairers learn the trade primarily on the job. Mechanical aptitude is desirable, and those who work in customers' homes must be courteous and tactful.

Employers prefer to hire people with formal training in appliance repair and electronics, and many repairers complete one- or two-year formal training programs in appliance repair and related subjects in high schools, private vocational schools, and community colleges. Courses in basic electricity and electronics are becoming increasingly necessary as more manufacturers are installing circuit boards and other electronic control systems in home appliances.

Regardless of whether their basic skills are developed through formal training or on the job, trainees usually get additional training from their employer. In shops that fix portable appliances, they work on a single type of appliance, such as vacuum cleaners, until they master its repair. Then they move on to others, until they can repair all those handled by the shop. In companies that repair major appliances, beginners assist experienced repairers on service visits. They may also study on their own. They learn to read schematic drawings, analyze problems, determine whether to repair or replace parts, and follow proper safety procedures. Up to three years of on-the-job training may be needed to become skilled in all aspects of repair of the more complex appliances.

Some appliance and power tool manufacturers and department store chains have formal training programs which include home study and shop classes, where trainees work with demonstration appliances and other training equipment. Many repairers receive supplemental instruction through two- or three-week seminars conducted by appliance and power tool manufacturers. Experienced repairers also often attend training classes and study service manuals.

The Environmental Protection Agency (EPA) has mandated that all repairers who purchase or work with refrigerants must be certified in its proper handling. To become certified to purchase and handle refrigerants, repairers must pass a written examination. Exams are administered by organizations approved by the Environmental Protection Agency, such as trade schools, unions, and employer associations. Though no formal training is required for certification, many of these organizations offer training programs designed to prepare workers for the certification examination.

To protect consumers, some states and areas require repairers to be licensed or registered. Applicants for licensure must meet standards of education, training, and experience; they also may have to pass an examination, which can include a written examination, a hands-on practical test, or a combination of both.

Repairers in large shops or service centers may be promoted to supervisor, assistant service manager, or service manager. A few advance to managerial positions such as regional service manager or parts manager for appliance or tool manufacturers. Preference is given to those who demonstrate technical competence and show an ability to get along with coworkers and customers. Experienced repairers who have sufficient funds and knowledge of small business management may open their own repair shop.

## Job Outlook

Employment of home appliance and power tool repairers is expected to decline slightly through the year 2005. Although the number of home appliances and power tools in use is expected to increase as the number of households and businesses grows and new and improved appliances and tools are introduced, increasing use of electronic parts such as solid-state circuitry, microprocessors, and sensing devices in appliances reduce the frequency of repairs. Nevertheless, prospects should continue to be good for well-trained repairers, particularly those with a strong background in electronics. Most people with the electronics training needed to repair appliances go into other repairer occupations.

Employment is relatively steady because the demand for appliance repair services continues even during economic downturns.

## Earnings

Home appliance and power tool repairers who usually worked full-time had median earnings of about $427 a week in 1994. The middle 50 percent earned between $308 and $674 a week. The lowest paid 10 percent earned $249 a week or less, while the highest paid 10 percent earned $838 a week or more. Earnings of home appliance and power tool repairers vary widely according to skill level, geographic location, and the type of equipment serviced. Trainees usually earn less and senior technicians more. Earnings tend to be highest in large firms and for those servicing gas appliances. Repairers are compensated when working overtime, weekends, or holidays. Many receive commission in addition to their hourly wage salary.

Many larger dealers and service stores offer benefits such as health insurance coverage, sick leave, and retirement and pension programs. Some home appliance and power tool repairers belong to the International Brotherhood of Electrical Workers.

## Related Occupations

Other workers who service electrical and electronic equipment include heating, air-conditioning, and refrigeration mechanics; pinsetter mechanics; office machine and cash register servicers; electronic home entertainment equipment repairers; and vending machine servicers and repairers.

## Related *D.O.T.* Jobs

These job titles are related to or more specific than the more general description above. They will help you identify job options you may not otherwise discover. These descriptions are in the current edition of the *Dictionary of Occupational Titles* and classified by numerical order.

637.261-010 AIR-CONDITIONING INSTALLER-SERVICER, WINDOW UNIT; 637.261-018 GAS-APPLIANCE SERVICER; 723.381-010 ELECTRICAL-APPLIANCE REPAIRER; 723.381-014 VACUUM CLEANER REPAIRER; 723.584-010 APPLIANCE REPAIRER; 729.281-022 ELECTRIC-TOOL REPAIRER; 827.261-010 ELECTRICAL-APPLIANCE SERVICER; 827.261-014 ELECTRICAL-APPLIANCE-SERVICER APPRENTICE; 827.661-010 HOUSEHOLD-APPLIANCE INSTALLER

## Sources of Additional Information

For information about jobs in the home appliance and power tool repair field, contact local appliance repair shops, appliance dealers, and utility companies, or the local office of the state employment service.

For general information about the work of home appliance repairers contact:

❏ Appliance Service News, P.O. Box 789, Lombard, IL 60148.

❏ National Association of Service Dealers, 10 East 22nd St., Suite 310, Lombard, IL 60148.

❏ Service Dealers Newsletter, 1400 Easton Rd., Roslyn, PA 19001.

❏ Professional Service Association, 71 Columbia St., Cohoes, NY 12047.

# Homemaker-Home Health Aides

## Nature of the Work

Homemaker-home health aides help elderly, disabled, and ill persons live in their own homes instead of in a health facility. Most work with elderly or disabled clients who need more extensive care than family or friends can provide. Some homemaker-home health aides work with families in which a parent is incapacitated and small children need care. Others help discharged hospital patients who have relatively short-term needs. These workers are sometimes called home care aides and personal care attendants.

Homemaker-home health aides provide housekeeping services, personal care, and emotional support for their clients. They clean clients' houses, do laundry, and change bed linens. Aides may also plan meals (including special diets), shop for food, and cook.

Home health aides provide personal care services, also known as *hands-on care* because they physically touch the patient. These aides help clients move from bed, bathe, dress, and groom. They also check pulse, temperature, and respiration; help with simple prescribed exercises; and assist with medication routines. Occasionally, they change nonsterile dressings, use special equipment such as a hydraulic lift, give massages and alcohol rubs, or assist with braces and artificial limbs. Some accompany clients outside the home, serving as guide, companion, and aide.

Homemaker-home health aides also provide instruction and psychological support. For example, they assist in toilet training a severely mentally handicapped child or just listen to clients talk about their problems. Aides keep records of services performed and of the client's condition and progress.

In home care agencies, homemaker-home health aides are supervised by a registered nurse, a physical therapist, or a social worker, who assigns them specific duties. Aides report changes in the client's condition to the supervisor or case manager. Homemaker-home health aides also participate in case reviews, consulting with the team caring for the client—registered nurses, therapists, and other health professionals.

## Working Conditions

The homemaker-home health aide's daily routine may vary. Aides may go to the same home every day for months or even years. However, most aides work with a number of different clients, each job lasting a few hours, days, or weeks. Aides often go to four or five clients on the same day.

Surroundings differ from case to case. Some homes are neat and pleasant, while others are untidy or depressing. Some clients are angry, abusive, depressed, or otherwise difficult; others are pleasant and cooperative.

Homemaker-home health aides generally work on their own with periodic visits by their supervisor. They get detailed instructions explaining when to visit clients and what services to perform. Many aides work part-time, and weekend hours are common.

Most aides generally travel by public transportation, but some need a car. In any event, they are responsible for getting to the client's home. Aides may spend a good portion of the working day traveling from one client to another.

## Employment

Homemaker-home health aides held about 598,000 jobs in 1994. Most aides are employed by homemaker-home health agencies, home health agencies, visiting nurse associations, residential care facilities with home health departments, hospitals, public health and welfare departments, community volunteer agencies, and temporary help firms. Self-employed aides have no agency affiliation or supervision, and accept clients, set fees, and arrange work schedules on their own.

## Training, Other Qualifications, and Advancement

In some states, this occupation is open to individuals with no formal training. On-the-job training is generally provided. Other states may require formal training, depending on federal or state law.

The federal government has enacted guidelines for home health aides whose employers receive reimbursement from Medicare. Federal law requires home health aides to pass a competency test covering 12 areas: communication skills; observation, reporting, and documentation of patient status and the care or services furnished; reading and recording vital signs; basic infection control procedures; basic elements of body function and changes; maintenance of a clean, safe, and healthy environment; recognition of and procedures for emergencies; the physical, emotional, and developmental characteristics of the patients served; personal hygiene and grooming; safe transfer techniques; normal range of motion and positioning; and basic nutrition.

A home health aide may also take training before taking the competency test. Federal law suggests at least 75 hours of classroom and practical training supervised by a registered nurse. Training and testing programs may be offered by the employing agency, but they must meet the standards of the Health Care Financing Administration. Training programs vary depending upon state regulations. Thirteen states have specific laws on personal care services.

The Foundation for Hospice and Home Care offers a National Homemaker-Home Health Aide certification. The certification is a voluntary demonstration that the individual has met industry standards.

Successful homemaker-home health aides like to help people and do not mind hard work. They should be responsible, compassionate, emotionally stable, and cheerful. Aides should also be tactful, honest, and discreet since they work in private homes.

Homemaker-home health aides must be in good health. A physical examination including state regulated tests like those for tuberculosis may be required.

Advancement is limited. In some agencies, workers start out performing homemaker duties, such as cleaning. With experience and training, they may take on personal care duties. The most experienced aides assist with medical equipment such as ventilators, which help patients breathe.

## Job Outlook

A large number of job openings is expected for homemaker-home health aides, due to very rapid growth and very high turnover. Homemaker-home health aides is expected to be one of the fastest growing occupations through the year 2005—more than doubling in employment size.

The number of people in their seventies and beyond is projected to rise substantially. This age group is characterized by mounting health problems that require some assistance. Also, there will be an increasing reliance on home care for patients of all ages. This trend reflects several developments: Efforts to contain costs by moving patients out of hospitals and nursing facilities as quickly as possible; the realization that treatment can be more effective in familiar surroundings rather than clinical surroundings; and the development of portable medical equipment for in-home treatment.

In addition to jobs created by the increase in demand for these workers, replacement needs are expected to produce numerous openings. Turnover is high, a reflection of the relatively low skill requirements, low pay, and high emotional demands of the work. For these same reasons, many people are unwilling to do this kind of work. Therefore, persons who are interested in this work and suited for it should have excellent job opportunities, particularly those with experience or training as homemaker-home health aides or nursing aides.

### Earnings

Earnings for homemaker-home health aides vary considerably. According to a National Association for Home Care survey of home care aides who work in Medicare-certified agencies, beginning aides' average starting hourly wage ranged from $4.90 to $6.86 in May 1994. More experienced aides' average starting hourly wage ranged from $5.69 to $8.11. Wages were somewhat higher in the Northeast and West and somewhat lower in the Midwest and South. Some aides are paid on a salary or per-visit basis.

Most employers give slight pay increases with experience and added responsibility. Aides usually are paid only for the time worked in the home. They normally are not paid for travel time between jobs. Most employers hire only on-call hourly workers and provide no benefits.

### Related Occupations

Homemaker-home health aide is a service occupation that combines duties of health workers and social service workers. Workers in related occupations that involve personal contact to help or instruct others include attendants in children's institutions, childcare attendants in schools, child monitors, companions, nursing aides, nursery school attendants, occupational therapy aides, nursing aides, physical therapy aides, playroom attendants, and psychiatric aides.

### Related *D.O.T.* Jobs

These job titles are related to or more specific than the more general description above. They will help you identify job options you may not otherwise discover. These descriptions are in the current edition of the *Dictionary of Occupational Titles* and classified by numerical order.

309.354-010 HOMEMAKER; 354.377-014 HOME ATTENDANT

### Sources of Additional Information

General information about training and referrals to state and local agencies about opportunities for homemaker-home health aides, a list of relevant publications, and information on national certification are available from:

❑ Foundation for Hospice and Homecare/National Certification Program, 519 C St. NE., Washington, DC 20002.

# Industrial Machinery Repairers

### Nature of the Work

Industrial machinery repairers maintain and repair machinery found in a plant or factory. This must be done accurately and quickly because an idle machine will delay production. In addition, a machine that is not properly repaired and maintained may damage the final product and injure the operator. All these factors cost companies money.

Industrial machinery repairers—often called maintenance mechanics—spend much of their time doing preventive maintenance. This includes keeping machines and their parts well oiled, greased, and cleaned. Repairers regularly inspect machinery and check performance. For example, they adjust and calibrate automated manufacturing equipment such as industrial robots and rebuild components of other industrial machinery. By keeping complete and up-to-date records, mechanics try to anticipate trouble and service equipment before factory production is interrupted.

Maintenance mechanics must be able to spot minor problems and correct them before they become major ones. For example, after hearing a vibration from a machine, the mechanic must decide whether it is due to worn belts, weak motor bearings, or some other problem. Computerized maintenance-management, vibration analysis techniques, and self-diagnostic systems are making this task easier. Self-diagnostic features on new industrial machinery can determine the cause of a malfunction and, in some cases, can alert the mechanic to potential trouble spots before symptoms develop.

After diagnosing the problem, the mechanic disassembles the equipment and repairs or replaces the necessary parts. The final step is to test the machine to ensure that it is running smoothly. When repairing electronically controlled machinery, maintenance mechanics may work closely with electronic repairers or electricians who maintain the machine's electronic parts. However, industrial machinery repairers increasingly need electronic skills to repair sophisticated equipment on their own.

A wide range of tools may be used when doing preventive maintenance or making repairs. For example, repairers may use a screwdriver and wrench to adjust an engine, or a hoist to lift a printing press off the ground. When replacements for broken or defective parts are not readily available, or when a machine must be quickly returned to production, repairers may sketch a part that can be fabricated by the plant's machine shop. Repairers use catalogs to order replacement parts and often follow blueprints and engineering specifications to maintain and fix equipment.

Some of the industrial machinery repairer's duties may be performed by millwrights.

### Working Conditions

Working conditions for repairers who work in manufacturing are similar to those of production workers. However, they often work underneath or above large machinery in cramped conditions or on the top of a ladder. These workers are subject to common shop injuries such as cuts and bruises and use protective equipment such as hard hats, protective glasses, and safety belts.

Because factories and other organizations cannot afford breakdowns in industrial machinery, industrial machinery repairers may be called to the plant at night or on weekends for emergency repairs. Overtime is common among industrial machinery repairers—half work more than 40 hours a week.

## Employment

Industrial machinery repairers held about 464,000 jobs in 1994. About 7 of every 10 worked in manufacturing industries, primarily food processing, textile mill products, chemicals, fabricated metal products, and primary metals. Others worked for government agencies, public utilities, mining companies, and any other business that relies on machinery.

Because industrial machinery repairers work in a wide variety of plants, they are employed in every part of the country. Employment is concentrated, however, in heavily industrialized areas.

## Training, Other Qualifications, and Advancement

Many workers learn their trade through a 4-year apprenticeship program that combines classroom instruction with on-the-job-training. These programs are usually sponsored by a local trade union. Other workers start as helpers and pick up the skills of the trade informally and by taking courses offered by machinery manufacturers and community colleges.

Repairers learn from experienced repairers how to operate, disassemble, repair, and assemble machinery. Classroom instruction focuses on subjects such as shop mathematics, blueprint reading, and welding. In addition, electronics and computer training are an increasingly important part of the apprenticeship program.

Most employers prefer to hire those who have completed high school. However, opportunities do exist for those without a high school diploma. High school courses in mechanical drawing, mathematics, blueprint reading, physics, and electronics are useful.

Mechanical aptitude and manual dexterity are important characteristics for workers in this trade. Good physical condition and agility are also necessary because repairers sometimes have to lift heavy objects or climb to reach equipment located high above the floor.

Opportunities for advancement are limited. Industrial machinery repairers advance either by working with more complicated equipment or by becoming a supervisor. Some of the most highly skilled repairers can be promoted to master mechanic or can become a machinist or a tool and die maker.

## Job Outlook

Employment of industrial machinery repairers is expected to grow more slowly than the average for all occupations through the year 2005. As more firms introduce automated production equipment, industrial machinery mechanics will be needed to insure that these machines are well-maintained and consistently in operation. This growth will be moderated, however, by the self-diagnostic capabilities and growing reliability of many new machines that help to reduce the need for repairs. Most job openings will result from the need to replace repairers who transfer to other occupations or leave the labor force. Qualified applicants should find ample employment opportunities as older workers retire.

Unlike many other manufacturing occupations, industrial machinery repairers are not usually affected by seasonal changes in production. During slack periods, when some plant workers are laid off, repairers often are retained to do major overhaul jobs. Although these workers may face layoff or a reduced workweek when economic conditions are particularly severe, they generally are less affected than other workers because machines have to be maintained regardless of the level of production.

## Earnings

Median weekly earnings of full-time industrial machinery repairers were about $530 in 1994; the middle 50 percent earned between $410 and $720 weekly. The lowest 10 percent earned less than $310, while the top 10 percent earned more than $950. Earnings vary by industry and geographic region. In addition to wages, most of these workers receive benefits such as health and life insurance, pension plans, annual leave, and sick days.

Labor unions to which some industrial machinery repairers belong include the United Steelworkers of America; the United Automobile, Aerospace and Agricultural Implement Workers of America; the International Association of Machinists and Aerospace Workers; and the International Union of Electronic, Electrical, Salaried, Machine, and Furniture Workers.

## Related Occupations

Other occupations that involve repairing machinery include aircraft mechanics and engine specialists; elevator installers and repairers; machinists; millwrights; and automotive and motorcycle, diesel, farm equipment, general maintenance, mobile heavy equipment, and heating, air-conditioning, and refrigeration mechanics.

## Related *D.O.T.* Jobs

These job titles are related to or more specific than the more general description above. They will help you identify job options you may not otherwise discover. These descriptions are in the current edition of the *Dictionary of Occupational Titles* and classified by numerical order.

There are too many *D.O.T.* titles to list here. Most are variations related to a specific industry, and we have included a small number of representative *D.O.T.* titles as examples. Complete lists are available in various career software published by JIST or directly from the U.S. Department of Labor.

549.685-042 UTILITY OPERATOR III; 601.281-030 TOOL AND FIXTURE REPAIRER; 620.281-046 MAINTENANCE MECHANIC; 623.281-010 DECK ENGINEER; 623.281-030 MACHINIST, OUTSIDE; 623.281-034 MAINTENANCE MECHANIC, ENGINE; 626.381-018 HYDRAULIC-PRESS SERVICER; 626.384-010 REPAIRER, WELDING EQUIPMENT; 627.261-022 MACHINIST, LINOTYPE; 628.281-010 MACHINE FIXER; 629.261-018 POWDER-LINE REPAIRER; 629.261-022 ELECTRONIC-PRODUCTION-LINE-MAINTENANCE MECHANIC; 629.280-010 MAINTENANCE MECHANIC; 629.281-034 PUMP MECHANIC; 630.261-014 OVEN-EQUIPMENT REPAIRER; 630.281-022 REPAIRER; 630.281-026 REPAIRER; 630.281-038 TREATMENT-PLANT MECHANIC; 631.261-014 POWERHOUSE MECHANIC

## Sources of Additional Information

Information about employment and apprenticeship opportunities in this field may be obtained from local offices of the state employment service or from:

❑ The Association for Manufacturing Technology, 7901 Westpark Dr., McLean, VA 22102.

❑ Associated General Contractors of America, 1957 E St. NW, Washington, DC 20006.

# Industrial Production Managers

## Nature of the Work

Industrial production managers coordinate the resources and activities required to produce millions of goods every year in the United States. Due to the wide variety of these goods and differences among factories, managers' duties vary from plant to plant. In general, industrial production managers share many of the same major functions, regardless of the industry. These functions include responsibility for production scheduling, staffing, equipment, quality control, inventory control, and the coordination of production activities with those of other departments.

The primary mission of industrial production managers is planning the production schedule within budgetary limitations and time constraints. This entails analyzing the plant's personnel and capital resources and selecting the best way to meet the production quota. Industrial production managers determine which machines will be used, whether overtime or extra shifts are necessary, and the sequence of production. They also monitor the production run to make sure that it stays on schedule and correct any problems that may arise.

Industrial production managers also monitor product standards. When quality drops below the established standard, they must determine why standards aren't being maintained and how to improve the product. If the problem is poor work, the manager may implement better training programs, reorganize the manufacturing process, or institute employee suggestion or involvement programs. If the cause is substandard materials, the manager works with the purchasing department to improve the quality of the product's components.

Working with the purchasing department, the production manager ensures that plant inventories are maintained at their optimal level. This is vital to a firm's operation because maintaining the inventory of materials necessary for production ties up the firm's financial resources, yet insufficient quantities of materials cause delays in production. A breakdown in communications between these departments can cause slowdowns and a failure to meet production schedules. Because the work of many departments is dependent upon others, managers work closely with heads of other departments such as sales, purchasing, and traffic to plan and implement companies' goals, policies, and procedures. Production managers also work closely with, and act as a liaison between, executives and first-line supervisors.

Production managers usually report to the plant manager or the vice president for manufacturing. In many plants, one production manager is responsible for all production. In large plants with several operations—aircraft assembly, for example—there are managers in charge of each operation, such as machining, assembly, or finishing.

Computers play an integral role in the coordination of the production process by providing up-to-date data on inventory, work-in-progress, and product standards. Industrial production managers analyze these data and, working with upper management and other departments, determine if adjustments need to be made.

As the trend toward a flatter management structure and worker empowerment continues, production managers will increasingly perform the role of facilitators. Instead of independently making decisions and giving and taking orders, production managers will review and discuss recommendations with subordinates and superiors in the hopes of improving productivity. Because of the additional duties resulting from corporate downsizing, production managers are delegating more authority and responsibility to first-line supervisors.

## Working Conditions

Most industrial production managers divide their time between the shop floor and their office. While on the floor, they must follow established health and safety practices and wear the required protective clothing and equipment. The time in the office—often located on or near the production floor—is usually spent meeting with subordinates or other department managers, analyzing production data, and writing and reviewing reports.

Most industrial production managers work more than 40 hours a week, especially when production deadlines must be met. In facilities that operate around the clock, managers may have to work shifts or may be called at any hour to deal with emergencies. This could mean going to the plant to resolve the problem, regardless of the hour, and staying until the situation is under control. Dealing with production workers as well as superiors when working under the pressure of production deadlines or emergency situations can be stressful. In addition, restructuring has eliminated levels of management and support staff. As a result, production managers now have to accomplish more with less, and this has greatly increased job-related stress.

## Employment

Industrial production managers held about 206,000 jobs in 1994. Although employed throughout manufacturing industries, about one-half are employed in industrial machinery and equipment, transportation equipment, electronic and electrical equipment, fabricated metal products, and food products manufacturing. Production managers work in all parts of the country, but jobs are most plentiful in areas where manufacturing is concentrated.

## Training, Other Qualifications, and Advancement

Because of the diversity of manufacturing operations and job requirements, there is no standard preparation for this occupation. Many industrial production managers have a college degree in business administration or industrial engineering. Some have a master's degree in business administration (MBA). Others are former production line supervisors who have been promoted. Although many employers prefer candidates to have a degree in business or engineering, some companies hire liberal arts graduates.

As production operations become more sophisticated, an increasing number of employers are looking for candidates with

MBAs. This, combined with an undergraduate degree in engineering, is considered particularly good preparation. Companies also are placing greater importance on a candidate's personality. Because the job demands technical knowledge and the ability to compromise, persuade, and negotiate, successful production managers must be well-rounded and have excellent communication skills.

Those who enter the field directly from college or graduate school often are unfamiliar with the firm's production process. As a result, they may spend their first few months on the job in the company's training program. These programs familiarize trainees with the production line, company policies and procedures, and the requirements of the job. In larger companies, they may also include assignments to other departments, such as purchasing and accounting.

Blue-collar worker supervisors who advance to production manager positions already have an intimate knowledge of the production process and the firm's organization. To be selected for promotion, these workers must have demonstrated leadership qualities, and often take company-sponsored courses in management skills and communications techniques. Some companies hire college graduates as blue-collar worker supervisors and then promote them.

Once in their job, industrial production managers must stay abreast of new production technologies and management practices. To do this, they belong to professional organizations and attend trade shows where new equipment is displayed; they also attend industry conferences and conventions where changes in production methods and technological advances are discussed.

Although certification in production management and inventory control is not required for most positions, it demonstrates an individual's knowledge of the production process and related areas. Various certifications are available through the American Production and Inventory Control Society. To be certified in production and inventory management, candidates must pass a series of examinations that test their knowledge of inventory management, just-in-time systems, production control, capacity management, and materials planning.

Industrial production managers with a proven record of superior performance may advance to plant manager or vice president for manufacturing. Others transfer to jobs at larger firms with more responsibilities. Opportunities also exist as consultants.

### Job Outlook

Employment of industrial production managers is expected to decline slightly through the year 2005. Although manufacturing output is expected to rise significantly, the trend toward smaller management staffs and the lack of growth in production worker employment will limit demand for production managers. The widening use of computers for scheduling and planning is also making production managers more productive, allowing fewer of them to accomplish the same amount of work. Nevertheless, some openings will result from the need to replace workers who transfer to other occupations or leave the labor force. Many of these openings, however, may be filled through internal promotions.

Opportunities should be best for those with college degrees in industrial engineering or business administration, and those

with MBAs and undergraduate engineering degrees. Employers also are likely to seek candidates who have excellent communication skills, and who are personable, flexible, and eager to participate in ongoing training.

### Earnings

Salaries of industrial production managers vary significantly by industry and plant size. According to Abbott, Langer, and Associates, the average salary for all production managers was $63,000 in 1994. In addition to salary, industrial production managers usually receive bonuses based on job performance.

Benefits for industrial production managers tend to be similar to those offered many workers—vacation and sick leave, health and life insurance, and retirement plans.

### Related Occupations

Industrial production managers oversee production staff and equipment, insure that production goals and quality standards are being met, and implement company policies. Individuals with similar functions include materials, operations, purchasing, and traffic managers.

Other occupations requiring similar training and skills are sales engineer, manufacturers' sales representative, and industrial engineer.

### Related *D.O.T.* Jobs

These job titles are related to or more specific than the more general description above. They will help you identify job options you may not otherwise discover. These descriptions are in the current edition of the *Dictionary of Occupational Titles* and classified by numerical order.

180.167-054 SUPERINTENDENT; 181.117-010 MANAGER, BULK PLANT; 182.167-022 SUPERINTENDENT, CONCRETE-MIXING PLANT; 183.117-010 MANAGER, BRANCH; 183.117-014 PRODUCTION SUPERINTENDENT; 183.161-014 WINE MAKER; 183.167-010 BREWING DIRECTOR; 183.167-014 GENERAL SUPERINTENDENT, MILLING; 183.167-018 GENERAL SUPERVISOR; 183.167-022 GENERAL SUPERVISOR; 183.167-026 MANAGER, FOOD PROCESSING PLANT; 183.167-034 SUPERINTENDENT, CAR CONSTRUCTION; 183.167-038 SUPERINTENDENT, LOGGING; 188.167-094 SUPERINTENDENT, INDUSTRIES, CORRECTIONAL FACILITY; 189.117-042 DIRECTOR, QUALITY ASSURANCE; 189.167-042 SUPERINTENDENT, LABOR UTILIZATION; 189.167-046 SUPERINTENDENT, MAINTENANCE

### Sources of Additional Information

Information on industrial production management can be obtained from:

❑ National Management Association, 2210 Arbor Blvd., Dayton, OH 45439.

❑ American Management Association, 135 W. 50th St., New York, NY 10020.

## Inspectors and Compliance Officers, Except Construction

### Nature of the Work

Inspectors and compliance officers enforce a wide range of laws, regulations, policies, or procedures, and advise on standards that protect the public. They inspect and enforce rules on matters such as health, safety, food, immigration, licensing, interstate commerce, or international trade. Inspectors' duties vary widely, depending upon their employer.

*Agricultural chemicals inspectors* protect American agriculture by inspecting establishments where agricultural service products, such as livestock feed and remedies, fertilizers, and pesticides are manufactured, sold, or used. They may visit processing plants, distribution warehouses, sales outlets, agricultural service organizations, and farmers to collect product samples for analysis. They call on dealers to determine that licensing requirements have been met. They then prepare reports for supervisors and for use as evidence in legal actions.

*Agricultural commodity graders* apply quality standards to aid the buying and selling of commodities and to insure that retailers and consumers know the quality of the products they purchase. Although this grading is not required by law, buyers generally will not purchase ungraded commodities. Graders usually specialize in an area such as eggs and egg products, meat, poultry, processed or fresh fruits and vegetables, grain, tobacco, cotton, or dairy products. They examine product samples to determine quality and grade, and issue official grading certificates. Graders also may inspect the plant and equipment to maintain sanitation standards.

*Attendance officers* investigate continued absences of pupils from public schools.

*Aviation safety inspectors* ensure that Federal Aviation Administration (FAA) regulations which govern the quality and safety of aircraft equipment, aircraft operations, and personnel are maintained. Aviation safety inspectors may inspect aircraft and equipment manufacturing, maintenance and repair, or flight procedures. They may work in the areas of flight operations, maintenance, or avionics, and usually specialize in either commercial or general aviation aircraft. They also examine and certify aircraft pilots, pilot examiners, flight instructors, repair stations, schools, and instructional materials.

*Bank examiners* investigate financial institutions to enforce federal and state laws and regulations governing the institution's operations and solvency. Examiners schedule audits, determine actions to protect the institution's solvency and the interests of shareholders and depositors, and recommend acceptance or rejection of applications for mergers, acquisitions, establishment of a new institution, or acceptance in the Federal Reserve System.

*Consumer safety inspectors* inspect food, feeds and pesticides, weights and measures, biological products, cosmetics, drugs and medical equipment, as well as radiation emitting products. Some are proficient in several areas. Working individually or in teams under a senior inspector, they check on firms that produce, handle, store, or market the products they regulate. They ensure that standards are maintained and respond to consumer complaints by questioning employees, vendors, and others to obtain evidence. Inspectors look for inaccurate product labeling, and for decomposition or chemical or bacteriological contamination that could result in a product becoming harmful to health. They may use portable scales, cameras, ultraviolet lights, thermometers, chemical testing kits, radiation monitors, or other equipment to find violations. They may send product samples collected as part of

their examinations to laboratories for analysis.

After completing their inspection, inspectors discuss their observations with plant managers or officials and point out areas where corrective measures are needed. They write reports of their findings and, when necessary, compile evidence that may be used in court if legal action must be taken.

*Customs inspectors* enforce laws governing imports and exports. Stationed in the United States and overseas at airports, seaports, and border crossing points, they examine, count, weigh, gauge, measure, and sample commercial and noncommercial cargoes entering and leaving the United States to determine admissibility and the amount of duties that must be paid. They insure that all cargo is properly described on accompanying importers' declarations to determine the proper duty and interdict contraband. They inspect baggage and articles carried by passengers and crew members to insure that all merchandise is declared, proper duties are paid, and contraband is not present. They also ensure that people, ships, planes, and anything used to import or export cargo comply with all appropriate entrance and clearance requirements.

*Dealer compliance representatives* inspect franchised establishments to ascertain compliance with the franchiser's policies and procedures. They may suggest changes in financial and other operations.

*Environmental health inspectors,* or sanitarians, who work primarily for state and local governments, ensure that food, water, and air meet government standards. They check the cleanliness and safety of food and beverages produced in dairies and processing plants, or served in restaurants, hospitals, and other institutions. They often examine the handling, processing, and serving of food for compliance with sanitation rules and regulations and oversee the treatment and disposal of sewage, refuse, and garbage. In addition, inspectors may visit pollution sources and test for pollutants by collecting air, water, or waste samples for analysis. They try to determine the nature and cause of pollution and initiate action to stop it.

In large local and state health or agriculture departments, environmental health inspectors may specialize in milk and dairy products, food sanitation, waste control, air pollution, water pollution, institutional sanitation, or occupational health. In rural areas and small cities, they may be responsible for a wide range of environmental health activities.

*Equal opportunity representatives* ascertain and correct unfair employment practices through consultation with and mediation between employers and minority groups.

Federal and state laws require *food inspectors* to inspect meat, poultry, and their byproducts to ensure that they are safe for public consumption. Working on site, frequently as part of a team, they inspect meat and poultry slaughtering, processing, and packaging operations. They also check for correct product labeling and proper sanitation.

*Immigration inspectors* interview and examine people seeking to enter the United States and its territories. They inspect passports to determine whether people are legally eligible to enter and to verify their citizenship status and identity. Immigration inspectors also prepare reports, maintain records, and process applications and petitions for immigration or temporary residence in the United States.

*Logging operations inspectors* review contract logging operations. They prepare reports and issue remedial instructions for violations of contractual agreements and of fire and safety regulations.

*Mine safety and health inspectors* work to ensure the health and safety of miners. They visit mines and related facilities to obtain information on health and safety conditions and to enforce safety laws and regulations. They discuss their findings with the management of the mine and issue citations describing violations and hazards that must be corrected. Mine inspectors also investigate and report on mine accidents and may direct rescue and firefighting operations when fires or explosions occur.

*Motor vehicle inspectors* verify the compliance of automobiles and trucks with state requirements for safe operation and emissions. They inspect truck cargoes to assure compliance with legal limitations on gross weight and hazardous cargoes.

*Occupational safety and health inspectors* visit places of employment to detect unsafe machinery and equipment or unhealthy working conditions. They discuss their findings with the employer or plant manager and order that violations be promptly corrected in accordance with federal, state, or local government safety standards and regulations. They interview supervisors and employees in response to complaints or accidents, and may order suspension of activity posing threats to workers.

*Park rangers* enforce laws and regulations in state and national parks. Their duties range from registering vehicles and visitors, collecting fees, and providing information regarding park use and points of interest, to patrolling areas to prevent fire, participating in first aid and rescue activities, and training and supervising other park workers. Some rangers specialize in snow safety and avalanche control. With increasing numbers of visitors to our national parks, some rangers specialize as law enforcement officers.

*Postal inspectors* observe the functioning of the postal system and enforce laws and regulations. As law enforcement agents, postal inspectors have statutory powers of arrest and the authority to carry firearms. They investigate criminal activities such as theft and misuse of the mail. In instances of suspected mismanagement or fraud, inspectors conduct management or financial audits. They also collaborate with other government agencies, such as the Internal Revenue Service, as members of special task forces.

*Quality control inspectors and coordinators* inspect products manufactured or processed by private companies for government use to ensure compliance with contract specifications. They may specialize in specific products such as lumber, machinery, petroleum products, paper products, electronic equipment, or furniture. Others coordinate the activities of workers engaged in testing and evaluating pharmaceuticals in order to control quality of manufacture and ensure compliance with legal standards.

*Railroad inspectors* verify the compliance of railroad systems and equipment with federal safety regulations. They investigate accidents and review railroads' operating practices.

*Revenue officers* investigate and collect delinquent tax returns from individuals or businesses. They investigate leads from various sources. They attempt to resolve tax problems with taxpayers and recommend penalties, collection actions, and recommend criminal prosecutions when necessary.

*Securities compliance examiners* implement regulations concerning securities and real estate transactions. They investigate applications for registration of securities sales and complaints of irregular securities transactions, and recommend necessary legal action.

*Travel accommodations raters* inspect hotels, motels, restaurants, campgrounds, and vacation resorts. They evaluate travel and tourist accommodations for travel guide publishers and organizations such as tourism promoters and automobile clubs.

Other inspectors and compliance officers include coroners, customs import specialists, code inspectors, mortician investigators, and dealer-compliance representatives. Closely related work is done by construction and building inspectors.

## Working Conditions

Inspectors and compliance officers meet all kinds of people and work in a variety of environments. Their jobs often involve considerable field work, and some inspectors travel frequently. They are generally furnished with an automobile or are reimbursed for travel expenses.

Inspectors may experience unpleasant, stressful, and dangerous working conditions. For example, mine safety and health inspectors often are exposed to the same hazards as miners. Some food inspectors examine and inspect the livestock slaughtering process in slaughterhouses and frequently come in contact with unpleasant conditions. Customs inspectors have to put up with an irritated public when they search individuals, luggage, and cargo, in addition to the danger inherent to making an occasional arrest. Park rangers often work outdoors—in many cases, on rugged terrain—in very hot or bitterly cold weather for extended periods.

Many inspectors work long and often irregular hours. Even those inspectors not engaged in some form of law enforcement may find themselves in adversarial roles when the organization or individual being inspected objects.

## Employment

Inspectors and compliance officers held about 157,000 jobs in 1994. State governments employed 34 percent, the federal government—chiefly the Departments of Defense, Labor, Treasury, Agriculture, and Justice—employed 29 percent, and local governments employed 18 percent. The remaining 19 percent were employed in the U.S. Postal Service and throughout the private sector—primarily in education, hospitals, insurance companies, labor unions, and manufacturing firms.

Most consumer safety inspectors on the federal level work for the U.S. Food and Drug Administration, but the majority of these inspectors work for state governments. Most food inspectors and agricultural commodity graders are employed by the U.S. Department of Agriculture. Many health inspectors work for state and local governments. Compliance inspectors are employed primarily by the Treasury, Justice, and Labor departments on the federal level, as well as by state and local governments. The Department of Defense employs the most quality assurance inspectors. The Treasury Department employs internal revenue officers and customs inspectors. Aviation safety inspectors work for the Federal Aviation Administration. The Environmental Protection Agency employs inspectors to verify compliance with pollution control and other laws. The U.S. Department of Labor and many state governments employ occupational safety and health inspectors, equal-opportunity officers, and mine safety and health inspectors. Immigration inspectors are employed by the U.S. Department of Justice, while the U.S. Department of Interior employs park rangers. Immigration and customs inspectors work in the United States and overseas at airports, seaports, and border crossing points.

### Training, Other Qualifications, and Advancement

Because of the diversity of the functions they perform, qualifications for inspector and compliance officer jobs differ greatly. Requirements include a combination of education, experience, and often a passing grade on a written examination. Employers may require college training, including courses related to the job. The following examples illustrate the range of qualifications for various inspector jobs.

Postal inspectors must have a bachelor's degree and one year's work experience. It is desirable that they have one of several professional certifications, such as that of certified public accountant. They also must pass a background suitability investigation, and meet certain health requirements, undergo a drug screening test, possess a valid state driver's license, and be a U.S. citizen between 21 and 36 years of age when hired.

Aviation safety inspectors working in operations must be pilots with varying certificates, ratings, and numbers of flight hours to their credit. Maintenance and avionics inspectors must have considerable experience in aviation maintenance and knowledge of industry standards and relevant federal laws. In addition, FAA medical certificates are required. Some also are required to have an FAA flight instructor rating. Many aviation safety inspectors have had flight and maintenance training in the Armed Forces. No written examination is required.

Applicants for positions as mine safety and health inspectors generally must have experience in mine safety, management, or supervision. Some may possess a skill such as that of an electrician (for mine electrical inspectors). Applicants must meet strict medical requirements and be physically able to perform arduous duties efficiently. Many mine safety inspectors are former miners.

Applicants for internal revenue officer jobs must be a U.S. citizen and have a bachelor's degree or three years of experience in business, legal, or financial, or investigative practices.

Park rangers need at least two years of college with at least 12 credits in science and criminal justice, although some start as part-time, seasonal workers with the U.S. Forest Service. Most positions require a bachelor's degree.

Environmental health inspectors, called sanitarians in many states, sometimes must have a bachelor's degree in environmental health or in the physical or biological sciences. In most states, they are licensed by examining boards.

All inspectors and compliance officers are trained in the applicable laws or inspection procedures through some combination of classroom and on-the-job training. In general, people who want to enter this occupation should be able to accept responsibility and like detailed work. Inspectors and compliance officers should be neat and personable and able to express themselves well orally and in writing.

Federal government inspectors and compliance officers whose job performance is satisfactory advance through their career ladder to a specified full performance level. For positions above this level (usually supervisory positions), advancement is competitive, based on agency needs and individual merit. Advancement opportunities in state and local governments and the private sector are often similar to those in the federal government.

Some civil service specifications, including those for mine inspectors, aviation safety inspectors, and agricultural commodity graders, rate applicants solely on their experience and education. Others require a written examination.

### Job Outlook

Employment of inspectors and compliance officers is expected to grow about as fast as the average for all occupations through the year 2005, reflecting a balance of growing public demand for a safe environment and quality products against the desire for smaller government and fewer regulations. Modest employment growth, particularly in local government, should stem from the expansion of regulatory and compliance programs in solid and hazardous waste disposal and water pollution. In private industry, employment growth will reflect industry growth, due to continuing self-enforcement of government and company regulations and policies, particularly among franchise operations in various industries. Job openings will also arise from the need to replace those who transfer to other occupations, retire, or leave the labor force for other reasons.

Employment of inspectors and compliance officers is seldom affected by general economic fluctuations. Federal, state, and local governments—which employ most inspectors—provide workers with considerable job security. As a result, inspectors are less likely to lose their jobs than many other workers.

### Earnings

The median weekly salary of inspectors and compliance officers, except construction, was about $667 in 1994. The lowest 10 percent earned less than $388; the highest 10 percent earned over $1,130. In the federal government, the annual starting salaries for inspectors varied substantially in 1995—from $18,700 to $41,100—depending upon the nature of the inspection or compliance activity. Beginning salaries were slightly higher in selected areas where the prevailing local pay level was higher. The following tabulation presents 1995 average salaries for selected inspectors and compliance officers in the federal government in nonsupervisory, supervisory, and managerial positions.

| | |
|---|---|
| Aviation safety inspectors | $62,970 |
| Highway safety inspectors | 59,750 |
| Railroad safety inspectors | 52,790 |
| Equal opportunity compliance officials | 52,420 |
| Mine safety and health inspectors | 51,850 |
| Internal revenue agent | 50,720 |
| Environmental protection specialists | 49,170 |
| Import specialists | 47,550 |

| Alcohol, tobacco, and firearms inspectors | 47,050 |
|---|---|
| Safety and occupational health managers | 46,730 |
| Quality assurance inspectors | 43,970 |
| Customs inspectors | 39,050 |
| Agricultural commodity graders | 36,040 |
| Immigration inspectors | 35,540 |
| Securities compliance examiners | 35,400 |
| Consumer safety inspectors | 31,700 |
| Food inspectors | 31,280 |
| Environmental protection assistants | 26,630 |

Most inspectors and compliance officers work for federal, state, and local governments and in large private firms, all of which generally offer more generous benefits than do smaller firms.

### Related Occupations

Inspectors and compliance officers are responsible for seeing that laws and regulations are obeyed. Construction and building inspectors, fire marshals, federal, state, and local law enforcement professionals, corrections officers, and fish and game wardens also enforce laws and regulations.

### Related *D.O.T.* Jobs

These job titles are related to or more specific than the more general description above. They will help you identify job options you may not otherwise discover. These descriptions are in the current edition of the *Dictionary of Occupational Titles* and classified by numerical order.

There are too many *D.O.T.* titles to list here. Most are variations related to a specific industry, and we have included a small number of representative *D.O.T.* titles as examples. Complete lists are available in various career software published by JIST or directly from the U.S. Department of Labor.

079.117-018 SANITARIAN; 079.161-010 INDUSTRIAL HYGIENIST; 168.161-010 CORONER; 168.167-018 HEALTH OFFICER, FIELD; 168.167-022 IMMIGRATION INSPECTOR; 168.261-010 RADIATION-PROTECTION SPECIALIST; 168.264-014 SAFETY INSPECTOR; 168.267-022 CUSTOMS INSPECTOR; 168.267-042 FOOD AND DRUG INSPECTOR; 168.267-054 INSPECTOR, INDUSTRIAL WASTE; 168.267-086 HAZARDOUS-WASTE MANAGEMENT SPECIALIST; 168.267-098 PESTICIDE-CONTROL INSPECTOR; 168.267-110 SANITATION INSPECTOR; 168.267-114 EQUAL OPPORTUNITY OFFICER; 169.167-042 PARK RANGER; 187.117-050 PUBLIC HEALTH SERVICE OFFICER; 188.167-074 REVENUE OFFICER; 188.167-090 SPECIAL AGENT, CUSTOMS

### Sources of Additional Information

Information on federal government jobs is available from offices of the state employment service, area offices of the U.S. Office of Personnel Management, and Federal Job Information Centers in large cities throughout the country. For information on a career as a specific type of federal inspector or compliance officer, a federal department or agency that employs them may also be contacted directly.

Information about state and local government jobs is available from state civil service commissions, usually located in each state capital, or from local government offices.

Information about jobs in private industry is available from the State Employment Service, which is listed under "Job Service" or "Employment" in the state government section of local telephone directories.

# Inspectors, Testers, and Graders

### Nature of the Work

Inspectors, testers, and graders ensure that your food won't make you sick, your car will run when you buy it, and your pants won't split the first time you wear them. These workers monitor quality standards for virtually all manufactured products, including foods, textiles, clothing, glassware, motor vehicles, electronic components, computers, and structural steel.

Inspectors visually check products and may also listen to, feel, smell, or even taste them. They verify dimensions, color, weight, texture, strength, or other physical characteristics of objects, and look for imperfections such as cuts, scratches, bubbles, missing pieces, misweaves, or crooked seams. Many inspectors use micrometers, electronic equipment, calipers, alignment gauges, and other instruments to check and compare the dimensions of parts against the parts' specifications. Those testing electrical devices may use voltmeters, ammeters, and oscilloscopes to test the insulation, current flow, and resistance. Machinery testers generally check that parts fit and move correctly and are properly lubricated, check the pressure of gases and the level of liquids, test the flow of electricity, and do a test run to check for proper operation. Some jobs involve only a quick visual inspection; others require a much longer detailed one. Senior inspectors may also set up tests and test equipment.

Inspectors, testers, and graders are involved at every stage of the production process. Some inspectors examine materials received from a supplier before sending them to the production line. Others inspect components, subassemblies, and assemblies or perform a final check on the finished product.

Inspectors mark, tag, or note problems. They may reject defective items outright, send them for rework, or, in the case of minor problems, fix them themselves. If the product checks out, they may screw on a nameplate, tag it, stamp a serial number, or certify it in some other way. Inspectors, testers, and graders record the results of their inspections, compute the percentage of defects and other statistical parameters, prepare inspection and test reports, notify supervisors of problems, and help analyze and correct problems in the production process. They also calibrate precision instruments used in inspection work.

The recent emphasis on quality control in manufacturing has meant that inspection is becoming more fully integrated into the production process. Many machines are now self-monitoring to ensure that the product is produced within quality standards. Inspectors still test products to ensure that they meet specifications, but, with the help of these machines, they direct the production line to adjust the machinery before the manufacturing line produces unusable parts. Also, many firms have automated inspection with the help of advanced vision systems, using machinery installed at one or several points in the production process. The inspectors in these firms generally are trained to operate this equipment.

## Working Conditions

Working conditions vary from industry to industry. Some inspectors examine similar products for an entire shift; others examine a variety of items. Most remain at one work station, but some travel from place to place to do inspections. Some are on their feet all day; others sit. In some industries, inspectors are exposed to the noise and grime of machinery; in others, they work in a clean, quiet environment. Some may have to lift heavy objects.

Some inspectors work evenings, nights, or weekends. In these cases, shift assignments generally are made on the basis of seniority. Overtime may be required to meet production goals.

## Employment

Inspectors, testers, and graders held about 654,000 jobs in 1994. More than three out of four worked in manufacturing industries, including industrial machinery and equipment, motor vehicles and equipment, primary and fabricated metals industries, electronic components and accessories, textiles, apparel, and aircraft and parts. Others worked in temporary help services, communications and utilities, wholesale trade, engineering and management services, and government agencies. Although they are employed throughout the country, most jobs are in large metropolitan areas where many large factories are located.

## Training, Other Qualifications, and Advancement

A high school diploma is helpful and may be required for some jobs. Simple jobs are generally filled by beginners with a few days of training. More complex ones are filled by experienced assemblers, machine operators, or mechanics who already have a thorough knowledge of the products and production processes. Inspectors, testers, and graders also need mechanical aptitude, good hand-eye coordination, and good vision.

In-house training for new inspectors may cover the use of special meters, gauges, computers, or other instruments; quality control techniques; blueprint reading; and reporting requirements. There are some postsecondary training programs in testing, but many employers prefer to train inspectors themselves.

Advancement for these workers frequently takes the form of higher pay. However, they also may advance to inspector of more complex products, supervisor, or quality control technician.

## Job Outlook

Individuals wishing to become inspectors, testers, or graders may face competition. Although the occupation is large, giving rise to a large number of openings due to normal turnover, some jobs may be available only to those having experience with the production process. Also, like many other occupations concentrated in manufacturing, employment of these workers is projected to decline through the year 2005.

Even though the volume of manufactured goods will grow, employment of inspectors, testers, and graders will not grow for several reasons. Manufacturers are taking steps to improve production methods by using computers and statistical analysis to control the production process. In some cases, machines alert workers when items approach limits so that problems can be corrected before defects occur. This growing emphasis on quality will drive down the number of defective parts and help to reduce the demand for inspectors. In addition, assemblers, machine op-

erators, and other production workers are becoming responsible for quality control in many firms, and they are correcting problems as they occur. As these responsibilities shift from inspectors to other workers, fewer inspectors, testers, and graders will be needed. Moreover, automated inspecting machinery is improving inspectors' speed and accuracy, resulting in higher productivity and adversely affecting employment of these workers.

In many industries, however, automation is not being aggressively pursued as an alternative to manual inspection. When key inspection elements are size oriented, such as length, width, or thickness, automation may play some role in the future. But when taste, smell, texture, appearance, or product performance are important, inspection will probably continue to be done by humans.

## Earnings

Inspectors, testers, and graders had median weekly earnings of about $430 in 1994. The middle 50 percent earned between $310 and $590 a week. The lowest 10 percent earned less than $240 a week; the highest 10 percent earned more than $780. In addition to these earnings, most inspectors, testers, and graders receive benefits including health and life insurance, pension plans, paid vacations, and sick leave.

## Related Occupations

Other workers who inspect products or services are construction and building inspectors and inspectors and compliance officers, except construction, which includes consumer safety, environmental health, agricultural commodity, immigration, customs, postal, motor vehicle, safety, and other inspectors.

## Related *D.O.T.* Jobs

These job titles are related to or more specific than the more general description above. They will help you identify job options you may not otherwise discover. These descriptions are in the current edition of the *Dictionary of Occupational Titles* and classified by numerical order.

There are too many *D.O.T.* titles to list here. Most are variations related to a specific industry, and we have included a small number of representative *D.O.T.* titles as examples. Complete lists are available in various career software published by JIST or directly from the U.S. Department of Labor.

194.387-010 QUALITY-CONTROL INSPECTOR; 194.387-014 RECORD TESTER; 369.687-014 CHECKER; 379.364-010 AUTOMOBILE TESTER; 529.367-030 YIELD-LOSS INSPECTOR; 529.487-010 SPECIAL TESTER; 529.684-014 INGREDIENT SCALER; 529.685-274 X-RAY INSPECTOR; 529.687-098 GRADER; 529.687-174 SALVAGE INSPECTOR; 529.687-226 INSPECTOR, PROCESSING; 539.367-014 WATER-QUALITY TESTER; 550.587-014 SAMPLE COLLECTOR; 953.367-014 GAS-METER CHECKER; 589.387-010 INSPECTOR AND SORTER; 601.281-022 INSPECTOR, TOOL; 706.387-014 MACHINE TESTER; 726.381-010 ELECTRONICS INSPECTOR; 729.281-038 RELAY TESTER; 736.381-018 PROCESS INSPECTOR; 739.687-082 EXAMINER; 806.367-018 QUALITY ASSURANCE MONITOR; 976.267-010 QUALITY-CONTROL TECHNICIAN

## Sources of Additional Information

For general information about this occupation, contact:

❏ The National Tooling and Machining Association, 9300 Livingston Rd., Fort Washington, MD 20744.

❑ The American Society for Quality Control, 611 East Wisconsin Ave., Milwaukee, WI 53202-4606.

# Insulation Workers

## Nature of the Work

Properly insulated buildings reduce energy consumption by keeping heat in during the winter and out in the summer. Refrigerated storage rooms, vats, tanks, vessels, boilers, and steam and hot water pipes also are insulated to prevent the wasteful transfer of heat. Insulation workers install this insulating material.

Insulation workers cement, staple, wire, tape, or spray insulation. When covering a steam pipe, for example, insulation workers measure and cut sections of insulation to the proper length, stretch it open along a cut that runs the length of the material, and slip it over the pipe. They fasten the insulation with adhesive, staples, tape, or wire bands. Sometimes they wrap a cover of aluminum, plastic, or canvas over it and cement or band the cover in place. Sometimes insulation workers screw on sheet metal around insulated pipes to protect the insulation from weather conditions or physical abuse.

When covering a wall or other flat surface, workers may use a hose to spray foam insulation onto a wire mesh. The wire mesh provides a rough surface to which the foam can cling and adds strength to the finished surface. Workers may then install drywall or apply a final coat of plaster for a finished appearance.

In attics or exterior walls of uninsulated buildings, workers blow in loose-fill insulation. A helper feeds a machine with shredded fiberglass, cellulose, or rock wool insulation while another worker blows the insulation from the compressor hose into the space being filled.

In new construction or major renovations, insulation workers staple fiberglass or rockwool batts to exterior walls and ceilings before drywall, paneling, or plaster walls are put in place. In major renovations of old buildings or when putting new insulation around pipes and industrial machinery, insulation workers often must first remove the old insulation. In the past, asbestos—now known to cause cancer in humans—was used extensively in walls and ceilings and for covering pipes, boilers, and various industrial equipment. Because of this danger, U.S. Environmental Protection Agency regulations require that asbestos be removed before a building undergoes major renovations or is demolished. When removing asbestos, insulation workers must follow carefully prescribed asbestos removal techniques and work practices. First they seal and depressurize the area that contains the asbestos, then they remove it using hand tools and special filtered vacuum cleaners and air-filtration devices.

Insulation workers use common handtools—trowels, brushes, knives, scissors, saws, pliers, and stapling guns. They use power saws to cut insulating materials, welding machines to join sheet metal or secure clamps, and compressors for blowing or spraying insulation.

## Working Conditions

Insulation workers generally work indoors. They spend most of the workday on their feet, either standing, bending, or kneeling. Sometimes they work from ladders or in tight spaces. However, the work is not strenuous; it requires more coordination than strength. Insulation work is often dusty and dirty. The minute particles from insulation materials, especially when blown, can irritate the eyes, skin, and respiratory system. Removing cancer-causing asbestos insulation is a hazardous task and is done by specially trained workers. To protect themselves from the dangers of asbestos and irritants, workers follow strict safety guidelines, wear protective suits, masks, and respirators, take decontamination showers, and keep work areas well ventilated.

## Employment

Insulation workers held about 64,0000 jobs in 1994; most worked for insulation or other construction contractors. Others worked for the federal government, in wholesale and retail trade, in shipbuilding, and in other manufacturing industries that have extensive installations for power, heating, and cooling. Most worked in urban areas. In less populated areas, insulation work may be done by carpenters, heating and air-conditioning installers, or drywall installers.

## Training, Other Qualifications, and Advancement

Most insulation workers learn their trade informally on the job, although some workers complete formal apprenticeship programs. For entry jobs, insulation contractors prefer high school graduates who are in good physical condition and are licensed to drive. High school courses in blueprint reading, shop math, sheetmetal layout, and general construction provide a helpful background. Applicants seeking apprenticeship positions must have a high school diploma or its equivalent, and be at least 18 years old.

Trainees are assigned to experienced insulation workers for instruction and supervision. They begin with simple tasks, such as carrying insulation or holding material while it is fastened in place. On-the-job training can take up to two years, depending on the work. Learning to install insulation in homes generally requires less training than insulation application in commercial and industrial settings. As they gain experience, trainees receive less supervision, more responsibility, and higher pay.

In contrast, trainees in formal apprenticeship programs receive in-depth instruction in all phases of insulation. Apprenticeship programs may be provided by a joint committee of local insulation contractors and the local union of the International Association of Heat and Frost Insulators and Asbestos Workers, to which many insulation workers belong. Programs normally consist of four years of on-the-job training coupled with classroom instruction, and trainees must pass practical and written tests to demonstrate a knowledge of the trade.

Insulation workers who work with asbestos usually have to be licensed. Although licensure requirements vary from area to area, most states require asbestos removal workers to complete a three-day training program in compliance with the 1986 Asbestos Hazard Emergency Act (AHERA). The National Asbestos Council (NAC) provides this training in more than 100 locations. This program emphasizes "hands-on" training. Typically, students build a decontamination unit, handle a respirator and filtered vacuum cleaners, and perform simulated asbestos removal. In addition, they receive classroom instruction on a wide variety of topics, such as government regulations, health effects and worker protection, sampling for asbestos, and work practices. NAC also offers a two-day course on compliance with Occupational Safety and Health Administration (OSHA) regulations governing industrial asbestos removal in plants and factories, and an annual AHERA recertification program.

Skilled insulation workers may advance to supervisor, shop superintendent, insulation contract estimator, or set up their own insulation or asbestos abatement business.

### Job Outlook

Employment of insulation workers is expected to increase about as fast as the average for all occupations through the year 2005, reflecting the demand for insulation associated with new construction and renovation as well as the demand for asbestos removal in existing structures. Concerns about the efficient use of energy to heat and cool buildings will result in growth in demand for insulation workers in the construction of new residential, industrial, and commercial buildings. In addition, renovation and efforts to improve insulation in existing structures also will increase demand.

Asbestos removal also will provide many jobs for insulation workers, not only because insulation workers often remove asbestos, but because they replace it with another insulating material. The 1986 Asbestos Hazard Emergency Act requires that all public and private schools have an asbestos management plan. Federal regulations also require that asbestos be removed from buildings that are to be demolished or undergo major renovations. In addition, many banks require that buildings be free of asbestos before a real estate loan will be granted. All these regulatory requirements are expected to stimulate asbestos removal and employment growth. The need to maintain, remove, and replace asbestos insulation on old pipes, boilers, and a variety of equipment in chemical and refrigeration plants and petroleum refineries will also add to employment requirements.

Despite this growth in demand, replacement needs will account for most job openings. This occupation has the highest turnover of all the construction trades. Each year thousands of jobs will become available as insulation workers transfer to other occupations or leave the labor force. Since there are no strict training requirements for entry, many people with limited skills work as insulation workers for a short time and then move on to other types of work, creating many job openings.

Insulation workers in the construction industry may experience periods of unemployment because of the short duration of many construction projects and the cyclical nature of construction activity. Workers employed in industrial plants generally have more stable employment because maintenance and repair must be done on a continuing basis. Unlike other construction occupations, insulation workers usually do not lose work time when weather conditions are poor. Most insulation is applied after buildings are enclosed.

### Earnings

Median weekly earnings for insulation workers who worked full-time were $485 in 1994. The middle 50 percent earned between $337 and $653. The lowest 10 percent earned less than $276, and the top 10 percent earned more than $819.

According to the *Engineering News Record*, union insulation workers received an average hourly wage of $30.20 in 1994,

including benefits. Wages ranged from a low of $20.38 an hour in New Orleans to a high of $46.67 in New York City. Insulation workers doing commercial and industrial work earn substantially more than those working in residential construction, which does not require as much skill.

### Related Occupations

Insulation workers combine a knowledge of insulation materials with the skills of cutting, fitting, and installing materials. Workers in occupations involving similar skills include carpenters, carpet installers, drywall applicators, floor layers, roofers, and sheetmetal workers.

### Related *D.O.T.* Jobs

These job titles are related to or more specific than the more general description above. They will help you identify job options you may not otherwise discover. These descriptions are in the current edition of the *Dictionary of Occupational Titles* and classified by numerical order.

863.364-010 INSULATION-WORKER APPRENTICE; 863.364-014 INSULATION WORKER; 863.381-010 CORK INSULATOR, REFRIGERATION PLANT; 863.381-014 PIPE COVERER AND INSULATOR; 863.664-010 BLOWER INSULATOR; 863.685-010 INSULATION-POWER-UNIT TENDER

### Sources of Additional Information

For information about training programs or other work opportunities in this trade, contact a local insulation contractor; a local of the International Association of Heat and Frost Insulators and Asbestos Workers; the nearest office of the state employment service or state apprenticeship agency, or:

❏ National Insulation and Abatement Contractors Association, 99 Canal Center Plaza, Suite 222, Alexandria, VA 22314.

❏ Insulation Contractors Association of America, 1321 Duke St., Suite 303, Alexandria, VA 22314.

# Janitors and Cleaners and Cleaning Supervisors

### Nature of the Work

Janitors and cleaners—also called building custodians, executive housekeepers, or maids—keep office buildings, hospitals, stores, apartment houses, hotels, and other types of buildings clean and in good condition. Some only do cleaning; others have a wide range of duties. They may fix leaky faucets, empty trash cans, do painting and carpentry, replenish bathroom supplies, mow lawns, and see that heating and air-conditioning equipment works properly. On a typical day, janitors may wet- or dry-mop floors, clean bathrooms, vacuum carpets, dust furniture, make minor repairs, and exterminate insects and rodents. In hospitals, where they are mostly known as maids or housekeepers, they may also wash bed frames, brush mattresses, make beds, and disinfect and sterilize equipment and supplies using germicides and sterilizing equipment. In hotels, aside from cleaning and maintaining the premises, they may deliver ironing boards, cribs, and rollaway beds to guests' rooms.

Janitors and cleaners use various equipment, tools, and cleaning materials. For one job, they may need a mop and bucket; for another, an electric polishing machine and a special cleaning solution. Improved building materials, chemical cleaners, and power equipment have made many tasks easier and less time consuming, but janitors must learn proper use of equipment and cleaners to avoid harming floors, fixtures, and themselves.

Cleaning supervisors coordinate, schedule, and supervise the activities of janitors and cleaners. They assign tasks and inspect building areas to see that work has been done properly; issue supplies and equipment; inventory stocks to ensure adequate supplies; screen and hire job applicants; and recommend promotions, transfers or dismissals. They also train new and experienced employees. Supervisors may prepare reports concerning room occupancy, hours worked, and department expenses. Some also perform cleaning duties.

## Working Conditions

Because most office buildings are cleaned while they are empty, many cleaners work evening hours. Some, however, such as school and hospital custodians, work in the daytime. When there is a need full-time janitors and cleaners and supervisors worked about 40 hours for 24-hour maintenance, janitors may be assigned to shifts. Most a week. Part-time cleaners usually work in the evenings and on weekends.

Janitors and cleaners usually work inside heated, well-lit buildings. However, sometimes they work outdoors sweeping walkways, mowing lawns, or shoveling snow. Working with machines can be noisy, and some tasks, such as cleaning bathrooms and trash rooms, can be dirty and unpleasant. Janitors may suffer cuts, bruises, and burns from machines, handtools, and chemicals. They spend most of their time on their feet, sometimes lifting or pushing heavy furniture or equipment. Many tasks, such as dusting or sweeping, require constant bending, stooping, and stretching. As a result, janitors may also suffer back injuries and sprains.

## Employment

Janitors and cleaners, including cleaning supervisors, held 3,168,000 jobs in 1994. More than one-third worked part-time (less than 35 hours a week).

Janitors and cleaners held about 19 jobs out of 20. They worked in every type of establishment. One in five worked for a firm supplying building maintenance services on a contract basis. About one in six worked in a school, including colleges and universities. One in eight worked in a hotel. Others were employed by hospitals, restaurants, operators of apartment buildings, office buildings, and other types of real estate, churches and other religious organizations, manufacturing firms, and government agencies.

Supervisors held about 1 job in 20. About 30 percent each were in hotels and hospitals. Others were employed by firms supplying building maintenance services on a contract basis, nursing care facilities, and educational facilities.

Although cleaning jobs can be found in all cities and towns, most are located in highly populated areas where there are many office buildings, schools, apartment houses, and hospitals.

## Training, Other Qualifications, and Advancement

No special education is required for most cleaning jobs, but beginners should know simple arithmetic and be able to follow instructions. High school shop courses are helpful for jobs that involve repair work.

Most janitors and cleaners learn their skills on the job. Usually, beginners work with an experienced cleaner, doing routine cleaning. They are given more complicated work as they gain experience.

In some cities, programs run by unions, government agencies, or employers teach janitorial skills. Students learn how to clean buildings thoroughly and efficiently, how to select and safely use various cleansing agents, and how to operate and maintain machines, such as wet and dry vacuums, buffers, and polishers. Students learn to plan their work, to follow safety and health regulations, to interact positively with people in the buildings they clean, and to work without supervision. Instruction in minor electrical, plumbing, and other repairs may also be given. Those who come in contact with the public should have good communication skills. Employers usually look for dependable, hard-working individuals who are in good health, follow directions well, and get along with other people.

Janitors and cleaners usually find work by answering newspaper advertisements, applying directly to organizations where they would like to work, contacting local labor unions, or contacting state employment service offices.

Advancement opportunities for janitorial workers usually are limited in organizations where they are the only maintenance worker. Where there is a large maintenance staff, however, janitors can be promoted to supervisor and to area supervisor or manager. A high school diploma improves the chances for advancement. Some janitors set up their own maintenance business.

Supervisors usually move up through the ranks. In many establishments, they are required to take some in-service training to perfect housekeeping techniques and procedures, and to enhance supervisory skills.

## Job Outlook

The occupation of janitors and cleaners is easy to enter because there are few requirements for formal education and training, turnover is high, and part-time and temporary jobs are plentiful. The need to replace workers who transfer to other occupations or leave the labor force will create most job openings.

Employment of building janitors and cleaners and cleaning supervisors is expected to grow about as fast as the average for all occupations through the year 2005 as the number of office buildings, apartment houses, schools, factories, hospitals, and other buildings increases. Businesses providing janitorial and cleaning services on a contract basis are expected to be one of the fastest growing employers of janitors and cleaners and cleaning supervisors as firms try to reduce costs by hiring independent contractors.

New technology is expected to have little effect on employment of janitors and cleaners. Robots now under development are limited to performing a single cleaning task and may not be usable in many places, particularly cluttered areas such as hotel and hospital rooms.

## Earnings

Janitors and cleaners who usually worked full-time averaged about $293 a week in 1994; the middle 50 percent earned between $219 and $401. Ten percent earned less than $178; 10 percent earned more than $527. Maids and housekeepers who usually worked full-time averaged about $246 a week in 1994, with the middle 50 percent earning between $198 and $312. Ten percent earned less than $162 and 10 percent earned more than $407.

Cleaning supervisors who usually worked full-time averaged about $361 a week in 1994; the middle 50 percent earned between $281 and $501. Ten percent earned less than $210 and 10 percent earned more than $686.

According to a survey of workplaces in 160 metropolitan areas, janitors had median earnings of $270 for a 40-hour week in 1993. The middle half earned between $206 and $374 a week.

Most building service workers receive paid holidays and vacations and health insurance.

## Related Occupations

Private household workers have job duties similar to janitors and cleaners. Workers who specialize in one of the many job functions of janitors and cleaners include refuse collectors, floor waxers, street sweepers, window cleaners, gardeners, boiler tenders, pest controllers, and general maintenance repairers.

## Related *D.O.T.* Jobs

These job titles are related to or more specific than the more general description above. They will help you identify job options you may not otherwise discover. These descriptions are in the current edition of the *Dictionary of Occupational Titles* and classified by numerical order.

321.137-010 HOUSEKEEPER; 321.137-014 INSPECTOR; 323.137-010 SUPERVISOR, HOUSECLEANER; 323.687-018 HOUSECLEANER; 350.137-026 STEWARD/STEWARDESS, THIRD; 358.687-010 CHANGE-HOUSE ATTENDANT; 381.137-010 SUPERVISOR, JANITORIAL SERVICES; 381.687-014 CLEANER, COMMERCIAL OR INSTITUTIONAL; 381.687-018 CLEANER, INDUSTRIAL; 381.687-022 CLEANER, LABORATORY EQUIPMENT; 381.687-026 CLEANER, WALL; 381.687-030 PATCH WORKER; 381.687-034 WAXER, FLOOR; 382.664-010 JANITOR; 389.667-010 SEXTON; 389.683-010 SWEEPER-CLEANER, INDUSTRIAL; 389.687-014 CLEANER, WINDOW; 739.687-198 VENETIAN-BLIND CLEANER AND REPAIRER; 891.687-010 CHIMNEY SWEEP; 891.687-018 PROJECT-CREW WORKER; 952.687-010 HYDROELECTRIC-PLANT MAINTAINER

## Sources of Additional Information

Information about janitorial jobs may be obtained from a local state employment service office.

For information about education and training or starting a janitorial company, contact:

❑ Building Service Contractors Association International, 10201 Lee Hwy., Suite 225, Fairfax, VA 22030.

For information about careers in executive housekeeping, contact:

❑ National Executive Housekeepers Association, Inc., 1001 Eastwind Dr., Suite 301, Westerville, OH 43081-3361.

# Jewelers

## Nature of the Work

Jewelers make, repair, and adjust rings, necklaces, bracelets, earrings, and other jewelry. Using drills, pliers, jeweler's soldering torches, saws, jeweler's lathes, and a variety of other handtools, they mold and shape metal and set gemstones. Jewelers also may use chemicals and polishing compounds, such as flux for soldering and tripoli and rouge for finishing.

Jewelers usually specialize in one or more areas of the jewelry field—buying, design, gem cutting, repair, sales, or appraisal. In small retail or repair shops, they may be involved in all aspects of the work. Regardless of the type of establishment or work setting, however, their work requires a high degree of skill and attention to detail. Those working in retail jewelry stores, in addition to their primary responsibility to sell jewelry, may spend some time repairing or adjusting it. In other cases, retailers send jewelry to specialized jewelry repair shops. Typical work includes enlarging or reducing rings, resetting stones, and replacing broken clasps and mountings. Some jewelers also design or make their own jewelry. Following their own designs or those created by designers or customers, they begin by shaping the metal or by carving wax to make a model for casting the metal. The individual parts are then soldered together, and the jeweler may mount a diamond or other gem or may engrave a design into the metal.

Jewelers who own or manage stores or shops hire and train employees; order, market, and sell merchandise; and perform other managerial duties. In manufacturing, jewelers usually specialize in a single operation. Some may make models or tools for the jewelry that is to be produced. Others do finishing work, such as setting stones, polishing, or engraving. A growing number of jewelers use lasers for cutting and improving the quality of stones.

Technology has not yet greatly affected the jewelry industry. However, some manufacturing firms use CAD/CAM (computer-aided design and manufacturing) to facilitate product design and automate some steps in mold and model making. Use of such systems should increase in the future as they become more affordable for smaller companies. In retail stores, computers are used mainly for inventory control; some jewelers use computers to design and create customized pieces according to their customers' wishes. With the aid of computers, customers visualize different combinations of styles, cuts, shanks, sizes, and stones to create their own pieces.

## Working Conditions

Jewelers usually do most of their work seated in comfortable surroundings, and the trade involves few physical hazards. While the work is not physically strenuous, there is a lot of work with detail and intricate designs which may be tiring to some. Caution must be taken because the chemicals, sawing and drilling tools, and torches a jeweler uses can cause serious injury. In addition, doing delicate work on precious stones or metals while trying to satisfy demands for speed and quality from customers and employers can cause stress, and bending over a workbench for long periods can be uncomfortable. In the future, the use of computers may ease some of these conditions since applications like CAD/CAM greatly increase the speed and accuracy of the design and manufacturing process.

Because many of the materials with which they work are very valuable, those working in retail stores must observe strict security procedures. These may include locked doors that are only opened by a buzzer, barred windows, burglar alarms, and the presence of armed guards.

In repair shops, jewelers generally work alone with little supervision. In retail stores, on the other hand, they may talk with customers about repairs, perform custom design work, and even do some sales work.

## Employment

Jewelers held about 30,000 jobs in 1994. About 35 percent of all jewelers were self-employed; many operated their own store or repair shop, and some specialized in designing and creating custom jewelry.

Nearly 55 percent of all salaried jewelers worked in retail establishments, while another 30 percent were employed in manufacturing plants. Although jewelry stores and repair shops can be found in every city and many small towns, most job opportunities are in larger metropolitan areas. Many jewelers employed in manufacturing work in New York, California, or Rhode Island.

## Training, Other Qualifications, and Advancement

Jewelers' skills usually are learned in technical schools, through correspondence courses, or informally on the job. Some aspiring jewelers begin working as clerks in department stores and transfer to jobs in jewelry shops or manufacturing firms after gaining experience. Colleges and art schools also offer programs which can lead to a bachelor's or master's degree of fine arts in jewelry design. Formal training in the basic skills of the trade enhances one's employment and advancement opportunities. Many employers prefer well-rounded jewelers with design, repair, and sales skills.

For those interested in working in a jewelry store or repair shop, technical schools or courses offered by local colleges are the best sources of training. In these programs, which vary in length from six months to two years, students learn the use and care of jewelers' tools and machines and basic jewelry making and repairing skills, such as design, casting, stone setting, and polishing. Technical school courses also cover topics like blueprint reading, math, and shop theory. Most employers feel that graduates need several more years of supervised on-the-job training to refine their repair skills and to learn more about the operation of the store or shop. In addition, some employers encourage workers to improve their skills by enrolling in short-term technical school courses such as sample making, wax carving, or gemology. Many employers pay all or part of the cost of this additional training.

The Gemological Institute of America offers programs lasting about six months, and self-paced correspondence courses lasting several years, leading to a gemologist diploma and a jeweler diploma. These advanced programs cover a wide range of topics including appraisal, evaluating diamonds and colored stones, identifying gems, and designing jewelry.

In jewelry manufacturing plants, workers traditionally have developed their skills through apprenticeships and informal on-the-job training. This training may last three to four years, depending on the difficulty of the specialty. Training usually focuses on casting, stone setting, model making, or engraving. In recent years, a growing number of technical schools and colleges have begun to offer training designed for jewelers working in manufacturing. Like employers in retail trade, those in manufacturing prefer graduates of these programs because they are familiar with the production process, allowing less in-house training.

To enter most technical school or college programs, a high school diploma or its equivalent is required. Courses in art, math, mechanical drawing, and chemistry are useful. Since computer-aided design is increasingly used in the jewelry field, it is recommended that students—especially those interested in design and manufacturing—obtain training in CAD.

The precise and delicate nature of jewelry work requires finger and hand dexterity, good hand-eye coordination, patience, and concentration. Artistic ability and fashion consciousness are major assets, because jewelry must be stylish and attractive. Those who work in jewelry stores have frequent contact with customers and should be neat, personable, and knowledgeable about the merchandise. In addition, employers require someone of good character because jewelers work with very valuable materials.

Advancement opportunities are limited and greatly dependent on an individual's skill and initiative. In manufacturing, some jewelers advance to supervisory jobs, such as master jeweler or head jeweler, but for most, advancement takes the form of higher pay for doing the same job. Jewelers who work in jewelry stores or repair shops may become salaried managers; some open their own businesses.

For those interested in starting their own business, a substantial financial investment is needed to acquire the necessary inventory. Also, because the jewelry business is highly competitive, jewelers who plan to open their own store should have experience in selling, as well as knowledge of marketing and business management. Courses in these areas often are available from technical schools and community colleges.

## Job Outlook

Employment of jewelers is expected to increase more slowly than the average for all occupations through the year 2005. Traditionally, job opportunities for jewelers depended largely on jewelry sales and on demand for jewelry repair services. Now, however, non-traditional jewelry marketers such as discount stores, mail-order catalogue companies, and television shopping networks have limited the growth of sales made by traditional jewelers, limiting job opportunities because these types of establishments require few if any jewelers.

Because the demand for jewelry is largely affected by the amount of disposable income people have, the increasing number of affluent individuals, working women, double-income households, and fashion conscious men are expected to keep jewelry sales strong.

Jewelers have a relatively strong attachment to their occupations—reflecting the large proportion of self-employed workers. Nevertheless, job openings will largely result from the need to replace jewelers who transfer to other occupations, retire, or leave the labor force for other reasons.

Opportunities in jewelry stores and repair shops will be best for graduates from jeweler or gemologist training programs. Demand for repair workers will be strong because maintaining and repairing jewelry is an ongoing process, even during economic slowdowns. In fact, demand for jewelry repair may increase during recessions as people repair or restore existing pieces rather than purchase new ones.

Increasing automation within jewelry manufacturing will adversely affect employment of low-skilled occupations, like assembler and polisher. Automation will have a lesser impact on more creative, highly skilled positions, such as mold and model maker. Because of recent international trade agreements, exports are steadily increasing as manufacturers become more competitive in foreign markets.

## Earnings

Median weekly earning of jewelers in all industries were $400 in 1994. Depending on the employer, jewelers may receive commissions on what they sell or bonuses for outstanding work. According to the *Jewelers' Circular-Keystone* annual salary survey, the median salary of jewelers in retail stores was approximately $25,700 in 1993, while the median annual salary of jewelry repair workers was $26,200.

For those in manufacturing, earnings of experienced, unionized jewelry workers averaged between $12 and $17 an hour in 1994, according to the limited information available. According to the Manufacturing Jewelers and Silversmiths of America, the median average hourly wage of jewelers in companies with more than 10 employees was $11.64 in 1994. Beginners in jewelry factories generally start at considerably less than experienced workers; as they become more proficient, they receive periodic raises.

Most jewelers enjoy a variety of fringe benefits including reimbursement from their employers for work-related courses and discounts on jewelry purchases.

## Related Occupations

Other skilled workers who do similar jobs include polishers, dental laboratory technicians, gem cutters, hand engravers, and watch makers and repairers.

## Related *D.O.T.* Jobs

These job titles are related to or more specific than the more general description above. They will help you identify job options you may not otherwise discover. These descriptions are in the current edition of the *Dictionary of Occupational Titles* and classified by numerical order.

199.281-010 GEMOLOGIST; 700.281-010 JEWELER; 700.281-014 JEWELER APPRENTICE; 700.281-022 SILVERSMITH II; 700.381-030 LOCKET MAKER; 700.381-042 RING MAKER; 700.381-046 SAMPLE MAKER I

## Sources of Additional Information

Information on job opportunities and training programs for jewelers is available from:

❑ Gemological Institute of America, 1660 Stewart St., Santa Monica, CA 90404.

General career information is available from:

❑ Jewelers of America, 1185 Avenue of the Americas, New York, NY 10036.

❑ Manufacturing Jewelers and Silversmiths of America, 1 State St., 6th Floor, Providence, RI 02908-5035.

To receive a list of technical schools accredited by the Accrediting Commission of Career Schools and Colleges of Technology that have programs in jewelry design, contact:

❑ Accrediting Commission of Career Schools and Colleges of Technology, 2101 Wilson Blvd., Suite 302, Arlington, VA 22201.

# Library Technicians

## Nature of the Work

Library technicians help librarians acquire, prepare, and organize material, and assist users in finding materials and information. Technicians in small libraries handle a wide range of duties; those in large libraries usually specialize.

Depending on the employer, library technicians may have other titles, such as library technical assistants. Library technicians assist in the use of public catalogues, direct library users to standard references, organize and maintain periodicals, prepare volumes for binding, handle interlibrary loan requests, prepare invoices, perform routine cataloguing and coding of library materials, retrieve information from computer databases, and supervise other support staff.

The widespread use of computerized information storage and retrieval systems has resulted in technicians handling more technical and user services, such as entering catalogue information into the library's computer, that were once performed by librarians. Technicians may assist with customizing databases. In addition, technicians may instruct patrons how to use computer systems to access data. The increased use of automation has cut down on the amount of clerical work performed by library technicians. Many libraries now offer self-service registration and circulation with computers, decreasing the time that library technicians spend manually recording and inputting records.

Some library technicians operate and maintain audiovisual equipment, such as projectors, tape recorders, and videocassette recorders, and assist library users with microfilm or microfiche readers. They may also design posters, bulletin boards, or displays.

Those in school libraries teach students to use the library and media center and encourage them to do so. They also help teachers obtain instructional materials and assist students with special assignments. Some work in special libraries maintained by government agencies, corporations, law firms, advertising agencies, museums, professional societies, medical centers, and research laboratories, where they conduct literature searches, compile bibliographies, and prepare abstracts, usually on subjects of particular interest to the organization.

## Working Conditions

Technicians who work with users answer questions and provide assistance. Those who prepare library materials sit at desks or computer terminals for long periods and may develop headaches or eyestrain from working with video display terminals. Some duties like calculating circulation statistics can be repetitive and boring. Others, such as performing computer searches using local and regional library networks and cooperatives, can be interesting and challenging.

Library technicians in school libraries work regular school hours. Those in public libraries and college and university (academic) libraries may work weekends, evenings and some holidays. Library technicians in special libraries usually work normal business hours, although they are often called upon to work overtime.

Library technicians usually work under the supervision of a professional librarian, although they may work independently in certain situations.

## Employment

Library technicians held about 75,000 jobs in 1994. Most worked in school, academic, or public libraries. Some worked in hospitals and religious organizations. The federal government, primarily the Department of Defense and the Library of Congress, and state and local governments also employed library technicians.

## Training, Other Qualifications, and Advancement

Training requirements for library technicians vary widely, ranging from a high school diploma to specialized postsecondary training. Some libraries require that technicians have a bachelor's degree. Some employers hire individuals with work experience or other training; others train inexperienced workers on the job. Given the widespread use of automation in libraries, computer skills are needed for many jobs. Knowledge of databases, library automation systems, on-line library systems, on-line public access systems, and circulation systems is valuable.

Some two-year colleges offer an associate of arts degree in library technology. Programs include both liberal arts and library-related study. Students learn about library and media organization and operation and how to order, process, catalogue, locate, and circulate library materials, and work with library automation. Libraries and associations offer continuing education courses to keep technicians abreast of new developments in the field.

Library technicians usually advance by assuming added responsibilities. For example, technicians may start at the circulation desk, checking books in and out. After gaining experience, they may be responsible for storing and verifying information. As they advance, they may become involved in budget and personnel matters in their department. Some library technicians advance to supervisory positions and are in charge of the day-to-day operation of their department.

## Job Outlook

Employment of library technicians is expected to grow about as fast as the average for all occupations through the year 2005. Additional job openings will result from the need to replace library technicians who transfer to other fields or leave the labor force. Willingness to relocate enhances an aspiring library technician's job prospects.

The increasing use of library automation may spur job growth among library technicians. Computerized information systems have simplified certain tasks, such as descriptive cataloguing, which can now be handled by technicians instead of librarians. For instance, technicians can now easily retrieve information from a central database and store it in the library's own computer. Although budgetary constraints may dampen employment growth of library technicians in school, public, and college and university libraries, libraries may use technicians to perform some librarian duties in order to stretch shrinking budgets. Growth in the number of professional and other workers who use special libraries should result in relatively fast employment growth among library technicians in special libraries.

## Earnings

Salaries for library technicians vary widely, depending on the type of library and geographic location. Salaries of library technicians in the federal government averaged $25,100 in 1995.

## Related Occupations

Library technicians perform organizational and administrative duties. Workers in other occupations with similar duties include library clerks, information clerks, record clerks, medical record technicians, and title searchers. Library technicians also assist librarians. Other workers who assist professional workers include museum technicians, teacher aides, legal assistants, and engineering and science technicians.

## Related *D.O.T.* Jobs

These job titles are related to or more specific than the more general description above. They will help you identify job options you may not otherwise discover. These descriptions are in the current edition of the *Dictionary of Occupational Titles* and classified by numerical order.

100.367-018 LIBRARY TECHNICAL ASSISTANT

## Sources of Additional Information

Information about a career as a library technician and a directory of schools offering training programs in this field can be obtained from:

❑ Council on Library/Media Technology, P.O. Box 951, Oxon Hill, MD 20750.

For information on training programs for library/media technical assistants, write to:

❑ American Library Association, Office for Library Personnel Resources, 50 East Huron St., Chicago, IL 60611.

Information on schools receiving federal financial assistance for library training is available from:

❑ Office of Educational Research and Improvement, Library Programs, Library Development Staff, U.S. Department of Education, 555 New Jersey Ave. NW, Washington, DC 20208-5571.

Those interested in a position as a library technician in the federal service should write to:

❑ Office of Personnel Management, 1900 E St. NW, Washington, DC 20415.

Information concerning requirements and application procedures for positions in the Library of Congress may be obtained directly from:

❑ Personnel Office, Library of Congress, Washington, DC 20540.

State library agencies can furnish information on requirements for technicians, and general information about career prospects in the state. Several of these agencies maintain job hotlines which report openings for library technicians.

State departments of education can furnish information on requirements and job opportunities for school library technicians.

# Licensed Practical Nurses

## Nature of the Work

Licensed practical nurses (L.P.N.s), or licensed vocational nurses (L.V.N.s) as they are called in Texas and California, care for the sick, injured, convalescing, and handicapped, under the direction of physicians and registered nurses.

Most L.P.N.s provide basic bedside care. They take vital signs such as temperature, blood pressure, pulse, and respiration. They also treat bedsores, prepare and give injections and enemas, apply dressings, give alcohol rubs and massages, apply ice packs and hot water bottles, and insert catheters. L.P.N.s observe patients and report adverse reactions to medications or treatments. They may collect samples from patients for testing and perform routine laboratory tests. They help patients with bathing, dressing, and personal hygiene, feed them and record food and liquid intake and output, keep them comfortable, and care for their emotional needs. In states where the law allows, they may administer prescribed medicines or start intravenous fluids. Some L.P.N.s help deliver, care for, and feed infants. Some experienced L.P.N.s supervise nursing assistants and aides.

L.P.N.s in nursing homes, in addition to providing routine bedside care, may also help evaluate residents' needs, develop care plans, and supervise nursing aides. In doctors' offices and clinics, including health maintenance organizations, they may also make appointments, keep records, and perform other clerical duties. L.P.N.s who work in private homes may also prepare meals and teach family members simple nursing tasks.

## Working Conditions

Most licensed practical nurses in hospitals and nursing homes work a 40-hour week, but because patients need round-the-clock care, some work nights, weekends, and holidays. They often stand for long periods and help patients move in bed, stand, or walk. They also face the stress of working with sick patients and their families.

L.P.N.s may face hazards from caustic chemicals, radiation, and infectious diseases such as AIDS and hepatitis. L.P.N.s also are subject to back injuries when moving patients and shock from electrical equipment. They often face heavy workloads. In addition, the people they take care of may be confused, irrational, agitated, or uncooperative.

## Employment

Licensed practical nurses held about 702,000 jobs in 1994. About a quarter worked part-time. Two out of five L.P.N.s worked in hospitals, about one-quarter worked in nursing homes, and over a tenth in doctors' offices and clinics. Others worked for temporary help agencies, home health care services, or government agencies.

## Training, Other Qualifications, and Advancement

All states require L.P.N.s to pass a licensing examination after completing a state-approved practical nursing program. A high school diploma is usually required for entry, but some programs accept people without a diploma.

In 1993, approximately 1,098 state-approved programs provided practical nursing training. Almost 6 out of 10 students were enrolled in technical or vocational schools, while 3 out of 10 were in community and junior colleges. Others were in high schools, hospitals, and colleges and universities.

Most practical nursing programs last about one year and include both classroom study and supervised clinical practice (patient care). Classroom study covers basic nursing concepts and patient-care related subjects, including anatomy, physiology, medical-surgical nursing, pediatrics, obstetrics, psychiatric nursing, administration of drugs, nutrition, and first aid. Clinical practice is usually in a hospital, but sometimes includes other settings.

L.P.N.s should have a caring, sympathetic nature. They should be emotionally stable because work with the sick and injured can be stressful. As part of a health care team, they must be able to follow orders and work under close supervision.

## Job Outlook

Job prospects for L.P.N.s are expected to be good if the current balance between jobs and job seekers continues. Over the past few years, the number of graduates from L.P.N. training programs has increased in pace with the need for additional workers. However, if enrollments in L.P.N. training programs level off or decline as they have on a cyclical basis in the past, job prospects will be even better.

Employment of L.P.N.s is expected to increase faster than the average for all occupations through the year 2005 in response to the long-term care needs of a rapidly growing population of very old people and to the general growth of health care. As in most other occupations, replacement needs will be the main source of job openings.

Employment in nursing homes is expected to grow much faster than the average. Nursing homes will offer the most new jobs for L.P.N.s as the number of aged and disabled persons in need of long-term care rises rapidly. In addition to caring for the aged, nursing homes will be called on to care for the increasing number of patients who have been released from the hospital and have not yet recovered enough to return home.

Much faster than average growth is also expected in home health care services. This is in response to a growing number of older persons with functional disabilities, consumer preference for care in the home, and technological advances which make it possible to bring increasingly complex treatments into the home.

An increasing proportion of sophisticated procedures, which once were performed only in hospitals, are being performed in physicians' offices and clinics, including health maintenance organizations, ambulatory surgicenters, and emergency medical centers—thanks largely to advances in technology. As a result, employment is projected to grow much faster than average in these places as health care in general expands.

Employment of L.P.N.s in hospitals is expected to show only a small increase, largely because the number of inpatients, with whom most work, is not expected to increase much.

## Earnings

Median weekly earnings of full-time salaried L.P.N.s were $450 in 1994. The middle 50 percent earned between $383 and $537. The lowest 10 percent earned less than $316; the top 10 percent, more than $636.

According to a University of Texas Medical Branch survey of hospitals and medical centers, the median annual salary of L.P.N.s, based on a 40-hour week and excluding shift or area differentials, was $23,394 in October 1994. The average minimum salary was $19,122 and the average maximum was $28,234.

According to the Buck Survey conducted by the American Health Care Association, staff L.P.N.s in chain nursing homes had median annual earnings of about $23,900 in 1994. The middle 50 percent earned between $21,500 and $27,100.

## Related Occupations

L.P.N.s work closely with people while helping them. So do emergency medical technicians, social service aides, human service workers, and teacher aides.

## Related *D.O.T.* Jobs

These job titles are related to or more specific than the more general description above. They will help you identify job options you may not otherwise discover. These descriptions are in the current edition of the *Dictionary of Occupational Titles* and classified by numerical order.

079.374-014 NURSE, LICENSED PRACTICAL

## Sources of Additional Information

A list of state-approved training programs and information about practical nursing are available from:

- ❑ Communications Department, National League for Nursing, 350 Hudson St., New York, NY 10014.
- ❑ National Association for Practical Nurse Education and Service, Inc., 1400 Spring St., Suite 310, Silver Spring, MD 20910.

For information on nursing careers in long-term care, write to:

- ❑ American Health Care Association, 1201 L St. NW, Washington, DC 20005.

# Line Installers and Cable Splicers

## Nature of the Work

Vast networks of wires and cables transmit the electric power produced in generating plants to individual customers, connect telephone central offices to customers' telephones and switchboards, and extend cable television to residential and commercial customers. These networks are constructed and maintained by line installers and cable splicers and their helpers.

To install new electric power or telephone lines, line installers or line erectors install poles and terminals, erect towers, and place wires and cables. They usually use power equipment to dig holes and set poles. Line installers climb the poles or use truck-mounted buckets (aerial work platforms) and use handtools

to attach the cables. When working with electric power lines, installers bolt or clamp insulators onto the pole before attaching the cable. They may also install transformers, circuit breakers, switches, or other equipment. To bury underground cable, they use trenchers, plows, and other power equipment.

Line installers also lay cable television lines underground or hang them on poles with telephone and utility wires. These lines transmit broadcast signals from microwave towers to customers' homes. Installers place wiring in the house, connect the customers' television sets to it, and check that the television signal is strong.

After telephone line installers place cables in position, cable splicers, also referred to as cable splicing technicians, complete the line connections. (Electric power line workers install and splice the cables simultaneously.) Splicers connect individual wires or fibers within the cable and rearrange wires when lines have to be changed. They first read and interpret service orders and circuit diagrams to determine splicing specifications. Splices are then made by joining wires and cables with small handtools, epoxy, or mechanical equipment. At each splice, they place insulation over the conductor, and seal the splice with some type of moisture proof covering. They may fill the cable sheathing on critical transmission routes with compressed air so that leaks in the sheathing can be monitored and repaired. Splicers work on poles, aerial ladders and platforms, in manholes, or in basements of large buildings.

Fiber optic cables are being used to replace worn or obsolete copper cables. These tiny hair-thin strands of glass are able to carry more signals per cable because they transmit pulses of light instead of electricity. Splices of fiber optic cables are completed in a van positioned near the splice point. These vans house workshops that contain all the necessary equipment, such as machines that heat the glass fibers so they can be joined.

Line installers and cable splicers also maintain and repair telephone, power, and cable television lines. They periodically make sure lines are clear of tree limbs or other obstructions that could cause problems and check insulation on cables and other equipment on line poles. When bad weather or earth quakes break wires or cables, knock poles down, or cause underground ducts to collapse, they make emergency repairs.

## Working Conditions

Because telephone, electric, and television cables are strung from utility poles or are underground, line installers and cable splicers must climb and lift or work in stooped and cramped positions. They usually work outdoors in all kinds of weather and are subject to 24-hour call. Most usually work a 40-hour week, but, for example, when severe weather damages transmission and distribution lines, they may work long and irregular hours to restore service. At times, they may travel to distant locations—and occasionally stay for a lengthy period to help restore damaged facilities or build new ones.

Line installers and cable splicers face many situations in which safety procedures must be followed. They wear safety equipment when entering manholes and test for the presence of gas before going underground. They may be exposed to hazardous chemicals from the solvents and plugging compounds that they use when splicing cables.

Electric power line workers have the most hazardous jobs. They typically work at higher elevations because the electric cable is always above telephone and cable television lines. Moreover, the voltages in electric power lines are lethal.

## Employment

Line installers and cable splicers held about 302,000 jobs in 1994. More than half were telephone and cable television line installers and repairers. Nearly all worked for telephone, cable television companies, or electric power companies, or for construction companies specializing in power line, telephone, and cable television construction.

## Training, Other Qualifications, and Advancement

Line installers are often hired as helpers or ground workers. Most employers prefer high school graduates. Many employers test applicants for basic verbal, arithmetic, and abstract reasoning skills. Some employers test for physical ability such as balance, coordination, and strength and mechanical aptitude. Because the work entails a lot of climbing, applicants should have stamina and must be unafraid of heights. Knowledge of basic electricity and training in installing telephone systems obtained in the Armed Forces or vocational education programs may be helpful. The ability to distinguish colors is necessary because wires and cables usually are coded by color. Motivation, self-discipline, and the ability to work as part of a team are needed to work efficiently and safely.

Line installers and cable splicers in electric companies and construction firms specializing in cable installation generally complete a formal apprenticeship program. These are administered jointly by the employer and the union representing the workers, either the International Brotherhood of Electrical Workers or the Communications Workers of America. These programs last several years and combine formal instruction with on-the-job training. Workers in telephone companies generally receive several years of informal on-the-job training, in some cases learning other skills like telephone installation and repair. They may also attend training provided by equipment manufacturers.

A growing number of employers are using computer-assisted instruction, video cassettes, movies, or "programmed" workbooks. Some training facilities are equipped with poles, cable-supporting clamps, and other fixtures, to simulate working conditions as closely as possible. Trainees learn to work on poles while keeping their hands free. In one exercise, for example, they play catch with a basketball while on the poles.

Formal training includes instruction in electrical codes, blueprint reading, and basic electrical theory. Afterwards trainees learn on the job and work with a crew of experienced line installers under a line supervisor. Line installers and cable splicers receive training throughout their careers to qualify for more difficult assignments and to keep up with technological changes.

Since deregulation of the telephone industry, many telephone companies have reduced the scope of their training programs in order to reduce their costs and to remain competitive. Increasingly, workers are responsible for their own training, which is provided by community colleges and postsecondary vocational schools.

For installers in the telephone industry, advancement may come about through promotion to splicer. Splicers can advance to engineering assistants or may move into other kinds of work, such as sales. Promotion to a supervisory position also is possible. In the electric industry, promotion is usually to a supervisory position.

## Job Outlook

Job seekers are expected to face competition. Because prerequisite skills and training are minimal, and earnings are above average, applicants outnumber available job openings. Employment growth is not expected to provide many opportunities; most will result from the need to replace the larger than average number of older workers reaching retirement age. Job prospects will be best for electrical line workers employed by electric utilities and construction firms because the effects of new technology are expected to be less than for telephone line workers. In telephone companies, those who combine knowledge of line installation, fiber optic or copper cable splicing, and repair of many types of equipment should enjoy better prospects.

Overall employment of line installers and cable splicers is expected to show little or no growth through the year 2005. Technological advances will result in divergent trends within this occupation. Employment of electrical power line installers is expected to grow more slowly than the average for all occupations as the demand for electricity grows and the need to maintain existing lines continues. Employment of telephone and cable television line installers and repairers, however, is expected to decline despite growth in telephone and cable television usage. Layoffs of telephone line workers have already occurred, due to increased efficiency being built into telephone systems. New ways of transmitting information—satellites, microwave towers, and underground fiber optic cable, for example—are not as vulnerable to adverse weather conditions as aerial wires, and fewer workers are needed to maintain them. Fiber optic cables will continue to replace copper cables, and this will generate short-term demand for installers. Also, some will be needed to install the infrastructure for the new telecommunications system. Telephone, cable, and even utility companies are converting more of their networks to fiber optics which makes it possible to carry voice, data, and video signals over the same lines to a wide range of customers. Over the longer term, however, employment will fall as the conversion to fiber optics is completed and as maintenance requirements are reduced. Improved splicing techniques as well as new power tools and equipment also will continue to improve the efficiency of cable splicers. Finally, most areas of the country that can economically be served by cable television have already been wired, and fewer installers will be needed.

## Earnings

Pay rates for line installers and cable splicers vary greatly across the country and depend on length of service; specific information may be obtained from local telephone, electric power, and cable television companies. It generally takes about five years to go from the bottom to the top of the pay scale. In 1994, line installers and repairers who worked full-time earned a median weekly wage of $712. The middle 50 percent earned between $501 and $887. The bottom 10 percent earned less than $337; the top 10 percent earned more than $1,089 a week.

Line installers and cable splicers employed by AT&T and the Bell Operating Companies and represented by the Communications Workers of America and the International Brotherhood of Electrical Workers earned between $469 and $1,063 a week in 1994. Because of low job turnover in these occupations, many workers earn salaries near the top of the pay scale.

Most line installers and cable splicers belong to unions, principally the Communications Workers of America and the International Brotherhood of Electrical Workers. For these workers, union contracts set wage rates, wage increases, and the time needed to advance from one step to the next. These contracts require extra pay for overtime and for all work on Sundays and holidays. Most contracts provide for additional pay for night work. Time in service determines the length of paid vacations. Depending on the locality, there are 9 to 12 holidays a year.

### Related Occupations

Workers in other skilled crafts and trades who work with tools and machines include communications equipment mechanics, biomedical equipment technicians, telephone installers and repairers, electricians, and sound technicians.

### Related *D.O.T.* Jobs

These job titles are related to or more specific than the more general description above. They will help you identify job options you may not otherwise discover. These descriptions are in the current edition of the *Dictionary of Occupational Titles* and classified by numerical order.

821.261-010 CABLE TELEVISION LINE TECHNICIAN; 821.261-014 LINE MAINTAINER; 821.261-022 SERVICE RESTORER, EMERGENCY; 821.261-026 TROUBLE SHOOTER II; 821.281-010 CABLE TELEVISION INSTALLER; 821.361-010 CABLE INSTALLER-REPAIRER; 821.361-018 LINE ERECTOR; 821.361-022 LINE INSTALLER, STREET RAILWAY; 821.361-026 LINE REPAIRER; 821.361-030 LINE-ERECTOR APPRENTICE; 821.361-038 TOWER ERECTOR; 821.684-022 TROLLEY-WIRE INSTALLER; 821.687-010 STEEL-POST INSTALLER; 822.381-014 LINE INSTALLER-REPAIRER; 823.261-014 RADIO INTERFERENCE INVESTIGATOR; 829.361-010 CABLE SPLICER; 829.361-014 CABLE-SPLICER APPRENTICE; 959.367-010 ELECTRIC POWER LINE EXAMINER

### Sources of Additional Information

For more details about employment opportunities, contact the telephone or electric power company in your community or local offices of the unions that represent these workers. For general information on line installer and cable splicer jobs, write to:

❏ Communications Workers of America, 501 3rd St. NW, Washington, DC 20001.

For additional information on the telephone industry and career opportunities contact:

❏ United States Telephone Association, 1401 H St. NW, Suite 600, Washington, DC 20005-2136.

For information on employment and training contact:

❏ Utility Workers Union of America, 815 16th. St. NW, Washington, DC 20006.

❏ International Brotherhood of Electrical Workers, 1125 15th. St. NW, Room 807, Washington, DC 20005.

# Machinists and Tool Programmers

### Nature of the Work

Machinists use machine tools such as lathes, drill presses, and milling machines to produce precision metal parts. Although they may produce large quantities of one part, machinists usually produce small batches or one-of-a-kind items. They use their knowledge of the working properties of metals—such as steel, cast iron, aluminum, and brass—and their skill with machine tools to plan and carry out the operations needed to make machined products that meet precise specifications.

Machinists first review blueprints or written specifications for a job. Next, they calculate where to cut or bore into the work piece, how fast to feed the metal into the machine, and how much metal to remove. They then select tools and materials for the job, plan the sequence of cutting and finishing operations, and mark the metal stock to show where these cuts should be made.

After this layout work is completed, machinists perform the necessary machining operations. They position the metal stock on the machine tool—drill presses, lathes, milling machines, or others—set the controls, and make the cuts. Today, new machinery allows various functions to be performed with one set-up, which reduces the need for additional, labor-intensive set-ups, saving time and money. During the machining process, they must constantly monitor the feed and speed of the machine. Machinists must also ensure that the work piece is being properly lubricated and cooled because the machining of metal products generates a significant amount of heat.

Some machinists, often called production machinists, may produce large quantities of one part, especially parts requiring complex operations and great precision. For unusually sophisticated procedures, expensive machinery is used. Usually, however, large numbers of parts requiring more routine operations are produced by metalworking machine operators. Other machinists do maintenance work—repairing or making new parts for existing machinery. For example, to repair a broken part, maintenance machinists may refer to blueprints and perform the same machining operations that were needed to create the original part.

Increasingly, the machine tools used to produce metal parts are numerically controlled (NC)—that is, they contain an electronic controller that directs the machine's operations. Most NC machines today are computer numerically controlled (CNC), which means that the controllers are computers. The controller "reads" a program—a coded list of the steps necessary to perform a specific machining job—and runs the machine tool's mechanisms through the steps.

The introduction of computer numerically controlled machines has greatly changed the nature of the work and productivity of machinists. These machines enable machinists to be more productive and to produce parts with a level of precision that is not possible with traditional machining techniques. Furthermore, because precise movements are recorded in the program, they allow this high level of precision to be consistently repeated.

The quality of the products these machines produce depends largely on the programs, which may be produced by machinists or by tool programmers—workers who specialize in programming machine tools. Tool programmers begin as machinists do—

by analyzing blueprints, computing the size and position of the cuts, determining the sequence of machine operations, selecting tools, and calculating the machine speed and feed rates. They then write the program in the language of the machine's controller and store it. Skilled machinists may also do programming. In fact, as computer software becomes more user friendly and CNC machines are used more widely, machinists are expected to perform this function more and more.

Machinists may work alone or with tool programmers to check new programs to ensure that machinery will function properly and the output will meet specifications. Because a problem with the program could damage the costly machinery and cutting tools, computer simulations may be used instead of a trial run to check the program. If errors are found, the program must be changed and retested until the problem is resolved. Some programs are modified for use on other jobs with similar specifications, thereby reducing the time and effort needed to start production of a part. A growing number of firms employ computer-aided design (CAD) systems to assist in writing programs.

## Working Conditions

Most machine shops are well lighted and ventilated. Nevertheless, working around high-speed machine tools presents certain dangers, and workers must follow safety precautions. Machinists must wear protective equipment such as safety glasses to shield against bits of flying metal and earplugs to protect against machinery noise. They must also exercise caution when handling hazardous coolants and lubricants. The job requires stamina because machinists stand most of the day and may lift moderately heavy work pieces.

Some tool programmers work in offices that are near, but separate from, the shop floor. These work areas are usually clean, well lighted, and free of machine noise.

Most machinists and tool programmers work a 40-hour week. Evening and weekend shifts are becoming more common as companies invest in more expensive machinery. Overtime is common during peak production periods.

## Employment

Machinists and tool programmers held about 376,000 jobs in 1994. Most machinists worked in small machining shops or in manufacturing firms that produce durable goods such as metal-working and industrial machinery, aircraft, or motor vehicles. Maintenance machinists work in most industries that use production machinery. Although machinists and tool programmers work in all parts of the country, jobs are most plentiful in areas where manufacturing is concentrated.

## Training, Other Qualifications, and Advancement

A high school or vocational school education, including mathematics, blueprint reading, metalworking, and drafting, is desirable for becoming a machinist or tool programmer. A basic knowledge of computers and electronics is helpful because of the increased use of computer-controlled machine tools. Experience with machine tools also is helpful. In fact, many of the people who enter these occupations have previously worked as machine tool operators or setters.

Machinist training varies from formal apprenticeship and postsecondary programs to informal on-the-job training. Apprentice programs consist of shop training and related classroom instruction. In shop training, apprentices learn filing, handtapping, and dowel fitting, as well as the operation of various machine tools. Classroom instruction includes math, physics, blueprint reading, mechanical drawing, and shop practices. In addition, as machine shops have increased their use of computer-controlled equipment, training in the operation and programming of numerically controlled machine tools has become essential. A growing number of machinists and tool programmers receive most of their formal training from community colleges.

Qualifications for tool programmers vary widely depending upon the complexity of the job. Basic requirements parallel those of machinists. Employers often prefer skilled machinists, tool and die makers, or those with technical school training. For some specialized types of programming, such as with complex parts for the aerospace or shipbuilding industries, employers may prefer individuals with a degree in engineering.

For those entering tool programming directly, a basic knowledge of computers and electronics is necessary and experience with machine tools is extremely helpful. Classroom training includes an introduction to numerical control and the basics of programming and then advances to more complex topics such as computer-aided design. Trainees start writing simple programs under the direction of an experienced programmer. Although machinery manufacturers are trying to standardize programming languages, currently there are numerous languages in use. Because of this, tool programmers must be able to learn and adapt to new programming languages.

Established workers may also take courses to update their skills and to learn the latest technology and equipment. Some employers offer tuition reimbursement for job-related courses. In addition, when new machinery is introduced, workers receive training in its operation—usually from a representative of the equipment manufacturer.

Persons interested in becoming a machinist or tool programmer should be mechanically inclined. They also should be able to work independently and do highly accurate work that requires concentration as well as physical effort.

Workers may advance in several ways. Experienced machinists may become tool programmers; some move into supervisory or administrative positions in their firms; and a few may open their own shops.

## Job Outlook

Employment of machinists and tool programmers is expected to decline slightly through the year 2005. Nevertheless, job opportunities will be good, as employers continue to report difficulties in attracting workers to machining and tool programming occupations. Therefore, candidates with the necessary mechanical and mathematical aptitudes should encounter ample demand for their skills. Many job openings also will arise each year from the need to replace experienced machinists and programmers who transfer to other occupations or retire. The number of openings for machinists is expected to be far greater than the number of openings for tool programmers, primarily because the occupation is larger.

Automation is the major factor in the employment decline projected for machinists and tool programmers. The use of computer-controlled machine tools, for example, reduces the time required for machining operations and increases worker productivity. This allows fewer machinists to accomplish the same amount of work previously performed by more workers. Advanced machine tool technology is allowing some programming to be performed on the shop floor by machinists, tool and die makers, and machine operators. These simplified controls are one of the main factors behind the slight employment decline expected for tool programmers in the coming years.

Employment levels in these occupations is influenced by economic cycles; as the demand for machined goods falls, machinists and tool programmers involved in production may be laid off or be forced to work fewer hours. Employment of machinists involved in plant maintenance, however, is often more stable because proper maintenance and repair of costly equipment remain vital concerns even when production levels fall.

### Earnings

Earnings of machinists compare favorably with those of other skilled workers. In 1994, median weekly earnings for machinists were about $520. Most earned between $400 and $690. The lowest paid ten percent of all machinists had median weekly earnings of less than $300; the 10 percent with the highest earnings made more than $880 a week. In addition to their hourly wage, most workers receive typical benefits such as health and life insurance, a pension plan, paid vacations, and sick leave.

### Related Occupations

Occupations most closely related to that of machinist and tool programmer are the other machining occupations. These include tool and die maker, tool and die designer, tool planner, and instrument maker. Workers in other occupations that require precision and skill in working with metal include blacksmiths, gunsmiths, locksmiths, metal patternmakers, and welders.

Tool programmers apply their knowledge of machining operations, metals, blueprints, and machine programming to write programs that run machine tools. Computer programmers also write detailed instructions for a machine—in this case a computer.

### Related *D.O.T.* Jobs

These job titles are related to or more specific than the more general description above. They will help you identify job options you may not otherwise discover. These descriptions are in the current edition of the *Dictionary of Occupational Titles* and classified by numerical order.

007.167-018 TOOL PROGRAMMER, NUMERICAL CONTROL; 600.260-022 MACHINIST, EXPERIMENTAL; 600.280-022 MACHINIST; 600.280-026 MACHINIST APPRENTICE; 600.280-030 MACHINIST APPRENTICE, AUTOMOTIVE; 600.280-034 MACHINIST, AUTOMOTIVE; 600.280-042 MAINTENANCE MACHINIST; 600.281-010 FLUID-POWER MECHANIC; 600.380-010 FIXTURE MAKER; 609.262-010 TOOL PROGRAMMER, NUMERICAL CONTROL; 714.281-018 MACHINIST, MOTION-PICTURE EQUIPMENT

### Sources of Additional Information

For general information about this occupation, contact:

❑ The Association for Manufacturing Technology, 7901 Westpark Dr., McLean, VA 22102.

❑ The National Tooling and Machining Association, 9300 Livingston Rd., Fort Washington, MD 20744.

❑ The Tooling and Manufacturing Association, ATTN: Education Department, 1177 South Dee Rd., Park Ridge, IL 60068.

❑ Precision Metalforming Association, 27027 Chardon Rd., Richmond Heights, OH 44143.

# Material Moving Equipment Operators

### Nature of the Work

Material moving equipment operators use machinery to move construction materials, manufactured goods, earth, logs, petroleum products, grain, coal, and other heavy materials. Generally they move materials over short distances—around a construction site, factory, warehouse, or on or off trucks and ships. Operators control equipment by moving levers or foot pedals, operating switches, or turning dials. They may also set up and inspect equipment and make adjustments and minor repairs.

Material moving equipment operators usually are classified by the type of machines they operate. Those who operate bulldozers, cranes, loaders, and similar equipment are often called *construction equipment operators* even though they work in the mining, logging, utilities, and other industries as well as the construction industry. Others operate industrial trucks and tractors and similar equipment in manufacturing plants and warehouses. Some operate many kinds of equipment; others only one.

*Crane and tower operators* lift and move materials, machinery, or other heavy objects using mechanical or hydraulic booms and tower and cable equipment. Although some cranes are used on construction sites, most are used in manufacturing and other industries.

*Excavation and loading machine operators* run and tend machinery equipped with scoops, shovels, or buckets to excavate earth at construction sites and to load and move loose materials, mainly in the construction and mining industries.

*Grader, dozer, and scraper operators* remove, distribute, level, and grade earth with vehicles equipped with blades. In addition to the familiar bulldozers, they operate trench excavators, road graders, and similar equipment. Although many work in the construction industry, grader, dozer, and scraper operators also work for state and local governments, mainly in maintenance and repair work.

*Hoist and winch operators* lift and pull loads by using power-operated equipment. Most work in loading operations in construction, manufacturing, logging, transportation and public utilities, and mining.

*Operating engineers* are qualified to operate more than one type of the construction equipment discussed above. Although the term operating engineer often is applied to many construction equipment operators, many work for state and local governments.

*Industrial truck and tractor operators* drive and control industrial trucks or tractors. A typical industrial truck, often called a forklift or lift truck, has a hydraulic lifting mechanism and forks. Industrial truck operators use these to carry loads on a skid or pallet around a factory or warehouse. Industrial tractor operators pull trailers loaded with materials, goods, or equipment within factories and warehouses, or around outdoor storage areas.

Other material moving equipment operators tend air compressors or pumps at construction sites. Some operate oil or natural gas pumps and compressors at oil and gas wells and on oil and gas pipelines, and others operate ship loading and unloading equipment, conveyors, hoists, and other kinds of specialized material handling equipment such as mine or railroad tank car unloading equipment.

Material moving equipment operators may keep records of materials moved, and do some manual loading and unloading. They also may clean, fuel, and service their equipment.

## Working Conditions

Many material moving equipment operators work outdoors, in hot and cold weather, and sometimes in rain or snow. Industrial truck and tractor operators work mainly indoors, in warehouses or manufacturing plants. Some machines, particularly bulldozers and scrapers, are noisy and shake or jolt the operator. To avoid injury while operating an industrial truck, operators must take care to avoid roll-overs, collisions, and other accidents as well as protect materials and equipment from damage. While operating a bulldozer, care must be taken to keep it from overturning on a steep slope. However, these jobs have become much safer with the adoption of overhead guards on forklift trucks and roll bars on construction machinery. As with most machinery, most accidents can be avoided when proper operating procedures and safety practices are observed.

## Employment

Material moving equipment operators held nearly 1,061,000 jobs in 1994. They were distributed among the detailed occupations of this group as follows:

| | |
|---|---|
| Industrial truck and tractor operators .................... | 464,000 |
| Operating engineers ............................................. | 146,000 |
| Grader, dozer, and scraper operators .................... | 108,000 |
| Excavation and loading machine operators ........... | 88,000 |
| Crane and tower operators ..................................... | 45,000 |
| Hoist and winch operators ....................................... | 9,000 |
| All other material moving equipment operators .. | 201,000 |

The largest proportion—one-third—of material moving equipment operators worked in manufacturing; most of these were industrial truck and tractor operators. More than one-fifth worked in the construction industry. Significant numbers also worked in state and local governments and in the trucking and warehousing, wholesale trade, and mining industries. A few material moving equipment operators were self-employed.

Material moving equipment operators work in every section of the country. Some work in remote locations on large construction projects, such as highways and dams, or in factory or mining operations.

## Training, Other Qualifications, and Advancement

Operation of material moving equipment is usually learned on the job. Operators need a good sense of balance, the ability to judge distance, and good eye-hand-foot coordination. Employers of material moving equipment operators prefer to hire high school graduates, although, for some equipment, persons with less education may occasionally be accepted. Mechanical aptitude and high school training in automobile mechanics are helpful because workers may perform some maintenance on their machines. Experience operating mobile equipment, such as farm tractors or heavy equipment in the Armed Forces, is an asset.

Beginning material moving equipment operators handle light equipment under the guidance of an experienced operator. Later, they may operate heavier equipment such as bulldozers and cranes. Some construction equipment operators, however, are trained in formal three-year apprenticeship programs administered by union-management committees of the International Union of Operating Engineers and the Associated General Contractors of America. Because apprentices learn to operate a wider variety of machines than other beginners, they usually have better job opportunities. Apprenticeship programs consist of at least three years or 6,000 hours of on-the-job training and 144 hours a year of related classroom instruction.

Private vocational schools offer instruction in the operation of certain types of construction equipment. Completion of such a program may help a person get a job as a trainee or apprentice. However, persons considering such training should check the reputation of the school among employers in the area.

## Job Outlook

Employment of material moving equipment operators is expected to increase more slowly than the average for all occupations through the year 2005 as equipment improvements, including the growing automation of material handling in factories and warehouses, make operators more productive.

Opportunities for individuals who wish to become material moving equipment operators are related to the outlook of the industries in which they are employed. The majority of these workers are employed in construction and manufacturing industries; employment in construction is expected to grow more slowly than the average for all occupations, while jobs in manufacturing are expected to decline. Despite the projected slow growth, this is a large occupation with many opportunities arising from the need to replace experienced workers who transfer to other occupations or leave the labor force. However, both construction and manufacturing are very sensitive to changes in economic conditions, so the number of job openings for material moving equipment operators in these industries may fluctuate widely from year to year.

Excavation and loading machine operators is the only occupation in this group that is expected to increase about as fast as the average for all occupations. Their growth is expected to stem from increased spending on improving the nation's infrastructure of highways, bridges, and dams. The majority of excavation and loading machine operators work in mining and construction, the sector that constructs and maintains most of these facilities.

Employment of crane and tower operators and hoist and winch operators is expected to decline as more precise computerized controls and robotics allow many of these jobs to be automated. All of the remaining material moving equipment operating occupations are projected to grow more slowly than the average for all occupations, including industrial truck and tractor operators, the largest occupation in the group.

Growth of industrial truck and tractor operators—the largest occupation in this group—will be slower than average for all occupations due to productivity increases resulting from improved maneuverability and efficiency of industrial trucks and tractors. In addition, although the volume of goods to be moved will increase as the economy grows, fewer operator jobs will result as material handling systems in large factories and warehouses will continue to become more automated. Some systems use computerized dispatching or onboard data communication devices to enable industrial truck and tractor operators to move goods more efficiently. In other systems, some industrial trucks and tractors may be replaced by computer-controlled conveyor systems, overhead handling systems, and automated vehicles that don't require operators.

### Earnings

Earnings for material moving equipment operators vary considerably. In 1994, median earnings of all material moving equipment operators were $459 a week; the middle 50 percent earned between $339 and $608. Ten percent earned less than $265 and 10 percent more than $839. Median weekly earnings of crane and tower operators were $535 in 1994; excavation and loading machine operators, $454; grader, dozer, and scraper operators, $497; industrial truck and tractor operators, $425; operating engineers, $527; hoist and winch operators, $514; and other material moving equipment operators, $463. Pay scales generally are higher in metropolitan areas. Annual earnings of some workers may be lower than weekly rates would indicate because the amount of time they work can be limited by bad weather.

### Related Occupations

Other workers who operate mechanical equipment include truck and bus drivers, manufacturing equipment operators, and farmers.

### Related *D.O.T.* Jobs

These job titles are related to or more specific than the more general description above. They will help you identify job options you may not otherwise discover. These descriptions are in the current edition of the *Dictionary of Occupational Titles* and classified by numerical order.

There are too many *D.O.T.* titles to list here. Most are variations related to a specific industry, and we have included a small number of representative *D.O.T.* titles as examples. Complete lists are available in various career software published by JIST or directly from the U.S. Department of Labor.

524.565-010 TROLLEY OPERATOR; 559.684-034 UTILITY WORKER, PRODUCTION; 850.663-010 DREDGE OPERATOR; 850.663-022 MOTOR-GRADER OPERATOR; 850.683-010 BULLDOZER OPERATOR I; 850.683-018 DRAGLINE OPERATOR; 850.683-030 POWER-SHOVEL OPERATOR; 850.683-038 SCRAPER OPERATOR; 859.683-010 OPERATING ENGINEER; 919.664-010 TEAMSTER; 921.565-010 CEMENT LOADER; 921.683-042 FRONT-END LOADER OPERATOR; 921.683-046 HYDRAULIC-BOOM OPERATOR; 921.683-050 INDUSTRIAL-TRUCK OPERATOR; 921.683-082 WINCH DRIVER; 921.685-042 ELECTRIC-FORK OPERATOR; 929.583-010 YARD WORKER; 932.363-010 HOIST OPERATOR; 932.683-018 MECHANICAL-SHOVEL OPERATOR; 954.362-010 DITCH RIDER

### Sources of Additional Information

For further information about apprenticeships or work opportunities for construction equipment operators, contact a local of the International Union of Operating Engineers; a local apprenticeship committee; or the nearest office of the state apprenticeship agency. In addition, the local office of the state employment service may provide information about apprenticeship and other training programs.

For general information about the work of construction equipment operators, contact:

❑ Associated Builders and Contractors, National Center for Construction Education and Research, 1300 North 17th St., Rosslyn, VA 22209.

❑ Associated General Contractors of America, Inc., 1957 E St. NW, Washington, DC 20006.

❑ International Union of Operating Engineers, 1125 17th St. NW, Washington, DC 20036.

Information on industrial truck and tractor operators is available from:

❑ Industrial Truck Association, 1750 K St. NW, Suite 460, Washington, DC 20006.

# Medical Assistants

### Nature of the Work

Medical assistants perform routine clinical and clerical tasks to keep the offices of physicians, podiatrists, chiropractors, and optometrists running smoothly. Medical assistants should not be confused with physician assistants who examine, diagnose and treat patients, under the direct supervision of a physician.

The duties of medical assistants vary from office to office, depending on office location, size, and specialty. In small practices, medical assistants are usually "generalists," handling both clerical and clinical duties and reporting directly to an office manager, physician, or other health practitioner. Those in large practices tend to specialize in a particular area under the supervision of department administrators.

Medical assistants perform many clerical duties. They answer telephones, greet patients, update and file patient medical records, fill out insurance forms, handle correspondence, schedule appointments, arrange for hospital admission and laboratory services, and handle billing and bookkeeping.

Clinical duties vary according to state law and include taking medical histories and recording vital signs, explaining treatment procedures to patients, preparing patients for examination, and assisting during the examination. Medical assistants collect and prepare laboratory specimens or perform basic laboratory tests on the premises, dispose of contaminated supplies, and sterilize medical instruments. They instruct patients about medication and special diets, prepare and administer medications as directed by a physician, authorize drug refills as directed, telephone prescriptions to a pharmacy, draw blood, prepare patients for x-rays, take electrocardiograms, remove sutures, and change dressings.

Medical assistants may also arrange examining room instruments and equipment, purchase and maintain supplies and equipment, and keep waiting and examining rooms neat and clean.

Assistants who specialize have additional duties. *Podiatric medical assistants* make castings of feet, expose and develop x-rays, and assist podiatrists in surgery. *Ophthalmic medical assistants* help ophthalmologists provide medical eye care. They administer diagnostic tests, measure and record vision, and test the functioning of eyes and eye muscles. They also show patients how to use eye dressings, protective shields, and safety glasses, and how to insert, remove, and care for contact lenses. Under the direction of the physician, they may administer medications, including eye drops. They also maintain optical and surgical instruments and assist the ophthalmologist in surgery.

## Working Conditions

Medical assistants work in well-lighted, clean environments. They constantly interact with other people, and may have to handle several responsibilities at once.

Most full-time medical assistants work a regular 40-hour week. Some work part-time, evenings or weekends.

## Employment

Medical assistants held about 206,000 jobs in 1994. Seven in 10 jobs were in physicians' offices, and more than 1 in 10 were in offices of other health practitioners such as chiropractors, optometrists, and podiatrists. The rest were in hospitals, nursing homes, and other health care facilities.

## Training, Other Qualifications, and Advancement

Medical assisting is one of the few health occupations open to individuals with no formal training. Although formal training in medical assisting is available, such training—while generally preferred—is not always required. Some medical assistants are trained on the job. Applicants usually need a high school diploma or the equivalent. Recommended high school courses include mathematics, health, biology, typing, bookkeeping, computers, and office skills. Volunteer experience in the health care field is also helpful.

Formal programs in medical assisting are offered in vocational-technical high schools, postsecondary vocational schools, community and junior colleges, and in colleges and universities. College-level programs usually last either one year, resulting in a certificate or diploma, or two years, resulting in an associate degree. Vocational programs can take up to one year and lead to a diploma or certificate. Courses cover anatomy, physiology, and medical terminology as well as typing, transcription, recordkeeping, accounting, and insurance processing. Students learn laboratory techniques, clinical and diagnostic procedures, pharmaceutical principles and medication administration, and first aid. They study office practices, patient relations, and medical law and ethics. Some accredited programs include an internship that provides practical experience in physicians' offices, hospitals, or other health care facilities.

Two agencies recognized by the U.S. Department of Education accredit programs in medical assisting: the Commission on Accreditation of Allied Health Education Programs (CAAHEP) and the Accrediting Bureau of Health Education Schools (ABHES). In 1995, there were 221 medical assisting programs accredited by CAAHEP and 162 accredited by ABHES. The Joint Review Committee for Ophthalmic Medical Personnel has approved 16 programs in ophthalmic medical assisting.

Although there is no licensing for medical assistants, some states require them to take a test or a short course before they can take x-rays, draw blood, or give injections. Employers prefer to hire experienced workers or certified applicants who have passed a national examination, indicating that the medical assistant meets certain standards of competence. The American Association of Medical Assistants awards the Certified Medical Assistant credential; the American Medical Technologists awards the Registered Medical Assistant credential; the American Society of Podiatric Medical Assistants awards the Podiatric Medical Assistant Certified credential; and the Joint Commission on Allied Health Personnel in Ophthalmology awards the Ophthalmic Medical Assistant credential at three levels: Certified Ophthalmic Assistant, Certified Ophthalmic Technician, and Certified Ophthalmic Medical Technologist.

Because medical assistants deal with the public, they must be neat and well-groomed and have a courteous, pleasant manner. Medical assistants must be able to put patients at ease and explain physicians' instructions. They must respect the confidential nature of medical information. Clinical duties require a reasonable level of manual dexterity and visual acuity.

Medical assistants may be able to advance to office manager. They may qualify for a wide variety of administrative support occupations, or may teach medical assisting. Some, with additional education, enter other health occupations such as nursing and medical technology.

## Job Outlook

Employment of medical assistants is expected to grow much faster than the average for all occupations through the year 2005 as the health services industry expands due to technological advances in medicine, and a growing and aging population.

Employment growth will be driven by growth in the number of group practices, clinics, and other health care facilities that need a high proportion of support personnel, particularly the flexible medical assistant who can handle both clinical and clerical duties. Medical assistants primarily work in outpatient settings, where faster than average growth is expected.

In view of the preference of many physicians for trained personnel, job prospects should be excellent for medical assistants with formal training or experience, particularly those with certification.

## Earnings

The earnings of medical assistants vary widely, depending on experience, skill level, and location. According to a 1995 survey by the Health Care Group, average hourly wages for medical assistants with less than two years of experience ranged from $7.51 to $10.20. Average hourly wages for medical assistants with more than five years of experience ranged from $9.60 to $13.12. Wages were higher in the Northeast and West and lower in the Midwest and South.

## Related Occupations

Workers in other medical support occupations include medical secretaries, hospital admitting clerks, pharmacy helpers, medical record clerks, dental assistants, occupational therapy aides, and physical therapy aides.

## Related *D.O.T.* Jobs

These job titles are related to or more specific than the more general description above. They will help you identify job options you may not otherwise discover. These descriptions are in the current edition of the *Dictionary of Occupational Titles* and classified by numerical order.

078.361-038 OPHTHALMIC TECHNICIAN; 078.364-014 ECHOCARDIOGRAPH TECHNICIAN; 079.362-010 MEDICAL ASSISTANT; 079.364-010 CHIROPRACTOR ASSISTANT; 079.364-014 OPTOMETRIC ASSISTANT; 079.374-018 PODIATRIC ASSISTANT; 355.667-010 MORGUE ATTENDANT

## Sources of Additional Information

Information about career opportunities, CAAHEP-accredited educational programs in medical assisting, and the Certified Medical Assistant exam is available from:

❏ The American Association of Medical Assistants, 20 North Wacker Dr., Suite 1575, Chicago, IL 60606-2903.

Information about career opportunities and the Registered Medical Assistant certification exam is available from:

❏ Registered Medical Assistants of American Medical Technologists, 710 Higgins Rd., Park Ridge, IL 60068-5765.

For a list of ABHES-accredited educational programs in medical assisting, write:

❏ Accrediting Bureau of Health Education Schools, 2700 South Quincy St., Suite 210, Arlington, VA 22206.

Information about career opportunities, training programs, and the Certified Ophthalmic Assistant exam is available from:

❏ Joint Commission on Allied Health Personnel in Ophthalmology, 2025 Woodlane Dr., St. Paul, MN 55125-2995.

Information about careers for podiatric assistants is available from:

❏ American Society of Podiatric Medical Assistants, 2124 S. Austin Blvd., Cicero, IL 60650.

# Medical Record Technicians

## Nature of the Work

When you enter a hospital, you see a whirl of white coats of physicians, nurses, radiologic technologists, and others. Every time these health care personnel treat a patient, they record what they observed and did to the patient. This record includes information the patient provides about their symptoms and medical history, and also the results of examinations, reports of x-rays and laboratory tests, and diagnoses and treatment plans. Medical record technicians organize and evaluate these records for completeness and accuracy.

When assembling a patient's medical record, technicians, who may also be called health information technicians, first make sure that the medical chart is complete. They ensure that all forms are present and properly identified and signed, and that all necessary information is on a computer file. Sometimes, they talk to physicians or others to clarify diagnoses or get additional information.

Technicians assign a code to each diagnosis and procedure. They consult a classification manual and rely, too, on their knowledge of disease processes. Technicians then use a software program to assign the patient to one of several hundred "diagnosis-related groups" or DRGs. The DRG determines the amount the hospital will be reimbursed if the patient is covered by Medicare or other insurance programs that use the DRG system. Technicians who specialize in coding are called medical record coders, coder/abstractors, or coding specialists.

Technicians also use computer programs to tabulate and analyze data to help improve patient care, to control costs, to be used in legal actions, or to respond to surveys. *Tumor registrars* compile and maintain records of patients who have cancer to provide information to physicians and for research studies.

Medical record technicians' duties vary with the size of the facility. In large to medium facilities, technicians may specialize in one aspect of medical records or supervise medical record clerks and transcribers while a *medical record administrator* manages the department.

## Working Conditions

Medical record technicians generally work a 40-hour week. Some overtime may be required. In hospitals where medical record departments are open 18 to 24 hours a day, seven days a week, they may work on day, evening, and night shifts.

They work in pleasant and comfortable offices. Medical record technician is one of the few health occupations in which there is little or no contact with patients. Accuracy is essential, and this demands concentration and close attention to detail. Medical record technicians who work at video display terminals for prolonged periods may experience eyestrain and muscle pain.

## Employment

Medical record technicians held about 81,000 jobs in 1994. About one half of the jobs were in hospitals. Most of the remainder were in nursing homes, medical group practices, health maintenance organizations, and clinics.

In addition, insurance, accounting, and law firms that deal in health matters employ medical record technicians to tabulate and analyze data from medical records. Public health departments hire technicians to supervise data collection from health care institutions and to assist in research.

Some self-employed medical record technicians are consultants to nursing homes and physicians' offices.

## Training, Other Qualifications, and Advancement

Medical record technicians entering the field usually have formal training in a two-year associate degree program offered at community and junior colleges. Courses include medical terminology and diseases, anatomy and physiology, legal aspects of medical records, coding and abstraction of data, statistics, databases, quality assurance methods, and computers as well as general education. Applicants can improve their chances of admission into a program by taking biology, chemistry, health and computer courses in high school.

Technicians may also gain training through an Independent Study Program in Medical Record Technology offered by the American Health Information Management Association (AHIMA). Hospitals sometimes advance promising medical record clerks to jobs as medical record technicians, although this practice may be less common in the future. Advancement generally requires two to four years of job experience and completion of the hospital's in-house training program.

Most employers prefer to hire Accredited Record Technicians (ART). Accreditation is obtained by passing a written examination offered by the AHIMA. To take the examination, a person must be a graduate of a two-year associate degree program accredited by the Commission on Accreditation of Allied Health Education Programs (CAAHEP) of the American Medical Association, or a graduate of the Independent Study Program in Medical Record Technology who has also obtained 30 semester hours of academic credit in prescribed areas. Technicians who have received training in non-CAAHEP accredited programs or on the job are not eligible to take the examination. In 1995, CAAHEP accredited 134 programs for medical record technicians.

Experienced medical record technicians generally advance in one of two ways: by specializing or managing. Many senior medical record technicians specialize in coding, particularly Medicare coding, or in tumor registry.

In large medical record departments, experienced technicians may become section supervisors, overseeing the work of the coding, correspondence, or discharge sections, for example. Senior technicians with ART credentials may become director or assistant director of a medical record department in a small facility. However, in larger institutions the director is a medical records administrator, with a bachelor's degree in medical record administration.

## Job Outlook

Job prospects for formally trained technicians should be very good. Employment of medical record technicians is expected to grow much faster than the average for all occupations through the year 2005 due to rapid growth in the number of medical tests, treatments, and procedures and because medical records will be increasingly scrutinized by third-party payers, courts, and consumers.

Hospitals will continue to employ the most medical record technicians, but growth will not be as fast as in other areas. The need for detailed records in offices and clinics of doctors of medicine should result in faster employment growth in large group practices and offices of specialists. Rapid growth is also expected in health maintenance organizations, nursing homes, and home health agencies.

## Earnings

According to a 1994 survey by American Health Consultant's, the median annual salary for accredited record technicians was $36,700 a year. The average annual salary for medical record technicians in the federal government in nonsupervisory, supervisory, and managerial positions was $23,779 in 1995.

## Related Occupations

Medical record technicians need a strong clinical background to analyze the contents of medical records. Other occupations that require a knowledge of medical terminology, anatomy, and physiology without directly touching the patient are medical secretaries, medical transcribers, medical writers, and medical illustrators.

## Related *D.O.T.* Jobs

These job titles are related to or more specific than the more general description above. They will help you identify job options you may not otherwise discover. These descriptions are in the current edition of the *Dictionary of Occupational Titles* and classified by numerical order.

079.362-014 MEDICAL RECORD TECHNICIAN; 079.362-018 TUMOR REGISTRAR

## Sources of Additional Information

Information on careers in medical record technology, including the Independent Study Program, and a list of CAAHEP-accredited programs is available from:

❑ American Health Information Management Association, 919 N. Michigan Ave., Suite 1400, Chicago, IL 60611.

# Metalworking and Plastics-Working Machine Operators

## Nature of the Work

Consider the parts of a toaster—the metal or plastic housing or the lever that lowers the toast, for example. These parts, and many other metal and plastic products, are produced by metalworking and plastics-working machine operators. In fact, manual and numerical control machine tool operators in the metalworking and plastics industries play a major part in producing most of the consumer products on which we rely daily.

These workers can be separated into two groups—those who set up machines for operation and those who tend the machines during production. Set-up workers prepare the machines prior to production and may adjust the machinery during operation. Operators and tenders, on the other hand, primarily monitor the machinery during operation, sometimes loading or unloading the machine or making minor adjustments to the controls. Many workers do both—set up and operate the equipment. Because the set-up process requires an understanding of the entire production process, setters usually have more training and are more highly skilled than those who simply operate or tend the machinery.

Setters, operators, tenders, and set-up operators are usually identified by the type of machine with which they work. Some examples of specific titles are screw machine operator, plastics-molding machine set-up operator, punch press operator, and lathe tender. Although some workers specialize in one or two types of machinery, many are trained to set up or operate a variety of machines. Job duties usually vary based on the size of the firm as well as on the type of machine being operated.

Metalworking machine setters and operators set up and tend machines that cut and form all types of metal parts. Traditionally, set-up workers plan and set up the sequence of operations according to blueprints, layouts, or other instructions. They adjust speed, feed, and other controls, choose the proper coolants and lubricants, and select the instruments or tools for each operation. Using micrometers, gauges, and other precision measuring instruments, they may compare the completed work with the tolerance limits stated in the specifications.

Although there are many different types of metalworking machine tools that require specific knowledge and skills, most operators perform similar tasks. Whether tending grinding machines that remove excess material from the surface of machined products or presses that extrude metal through a die to form wire, operators usually perform simple, repetitive operations that can be learned quickly. Typically, these workers place metal stock in a machine on which the operating specifications have already been set. They may watch one or more machines and make minor adjustments according to their instructions. Regardless of the type of machine they operate, machine tenders usually depend on skilled set-up workers for major adjustments when the machines are not functioning properly.

Plastics working machine operators set up and tend machines that transform plastic compounds—chemical based products that can be produced in powder, pellet, or syrup form—into a wide variety of consumer goods such as toys, tubing, and auto parts. These products are produced by various methods, of which injection molding is the most common. The injection molding machine heats a plastic compound and forces it into a mold. After the part has cooled and hardened, the mold opens and the part is released. Many common kitchen products are produced using this method. To produce long parts such as pipes or window frames, on the other hand, an extruding machine is usually employed. These machines force a plastic compound through a die that contains an opening of the desired shape of the final product. Yet another type of plastics working technique is blow molding. Blow-molding machines force hot air into a mold which contains a plastic tube. As the air moves into the mold, the plastic tube is inflated to the shape of the mold and a plastic container is formed. The familiar two-liter soft drink bottles are produced using this method.

Regardless of the process used, plastics-working machine operators check the materials feed, the temperature and pressure of the machine, and the rate at which the product hardens. Depending on the type of equipment in use, they may also load material into the machine, make minor adjustments to the machinery, or unload and inspect the finished products. Plastics-working machine operators also remove clogged material from molds or dies. Because molds and dies are quite costly, operators must exercise proper care to avoid damaging them.

Metalworking and plastics-working machine operators are increasingly being called upon to work with numerically controlled (NC) equipment. These machine tools have two major components—an electronic controller and a machine tool. Almost all NC machines today are computer numerically controlled (CNC), which means that the controllers are computers. The controller directs the mechanisms of the machine tool through the positioning and machining described in the program or instruc-

tions for the job. A program could contain, for example, commands that cause the controller to move a drill bit to certain spots on a work piece and drill a hole at each spot.

Each type of CNC machine tool, such as a milling machine, a lathe, or a punch press, performs a specific task. A part may be worked on by several machines before it is finished. CNC machines are often used in computer-integrated manufacturing (CIM) systems. In these systems, automated material handling equipment moves work pieces through a series of work stations where machining processes are computer numerically controlled. In some cases, the work piece is stationary and the tools change automatically. Although the machining is done automatically, numerically controlled machine tools must be set up and used properly in order to obtain the maximum benefit from their use. These tasks are the responsibility of numerical-control machine-tool operators or, in some instances, machinists.

Like the duties of manual metal and plastics machine operators, the duties of numerical-control machine-tool operators vary. In some shops, operators tend just one machine. More likely, however, they tend a number of machines or do some programming. As a result, the skill requirements of these workers vary from job to job. Although there are many variations in operators' duties, they generally involve many of the tasks described below.

Working from given instructions, operators load programs that are usually stored on disks into the controller. They also securely position the work piece, attach the necessary tools, and check the coolants and lubricants. Many numerically controlled machines are equipped with automatic tool changers, so operators may also load several tools in the proper sequence. In addition, heat generated by machining could damage the cutting tools and the part being machined, so operators must ensure that the proper coolants and lubricants are being used. This entire process may require a few minutes or several hours, depending on the size of the work piece and the complexity of the job.

A new program must be "debugged," or adjusted, to obtain the desired results. If the tool moves to the wrong position or makes a cut that is too deep, for example, the program must be changed so that the job is done properly. NC operators rarely debug programs. More often, a machinist or tool programmer will perform this function, occasionally with the assistance of a computer automated design program that simulates the operation of machine tools. A new generation of machine tool technology called direct numerical control allows operators to make changes to the program and enter new specifications using minicomputers on the shop floor.

Because numerically controlled machine tools are very expensive, an important duty of operators is to monitor the machinery to prevent situations that could result in costly damage to the cutting tools or other parts. The extent to which the operator performs this function depends on the type of job as well as the type of equipment being used. Some numerically controlled machine tools automatically monitor and adjust machining operations. When the job has been properly set up and the program has been checked, the operator may only need to monitor the machine as it operates. These operators often set up and monitor more than one machine. Other jobs require frequent loading and unloading, tool changing, or programming. Operators may check the finished part using micrometers, gauges, or other precision inspection equipment to ensure that it meets specifications. Increasingly, however, this function is being performed by numerically controlled machine tools that are able to inspect products as they are being produced.

CNC machines are changing the nature of the work that machine setters and operators perform. For example, computer-controlled machines simplify set-ups by using formerly tested computer programs for new work pieces. If a work piece is similar to one previously produced, small adjustments can be made to the old program instead of developing a new program from scratch. Also, operators of this equipment have less physical interaction with the machinery or materials. They primarily act as "trouble-shooters," monitoring machines on which the loading, forming, and unloading processes are often controlled by computers.

## Working Conditions

Most metalworking and plastics-working machine operators work in areas that are clean, well lit, and well ventilated. Regardless of setting, all of these workers operate powerful, high-speed machines that can be dangerous if strict safety rules are not observed. Most operators wear protective equipment such as safety glasses and earplugs to protect against flying particles of metal or plastic and noise from the machines. Other required equipment varies by work setting and by machine. For example, workers in the plastics industry who work near materials that emit dangerous fumes or dust must wear face masks or self-contained breathing apparatuses.

Most metal and plastics working machine operators work a 40-hour week, but overtime is common during periods of increased production. Because many metalworking and plastics working shops operate more than one shift daily, some operators work nights and weekends.

The work requires stamina because operators are on their feet much of the day and may do moderately heavy lifting. Approximately one-third of these workers are union members; the metalworking industries have a higher rate of unionization than the plastics industry.

## Employment

Metalworking and plastics-working machine operators held about 1,445,000 jobs in 1994. Of these, 1,370,000 were manual machine operators, and 75,000 were NC machine operators. Eight out of every 10 of these workers are found in five manufacturing industries—fabricated metal products, industrial machinery and equipment, miscellaneous plastic products, transportation equipment, and primary metals. The following tabulation shows the distribution of employment of metalworking and plastics-working machine operators by detailed occupation.

| | |
|---|---|
| Machine tool cutting and forming machine setters and operators | 709,000 |
| Molding machine setters and operators | 205,000 |
| Sheetmetal workers and duct installers | 116,000 |
| Combination machine tool setters and operators | 106,000 |
| Numerical control machine operators | 75,000 |
| Metal fabricators, structural metal products | 44,000 |

| | |
|---|---|
| Plating machine setters and operators | 42,000 |
| Heat treating machine setters and operators | 20,000 |
| All other metal and plastics working machine operators | 128,000 |

## Training, Other Qualifications, and Advancement

Most metalworking and plastics-working machine operators learn their skills on the job. Trainees begin by observing and assisting experienced workers, often in formal training programs. Under supervision they may supply material, start and stop the machine, or remove finished products from the machine. As part of their training they advance to more difficult tasks like adjusting feed speeds, changing cutting tools, or inspecting a finished product for defects. Eventually they become responsible for their own machine or machines.

The complexity of equipment largely determines the time required to become an operator. Most operators learn the basic machine operations and functions in a few weeks, but they may need several years to become a skilled operator or to advance to the more highly skilled job of set-up operator.

Although set-up operators perform many of the same tasks as skilled machine operators, they also need to have a thorough knowledge of the machinery and of the products being produced. Set-up operators often study blueprints, plan the sequence of work, make the first production run, and determine which adjustments need to be made. Strong analytical abilities are particularly important to perform this job. Some companies have formal training programs for set-up operators that combine classroom instruction with on-the-job training.

CNC machine tool operators undergo similar training. Working under a supervisor or an experienced operator, trainees learn to set up and run one or more kinds of numerically controlled machine tools. They usually learn the basics of their jobs within a few months. However, the length of the training period varies with the number and complexity of the machine tools the operator will run and with the individual's ability. If the employer expects operators to write programs, trainees may attend programming courses offered by machine tool manufacturers or technical schools. These courses usually last a couple of weeks.

Although no special education is required for most operating jobs, employers prefer to hire applicants with good basic skills. Many require employees to have a high school education and to read, write, and speak English. This is especially true for numerical control machine operators, who may need to be retrained often in order to learn to operate new equipment. Because machinery is becoming more complex and shop floor organization is changing, employers increasingly look for persons with good communication and interpersonal skills. Mechanical aptitude, manual dexterity, and experience working with machinery are also pluses. Those interested in becoming a metalworking or plastics-working machine operator can improve their employment opportunities by completing high school courses in shop, mathematics, and blueprint reading and by gaining a working knowledge of the properties of metals and plastics.

Advancement for operators usually takes the form of higher pay, although there are some limited opportunities for operators to advance to new positions as well. For example, they can become multiple machine operators, set-up operators, or trainees for the more highly skilled positions of machinist or tool and die maker. Manual machine operators can move on to CNC equipment when it is introduced into their establishments. Some set-up workers and CNC operators may advance to supervisory positions. CNC operators who have substantial training in numerical control programming may advance to the higher paying job of tool programmer.

## Job Outlook

Overall employment of metalworking and plastics-working machine operators is expected to decline through the year 2005. This decline is likely to affect metalworking machine operators more than those working with plastics machines. In addition, setters and more highly skilled operators are more likely to be retained by firms than are semi-skilled operators and tenders. In spite of the overall employment decline, however, a large number of jobs will become available each year as current operators and setters transfer to other occupations or leave the labor force.

A major factor driving the employment decline is the increasing productivity resulting from computer-controlled equipment. In order to remain competitive, many firms are adopting this technology to improve quality and lower production costs. Computer-controlled equipment allows operators to simultaneously tend a greater number of machines and often makes set-up easier, thereby reducing the amount of time set-up workers spend on each machine. For these reasons, employment of CNC machine operators is expected to increase in the future despite the decline in machine operators as a whole. Lower-skilled positions like manual machine tool operators and tenders are more likely to be eliminated by increasing automation than those of setters and set-up operators, whose higher skills are more in demand and whose job functions are less easily automated.

The demand for metalworking and plastics-working machine operators largely mirrors the demand for the parts they produce. In recent years, plastic products have been substituted for metal goods in many consumer and manufacturing products. Although the rate of substitution may slow in the future, this process is likely to continue and should result in a relatively stronger demand for machine operators in plastics than in metalworking. Both industries, however, face stiff foreign competition that is limiting the demand for domestically-produced parts. One way that larger U.S. producers have responded to this competition is by moving production operations to other countries in order to reduce labor costs. These moves are likely to continue and will further reduce employment opportunities for metalworking and plastics-working machine tool operators in the United States.

Workers with a thorough background in machine operations, exposure to a variety of machines, and a good working knowledge of the properties of metals and plastics will be best able to adjust to this changing environment. In addition, new shop floor arrangements will reward workers with good basic mathematics and reading skills, good communication skills, flexibility, and the ability and willingness to learn new tasks. Those interested in working with CNC machine tools will most likely need to have a high school education and should be familiar with several types of machines and operating systems.

## Earnings

Median weekly earnings for most metalworking and plastics-working machine operators were about $420 in 1994. The middle 50 percent earned between $310 and $570. The top 10 percent earned over $760 and the bottom 10 percent earned less than $240. Metal and plastics molding, plating, heat-treating, and other processing machine operators earned somewhat less, about $390 a week. In addition to wages, most machine operators receive benefits such as health and life insurance, pension plans, paid vacation, and sick leave.

Earnings of production workers vary considerably by industry. The following tabulation shows 1994 average weekly wages for production workers in manufacturing industries where employment of metal-working and plastics-working machine operators is concentrated.

| | |
|---|---|
| Transportation equipment | $730 |
| Primary metals industries | 640 |
| Industrial machinery and equipment | 570 |
| Fabricated metal products | 510 |
| Rubber and miscellaneous plastics products | 450 |

## Related Occupations

Workers in occupations closely related to metalworking and plastics-working machine occupations include machinists, tool and die makers, extruding and forming machine operators producing synthetic fibers, woodworking machine operators, and metal patternmakers. Numerical-control machine-tool operators may program CNC machines or alter existing programs, which are functions closely related to those performed by NC machine tool programmers.

## Related *D.O.T.* Jobs

These job titles are related to or more specific than the more general description above. They will help you identify job options you may not otherwise discover. These descriptions are in the current edition of the *Dictionary of Occupational Titles* and classified by numerical order.

There are too many *D.O.T.* titles to list here. Most are variations related to a specific industry, and we have included a small number of representative *D.O.T.* titles as examples. Complete lists are available in various career software published by JIST or directly from the U.S. Department of Labor.

500.380-010 PLATER; 501.362-010 COATING-MACHINE OPERATOR; 502.682-014 CASTING-MACHINE OPERATOR; 503.685-038 SANDBLAST OPERATOR; 509.684-010 ENAMELER; 509.685-054 TANK TENDER; 512.382-014 STOVE TENDER; 514.382-010 DIE-CASTING-MACHINE OPERATOR I; 514.682-014 PRESS OPERATOR, CARBON BLOCKS; 518.664-010 MOLD MAKER; 554.682-018 ROLL OPERATOR; 590.685-082 STRIPPER-ETCHER, PRINTED CIRCUIT BOARDS; 590.685-094 PLASMA ETCHER, PRINTED CIRCUIT BOARDS; 599.685-054 LACQUERER; 606.362-010 DRILL-PRESS OPERATOR, NUMERICAL CONTROL; 606.685-026 DRILL PRESS TENDER; 614.482-014 EXTRUDER OPERATOR; 615.685-030 PUNCH-PRESS OPERATOR; 619.685-062 MACHINE OPERATOR II; 715.685-030 GRINDER II; 979.682-026 ROUTER

## Sources of Additional Information

For general information about the metalworking trades, contact:

❑ The Association for Manufacturing Technology, 7901 Westpark Dr., McLean, VA 22102.

❑ The National Tooling and Machining Association, 9300 Livingston Rd., Fort Washington, MD 20744.

❑ The Tooling and Manufacturing Association, ATTN: Education Department, 1177 South Dee Rd., Park Ridge, IL 60068.

❑ The National Screw Machine Products Association, 6700 West Snowville Rd., Brecksville, OH 44141.

❑ The Precision Metalforming Association, 27027 Chardon Rd., Richmond Heights, OH 44143.

Information on educational programs in plastics technology and polymer sciences is available from:

❑ The Society of the Plastics Industry, Inc., 1275 K St. NW, Washington, DC 20005.

# Millwrights

## Nature of the Work

Millwrights install, repair, replace, and dismantle the machinery and heavy equipment used in almost every industry. These responsibilities require a wide range of skills—from blueprint reading and pouring concrete to diagnosing and solving mechanical problems.

The millwright's responsibilities begin when machinery arrives at the job site. The new equipment must be unloaded, inspected, and then moved into position. To lift and move light machinery, millwrights may use rigging and hoisting devices such as pulleys and cables. In other cases, they require the assistance of hydraulic lift-truck or crane operators to position the machinery. Because millwrights often decide what device to use for moving machinery, they must know the load-bearing properties of ropes, cables, hoists, and cranes.

New machinery sometimes requires a new foundation. Millwrights either personally prepare the foundation or supervise its construction, so they must know how to read blueprints and work with building materials such as concrete, wood, and steel.

When assembling machinery, millwrights fit bearings, align gears and wheels, attach motors, and connect belts according to the manufacturer's blueprints and drawings. Precision leveling and alignment are important in the assembly process; millwrights must have good mathematical skills so that they can measure angles, material thickness, and small distances with tools such as squares, calipers, and micrometers. When a high level of precision is required, devices such as lasers may be used. They also use hand and power tools, cutting torches, welding machines, and soldering guns. Some millwrights use metalworking equipment such as lathes or grinders to modify parts to specifications.

The increasing level of automation found in most industries means that there are more sophisticated machines for millwrights to install and maintain. This machinery often requires special care and knowledge, so millwrights often work closely with computer or electronic experts, electricians, engineers, and manufacturer's representatives to install it.

In addition to installing and dismantling machinery, many millwrights repair and maintain equipment. This includes preventive maintenance, such as lubrication, and fixing or replacing worn parts.

## Working Conditions

Working conditions of millwrights vary by industry. Those employed in manufacturing often work in a typical shop setting and use protective equipment to avoid common hazards. For example, injuries from falling objects or machinery are avoided by protective de-vices such as safety belts, protective glasses, and hard hats. Those in construction may work outdoors in uncomfortable weather conditions.

Millwrights may work independently or as part of a team. They must work quickly and precisely because non-functioning machinery costs a company time and money. Most millwrights work overtime; nearly two-thirds report working more than 40 hours during a typical week.

## Employment

Millwrights held about 77,000 jobs in 1994. Most worked in manufacturing, primarily in durable goods industries such as motor vehicles and equipment and basic steel products. Millwrights found in other sectors were employed primarily by construction firms and machining and equipment wholesalers. Many of these workers are contractors.

Although millwrights work in every state, employment is concentrated in heavily industrialized areas.

## Training, Other Qualifications, and Advancement

Millwrights receive their training from a formal apprenticeship program, a community college, or informally on the job. Apprenticeship programs normally last four years and combine on-the-job training with classroom instruction. Apprenticeship programs include training in dismantling, moving, erecting, and repairing machinery. Apprentices may also work with concrete and receive instruction in related skills such as carpentry, welding, and sheetmetal work. Classroom instruction is given in mathematics, blueprint reading, hydraulics, electricity, and increasingly, computers or electronics.

Most employers prefer applicants with a high school diploma and some vocational training or experience. Courses in science, mathematics, mechanical drawing, and machine shop practice are useful. Because millwrights assemble and disassemble complicated machinery, mechanical aptitude is very important.

Strength and agility also are important because the work can require a considerable amount of lifting and climbing. Millwrights need good interpersonal and communication abilities in order to work as part of a team and give detailed instructions to others.

Advancement for millwrights usually takes the form of higher wages. Some advance to supervisor.

## Job Outlook

Employment of millwrights is projected to decline through the year 2005, due in part to an expected downturn in new industrial construction. When construction activity falls, jobs are scarce, and even experienced millwrights may face layoffs or shortened workweeks. In coming years, new industrial construction is expected to be insufficient to maintain existing employment levels. In addition, some of the duties of millwrights are being transferred to other workers, such as electronic technicians and industrial machinery mechanics, as new automation becomes more complicated and involves more electronic components. Finally, millwrights are becoming more productive through technologies like hydraulic torque wrenches, ultrasonic measuring tools, and laser shaft alignment that allow fewer of these workers to perform a greater amount of work.

Although employment is expected to decline, millwrights will still be needed to maintain and repair existing machinery, to dismantle old machinery, and to install and maintain new equipment. Workers with these skills will encounter a number of job openings that will arise annually as experienced millwrights transfer to other occupations or leave the labor force.

### Earnings

Median weekly earnings of full-time millwrights were about $700 in 1994; the middle 50 percent earned between $520 and $880. The lowest 10 percent earned less than $380, while the top 10 percent earned more than $1,290. Earnings vary by industry and geographic location. Two-thirds of millwrights belong to labor unions, one of the highest rates of membership in the economy. Typical benefits for these workers include health and life insurance, pension plans, paid vacation, and sick leave.

### Related Occupations

To set up machinery for use in a plant, millwrights must know how to use hoisting devices and how to assemble, disassemble, and in some cases repair machinery. Other workers with similar job duties are industrial machinery repairers, mobile heavy equipment mechanics, aircraft mechanics and engine specialists, diesel mechanics, farm equipment mechanics, ironworkers, and machine assemblers.

### Related *D.O.T.* Jobs

These job titles are related to or more specific than the more general description above. They will help you identify job options you may not otherwise discover. These descriptions are in the current edition of the *Dictionary of Occupational Titles* and classified by numerical order.

638.261-010 AUTOMATED EQUIPMENT ENGINEER-TECHNICIAN; 638.261-014 MACHINERY ERECTOR; 638.261-018 MANUFACTURER'S SERVICE REPRESENTATIVE; 638.261-026 FIELD SERVICE TECHNICIAN; 638.281-018 MILLWRIGHT; 638.281-022 MILLWRIGHT APPRENTICE

### Sources of Additional Information

For further information on apprenticeship programs, write to the Apprenticeship Council of your state's labor department, local offices of your state employment service, or local firms that employ millwrights. In addition, you may contact:

❑ The United Brotherhood of Carpenters and Joiners of America, 101 Constitution Ave. NW, Washington DC 20001.

❑ Association for Manufacturing Technology, 7901 Westpark Dr., McLean, VA 22102.

❑ Associated General Contractors of America, 1957 E St. NW, Washington, DC 20006.

# Mobile Heavy Equipment Mechanics

### Nature of the Work

Mobile heavy equipment is indispensable to construction, logging, surface mining, and other industrial activities. Mobile heavy equipment mechanics service and repair the engines, transmissions, hydraulics, electrical systems, and other components of equipment such as motor graders, trenchers and backhoes, crawler-loaders, and stripping and loading shovels.

Mobile heavy equipment mechanics perform routine maintenance on the diesel engines that power most heavy equipment, and, if an operator reports a malfunction, they search for its cause. First, they inspect and operate the equipment to diagnose the nature of the repairs required. If necessary, they may partially dismantle the engine, examining parts for damage or excessive wear. Then they repair, replace, clean, and lubricate the parts as necessary, and reassemble and test the engine for operating efficiency. If repairs to the drive train are needed, mechanics remove and repair the transmission or differential.

Many types of mobile heavy equipment use hydraulics to raise and lower movable parts such as scoops, shovels, log forks, or scraper blades. Repairing malfunctioning hydraulic components is an important responsibility of mobile heavy equipment mechanics. When hydraulics loses power, mechanics examine them for hydraulic fluid leaks and replace ruptured hoses or worn gaskets on fluid reservoirs. Occasionally, more extensive repairs are required, such as replacing a defective hydraulic pump.

Mobile heavy equipment mechanics perform a variety of other types of repairs. They diagnose and correct electrical problems and replace defective electronic components. They also disassemble and repair crawler undercarriages and track assemblies. Occasionally, mechanics weld broken body and structural parts, using electric or gas welders.

Many mechanics work in small repair shops of construction contractors, logging and mining companies, and local government road maintenance departments. They typically perform routine maintenance and minor repairs necessary to keep the equipment in operation. Mechanics in larger repair shops—particularly those of mobile heavy equipment dealers and the federal government—perform more difficult repairs, such as rebuilding or replacing engines, repairing hydraulic fluid pumps, or correcting electrical problems. Mechanics in some large shops specialize in one or two types of work, such as hydraulics or electrical systems.

Mobile heavy equipment mechanics use a variety of tools in their work, including common handtools such as pliers, wrenches, and screwdrivers and power tools such as pneumatic wrenches. They use micrometers and gauges to measure wear on parts, and a variety of testing equipment. For example, they use tachometers and dynamometers to locate engine malfunctions; when working on electrical systems, they use ohmmeters, ammeters, and voltmeters.

## Working Conditions

Most mobile heavy equipment repair shops are well ventilated, lighted, and heated. Many mechanics work indoors in shops, but others work as field service mechanics and spend much of their time away from the shop working outdoors. When mobile heavy equipment breaks down at a construction site, it may be too difficult or expensive to bring it into a repair shop, so a field service mechanic is sent to the job site to make repairs. Generally, the more experienced mobile heavy equipment mechanics specialize in field service; they usually drive specially equipped trucks and sometimes must travel many miles to reach disabled machinery. For many mechanics, the independence and challenge of field work outweigh the occasional long hours or bad weather, but other mechanics are more comfortable with the routine of shop work and the opportunity to work as part of a team.

Mechanics handle greasy and dirty parts and often work in awkward or cramped positions. They sometimes must lift heavy tools and parts, and must be careful to avoid burns, bruises, and cuts from hot engine parts and sharp edges of machinery. However, serious accidents may be prevented when the shop is kept clean and orderly and safety practices are observed.

## Employment

Mobile heavy equipment mechanics held about 101,000 jobs in 1994. Over half worked for mobile heavy equipment dealers and construction contractors. About one-fifth were employed by federal, state, and local governments; the Department of Defense is the primary federal employer. Other mobile heavy equipment mechanics worked for surface mine operators, public utility companies, logging camps and contractors, and heavy equipment rental and leasing companies. Still others repaired equipment for machinery manufacturers, airlines, railroads, steel mills, and oil and gas field companies. About 1 in 20 mobile heavy equipment mechanics was self-employed.

Mobile heavy equipment mechanics are employed in every section of the country, but most work near cities and towns, where most construction takes place.

## Training, Other Qualifications, and Advancement

For trainee jobs, employers hire persons with mechanical aptitude who are high school graduates and at least 18 years of age. They seek persons knowledgeable about the fundamentals of diesel engines, transmissions, electrical systems, and hydraulics. Although some persons are able to acquire these skills on their own or by working as helpers to experienced mechanics, most employers prefer to hire graduates of formal training programs in diesel or heavy equipment mechanics.

Training programs in diesel and heavy equipment mechanics are given by vocational and technical schools and community and junior colleges. Training in the fundamentals of electronics is also essential because new mobile heavy equipment increasingly features electronic controls and sensing devices. Some one- to two-year programs lead to a certificate of completion; others lead to an associate degree if they are supplemented with additional academic courses. These programs provide a foundation in the basics of diesel and heavy equipment technology, including hydraulics, and enable trainee mechanics to advance more rapidly to the journey, or experienced worker, level.

Through a combination of formal and on-the-job training, trainee mechanics acquire the knowledge and skills to efficiently service and repair the particular types of equipment handled by the shop. Beginners are assigned relatively simple service and repair tasks. As they gain experience and become more familiar with the equipment, they are assigned increasingly difficult jobs, and are exposed to a greater variety of equipment.

Many employers send trainee mechanics to training sessions conducted by heavy equipment manufacturers. These sessions, which typically last up to one week, provide intensive instruction in the repair of a manufacturer's equipment. Some sessions focus on particular components found in all of the manufacturer's equipment, such as diesel engines, transmissions, axles, and electrical systems. Other sessions focus on particular types of equipment, such as crawler-loaders and crawler-dozers. As they progress, trainees may periodically attend additional training sessions. Experienced mechanics also occasionally attend training sessions to gain familiarity with new technology or with types of equipment they may never have repaired.

High school courses in automobile mechanics, physics, chemistry, and mathematics provide an essential foundation for a career as a mechanic. Good reading and basic mathematics skills and a basic understanding of scientific principles are needed to help a mechanic learn important job skills and to keep abreast of new technology through the study of technical manuals. Experience working on diesel engines and heavy equipment acquired in the Armed Forces also is valuable.

Mobile heavy equipment mechanics usually must buy their own handtools, although employers furnish power tools and test equipment. Trainee mechanics are expected to accumulate their own tools as they gain experience. Many experienced mechanics have thousands of dollars invested in tools.

Experienced mechanics may advance to field service jobs, where they have greater opportunity to tackle problems independently and earn overtime pay. Mechanics who have leadership ability may become shop supervisors or service managers. Some mechanics open their own repair shops.

## Job Outlook

Opportunities should generally be good for persons who have completed formal training programs in diesel or heavy equipment mechanics. Persons without formal training are expected to encounter growing difficulty entering this occupation.

Employment of mobile heavy equipment mechanics is expected to grow more slowly than the average for all occupations through the year 2005. Increasing numbers of mechanics will be required in repair shops of equipment dealers and rental and leasing companies as the growing complexity of mobile heavy equipment necessitates more repairs being done by professionals. More mechanics also will be needed by all levels of government to service construction equipment that repairs and maintains the country's system of highways and bridges. But employment of mechanics will increase more slowly at the federal level as defense-related spending is trimmed. Employment of mechanics by construction contractors will increase more slowly as more of the equipment in use is rented or leased.

As the economy expands, growth of construction activity should result in the use of more mobile heavy equipment, which would increase the necessity for periodic service and repair. Various kinds of equipment will be needed in increasing numbers to grade construction sites, excavate basements, lay water and sewer lines, and put in streets. In addition, construction of new highways and bridges and repair or rebuilding of existing ones will also require more mechanics for servicing the equipment.

Since construction and mining are sensitive to changes in the level of economic activity, mobile heavy equipment may be idled during downturns. In addition, winter is traditionally the slack season for construction activity, particularly in colder regions. Fewer mechanics may be needed during periods when equipment is used less intensively, but employers usually try to retain experienced workers. However, employers may be reluctant to hire inexperienced workers during slack periods.

## Earnings

Median weekly earnings of mobile heavy equipment mechanics were about $554 in 1994. The middle 50 percent earned from around $409 to $684 a week; the lowest 10 percent earned less than $322 a week, and the top 10 percent earned over $864 a week in 1994.

Some mobile heavy equipment mechanics are members of unions. The unions include the International Association of Machinists and Aerospace Workers; the International Union of Operating Engineers; and the International Brotherhood of Teamsters.

## Related Occupations

Workers in other occupations who repair and service diesel-powered vehicles and heavy equipment include rail car repairers and diesel, farm equipment, and mine machinery mechanics.

## Related *D.O.T.* Jobs

These job titles are related to or more specific than the more general description above. They will help you identify job options you may not otherwise discover. These descriptions are in the current edition of the *Dictionary of Occupational Titles* and classified by numerical order.

620.261-022 CONSTRUCTION-EQUIPMENT MECHANIC; 620.281-042 LOGGING-EQUIPMENT MECHANIC; 620.381-014 MECHANIC, ENDLESS TRACK VEHICLE

## Sources of Additional Information

More details about work opportunities for mobile heavy equipment mechanics may be obtained from local mobile heavy equipment dealers, construction contractors, surface mining companies, and government agencies. Local offices of the state employment service may also have information on work opportunities and training programs.

# Motorcycle, Boat, and Small-Engine Mechanics

## Nature of the Work

Although the engines that power motorcycles, boats, and lawn and garden equipment are usually smaller than those that power automobiles and trucks, they have many things in common, including breakdowns. Motorcycle, boat, and small-engine mechanics repair and service power equipment ranging from chain saws to yachts.

Small engines, like larger engines, require periodic servicing to minimize the possibility of breakdowns and keep them operating at peak efficiency. At routine intervals, mechanics adjust, clean, lubricate, and, when necessary, replace worn or defective parts such as spark plugs, ignition points, valves, and carburetors. Routine maintenance is normally a major part of the mechanic's work.

When breakdowns occur, mechanics diagnose the cause and repair or replace the faulty parts. The mark of a skilled mechanic is the ability to diagnose mechanical, fuel, and electrical problems and to make repairs in a minimum amount of time. A quick and accurate diagnosis requires problem-solving ability as well as a thorough knowledge of the equipment's operation. The mechanic first obtains a description of the symptoms of the problem from the owner, and then, if possible, operates the equipment to observe the symptoms. The mechanic may have to use special diagnostic testing equipment and disassemble some components for further examination. After pinpointing the cause of the problem, the needed adjustments, repairs, or replacements are made. Some jobs require only the adjustment or replacement of a single item, such as a carburetor or fuel pump, and may be completed in less than an hour. In contrast, a complete engine overhaul may require a number of hours, because the mechanic must disassemble and reassemble the engine to replace worn valves, pistons, bearings, and other internal parts.

Motorcycle, boat, and small-engine mechanics use common handtools such as wrenches, pliers, and screwdrivers, as well as power tools such as drills and grinders. Engine analyzers, compression gauges, ammeters and voltmeters, and other testing devices help mechanics locate faulty parts and tune engines. Hoists may be used to lift heavy equipment such as motorcycles, snowmobiles, or boats. Mechanics often refer to service manuals for detailed directions and specifications while performing repairs.

Mechanics usually specialize in the service and repair of one type of equipment, although they may work on closely related products. *Motorcycle mechanics* repair and overhaul motorcycles, motor scooters, mopeds, and all-terrain vehicles. Besides engines, they may work on transmissions, brakes, and ignition systems, and make minor body repairs. Because many motorcycle mechanics work for dealers that service only the products they sell, mechanics may specialize in servicing only a few of the many makes and models of motorcycles.

*Motorboat mechanics* repair and adjust the engines and electrical and mechanical equipment of inboard and outboard marine engines. Most small boats have portable outboard engines that can be removed and brought into the repair shop. Larger craft, such as cabin cruisers and commercial fishing boats, are powered by diesel or gasoline inboard or inboard-outdrive engines, which are only removed for major overhauls. Motorboat mechanics may also work on propellers, steering mechanisms, marine plumbing, and other boat equipment.

*Small-engine mechanics* service and repair outdoor power equipment such as lawnmowers, garden tractors, edge trimmers, and chain saws. They also may occasionally work on portable generators, go-carts, and snowmobiles.

## Working Conditions

Motorcycle, boat, and small-engine mechanics usually work in repair shops that are well lighted and ventilated, but which are sometimes noisy when engines are being tested. However, motorboat mechanics may work outdoors in all weather when repairing inboard engines aboard boats; they may have to work in cramped or awkward positions to reach a boat's engine.

In northern states, motorcycles, boats, lawnmowers, and other equipment are used less, or not at all, during the winter, and mechanics may work fewer than 40 hours a week; many mechanics are only hired temporarily during the busy spring and summer seasons. Some of the winter slack is taken up by scheduling time-consuming engine overhauls and working on snowmobiles and snow blowers. Many mechanics may work considerably more than 40 hours a week when the weather is warmer in the spring, summer, and fall.

## Employment

Motorcycle, boat, and small-engine mechanics held almost 46,000 jobs in 1994. About 11,000 were motorcycle mechanics, while the remainder specialized in the repair of boats or outdoor power equipment such as lawnmowers, garden tractors, and chain saws. More than one-quarter of all motorcycle, boat, and small-engine mechanics worked for dealers of boats, motorcycles, and miscellaneous vehicles. Others were employed by independent repair shops, marinas and boat yards, equipment rental companies, and hardware and lawn and garden stores. Nearly one-third were self-employed.

## Training, Other Qualifications, and Advancement

Due to the increasing complexity of motorcycles, most employers prefer to hire motorcycle mechanics who are graduates of formal training programs. However, because technology has not had as great an impact on boat and outdoor power equipment, most boat and small-engine mechanics learn their skills on the job. For trainee jobs, employers hire persons with mechanical aptitude who are knowledgeable about the fundamentals of small two- and four-cycle engines. Many trainees develop an interest in mechanics and acquire some basic skills through working on automobiles, motorcycles, boats, or outdoor power equipment as a hobby, or through mechanic vocational training in high school, vocational and technical schools, or community colleges. A growing number also prepare for their careers by completing training programs in motorcycle, marine, or small-engine mechanics, but only a relatively small number of such specialized programs exist.

Trainees begin by learning routine service tasks under the guidance of experienced mechanics, such as replacing ignition points and spark plugs, or taking apart, assembling, and testing new equipment. Equipment manufacturers' service manuals are an important training tool. As trainees gain experience and proficiency, they progress to more difficult tasks, such as diagnosing the cause of breakdowns or overhauling engines. Up to three years of training on the job may be necessary before an inexperienced beginner becomes skilled in all aspects of the repair of some motorcycle and boat engines.

Employers sometimes send mechanics and trainees to special training courses conducted by motorcycle, boat, and outdoor power equipment manufacturers or distributors. These courses, which can last as long as two weeks, are designed to upgrade the worker's skills and provide information on repairing new models.

Most employers prefer to hire high school graduates for trainee mechanic positions, but will accept applicants with less education if they possess adequate reading, writing, and arithmetic skills. Many equipment dealers employ students part-time and during the summer to help assemble new equipment and perform minor repairs. Helpful high school courses include small-engine repair, automobile mechanics, science, and business arithmetic.

Knowledge of basic electronics is increasingly desirable for motorcycle, boat, and small-engine mechanics. Electronics are increasingly being used in engine controls, instrument displays, and a variety of other components of motorcycles, boats, and outdoor power equipment. Mechanics should be familiar with at least the basic principles of electronics in order to recognize when an electronic malfunction may be responsible for a problem, and be able to test and replace electronic components.

Motorcycle, boat, and small-engine mechanics are sometimes required to furnish their own handtools. Employers generally provide some tools and test equipment, but beginners are expected to gradually accumulate handtools as they gain experience. Some experienced mechanics have thousands of dollars invested in tools.

Some mechanics are able to use skills learned through repairing motorcycles, boats, and outdoor power equipment to advance to higher paying jobs as automobile, truck, or heavy equipment mechanics. In larger shops, mechanics with leadership ability can advance to supervisory positions such as shop supervisor or service manager. Mechanics who are able to raise enough capital may open their own repair shops or equipment dealerships.

## Job Outlook

Employment of motorcycle, boat, and small-engine mechanics is expected to grow more slowly than the average for all occupations through the year 2005. The majority of job openings are expected to occur because many experienced motorcycle, boat, and small-engine mechanics leave each year to transfer to other occupations, retire, or stop working for other reasons. Job prospects should be especially favorable for persons who complete mechanic training programs.

Growth of personal disposable income over the 1994-2005 period should provide consumers with more discretionary dollars to buy boats, lawn and garden power equipment, and motorcycles—requiring more mechanics to keep the growing amount of equipment in operation. However, growth in the demand for mechanics will be slowed by design improvements that should continue to make equipment more reliable and lengthen intervals between routine service.

Employment of motorcycle mechanics should increase slowly as the popularity of motorcycles rebounds. Beginning in the late 1990s, the number of persons between the ages of 18 and 24 should begin to grow. Motorcycle usage should continue to be popular with persons in this age group, who historically have the greatest proportion of motorcycle enthusiasts. Motorcycles have also been increasing in popularity with persons between the ages of 25 and 40, a group with more disposable income to spend on recreational equipment such as motorcycles and boats.

Recreational boating is expected to continue to be popular, and construction of new single-family houses will result in an increase in the lawn and garden equipment in operation, increasing the need for mechanics. However, equipment growth will be slowed by trends toward smaller lawns and contracting out their maintenance to lawn service firms.

### Earnings

Motorcycle, boat, and small-engine mechanics who usually worked full-time had median earnings of about $407 a week in 1994. The middle 50 percent earned between $286 and $516 a week. The lowest paid 10 percent earned less than $202 a week, while the highest paid 10 percent earned over $644 a week.

Motorcycle, boat, and small-engine mechanics tend to receive few fringe benefits in small shops, but those employed in larger shops often receive paid vacations and sick leave and health insurance. Some employers also pay for work-related training and provide uniforms.

### Related Occupations

The work of motorcycle, boat, and small-engine mechanics is closely related to that of mechanics and repairers who work on other types of mobile equipment powered by internal combustion engines. Related occupations include automotive mechanic, diesel mechanic, farm equipment mechanic, and mobile heavy equipment mechanic.

### Related *D.O.T.* Jobs

These job titles are related to or more specific than the more general description above. They will help you identify job options you may not otherwise discover. These descriptions are in the current edition of the *Dictionary of Occupational Titles* and classified by numerical order.

620.281-054 MOTORCYCLE REPAIRER; 620.684-026 MOTORCYCLE SUBASSEMBLY REPAIRER; 623.261-010 EXPERIMENTAL MECHANIC, OUTBOARD MOTORS; 623.261-014 OUTBOARD-MOTOR TESTER; 623.281-038 MOTORBOAT MECHANIC; 623.281-042 OUTBOARD-MOTOR MECHANIC; 625.281-018 ENGINE REPAIRER, SERVICE; 625.281-026 GAS-ENGINE REPAIRER; 625.281-030 POWER-SAW MECHANIC; 625.281-034 SMALL-ENGINE MECHANIC; 625.381-010 ENGINE REPAIRER, PRODUCTION; 721.281-022 MAGNETO REPAIRER

### Sources of Additional Information

For more details about work opportunities, contact local motorcycle, boat, and lawn and garden equipment dealers, and boat yards and marinas. Local offices of the state employment service also may have information about employment and training opportunities.

General information about motorcycle mechanic careers may be obtained from:

❏ Motorcycle Mechanics Institute, 2844 West Deer Valley Rd., Phoenix, AZ 85027.

General information about motorboat mechanic careers may be obtained from:

❏ Marine Mechanics Institute, 2844 West Deer Valley Rd., Phoenix, AZ 85027.

# Musical Instrument Repairers and Tuners

### Nature of the Work

Musical instruments are a source of entertainment and recreation for millions of people. Maintaining these instruments so they perform properly is the job of musical instrument repairers and tuners. The occupation includes piano tuners and repairers (often called piano technicians); pipe-organ tuners and repairers; and brass, woodwind, percussion, or string instrument repairers.

*Piano tuners* adjust piano strings to the proper pitch. A string's pitch is the frequency at which it vibrates—and produces sound—when it is struck by one of the piano's wooden hammers. Tuners first adjust the pitch of the "A" string. Striking the key, the tuner compares the string's pitch with that of a tuning fork. Using a tuning hammer (also called a tuning lever or wrench), the tuner turns a steel pin to tighten or loosen the string until its pitch matches that of the tuning fork. The pitch of each of the other strings is set in relation to the "A" string. The standard 88-key piano has 230 strings and can be tuned in about an hour and a half.

A piano has thousands of wooden, steel, iron, ivory, and felt parts which can be plagued by an assortment of problems. It is the task of *piano repairers* to locate and correct these problems. In addition to repair work, piano repairers may also tune pianos.

To diagnose problems, repairers talk with customers before partially dismantling a piano to inspect its parts. Repairers may realign moving parts, replace old or worn ones, or completely rebuild pianos. Repairers use common handtools as well as special ones, such as regulating, repining, and restringing tools.

Some piano tuners service pianos that have built-in computers that control humidity, assist in recording, or allow the piano to operate as an automatic player-piano. Piano repair work will increasingly require some knowledge of electronics, as sales of sophisticated pianos increase, and people decide to upgrade their older pianos.

*Pipe-organ repairers* tune, repair, and install organs that make music by forcing air through flue pipes or reed pipes. The flue pipe sounds when a current of air strikes a metal lip in the side of the pipe. The reed pipe sounds when a current of air vibrates a brass reed inside the pipe.

To tune an organ, repairers first match the pitch of the "A" pipes with that of a tuning fork. The pitch of other pipes is set by comparing it to that of the "A" pipes. To tune a flue pipe, repairers move the metal slide that increases or decreases the pipe's "speaking length." To tune a reed pipe, the tuner alters the length of the brass reed. Most organs have hundreds of pipes, so often a day or more is needed to completely tune an organ.

Pipe-organ repairers locate problems, repair or replace worn parts, and clean pipes. Repairers also assemble organs on site in churches and auditoriums, following manufacturer's blueprints. They use hand and power tools to install and connect the air chest, blowers, air ducts, pipes, and other components. They may work in teams or be assisted by helpers. Depending on the size of the organ, a job may take several weeks or even months.

*Violin repairers* adjust and repair bowed instruments, such as violins, violas, and cellos, using a variety of handtools. They find defects by inspecting and playing instruments. They remove cracked or broken sections, repair or replace defective parts, and restring instruments. They also fill in scratches with putty, sand rough spots, and apply paint or varnish.

*Guitar repairers* inspect and play the instrument to determine defects. They replace levels using handtools, and fit wood or metal parts. They reassemble and string guitars.

Brass and woodwind instruments include trumpets, cornets, French horns, trombones, tubas, clarinets, flutes, saxophones, oboes, and bassoons. *Brass and wind instrument repairers* clean, adjust, and repair these instruments. They move mechanical parts or play scales to find defects. They may unscrew and remove rod pins, keys, and pistons, and remove soldered parts using gas torches. They repair dents in metal instruments using mallets or burnishing tools. They fill cracks in wood instruments by inserting pinning wire and covering them with filler. Repairers also inspect instrument keys and replace worn pads and corks.

*Percussion instrument repairers* work on drums, cymbals, and xylophones. In order to repair a drum, they remove drum tension rod screws and rods by hand or by using a drum key. They cut new drumheads from animal skin, stretch the skin over rimhoops and tuck it around and under the hoop using hand tucking tools. To prevent a crack in a cymbal, gong or similar instrument from advancing repairers may operate a drill press or hand power drill to drill holes at the inside edge of the crack. Another technique they may use involves cutting out sections around the cracks using shears or grinding wheels. They also replace the bars and wheels of xylophones.

## Working Conditions

Although they may suffer small cuts and bruises, the work of musical instrument repairers and tuners is relatively safe. Most brass, woodwind, percussion, and string instrument repairers work in repair shops or music stores. Piano and organ repairers and tuners usually work on instruments in homes, schools, and churches and may spend several hours a day driving. Salaried repairers and tuners work out of a shop or store; the self-employed generally work out of their homes.

## Employment

Musical instrument repairers and tuners held about 9,702 jobs in 1994. Most worked on pianos. About two-thirds were self-employed. Eight of 10 wage and salary repairers and tuners worked in music stores, and most of the rest worked in repair shops or for musical instrument manufacturers.

## Training, Other Qualifications, and Advancement

For musical instrument repairer and tuner jobs, employers prefer people with post high school training in music repair technology. Some musical instrument repairers and tuners learn their trade on the job as apprentices or assistants, but employers willing to provide on-the-job training are difficult to find. A few music stores, large repair shops, and self-employed repairers and tuners hire inexperienced people as trainees to learn how to tune and repair instruments under the supervision of experienced workers. Trainees may sell instruments, clean up, and do other routine work. Usually two to five years of training and practice are needed to become fully qualified.

A small number of technical schools and colleges offer courses in piano technology or brass, woodwind, string, and electronic musical instrument repair. A few music repair schools offer one- or two-year courses. There are also home-study (correspondence school) courses in piano technology. Graduates of these courses generally refine their skills by working for a time with an experienced tuner or technician.

Music courses help develop the student's ear for tonal quality. The ability to play an instrument is helpful. Knowledge of woodworking is useful for repairing instruments made of wood.

Repairers and tuners need good hearing, mechanical aptitude, and manual dexterity. For those dealing directly with customers, a neat appearance and a pleasant, cooperative manner are important.

Musical instrument repairers keep up with developments in their fields by studying trade magazines and manufacturers' service manuals. The Piano Technicians Guild helps its members improve their skills through training conducted at local chapter meetings and at regional and national seminars. Guild members also can take a series of tests to earn the title Registered Piano Technician. The National Association of Professional Band Instrument Repair Technicians offers similar programs, scholarships, and a trade publication. Its members specialize in the repair of woodwind, brass, string and percussion instruments. Repairers and technicians who work for large dealers, repair shops, or manufacturers can advance to supervisory positions or go into business for themselves.

## Job Outlook

Musical instrument repairer and tuner jobs are expected to increase about as fast as the average for all occupations through the year 2005. Replacement needs will provide the most job opportunities as many repairers and tuners near retirement age. Nonetheless, due to its small size the number of openings due to both growth and replacement needs is very low relative to other occupations. Because training is difficult to get—there are only a few schools that offer training programs and few experienced workers are willing to take on apprentices—opportunities for those who do get training should be excellent.

Several competing factors are expected to influence the demand for musical instrument repairers and tuners. Although the number of people employed as musicians will increase, the number of students of all ages playing musical instruments is expected to grow slowly. Yet, consumers should continue to buy more expensive instruments, so they should be willing to spend more on tuning and repairs to protect their value.

## Earnings

According to the limited information available, repairers and tuners employed full-time by retail music stores averaged about $26,550 in 1994. Repairers and tuners who worked full-time plus supervised at least one other technician averaged $34,250.

## Related Occupations

Musical instrument repairers need mechanical aptitude and manual dexterity. Electronic home entertainment equipment repairers, vending machine servicers and repairers, home appliance and power tool repairers, and computer and office machine repairers all require similar talents.

## Related *D.O.T.* Jobs

These job titles are related to or more specific than the more general description above. They will help you identify job options you may not otherwise discover. These descriptions are in the current edition of the *Dictionary of Occupational Titles* and classified by numerical order.

730.281-014 ACCORDION REPAIRER; 730.281-026 FRETTED-INSTRUMENT REPAIRER; 730.281-038 PIANO TECHNICIAN; 730.281-050 VIOLIN REPAIRER; 730.281-054 WIND-INSTRUMENT REPAIRER; 730.361-010 PIANO TUNER; 730.361-014 PIPE-ORGAN TUNER AND REPAIRER; 730.381-010 ACCORDION TUNER; 730.381-026 HARP REGULATOR; 730.381-034 METAL-REED TUNER; 730.381-038 ORGAN-PIPE VOICER; 730.381-042 PERCUSSION-INSTRUMENT REPAIRER; 730.381-058 TUNER, PERCUSSION; 730.681-010 PIANO REGULATOR-INSPECTOR; 730.684-022 BOW REHAIRER; 730.684-026 CHIP TUNER; 730.684-094 TONE REGULATOR

## Sources of Additional Information

Details about job opportunities may be available from local music instrument dealers and repair shops.

For general information about piano technicians and a list of schools offering courses in piano technology, write to:

❏ Piano Technicians Guild, 3930 Washington St., Kansas City, MO 64111-2963.

For general information on musical instrument repair, write to:

❏ National Association of Professional Band Instrument Repair Technicians (NAPBIRT), P.O. Box 51, Normal, IL 61761.

# Nuclear Medicine Technologists

## Nature of the Work

In nuclear medicine, radionuclides—unstable atoms that emit radiation spontaneously—are used to diagnose and treat disease. Radionuclides are purified and compounded like other drugs to form radiopharmaceuticals. Nuclear medicine technologists administer these radiopharmaceuticals to patients, then monitor the characteristics and functions of tissues or organs in which they localize. Abnormal areas show higher or lower concentrations of radioactivity than normal.

Nuclear medicine technologists operate cameras that detect and map the radioactive drug in the patient's body to create an image on photographic film. Radiologic technologists also operate diagnostic imaging equipment, but their equipment creates an image by projecting an x-ray through the patient.

Nuclear medicine technologists explain test procedures to patients. They prepare a dosage of the radiopharmaceutical and administer it by mouth, injection, or other means. When preparing radiopharmaceuticals, technologists adhere to safety standards that keep the radiation dose to workers and patients as low as possible.

Technologists position patients and start a gamma scintillation camera, or scanner, which creates images of the distribution of a radiopharmaceutical as it passes through or localizes in the patient's body. Technologists produce the images on a computer screen or on film for a physician to interpret. Some nuclear medicine studies, such as cardiac function studies, are processed with the aid of a computer.

Nuclear medicine technologists also perform radioimmunoassay studies which assess the behavior of a radioactive substance inside the body. For example, technologists may add radioactive substances to blood or serum to determine levels of hormones or therapeutic drug content.

Technologists keep patient records and record the amount and type of radionuclides received, used, and disposed of.

## Working Conditions

Nuclear medicine technologists generally work a 40-hour week. This may include evening or weekend hours in departments which operate on an extended schedule. Opportunities for part-time and shift work are also available. In addition, technologists in hospitals may be on-call duty on a rotational basis.

Because technologists are on their feet much of the day, and may lift or turn disabled patients, physical stamina is important.

Although there is potential for radiation exposure in this field, it is kept to a minimum by the use of shielded syringes, gloves, and other protective devices. Technologists also wear badges that measure radiation levels. Because of safety programs, however, badge measurements rarely exceed established safety levels.

## Employment

Nuclear medicine technologists held about 13,000 jobs in 1994. About 9 out of 10 jobs were in hospitals. The rest were in physicians' offices and clinics, including imaging centers.

## Training, Other Qualifications, and Advancement

Nuclear medicine technology programs range in length from one to four years and lead to a certificate, associate degree, or bachelor's degree. Generally, certificate programs are offered in hospitals; associate programs in community colleges; and bachelor's programs in four-year colleges and in universities. Courses cover physical sciences, the biological effects of radiation exposure, radiation protection and procedures, the use of radiopharmaceuticals, imaging techniques, and computer applications. Associate and bachelor's programs also cover liberal arts.

One-year certificate programs are for health professionals, especially radiologic technologists and ultrasound technologists wishing to specialize in nuclear medicine. They also attract medical technologists, registered nurses, and others who wish to change fields or specialize. Others interested in the nuclear medicine technology field have three options: a two-year certificate program, a two-year associate program, or a four-year bachelor's program.

The Joint Review Committee on Education Programs in Nuclear Medicine Technology accredits most formal training programs in nuclear medicine technology. In 1994, there were 120 accredited programs.

All nuclear medicine technologists must meet the minimum federal standards on the administration of radioactive drugs and the operation of radiation detection equipment. In addition, about half of all states require technologists to be licensed. Technologists also may obtain voluntary professional certification or registration. Registration or certification is available from the

American Registry of Radiologic Technologists and from the Nuclear Medicine Technology Certification Board. Most employers prefer to hire certified or registered technologists.

Technologists may advance to supervisor, then to chief technologist, and to department administrator or director. Some technologists specialize in a clinical area such as nuclear cardiology or computer analysis or leave patient care to take positions in research laboratories. Some become instructors or directors in nuclear medicine technology programs, a step that usually requires a bachelor's degree or a master's in nuclear medicine technology. Others leave the occupation to work as sales or training representatives for health equipment and radiopharmaceutical manufacturing firms, or as radiation safety officers in regulatory agencies or hospitals.

## Job Outlook

Job prospects for nuclear medicine technologists are expected to be good. The number of openings each year, however, will be very low because the occupation is small.

Employment of nuclear medicine technologists is expected to grow faster than the average for all occupations through the year 2005. Substantial growth in the number of middle-aged and older persons will spur demand for diagnostic procedures, including nuclear medicine tests. Furthermore, technological innovations seem likely to increase the diagnostic uses of nuclear medicine. One example is the use of radiopharmaceuticals in combination with monoclonal antibodies to detect cancer at far earlier stages than is customary today, and without resorting to surgery. Another is the use of radionuclides to examine the heart's ability to pump blood. Wider use of nuclear medical imaging to observe metabolic and biochemical changes for neurology, cardiology, and oncology procedures, will also spur demand for nuclear medicine technologists.

Cost considerations will affect the speed with which new applications of nuclear medicine grow. Some promising nuclear medicine procedures, such as positron emission tomography, are extremely costly, and hospitals contemplating them will have to consider equipment costs, reimbursement policies, and the number of potential users.

## Earnings

According to a University of Texas Medical Branch survey of hospitals and medical centers, the median annual salary of nuclear medicine technologists, based on a 40-hour week and excluding shift or area differentials, was $35,027 in October 1994. The average minimum salary was $28,044 and the average maximum was $41,598.

## Related Occupations

Nuclear medical technologists operate sophisticated equipment to help physicians and other health practitioners diagnose and treat patients. Radiologic technologists, diagnostic medical sonographers, cardiovascular technologists, electroneurodiagnostic technologists, clinical laboratory technologists, perfusionists, and respiratory therapists also perform similar functions.

## Related *D.O.T.* Jobs

These job titles are related to or more specific than the more general description above. They will help you identify job op-tions you may not otherwise discover. These descriptions are in the current edition of the *Dictionary of Occupational Titles* and classified by numerical order.

078.361-018 NUCLEAR MEDICINE TECHNOLOGIST

## Sources of Additional Information

Additional information on a career as a nuclear medicine technologist is available from:

❑ The Society of Nuclear Medicine-Technologist Section, 1850 Samuel Morse Dr., Reston, VA 22090.

For information on a career as a nuclear medicine technologist, enclose a stamped, self-addressed business size envelope with your request to:

❑ American Society of Radiologic Technologists, 15000 Central Ave., SE, Albuquerque, NM 87123-3917.

For a list of accredited programs in nuclear medicine technology, write to:

❑ Joint Review Committee on Educational Programs in Nuclear Medicine Technology, 1144 West 3300 South, Salt Lake City, UT 84119-3330.

Information on certification is available from:

❑ Nuclear Medicine Technology Certification Board, 2970 Clairmont Rd., Suite 610, Atlanta, GA 30329.

# Nursing Aides and Psychiatric Aides

## Nature of the Work

Nursing aides and psychiatric aides help care for physically or mentally ill, injured, disabled, or infirm individuals confined to hospitals, nursing or residential care facilities, and mental health settings.

Nursing aides, also known as nursing assistants or hospital attendants, work under the supervision of nursing and medical staff. They answer patients' call bells, deliver messages, serve meals, make beds, and help patients eat, dress, and bathe. Aides may also provide skin care to patients, take temperatures, pulse, respiration, and blood pressure, and help patients get in and out of bed and walk. They may also escort patients to operating and examining rooms, keep patients' rooms neat, set up equipment, or store and move supplies. Aides observe patients' physical, mental, and emotional conditions and report any change to the nursing or medical staff.

Nursing aides employed in nursing homes are often the principal caregivers, having far more contact with residents than other members of the staff do. Since some residents may stay in a nursing home for months or even years, aides develop ongoing relationships with them and respond to them in a positive, caring way.

Psychiatric aides are also known as mental health assistants and psychiatric nursing assistants. They care for mentally impaired or emotionally disturbed individuals. They work under a team that may include psychiatrists, psychologists, psychiatric nurses, social workers, and therapists. In addition to helping patients dress, bathe, groom, and eat, psychiatric aides socialize with them and lead them in educational and recreational activities. Psychiatric aides may play games such as cards with the patients, watch television with them, or participate in group activities such as sports or field trips. They observe patients and report any signs which might be important for the professional staff to know. They accompany patients to and from wards for examination and treatment. Because they have the closest contact with patients, psychiatric aides have a great deal of influence on patients' outlook and treatment.

## Working Conditions

Most full-time aides work about 40 hours a week, but because patients need care 24 hours a day, some aides work evenings, nights, weekends, and holidays. Many work part-time. Aides spend many hours standing and walking. Since they may have to move partially paralyzed patients in and out of bed or help them stand or walk, aides must guard against back injury.

Nursing aides often have unpleasant duties; they empty bed pans and change soiled bed linens. They also care for disoriented and irritable patients. Psychiatric aides must be prepared to care for patients whose disease may cause violent behavior. While their work can be emotionally demanding, many aides gain satisfaction from assisting those in need.

## Employment

Nursing aides held about 1,265,000 jobs in 1994, and psychiatric aides held about 105,000 jobs. About one-half of all nursing aides worked in nursing homes, and about one-fourth worked in hospitals. Some worked in residential care facilities, such as halfway houses and homes for the aged or disabled, or in private households. Most psychiatric aides worked in state and county mental institutions, psychiatric units of general hospitals, private psychiatric facilities and community mental health centers.

## Training, Other Qualifications, and Advancement

In many cases, neither a high school diploma nor previous work experience is necessary for a job as a nursing or psychiatric aide. A few employers, however, require some training or experience. Hospitals may require experience as a nursing aide or home health aide. Nursing homes often hire inexperienced workers who must complete a minimum of 75 hours of mandatory training and pass a competency evaluation program within four months of employment. Aides who complete the program are placed on the state registry of nursing aides. Some states require psychiatric aides to complete a formal training program.

These occupations can offer individuals an entry into the world of work. The flexibility of night and weekend hours also provides high school and college students a chance to work during the school year.

Nursing aide training is offered in high schools, vocational-technical centers, some nursing homes, and community colleges. Courses cover body mechanics, nutrition, anatomy and physiology, infection control, communication skills, and resident rights. Personal care skills such as how to help patients bathe, eat, and groom are also taught.

Some facilities, other than nursing homes, provide classroom instruction for newly hired aides, while others rely exclusively on informal on-the-job instruction from a licensed nurse or an experienced aide. Such training may last several days to a few months. From time to time, aides may also attend lectures, workshops, and in-service training.

Applicants should be healthy, tactful, patient, understanding, emotionally stable, dependable, and have a desire to help people. They should also be able to work as part of a team, and be willing to perform repetitive, routine tasks.

Opportunities for advancement within these occupations are limited. To enter other health occupations, aides generally need additional formal training. Some employers and unions provide opportunities by simplifying the educational paths to advancement. Experience as an aide can also help individuals decide whether to pursue a career in the health care field.

## Job Outlook

Job prospects for nursing aides should be good through the year 2005. Employment of nursing aides is expected to grow faster than the average for all occupations in response to an emphasis on rehabilitation and the long-term care needs of a rapidly growing population of those 75 years old and older. Employment will increase as a result of the expansion of nursing homes and other long-term care facilities for people with chronic illnesses and disabling conditions, many of whom are elderly. Also increasing employment of nursing aides will be modern medical technology which, while saving more lives, increases the need for the extended care provided by aides. As a result, nursing and personal care facilities are expected to grow very rapidly and to provide most of the new jobs for nursing aides.

Employment of psychiatric aides is expected to grow about as fast as the average for all occupations. Employment will rise in response to the sharp increase in the number of older persons—many of whom will require mental health services. Employment of aides in private psychiatric facilities and community mental health centers is likely to grow because of increasing public acceptance of formal treatment for drug abuse and alcoholism, and a lessening of the stigma attached to those receiving mental health care. While employment in private psychiatric facilities may grow, employment in public mental hospitals is likely to be stagnant due to constraints on public spending.

Replacement needs will constitute the major source of openings for aides. Turnover is high, a reflection of modest entry requirements, low pay, and lack of advancement opportunities.

## Earnings

Median weekly earnings of full-time salaried nursing aides and psychiatric aides were $275 in 1994. The middle 50 percent earned between $214 and $356. The lowest 10 percent earned less than $175; the top 10 percent, more than $482.

According to a University of Texas Medical Branch survey of hospitals and medical centers, the median annual salary of nursing aides, based on a 40-hour week and excluding shift or area differentials, was $14,612 in October 1994.

According to the Buck Survey conducted by the American Health Care Association, nursing aides in chain nursing homes had median annual earnings of about $12,800 in 1994. The middle 50 percent earned between $11,600 and $14,400.

Aides in hospitals generally receive at least one week's paid vacation after one year of service. Paid holidays and sick leave, hospital and medical benefits, extra pay for late-shift work, and pension plans also are available to many hospital and some nursing home employees.

## Related Occupations

Nursing aides and psychiatric aides help people who need routine care or treatment. So do homemaker-home health aides, childcare attendants, companions, occupational therapy aides, and physical therapy aides.

## Related *D.O.T.* Jobs

These job titles are related to or more specific than the more general description above. They will help you identify job options you may not otherwise discover. These descriptions are in the current edition of the *Dictionary of Occupational Titles* and classified by numerical order.

354.374-010 NURSE, PRACTICAL; 354.377-010 BIRTH ATTENDANT; 354.677-010 FIRST-AID ATTENDANT; 355.377-014 PSYCHIATRIC AIDE; 355.377-018 MENTAL-RETARDATION AIDE; 355.674-014 NURSE ASSISTANT; 355.674-018 ORDERLY; 355.677-014 TRANSPORTER, PATIENTS

## Sources of Additional Information

For information on nursing careers in long-term care, write:

❏ American Health Care Association, 1201 L St. NW, Washington, DC 20005.

Information about employment also may be obtained from local hospitals, nursing homes, psychiatric facilities, and state boards of nursing.

# Occupational Therapy Assistants and Aides

## Nature of the Work

Occupational therapy assistants and aides work under the direction of occupational therapists to provide rehabilitative services to patients suffering from mental, physical, emotional, or developmental impairments. The ultimate goal is to improve patients' quality of life by assisting them in overcoming limitations. For example, they help injured workers reenter the labor force by improving their motor skills or help persons with learning disabilities increase their independence by teaching them to prepare meals or use public transportation.

*Occupational therapy assistants* help patients with the rehabilitative activities and exercises that are outlined in the treatment plan devised by the occupational therapist. The activities range from teaching the patient the proper method of moving from a bed into a wheelchair, to the best way to stretch and limber the muscles of the hand. Assistants monitor the individual to ensure the patient is performing the activities correctly and to provide encouragement. They also record their observations with regard to the patient's progress for use by the occupational therapist. If the treatment is not having the intended effect or the client is not improving as expected, the treatment program may be altered to obtain better results. They also document billing of the patient's health insurance provider.

*Occupational therapy aides* typically prepare materials and assemble equipment used during treatment and are responsible for a range of clerical tasks. Their duties may include scheduling appointments, answering the telephone, restocking or ordering depleted supplies, and filling out insurance forms or other paperwork. Aides are not licensed, so by law they are not allowed to perform as wide a range of tasks as occupational therapy assistants.

## Working Conditions

Occupational therapy assistants and aides usually work during the day, but may occasionally work evenings or weekends in order to accommodate the patient's schedule. They should be in good physical shape because they are on their feet for long periods of time and may be asked to help lift and move patients or equipment.

Assistants and aides must be responsible, patient, willing to take directions, and work as part of a team. Furthermore, they should be caring and want to help people who are not able to help themselves. The job can be rewarding and assistants and aides often feel a sense of accomplishment when patients show improvement or recover.

## Employment

Occupational therapy assistants and aides held 16,000 jobs in 1994. Over one-third worked in hospitals and about one in four worked in nursing and personal care facilities. The rest worked primarily in offices of occupational therapists and other offices operated by health practitioners. A small, but increasing number of assistants and aides work in the home health services industry and provide care in patients' homes.

## Training, Other Qualifications, and Advancement

Occupational therapy assistants need an associate degree from an accredited community college or technical school. There were 77 accredited occupational therapy assistant programs in the United States in 1993. The first year of study typically involves an introduction to health care, and basic medical terminology, anatomy, and physiology. In the second year, courses are more rigorous and usually include occupational theory courses in areas like mental health, gerontology and pediatrics. Students also must complete supervised fieldwork in a clinic. Applicants to occupational therapy assistant programs can improve their chances of admission by taking high school courses in biology and health, and by performing volunteer work in nursing homes, occupational or physical therapist's offices, or elsewhere in the health care field.

After students receive their associate degrees, they may have to take a state licensure exam to prove their competence. Thirty-seven states, Puerto Rico, and the District of Columbia required occupational therapy assistants to be licensed in 1994.

Occupational therapy aides usually receive most of their training on the job. Qualified applicants must have a high school diploma, strong interpersonal skills, and a desire to help people in need. Applicants may increase their chances of getting a job by volunteering their services, thus displaying initiative and their aptitude to the employer.

## Job Outlook

Opportunities for job seekers should be favorable. Employment of occupational therapy assistants and aides is expected to grow much faster than the average for all occupations through

2005. Although the occupation is expected to be one of the fastest growing in the economy, the number of job openings will be low because the occupation is small.

Growth will result from an aging population, especially the baby boom cohort, that will need more occupational therapy services. Demand will also result from advances in medicine that allow more people with critical problems to survive, but then need rehabilitative therapy. Furthermore, employers seeking to reduce health care costs are expected to hire more occupational therapy assistants and aides for tasks currently being performed by more highly paid occupational therapists.

### Earnings

According to a membership survey of the American Occupational Therapy Association, the median annual income for occupational therapy assistants was about $25,300 in 1993. Based on limited information, occupational therapy aides usually start between $6.00 and $7.00 an hour. Starting salaries for both occupations tend to be lower in hospitals and higher in privately owned practices and nursing homes.

### Related Occupations

Occupational therapy assistants and aides work under the direction of occupational therapists. Other occupations in the health care field that work closely with and are supervised by professionals include dental assistants, medical assistants, optometric assistants, pharmacy assistants, and physical therapy assistants and aides.

### Related *D.O.T.* Jobs

These job titles are related to or more specific than the more general description above. They will help you identify job options you may not otherwise discover. These descriptions are in the current edition of the *Dictionary of Occupational Titles* and classified by numerical order.

076.364-010 OCCUPATIONAL THERAPY ASSISTANT; 355.377-010 OCCUPATIONAL THERAPY AIDE

### Sources of Additional Information

Information on a career as an occupational therapy assistant or aide, and a list of accredited programs can be obtained from:

❏ The American Occupational Therapy Association, 4720 Montgomery Lane., P.O. Box 31220, Bethesda, MD 20824-1220.

# Ophthalmic Laboratory Technicians

### Nature of the Work

Ophthalmic laboratory technicians—also known as manufacturing opticians, optical mechanics, or optical goods workers—make prescription eyeglass lenses. Prescription lenses are curved in such a way that light is correctly focused onto the retina of the patient's eye, improving vision. Some ophthalmic laboratory technicians manufacture lenses for other optical instruments, such as telescopes and binoculars. Ophthalmic laboratory technicians cut, grind, edge, and finish lenses according to specifications provided by dispensing opticians, optometrists, or ophthalmologists, and may insert lenses into frames to produce finished glasses.

Ophthalmic laboratory technicians should not be confused with workers in other vision care occupations. Ophthalmologists and optometrists are "eye doctors" who examine eyes, diagnose and treat vision problems, and prescribe corrective lenses. Ophthalmologists also perform eye surgery. Dispensing opticians, who may also do work described here, help patients select frames and lenses, and adjust finished eyeglasses.

Ophthalmic laboratory technicians read prescription specifications, then select standard glass or plastic lens blanks and mark them to indicate where the curves specified on the prescription should be ground. They place the lens into the lens grinder, set the dials for the prescribed curvature, and start the machine. After a minute or so, the lens is ready to be "finished" by a machine which rotates the lens against a fine abrasive to grind it and smooth out rough edges. The lens is then placed in a polishing machine with an even finer abrasive, to polish it to a smooth, bright finish.

Next, the technician examines the lens through a lensometer, an instrument similar in shape to a microscope, and makes sure the degree and placement of the curve is correct. The technician then cuts the lenses and bevels the edges to fit the frame, dips each lens into dye if the prescription calls for tinted or coated lenses, polishes the edges, and assembles the lenses and frame parts into a finished pair of glasses.

In small laboratories, technicians generally handle every phase of the operation. In large ones, technicians may specialize in one or more steps, assembly-line style.

### Working Conditions

Ophthalmic laboratory technicians work in relatively clean and well-lighted laboratories and have limited contact with the public. Surroundings are relatively quiet despite the humming of machines. At times, technicians may need to wear goggles to protect their eyes, and may spend a great deal of time standing.

Most ophthalmic laboratory technicians work a five-day, 40-hour week, which may include weekends, evenings, or occasionally some overtime. Some work part-time.

Ophthalmic laboratory technicians need to take precautions against the hazards associated with cutting glass, handling chemicals, and working near machinery.

### Employment

Ophthalmic laboratory technicians held about 19,000 jobs in 1994. More than half of these jobs were in optical laboratories. These laboratories manufacture eye wear for dispensing by retail stores that sell but do not fabricate prescription glasses, and by ophthalmologists and optometrists. Most of the rest were in retail stores that manufacture and sell prescription glasses—primarily chains of optical goods stores or independent retailers.

### Training, Other Qualifications, and Advancement

Nearly all ophthalmic laboratory technicians learn their skills on the job. Employers filling trainee jobs prefer applicants who are high school graduates. Courses in science and mathematics are valuable; manual dexterity and the ability to do precision work is essential.

Technician trainees start on simple tasks such as marking or blocking lenses for grinding, then progress to lens grinding, lens cutting, edging, beveling, and eyeglass assembly. Depending on the individual's aptitude, it may take 6 to 18 months to become proficient in all phases of the work.

Some ophthalmic laboratory technicians learn their trade in the Armed Forces. Others attend the few programs in optical technology offered by vocational-technical institutes or trade schools. These programs have classes in optical theory, surfacing and lens finishing, and the reading and applying of prescriptions. Programs vary in length from six months to one year, and award certificates or diplomas.

Ophthalmic laboratory technicians can become supervisors and managers. Some technicians become dispensing opticians, although further education or training may be required.

## Job Outlook

Employment of ophthalmic laboratory technicians is expected to increase about as fast as the average for all occupations through the year 2005 due to rising demand for corrective lenses. Nonetheless, most job openings will come from the need to replace technicians who transfer to other occupations or leave the labor force. Relatively few opportunities will occur in any year because the occupation is small.

Demographic trends make it likely that many more Americans will wear glasses in the years ahead. Not only will the population grow, but the number of middle-aged and older adults will grow particularly rapidly. Middle age is a time when many people use corrective lenses for the first time, and older persons require appreciably more vision care than the rest of the population.

The public's heightened awareness of vision care should also increase demand for corrective lenses. The emergence of eye wear as a fashion item—eye wear now comes in an assortment of attractive shapes and colors—has been enticing many people to purchase two or three pair of glasses rather than just one. Most new jobs for ophthalmic laboratory technicians will be in retail optical chains that manufacture prescription glasses on the premises and provide fast service.

## Earnings

Earnings vary greatly according to geographical region. According to the Opticians Association of America, the beginning average salary for laboratory technicians in retail optical stores was $14,185 in 1994. Those with 3 to 5 years of experience averaged $17,913; 6 to 10 years, $22,873; and 11 years or more, $23,980. Trainees may start at the minimum wage.

## Related Occupations

Workers in other precision production occupations include biomedical equipment technicians, dental laboratory technicians, orthodontic technicians, orthotics technicians, prosthetics technicians, and instrument repairers.

## Related *D.O.T.* Jobs

These job titles are related to or more specific than the more general description above. They will help you identify job options you may not otherwise discover. These descriptions are in the current edition of the *Dictionary of Occupational Titles* and classified by numerical order.

711.381-010 OPTICAL-INSTRUMENT ASSEMBLER; 713.381-010 LENS-MOLD SETTER; 713.681-010 LENS MOUNTER II; 716.280-010 OPTICIAN APPRENTICE; 716.280-014 OPTICIAN; 716.280-018 OPTICIAN; 716.381-014 LAY-OUT TECHNICIAN; 716.382-010 LATHE OPERATOR, CONTACT LENS; 716.382-014 OPTICAL-ELEMENT COATER; 716.382-018 PRECISION-LENS GRINDER; 716.382-022 PRECISION-LENS-GRINDER APPRENTICE; 716.462-010 PRECISION-LENS CENTERER AND EDGER; 716.681-010 BLOCKER AND CUTTER, CONTACT LENS; 716.681-018 LENS POLISHER, HAND; 716.682-018 PRECISION-LENS POLISHER

## Sources of Additional Information

For general information about a career as an ophthalmic laboratory technician and for a list of accredited programs in ophthalmic laboratory technology, contact:

❑ Commission on Opticianry Accreditation, 10111 Martin Luther King, Jr. Hwy., Suite 100, Bowie, MD 20720-4299.

# Painters and Paperhangers

## Nature of the Work

Paint and wall coverings make surfaces clean, attractive and bright. In addition, paints and other sealers protect outside walls from wear caused by exposure to the weather. Although some people do both painting and paper hanging, each requires different skills.

*Painters* apply paint, stain, varnish, and other finishes to buildings and other structures. They choose the right paint or finish for the surface to be covered, taking into account customers' wishes, durability, ease of handling, and method of application. They first prepare the surfaces to be covered so the paint will adhere properly. This may require removing the old coat by stripping, sanding, wire brushing, burning, or water and abrasive blasting. Painters also wash walls and trim to remove dirt and grease, fill nail holes and cracks, sandpaper rough spots, and brush off dust. On new surfaces, they apply a primer or sealer to prepare them for the finish coat. Painters also mix paints and match colors, relying on knowledge of paint composition and color harmony.

There are several ways to apply paint and similar coverings. Painters must be able to choose the right paint applicator for each job, depending on the surface to be covered, the characteristics of the finish, and other factors. Some jobs only need a good bristle brush with a soft, tapered edge; others require a dip or fountain pressure roller; still others can best be done using a paint sprayer. Many jobs need several types of applicators. The right tools for each job not only expedite the painter's work but also produce the most attractive surface.

When working on tall buildings, painters erect scaffolding, including "swing stages," scaffolds suspended by ropes or cables attached to roof hooks. When painting steeples and other conical structures, they use a "bosun chair," a swinglike device.

*Paperhangers* cover walls and ceilings with decorative wall coverings made of paper, vinyl, or fabric. They first prepare the surface to be covered by applying "sizing," which seals the surface and makes the covering stick better. When redecorating, they may first remove the old covering by soaking, steaming, or applying solvents. When necessary, they patch holes and take care of other imperfections before hanging the new wall covering.

After the surface has been prepared, paperhangers must prepare the paste or other adhesive. Then they measure the area to be covered, check the covering for flaws, cut the covering into strips of the proper size, and closely examine the pattern to match it when the strips are hung.

The next step is to brush or roll the adhesive onto the back of the covering, then to place the strips on the wall or ceiling, making sure the pattern is matched, the strips are hung straight, and the edges butted together to make tight, closed seams. Finally, paperhangers smooth the strips to remove bubbles and wrinkles, trim the top and bottom with a razor knife, and wipe off any excess adhesive.

## Working Conditions

Most painters and paperhangers work 40 hours a week or less; about one in six works part-time. Painters and paperhangers must stand for long periods. Their jobs also require a considerable amount of climbing and bending. These workers must have stamina because much of the work is done with their arms raised overhead. Painters often work outdoors, but seldom in wet, cold, or inclement weather.

Painters and paperhangers risk injury from slips or falls off ladders and scaffolds. They may sometimes work with materials that can be hazardous if masks are not worn or if ventilation is poor. Some painting jobs can leave a worker covered with paint.

## Employment

Painters and paperhangers held about 439,000 jobs in 1994; most were painters. The majority of painters and paperhangers work for contractors engaged in new construction, repair, restoration, or remodeling work. In addition, organizations that own or manage large buildings, such as apartment complexes, employ maintenance painters, as do some schools, hospitals, and factories.

Self-employed independent painting contractors accounted for almost half of all painters and paperhangers, about twice the proportion of building trades workers in general.

## Training, Other Qualifications, and Advancement

Painting and paper hanging are learned through apprenticeship or informal, on-the-job instruction. Although training authorities recommend completion of an apprenticeship as the best way to become a painter or paperhanger, most painters learn the trade informally on the job as a helper to an experienced painter. Few opportunities for informal training exist for paperhangers because few paperhangers have a need for helpers.

The apprenticeship for painters and paperhangers consists of three to four years of on-the-job training, in addition to 144 hours of related classroom instruction each year. Apprentices receive instruction in color harmony, use and care of tools and equipment, surface preparation, application techniques, paint mixing and matching, characteristics of different finishes, blueprint reading, wood finishing, and safety.

Whether a painter learns the trade through a formal apprenticeship or informally as a helper, on-the-job instruction covers similar skill areas. Under the direction of experienced workers, trainees carry supplies, erect scaffolds, and do simple painting and surface preparation tasks while they learn about paint and painting equipment. Within two or three years, trainees learn to prepare surfaces for painting and paper hanging, to mix paints, and to apply paint and wall coverings efficiently and neatly. Near the end of their training, they may learn decorating concepts, color coordination, and cost-estimating techniques.

Apprentices or helpers generally must be at least 16 years old and in good physical condition. A high school education or its equivalent that includes courses in mathematics is generally required to enter an apprenticeship program. Applicants should have manual dexterity and a good color sense.

Painters and paperhangers may advance to supervisory or estimating jobs with painting and decorating contractors. Many establish their own painting and decorating businesses.

## Job Outlook

Employment of painters and paperhangers is expected to grow about as fast as the average for all occupations through the year 2005 as the level of new construction increases and the stock of buildings and other structures that require maintenance and renovation grows. In addition to job openings created by rising demand for the services of these workers, many tens of thousands of jobs will become available each year as painters and paperhangers transfer to other occupations or leave the labor force. There are no strict training requirements for entry, so many people with limited skills work as painters or paperhangers for a short time and then move on to other types of work, creating many job openings. Many fewer openings will occur for paperhangers because the number of these jobs is comparatively small.

Prospects for persons seeking jobs as painters or paperhangers should be quite favorable, due to the high turnover. Since there are no strict training requirements, a significant number of people work as painter for a short time and transfer to something else or work part-time. Despite the favorable overall conditions, job seekers considering these occupations should expect some periods of unemployment because many construction projects are of the short duration and construction activity is cyclical and seasonal in nature. Remodeling, restoration, and maintenance projects, however, often provide many jobs for painters and paperhangers even when new construction activity declines. The most versatile painters and paperhangers generally are most able to keep working steadily during downturns in the economy.

## Earnings

Median weekly earnings for painters who were not self-employed were about $381 in 1994. Most earned between $288 and $516 weekly, while the top 10 percent earned over $721 a week. In general, paperhangers earn more than painters. Earnings for painters may be reduced on occasion because of bad weather and the short-term nature of many construction jobs.

Hourly wage rates for apprentices usually start at 40 to 50 percent of the rate for experienced workers and increase periodically.

Some painters and paperhangers are members of the International Brotherhood of Painters and Allied Trades. Some maintenance painters are members of other unions.

## Related Occupations

Painters and paperhangers apply various coverings to decorate and protect wood, drywall, metal, and other surfaces. Other occupations in which workers apply paints and similar finishes include billboard posterers, metal sprayers, undercoaters, and transportation equipment painters.

## Related *D.O.T.* Jobs

These job titles are related to or more specific than the more general description above. They will help you identify job options you may not otherwise discover. These descriptions are in the current edition of the *Dictionary of Occupational Titles* and classified by numerical order.

840.381-010 PAINTER; 840.381-014 PAINTER APPRENTICE, SHIPYARD; 840.381-018 PAINTER, SHIPYARD; 840.681-010 PAINTER, STAGE SETTINGS; 840.684-010 GLASS TINTER; 841.381-010 PAPERHANGER

## Sources of Additional Information

For details about painting and paper hanging apprenticeships or work opportunities, contact local painting and decorating contractors; a local of the International Brotherhood of Painters and Allied Trades; a local joint union-management apprenticeship committee; or an office of the state apprenticeship agency or state employment service.

For general information about the work of painters and paperhangers, contact:

❏ Associated Builders and Contractors, 1300 North 17th St., Rosslyn, VA 22209.

❏ International Brotherhood of Painters and Allied Trades, 1750 New York Ave. NW, Washington, DC 20006.

❏ Home Builders Institute, National Association of Home Builders, 1201 15th St. NW, Washington, DC 20005.

# Painting and Coating Machine Operators

## Nature of the Work

Paints and coatings are an important part of most products. In manufacturing, everything from cars to candy is covered by either paint, plastic, varnish, chocolate, or some special coating solution. Often the paints and coatings are merely intended to enhance the products' appeal to consumers, as with the chocolate coating on candy. More often, however, the protection provided by the paint or coating is essential to the product, as with the coating of insulating material covering wires and other electrical and electronic components. Many paints and coatings have dual purposes, such as the paint finish on an automobile, which heightens the visual appearance of the vehicle while providing protection from corrosion.

Painting and coating machine operators control the machinery and equipment that applies these paints and coatings to a wide range of manufactured products. These workers use several basic methods to apply paints and coatings to manufactured articles. For example, dippers immerse racks or baskets of articles in vats of paint, liquid plastic, or other solutions using a power hoist. Tumbling barrel painters deposit articles of porous materials in a barrel of paint, varnish, or other coating, which is then rotated to ensure thorough coverage.

Commonly, paints and coatings are applied by spraying the article with a solution. Spray-machine operators use spray guns to coat metal, wood, ceramic, fabric, paper, and food products with paint and other coating solutions. Following a formula, operators fill the equipment's tanks with a mixture of paints or chemicals, adding prescribed amounts or proportions. They screw nozzles onto the spray guns and adjust them to obtain the proper dispersion of the spray, and hold or position the guns to direct the spray onto the article. The pressure of the spray is regulated by adjusting valves. Operators check the flow and viscosity of the paint or solution and visually inspect the quality of the coating. They may also regulate the temperature and air circulation in drying ovens.

In response to concerns about air pollution and worker safety, manufacturers are increasingly using new types of paints and coatings on their products instead of high-solvent paints. Water-based paints and powder coatings are two of the most common. These compounds do not emit as many volatile organic compounds into the air and can be applied to a wide variety of products. Powder coatings are sprayed much like liquid paints and heated to melt and cure the coating.

The switch to new types of paints is often accompanied by a conversion to newer, more automated painting equipment that the operator sets and monitors. Operators position the automatic spray guns, set the nozzles, and synchronize the action of the guns with the speed of the conveyor carrying articles through the machine and drying ovens. The operator may also add solvents or water to the paint vessel that prepares the paint for application. During operation, the operator attends the painting machine, observes gauges on the control panel and randomly checks articles for evidence of any variation of the coating from specifications. The operator then "touches up" spots where necessary, using a spray gun.

Painting and coating machine operators use various types of spray machines to coat a wide range of products. Often their job title reflects the specialized nature of the machine or the coating being applied. For example, paper coating machine operators spray "size" on rolls of paper to give it its gloss or finish. Silvering applicators spray silver, tin, and copper solutions on glass in the manufacture of mirrors. Enrobing machine operators coat, or "enrobe," confectionery, bakery, and other food products with melted chocolate, cheese, oils, sugar, or other substances.

Although the majority of painting and coating machine operators are employed in manufacturing, the best known group of them work in automotive body repair and paint shops refinishing old and damaged cars, trucks, and buses. Automotive painters are among the most highly skilled manual spray operators because they often have to mix paint to match the original color, which can be very difficult, particularly if the color has faded.

To prepare a vehicle for painting, automotive painters or their helpers use power sanders and sandpaper to remove the original paint or rust, and then fill small dents and scratches with body filler. They also remove or mask parts they do not want painted, such as chrome trim, headlights, windows, and mirrors. Automotive painters use a spray gun to apply several coats of paint. They apply lacquer, enamel, or water-based primers to vehicles with metal bodies, and flexible primers to newer vehicles with plastic body parts. Controlling the spray gun by hand, they apply successive coats until the finish of the repaired sections of the vehicle matches that of the original undamaged portions. To speed drying between coats, they may place the freshly painted vehicle under heat lamps or in a special infrared oven. After each coat of primer dries, they sand the surface to remove any irregularities and to improve the adhesion of the next coat. Final sanding of the primers may be done by hand with a fine grade of sandpaper. A sealer is then applied and allowed to dry, followed by the final topcoat. When lacquer is used, painters or their helpers usually polish the finished surface after the final coat has dried; enamel dries to a high gloss and usually is not polished.

## Working Conditions

Painting and coating machine operators work indoors and may be exposed to dangerous fumes from paint and coating solutions. Many operators wear masks or respirators that cover their nose and mouth, and painting is usually done in special ventilated booths that protect the operators from these hazards. The Clean Air Act of 1990 has led to a decrease in workers' exposure to hazardous chemicals by regulating emissions of volatile organic compounds from paints and other chemicals.

Operators have to stand for long periods of time and, when using a spray gun, they may have to bend, stoop, or crouch in uncomfortable positions to reach all parts of the article. Most operators work a normal 40-hour week, but self-employed automotive painters sometimes work more than 50 hours a week, depending on the number of vehicles customers bring in to be repainted.

## Employment

Painting and coating machine operators held about 155,000 jobs in 1994. Eighty percent worked in manufacturing establishments—in the production of fabricated metal products, motor vehicles and related equipment, industrial machines, household and office furniture, and plastics, wood, and paper products, for example. Other workers included automotive painters employed by independent automotive repair shops and body repair and paint shops operated by retail automotive dealers. Five percent of painting and coating machine operators were self-employed; most of these were automotive painters.

## Training, Other Qualifications, and Advancement

Most painting and coating machine operators acquire their skills on the job, usually by watching and helping experienced operators. For most operators, training lasts from a few days to several months. However, becoming skilled in all aspects of automotive painting usually requires one to two years of on-the-job training.

Most automotive painters start as helpers and gain their skills informally by working with experienced painters. Beginning helpers usually remove trim, clean and sand surfaces to be painted, mask surfaces that they do not want painted, and polish finished work. As helpers gain experience, they progress to more complicated tasks, such as mixing paint to achieve a good match and using spray guns to apply primer coats or final coats to small areas.

Painters should have keen eyesight and a good color sense. Completion of high school is generally not required but is advantageous. Additional instruction is offered at many community colleges and vocational or technical schools. Such programs enhance one's employment prospects and can speed promotion to the next level.

Some employers sponsor training programs to help their workers become more productive. This training is available from manufacturers of chemicals, paints, or equipment or from other private sources. It may include safety and quality tips and knowledge of products, equipment, and general business practices. Some automotive painters are sent to technical schools to learn the intricacies of mixing and applying different types of paint.

Voluntary certification by ASE (the National Institute for Automotive Service Excellence) is recognized as the standard of achievement for automotive painters. For certification, painters must pass a written examination and have at least two years of experience in the field. High school, trade or vocational school, or community or junior college training in automotive painting and refinishing may substitute for up to one year of experience. To retain certification, painters must retake the examination at least every five years.

Experienced painting and coating machine operators with leadership ability may advance to supervisory jobs. Those who acquire practical experience or college or other formal training may become sales or technical representatives to large customers or for chemical or paint companies. Some automotive painters open their own shops.

## Job Outlook

Little change is expected in the employment of painting and coating machine operators through the year 2005, as technological improvements enable these operators to work more productively. Nevertheless, several thousand jobs will become available each year as employers replace experienced operators who transfer to other occupations or leave the labor force.

In manufacturing, employment of painting and coating machine operators is expected to decline, reflecting the increasing automation of paint and coating application. Improvements in the capabilities of industrial robots allow them to move and aim spray guns more like humans. As the cost of these machines continues to fall, they will be more widely used. The Clean Air Act of 1990, which sets limits on the emissions of ozone-forming volatile organic compounds, also is reducing the demand for operators in manufacturing. As firms switch to water-based and powder coatings to comply with the law, many are upgrading their equipment to increase the efficiency of the painting process. In fact, the powder coating process alone is much more efficient for work on assembly lines than liquid sprays because no drying time is required between coats and fewer operators are needed for touch-up painting. The expected employment decline resulting from these trends will be moderated, however, as painting and coating machine operators assume emissions monitoring and recording responsibilities.

Employment of these workers in the auto repair industry will grow slowly, as the improved quality of car finishes and the increasing use of nonrusting alloys slow the growth in demand for refinishing services. The employment outlook for skilled automotive painters, however, should remain bright.

The number of job openings for painting and coating machine operators may fluctuate from year to year due to cyclical changes in economic conditions. When demand for manufactured goods slackens, production may be suspended or reduced, and workers may be laid off or face a shortened workweek. Automotive painters, on the other hand, can expect relatively steady work because automobiles damaged in accidents require repair and refinishing regardless of the state of the economy.

## Earnings

Painting and coating machine operators who usually worked full-time had median weekly earnings of $370 in 1994. The middle 50 percent had usual weekly earnings between $280 and $560, while the highest 10 percent earned more than $750 weekly. Beginning automotive painter apprentices usually start at about half the hourly rate of fully qualified painters. As they progress, their wages gradually approach those of experienced automotive painters. Helpers start at lower wage rates than beginning apprentices.

Many automotive painters employed by automobile dealers and independent repair shops receive a commission based on the labor cost charged to the customer. Under this method, earnings depend largely on the amount of work a painter does and how fast it is completed. Employers frequently guarantee commissioned painters a minimum weekly salary. Helpers and apprentices usually receive an hourly rate until they become sufficiently skilled to work on a commission basis. Trucking companies, bus lines, and other organizations that repair their own vehicles usually pay by the hour.

Many painting and coating machine operators belong to unions, including the International Association of Machinists and Aerospace Workers; the International Brotherhood of Painters and Allied Trades; the International Union, United Automobile, Aerospace and Agricultural Implement Workers of America; the Sheet Metal Workers' International Association; and the International Brotherhood of Teamsters. Most union operators work for manufacturers and the larger automobile dealers.

## Related Occupations

Other occupations in which workers apply paints and coatings include construction and maintenance painters, electrolytic metal platers, and hand painting, coating, and decorating occupations.

## Related *D.O.T.* Jobs

These job titles are related to or more specific than the more general description above. They will help you identify job options you may not otherwise discover. These descriptions are in the current edition of the *Dictionary of Occupational Titles* and classified by numerical order.

There are too many *D.O.T.* titles to list here. Most are variations related to a specific industry, and we have included a small number of representative *D.O.T.* titles as examples. Complete lists are available in various career software published by JIST or directly from the U.S. Department of Labor.

524.382-010 COATING-MACHINE OPERATOR; 524.382-014 ENROBING-MACHINE OPERATOR; 524.665-010 SANDING-MACHINE OPERATOR; 534.685-022 PAPER COATER; 534.685-030 VARNISHING-MACHINE OPERATOR; 554.362-010 CALENDER OPERATOR; 554.382-010 COATER; 554.384-010 DYER; 554.685-026 SIZING-MACHINE OPERATOR; 559.685-170 SPREADING-MACHINE OPERATOR; 561.585-010 STAIN APPLICATOR; 573.685-018 GLAZING-MACHINE OPERATOR; 574.582-010 SILVERING APPLICATOR; 574.682-014 SPRAY-MACHINE OPERATOR; 584.382-010 COATING-MACHINE OPERATOR I; 599.685-030 DIPPER AND BAKER; 845.381-018 PAINT SPRAYER, SANDBLASTER

## Sources of Additional Information

For more details about work opportunities, contact local manufacturers, automotive-body repair shops, automotive dealers, and vocational schools; locals of the unions previously mentioned; or the local office of the state employment service. The state employment service also may be a source of information about training programs.

For general information about a career as an automotive painter, write to:

❑ Automotive Service Industry Association, 25 Northwest Point, Suite 425, Elk Grove Village, IL 60007-1035.

❑ Automotive Service Association, Inc., P.O. Box 929, Bedford, TX 76021-0929.

Information on how to become a certified automotive painter is available from:

❑ National Institute for Automotive Service Excellence (ASE), 13505 Dulles Technology Dr., Herndon, VA 22071-3415.

# Paralegals

## Nature of the Work

Not all legal work requires a law degree. Lawyers are often assisted in their work by paralegals or legal assistants. Paralegals perform many of the same tasks as lawyers, except for those tasks considered to be the practice of law.

Paralegals work under the direct supervision of lawyers. Although the lawyers assume responsibility for the legal work, they often delegate many of the tasks they perform to paralegals. Paralegals are prohibited from setting legal fees, giving legal advice, and presenting cases in court.

Paralegals generally do the background work for lawyers. To help prepare cases for trial, paralegals investigate the facts of cases ensuring all relevant information is uncovered. Paralegals may conduct legal research to identify the appropriate laws, judicial decisions, legal articles, and other materials that may be relevant to assigned cases. After organizing and analyzing all the information, paralegals may prepare written reports that attorneys use in determining how cases should be handled. Should attorneys decide to file lawsuits on behalf of clients, paralegals may help prepare the legal arguments, draft pleadings and motions to be filed with the court, obtain affidavits, and assist the attorneys during trials. Paralegals also keep files of all documents and correspondence important to cases.

Besides litigation, paralegals may also work in areas such as bankruptcy, corporate law, criminal law, employee benefits, patent and copyright law, and real estate. They help draft documents such as contracts, mortgages, separation agreements, and trust instruments. They may help prepare tax returns and plan estates. Some paralegals coordinate the activities of the other law office employees and keep the financial records for the office.

Paralegals who work for corporations help attorneys with such matters as employee contracts, shareholder agreements, stock option plans, and employee benefit plans. They may help prepare and file annual financial reports, maintain corporate minute books and resolutions, and help secure loans for the corporation. Paralegals may also review government regulations to ensure the corporation operates within the law.

The duties of paralegals who work in government vary depending on the agency with whom they are employed. Generally, paralegals in government analyze legal material for internal use, maintain reference files, conduct research for attorneys, collect and analyze evidence for agency hearings, and prepare informative or explanatory material on the law, agency regulations, and agency policy for general use by the agency and the public.

Paralegals employed in community legal service projects help the poor, the aged, and others in need of legal assistance. They file forms, conduct research, and prepare documents. When authorized by law, they may represent clients at administrative hearings.

Some paralegals, usually those in small and medium-sized law firms, perform a variety of duties. They may research judicial decisions on improper police arrests or help prepare a mortgage contract. Paralegals must have a general knowledge of the law to perform these duties.

Some paralegals employed by large law firms, government agencies, and corporations, specialize in one aspect of the law, including real estate, estate planning, family law, labor law, litigation, and corporate law. Even within specialties, functions often are broken down further so paralegals may deal with a specific area of the specialty. For example, paralegals specializing in labor law may deal exclusively with employee benefits.

A growing number of paralegals use computers in their work. Computer software packages and on-line legal research are increasingly used to search legal literature stored in computer databases and on CD-ROM. In litigation that involves many supporting documents, paralegals may use computers to organize and index the material. They may also use computer software packages to perform tax computations and explore the consequences of possible tax strategies for clients.

## Working Conditions

Paralegals do most of their work at desks in offices and law libraries. Occasionally, they travel to gather information and perform other duties.

Paralegals employed by corporations and government work a standard 40-hour week. Although most paralegals work year round, some are temporarily employed during busy times of the year, then released when the workload diminishes. Paralegals who work for law firms sometimes work very long hours when they are under pressure to meet deadlines. Some law firms reward such loyalty with bonuses and additional time off.

Paralegals handle many routine assignments, particularly when they are inexperienced. Some find that these assignments offer little challenge and become frustrated with their duties. However, paralegals usually assume more responsible and varied tasks as they gain experience. Furthermore, as new laws and judicial interpretations emerge, paralegals are exposed to many new legal problems that make their work more interesting and challenging.

## Employment

Paralegals held about 111,000 jobs in 1994. Private law firms employed the vast majority; most of the remainder worked for the various levels of government. Paralegals are found in nearly every federal government agency; the Departments of Justice, Treasury, Interior, and Health and Human Services, and the General Services Administration are the largest employers. State and local governments and publicly funded legal service projects employ paralegals as well. Banks, real estate development companies, and insurance companies also employ small numbers of paralegals. Some paralegals own their own businesses; as freelance legal assistants they contract their services to attorneys or corporate legal departments.

## Training, Other Qualifications, and Advancement

There are several ways to enter the paralegal profession. Employers generally require formal paralegal training; several types of training programs are acceptable. Increasingly employers prefer to hire either graduates of four-year paralegal programs, or persons with bachelor's degrees who have earned paralegal certificates through short-term programs after graduation. However, some employers prefer to train their paralegals on the job, promoting experienced legal secretaries or hiring college graduates with no legal experience. Other entrants have experience in a technical field that is useful to law firms, such as a background in tax preparation for tax and estate practice or nursing or health administration for personal injury practice.

More than 800 formal paralegal training programs are offered by four-year colleges and universities, law schools, community and junior colleges, business schools, and proprietary schools. In 1995, about 200 programs had been approved by the American Bar Association (ABA). Although this approval is neither required nor sought by many programs, graduation from an ABA-approved program can enhance one's employment opportunities. The requirements for admission to formal training programs vary widely. Some require some college courses or a bachelor's degree. Others accept high school graduates or those with legal experience. A few schools require standardized tests and personal interviews.

Some paralegal programs are completed in two years, while others take as long as four years and award a bachelor's degree upon completion. Certificate programs take only a few months to complete, but require a bachelor's degree for admission. Programs typically include general courses on the law and legal research techniques, in addition to courses covering specialized areas of the law, such as real estate, estate planning and probate, litigation, family law, contracts, and criminal law. Many employers prefer applicants with training in a specialized area of the law. Programs increasingly include courses introducing students to the legal applications of computers. Many paralegal training programs include an internship in which students gain practical experience by working for several months in a law office, corporate legal department, or government agency. Experience gained in internships is an asset when seeking a job after graduation. Depending on the program, graduates may receive a certificate, an associate degree, or a bachelor's degree.

The quality of paralegal training programs varies; the better programs generally emphasize job placement. Prospective students should examine the experiences of recent graduates of programs in which they are considering enrolling.

Paralegals need not be certified, but the National Association of Legal Assistants has established standards for voluntary certification which require various combinations of education and experience. Paralegals who meet these standards are eligible to take a two-day examination given each year at several regional testing centers by the Certifying Board of Legal Assistants of the National Association of Legal Assistants. Those who pass this examination may use the designation Certified Legal Assistant (CLA). This designation is a sign of competence in the field and may enhance employment and advancement opportunities. The Paralegal Advanced Competency Exam, administered through the National Federation of Paralegal Associations to qualified paralegals, offers a similar level of professional recognition.

Paralegals must be able to handle legal problems logically and communicate, both orally and in writing, their findings and opinions to their supervising attorney. They must understand legal terminology and have good research and investigative skills. Familiarity with the operation and applications of computers in legal research and litigation support is increasingly important. Paralegals must always stay abreast of new developments in the law that affect their area of practice.

Because paralegals often deal with the public, they must be courteous and uphold the high ethical standards of the legal profession. A few states and the National Federation of Paralegal Associations have established ethical guidelines which paralegals must follow.

Experienced paralegals usually are given progressively more responsibilities and less supervision. In large law firms, corporate legal departments, and government agencies, experienced paralegals may supervise other paralegals and clerical staff and delegate work assigned by the attorneys. Advancement opportunities include promotion to managerial and other law-related positions within the firm or corporate legal department. However, some paralegals find it easier to move to another law firm when seeking increased responsibility or advancement.

## Job Outlook

Employment of paralegals is expected to grow much faster than the average for all occupations through the year 2005. Job opportunities are expected to expand as more employers become aware that paralegals are able to do many legal tasks for lower salaries than lawyers. Both law firms and other employers with legal staffs should continue to emphasize hiring paralegals so that the cost, availability, and efficiency of legal services can be improved.

New jobs created by rapid employment growth will create most of the job openings for paralegals in the future. Other job openings will arise as people leave the occupation. Although the number of job openings for paralegals is expected to increase significantly through the year 2005, so will the number of people pursuing this career. Thus, keen competition for jobs should continue as the growing number of graduates from paralegal education programs keeps pace with employment growth. Still, job prospects are expected to be favorable for persons with bachelor's degrees who graduate from well regarded paralegal training programs.

Private law firms will continue to be the largest employers of paralegals as a growing population demands additional legal services. The growth of prepaid legal plans should also contribute to the demand for the services of law firms. A growing array of other organizations, such as corporate legal departments, insurance companies, real estate and title insurance firms, and banks will also hire paralegals.

Job opportunities for paralegals will expand even in the public sector. Community legal service programs—which provide assistance to the poor, aged, minorities, and middle-income families—operate on limited budgets. They will seek to employ additional paralegals in order to minimize expenses and serve the most people. Federal, state, and local government agencies, consumer organizations, and the courts should continue to hire paralegals in increasing numbers.

To a limited extent, paralegal jobs are affected by the business cycle. During recessions, demand declines for some discretionary legal services, such as planning estates, drafting wills, and handling real estate transactions. Corporations are less inclined to initiate litigation when falling sales and profits lead to fiscal belt tightening. As a result, full-time paralegals employed in offices adversely affected by a recession may be laid off or have their work hours reduced. On the other hand, during recessions, corporations and individuals are more likely to face other legal problems, such as bankruptcies, foreclosures, and divorces, that require legal assistance. Furthermore, the continuous emergence of new laws and judicial interpretations of existing ones creates new business for lawyers and paralegals without regard to the business cycle.

## Earnings

Earnings of paralegals vary greatly. Salaries depend on the education, training, and experience the paralegal brings to the job, the type and size of employer, and the geographic location of the job. Generally, paralegals who work for large law firms or in large metropolitan areas earn more than those who work for smaller firms or in less populated regions.

Paralegals had an average annual salary of about $31,700 in 1993, according to a compensation survey by Kenneth Leventhal & Company for the National Federation of Paralegal Associations. Starting salaries of entry-level paralegals ranged from a low of $14,000 to a high of $32,000 an year, according to the same survey. In addition to a salary, many paralegals received an annual bonus, which averaged more than $1,600 in 1993. Employers of the majority of paralegals provided life and health insurance benefits and contributed to a retirement plan on their behalf.

Paralegal Specialists hired by the federal government in 1994 started at about $20,000 or $25,200 a year, depending on their training and experience. The average annual salary of paralegals who worked for the federal government in 1995 was about $39,800.

## Related Occupations

Several other occupations also call for a specialized understanding of the law and the legal system but do not require the extensive training of a lawyer. Some of these are abstractors, claim examiners, compliance and enforcement inspectors, occupational safety and health workers, patent agents, police officers, and title examiners.

## Related *D.O.T.* Jobs

These job titles are related to or more specific than the more general description above. They will help you identify job options you may not otherwise discover. These descriptions are in the current edition of the *Dictionary of Occupational Titles* and classified by numerical order.

119.267-022 LEGAL INVESTIGATOR; 119.267-026 PARALEGAL

## Sources of Additional Information

General information on a career as a paralegal and the *Guide for Legal Assistant Education Programs* by the American Bar Association may be purchased for $7.50 from:

❏ Standing Committee on Legal Assistants, American Bar Association, 750 North Lake Shore Dr., Chicago, IL 60611.

For information on certification of paralegals, schools that offer training programs in a specific state, and standards and guidelines for paralegals, contact:

❏ National Association of Legal Assistants, Inc., 1516 South Boston St., Suite 200, Tulsa, OK 74119.

Information on a career as a paralegal, schools that offer training programs, the Paralegal Advanced Competency Exam, and local paralegal associations can be obtained from:

❏ National Federation of Paralegal Associations, P.O. Box 33108, Kansas City, MO 64114; or on the Internet http://www.paralegals.org.

Information on paralegal training programs, including the pamphlet "How to Choose a Paralegal Education Program" may be obtained from:

❏ American Association for Paralegal Education, P.O. Box 40244, Overland Park, KS 66204; (913) 381-4458.

# Photographers and Camera Operators

## Nature of the Work

Photographers and camera operators use cameras to capture the special feeling or mood that sells products, provides entertainment, highlights news stories, or brings back memories.

Photographers use a wide variety of cameras that can accept lenses designed for close-up, medium-range, or distance photography. Some cameras also offer adjustment settings that allow the photographer greater creative and technical control over the picture-taking process. In addition to cameras and film, photographers and camera operators use an array of equipment, from filters, tripods, and flash attachments to specially constructed motorized vehicles and lighting equipment.

Photography increasingly involves the use of computers. A photographer may take a picture, scan it to digital form, and, using a computer, manipulate it to create a desired effect. The images may be stored on a compact disk (CD) in the same way that music is stored on a CD. Currently, some photographers use this technology to create an electronic portfolio. However, due to inferior image quality and high cost, this technology has not been widely adopted.

Camera operators generally use 35- or 16-millimeter cameras or video cameras to film commercial motion pictures and documentary or industrial films. Some film events for television news, or film private ceremonies and special events.

Making commercial quality photographs and movies requires technical expertise and creativity. Composing a picture includes choosing and presenting a subject to achieve a particular effect and selecting equipment to accomplish the desired goal. By creatively using lighting, lenses, film, filters, and camera settings, photographers and camera operators produce pictures that capture a mood or tell a story. For example, photographers and camera operators may enhance the subject's appearance with lighting or by drawing attention to a particular aspect by blurring the background.

Some photographers develop and print their own photographs, especially those requiring special effects, but this requires a fully equipped darkroom and the technical skill to operate it. As a result, many professional photographers send their film to laboratories for processing. This is especially true for color film, which requires very expensive equipment and exacting conditions for processing and printing.

Most photographers specialize in commercial, portrait, or media photography. Some specialize in weddings or school photographs. Portrait photographers take pictures of individuals or groups of people and often work in their own studios. Portrait photographers who are business owners arrange for advertising, schedule appointments, set and adjust equipment, develop and retouch negatives, and mount and frame pictures. They also hire and train employees, purchase supplies, keep records, and bill customers.

Self-employed photographers may license the use of their photographs through stock photo agencies. These agencies grant magazines and other customers the right to purchase the use of a photograph, and, in turn, pay the photographer on a commission basis. Stock photo agencies require an application from the photographer and a sizable portfolio. Once accepted, a large number of new submissions are generally required each year. Photographers frequently have their photos placed on CDs for this purpose.

Commercial and industrial photographers take pictures of such subjects as manufactured articles, buildings, livestock, landscapes, and groups of people. Their work is used in a wide variety of mediums, such as reports, advertisements, and catalogs. Industrial photographers use photographs or videotapes for analyzing engineering projects, publicity, or as records of equipment development or deployment, such as the placement of an off-shore oil rig. Automobile manufacturers hire photographers every year to publicize their new models. Companies use photographs in publications to report to stockholders or to advertise company products or services. This photography frequently is done on location.

Scientific photographers provide illustrations and documentation for scientific publications, research reports, and textbooks. They usually specialize in a field such as engineering, medicine, biology, or chemistry. Some use photographic or video equipment as research tools. For example, biomedical photographers use photomicrography, photographs of small objects magnified many times to obtain information not visible under normal conditions, and time-lapse photography, where time is stretched or condensed. Biomedical photographers record medical procedures such as surgery.

Photojournalists photograph newsworthy events, places, people, and things for newspapers, journals, magazines, or television. Some are salaried staff, while others are independent and known as freelance photographers.

Photography also is an art medium. Some photographers sell their photographs as artwork, placing even greater emphasis on self-expression and creativity, in addition to technical proficiency. Unlike other specializations, however, very few artistic photographers are successful enough to support themselves in this manner.

Many camera operators are employed by independent television stations, local affiliates, or networks. They often cover news events as part of a reporting team.

Camera operators employed in the entertainment field use motion picture cameras to film movies, television programs, and commercials. Some camera operators specialize in filming cartoons or other special effects for television and movies.

## Working Conditions

Working conditions for photographers and camera operators vary considerably. Photographers employed in government, commercial studios, and advertising agencies usually work a five-day, 40-hour week. News photographers and camera operators often work long and irregular hours and must be available on short notice.

Self-employment allows for greater autonomy, freedom of expression, and flexible scheduling. However, income is uncertain and necessitates a continuous, time consuming, and sometimes stressful search for new clients. Some photographers hire an assistant solely for this responsibility.

Portrait photographers often work in their own studios but may travel to take photographs at schools and other places and weddings and other events. Press and commercial photographers and camera operators frequently travel locally or overnight; some travel to distant places for long periods of time. Their work may put them in uncomfortable or even dangerous surroundings. This is especially true for photojournalists covering natural disasters, civil strife, or military conflicts.

Some photographers and camera operators wait long hours in all kinds of weather for an event to take place and stand or walk for long periods while carrying heavy equipment. Photographers often work under severe time restrictions to meet deadlines and satisfy customers.

## Employment

Photographers and camera operators held about 139,000 jobs in 1994. About 4 out of 10 were self-employed, a much higher proportion than the average for all occupations. Some self-employed photographers contracted with advertising agencies, magazines, or others to do individual projects at a predetermined fee, while others operated portrait studios or provided photographs to stock photo agencies.

Most salaried photographers worked in portrait or commercial photography studios. Others were employed by newspapers, magazines, advertising agencies, and government agencies. Most camera operators were employed in television broadcasting or in motion picture studios; relatively few were self-employed. Most photographers and camera operators worked in metropolitan areas.

## Training, Other Qualifications, and Advancement

Employers usually seek applicants with a good technical understanding of photography who are imaginative and creative. Entry-level positions in photojournalism and in industrial, scientific, or technical photography are likely to require a college degree in photography with courses in the specific field being photographed, such as industrial products or botany. Camera operators generally acquire their skills through formal postsecondary training at colleges, photographic institutes, universities, or through on-the-job training. Those in entry-level jobs, including photography and cinematography assistants, learn to set up lights and cameras. They may receive routine assignments requiring few camera adjustments or decisions on what subject matter to capture. With increasing experience, they may advance to more demanding assignments. Photography assistants often learn to mix chemicals, develop film, print photographs, and the various skills vital to running their own business.

Individuals interested in this occupation should subscribe to photographic newsletters and magazines, join camera clubs, and seek work in camera stores or photo studios. Individuals also should decide on an area of interest and specialize in it. Completing a course of study at a private photographic institute, university, or community college provides many of the necessary skills to be successful. Summer or part-time work for a photographer, network, newspaper, or magazine is an excellent way to gain experience and eventual entry to this field.

Many sources, including universities, community and junior colleges, vocational-technical institutes, and private trade and technical schools, offer courses in photography. Courses in cinematography are most often offered by photography institutes and universities. Many photographers enhance their technical expertise by attending seminars.

Basic courses in photography cover equipment, processes, and techniques. Bachelor's degree programs provide a well-rounded education, including business courses. Art schools offer useful training in design and composition, but may be weak in the technical and commercial aspects of photography.

Photographers who wish to operate their own business need business skills as well as talent. They must know how to submit bids; write contracts; hire models, if needed; get permission to take on-site photographs at locations normally not open to the public; get clearances to use photographs of people; price photographs; and keep financial records. They should develop an individual style of photography to differentiate themselves from the competition. Some self-employed photographers enter the field by submitting unsolicited photographs to magazines or art directors at advertising agencies.

Photographers and camera operators need good eyesight, artistic ability, and manual dexterity. They should be patient, accurate, and enjoy working with detail. They should be able to work alone or with others, as photographers frequently deal with clients, graphic designers, and advertising and publishing specialists. Knowledge of mathematics, physics, and chemistry is helpful for understanding the workings of lenses, films, light sources, and developing processes.

Commercial photographers must be imaginative and original. Portrait photographers need the ability to help people relax in front of the camera. Photojournalists must not only be good with a camera but also understand the story behind an event so that their pictures match the story. They must be decisive in recognizing a potentially good photograph and act quickly to capture it. This requires journalistic skills and explains why such employers increasingly look for individuals with a four-year degree in photojournalism or journalism with an emphasis on photography.

Camera operators can become directors of photography for movie studios, advertising agencies, or television programs. Magazine and news photographers may become photography editors. A few photographers and camera operators become teachers and provide instruction in their own area of expertise.

### Job Outlook

Photography, particularly commercial photography and photojournalism, is a highly competitive field because there are more people who want to be photographers than there is employment to support them. Only the most skilled and those with the best business ability, and who have developed the best reputations in the industry, are able to find salaried positions or attract enough work to support themselves as self-employed photographers. Many have full-time jobs in other fields and take photographs or videos of weddings and other events on weekends.

Employment of photographers is expected to grow faster than the average for all occupations through the year 2005. The growing demand for visual images in education, communication, entertainment, marketing, research and development, and other areas should spur demand for photographers. Demand for portrait photographers should increase as the population grows.

Digital cameras use electronic memory rather than a film negative to record the image, which, in turn, can be transmitted instantly via a computer modem and telephone lines. For this reason, they are used widely by news photographers. However, these cameras are much more expensive than conventional cameras, and are not capable of producing an equally clear image, or one where the subject is in motion. As the technology improves and the prices drop, however, they may be more widely used, increasing demand for commercial photographers with a high degree of computer skills.

Employment of camera operators also is expected to grow more slowly than the average for all occupations through the year 2005, even though businesses are making greater use of videos for training films, business meetings, sales campaigns, and public relations work. Expansion of the entertainment industry will create additional openings, but competition will be keen for what generally is regarded as an exciting field.

### Earnings

The median annual earnings for salaried photographers and camera operators who worked full-time were about $25,100 in 1994. The middle 50 percent earned between $16,300 and $39,200. The top 10 percent earned more than $46,300, while the lowest 10 percent earned less than $12,400.

Most salaried photographers work full-time and earn more than the majority of self-employed photographers, who work part-time, but some self-employed photographers have very high earnings. Earnings are affected by the number of hours worked, skills, marketing ability, and general business conditions.

Unlike photojournalists and commercial photographers, very few artistic photographers are successful enough to support themselves solely through this specialty.

### Related Occupations

Other jobs requiring visual arts talents include illustrators, designers, painters, sculptors, and photo editors.

### Related *D.O.T.* Jobs

These job titles are related to or more specific than the more general description above. They will help you identify job options you may not otherwise discover. These descriptions are in the current edition of the *Dictionary of Occupational Titles* and classified by numerical order.

143.062-010 DIRECTOR OF PHOTOGRAPHY; 143.062-014 PHOTOGRAPHER, AERIAL; 143.062-018 PHOTOGRAPHER, APPRENTICE; 143.062-022 CAMERA OPERATOR; 143.062-026 PHOTOGRAPHER, SCIENTIFIC; 143.062-030 PHOTOGRAPHER, STILL; 143.062-034 PHOTOJOURNALIST; 143.260-010 OPTICAL EFFECTS CAMERA OPERATOR; 143.362-010 BIOLOGICAL PHOTOGRAPHER; 143.362-014 OPHTHALMIC PHOTOGRAPHER; 143.382-010 CAMERA OPERATOR, ANIMATION; 143.382-014 PHOTOGRAPHER, FINISH; 143.457-010 PHOTOGRAPHER

### Sources of Additional Information

Career information on photography is available from:

❏ Professional Photographers of America, Inc., 57 Forsythe Street, Suite 1600, Atlanta, GA 30303

For reprints of a publication describing the work of various types of photographers and lists of colleges and universities offering courses or a degree in photography, write to:

❏ American Society of Media Photographers, Washington Rd., Suite 502, Princeton Junction, NJ 08550-1033.

# Photographic Process Workers

### Nature of the Work

Most photographers, both amateur and professional, rely on photo processing workers to develop their film, make prints or slides, and do related tasks such as enlarging or retouching photographs. Photographic processing machine operators and tenders operate various machines, such as motion picture film printing machines, photographic printing machines, film developing machines, and mounting presses. Precision photographic process workers perform more delicate tasks, such as retouching photographic negatives and prints to emphasize or correct specific features. They may restore damaged and faded photographs, and may color or shade drawings to create photographic likenesses using an airbrush. They also may color photographs, using oil colors to produce natural, lifelike appearances according to specifications.

The following jobs are examples of the work that machine operators perform. *Film process technicians* develop exposed photographic film or sensitized paper in a series of chemical and water baths to produce negative or positive images. They first mix the developing and fixing solutions, following a formula. They then immerse the exposed film in a developer solution to bring out the latent image, immerse the negative in stop-bath to halt the developer action, immerse it in hyposolution to fix the image, and finally immerse it in water to remove chemicals. The worker then dries the films. In some cases, these steps may be performed by hand.

*Color printer operators* control equipment which produces color prints from the negatives. They read customer instructions to determine processing requirements. They load the rolls into color printing equipment, examine the negatives to determine equipment control settings, set the controls, and produce a specified number of prints. They inspect the finished prints for defects, and remove any that are found, finally inserting the processed negatives and prints into an envelope for return to the customer.

*Paper process technicians* develop strips of exposed photographic paper; *takedown sorters* sort processed film; and *automatic mounters* operate equipment that cuts and mounts slide film into individual transparencies.

*Precision photographic process workers,* also known as digital imaging technicians, may take a conventional negative and, using a computer, vary the contrast of images, remove unwanted background, or even combine features from several different photographs. Precision photographic process workers in portrait studios, on the other hand, deal in very high volume, and tend to work directly on the photo negative, rather than on a computer. These workers include *airbrush artists,* who restore damaged and faded photographs; *photographic retouchers*, who alter photographic negatives and prints to accentuate the subject; *colorists*, who apply oil colors to portrait photographs to create natural, lifelike appearances; and *photographic spotters*, who spot out imperfections on photographic prints.

## Working Conditions

In recent years, more commercial photographic processing has been done on computers than in darkrooms, and this trend is expected to continue. Work generally is performed in clean, appropriately lighted, well-ventilated, and air-conditioned offices, photo-finishing laboratories, or one-hour mini-labs. At peak times, portrait studios hire individuals who work at home retouching negatives.

Photographic process machine operators must do repetitious work at a rapid pace without any loss of accuracy. Precision process workers do detailed tasks, such as airbrushing and spotting, which may contribute to eye fatigue.

Some photographic process workers are continuously exposed to the chemicals and fumes associated with developing and printing. These workers must wear rubber gloves and aprons and take precautions against chemical hazards.

Many photo laboratory employees work a 40-hour week, including weekends, and may work overtime during peak seasons.

## Employment

Photographic process workers held about 57,000 jobs in 1994. Photo-finishing laboratories and 1-hour mini-labs employed about two-thirds. About 3 out of 10 worked for portrait studios and commercial laboratories that specialize in processing the work of professional photographers for advertising and other industries.

Employment fluctuates over the course of the year; peak periods include school graduation, summer vacation, and Christmas time.

## Training, Other Qualifications, and Advancement

Most photographic process machine operators receive on-the-job training from manufacturers' representatives, company management, and more experienced workers. New employees gradually learn to use the machines and chemicals that develop and print film.

Employers prefer applicants who are high school graduates or those who have some experience or knowledge in the field. As preparation for precision work, proficiency in mathematics, art, chemistry, and computer science, as well as photography courses that include instruction in film processing are valuable. Such courses are available through high schools, vocational-technical institutes, private trade schools, and colleges and universities.

On-the-job training in photographic processing occupations can range from just a few hours for print machine operators to years for precision workers like airbrush artists, spotters, and negative retouchers. Some workers attend periodic training seminars to maintain a high level of skill. Manual dexterity, good hand-eye coordination, and good vision, including normal color perception, are important qualifications for precision photographic process workers. They must be comfortable with computers and able to adapt to technological advances.

Photographic process machine workers can advance from jobs as machine operators to supervisory positions in laboratories. Precision photographic process workers generally earn more as their skill level and the complexity of tasks they can perform increases.

## Job Outlook

Employment of photographic process workers is expected to in-crease about as fast as the average for all occupations through the year 2005. Most openings will result from replacement needs, which tend to be higher for machine operators than for precision process workers.

Digital cameras, which use electronic memory rather than a film negative to record the image, are now available. However, these cameras are much more expensive than conventional cameras, and generally are not capable of producing an equally sharp image. Also, traditional photo development will coexist, rather than compete directly, with electronic photography for many years. As this technology improves and the prices decline, photographic process machine operators may be displaced.

Technological change is unlikely to affect demand for precision photographic process workers because the adjustments they make to pictures need to be done to digital images as well as to negatives. No matter what improvements occur in camera technology, there always will be some images which require precise manipulation.

Because photographic processing services are luxuries for most consumers, the number of job openings decreases during recessions.

## Earnings

Earnings of photographic process workers vary greatly depending on skill level, experience, and geographic location. Median earnings for full-time photographic process workers in 1994 were about $327 a week. The middle 50 percent earned between $245 and $469 a week. The lowest 10 percent earned less than $201 a week while the highest 10 percent earned more than $611.

## Related Occupations

Precision photographic process workers need a specialized knowledge of the photo-developing process. Other workers who apply specialized technical knowledge include chemical laboratory technicians, crime laboratory analysts, food testers, medical laboratory assistants, metallurgical technicians, quality control technicians, engravers, and some of the printing occupations, such as photolithographer.

Photographic process machine operators perform work similar to that of other machine operators, such as computer and peripheral equipment operators and printing press operators.

## Related D.O.T. Jobs

These job titles are related to or more specific than the more general description above. They will help you identify job options you may not otherwise discover. These descriptions are in the current edition of the *Dictionary of Occupational Titles* and classified by numerical order.

There are too many *D.O.T.* titles to list here. Most are variations related to a specific industry, and we have included a small number of representative *D.O.T.* titles as examples. Complete lists are available in various career software published by JIST or directly from the U.S. Department of Labor.

970.281-010 AIRBRUSH ARTIST; 970.281-018 PHOTOGRAPH RE-TOUCHER; 970.381-010 COLORIST, PHOTOGRAPHY; 970.381-034 SPOTTER, PHOTOGRAPHIC; 976.361-010 REPRODUCTION TECHNICIAN; 976.381-010 FILM LABORATORY TECHNICIAN I; 976.382-010 CAMERA OPERATOR, TITLE; 976.382-018 FILM DEVELOPER; 976.384-010 PHOTO TECHNICIAN; 976.681-010 DEVELOPER; 976.682-010 FILM PRINTER; 976.685-014 DEVELOPER, AUTOMATIC; 976.685-018 FILM LABORATORY TECHNICIAN II; 976.685-022 MOUNTER, AUTOMATIC; 976.685-026 PRINT DEVELOPER, AUTOMATIC; 976.685-030 UTILITY WORKER, FILM PROCESSING; 976.685-034 DEVELOPER, PRINTED CIRCUIT BOARD PANELS; 976.685-038 PHOTOGRAPHIC PROCESSOR, SEMICONDUCTOR WAFERS; 979.384-010 SCREEN MAKER, PHOTO-GRAPHIC PROCESS

## Sources of Additional Information

For information about employment opportunities in photographic laboratories and schools that offer degrees in photographic technology, write to:

❑ Photo Marketing Association International, 3000 Picture Place, Jackson, MI 49201.

# Physical Therapy Assistants and Aides

## Nature of the Work

Physical therapy assistants and aides prepare patients both physically and psychologically for therapy under the watchful eye of a licensed physical therapist. The objective of physical therapy is two-fold: first prevent permanent disability from injury or ill-ness, and second to have patients resume their regular activities as soon as they are physically capable. Physical therapy assistants and aides work toward these objectives by administering rehabilitation plans that are developed by a licensed physical therapist.

*Physical therapy assistants* instruct patients in a wide variety of treatments that may encompass manual exercises on a treadmill, stationary bike, or weight lifting equipment. For patients whose therapy requires non-weight bearing exercise, their treatment often includes exercises in a swimming pool. Other forms of treatment administered by the physical therapy assistant involve massages, electrical stimulation, paraffin baths, hot/cold packs and traction. Assistants may also measure a patient's size, flexibility, and range of motion. They may also use ultrasound equipment to evaluate discomfort patients are experiencing with a knee or elbow. Physical therapists may use this data to fit the patient with an orthopedic brace, prostheses, or other support device. Assistants monitor the patient's progress during treatment and report all abnormalities and achievements to the physical therapist for periodic evaluation.

*Physical therapy aides* help make therapy sessions productive. They are usually responsible for keeping the treatment area clean and organized, and preparing for each patient's therapy. When patients needs assistance to or from the treatment area, aides may push them in a wheelchair, or provide them with a shoulder to lean on. Aides encourage patients during therapy sessions, and watch to see that exercises are performed correctly so as to attain the maximum benefit and to guard against further injury. Aides consult with the therapist or assistant if patients are experiencing difficulty with the treatment. Because they are not licensed, aides perform a smaller range of tasks than physical therapy assistants.

The duties of assistants and aides include some clerical tasks such as ordering depleted supplies, maintaining patient records, answering the phones, and filling out insurance forms and other paperwork. Records kept by the assistant or aide keep the therapist abreast of progress and any problems that may develop during treatment. The extent to which an aide, or even an assistant, performs clerical tasks depends on the size and location of the facility.

## Working Conditions

The hours and days that physical therapy assistants and aides work vary depending on the facility and whether they are full-time or part-time employees. In 1994, approximately four out of five assistants worked in a full-time, salaried capacity. Many private physical therapy offices have evening and weekend office hours to help coincide with patients' personal schedules.

Physical therapy assistants and aides need to have a moderate degree of strength due to the physical exertion required in assisting patients with their treatment. For example, constant kneeling, stooping and standing for long periods of time are all part of the job. In some cases assistants may need to help lift patients, therefore physical therapy programs strongly recommend against anyone prone to back problems becoming a physical therapy assistant.

## Employment

Physical therapy assistants and aides held 78,000 jobs in

1994. They work alongside physical therapists in a variety of settings. Over half of all assistants and aides work in hospitals or private physical therapy offices. Others work in clinics, nursing homes, schools and even inside patients' homes. In sports medicine, they may work part of the time on the sidelines of sporting events, or in swimming pools performing aqua therapy.

### Training, Other Qualifications, and Advancement

Physical therapy assistants typically have earned an associate degree from an accredited physical therapist assistant program. As of January 1996, 41 states and Puerto Rico required assistants to be certified or licensed. Other requirements include certification in CPR and First Aid, and a minimum number of hours of clinical experience.

According to the American Physical Therapy Association (APTA), there were 173 accredited physical therapist assistant programs in the United States, with another 54 in development as of June 1995. Accredited physical therapy assistant programs are designed to last two years, or four semesters, and culminate in an associate degree. Admission into physical therapist assistant programs is competitive and it is not unusual for colleges to have long waiting lists of prospective candidates. The programs are divided into academic study and hands-on clinical experience. Academic coursework initially includes algebra, anatomy and physiology, biology, chemistry, and psychology. Before students embark on their clinical field experience in a hospital or private clinic, many programs require that students complete a semester of anatomy and physiology and have certifications in CPR and First Aid. Both educators and prospective employers view clinical experience as an integral part of ensuring that students understand the responsibilities of a physical therapy assistant.

Employers typically require physical therapy aides to have a high school diploma, strong interpersonal skills, and a desire to assist people in need. Most employers provide aides clinical training on the job.

### Job Outlook

Physical therapy assistants and aides is expected to be one of the fastest growing occupations through the year 2005. Opportunities should be especially favorable for assistants unless the number of new graduates increases significantly. Reports consistently indicate employers currently are having difficulty finding qualified candidates for job openings.

Demand for physical therapy assistants and aides will continue to rise as the median age of Americans increases. The elderly consume a disproportionate share of physical therapy services. As the baby boom generation ages, demand for services associated with geriatric medicine will grow significantly. Older patients often need more assistance in their treatment, making the roles of assistants and aides vital.

Shortages of physical therapists in many areas makes hiring licensed assistants an attractive alternative. After a patient is evaluated and a treatment plan is designed by the physical therapist, the patient can be turned over to an assistant. The licensed assistant can administer many aspects of the treatment prescribed by the therapist. By increasing the role of physical therapy assistants relative to physical therapists, more patients receive care and labor costs are substantially lower.

While the number of accredited programs has increased,

enrollment in each has not thus limiting the growth in newly trained assistants. The size of many programs has been limited because of the difficulties in recruiting qualified instructors—educational institutions are often outbid for their services by other employers.

### Earnings

According to the limited information available, starting salaries for physical therapy assistants average about $22,500 a year. Starting salaries of assistants working in hospitals tended to be lower than those in private practice. As an inducement, many hospitals offer assistants a structured path of advancement and a chance to work with a varied patient population. In private practice, experienced physical therapy assistants earn, on average, about $24,000 a year.

### Related Occupations

Physical therapy assistants and aides work under the supervision of physical therapists. Other occupations in the health care field that work under the supervision of professionals include dental, medical, occupational therapy, optometric, recreational therapy, and pharmacy assistants.

### Related *D.O.T.* Jobs

These job titles are related to or more specific than the more general description above. They will help you identify job options you may not otherwise discover. These descriptions are in the current edition of the *Dictionary of Occupational Titles* and classified by numerical order.

076.224-010 PHYSICAL THERAPY ASSISTANT; 355.354-010 PHYSICAL THERAPY AIDE

### Sources of Additional Information

Information on a career as a physical therapy assistant or aide, and a list of schools offering accredited programs can be obtained from:

❑ The American Physical Therapy Association, 1111 North Fairfax Street, Alexandria, VA 22314-1488.

# Plasterers

### Nature of the Work

Plastering—one of the oldest crafts in the building trades—is enjoying a resurgence in popularity because of the introduction of newer, less costly materials and techniques. Plasterers apply plaster to interior walls and ceilings to form fire-resistant and relatively soundproof surfaces. They also apply plaster veneer over drywall to create smooth or textured abrasion-resistant finishes. They apply durable plasters such as polymer-based acrylic finishes and stucco to exterior surfaces, and install prefabricated exterior insulation systems over existing walls for good insulation and interesting architectural effects. In addition, they cast ornamental designs in plaster. Drywall workers and lathers—a related occupation—use drywall instead of plaster when erecting interior walls and ceilings.

When plasterers work with interior surfaces such as cinder block and concrete, they first apply a brown coat of gypsum plaster that provides a base, followed by a second or finish coat—also called "white coat"—which is a lime-based plaster. When plastering metal lath (supportive wire mesh) foundations, they apply a preparatory or "scratch coat" with a trowel. They spread this rich plaster mixture into and over the metal lath. Before the plaster sets, they scratch its surface with a rake-like tool to produce ridges so the subsequent brown coat will bond to it tightly.

Laborers prepare a thick, smooth plaster for the brown coat. Plasterers spray or trowel this mixture onto the surface, then finish by smoothing it to an even, level surface.

For the finish coat, plasterers prepare a mixture of lime, plaster of Paris, and water. They quickly apply this onto the brown coat using a "hawk"—a light, metal plate with a handle—trowel, brush, and water. This mixture, which sets very quickly, produces a very smooth, durable finish.

Plasterers also work with a plaster material that can be finished in a single coat. This thin-coat or gypsum veneer plaster is made of lime and plaster of Paris and is mixed with water at the job site. It provides a smooth, durable, abrasion resistant finish on interior masonry surfaces, special gypsum base board, or drywall prepared with a bonding agent.

Plasterers create decorative interior surfaces as well. They do this by pressing a brush or trowel firmly against the wet plaster surface and using a circular hand motion to create decorative swirls.

For exterior work, plasterers usually apply a mixture of Portland cement, lime, and sand (stucco) over cement, concrete, masonry, and lath. Stucco is also applied directly to a wire lath with a scratch coat followed by a brown coat and then a finish coat. Plasterers may also embed marble or gravel chips into the finish coat to achieve a pebblelike, decorative finish.

Increasingly, plasterers apply insulation to the exteriors of new and old buildings. They cover the outer wall with rigid foam insulation board and reinforcing mesh and then trowel on a polymer-based or polymer-modified base coat. They apply an additional coat of this material with a decorative finish.

Plasterers sometimes do complex decorative and ornamental work that requires special skill and creativity. For example, they mold intricate wall and ceiling designs. Following an architect's blueprint, they pour or spray a special plaster into a mold and allow it to set. Workers then remove the molded plaster and put it in place according to the plan.

## Working Conditions

Most plastering jobs are indoors; however, plasterers work outside when applying stucco or exterior wall insulation and decorative finish systems. Because plaster can freeze, heat is usually necessary to complete plastering jobs in cold weather. Sometimes plasterers work on scaffolds high above the ground.

Plastering is physically demanding, requiring considerable standing, bending, lifting, and reaching overhead. The work can be dusty and dirty; plaster materials also soil shoes and clothing and can irritate skin and eyes.

## Employment

Plasterers held about 30,000 jobs in 1994. Most plasterers work on new construction, particularly where special architectural and lighting effects are part of the work. Some repair and renovate older buildings. Many plasterers are employed in Florida, California, and the Southwest, where exterior plasters with decorative finishes are very popular.

Most plasterers work for independent contractors. About one in five plasterers is self-employed.

## Training, Other Qualifications, and Advancement

Although most employers recommend apprenticeship as the best way to learn plastering, many people learn the trade by working as helpers to experienced plasterers. Those who learn the trade informally as helpers usually start by carrying materials, setting up scaffolds, and mixing plaster. Later they learn to apply the scratch, brown, and finish coats.

Apprenticeship programs, sponsored by local joint committees of contractors and unions, generally consist of two or three years of on-the-job training, in addition to at least 144 hours annually of classroom instruction in drafting, blueprint reading, and mathematics for layout work.

In the classroom, apprentices start with a history of the trade and the industry. They also learn about the uses of plaster, estimating materials and costs, and casting ornamental plaster designs. On the job, they learn about lath bases, plaster mixes, methods of plastering, blueprint reading, and safety. They also learn how to use various tools, such as hand and powered trowels, floats, brushes, straightedges, power tools, plaster-mixing machines, and piston-type pumps. Some apprenticeship programs also allow individuals to obtain training in related occupations such as cement masonry and bricklaying.

Applicants for apprentice or helper jobs generally must be at least 17 years old, be in good physical condition, and have manual dexterity. Applicants who have a high school education are preferred. Courses in general mathematics, mechanical drawing, and shop provide a useful background.

Plasterers may advance to supervisors, superintendents, or estimators for plastering contractors, or may become self-employed contractors.

## Job Outlook

Employment of plasterers is expected to increase about as fast as the average for all occupations through the year 2005. In addition to job openings due to rising demand for plastering work, additional jobs will open up as plasterers transfer to other occupations or leave the labor force.

In past years, employment of plasterers declined as more builders switched to drywall construction. This decline has halted, however, and employment of plasterers is expected to continue growing as a result of greater appreciation for the durability and attractiveness that troweled finishes provide. Thin-coat plastering—or veneering—in particular, is gaining greater acceptance as more builders recognize its ease of application, durability, quality of finish, and fire-retarding qualities. An increasing use of prefabricated wall systems and new polymer-based or polymer-modified acrylic exterior insulating finishes are also gaining popularity, not only because of their durability, attractiveness, and insulating properties, but also because of their lower cost. These wall systems and finishes are growing in popularity particularly in the South and Southwest regions of the country. In addition, plasterers will be needed to renovate plaster work in older structures and create special architectural effects such as curved surfaces, which are not practical with drywall materials.

Most plasterers work in construction, where prospects fluctuate from year to year due to changing economic conditions. Bad weather affects plastering less than other construction trades because most work is indoors. On exterior surfacing jobs, however, plasterers may lose time because materials cannot be applied under wet or freezing conditions. Best employment opportunities should continue to be in Florida, California, and the Southwest, where exterior plaster and decorative finishes are expected to remain popular.

## Earnings

Median weekly earnings for plasterers working full-time were about $385 a week in 1994. The middle 50 percent earned between $260 and $489 a week. The top 10 percent earned more than $626 and the lowest 10 percent less than $237 a week.

According to the limited information available, average hourly earnings—including benefits—for plasterers who belonged to a union and worked full-time ranged between $15.80 and $37.63 in 1994. Plasterers in New York, Boston, Chicago, San Francisco, Los Angeles, and other large cities received the higher hourly earnings. Apprentice wage rates start at about half the rate paid to experienced plasterers. Annual earnings for plasterers and apprentices may be less than the hourly rate would indicate because poor weather and periodic declines in construction activity may limit their work time.

Many plasterers are members of unions. They are represented by the Operative Plasterers' and Cement Masons' International Association of the United States and Canada, or the International Union of Bricklayers and Allied Craftsmen.

## Related Occupations

Other construction workers who use a trowel as their primary tool include drywall finishers, bricklayers, concrete masons, marble setters, stonemasons, terrazzo workers, and tilesetters.

## Related *D.O.T.* Jobs

These job titles are related to or more specific than the more general description above. They will help you identify job options you may not otherwise discover. These descriptions are in the current edition of the *Dictionary of Occupational Titles* and classified by numerical order.

842.361-018 PLASTERER; 842.361-022 PLASTERER APPRENTICE; 842.361-026 PLASTERER, MOLDING; 842.381-014 STUCCO MASON

## Sources of Additional Information

For information about apprenticeships or other work opportunities, contact local plastering contractors; locals of the unions previously mentioned; a local joint union-management apprenticeship committee; or the nearest office of the state apprenticeship agency or the state employment service.

For general information about the work of plasterers, contact:

❑ International Union of Bricklayers and Allied Craftsmen, 815 15th St. NW, Washington, DC 20005.

❑ Operative Plasterers' and Cement Masons' International Association of the United States and Canada, 1125 17th St. NW, Washington, DC 20036.

# Plumbers and Pipefitters

## Nature of the Work

Most people are familiar with plumbers who come to their home to unclog a drain or install an appliance. In addition to these activities, however, plumbers and pipefitters install, maintain, and repair many different types of pipe systems. For example, some systems move water to a municipal water treatment plant, and then to residential, commercial, and public buildings. Others dispose of waste. Some bring in gas for stoves and furnaces. Others supply air-conditioning. Pipe systems in power plants carry the steam that powers huge turbines. Pipes also are used in manufacturing plants to move material through the production process.

Although plumbing and pipefitting sometimes are considered a single trade, workers generally specialize in one or the other. *Plumbers* install and repair the water, waste disposal, drainage, and gas systems in homes and commercial and industrial buildings. They also install plumbing fixtures—bathtubs, showers, sinks, and toilets—and appliances such as dishwashers and water heaters. *Pipefitters* install and repair both high and low-pressure pipe systems that are used in manufacturing, in the generation of electricity, and in heating and cooling buildings. They also install automatic controls that are increasingly being used to regulate these systems. Some pipefitters specialize in only one type of system. *Steamfitters*, for example, install pipe systems that move liquids or gases under high pressure. *Sprinkler fitters* install automatic fire sprinkler systems in buildings.

Plumbers and pipefitters use many different materials and construction techniques, depending on the type of project. Residential water systems, for example, use copper, steel, and increasingly plastic pipe that can be handled and installed by one or two workers. Municipal sewerage systems, on the other hand, are made of large cast iron pipes; installation normally requires crews of pipefitters. Despite these differences, all plumbers and pipefitters must be able to follow building plans or blueprints and instructions from supervisors, lay out the job, and work efficiently with the materials and tools of the trade.

When construction plumbers install piping in a house, for example, they work from blueprints or drawings that show the planned location of pipes, plumbing fixtures, and appliances. They lay out the job to fit the piping into the structure of the house with the least waste of material and within the confines of the structure. They measure and mark areas where pipes will be installed and connected. They check for obstructions, such as electrical wiring, and, if necessary, plan the pipe installation around the problem.

Sometimes plumbers have to cut holes in walls, ceilings, and floors of a house. For some systems, they may have to hang steel supports from ceiling joists to hold the pipe in place. To assemble the system, plumbers cut and bend lengths of pipe using saws, pipe cutters, and pipe-bending machines. They connect lengths of pipe with fittings; the method depends on the type of pipe used. For plastic pipe, plumbers connect the sections and fittings with adhesives. For copper pipe, they slide fittings over the end of the pipe and solder the fitting in place with a torch.

After the piping is in place in the house, plumbers install

the fixtures and appliances and connect the system to the outside water or sewer lines. Using pressure gauges, they check the system to insure that the plumbing works properly.

## Working Conditions

Because plumbers and pipefitters frequently must lift heavy pipes, stand for long periods, and sometimes work in uncomfortable or cramped positions, they need physical strength as well as stamina. They may have to work outdoors in inclement weather. They also are subject to falls from ladders, cuts from sharp tools, and burns from hot pipes or from soldering equipment.

Plumbers and pipefitters engaged in construction generally work a standard 40-hour week; those involved in maintaining pipe systems, including those who provide maintenance services under contract, may have to work evening or weekend shifts, as well as be on-call. These maintenance workers may spend quite a bit of time traveling to and from work sites.

## Employment

Plumbers and pipefitters held about 375,000 jobs in 1994. About two-thirds worked for mechanical and plumbing contractors engaged in new construction, repair, modernization, or maintenance work. Others did maintenance work for a variety of industrial, commercial, and government employers. For example, pipefitters were employed as maintenance personnel in the petroleum and chemical industries, where manufacturing operations require the moving of liquids and gases through pipes. One of every five plumbers and pipefitters is self-employed.

Jobs for plumbers and pipefitters are distributed across the country in about the same proportion as the general population.

## Training, Other Qualifications, and Advancement

Virtually all plumbers undergo some type of apprenticeship training. Many programs are administered by local union-management committees made up of members of the United Association of Journeymen and Apprentices of the Plumbing and Pipefitting Industry of the United States and Canada, and local employers who are members of either the Mechanical Contractors Association of America, Inc., the National Association of Plumbing-Heating-Cooling Contractors, or the National Fire Sprinkler Association, Inc.

Nonunion training and apprenticeship programs are administered by local chapters of the Associated Builders and Contractors, the National Association of Plumbing-Heating-Cooling Contractors, the American Fire Sprinkler Association, and the Home Builders Institute of the National Association of Home Builders.

Apprenticeships—both union and nonunion—consist of four to five years of on-the-job training, in addition to at least 144 hours annually of related classroom instruction. Classroom subjects include drafting and blueprint reading, mathematics, applied physics and chemistry, safety, and local plumbing codes and regulations. On the job, apprentices first learn basic skills such as identifying grades and types of pipe, the use of the tools of the trade, and the safe unloading of materials. As apprentices gain experience, they learn how to work with various types of pipe and install different piping systems and plumbing fixtures. Apprenticeship gives trainees a thorough knowledge of all aspects of the trade. Although most plumbers are trained through apprenticeship, some still learn their skills informally on the job.

Applicants for union or nonunion apprentice jobs must be 18 years old and in good physical condition. Apprenticeship committees may require applicants to have a high school diploma or its equivalent. Armed Forces training in plumbing and pipefitting is considered very good preparation. In fact, persons with this background may be given credit for previous experience when entering a civilian apprenticeship program. Secondary or postsecondary courses in shop, plumbing, general mathematics, drafting, blueprint reading, and physics also are good preparation.

Although there are no uniform national licensing requirements, most communities require plumbers to be licensed. Licensing requirements vary from area to area, but most localities require workers to pass an examination that tests their knowledge of the trade and of local plumbing codes.

Some plumbers and pipefitters may become supervisors for mechanical and plumbing contractors. Others go into business for themselves.

## Job Outlook

Job opportunities for skilled plumbers and pipefitters are expected to be good as the growth in demand outpaces the supply of workers trained in this craft. Employment of plumbers and pipefitters is expected to grow more slowly than the average for all occupations through the year 2005. However, the pool of young workers available to enter training programs will also be increasing slowly and many in that group are reluctant to seek training for jobs that may be strenuous and have uncomfortable working conditions.

Construction activity—residential, industrial, and commercial—is expected to grow slowly over the next decade. Demand for plumbers will stem from building renovation, including the increasing installation of sprinkler systems; repair and maintenance of existing residential systems, and maintenance activities for places that have extensive systems of pipes, such as power plants, water and wastewater treatment plants, pipelines, office buildings, and factories. However, the growing use of plastic pipe and fittings, which are much easier to use; more efficient sprinkler systems; and other technologies will mean that employment will not grow as fast as it has in past years. In addition, several thousand positions will become available each year from the need to replace experienced workers who leave the occupation.

Traditionally, many organizations with extensive pipe systems have employed their own plumbers or pipefitters to maintain their equipment and keep everything running smoothly. But, in order to reduce their labor costs, many of these firms no longer employ a full-time in-house plumber or pipefitter. Instead, when they need one they rely on workers provided, under service contracts, by plumbing and pipefitting contractors.

All construction projects provide only temporary employment, so when a project ends, plumbers and pipefitters working on it may experience short bouts of unemployment. Because construction activity varies from area to area, job openings, as well as apprenticeship opportunities, fluctuate with local economic conditions. However, employment of plumbers and pipefitters generally is less sensitive to changes in economic conditions than some of the other construction trades. Even when construction activity declines, maintenance, rehabilitation, and replacement of existing piping systems, as well as the growing installation of fire sprinkler systems, provide many jobs for plumbers and pipefitters.

### Earnings

Median weekly earnings for plumbers and pipefitters who were not self-employed were $530 in 1994. The middle 50 percent earned between $373 and $742 weekly. The lowest 10 percent earned less than $284; the highest 10 percent earned more than $970 a week.

In 1993, the median hourly wage rate for maintenance pipefitters in 160 metropolitan areas were about $18.70. The middle 50 percent earned between about $16.90 and $20.90 an hour. In comparison, the average wage for all nonsupervisory and production workers in private industry, except farming, was $10.80. In general, wage rates tend to be higher in the Midwest and West than in the Northeast and South.

Apprentices usually begin at about 50 percent of the wage rate paid to experienced plumbers or pipefitters. This increases periodically as they improve their skills. After an initial waiting period, apprentices receive the same benefits as experienced plumbers and pipefitters.

Many plumbers and pipefitters are members of the United Association of Journeymen and Apprentices of the Plumbing and Pipefitting Industry of the United States and Canada.

### Related Occupations

Other occupations in which workers install and repair mechanical systems in buildings are boilermakers, stationary engineers, electricians, elevator installers, industrial machinery repairers, millwrights, sheetmetal workers, and heating, air-conditioning, and refrigeration mechanics.

### Related *D.O.T.* Jobs

These job titles are related to or more specific than the more general description above. They will help you identify job options you may not otherwise discover. These descriptions are in the current edition of the *Dictionary of Occupational Titles* and classified by numerical order.

862.261-010 PIPE FITTER; 862.281-010 COPPERSMITH; 862.281-014 COPPERSMITH APPRENTICE; 862.281-022 PIPE FITTER; 862.281-026 PIPE FITTER APPRENTICE; 862.361-014 GAS-MAIN FITTER; 862.361-018 PIPE FITTER, DIESEL ENGINE I; 862.361-022 STEAM SERVICE INSPECTOR; 862.381-014 INDUSTRIAL-GAS FITTER; 862.381-022 PIPE FITTER, DIESEL ENGINE II; 862.381-030 PLUMBER; 862.381-034 PLUMBER APPRENTICE; 862.681-010 PLUMBER; 862.682-010 PIPE CUTTER; 862.684-034 WATER-SOFTENER SERVICER-AND-INSTALLER

### Sources of Additional Information

For information about apprenticeships or work opportunities in plumbing and pipefitting, contact local plumbing, heating, and air-conditioning contractors; a local or state chapter of the National Association of Plumbing, Heating, and Cooling Contractors; a local chapter of the Mechanical Contractors Association; a local of the United Association of Journeymen and Apprentices of the Plumbing and Pipefitting Industry of the United States and Canada; or the nearest office of the state employment service or state apprenticeship agency. This information is also available from:

❏ The Home Builders Institute, National Association of Home Builders, 1201 15th St. NW, Washington, DC 20005.

For general information about the work of plumbers, pipefitters, and sprinkler fitters, contact:

❏ National Association of Plumbing-Heating-Cooling Contractors, P.O. Box 6808, Falls Church, VA 22046.

❏ Associated Builders and Contractors, 1300 North 17th St., Rosslyn, VA 22209.

❏ National Fire Sprinkler Association, P.O. Box 1000, Patterson, NY 12563.

❏ American Fire Sprinkler Association, Inc., 12959 Jupiter Rd., Suite 142, Dallas, TX 75238-3200.

❏ Mechanical Contractors Association of America, 1385 Piccard Dr., Rockville, MD 20850.

# Police, Detectives, and Special Agents

### Nature of the Work

Police officers, detectives, and special agents are responsible for enforcing statutes, laws, and regulations designed to protect life and property. Many law enforcement officers spend much of their time interviewing witnesses and suspects, apprehending fugitives and criminals, collecting evidence, and providing testimony in court. After being incarcerated, many individuals are held under the care of correctional officers. Others spend most of their time patrolling a designated area to preserve the peace and to prevent crime. They resolve problems within the community and enforce laws governing motor vehicle operations. All law enforcement officers are required to file reports of their activities, often involving long hours of paperwork. In most jurisdictions, whether on or off duty, these officers are expected to exercise their authority whenever necessary.

In recent years, American voters have expressed their desire for government to place increasing emphasis on law enforcement efforts to reduce serious crime. As one response to serious crime, law enforcement officers are becoming more involved in community policing—building partnerships with the citizens of high-crime, urban neighborhoods, thus increasing public confidence in the police and mobilizing the public to help the police fight crime. Through the use of government, volunteer, and commercial resources, police encourage people in the community to help identify and solve recurring problems. This involves making the police officer a permanent, highly visible figure in the neighborhood rather than merely an officer reacting to a crime.

Police officers and detectives who work in small communities and rural areas have general law enforcement duties. In the course of a day's work, they may direct traffic at the scene of a fire, investigate a burglary, or give first aid to an accident victim. In large police departments and federal agencies, officers and special agents usually are assigned to a specific detail for a fixed length of time. Some may become experts in chemical and microscopic analysis, firearms identification, handwriting and fingerprint identification, or serve on mounted and motorcycle patrol, harbor patrol, canine corps, special weapons and tactics or emergency response teams, or task forces formed to combat specific types of crime.

*Sheriffs* and *deputy sheriffs* generally enforce the law in rural areas or places where there is no local police department. They may serve legal processes of courts. Sheriffs' duties resemble those of local or county police departments, but generally on a smaller scale. Most sheriffs' departments employ fewer than 25 sworn officers, and many employ fewer than 10.

Detectives and special agents work as plainclothes investigators, gathering facts and collecting evidence for criminal cases. They conduct interviews, examine records, observe the activities of suspects, and participate in raids or arrests.

Special agents employed by the U.S. Department of Justice work for the Drug Enforcement Administration, the Federal Bureau of Investigation, the U.S. Border Patrol, and the U.S. Marshals Service.

*Drug Enforcement Administration (DEA) special agents* specialize in enforcement of drug laws and regulations. Agents may conduct complex criminal investigations, carry out surveillance of criminals, and infiltrate illicit drug organizations using undercover techniques. They may work closely with confidential sources of information to collect evidence leading to the seizure of assets gained from the sale of illegal drugs.

*Federal Bureau of Investigation (FBI) special agents* are the government's principal investigators, responsible for investigating violations of more than 260 statutes. Agents may be required to do surveillance, monitor court-authorized wiretaps, examine business records to investigate white-collar crime, track the interstate movement of stolen property, collect evidence of espionage activities, or be assigned to sensitive undercover assignments designed to apprehend terrorists. Some special agents investigate violations of federal laws in connection with bank robberies, theft of government property, organized crime, espionage, sabotage, kidnapping, and terrorism. Agents with specialized training usually work on cases related to their background. For example, agents with an accounting background may investigate bank embezzlements or fraudulent bankruptcies.

*U.S. marshals and deputy marshals* provide security for federal courts, including judges, witnesses, and prisoners. They apprehend fugitives and operate the Special Operations Group (SOG)—a tactical unit which responds to high-threat and emergency situations. Some deputies provide security to the Department of Defense and the U.S. Air Force during movements of missiles between military facilities.

*U.S. Border Patrol special agents* are responsible for protecting more than 8,000 miles of international land and water boundaries. Their primary mission is to detect and prevent the smuggling and unlawful entry of undocumented aliens into the United States and to apprehend those persons found in violation of the immigration laws. The Border Patrol is the primary interdicting agency along the land borders between the ports of entry for illicit drugs and various contraband. They accomplish their mission through activities such as: tracking, traffic checks on roads and highways leading away from the border, and participating in various task force operations with other law enforcement agencies.

Special agents employed by the U.S. Department of the Treasury work for The Bureau of Alcohol, Tobacco, and Firearms, the U.S. Customs Service, Internal Revenue Service, and U.S. Secret Service.

*Bureau of Alcohol, Tobacco, and Firearms (BATF) special agents* investigate violations of federal explosives laws, including bombings and arson-for-profit schemes affecting interstate commerce. They may investigate suspected illegal sales, possession, or use of firearms. Other BATF agents investigate violations related to the illegal sale of liquor and interstate smuggling of untaxed cigarettes. These investigations involve surveillance, participation in raids, interviewing suspects, and searching for physical evidence.

*Customs agents* enforce laws to prevent smuggling of goods across U.S. borders.

*Internal Revenue Service special agents* collect evidence against individuals and companies that are evading the payment of federal taxes.

*U.S. Secret Service special agents* are charged with two main missions—protection and investigation. During the course of their careers, they may be assigned to protect the President, Vice President, and their immediate families, presidential candidates, ex-presidents, and foreign dignitaries visiting the United States. Secret Service agents also investigate counterfeiting, the forgery of government checks or bonds, and the fraudulent use of credit cards.

Special agents employed by the U.S. Department of State work for the Diplomatic Security Service. *Diplomatic Security Service special agents* advise ambassadors on security matters and manage a complex range of security programs overseas. In the United States, they investigate passport and visa fraud, conduct personnel security investigations, issue security clearances, and protect the Secretary of State and certain foreign dignitaries. They train foreign civilian police who then return to their own countries better able to fight terrorism.

Various other federal agencies employ special agents with sworn police powers and the authority to carry firearms and make arrests. These agencies generally evolved from the need for security for the agency's property and personnel. The largest such agency is the Federal Protective Service, which has personnel nationwide. Other examples include the U.S. Mint police, the Government Printing Service police, and the Central Intelligence Agency's Special Protective Service.

*State police officers* (sometimes called state troopers or highway patrol officers) patrol highways and enforce motor vehicle laws and regulations. They issue traffic citations to motorists who violate the law. At the scene of an accident, they may direct traffic, give first aid, and call for emergency equipment. They also write reports that may be used to determine the cause of the accident. In addition, state police officers may provide services to motorists on the highways, such as calling for road service for drivers with mechanical trouble.

State police also enforce criminal laws. They are frequently called upon to render assistance to officers of other law enforcement agencies. In rural areas that do not have a police force or a local representative from the sheriff's department, the state police are the primary law enforcement agency, investigating any crimes that occur, such as burglary or assault.

Most new police recruits begin their careers in an urban setting. They generally start on patrol duty, riding in a police vehicle. In smaller agencies, they may work alone; in larger agencies, they ride with experienced officers. Patrols generally cover an area such as old and congested business districts or outlying residential neighborhoods. Officers attempt to become thoroughly familiar with conditions throughout their patrol area and, while on patrol, remain alert for anything unusual. They note suspicious circumstances, such as open windows or lights in vacant buildings, as well as hazards to public safety. Officers on patrol enforce traffic regulations and also watch for stolen vehicles and wanted individuals. At regular intervals, officers report to police headquarters by radio, or by telephone when they are imparting information that is confidential, since scanners which pick up police radio communications are in popular usage.

Regardless of where they work, police, detectives, and special agents spend considerable time writing reports and maintaining records. They are called to testify in court when their arrests result in legal action. Some senior officers, such as chief inspectors, commanders, division and bureau chiefs, and agents-in-charge, are responsible for operation of geographic divisions of an agency, certain kinds of criminal investigations, and various agency functions. Such managers have administrative and supervisory duties.

## Working Conditions

Police, detectives, and special agents usually work a 40-hour week, but paid overtime work is common. Shift work is necessary because police protection must be provided around the clock. More junior officers frequently must work weekends, holidays, and nights. Police officers, detectives, and special agents are subject to call at any time their services are needed and may work long hours during criminal investigations.

The jobs of some special agents such as U.S. Secret Service and DEA special agents require extensive travel, often on very short notice.

Some police, detectives, and special agents with agencies such as the U.S. Border Patrol have to work outdoors for long periods in all kinds of weather. While police work is inherently dangerous, good training, team work, and equipment such as bullet-resistant vests minimize the number of injuries and fatalities. The risks associated with pursuing speeding motorists, apprehending criminals, and dealing with public disorders can be very stressful for the officer as well as for his or her family.

## Employment

Police, detectives, and special agents held about 682,000 jobs in 1994. About 81 percent were employed by local governments, primarily in cities with more than 25,000 inhabitants. Some cities have very large police forces, while hundreds of small communities employ fewer than 25 officers each. State police agencies employed about 13 percent of all police, detectives, and special agents; various federal agencies employed an additional 6 percent. There are about 17,000 federal, state, special (such as park police, transit police, and county police) and local police agencies in the nation.

## Training, Other Qualifications, and Advancement

Civil service regulations govern the appointment of police and detectives in practically all state and large city agencies and in many smaller ones. Candidates must be U.S. citizens, usually at least 20 years of age, and must meet rigorous physical and personal qualifications. Eligibility for appointment generally depends on performance in competitive written examinations as well as on education and experience. Physical examinations often include tests of vision, hearing, strength, and agility.

Because personal characteristics such as honesty, judgment, integrity, and a sense of responsibility are especially important in law enforcement work, candidates are interviewed by senior officers, and their character traits and background are investigated. In some agencies, candidates are interviewed by a psychiatrist or a psychologist, or given a personality test. Most applicants are subjected to lie detector examinations and drug testing. Some agencies subject sworn personnel to random drug testing as a condition of continuing employment. Although police, detectives, and special agents work independently, they must perform their duties in accordance with the law and departmental rules. They should enjoy working with people and meeting the public.

In larger police departments, where the majority of law enforcement jobs are found, applicants usually must have at least a high school education. A small but growing proportion of local, special, and state departments require some college training. Some agencies hire police science or criminal justice students as police interns or cadets; some police departments and virtually all federal agencies require a college degree. A few police departments accept applicants as recruits who have less than a high school education, but the number is declining.

The federal agency with the largest number of special agents is the FBI. To be considered for appointment as an FBI special agent, an applicant either must be a graduate of an accredited law school; be a college graduate with a major in accounting; or be a college graduate with either fluency in a foreign language or three years of full-time work experience. Applicants must be U.S. citizens, possess a valid driver's license, be between 23 and 37 years of age at the time of appointment, and be willing to accept an assignment anywhere in the United States. They also must be in excellent physical condition with at least 20/200 vision corrected to 20/40 in one eye and 20/20 in the other eye. All new agents undergo 16 weeks of training at the FBI academy on the U.S. Marine Corps base in Quantico, Virginia.

Applicants for special agent jobs with the U.S. Department of Treasury's Secret Service and BATF must have a bachelor's degree, or a minimum of three years' work experience which demonstrates the ability to deal effectively with individuals or groups, collect and assemble pertinent facts, and prepare clear and concise reports. Candidates must be in excellent physical condition and be under 37 years of age at the time they enter the agency unless they have previous qualifying federal law enforcement experience. Prospective special agents undergo 8 weeks of training at the Federal Law Enforcement Training Center in Glynco, Georgia, and another 8 to 11 weeks of specialized training with their particular agencies.

Applicants for special agent jobs with the U.S. Drug Enforcement Administration must be U.S. citizens, have a college degree in any field and either one year of experience conducting criminal investigations, one year of graduate school, or have achieved at least a 2.95 grade point average while in college. The minimum age for entry is 21 and the maximum age is 37 unless they have previous qualifying federal law enforcement experience. DEA special agents undergo 14 weeks of specialized training at the FBI Academy in Quantico, Virginia.

More and more, police departments are encouraging applicants to take postsecondary school training in law enforcement. Many entry-level applicants to police jobs have completed some formal postsecondary education and a significant number are college graduates. Many junior colleges, colleges, and universities offer programs in law enforcement or administration of justice. Other courses helpful in preparing for a career in law enforcement include accounting, finance, electrical engineering or computer science, and foreign languages. Physical education and sports are helpful in developing the competitiveness, stamina, and agility needed for law enforcement work. Knowledge of a foreign language is an asset in many agencies.

Some large cities hire high school graduates who are still in their teens as police cadets or trainees. They do clerical work and attend classes, and can be appointed to the regular force at the conclusion of their training, usually in one to two years, upon reaching the minimum age requirement.

Before their first assignments, officers usually go through a period of training. In small agencies, recruits often get on the job training with more experienced officers, rather than formal training. In state and large local departments, they get training at a police academy for 12 to 14 weeks, as mandated by the state. This training includes classroom instruction in constitutional law and civil rights, state laws and local ordinances, and accident investigation. Recruits also receive training and supervised experience in patrol, traffic control, use of firearms, self-defense, first aid, and handling emergencies.

Police officers usually become eligible for promotion after a probationary period ranging from six months to three years. In a large department, promotion may enable an officer to become a detective or specialize in one type of police work such as laboratory analysis of evidence, traffic control, communications, or working with juveniles. Promotions to sergeant, lieutenant, and captain usually are made according to a candidate's position on a promotion list, as determined by scores on a written examination and on-the-job performance, and are very competitive.

Continuing training helps police officers, detectives, and special agents improve their job performance. Through police department academies, regional centers for public safety employees established by the states, and federal agency training centers, instructors provide annual training in defensive tactics, firearms, use-of-force policies, sensitivity and communications skills, crowd-control techniques, legal developments that affect their work, and advances in law enforcement equipment. Many agencies pay all or part of the tuition for officers to work toward degrees in law enforcement, police science, administration of justice, or public administration, and pay higher salaries to those who earn such a degree.

## Job Outlook

The opportunity for public service through law enforcement work is attractive to many. The job is challenging and involves much personal responsibility. Furthermore, in many agencies, law enforcement officers may retire with a pension after 20 or 25 years of service, allowing them to pursue a second career while still in their 40s. Because of relatively attractive salaries and benefits, the number of qualified candidates exceeds the number of job openings in federal law enforcement agencies and in most state, local, and special police departments—resulting in increased hiring standards and selectivity by employers.

Competition is expected to remain keen for the higher paying jobs with state and federal agencies and police departments in more affluent areas. Persons having college training in police science, military experience, or both should have the best opportunities. Opportunities will be best in those urban communities whose departments offer relatively low salaries and where the crime rate is relatively high. Such departments are having difficulty attracting an adequate supply of high quality police officer candidates.

Competition is extremely keen for special agent positions with the Justice and Treasury Departments and other federal law enforcement agencies. Positions with these prestigious agencies tend to attract a far greater number of applicants than the number of job openings. Consequently, only the most highly qualified candidates obtain jobs.

Employment of police officers, detectives, and special agents is expected to increase faster than average for all occupations through the year 2005. A more security-conscious society and growing concern about drug-related crimes should contribute to the increasing demand for police services. At the local and state levels, growth is likely to continue as long as crime remains a serious concern. However, employment growth at the federal level will be tempered by continuing budgetary constraints faced by law enforcement agencies. Turnover in police, detective, and special agent positions is among the lowest of all occupations; nevertheless, the need to replace workers who retire, transfer to other occupations, or stop working for other reasons will be the source of most job openings.

The level of government spending determines the level of employment for police officers, detectives, and special agents. The number of job opportunities, therefore, can vary from year to year and from place to place. Layoffs, on the other hand, are rare because retirements enable most staffing cuts to be handled through attrition. Trained law enforcement officers who lose their jobs because of budget cuts usually have little difficulty finding jobs with other agencies.

## Earnings

In 1994, the median salary of nonsupervisory police officers and detectives was about $34,000 a year. The middle 50 percent earned between about $25,500 and $43,900; the lowest 10 percent were paid less than $17,900, while the highest 10 percent earned over $56,100 a year. Generally, salaries tend to be higher in urban, more affluent jurisdictions, which usually have best funded police departments.

Police officers and detectives in supervisory positions had a median salary of about $42,800 a year, also in 1994. The middle 50 percent earned between about $30,100 and $52,500; the lowest 10 percent were paid less than $19,800, while the highest 10 percent earned over $62,100 annually.

Sheriffs and other law enforcement officers had a median annual salary of about $26,800 in 1994. The middle 50 percent earned between about $20,800 and $37,200; the lowest 10 percent were paid less than $16,500, while the highest 10 percent earned over $48,600.

Federal law provides special salary rates to federal employees who serve in law enforcement. Additionally, many federal special agents receive administratively uncontrolled overtime (AUO)—equal to 25 percent of the agent's grade and step—awarded because of the large amount of overtime that these agents are expected to work. For example, in 1995 FBI agents started at a base salary of $31,200 a year, therefore earning $39,000 a year with AUO. Other Justice and Treasury Department special agents started at about $23,200 or $28,300 a year, therefore earning $29,000 or $35,400 per year including AUO, depending on their qualifications. Salaries of Justice and Treasury Department special agents progress to $66,800 including AUO, while supervisory agents started at $61,100 including AUO. Salaries were slightly higher in selected areas where the prevailing local pay level was higher. Since federal agents may be eligible for a special law enforcement benefits package, applicants should ask their recruiter for more information.

Total earnings for local, state, and special police detectives frequently exceed the stated salary due to payments for overtime, which can be significant. In addition to the common benefits—paid vacation, sick leave, and medical and life insurance—most police and sheriffs' departments provide officers with special allowances for uniforms and furnish weapons, handcuffs, and other required equipment. In addition, because police officers generally are covered by liberal pension plans, many retire at half-pay after 20 or 25 years of service.

### Related Occupations

Police, detectives, and special agents maintain law and order. Workers in related occupations include correctional officers, guards, fire marshals, and inspectors.

### Related *D.O.T.* Jobs

These job titles are related to or more specific than the more general description above. They will help you identify job options you may not otherwise discover. These descriptions are in the current edition of the *Dictionary of Occupational Titles* and classified by numerical order.

There are too many *D.O.T.* titles to list here. Most are variations related to a specific industry, and we have included a small number of representative *D.O.T.* titles as examples. Complete lists are available in various career software published by JIST or directly from the U.S. Department of Labor.

168.167-010 CUSTOMS PATROL OFFICER; 372.167-018 JAILER, CHIEF; 372.267-010 SPECIAL AGENT; 372.363-010 PROTECTIVE OFFICER; 375.137-034 COMMANDING OFFICER, POLICE; 375.163-014 PILOT, HIGHWAY PATROL; 375.167-022 DETECTIVE CHIEF; 375.167-050 COMMANDER, INTERNAL AFFAIRS; 375.263-014 POLICE OFFICER I; 375.263-018 STATE-HIGHWAY POLICE OFFICER; 375.264-010 POLICE OFFICER, CRIME PREVENTION; 375.267-014 DETECTIVE, NARCOTICS AND VICE; 375.267-018 INVESTIGATOR, NARCOTICS; 375.267-022 INVESTIGATOR, VICE; 375.267-034 INVESTIGATOR, INTERNAL AFFAIRS; 375.363-010 BORDER GUARD; 377.263-010 SHERIFF, DEPUTY; 377.267-010 DEPUTY UNITED STATES MARSHAL; 377.667-010 BAILIFF; 379.167-010 FISH AND GAME WARDEN; 379.263-014 PUBLIC-SAFETY OFFICER

### Sources of Additional Information

Information about entrance requirements may be obtained from federal, state, and local law enforcement agencies.

Further information about qualifications for employment as an FBI Special Agent is available from the nearest state FBI office; the address and phone number are listed in the local telephone directory.

Information about career opportunities, qualifications, and training to become a deputy marshal is available from:

❑ United States Marshals Service, Employment and Compensation Division, Field Staffing Branch, 600 Army Navy Dr., Arlington, VA 22202.

Information on careers as a DEA Special Agent may be obtained from:

❑ Drug Enforcement Administration, Special Agent Staffing Unit, Washington, DC 20537.

An overview of career opportunities, qualifications, and training for U.S. Secret Service Special Agents is available from:

❑ Secret Service, Personnel, 1800 G St. NW, Washington, DC 20223.

# Precision Assemblers

### Nature of the Work

Workers who put together the parts of manufactured products are called assemblers. In some instances, such as the building of a car, hundreds of assemblers work on a single product; in others, such as the assembly of a toy doll, a single assembler may be responsible for each product. Assembly work varies from simple, repetitive jobs that are relatively easy to learn to those requiring great precision and many months of experience and training. Precision assemblers are the highly experienced and trained workers who assemble complicated products.

The work of precision assemblers requires a high degree of accuracy. Workers must be able to interpret detailed specifications and instructions and apply independent judgment. Some experienced assemblers work with engineers and technicians, assembling prototypes or test products. Precision assemblers involved in product development must know how to read and interpret engineering specifications from text, drawings, and computer-aided drafting systems, and how to use a variety of tools and precision measuring instruments.

Precision assemblers may work on subassemblies or the final assembly of finished products or components of a vast array of products. For example, precision electrical and electronic equipment assemblers put together or modify prototypes or final assemblies of items such as missile control systems, radio or test equipment, computers, machine-tool numerical controls, radar, sonar, telemetering systems, and appliances. Precision electromechanical equipment assemblers prepare and test equipment or devices such as dynamometers, ejection seat mechanisms, magnetic drums, and tape drives. Precision machine builders construct, assemble, or rebuild engines and turbines, and office, agricultural, construction, oil field, rolling mill, textile, woodworking, paper, printing, and food wrapping machinery. Precision aircraft assemblers put together and install parts of airplanes, space vehicles, or missiles, such as wings or landing gear. Precision structural metal fitters align and fit structural metal parts according to detailed specifications prior to welding or riveting.

The manufacturing process is changing. Flexible manufacturing systems, which include the manufacturing applications of robotics, computers, programmable motion control, and various sensing technologies, are changing the way goods are made and affecting the jobs of those who make them. Precision assemblers have had to learn to use these machines and adapt to changes in work processes. The advent of cellular manufacturing in American firms, for example, has meant that the assembly line is more likely to be composed of "cells" that place a premium on communication and teamwork. As the United States manufacturing sector continues to evolve in the face of growing international competition, the nature of precision assembly will change along with it.

## Working Conditions

The conditions under which precision assemblers work depend on the manufacturing plant where they are employed. Electronics assemblers sit at tables in rooms that are clean, well lighted, and free from dust. Assemblers of aircraft and industrial machinery, however, usually come in contact with oil and grease, and their working areas may be quite noisy. They also may have to lift and fit heavy objects.

Most full-time assemblers work a standard 40-hour week, although overtime is fairly common. Work schedules of assemblers may vary at plants with more than one shift. In some plants, workers can accept or reject a certain job on a given shift, usually in order of seniority.

## Employment

Virtually all of the 324,000 precision assembler jobs in 1994 were in plants that manufacture durable goods. One-third of all jobs involved assembly of electronic and electrical machinery, equipment, and supplies, including electrical switches, welding equipment, electric motors, lighting equipment, household appliances, and radios and television sets. Nearly one-quarter of all jobs involved assembly of industrial machinery—diesel engines, steam turbine generators, farm tractors, mining and construction machinery, and office machines. Other industries employing many precision assemblers were transportation equipment (aircraft, autos, trucks, and buses) and instruments manufacturing.

The following tabulation lists the wage and salary employment of precision assemblers in 1994 by industry.

| | |
|---|---|
| Electronic and other electrical equipment manufacturing | 109,000 |
| Industrial machinery and equipment manufacturing | 81,000 |
| Transportation equipment manufacturing | 57,000 |
| Instruments and related products manufacturing | 57,000 |
| Fabricated metal products manufacturing | 15,000 |
| All other industries | 5,000 |

## Training, Other Qualifications, and Advancement

Precision assemblers often are promoted from the ranks of workers in less skilled jobs in the same firm. Sometimes, outside applicants may be hired if they possess suitable experience. The ability to do accurate work at a rapid pace is a key job requirement. A high school diploma is helpful but usually is not required.

For some precision assembly jobs, applicants need specialized training. For example, employers may require that applicants for electrical or electronic assembler jobs be technical school graduates or have equivalent military training.

Good eyesight, with or without glasses, is required for assemblers who work with small parts. In plants that make electrical and electronic products, which may contain many different colored wires, applicants often are tested for color vision.

As precision assemblers become more experienced, they may progress to jobs that require more skill and be given more responsibility. Experienced assemblers who have learned many assembly operations and understand the construction of a product may become product repairers. These workers fix assembled articles that operators or inspectors have identified as defective. Assemblers also can advance to quality control jobs or be promoted to supervisor. In some firms, assemblers can become trainees for one of the skilled trades. Those with a background in math, science, and computers may advance to programmers or operators of more highly automated production equipment.

## Job Outlook

Employment of precision assemblers is expected to decline through the year 2005, as increasing automation and internationalization of production will offset any increase in employment that would have resulted from industrial growth. As manufacturing firms strive for greater precision and productivity, jobs that can be performed more economically or more accurately by automated equipment will be upgraded or will disappear. Recent advancements have made robotics more applicable and affordable for manufacturing firms. The introduction of robots in these plants should continue to grow in coming years, raising the productivity of assembly workers and adversely affecting their employment.

The effects of automation will be felt more acutely in some industries than in others. Flexible manufacturing systems are expensive, and a large volume of repetitive work is required to justify their purchase. Also, where the assembly parts involved are irregular in size or location, new technology is only now beginning to make inroads. For example, much precision assembly in the aerospace industry is done in hard-to-reach locations unsuited for robots—inside airplane fuselages or gear boxes, for example—and replacement of these workers by automated processes will be slower and less comprehensive than replacement of other workers such as welders and painters. On the other hand, automation will continue to make more inroads in the precision assembly of electronic goods, where a third of these workers are employed.

An alternative to automation for many firms is sending their subassembly or component production functions to countries where labor costs are lower. This growing internationalization of production will be promoted by more liberal trade and investment. Although there will be some growth in exports of goods assembled in the United States as a result of this freer trade environment, growing imports and decisions by American corporations to relocate assembly in other nations will, on balance, lead to employment reductions for precision assemblers.

Despite the expected decline in employment, job openings will still arise as workers transfer to other occupations or leave the labor force. Moreover, the need for precision, independent judgment, and specialized knowledge will ensure the continued employment of many precision assemblers.

### Earnings

Earnings information is somewhat limited for precision assemblers. Full-time workers who assemble electrical and electronic equipment had median weekly earnings of about $330 in 1994. Most earned between $260 and $430; the lowest 10 percent earned less than $210 a week while the highest 10 percent earned over $590. In addition to earnings, most precision assemblers receive typical benefits such as health and life insurance, a pension plan, paid vacation, and sick leave.

Many precision assemblers are members of labor unions. These unions include the International Association of Machinists and Aerospace Workers; the United Electrical, Radio and Machine Workers of America; the United Automobile, Aerospace and Agricultural Implement Workers of America; the International Brotherhood of Electrical Workers; and the United Steelworkers.

### Related Occupations

Other occupations that involve operating machines and tools and assembling products include welders, ophthalmic laboratory technicians, and machine operators.

### Related *D.O.T.* Jobs

These job titles are related to or more specific than the more general description above. They will help you identify job options you may not otherwise discover. These descriptions are in the current edition of the *Dictionary of Occupational Titles* and classified by numerical order.

There are too many *D.O.T.* titles to list here. Most are variations related to a specific industry, and we have included a small number of representative *D.O.T.* titles as examples. Complete lists are available in various career software published by JIST or directly from the U.S. Department of Labor.

600.281-022 MACHINE BUILDER; 638.361-010 MACHINE ASSEMBLER; 710.281-010 ASSEMBLER AND TESTER, ELECTRONICS; 715.381-094 WATCH ASSEMBLER; 715.681-010 TIMING ADJUSTER; 722.381-010 ASSEMBLER; 729.281-042 WIRER; 801.261-010 ASSEMBLER, MINING MACHINERY; 801.261-014 FITTER I; 801.381-014 FITTER; 806.361-030 AIRCRAFT MECHANIC, ARMAMENT; 806.381-066 AIRCRAFT MECHANIC, PLUMBING AND HYDRAULICS; 806.381-078 INSTALLER, INTERIOR ASSEMBLIES; 806.381-082 PRECISION ASSEMBLER; 806.481-014 ASSEMBLER, INTERNAL COMBUSTION ENGINE; 820.381-014 TRANSFORMER ASSEMBLER I; 823.261-026 AVIONICS TECHNICIAN; 826.361-010 ASSEMBLER AND WIRER, INDUSTRIAL EQUIPMENT; 828.381-018 ASSEMBLER, ELECTROMECHANICAL

### Sources of Additional Information

Information about employment opportunities for assemblers is available from local offices of the state employment service and from locals of the unions mentioned earlier.

# Prepress Workers

### Nature of the Work

The printing process has three stages—prepress, press, and binding or finishing. Prepress workers prepare material for printing presses. They perform a variety of tasks involved with transforming text and pictures into finished pages and making printing plates of the pages.

As personal computers recently have come into more widespread use, advances in computer software and printing technology have begun to greatly change prepress work. Much of the typesetting and page layout work formerly done by prepress workers is increasingly done by customers on their computers. Customers are able to use their computers to send material to printers that looks more and more like the desired finished product. This change, called "desktop publishing," poses new challenges for the printing industry. Instead of receiving simple typed text from customers, prepress workers increasingly get the material on a computer disk, and instead of relying on prepress workers to suggest a format, customers are increasingly likely to have already settled on one by experimenting on their personal computers. The printing industry is rapidly moving toward complete "digital imaging," by which customers' material received on computer disks is converted directly into printing plates. Other aspects of prepress work experiencing innovation include digital color page makeup systems, electronic page layout systems, and off-press color proofing systems.

As electronic imaging becomes more prevalent, the use of film in printing will decline. Film, however, is still often the most economical and efficient data storage and retrieval medium currently in use. Today, electronic imaging is limited to more advanced printing shops, but as costs decline and quality improves, the process will become the method of choice in the industry.

Typesetting and page layout have been greatly affected by technological changes. Today, composition work is done with computers and "cold type" technology. The old "hot type" method of text composition—which used molten lead to create individual letters, paragraphs, and full pages of text—is nearly extinct. Cold type, which is any of a variety of methods that create type without molten lead, has traditionally used "phototypesetting" to ready text and pictures for printing. Although this method has many variations, all use photography to create positive images on paper. The images are assembled into page format and rephotographed to create film negatives from which the actual printing plates are made. However, newer cold type methods are coming into increasing use; these automate the photography or make printing plates directly from material in a computer.

In one common form of phototypesetting, text is entered into a computer programmed to hyphenate, space, and create columns of text. Keyboarding of text may be done by typesetters or data entry clerks at the printing establishment or, increasingly, by the author before the job is sent out for composition. The computer stores the text on magnetic tape, floppy disk, or hard disk. The magnetically coded text is then transferred to a typesetting machine which uses photography, a cathode-ray tube, or a laser to create an image on typesetting paper or film. Once it has been developed, the paper or film is sent to a lithographer who makes the actual printing plate.

In another type of phototypesetting, a computer produces text on special paper in the desired format. In newspapers, for example, text is printed in long columns. Workers called *paste-up artists* cut and arrange the columns of text and illustrations onto a special illustration board called a "mechanical." The special paper adheres easily to the board, yet is designed to allow easy removal and positioning. Once the text is arranged in final form, the board is sent to the camera department where a photographic negative used to create printing plates is produced. In small shops, *job printers* may be responsible for composition and page layout, reading proof for errors and clarity, correcting mistakes, and printing.

The most advanced method of typesetting, called "electronic pagination," is in growing commercial use. *Electronic pagination system operators* use a keyboard to enter and select the size and style of type, the column width, and appropriate spacing, and to store it in the computer. The computer then displays and arranges columns of type on a screen that resembles a television screen. An entire newspaper page—complete with artwork and graphics—can be made up on the screen exactly as it will appear in print. Operators transmit the pages for production into film and then into plates, or directly into plates, eliminating the role of paste-up artists.

New technologies are also affecting the roles of other composition workers. Improvements in desktop publishing software will allow customers to do more typesetting directly. Laser printers read text from computer memory and then "beam" it directly onto film, paper, or plates, bypassing the slower photographic process traditionally used.

After the material has been arranged and typeset, in traditional processes that use photography it is passed on to workers who further prepare it for the presses. *Camera operators* are generally classified as line camera operators, halftone operators, or color separation photographers. Line camera operators start the process of making a lithographic plate by photographing and developing film negatives or positives of the material to be printed. They adjust light and expose film for a specified length of time, and then develop film in a series of chemical baths. They may load unexposed film in machines that automatically develop and fix the image.

Normal continuous-tone photographs cannot be reproduced by most printing processes, so halftone camera operators separate the photograph into pictures that are made up of tiny dots, which can be reproduced. Color separation photography is more complex. In this process, camera operators produce four-color separation negatives from a continuous-tone color print or transparency which is being reproduced.

More of this separation work will be done electronically in the future on scanners. *Scanner operators* use computerized equipment to create film negatives or positives of photographs or art. The computer controls the color separation or the scanning process, correcting for mistakes, or compensating for deficiencies in the original color print or transparency. Operators review all work to determine if corrections to the original are necessary and adjust the equipment accordingly. They then use a densitometer to measure the density of the colored areas, and adjust the scanner to obtain the best results. An original color photograph or transparency is scanned for each color to be printed. Each scan produces a dotted image, or halftone, of the original in one of four primary colors—yellow, magenta, cyan, and black. The images are used to produce printing plates that print each of these colors, one at a time. The printing is done with primary process color inks which are transparent, creating "secondary" color combinations of red, green, blue, and black. These secondary colors can be combined to produce all the colors and hues of the original photograph. The computer controls the color separation or the scanning process, correcting for mistakes or compensating for deficiencies in the original color print or transparency.

Scanners which can perform color correction during the color separation procedure are rapidly replacing *lithographic dot etchers,* who retouch film negatives or positives by sharpening or reshaping images. They do the work by hand, using chemicals, dyes, and special tools. Dot etchers must know the characteristics of all types of paper and must produce fine shades of color. Like camera operators, they are usually assigned to only one phase of the work, and may have job titles such as dot etcher, retoucher, or letterer.

New technology is also eliminating the need for *strippers,* who cut the film to required size and arrange and tape the negatives onto "flats"—or layout sheets used by platemakers to make press plates. When completed, flats resemble large film negatives of the text in its final form. In large printing establishments like newspapers, arrangement is done automatically.

*Platemakers* use a photographic process to make printing plates. The film assembly or flat is placed on top of a thin metal plate treated with a light-sensitive chemical. Exposure to ultraviolet light activates the chemical in those parts not protected by the film's dark areas. The plate is then developed in a special solution that removes the unexposed nonimage area, exposing bare metal. The chemical on areas of the plate exposed to the light hardens and becomes water repellent. The hardened parts of the plate form the text.

A growing number of printing plants use lasers to directly convert electronic data to plates without any use of film. Entering, storing, and retrieving information from computer-aided equipment requires technical skills. In addition to operating and maintaining the equipment, lithographic platemakers must make sure that plates meet quality standards.

During the printing process, the plate is first covered with a thin coat of water. The water adheres only to the bare metal nonimage areas, and is repelled by the hardened areas that were exposed to light. Next, the plate comes in contact with a rubber roller covered with an oil-based ink. Because oil and water do not mix, the ink is repelled by the water-coated area and sticks to the hardened areas. The ink covering the hardened text is transferred to paper.

Technological changes will continue in the prepress area as hand work is automated. Although computers will perform a wider variety of tasks, printing will still involve text composition, page layout, and plate making, so printing will still require prepress workers. Computer skills will be increasingly important to prepress workers. These workers will, however, need to demonstrate a desire and an ability to benefit from the frequent retraining that rapidly changing technology necessitates.

### Working Conditions

Prepress workers usually work in clean, air-conditioned areas with little noise. Some workers, such as typesetters and compositors, may develop eyestrain from working in front of a video display terminal, as well as musculoskeletal problems, such as backaches. Lithographic artists and strippers may find working with fine detail tiring to the eyes. Platemakers, who work with toxic chemicals, face the hazard of skin irritations. Stress may be an important factor as workers are often subject to the pressures of shorter and shorter deadlines and tighter and tighter work schedules.

Prepress employees generally work an eight-hour day. Some workers—particularly those employed by newspapers—work night shifts, weekends, and holidays.

## Employment

Prepress workers held about 169,000 jobs in 1994. Employment was distributed as follows:

| Prepress precision workers | |
|---|---|
| Strippers, printing ...................................................... | 31,000 |
| Paste-up workers ....................................................... | 22,000 |
| Electronic pagination systems workers .................. | 18,000 |
| Camera operators ..................................................... | 15,000 |
| Job printers ............................................................... | 14,000 |
| Platemakers................................................................ | 13,000 |
| Compositors and typesetters................................... | 11,000 |
| Photoengravers ......................................................... | 7,000 |
| All other precision printing workers ...................... | 13,000 |
| **Prepress machine operators** | |
| Typesetting and composing machine operators ..... | 20,000 |
| Photoengraving and lithographic machine operators ................................................................. | 5,000 |

Most prepress jobs were found in firms that handle commercial or business printing and in newspaper plants. Commercial printing firms print newspaper inserts, catalogs, pamphlets, and advertisements, while business form establishments print material such as sales receipts and paper used in computers. Additional jobs are found in printing trade service firms and "in-plant" operations. Establishments in printing trade services typically perform custom compositing, platemaking, and related prepress services.

The printing and publishing industry is one of the most geographically dispersed in the United States, and prepress jobs are found throughout the country. However, job prospects may be best in large printing centers such as New York, Chicago, Los Angeles, Philadelphia, Washington, D.C., and Dallas.

## Training, Other Qualifications, and Advancement

The length of training required for prepress jobs varies by occupation. Some, such as typesetting, can be learned in only a few months, but they are the most likely to be automated. Others, such as stripping, require years of experience to master. Nevertheless, even workers in these occupations should expect to receive intensive retraining. Workers often start as helpers who are selected for on-the-job training programs once they demonstrate their reliability and interest in learning the job. They begin instruction with an experienced craft worker and advance based upon their demonstrated mastery of skills at each level of instruc-

tion. All workers should expect to be retrained from time to time to handle new, improved equipment.

Apprenticeship is another way to become a skilled prepress worker, although few apprenticeships have been offered in recent years. Apprenticeship programs emphasize a specific craft—such as camera operator, stripper, lithographic etcher, scanner operator, or platemaker—but apprentices are introduced to all phases of printing.

Generally, most employers prefer to hire high school graduates who possess good communication skills, both oral and written. Prepress workers need to be able to deal courteously with people because in small shops they may take customer orders. They may also need to add, subtract, multiply, divide, and compute ratios to estimate job costs. Persons interested in working for firms that use advanced printing technology need to know the basics of electronics and computers. Mathematical skills are also essential for operating many of the software packages used to run modern, computerized prepress equipment.

Prepress workers need manual dexterity, and they must be able to pay attention to detail and work independently. Good eyesight, including visual acuity, depth perception, field of view, color vision, and the ability to focus quickly, is an asset. Artistic ability is often a plus. Employers seek persons who are even-tempered and adaptable, important qualities for workers who often must meet deadlines and learn how to operate new equipment.

Formal graphic arts programs, offered by community and junior colleges and some four-year colleges, also introduce persons to the industry. These programs provide job-related training, and enrolling in one demonstrates an interest in the graphic arts, which may impress an employer favorably. Bachelor's degree programs in graphic arts are generally intended for students who may eventually move into management positions, and two-year associate degree programs are designed to train skilled workers.

Courses in various aspects of printing are also available at vocational-technical institutes, industry-sponsored update and retraining programs, and private trade and technical schools.

As workers gain experience, they advance to positions with greater responsibility. Some move into supervisory positions.

## Job Outlook

Employment of prepress workers is expected to decline through the year 2005. Demand for printed material should grow rapidly spurred by rising levels of personal income, increasing school enrollments, and higher levels of educational attainment. However, increased use of computers in typesetting and page layout should eliminate many prepress jobs.

New technologies are also expected to spur demand for printed materials by expanding markets, allowing advertising dollars currently allotted to nonprint media, such as television, to be spent on direct mail. Work previously requiring a week or more can now be completed in a few days. Much faster turnaround time will permit printers to compete with nonprint media for time-sensitive business, providing advertisers with specialty advertisements used to target specific market segments, for example.

Technological advances will have a varying effect on employment among the prepress occupations. Employment of electronic pagination system operators is expected to much grow much faster than average, reflecting the increasing proportion of page layout and design that will be performed using computers. In contrast, prepress machine operators are expected to decline sharply as the work that these workers perform manually is increasingly automated. Occupations that are expected to experience moderate declines as hand work becomes automated include paste-up workers, job printers, precision compositors and typesetters, photoengravers, platemakers, and camera operators.

Job prospects also will vary by industry, most notably for compositors and typesetters. Changes in technology have shifted many employment opportunities away from the traditional printing plants into advertising agencies, public relations firms, and large corporations. Many companies are turning to in-house typesetting or "desktop publishing" due to the advent of inexpensive personal computers with graphic capabilities. Corporations are finding it more profitable to print their own newsletters and other reports than to send them out to trade shops. In addition, press shops themselves have responded to desktop publishers' needs by sending their own staff into the field to help customers prepare a disk that will live up to the customer's expectations.

Compositors and typesetters should find competition extremely keen in the newspaper industry, currently their largest employer. Computerized equipment that allows reporters and editors to specify type and style and to format pages at a desktop computer terminal has already eliminated many typesetting and composition jobs, and more are certain to disappear in the years ahead.

Many new jobs for prepress workers are expected to emerge in commercial printing establishments. New equipment should reduce the time needed to complete a printing job, and allow commercial printers to make inroads into new markets that require fast turnaround. Because small establishments predominate, commercial printing should provide the best opportunities for inexperienced workers looking to gain a good background in all facets of printing.

Opportunities for prepress workers should also be good in the printing trade services industry. Despite the fact that companies may have their own typesetting and printing capabilities, they usually turn to professionals in printing trade services if quality and time are of the essence.

Most employers prefer to hire experienced prepress workers. However, among persons without experience, opportunities should be best for those with a computer background who have completed postsecondary programs in printing technology. Many employers prefer graduates of these programs because the comprehensive training they receive helps them learn the printing process and adapt more rapidly to new processes and techniques.

### Earnings

Wage rates for prepress workers vary according to occupation, level of experience and training, location and size of the firm, and whether they are union members. According to limited data available, the median earnings of full-time workers were $549 a week in 1994 for lithographers and photoengravers and $389 a week for typesetters and compositors.

Of the prepress workers who were unionized, scanner operators earned an hourly wage of $21.88 in 1995, and strippers earned $17.57 per hour, according to the Graphic Communica-

tions International Union, the principal union for prepress workers.

### Related Occupations

Prepress workers use artistic skills in their work. These skills are also essential for sign painters, jewelers, decorators, engravers, and graphic artists. Other workers who operate machines equipped with keyboards like typesetters include clerk-typists, computer terminal system operators, keypunch operators, and telegraphic-typewriter operators.

### Related *D.O.T.* Jobs

These job titles are related to or more specific than the more general description above. They will help you identify job options you may not otherwise discover. These descriptions are in the current edition of the *Dictionary of Occupational Titles* and classified by numerical order.

There are too many *D.O.T.* titles to list here. Most are variations related to a specific industry, and we have included a small number of representative *D.O.T.* titles as examples. Complete lists are available in various career software published by JIST or directly from the U.S. Department of Labor.

650.582-010 LINOTYPE OPERATOR; 650.582-018 PHOTO-COMPOSING MACHINE OPERATOR; 652.685-106 TYPEPROOF REPRODUCER; 970.381-030 RETOUCHER, PHOTO-ENGRAVING; 971.381-014 ETCHER, PHOTO-ENGRAVING; 971.381.022 PHOTO-ENGRAVER; 971.381-050 STRIPPER; 971.382-014 PHOTOGRAPHER, PHOTO-ENGRAVING; 972.281-010 DOT ETCHER; 972.282-010 SCANNER OPERATOR;; 972.381-010 LITHOGRAPHIC PLATEMAKER; 972.381-030 PASTE-UP ARTIST; 972.381-034 PROOFER, PREPRESS; 972.382-014 PHOTOGRAPHER, LITHOGRAPHIC; 972.687-010 PLATE INSPECTOR; 973.381-010 COMPOSITOR; 973.381-018 JOB PRINTER; 973.681-010 GALLEY STRIPPER; 979.382-018 PRINTER; 979.382-022 PANTOGRAPHER; 979.382-026 COMPUTER TYPESETTER KEY-LINER

### Sources of Additional Information

Details about apprenticeship and other training programs may be obtained from local employers such as newspapers and printing shops or from local offices of the state employment service.

For information on careers and training in printing and the graphic arts, write to:

❑ PIA-PrintED Accreditation Program for the Graphic Arts, 100 Daingerfield Rd., Alexandria, VA 22314.

❑ Education Council of the Graphic Arts Industry, 1899 Preston White Dr., Reston, VA 22091-4326.

❑ Graphic Communications International Union, 1900 L St. NW, Washington, DC 20212.

# Printing Press Operators

### Nature of the Work

Printing press operators prepare, operate, and maintain the printing presses in a pressroom. Duties of press operators vary according to the type of press they operate—offset, gravure, flexography, screen printing, or letterpress. Offset is the dominant printing process and is expected to remain so into the next century. Gravure and flexography should increase in use, but letterpress should continue being phased out. In addition to the major printing processes, plateless or nonimpact processes are coming into general use. Plateless processes—including electronic, electrostatic, and ink-jet printing—are used for copying, duplicating, and document and specialty printing, generally by quick and in-house printing shops.

To prepare presses for printing, press operators install and adjust the printing plate, mix fountain solution, adjust pressure, ink the presses, load paper, and adjust the press to the paper size. Press operators check that paper and ink meet specifications, and adjust control margins and the flow of ink to the inking rollers accordingly. They then feed paper through the press cylinders and adjust feed and tension controls.

While printing presses are running, press operators monitor their operation and keep the paper feeders well stocked. They make adjustments to correct uneven ink distribution, speed, and temperatures in the drying chamber, if the press has one. If paper jams or tears—which can happen with some offset presses—and the press stops, operators quickly correct the problem to minimize downtime. Similarly, operators working with other high-speed presses constantly look for problems, making quick corrections to avoid expensive losses of paper and ink. Throughout the run, operators also occasionally pull sheets to check for any printing imperfections.

In many shops, press operators perform preventive maintenance. They oil and clean the presses and make minor repairs to keep them running smoothly.

Press operators' jobs differ from one shop to another because of differences in the kinds and sizes of presses. Small commercial shops tend to have relatively small presses which print only one or two colors at a time and are operated by one person. Operators who work with large presses have assistants and helpers. Large newspaper, magazine, and book printers use giant "in-line web" presses that require a crew of several press operators and press assistants. These presses are fed paper in big rolls, called *webs*, up to 50 inches or more in width. Presses print the paper on both sides; trim, assemble, score, and fold the pages; and count the finished sections as they come off the press.

Most plants have or soon will have installed printing presses that have computers and sophisticated instruments to control press operations, making it possible to set up for jobs in much less time. Computers allow press operators to perform many of their tasks electronically. With this equipment, press operators monitor the printing process on a control panel that allows them to adjust the press electronically by pushing buttons.

## Working Conditions

Operating a press can be physically and mentally demanding, and sometimes tedious. Press operators are on their feet most of the time. Often, operators work under pressure to meet deadlines. Most printing presses are capable of high printing speeds, and adjustments must be made quickly to avoid waste. Pressrooms are noisy, and workers in certain areas wear ear protectors. Working with press machinery can be hazardous, but accidents can be avoided when safe work practices are observed. The danger of accidents is much less with newer computerized presses because operators make most adjustments from a control panel. Many press operators work evening, night, and overtime shifts.

## Employment

Press operators held about 244,000 jobs in 1994. Employment was distributed as follows:

| | |
|---|---|
| Printing press machine setters and operators | 113,000 |
| Offset lithographic press operators | 79,000 |
| Screen printing machine setters and set-up operators | 26,000 |
| Letterpress operators | 14,000 |
| All other printing press setters and set-up operators | 13,000 |

Most jobs were in newspaper plants or in firms that handle commercial or business printing. Commercial printing firms print newspaper inserts, catalogs, pamphlets, and the advertisements found in your mailbox, and business form establishments print items such as sales receipts and paper used in computers. Additional jobs were in the "in-plant" section of organizations and businesses that do their own printing—among them, banks, insurance companies, and government agencies.

The printing and publishing industry is one of the most geographically dispersed in the United States, and press operators can find jobs throughout the country. However, jobs are concentrated in large printing centers such as New York, Los Angeles, Chicago, Philadelphia, Washington, D.C., and Dallas.

## Training, Other Qualifications, and Advancement

Although completion of a formal apprenticeship or a postsecondary program in printing equipment operation continue to be the best way to learn the trade, most printing press operators are trained informally on the job working as assistants or helpers to experienced operators. Beginning press operators load, unload, and clean presses. With time, they move up to operating one-color sheet-fed presses and eventually advance to multicolor presses. Operators are likely to gain experience on many kinds of printing presses during the course of their career.

Apprenticeship, once the dominant method of preparing for this occupation, is becoming less prevalent with the growing importance of formal postsecondary programs in printing equipment operation offered by technical and trade schools and community and junior colleges. Apprenticeships for press operators in commercial shops take four years. In addition to on-the-job instruction, apprenticeships include related classroom or correspondence school courses. In contrast, although some postsecondary school programs require two years of study and award an associate degree, most programs can be completed in one year or less. Postsecondary courses in printing are increasingly important because they provide the theoretical knowledge needed to operate advanced equipment.

Persons who wish to become printing press operators need mechanical aptitude to make press adjustments and repairs and an ability to visualize color in order to work on color presses. Oral and writing skills also are required. Operators should be able to compute percentages, weights, and measures, and should possess adequate mathematical skills to calculate the amount of ink and paper needed to do a job. Because of technical developments in the printing industry, courses in chemistry, electronics, color theory, and physics are helpful.

Technological changes have had a tremendous effect on the skills needed by press operators. New presses require basic computer skills. Printing plants that change from sheet-fed offset presses to web-offset presses have to retrain the entire press crew because the skill requirements for the two types of presses are different. Web-offset presses, with their faster operating speeds, require faster decisions, monitoring of more variables, and greater physical effort. Even experienced operators periodically receive retraining and skill updating. In the future, workers are expected to need to retrain several times during their career.

Press operators may advance in pay and responsibility by taking a job working on a more complex printing press. For example, a one-color sheet-fed press operator may, through experience and demonstrated ability, become a four-color sheet-fed press operator. Others may advance to pressroom supervisor and become responsible for the work of the entire press crew.

## Job Outlook

Persons seeking jobs as printing press operators will face keen competition from experienced operators and prepress workers who have been displaced by new technology, particularly those who have completed retraining programs. Opportunities to become printing press operators are likely to be best for persons who qualify for formal apprenticeship training or who complete postsecondary training programs.

Employment of press operators is expected to grow more slowly than the average for all occupations through the year 2005. Although demand for printed materials will grow, employment growth will be slowed by the increasing use of new, more efficient computerized printing presses. However, employment growth will vary among various press operator jobs. Employment of offset, gravure, and flexographic operators will increase, while employment of letterpress operators will decline sharply. Most job openings will result from the need to replace operators who retire or leave the occupation.

Most new jobs will result from expansion of the printing industry as demand for printed material increases in response to demographic trends, U.S. expansion into foreign markets, and growing use of direct mail by advertisers. Demand for books and magazines will increase as school enrollments rise, and as substantial growth in the middle-aged and older population spurs adult education and leisure reading. Additional growth should stem from increasing foreign demand for domestic trade publications, professional and scientific works, and mass-market books such as paperbacks.

Much of the growth in commercial printing will be spurred by increased expenditures for print advertising materials to be mailed directly to prospective customers. New market research techniques are leading advertisers to increase spending on messages targeted to specific audiences and should continue to require the printing of a wide variety of newspaper inserts, catalogs, direct mail enclosures, and other kinds of print advertising.

Other printing, such as newspapers, books, and periodicals, will also provide jobs. Experienced press operators will fill most of these jobs because many employers are under severe pressure to meet deadlines and have limited time to train new employees.

## Earnings

The basic wage rate for a press operator depends on the type of press being run and the area of the country in which the work is located. Median weekly earnings of press operators who worked full-time were about $432 in 1994. The middle 50 percent earned between $307 and $605 a week. The lowest 10 percent earned $239 or less a week, while the highest 10 percent earned over $787 a week.

Fewer than one in five press operators belonged to a union.

## Related Occupations

Other workers who set up and operate production machinery include paper-making machine operators, shoe-making machine operators, bindery machine operators, and various precision machine operators.

## Related *D.O.T.* Jobs

These job titles are related to or more specific than the more general description above. They will help you identify job options you may not otherwise discover. These descriptions are in the current edition of the *Dictionary of Occupational Titles* and classified by numerical order.

651.362-010 CYLINDER-PRESS OPERATOR; 651.362-018 PLATEN-PRESS OPERATOR; 651.362-026 ROTOGRAVURE-PRESS OPERATOR; 651.362-030 WEB-PRESS OPERATOR; 651.382-010 ENGRAVING-PRESS OPERATOR; 651.382-014 LITHOGRAPH-PRESS OPERATOR, TINWARE; 651.382-030 STEEL-DIE PRINTER; 651.382-038 TRANSFER OPERATOR; 651.382-042 OFFSET-PRESS OPERATOR I; 651.582-010 PROOF-PRESS OPERATOR; 651.682-018 STRIPPER; 651.685-014 DESIGN PRINTER, BALLOON; 651.686-014 FEEDER; 651.686-018 JOGGER; 651.686-022 ROLL TENDER; 652.582-010 MARKER; 652.662-018 PRINT-LINE OPERATOR; 652.682-018 SCREEN-PRINTING-MACHINE OPERATOR; 652.682-030 STAMPING-PRESS OPERATOR; 652.685-038 INK PRINTER; 652.685-058 PRESS FEEDER; 652.685-062 PRINTER

## Sources of Additional Information

Details about apprenticeships and other training opportunities may be obtained from local employers such as newspapers and printing shops, local offices of the Graphic Communications International Union, local affiliates of Printing Industries of America, or local offices of the state employment service.

For general information about press operators, write to:

❑ Graphic Communications International Union, 1900 L St. NW, Washington, DC 20036.

For information on careers and training in printing and the graphic arts, write to:

❑ PIA-PrintED Accreditation Program for the Graphic Arts, 100 Daingerfield Rd., Alexandria, VA 22314.

❑ Education Council of the Graphic Arts Industry, 1899 Preston White Dr., Reston, VA 22091-4326.

# Private Detectives and Investigators

## Nature of the Work

Private detectives and investigators assist attorneys, government agencies, businesses, and the public with a variety of problems, such as gathering facts, tracing debtors, or conducting background investigations. The main job of private investigators and some private detectives is to obtain information and locate assets or individuals. Some private detectives protect stores and hotels from theft, vandalism, and disorder.

Private detectives working as general investigators have duties ranging from locating missing persons to exposing fraudulent workers' compensation claims. Some investigators specialize in one field, such as finance, where they might use accounting skills to investigate the financial standing of a company or locate funds stolen by an embezzler.

About half of all private investigators are self-employed or work for detective agencies. They specialize in missing persons, infidelity, and background investigations, including financial profiles and asset searches; physical surveillance; on-line computer database searches; and insurance investigations. They may obtain information, interview witnesses, and assemble evidence for litigation or criminal trials. They get cases from clients or are assigned to cases by the owner or manager of the firm.

Many investigators spend considerable time conducting surveillance, seeking to observe inconsistencies in a subject's behavior. For example, a person who has recently filed a workers' compensation claim that an injury has made walking difficult should not be able to jog or mow the lawn. If such behavior is observed, the investigator takes video or still photographs to document the activity and reports back to the supervisor or client.

"Stakeouts" are a common form of surveillance. On a stakeout, an investigator regularly observes a site, such as the home of a subject, until the desired evidence is obtained. The investigator sits in a car or other inconspicuous location. They are equipped with cameras—including still and video cameras—binoculars, and a citizen's band radio or a car phone.

Some investigations involve verification of facts, such as an individual's place of employment or income. This might involve a phone call or a visit to the workplace. In other investigations, especially in missing persons cases, the investigator interviews people to learn as much as possible about someone's previous movements. These interviews can be formal or informal and sometimes turn into confrontations if the person is uncooperative.

*Legal investigators* specialize in cases involving the courts and lawyers. To assist in preparing criminal defenses, investigators locate witnesses, interview police, gather and review evidence, take photographs, and testify in court. To assist attorneys in the preparation of litigation for injured parties, they interview prospective witnesses, collect information on the parties to the litigation, and search out testimonial, documentary, or physical evidence.

*Corporate investigators* work for companies other than investigative firms—often large corporations. In contrast to most private investigators, they report to a corporate chain of command. They conduct internal or external investigations. External investigations consist of preventing criminal schemes, thefts of company assets, and fraudulent deliveries of products by suppliers. In internal investigations, they ensure that expense accounts are not abused and catch employees who are stealing.

Investigators who specialize in finance may be hired to investigate the financial standing of companies or individuals. These investigators often work with investment bankers and lawyers.

They generally develop confidential financial profiles of individuals or companies who may be parties to large financial transactions. An asset search is a common type of such an investigation.

Private detectives and investigators who work for large retail stores or malls are responsible for loss control and asset protection. *Store detectives* safeguard the assets of retail stores by apprehending persons attempting to steal merchandise or destroy store property. They detect theft by shoplifters, vendor representatives, delivery personnel, and even store employees. Store detectives also conduct periodic inspections of stock areas, dressing rooms, and rest rooms, and sometimes assist in the opening and closing of the store. They may prepare loss prevention and security reports for management and testify in court against persons they apprehend.

Computers have changed the nature of this profession and have become an integral part of investigative work. They allow investigators to obtain massive amounts of information in a short period of time from the dozens of on-line data bases containing probate records, motor-vehicle registrations, credit reports, association membership lists, and other information.

## Working Conditions

Private investigators often work irregular hours. Early morning, evening, weekend, and holiday work is common. The irregular hours result from the need to conduct surveillance and contact people who may not be available during normal working hours. Investigators who work solely for insurance companies and corporate investigators have more normal work hours.

Many investigators spend much time away from their offices conducting interviews or doing surveillance, but some work in their office most of the day conducting computer searches and making phone calls. Corporate investigators often split their time between the office and the field; work done in the office generally consists of computer research.

When away from the office, the environment might range from plush boardrooms to seedy bars. Store and hotel detectives work mostly in the businesses they protect. Investigators generally work alone, but sometimes work with others during surveillance or stake-outs.

Much of the work that detectives and investigators do can be confrontational because the person being observed may not want to be observed. As a result, the job can be quite stressful and sometimes dangerous. Some investigators carry handguns, but most do not since it is difficult to obtain a permit to carry a concealed weapon in many jurisdictions. Owners of investigations firms have the added stress of having to deal with demanding and sometimes distraught clients.

## Employment

Private detectives and investigators held about 55,000 jobs in 1994. About 20 percent were self-employed. About 34 percent of wage and salary workers worked for detective agencies and about 40 percent were employed as store detectives in department or clothing and accessories stores. Others worked for hotels and other lodging places, legal services firms, and many other industries.

## Training, Other Qualifications, and Advancement

There are no formal education requirements for most private detective and investigator jobs, although most employers prefer high school graduates and many private detectives have college degrees. Some private detectives and investigators get their entry-level training on the job while working for insurance or collections companies or in the security industry. Many investigators enter from the military or law enforcement jobs and apply their experience as law enforcement officers, military police, or government agents. Other investigators enter from such diverse fields as finance, accounting, investigative reporting, insurance, and law. These individuals often can apply their prior work experience in a related investigation specialty.

The vast majority of states and the District of Colombia require that private investigators be licensed. Licensing requirements vary widely among the states, but, in most, the state police is the licensing authority. Some states have very liberal requirements, while others have stringent regulations. For example, the California Department of Consumer Affairs Bureau of Security and Investigative Services requires 6,000 hours of investigative experience, a background check, a qualifying score on a written examination, payment of a $50 application fee and a $32 fingerprint fee, and payment of an annual $175 license fee upon approval. In contrast, other states may have little or no licensing requirements. A growing number of states are enacting mandatory training programs for private investigators. In states that require licensing, a felony conviction generally disqualifies a candidate from being granted a license.

In most investigations firms, the screening process for potential employees includes a background check, consisting of confirmation of education, work experience, and criminal history, and interviews with references and others known to the applicant. Corporate and industrial security positions may require a criminal history check, a personal interview, an ethics interview, a practical test, verification of education claims, and license review as well as personal and employment references checks.

For private detective and investigator jobs, most employers look for individuals with ingenuity who are aggressive, persistent, and assertive. A candidate must not be afraid of being confrontational, should communicate well, and should be able to think on his or her feet. The courts are often the ultimate judge of a properly conducted investigation, so the investigator must be able to present the facts in a manner a jury will believe.

Training in subjects such as criminal justice are helpful to the aspiring private detective. Most corporate investigators must have a bachelor's degree, preferably in a business-related field. Some corporate investigators have Master of Business Administration or law degrees, while others are Certified Public Accountants.

Corporate investigators hired by larger companies may receive formal training from their employers on business practices, management structure, and various finance related topics. Interview and interrogation training is frequently included.

Most investigations firms are small, with little room for advancement. Usually there are no defined ranks or steps, so advancement is in terms of salary and assignment status. Many investigators work for an investigations firm in the beginning of their investigative careers and after a few years try to start their own investigations firms. Corporate and legal investigators may rise to supervisor or manager of the security or investigations department.

## Job Outlook

Employment of private detectives and investigators is expected to grow much faster than average for all occupations through the year 2005. In addition, job turnover should create many additional job openings, particularly among wage and salary workers. Nevertheless, competition is expected for the available openings because private detective and investigator careers are attractive to many.

Demand for private detectives and investigators is expected to be generated by increases in the size of the population, increased economic activity, and global and domestic competition. These forces are expected to produce increases in crime, litigation, and the need for confidential information of all kinds. As crime continues to increase, more firms will hire or contract for the service of private detectives. Drug abuse continues to be a problem in our society, contributing to the high crime rate, and some companies will hire private investigators to determine the extent of their internal drug problems. Additional private detectives and investigators will be needed to meet the needs for information associated with criminal defenses and litigation among companies and individuals. Greater financial activity also will increase the demand for investigators. In addition, as competition becomes more intense, growing numbers of companies will hire investigators to control internal and external financial losses, as well as to find out what their competitors are doing and to prevent industrial spying.

In spite of the rapid growth in employment of private detectives and investigators, competition should continue to be very intense for full-time, salaried job openings due to a large supply of workers qualified for these jobs. Many individuals leave law enforcement, military, and intelligence jobs in the public sector, often at a relatively young age, and decide to become private investigators. Opportunities should be best for entry-level jobs as store detectives or with detective agencies on a part-time basis. Persons seeking store detective jobs may find the best opportunities with private guard and security firms since some retail businesses are replacing their own workers with outside contract workers.

## Earnings

Earnings of private detectives and investigators vary greatly depending on their employer, specialty, and geographic area in which they work. According to a study by Abbott, Langer & Associates, private investigators averaged about $36,700 a year in 1993, and store detectives about $16,100.

According to other limited information, legal investigators earned an estimated $15,000 to $18,000 a year to start, and experienced legal investigators earned $20,000 to $35,000. Entry-level corporate investigators earned an estimated $40,000 to $45,000 annually, and experienced corporate investigators, $50,000 to $55,000.

Most private investigator bill their clients between $50 and $150 per hour to conduct investigations. Most private investigators, except for those working for large corporations, do not receive paid vacation or sick days, health or life insurance, retirement packages, or other benefits. Investigators are usually reimbursed for expenses and generally given a car allowance.

Most corporate investigators received health insurance, pension plans, profit-sharing plans, and paid vacation.

## Related Occupations

Private detectives and investigators often collect information and protect property and assets of companies. Others with related concerns include security guards, insurance claims examiners, inspectors, collectors, and law enforcement officers. Corporate investigators and investigators who specialize in conducting financial profiles and asset searches do work closely related to that of accountants and financial analysts.

## Related *D.O.T.* Jobs

These job titles are related to or more specific than the more general description above. They will help you identify job options you may not otherwise discover. These descriptions are in the current edition of the *Dictionary of Occupational Titles* and classified by numerical order.

189.167-054 SECURITY CONSULTANT; 343.367-014 GAMBLING MONITOR; 376.137-010 MANAGER, INTERNAL SECURITY; 376.267-010 INVESTIGATOR, CASH SHORTAGE; 376.267-014 INVESTIGATOR, FRAUD; 376.267-018 INVESTIGATOR, PRIVATE; 376.267-022 SHOPPING INVESTIGATOR; 376.367-010 ALARM INVESTIGATOR; 376.367-014 DETECTIVE I; 376.367-018 HOUSE OFFICER; 376.367-022 INVESTIGATOR; 376.367-026 UNDERCOVER OPERATOR; 376.667-014 DETECTIVE II

## Sources of Additional Information

Most states have associations for private detectives and investigators that provide career information. For information on local licensing requirements, contact your local state police headquarters.

# Radiologic Technologists

## Nature of the Work

Perhaps the most familiar use of the x-ray is the diagnosis of broken bones. However, medical uses of radiation go far beyond that. Radiation is used not only to produce images of the interior of the body, but to treat cancer as well. At the same time, the use of imaging techniques that do not involve x-rays, such as ultrasound and magnetic resonance scans, is growing rapidly. The term "diagnostic imaging" embraces these procedures as well as the familiar x-ray.

*Radiographers* produce x-ray films (radiographs) of parts of the human body for use in diagnosing medical problems. They prepare patients for radiologic examinations by explaining the procedure, removing articles such as jewelry, through which x-rays cannot pass, and positioning patients so that the correct parts of the body can be radiographed. To prevent unnecessary radiation exposure, technologists surround the exposed area with radiation protection devices, such as lead shields, or limit the size of the x-ray beam. Radiographers position radiographic equipment at the correct angle and height over the appropriate area of a patient's body. Using instruments similar to a measuring tape, technologists may measure the thickness of the section to be radiographed and set controls on the machine to produce radiographs of the appropriate density, detail, and contrast. They place the x-ray film under the part of the patient's body to be examined and make the exposure. They then remove the film and develop it.

Experienced radiographers may perform more complex imaging tests. For fluoroscopies, radiographers prepare a solution of contrast medium for the patient to drink, allowing the radiologist, a physician who interprets x-rays, to see soft tissues in the body. Some radiographers who operate computerized tomography scanners to produce cross sectional views of patients, are be called CT technologists. Others operate machines using giant magnets and radio waves rather than radiation to create an image and are be called magnetic resonance imaging technologists.

*Radiation therapy technologists*, also known as radiation therapists, prepare cancer patients for treatment and administer prescribed doses of ionizing radiation to specific body parts. They operate many kinds of equipment, including high-energy linear accelerators with electron capabilities. They position patients under the equipment with absolute accuracy in order to expose affected body parts to treatment while protecting the rest of the body from radiation.

They also check the patient's reactions for radiation side effects such as nausea, hair loss, and skin irritation. They give instructions and explanations to patients who are likely to be very ill. Radiation therapists, in contrast to other radiologic technologists, are likely to see the same patient a number of times during the course of treatment.

*Sonographers*, also known as ultrasound technologists, use nonionizing, high frequency sound waves into areas of the patient's body; the equipment then collects reflected echoes to form an image. The image is viewed on a screen and may be recorded on a printout strip or photographed for interpretation and diagnosis by physicians. Sonographers explain the procedure, record additional medical history, and then position the patient for testing. Viewing the screen as the scan takes place, sonographers look for subtle differences between healthy and pathological areas, and judge if the images are satisfactory for diagnostic purposes. Sonographers may specialize in neurosonography (the brain), vascular (blood flows), echocardiography (the heart), abdominal (the liver, kidneys, spleen, and pancreas), obstetrics/gynecology (the female reproductive system), and ophthalmology (the eye).

Radiologic technologists follow precisely physicians' instructions and regulations concerning use of radiation to ensure that they, patients, and coworkers are protected from overexposure.

In addition to preparing patients and operating equipment, radiologic technologists keep patient records and adjust and maintain equipment. They may also prepare work schedules, evaluate equipment purchases, or manage a radiology department.

## Working Conditions

Most full-time radiologic technologists work about 40 hours a week; they may have evening, weekend, or on-call hours.

Technologists are on their feet for long periods and may lift or turn disabled patients. They work at radiologic machines but may also do some procedures at patients' bedsides. Some radiologic technologists travel to patients in large vans equipped with sophisticated diagnostic equipment.

Radiation therapists are prone to emotional burn out because they regularly treat extremely ill and dying patients on a daily basis. Although potential radiation hazards exist in this occupation, they have been minimized by the use of lead aprons, gloves, and other shielding devices, as well as by instruments that monitor radiation exposure. Technologists wear badges that measure radiation levels in the radiation area, and detailed records are kept on their cumulative lifetime dose.

## Employment

Radiologic technologists held about 167,000 jobs in 1994. Most technologists were radiographers. Some were sonographers and radiation therapists. About one radiologic technologist in five worked part-time. About three of five jobs are in hospitals. The rest are in physicians' offices and clinics, including diagnostic imaging centers.

## Training, Other Qualifications, and Advancement

Preparation for this profession is offered in hospitals, colleges and universities, vocational-technical institutes, and the Armed Forces. Hospitals, which employ most radiologic technologists, prefer to hire those with formal training.

Formal training is offered in radiography, radiation therapy, and diagnostic medical sonography (ultrasound). Programs range in length from one to four years and lead to a certificate, associate degree, or bachelor's degree. Two-year programs are most prevalent.

Some one-year certificate programs are for individuals from other health occupations such as medical technologists and registered nurses who want to change fields or experienced radiographers who want to specialize in radiation therapy technology or sonography. A bachelor's or master's degree in one of the radiologic technologies is desirable for supervisory, administrative, or teaching positions.

The Joint Review Committee on Education in Radiologic Technology accredits most formal training programs for this field. They accredited 692 radiography programs, 125 radiation therapy programs. The Joint Review Committee on Education in Diagnostic Medical Sonography accredited 65 programs in sonography in 1995.

Radiography programs require, at a minimum, a high school diploma or the equivalent. High school courses in mathematics, physics, chemistry, and biology are helpful. The programs provide both classroom and clinical instruction in anatomy and physiology, patient care procedures, radiation physics, radiation protection, principles of imaging, medical terminology, positioning of patients, medical ethics, radiobiology, and pathology.

For training programs in radiation therapy and diagnostic medical sonography, applicants with a background in science, or experience in one of the health professions, generally are preferred. Some programs consider applicants with liberal arts backgrounds, however, as well as high school graduates with courses in math and science.

Radiographers and radiation therapists are covered by provisions of the Consumer-Patient Radiation Health and Safety Act of 1981, which aims to protect the public from the hazards of unnecessary exposure to medical and dental radiation by ensuring operators of radiologic equipment are properly trained. The act requires the federal government to set standards that the states, in turn, may use for accrediting training programs and certifying individuals who engage in medical or dental radiography.

By January 1995, 31 states required radiographers to be licensed, and 26 required radiation therapists to be licensed. (Puerto Rico requires a license for the practice of either specialty.)

Voluntary registration is offered by the American Registry of Radiologic Technologists (ARRT) in both radiography and radiation therapy. The American Registry of Diagnostic Medical Sonographers (ARDMS) certifies the competence of sonographers. To become registered, technologists must be graduates of an accredited program or meet other prerequisites and have passed an examination. Many employers prefer to hire registered technologists.

With experience and additional training, staff technologists may become specialists, performing CT scanning, ultrasound, angiography, and magnetic resonance imaging. Experienced technologists may also be promoted to supervisor, chief radiologic technologist, and—ultimately—department administrator or director. Depending on the institution, courses or a master's degree in business or health administration may be necessary for the director's position. Some technologists progress by becoming instructors or directors in radiologic technology programs; others take jobs as sales representatives or instructors with equipment manufacturers.

With additional education, available at major cancer centers, radiation therapy technologists can specialize as medical radiation dosimetrists. Dosimetrists work with health physicists and oncologists (physicians who specialize in the study and treatment of tumors) to develop treatment plans.

Radiographers and radiation therapists are required to fulfill 24 hours of continuing education every other year and provide documentation to prove that they are complying with these requirements.

## Job Outlook

While a significant increase in radiologic technologist employment is anticipated, job seekers are likely to face competition from many other qualified applicants for most openings. Reports of shortages of radiographers and radiation therapists that were common during the last decade no longer exist. As more people entered the field, the number of qualified applicants increased faster than the number of job openings. The imbalance that resulted caused competition for jobs to become intense. While reduced, the imbalance is expected to persist through the year 2005. Sonographers should experience somewhat better job opportunities than other radiologic technologist occupations as technology spawns many new ultrasound procedures.

Employment of radiologic technologists is expected to grow faster than the average for all occupations through 2005, as the health care industries grow, and because of the vast clinical potential of diagnostic imaging and therapeutic technology. Current as well as new uses of imaging equipment should increase the demand for radiologic technologists.

Radiation therapy will continue to be used—alone or in combination with surgery or chemotherapy—to treat cancer. More treatment of cancer is anticipated due to the aging of the population, educational efforts aimed at early detection, and improved ability to detect malignancies through radiologic procedures such as mammography.

Although physicians are enthusiastic about the clinical benefits of new technologies, the extent to which they are adopted depends largely on cost and reimbursement considerations. Some promising new technologies may not come into widespread use because they are too expensive and third-party payers may not be willing to pay for their use. But on the whole, it appears that radiologic procedures will be used more widely.

Hospitals will remain the principal employer of radiologic technologists. However, employment is expected to grow most rapidly in offices and clinics of physicians, including diagnostic imaging centers. Health facilities such as these are expected to grow very rapidly through 2005 due to the strong shift toward outpatient care, encouraged by third-party payers and made possible by technological advances that permit more procedures to be performed outside the hospital. Some jobs will also come from the need to replace technologists who leave the occupation.

## Earnings

In 1994, the median annual earnings for radiologic technologists who worked year-round full-time were $29,432. The middle 50 percent earned between $24,596 and $36,244 a week; 10 percent earned less than $20,696 a week; and 10 percent earned more than $49,036.

According to a University of Texas Medical Branch survey of hospitals and medical centers, the median salary for radiologic technologists, based on a 40-hour week and excluding shift or area differentials, was $27,008 in October 1994. The average minimum salary was $23,265 and the average maximum was $34,687. For radiation therapy technologists the median was $35,877 and for ultrasound technologists, $33,522.

## Related Occupations

Radiologic technologists operate sophisticated equipment to help physicians, dentists, and other health practitioners diagnose and treat patients. Workers in related occupations include radiation dosimetrists, nuclear medicine technologists, cardiovascular technologists and technicians, perfusionists, respiratory therapists, clinical laboratory technologists, and electroneurodiagnostic technologists.

## Related *D.O.T.* Jobs

These job titles are related to or more specific than the more general description above. They will help you identify job options you may not otherwise discover. These descriptions are in the current edition of the *Dictionary of Occupational Titles* and classified by numerical order.

078.361-034 RADIATION-THERAPY TECHNOLOGIST; 078.362-026 RADIOLOGIC TECHNOLOGIST; 078.362-046 SPECIAL PROCEDURES TECHNOLOGIST, ANGIOGRAM; 078.362-054 SPECIAL PROCEDURES TECHNOLOGIST, CT SCAN; 078.362-058 SPECIAL PROCEDURES TECHNOLOGIST, MAGNETIC RESONANCE IMAGING (MRI); 078.364-010 ULTRASOUND TECHNOLOGIST

## Sources of Additional Information

For career information, enclose a stamped, self-addressed business size envelope with your request to:

❏ American Society of Radiologic Technologists, 15000 Central Ave. SE., Albuquerque, NM 87123-3917.

❏ Society of Diagnostic Medical Sonographers, 12770 Coit Rd., Suite 508, Dallas, TX 75251.

❏ American Healthcare Radiology Administrators, 111 Boston Post Rd., Suite 215, P.O. Box 334, Sudbury, MA 01776.

For the current list of accredited education programs in radiography, radiation therapy technology, write to:

❏ Joint Review Committee on Education in Radiologic Technology, 20 N. Wacker St., Chicago, IL 60606-2901.

For a current list of accredited education programs in diagnostic medical sonography, write to:

❏ The Joint Review Committee on Education in Diagnostic Medical Sonography, 7108 S. Alton Way, Building C., Englewood, CO 80112.

For information on certification in sonography, contact:

❏ American Registry of Diagnostic Medical Sonographers, 600 Jefferson Plaza, Rockville, MD 20852-1150.

# Rail Transportation Workers

## Nature of the Work

Rail transportation workers operate our nation's trains, subways, and streetcars to facilitate the movement of passengers and cargo. Railroad transportation workers deliver travelers and freight to destinations throughout the nation while subway and streetcar operators provide passenger service within a single metropolitan area.

**Railroad transportation workers.** *Locomotive engineers* and *rail yard engineers* are among the most highly skilled workers on the railroad. They operate locomotives in yards, stations, and over the track between distant stations and yards. Locomotive engineers operate trains carrying cargo and passengers between stations, while rail yard engineers move cars within yards to assemble or disassemble trains. In addition to those engineers who work for railroads, some engineers called *dinkey operators* work at industrial plants or mines operating smaller engines that pull cars loaded with coal, rock, or supplies around the site.

Engineers operate the throttle to start and accelerate the train and use air brakes or dynamic brakes to slow and stop it. They monitor gauges and meters that measure speed, fuel, temperature, battery charge, and air pressure in the brake lines. Both on the road and in the yard, they watch for signals that indicate track obstructions, other train movements, and speed limits. They must have a thorough knowledge of the signal systems, yards, and terminals along their routes and be constantly aware of the condition and makeup of their train. This is extremely important because trains react differently to acceleration, braking, and curves, depending on the number of cars, the ratio of empty to loaded cars, and the amount of slack in the train.

Most engineers run diesel locomotives; a few run electric locomotives. Before and after each run, engineers check locomotives for mechanical problems. Minor adjustments are made on the spot, but major problems are reported to the engine shop supervisor. In an effort to reduce costs, most railroads are phasing out *assistant engineers*, also known as firers, who monitor locomotive instruments and signals and observe the track for obstructions. Most of these duties are now performed by brake operators.

*Road conductors* and *yard conductors* are in charge of the train and yard crews. Conductors assigned to freight trains record each car's contents and destination and make sure that cars are added and removed at the proper points along the route. Conductors assigned to passenger trains collect tickets and fares and assist passengers. At stops, they signal engineers when to pull out of the station.

Before a train leaves the terminal, the road conductor and engineer discuss instructions received from the dispatcher concerning the train's route, timetable, and cargo. While underway, conductors receive additional information by radio. This may include information about track conditions ahead or instructions to pull off at the next available stop to let another train pass. During the run, conductors use two-way radios to contact engineers. They pass on instructions received from dispatchers and remind engineers of stops, reported track conditions, and the presence of other trains.

While underway, conductors receive information from *brake operators* regarding any equipment problems, and they may arrange for defective cars to be removed from the train for repairs at the nearest station or stop. They inform dispatchers of any problems using a radio or wayside telephone.

Yard conductors supervise the crews that assemble and disassemble trains. Some cars are sent to special tracks for unloading, while the rest are moved to other tracks to await assemblage into trains destined for different cities. Conductors tell engineers where to move cars. They tell brake operators which cars to couple and uncouple and which switches to throw to divert the locomotive or cars to the proper track. In yards that have automatic classification systems, conductors use electrical remote controls to operate the track switches that route cars to the correct track.

Brake operators play a pivotal role in making locomotives and cars into trains. Working under the direction of conductors, they do the physical work involved in adding and removing cars at railroad stations and assembling and disassembling trains in railroad yards.

Freight train crews include either one or two brake operators—one in the locomotive with the engineer and another in the rear car. An increasing number of freight trains use only one brake operator because new visual instrumentation and monitoring devices have eliminated the need for operators outside the locomotive. Before departure, brake operators inspect the train to make sure that all couplers and air hoses are fastened, that hand brakes on all the cars are released, and that the air brakes are functioning properly. While underway, they regularly look for smoke, sparks, and other signs of sticking brakes, overheated axle bearings, and other potentially faulty equipment. They may make minor repairs to air hoses and couplers. In case of unexpected stops, brake operators set up signals to protect both ends of the train.

When freight trains approach an industrial site, the brake operator in the locomotive gets off the train and runs ahead to switch the train to the proper track. They uncouple the cars and throw track switches to route them to certain tracks if they are to be unloaded, or to an outgoing train if their final destination is further down the line. They also set hand brakes to secure cars.

Many smaller railroads operate with only two crew members—an engineer and a conductor. Most passenger trains no longer employ brake operators but employ *assistant conductors* to help conductors collect tickets and assist passengers.

**Subway and streetcar operators.** *Subway operators* control trains that transport passengers throughout a city and its suburbs. The trains usually run on tracks in underground tunnels, but some systems have lines that run in part on tracks on the surface or elevated above streets. Observing the system's signals, operators start, slow, or stop the subway train. They make announcements to riders, open and close the doors, and ensure that passengers get on and off the subway safely. Operators should have a basic understanding of the operating system and be able to recognize common equipment problems. When breakdowns or emergencies occur, operators contact their dispatcher or supervisor and may have to evacuate cars. To meet predetermined schedules, operators must control the amount of time spent at each station.

*Streetcar operators* drive electric-powered streetcars or trolleys that transport passengers. Streetcars run on tracks that may be recessed in city streets, so operators must observe traffic signals and cope with car and truck traffic. Operators start, slow, and stop their cars so passengers may board or alight. They collect fares, and issue change and transfers. They also answer questions from passengers concerning fares, schedules, and routes.

## Working Conditions

Because trains operate 24 hours a day, seven days a week, many rail transportation employees often work nights, weekends, and holidays. On some days subway operators may work multiple shifts. Undesirable shifts are assigned to persons who have the least seniority.

Most freight trains are unscheduled, and few workers on these trains have scheduled assignments. Instead, their names are placed on a list, and when their turn comes they are assigned to the next train, usually on short notice and often at odd hours. Because road service personnel often work on trains that operate between stations that are hundreds of miles apart, they may spend several nights a week away from home.

Freight and yard conductors and brake operators spend most of their time outdoors in all kinds of weather. The work of brake operators on local runs—where trains frequently stop at stations to pick up and deliver cars—is physically demanding. Climbing up and down and getting off moving cars is strenuous and can be dangerous.

## Employment

Rail transportation workers held about 86,000 jobs in 1994—including 26,000 conductors, 22,000 locomotive engineers, 19,000 brake operators, and 6,000 rail yard engineers and dinkey operators. Subway and streetcar operators accounted for over 12,000 jobs. Railroads employ about 82 percent of all rail transportation workers. The rest work for state and local governments as subway and streetcar operators, and for mining and manufacturing establishments that operate their own locomotives and rail cars to move ore, coal, and other bulk materials.

## Training, Other Qualifications, and Advancement

Most railroad transportation workers begin as trainees for either engineer or brake operator jobs. Railroads prefer that applicants have a high school education. Applicants must have good hearing, eyesight, and color vision, as well as good hand-eye coordination, manual dexterity, and mechanical aptitude. Physical stamina is required for brake operator jobs. Most employers require that applicants for railroad transportation jobs pass a physical examination and tests that screen for drug and alcohol use.

Railroads prefer that applicants for locomotive engineer jobs be at least 21 years old. Engineer jobs are frequently filled by workers with experience in other railroad operating occupations, such as brake operators or conductors. Most beginning engineers undergo a 6-month training program, which includes classroom and hands-on instruction in locomotive operation. At the end of the training period, aspiring engineers must pass qualifying tests covering locomotive equipment, air brake systems, fuel economy, train handling techniques, and operating rules and regulations.

On most railroads, brake operators begin by making several trips with conductors and experienced operators to become familiar with the job. On some railroads, however, new brake operators undergo extensive training, including instruction in signaling, coupling and uncoupling cars, throwing switches, and boarding moving trains.

As railroads need new engineers and brake operators, newly trained workers who have the most seniority are placed on the "extra board." Extra board engineers and brake operators work only when the railroad needs substitutes for regular workers who are absent because of vacation, illness, or other personal reasons. Extra board engineers and brake operators frequently must wait years until they accumulate enough seniority to get a regular assignment. Seniority rules also may allow workers with greater seniority to select their type of assignment. For example, an engineer may move from an initial regular assignment in yard service to road service.

Engineers undergo periodic physical examinations and drug and alcohol testing to determine their fitness to operate locomotives. Unannounced safety and efficiency tests are also given to judge their overall conduct of operations. In some cases, engineers who fail to meet these physical and conduct standards are restricted to yard service; in other instances, they may be disciplined, trained to perform other work, or discharged.

Conductor jobs generally are filled from the ranks of experienced brake operators who have passed tests covering signals, timetables, operating rules, and related subjects. Some companies require these tests be passed within the first few years of employment. Until permanent positions become available, new conductors are put on the extra board, where they substitute for experienced conductors who are absent. On most railroads, conductors on extra board may work as brake operators if there are not enough conductor runs available that month. Seniority usually is the main factor in determining promotion from brake operator to conductor and from extra board to a permanent position. Advancement to conductor jobs is limited because there are many more brake operators than conductors.

Most railroads maintain separate seniority lists for road service and yard service conductors. Conductors usually remain in one type of service for their entire career. On some railroads, however, conductors start in the yards, then move to freight service, and finally to passenger service. Some conductors advance to managerial or administrative positions.

For subway and streetcar operator jobs, subway transit systems prefer applicants to have a high school education. Some systems require subway operators to work as bus drivers for a specified period of time. Applicants must be in good health, articulate, and able to make quick, responsible judgments.

New operators generally are placed in training programs that last from a few weeks to six months. At the end of the period of classroom and on-the-job training, operators usually must pass qualifying examinations covering the operating system, troubleshooting, and evacuation and emergency procedures. Some operators with sufficient seniority can advance to station managers.

## Job Outlook

Competition for available opportunities is expected to be keen. Many persons qualify for rail transportation occupations because education beyond high school generally is not required and many more desire employment than can be hired because the pay is good and the work steady. While employment of railroad transportation workers is expected to decline for all occupations through the year 2005, employment of subway and streetcar operators is expected to grow faster than the average. The total number of new jobs, however, is not large. Also, relatively few opportunities resulting from replacement needs will occur because the attractive pay and job security results in relatively few rail transportation workers leaving their jobs.

Demand for railroad freight service will grow as the economy expands, but opportunities for railroad transportation workers will be limited because of ongoing reductions in the size of operating crews and improvements in the efficiency of railroad operations. Railroad freight service is expected to increase as the population and economy grow in size, and as intermodal freight transportation continues to become more efficient. Intermodal systems use trucks to pick-up and deliver the shippers' sealed trailers or containers, and trains to transport them long distance. Productivity and efficiency improvements cutting the time railroads need to deliver cargoes are also increasing shippers' use of railroads. In order to compete with other modes of transportation such as trucks, ships and barges, and aircraft, railroads are improving delivery times and on-time service while reducing shipping rates. As a result, businesses are expected to increasingly use railroads to carry their goods.

However, growth in the number of railroad transportation workers will be affected by innovations such as larger, faster, more fuel-efficient trains and computerized classification yards that make it possible to move passengers and freight more economically. Computers are used to keep track of freight cars, match empty cars with the closest loads, and dispatch trains. Computer-assisted devices alert engineers to train malfunctions, eliminating the need for brake operators in the rear car. Also, new work rules that allow trains to operate with two- or three-person crews instead of the traditional five-person crews are now becoming widespread. Many positions will not be filled as people leave the occupations, or the work will be restructured so that it can be done by other railroad employees. Employment opportunities for locomotive and yard engineers should be slightly better than other rail occupations because they should be less affected by technological changes and reductions in crew size. On the other hand, employment of brake operators should be the most adversely affected as visual instrumentation and monitoring devices eliminate the need for rear brake operators.

Subway and streetcar operator employment is expected to grow as cities build new rail systems and add new lines to existing systems. New construction is spurred by population growth in metropolitan areas that increases automobile traffic and makes streets and highways more congested. Improved rail systems offer an alternative to automobile transportation that can reduce road congestion and, by reducing automobile use, also contribute to government mandated improvements in air quality.

### Earnings

Earnings of railroad transportation workers vary by occupation, size of the train, and type of service. According to the Brotherhood of Locomotive Engineers, in 1993, passenger engineers averaged about $63,900 a year, through-freight engineers about $62,900, local way freight engineers about $60,800, and yard engineers about $47,700 a year.

According to the Association of American Railroads, in 1994, annual earnings of conductors averaged $41,000 for through-freight and $39,200 for local and way freight. Brake operators averaged about $28,300 for through-freight and $31,000 for local and way freight. Yard brake operators averaged about $24,800 in 1994, while passenger brake operators averaged $21,600.

According to the American Public Transit Association, in 1994, operators for commuter rail had hourly earnings of about $19.20; operators for heavy rail about $17.30; and operators for light rail, about $15.90.

Most rail transportation employees in yards work 40 hours a week and receive extra pay for overtime. Most railroad workers in road service are paid according to miles traveled or hours worked, whichever leads to higher earnings. Full-time employees have steadier work, more regular hours, and higher earnings than those assigned to the extra board.

Most railroad transportation workers are members of unions. Many different railroad unions represent various crafts on the railroads, but most railroad engineers are members of the Brotherhood of Locomotive Engineers, while most other railroad transportation workers are members of the United Transportation Union. Many subway operators are members of the Amalgamated Transit Union, while others belong to the Transport Workers Union of North America.

### Related *D.O.T.* Jobs

These job titles are related to or more specific than the more general description above. They will help you identify job options you may not otherwise discover. These descriptions are in the current edition of the *Dictionary of Occupational Titles* and classified by numerical order.

184.167-278 YARD MANAGER; 198.167-010 CONDUCTOR, PASSENGER CAR; 198.167-014 CONDUCTOR, PULLMAN; 198.167-018 CONDUCTOR, ROAD FREIGHT; 850.663-018 LOCK TENDER II; 910.362-010 TOWER OPERATOR; 910.363-010 FIRER, LOCOMOTIVE; 910.363-014 LOCOMOTIVE ENGINEER; 910.363-018 YARD ENGINEER; 910.364-010 BRAKER, PASSENGER TRAIN; 910.367-010 BRAKE COUPLER, ROAD FREIGHT; 910.367-022 LOCOMOTIVE OPERATOR HELPER; 910.382-010 CAR-RETARDER OPERATOR; 910.583-010 LABORER, CAR BARN; 910.664-010 YARD COUPLER; 910.667-026 SWITCH TENDER; 910.683-010 HOSTLER; 910.683-014 MOTOR OPERATOR; 910.683-022 TRANS-

FER-TABLE OPERATOR; 913.463-014 STREETCAR OPERATOR; 919.663-014 DINKEY OPERATOR; 919.683-018 RAIL-TRACTOR OPERATOR; 919.683-026 TRACKMOBILE OPERATOR; 932.664-010 BRAKE HOLDER

### Sources of Additional Information

Information on employment opportunities for railroad transportation workers may be obtained from the employment offices of the various railroads and rail transit systems, or state employment service offices.

For general information about career opportunities in passenger transportation, contact:

❏ American Public Transit Association, 1201 New York Ave. NW, Suite 400, Washington, DC 20005.

General information on rail transportation occupations and career opportunities as a locomotive engineer is available from:

❏ Brotherhood of Locomotive Engineers, 1370 Ontario Ave., Cleveland, OH 44113-1702.

# Roofers

### Nature of the Work

A leaky roof can damage ceilings, walls, and furnishings. To protect buildings and their contents from water damage, roofers repair and install roofs of tar or asphalt and gravel, rubber, thermoplastic, and metal; and shingles made of asphalt, slate, fiberglass, wood, tile, or other material. Repair and reroofing—replacing old roofs on existing buildings—provide many work opportunities for these workers. Roofers also may waterproof foundation walls and floors.

There are two types of roofs, flat and pitched (sloped). Most commercial, industrial, and apartment buildings have flat or slightly sloping roofs. Most houses have pitched roofs. Some roofers work on both types; others specialize.

Most flat roofs are covered with several layers of materials. Roofers first put a layer of insulation on the roof deck. Over the insulation, they then spread a coat of molten bitumen, a tar-like substance. Next, they install partially overlapping layers of roofing felt—a fabric saturated in bitumen—over the insulation surface and use a mop to spread hot bitumen over it and under the next layer. This seals the seams and makes the surface watertight. Roofers repeat these steps to build up the desired number of layers, called "plies." The top layer is either glazed to make a smooth finish, or has gravel embedded in the hot bitumen for a rough surface.

An increasing number of flat roofs are covered with a single-ply membrane of waterproof rubber or thermoplastic compounds. Roofers roll these sheets over the roof's insulation and seal the seams. Adhesive, mechanical fasteners, or stone ballasts hold the sheets in place. The building must be of sufficient strength to hold the ballast.

Most residential roofs are covered with shingles. To apply shingles, roofers first lay, cut, and tack 3-foot strips of roofing felt lengthwise over the entire roof. Then, starting from the bottom edge, they nail overlapping rows of shingles to the roof. Workers measure and cut the felt and shingles to fit intersecting roofs, and to fit around vent pipes and chimneys. Wherever two roof surfaces intersect or shingles reach a vent pipe or chimney, roofers cement or nail "flashing," strips of metal or shingle, over the joints to make them watertight. Finally, roofers cover exposed nail heads with roofing cement or caulking to prevent water leakage.

Some roofers also waterproof and damp-proof masonry and concrete walls and floors. To prepare surfaces for waterproofing, they hammer and chisel away rough spots or remove them with a rubbing brick before applying a coat of liquid waterproofing compound. They also may paint or spray surfaces with a waterproofing material or attach waterproofing membrane to surfaces. When damp-proofing, they usually spray a bitumen-based coating on interior or exterior surfaces.

## Working Conditions

Roofers' work is strenuous. It involves heavy lifting, as well as climbing, bending, and kneeling. Roofers risk injuries from slips or falls from scaffolds, ladders, or roofs, and burns from hot bitumen. In fact, of all construction industries, the roofing industry has the highest accident rate. Roofers work outdoors in all types of weather, particularly when making repairs. Roofs are extremely hot during the summer.

## Employment

Roofers held about 126,000 jobs in 1994. Almost all wage and salary roofers worked for roofing contractors. Nearly one-third of all roofers were self-employed. Many self-employed roofers specialize in residential work.

## Training, Other Qualifications, and Advancement

Most roofers acquire their skills informally by working as helpers for experienced roofers. They start by carrying equipment and material and erecting scaffolds and hoists. Within two or three months, they are taught to measure, cut, and fit roofing materials and then to lay asphalt or fiberglass shingles. Because some roofing materials are used infrequently, it can take several years to get experience working on all the various types of roofing applications.

Some roofers train through three-year apprenticeship programs administered by local union-management committees representing roofing contractors and locals of the United Union of Roofers, Water-proofers, and Allied Workers. The apprenticeship program generally consists of a minimum of 1,400 hours of on-the-job training annually, plus 144 hours of classroom instruction a year in subjects such as tools and their use, arithmetic, and safety. On-the-job training for apprentices is similar to that for helpers, except that the apprenticeship program is more structured. Apprentices also learn to damp-proof and waterproof walls.

Good physical condition and good balance are essential for roofers. A high school education or its equivalent is helpful, as are courses in mechanical drawing and basic mathematics. Most apprentices are at least 18 years old.

Roofers may advance to supervisor or estimator for a roofing contractor or become contractors themselves.

## Job Outlook

Jobs for roofers should be plentiful through the year 2005, primarily because of the need to replace workers who transfer to other occupations or who leave the labor force. Turnover is high;

roofing work is hot, strenuous, and dirty, and a significant number of workers treat roofing as a temporary job until something better comes along. Some roofers leave the occupation to go into other construction trades.

Employment of roofers is expected to increase about as fast as the average for all occupations through the year 2005. Roofs deteriorate faster than most other parts of buildings and periodically need to be repaired or replaced. About 75 percent of roofing work is repair and reroofing, a higher proportion than in most other construction work. As a result, demand for roofers is less susceptible to downturns in the economy than some of the other construction trades. In addition to repair and reroofing work on the growing stock of buildings, new construction of industrial, commercial, and residential buildings will add to the demand for roofers. However, many innovations and advances in materials, techniques, and tools have made roofers more productive and will restrict the growth of employment at least to some extent. Jobs should be easiest to find during spring and summer, when most roofing is done.

## Earnings

Median weekly earnings for roofers working full-time were about $371 a week in 1994. The middle 50 percent earned between $278 and $498 a week. The top 10 percent earned more than $630 weekly and the lowest 10 percent less than $219 a week.

According to the *Engineering News Record*, average hourly earnings—including benefits—for union roofers were $23.98 in 1994. Wages ranged from a low of $13.90 in Denver to a high of $38.58 in New York City. Apprentices generally start at about 40 percent of the rate paid to experienced roofers and receive periodic raises as they acquire the skills of the trade. Earnings for roofers are reduced on occasion because poor weather often limits the time they can work.

Some roofers are members of the United Union of Roofers, Water-proofers & Allied Workers.

## Related Occupations

Roofers use shingles, bitumen and gravel, single-ply plastic or rubber sheets, or other materials to waterproof building surfaces. Workers in other occupations who cover surfaces with special materials for protection and decoration include carpenters, concrete masons, drywall installers, floor covering installers, plasterers, terrazzo workers, and tilesetters.

## Related *D.O.T.* Jobs

These job titles are related to or more specific than the more general description above. They will help you identify job options you may not otherwise discover. These descriptions are in the current edition of the *Dictionary of Occupational Titles* and classified by numerical order.

866.381-010 ROOFER; 866.381-014 ROOFER APPRENTICE; 866.684-010 ROOFER APPLICATOR

## Sources of Additional Information

For information about roofing apprenticeships or work opportunities in this trade, contact local roofing contractors; a local of the Roofers union; a local joint union-management apprenticeship committee; or the nearest office of the state employment service or state apprenticeship agency.

For information about the work of roofers, contact:

❏ National Roofing Contractors Association, 10255 W. Higgins Rd., Rosemont, IL 60018.

❏ United Union of Roofers, Water-proofers and Allied Workers, 1125 17th St. NW, Washington, DC 20036.

# Science Technicians

## Nature of the Work

Science technicians use the principles and theories of science and mathematics to solve problems in research and development and to help invent and improve products. Their jobs are more practically oriented than those of scientists. Technicians set up, operate, and maintain laboratory instruments, monitor experiments, make observations, calculate and record results, and often develop conclusions. Those who work in production test products for proper proportions of ingredients or for strength and durability.

In recent years, as laboratory instrumentation and procedures have become more complex, the role of science technicians in research and development has expanded. In addition to performing routine tasks under the direction of scientists, many technicians also develop and adapt laboratory procedures to achieve the best results, interpret data, and devise solutions to problems. The increasing use of robotics to perform many routine tasks formerly done by technicians has freed technicians to operate other, more sophisticated laboratory equipment. Science technicians make extensive use of computers, computer-interfaced equipment, robotics, and high-technology industrial applications such as biological engineering.

*Agricultural technicians* work with agricultural scientists in food and fiber research, production, and processing. Some conduct tests and experiments to improve the yield and quality of crops or to increase the resistance of plants and animals to disease, insects, or other hazards. Other agricultural technicians do animal breeding and nutrition work.

*Biological technicians* work with biologists, studying living organisms. They may assist scientists who conduct medical research, helping to find a cure for cancer or AIDS, for example. Those who work in pharmaceutical companies help develop and manufacture medicinal and pharmaceutical preparations. Biological technicians also analyze organic substances such as blood, food, and drugs, and some examine evidence in criminal investigations. Biological technicians working in biotechnology labs use the knowledge and techniques gained from basic research by scientists, including gene splicing and recombinant DNA, and apply these techniques in product development.

*Chemical technicians* work with chemists and chemical engineers, developing and using chemicals and related products and equipment. Most do research and development, testing, or other laboratory work. For example, they might test packaging for design, materials, and environmental acceptability; assemble and operate new equipment to develop new products; monitor product quality; or develop new production techniques. Some chemical technicians collect and analyze samples of air and water to monitor pollution levels. Those who focus on basic research might produce compounds through complex organic synthesis.

*Nuclear technicians* operate nuclear test and research equipment, monitor radiation, and assist nuclear engineers and physicists in research. Some also operate remote control equipment to manipulate radioactive materials or materials to be exposed to radioactivity.

*Petroleum technicians* measure and record physical and geologic conditions in oil or gas wells using instruments lowered into wells or by analysis of the mud from wells. In oil and gas exploration, they collect and examine geological data or test geological samples to determine petroleum and mineral content. Some petroleum technicians, called scouts, collect information about oil and gas well drilling operations, geological and geophysical prospecting, and land or lease contracts.

Other science technicians collect weather information or assist oceanographers.

## Working Conditions

Science technicians work under a wide variety of conditions. Most work indoors, usually in laboratories, and have regular hours. Some occasionally work irregular hours to monitor experiments that can't be completed during regular working hours. Some, such as agricultural and petroleum technicians, perform much of their work outdoors, sometimes in remote locations, and some may be exposed to hazardous conditions. Chemical technicians sometimes work with toxic chemicals or radioactive isotopes; nuclear technicians may be exposed to radiation; and biological technicians sometimes work with disease-causing organisms or radioactive agents. However, there is little risk if proper safety procedures are followed.

## Employment

Science technicians held about 231,000 jobs in 1994. Over one-third worked in manufacturing, mostly in the chemical industry, but also in the food processing industry. About 15 percent worked in education services and another 15 percent worked in research and testing services.

In 1994, the federal government employed about 17,500 science technicians, mostly in the Departments of Defense, Agriculture, and Interior.

## Training, Other Qualifications, and Advancement

There are several ways to qualify for a job as a science technician. Most employers prefer applicants who have at least two years of specialized training. Many junior and community colleges offer associate degrees in a specific technology or a more general education in science and mathematics. A number of two-year associate degree programs are designed to provide easy transfer to a four-year college or university if desired. Technical institutes generally offer technician training but provide less theory and general education than junior or community colleges. The length of programs at technical institutes varies, although two-year associate degree programs are common. Some of these schools offer cooperative-education programs, allowing students the opportunity to work at a local company while attending classes in alternate terms. Many science technicians have a bachelor's degree in chemistry or biology, or have at least had several science and math courses in four-year colleges.

Two-year formal training programs that combine the teaching of scientific principles and theory with practical hands-on application in a laboratory setting with up-to-date equipment provide very good preparation for prospective science technicians. Graduates of four-year bachelor's degree programs in science who have completed internships or held summer jobs in laboratories are also well-qualified for science technician positions.

Persons interested in careers as science technicians should take as many high school science and math courses as possible. Science courses taken beyond high school, in an associate or bachelor's program, should be laboratory oriented, with an emphasis on "bench" skills. Because computers and computer-interfaced equipment are often used in research and development laboratories, technicians should have strong computer skills. Communication skills are important, since technicians are often asked to report their finding both verbally and in writing. Technicians should also be able to work well with others since they often are part of a team.

Technicians usually begin work as trainees in routine positions under the direct supervision of a scientist or experienced technician. Job candidates whose training or educational background encompasses extensive hands-on experience with a variety of laboratory equipment, including computers and related equipment, usually require a much shorter period of on-the-job training. As they gain experience, they take on more responsibility and carry out assignments under only general supervision. Some eventually become supervisors.

## Job Outlook

Employment of science technicians is expected to increase about as fast as the average for all occupations through the year 2005. Continued growth of scientific and medical research and development and the production of technical products should spur demand for all science technicians. The growing number of agricultural and medicinal products developed using biotechnology techniques will increase the need for biological technicians in particular. Employment growth will also be fueled by the demand for science technicians to work in environmental research and testing. Technicians will be needed to help regulate waste products, collect air and water samples to measure levels of pollutants, and clean up contaminated sites. However, growth of job openings will be moderated somewhat by an expected slowdown in overall employment growth in the chemical industry, where many chemical technicians are employed.

Job opportunities are expected to be very good for graduates of science technician training programs who are well-trained on the equipment currently in use in industrial and government laboratories. As the instrumentation and techniques used in industrial research and development laboratories becomes more complex, employers are seeking well trained individuals with highly developed technical and communication skills.

In addition to the projected growth, nearly as many job openings will arise from the need to replace technicians who retire or leave the labor force for other reasons.

## Earnings

Median annual earnings of science technicians were about $26,900 in 1994; the middle 50 percent earned between $19,600 and $37,300. Ten percent earned less than $14,700, and 10 percent earned over $46,800. At all income levels, chemical technicians earned significantly more than biological technicians.

In the federal government in 1995, science technicians could start at $14,900, $16,700, or $18,700, depending on their education and experience. Beginning salaries were slightly higher in selected areas of the country where the prevailing local pay level was higher. The average annual salary for biological science technicians in nonsupervisory, supervisory, and managerial positions employed by the federal government in 1995 was $23,790; for mathematical technicians, $26,640; for physical science technicians, $32,490; for geodetic technicians, $40,860; for hydrologic technicians, $28,850; and for meteorologic technicians, $36,750.

## Related Occupations

Other technicians who apply scientific principles at a level usually taught in two-year associate degree programs include engineering technicians, broadcast technicians, drafters, and health technologists and technicians. Some of the work of agricultural and biological technicians is related to that in agriculture and forestry occupations.

## Related *D.O.T.* Jobs

These job titles are related to or more specific than the more general description above. They will help you identify job options you may not otherwise discover. These descriptions are in the current edition of the *Dictionary of Occupational Titles* and classified by numerical order.

There are too many *D.O.T.* titles to list here. Most are variations related to a specific industry, and we have included a small number of representative *D.O.T.* titles as examples. Complete lists are available in various career software published by JIST or directly from the U.S. Department of Labor.

010.261-022 SURVEYOR, OIL-WELL DIRECTIONAL; 010.267-010 SCOUT; 012.261-010 AIR ANALYST; 015.261-010 CHEMICAL-RADIATION TECHNICIAN; 015.362-026 REACTOR OPERATOR, TEST-AND-RESEARCH; 019.261-030 LABORATORY TECHNICIAN; 020.162-010 MATHEMATICAL TECHNICIAN; 022.261-022 CHEMIST, WASTEWATER-TREATMENT PLANT; 022.281-010 ASSAYER; 022.281-018 LABORATORY TESTER; 024.381-010 LABORATORY ASSISTANT; 025.267-014 WEATHER OBSERVER; 029.261-010 LABORATORY TESTER; 029.261-014 POLLUTION-CONTROL TECHNICIAN; 029.261-018 TEST-ENGINE OPERATOR; 029.261-026 CRIMINALIST; 029.361-014 FOOD TESTER; 199.364-014 SCIENTIFIC HELPER; 408.181-010 TREE SURGEON; 559.384-010 LABORATORY ASSISTANT, CULTURE MEDIA; 930.167-010 TECHNICAL OPERATOR

## Sources of Additional Information

For information about a career as a chemical technician, contact:

❑ American Chemical Society, Education Division, Career Publications, 1155 16th St. NW, Washington, DC 20036.

# Sheetmetal Workers

## Nature of the Work

Sheetmetal workers make, install, and maintain air-conditioning, heating, ventilation, and pollution control duct systems; roofs; siding; rain gutters and downspouts; skylights; restaurant equipment; outdoor signs; and many other building parts and products made from metal sheets. They may also work with fiberglass and plastic materials. Although some workers specialize in fabrication, installation, or maintenance, most do all three jobs. (Workers employed in the mass production of sheetmetal products in manufacturing are not included in this section.)

Sheetmetal workers usually fabricate their products at a shop away from the construction site. They first study plans and specifications to determine the kind and quantity of materials they will need. They then measure, cut, bend, shape, and fasten pieces of sheet metal to make duct work, counter tops, and other custom products. In an increasing number of shops, sheetmetal workers use computerized metalworking equipment. This enables them to experiment with different layouts and to select the one that results in the least waste of material. They cut or form the parts with computer-controlled saws, lasers, shears, and presses.

In shops without computerized equipment and for products that cannot be made on such equipment, sheetmetal workers use hand calculators to make the required calculations and use tapes, rulers, and other measuring devices for layout work. They then cut or stamp the parts on machine tools.

Before assembling the pieces, sheetmetal workers check each part for accuracy and, if necessary, finish it by using hand, rotary, or squaring shears and hacksaws. After the parts have been inspected, workers fasten the seams and joints together with welds, bolts, cement, rivets, solder, specially formed sheetmetal drive clips, or other connecting devices. They then take the parts to the construction site where they further assemble the pieces as they install them. These workers install ducts, pipes, and tubes by joining them end to end and hanging them with metal hangers secured to a ceiling or a wall. They also use shears, hammers, punches, and drills to make parts at the work site or to alter parts made in the shop.

Some jobs are done completely at the job site. When installing a metal roof, for example, sheetmetal workers measure and cut the roofing panels that are needed to complete the job. They secure the first panel in place and interlock and fasten the grooved edge of the next panel into the grooved edge of the first. Then they nail or weld the free edge of the panel to the structure. This two-step process is repeated for each additional panel. Finally, they fasten machine-made molding at joints, along corners, and around windows and doors for a neat, finished effect.

In addition to installation, some sheetmetal workers specialize in testing, balancing, adjusting, and servicing existing air-conditioning and ventilation systems to make sure they are functioning properly and to improve their energy efficiency. Some sheetmetal workers also remove asbestos and toxic materials.

## Working Conditions

Sheetmetal workers usually work a 40-hour week. Those who fabricate sheetmetal products work in shops that are well lighted and well ventilated. They stand for long periods and lift heavy materials and finished pieces. Sheetmetal workers must follow safety practices because working around high-speed machines can be dangerous. They are subject to cuts from sharp metal, burns from soldering and welding, and falls from ladders and scaffolds. They generally wear safety glasses and must not wear jewelry or loose-fitting clothing that could easily get caught in a machine.

Those doing installation work do considerable bending, lifting, standing, climbing, and squatting, sometimes in close quarters or in awkward positions. Although installing duct systems and kitchen equipment is done indoors, the installation of siding, roofs, and gutters involves much outdoor work, requiring sheetmetal workers to work in all kinds of weather.

## Employment

Sheetmetal workers held about 100,00 wage and salary jobs in the construction industry in 1994. Three-fourths worked for plumbing, heating, and air-conditioning contractors; most of the rest worked for roofing and sheetmetal contractors; and a few worked for other special trade contractors and for general contractors engaged in residential and commercial building. Unlike many other construction trades, very few sheetmetal workers are self-employed.

Jobs for sheetmetal workers are distributed throughout the country in about the same proportion as the total population.

## Training, Other Qualifications, and Advancement

Sheetmetal contractors consider apprenticeship the best way to learn this trade. The apprenticeship program consists of four or five years of on-the-job training and a minimum of 144 hours per year of classroom instruction. Apprenticeship programs provide comprehensive instruction in both sheetmetal fabrication and installation. They are administered by local joint committees composed of the Sheet Metal Workers' International Association and local chapters of the Sheet Metal and Air-Conditioning Contractors National Association, or by local chapters of the Associated Builders and Contractors.

On the job, apprentices learn the basics of pattern layout and how to cut, bend, fabricate, and install sheet metal. They begin with basic ductwork and gradually advance to more difficult jobs, such as making more complex ducts, fittings, and decorative pieces. They also use materials such as fiberglass, plastics, and other non-metallic materials.

In the classroom, apprentices learn drafting, plan and specification reading, trigonometry and geometry applicable to layout work, the use of computerized equipment, welding, and the principles of heating, air-conditioning, and ventilating systems. Safety is stressed throughout the program. In addition, apprentices learn the relationship between sheetmetal work and other construction work.

A relatively small number of persons pick up the trade informally, usually by working as helpers to experienced sheetmetal workers. Most begin by carrying metal and cleaning up debris in a metal shop while they learn about materials and tools and their uses. Later, they learn to operate machines that bend or cut metal. In time, helpers go out on the job site to learn installation. Those who acquire their skills this way often take vocational school courses in mathematics or sheetmetal fabrication to supplement their work experience. To be promoted to the journey level, helpers usually must pass the same written examination as apprentices.

Applicants for jobs as apprentices or helpers should be in good physical condition and have mechanical and mathematical aptitude. Good eye-hand coordination, spatial and form perception, and manual dexterity are also important. Local apprenticeship committees require a high school education or its equivalent. Courses in Algebra, trigonometry, geometry, mechanical drawing, and shop provide a helpful background for learning the trade, as does work experience obtained in the Armed Services.

It is important that experienced sheetmetal workers keep abreast of new technological developments such as the growing use of computerized layout and laser cutting machines. Workers often take additional training provided by the union or by their employer in order to improve existing skills or to acquire new ones.

Sheetmetal workers may advance to supervisory jobs. Some take additional training in welding and do more specialized work. Others go into the contracting business for themselves. Because a sheetmetal contractor must have a shop with equipment to fabricate products, this type of contracting business is more expensive to start than other types of construction contracting.

### Job Outlook

Opportunities should be good for individuals who acquire for apprenticeship training. Employment of sheetmetal workers in construction is expected to increase about as fast as the average for all occupations reflecting the growth of that sector. Demand for sheetmetal installation should increase as more industrial, commercial, and residential structures are built. Growing demand for more energy-efficient air-conditioning, heating, and ventilation systems in the growing stock of older buildings, as well as other types of renovation and maintenance work, also should boost employment. In addition, the greater use of decorative sheetmetal products and increased architectural restoration are expected to add to the demand for sheetmetal workers. Despite this growth in demand, most job openings will result from the need to replace workers who leave the occupation.

Job prospects are expected to be good for skilled sheetmetal workers over the long run, although workers may experience periods of unemployment when construction projects end and when economic conditions reduce the amount of construction activity. Because local economic conditions can vary so widely, there can be shortages of experienced workers in some areas and an oversupply in other parts of the country. The availability of training slots also fluctuates with economic conditions, so the number of openings may vary from year to year and by geographic area. Nevertheless, employment of sheetmetal workers is less sensitive to declines in new construction than employment of some other construction workers, such as carpenters. Maintenance of existing equipment—which is less affected by economic fluctuations than new construction—makes up a large part of the work done by sheetmetal workers. Installation of new air-conditioning and heating systems in existing buildings also continues during construction slumps as individuals and businesses seek more energy-efficient equipment to cut utility bills. In addition, a large proportion of sheetmetal installation and maintenance is done indoors so these workers usually lose less work time due to bad weather than other construction workers.

### Earnings

Median weekly earnings for sheetmetal workers working full-time were about $444 a week in 1994. The middle 50 percent earned between $317 and $692 a week. The top 10 percent earned more than $914 and the lowest 10 percent less than $283 a week.

According to the Engineering News Record, average hourly earnings—including benefits—for union sheetmetal workers were $29.40 in 1994. Wages ranged from a low of $19.92 in Birmingham, Alabama, to a high of $46.69 in New York City. Apprentices generally start at about 40 percent of the rate paid to experienced workers. As they acquire more skills of the trade throughout the course of the apprenticeship program, they receive periodic increases until their pay approaches that of experienced workers. In addition, union workers in some areas receive supplemental wages from the union when they are on layoff or shortened workweeks. Many sheetmetal workers are members of the Sheet Metal Workers' International Association.

### Related Occupations

To fabricate and install sheetmetal products, sheetmetal workers combine metalworking skills and knowledge of construction materials and techniques. Other occupations in which workers lay out and fabricate metal products include layout workers, machinists, metal fabricators, metal patternmakers, shipfitters, and tool and die makers. Construction occupations requiring similar skills and knowledge include heating, air-conditioning, and refrigeration technicians and glaziers.

### Related *D.O.T.* Jobs

These job titles are related to or more specific than the more general description above. They will help you identify job options you may not otherwise discover. These descriptions are in the current edition of the *Dictionary of Occupational Titles* and classified by numerical order.

804.281-010 SHEET-METAL WORKER; 804.281-014 SHEET-METAL-WORKER APPRENTICE

### Sources of Additional Information

For more information about apprenticeships or other work opportunities, contact local sheetmetal contractors or heating, refrigeration, and air-conditioning contractors; a local of the Sheet Metal Workers; a local of the Sheetmetal and Air Conditioning Contractors Association; a local joint union-management apprenticeship committee; or the nearest office of the state employment service or apprenticeship agency.

For general information about sheetmetal workers, contact:

- ❏ The Sheet Metal National Training Fund, 601 N. Fairfax St., Suite 240, Alexandria, VA 22314.

- ❏ Associated Builders and Contractors, 1300 N. 17th St. NW, Rosslyn, VA 22209.

- ❏ The Sheetmetal and Air Conditioning Contractors Association, 4201 Lafayette Center Dr., Chantilly, VA 22021.

- ❏ The Sheet Metal Workers International Association, 1750 New York Ave. NW, Washington, DC 20006.

# Shoe and Leather Workers and Repairers

### Nature of the Work

Creating stylish and durable leather products is the job of precision shoe and leather workers; keeping them in good condition is the work of repairers. Among the workers who do leather work and repair are custom orthopedic shoemakers, saddle makers, and luggage makers. Although these workers produce different goods, their duties are actually quite similar.

Depending on the size of the factory or shop, a leather worker may perform one or more of the steps required to complete a product. In smaller factories or shops, workers generally perform several tasks, while those in larger facilities tend to specialize. However, most leather workers eventually learn the different skills involved in producing leather goods as they move from one task to another.

Leather workers must first check the leather for texture, color, and strength. They then place a pattern of the item being produced on the leather, trace the pattern onto the leather, cut along the outline, and sew the pieces together. Other steps may vary according to the type of good being produced.

*Orthopedic shoemakers*, for example, attach the insoles to shoe lasts (a wooden form shaped like a foot), affix the shoe uppers, and apply heels and outsoles. They shape the heels with a knife and then sand them on a buffing wheel for smoothness. Finally, they dye and polish the shoes. Custom shoe workers also may modify existing footwear for people with foot problems and special needs. This can involve preparing inserts, heel pads, and lifts from casts of customers' feet.

*Saddle makers* often apply leather dyes and liquid top coats to produce a gloss finish on a saddle. They may also decorate the saddle surface by hand stitching or by stamping the leather with decorative patterns and designs. *Luggage makers* fasten leather to a frame and attach handles and other hardware. They also cut and secure linings inside the frames and sew or stamp designs onto the luggage exterior.

*Shoe and leather repairers* use their knowledge of leatherworking to give worn leather goods extended wearability. The most common type of shoe repair is replacing soles and heels. Repairers place the shoe on a last and remove the old sole and heel with a knife or pliers or both. They attach new soles and heels to shoes either by stitching them in place or by using cement or nails. Other leather goods, suitcases or handbags, for example, may need seams to be re-sewn or handles and linings to be replaced.

Leather workers and repairers use handtools and machines. The most commonly used handtools are knives, hammers, awls (used to poke holes in leather to make sewing possible), and skivers (for splitting leather). Power-operated equipment includes sewing machines, heel nailing machines, hole punching machines, and sole stitchers.

Self-employed shoe repairers and owners of custom-made shoe and leather shops have managerial responsibilities in addition to their regular duties. They must maintain good relations with their customers, make business decisions, and keep accurate records.

## Working Conditions

Working conditions of leather workers vary according to the type of work performed, the size of the factory or business, and the practices of each individual shop.

Workers employed in custom leather goods manufacturing establishments generally work a regular 40-hour week. Those in repair shops work nights and weekends and often work irregular hours. For those who own their own repair shop, long hours are common. Although there are few health hazards if precautions are followed, work areas can be noisy and odors from leather dyes and stains are often present.

## Employment

Shoe and leather workers and repairers held about 24,000 jobs in 1994. Self-employed individuals, who typically own and operate small shoe repair shops or specialty leather manufacturing firms, held about 7,000 of these jobs. Of the remaining workers, about half were employed in the manufacture of footwear products, and an additional one-fifth were employed in production of leather goods such as luggage, handbags, and apparel. Another fifth worked in shoe repair and shoeshine shops.

## Training, Other Qualifications, and Advancement

Precision shoe and leather workers and repairers generally learn their craft on the job, either through in-house training programs or working as helpers to experienced workers. Helpers generally begin by performing simple tasks and then progress to more difficult projects like cutting or stitching leather. Trainees generally become fully skilled in six months to two years; the length of training varies according to the nature of the work and the aptitude and dedication of the individual.

A limited number of schools offer vocational training in shoe repair and leather work. These programs may last from six months to a year and impart basic skills including leather cutting, stitching, and dyeing. Students learn shoe construction, practice shoe repair, and study the fundamentals of running a small business. Graduates are encouraged to gain additional training by working with an experienced leather worker or repairer. National and regional associations also offer specialized training seminars and workshops in custom shoe making, shoe repair, and other leather work.

Manual dexterity and the mechanical aptitude to work with handtools and machines are important in the shoe repair and leatherworking occupations. Shoe and leather workers who produce custom goods should have artistic ability as well. These workers must have self-discipline to work alone under little supervision. In addition, leather workers and repairers who own shops will need to have a knowledge of business practices and management as well as a pleasant manner when dealing with customers.

Many individuals who begin as workers or repairers advance to salaried supervisory and managerial positions. Some may open their own shop or business.

## Job Outlook

Employment of shoe and leather workers is expected to decline through the year 2005. Inexpensive imports have made the cost of replacing shoes and leather goods cheaper or more convenient than repairing them, thus reducing the demand for shoe and leather repairers. These workers are also adversely affected by the rising cost of leather and higher rents in the high-traffic areas in which more shoe repairers are relocating. Some of the more expensive, fine leather products will continue to be repaired, however, and this demand will moderate the employment decline of shoe repairers. Consumers are also buying more comfort-soled leather shoes, which should also increase demand for the services provided by shoe repairers. In the future, though, most job openings in this occupation will arise from the need to replace experienced workers who transfer to other occupations or leave the workforce.

Prospects for workers employed in the manufacture and modification of custom-made molded or orthopedic shoes are better than those for most other leather workers. This is a result of substantial expected growth in the elderly population and an increasing emphasis on preventive foot care. The employment effects of these trends may be limited, however, since the demand for orthopedic footwear is increasingly fulfilled by manufactured shoes that are modified to specification instead of totally custom made.

## Earnings

Data on earnings of shoe and leather workers are very limited. Their earnings vary greatly depending upon the place of employment. Beginning workers often start near the minimum wage and can advance in just a few months. Owners of shoe repair and custom shoe manufacturing shops can earn substantially more.

## Related Occupations

Other workers who make or repair items using handtools and machinery include dressmakers, designers and patternmakers, and furriers.

## Related *D.O.T.* Jobs

These job titles are related to or more specific than the more general description above. They will help you identify job options you may not otherwise discover. These descriptions are in the current edition of the *Dictionary of Occupational Titles* and classified by numerical order.

365.361-010 LUGGAGE REPAIRER; 365.361-014 SHOE REPAIRER; 780.381-030 PAD HAND; 781.381-018 LEATHER STAMPER; 783.361-010 CUSTOM-LEATHER-PRODUCTS MAKER; 783.381-018 HARNESS MAKER; 783.381-022 LUGGAGE MAKER; 783.381-026 SADDLE MAKER; 788.261-010 ORTHOPEDIC-BOOT-AND-SHOE DESIGNER AND MAKER; 788.381-010 COBBLER; 788.381-014 SHOEMAKER, CUSTOM

## Sources of Additional Information

For information about the custom-made prescription shoe business, and about training opportunities in this field, contact:

❑ Pedorthic Footwear Association, 9861 Broken Land Pkwy., Suite 255, Columbia, MD 21046-1151.

For information about opportunities in shoe repair, contact:

❑ Shoe Service Institute of America, Educational Library, 5024-R Campbell Blvd., Baltimore, MD 21236-5974.

# Stationary Engineers

## Nature of the Work

Heating, air-conditioning, and ventilation systems are what keep large buildings comfortable all year long. Industrial plants often have facilities to provide electrical power, steam, or other services as well. Stationary engineers operate and maintain these systems, which can include boilers, air-conditioning and refrigeration equipment, diesel engines, turbines, generators, pumps, condensers, and compressors. These workers are called stationary engineers because the equipment they operate is similar to equipment operated by locomotive or marine engineers except it is not on a moving vehicle.

Stationary engineers start up, regulate, and shut down equipment. They ensure that it operates safely and economically and within established limits by monitoring attached meters, gauges, other instruments, and computerized controls. They manually control equipment, and if necessary, make adjustments. They use hand and power tools to perform repairs and maintenance ranging from a complete overhaul to replacing defective valves, gaskets, or bearings. They also record relevant events and facts concerning operation and maintenance in an equipment log. On steam boilers, for example, they observe, control, and record steam pressure, temperature, water level, power output, and fuel consumption. They watch and listen to machinery and routinely check safety devices, identifying and correcting any trouble that develops.

New building and plant systems are increasingly being run by stationary engineers using computers. These systems allow engineers to monitor, adjust, and diagnose systems from a central location or using a laptop computer linked into the buildings' communications network.

Stationary engineers also perform routine maintenance, such as lubricating moving parts, replacing filters, and removing soot and corrosion that can reduce operating efficiency. They test boiler water and add chemicals to prevent corrosion and harmful deposits. They also may check the air quality of the ventilation system and make adjustments to keep within mandated guidelines.

In a large building or industrial plant, a stationary engineer may be in charge of all mechanical systems in the building or an industrial power plant or engine room. Engineers may direct the work of assistant stationary engineers, turbine operators, boiler tenders, and air-conditioning and refrigeration operators and mechanics. In a small building or industrial plant, there may be only one stationary engineer.

## Working Conditions

Stationary engineers generally have steady year-round employment. They usually work a five-day, 40-hour week. Many work one of three daily eight-hour shifts, and weekend and holiday work often is required.

Engine rooms, power plants, and boiler rooms usually are clean and well lighted. Even under the most favorable conditions, however, some stationary engineers are exposed to high temperatures, dust, dirt, and high noise levels from the equipment. General maintenance duties may cause contact with oil and grease, as well as fumes or smoke. Workers spend much of their time on their feet; they also may have to crawl inside boilers and work in crouching or kneeling positions to inspect, clean, or repair equipment.

Because stationary engineers work around boilers as well as electrical and mechanical equipment, they must be alert to avoid burns, electric shock, and injury from moving parts. They also must be aware of exposure to hazardous materials such as asbestos and certain chemicals.

## Employment

Stationary engineers held about 30,000 jobs in 1994. They worked in a wide variety of places, including factories, hospitals, hotels, office and apartment buildings, schools, and shopping malls.

Stationary engineers work throughout the country, generally in the more heavily populated areas where large industrial and commercial establishments usually are located.

## Training, Other Qualifications, and Advancement

Most stationary engineers acquire their skills through a formal apprenticeship program or through informal on-the-job training which usually is supplemented by courses at trade or technical schools. In addition, a good background can be obtained in the Navy or the Merchant Marine because marine engineering plants are similar to many stationary power and heating plants. The increasing complexity of the equipment with which they work has made a high school diploma or its equivalent necessary; many stationary engineers have some college education.

Apprenticeship programs are sponsored by the International Union of Operating Engineers, the principal union to which stationary engineers belong. In selecting apprentices, most local labor-management apprenticeship committees prefer applicants who have received instruction in mathematics, computers, mechanical drawing, machine-shop practice, physics, and chemistry. Mechanical aptitude, manual dexterity, and good physical condition also are important.

An apprenticeship usually lasts four years. In addition to 8,000 hours of on-the-job training, apprentices receive 600 hours of classroom instruction in boiler design and operation, basic chemistry and water treatment, elementary physics, pneumatics, refrigeration and air conditioning, electricity and electronics, computer systems, and other technical subjects.

Those who acquire their skills on the job usually start as helpers to experienced stationary engineers or as boiler tenders. This practical experience may be supplemented by postsecondary vocational training in computerized controls and instrumentation. However, becoming a stationary engineer without going through a formal apprenticeship program usually requires many years of work experience.

Most large and some small employers encourage and pay for skill-improvement training for their employees. Training is almost always provided when new equipment is introduced, usually by a representative of the machinery manufacturer, or when regulations concerning some aspect of their duties change.

Most states and cities have licensing requirements for stationary engineers. Applicants usually must be at least 18 years of age, reside for a specified period in the state or locality, meet experience requirements, and pass a written examination. Because of regional differences in licensing requirements, a stationary engineer who moves from one state or city to another may have to pass an examination for a new license.

Generally, there are several classes of stationary engineer licenses, each specifying the type of equipment or the steam pressure or horsepower of the equipment the engineer can operate without supervision. A first-class license covers equipment of all types and capacities. A licensed first-class stationary engineer is qualified to run a large facility and to supervise others. An applicant for this license may be required to have a high school education, apprenticeship or on-the-job training, and several years of experience. Lower class licenses limit the types or capacities of equipment the engineer may operate without the supervision of a higher rated engineer.

Stationary engineers advance by being placed in charge of larger, more powerful, or more varied equipment. Generally, engineers advance to these jobs as they obtain higher class licenses. Some stationary engineers advance to boiler inspectors, chief plant engineers, building and plant superintendents, or building managers. A few obtain jobs as examining engineers or technical instructors.

## Job Outlook

Persons wishing to become stationary engineers may face competition because of the small number of openings expected through the year 2005. Although growing commercial and industrial development will increase the amount of equipment to be operated and maintained, automated systems and computerized controls will make newly installed equipment more efficient and reduce the number of stationary engineers needed. Therefore, employment of stationary engineers is expected to decline through the year 2005. Most of the job openings will arise from the need to replace experienced workers who transfer to other occupations or leave the labor force. Because turnover in this occupation is low, partly due to its high wages, relatively few replacement openings are expected.

Due to the increasing complexity of power-generating systems, job opportunities will be best for those with apprenticeship training or vocational school courses in computerized controls and instrumentation.

## Earnings

In 1994, the median weekly earnings for stationary engineers who worked full-time were about $591. The middle 50 percent earned between $430 and $758 a week; 10 percent earned less than $304 a week; and 10 percent earned more than $977.

## Related Occupations

Other workers who monitor and operate stationary machinery include nuclear reactor operators, power station operators, water and wastewater treatment plant operators, waterworks pump-station operators, chemical operators, and refinery operators.

## Related *D.O.T.* Jobs

These job titles are related to or more specific than the more general description above. They will help you identify job options you may not otherwise discover. These descriptions are in the current edition of the *Dictionary of Occupational Titles* and classified by numerical order.

950.362-014 REFRIGERATING ENGINEER; 950.382-010 BOILER OPERATOR; 950.382-018 GAS-ENGINE OPERATOR; 950.382-026 STATIONARY ENGINEER; 950.382-030 STATIONARY-ENGINEER APPRENTICE

## Sources of Additional Information

Information about training or work opportunities is available from local offices of state employment services, locals of the International Union of Operating Engineers, and from state and local licensing agencies.

Specific questions about the occupation should be addressed to:

❏ International Union of Operating Engineers, 1125 17th St. NW, Washington, DC 20036.

❏ National Association of Power Engineers, Inc., 1 Springfield St., Chicopee, MA 01013.

❏ Building Owners and Managers Institute International, 1521 Ritchie Hwy., Suite 3A, Arnold, MD 21403.

# Structural and Reinforcing Ironworkers

## Nature of the Work

Materials made from iron, steel, aluminum, and bronze are used extensively in the construction of highways, bridges, office buildings, power transmission towers, and other large buildings. These structures have frames made of steel columns, beams, and girders. In addition, reinforced concrete—concrete containing steel bars or wire fabric—is an important material in buildings, bridges, and other structures. The steel gives the concrete additional strength. Metal stairways, catwalks, floor gratings, ladders, and window frames, as well as lampposts, railings, fences, and decorative ironwork are used to make these structures more functional and attractive. Structural and reinforcing ironworkers fabricate, assemble, and install these products. These workers also repair, renovate, and maintain older buildings and structures such as steel mills, utility plants, automobile factories, highways, and bridges.

Before construction can begin, ironworkers must erect the steel frames and assemble the cranes and derricks that move structural steel, reinforcing bars, buckets of concrete, lumber, and other materials and equipment around the construction site. This equipment arrives at the construction site in sections. There it is lifted into position by a mobile crane. Ironworkers then connect the sections and set up the cables that do the hoisting.

Once this job has been completed, *structural ironworkers* begin to connect steel columns, beams, and girders according to blueprints and instructions from supervisors and superintendents. Structural steel, reinforcing rods, and ornamental iron generally are delivered to the construction site ready for erection—cut to the proper size with holes drilled for bolts and numbered for assembly. This work is done by ironworkers in fabricating shops located away from the construction site. There they lay out the raw steel received from a steel mill and cut, bend, drill, bolt, and weld each piece according to the specifications for that particular job. Ironworkers at the construction site unload and stack the fabricated steel so it can be hoisted easily when needed.

To hoist the steel, ironworkers attach cables from the crane or derrick. One worker directs the hoist operator with hand signals. Another worker holds a rope (tag line) attached to the steel to prevent it from swinging. The steel is hoisted into place in the framework, where several workers using spud wrenches position it with connecting bars and jacks. Workers use driftpins or the handle of a spud wrench—a long wrench with a pointed handle—to align the holes in the steel with the holes in the framework. Then they bolt the piece in place temporarily, check vertical and horizontal alignment with plumb bobs, laser equipment, transits, or levels and then bolt or weld it permanently in place.

*Reinforcing ironworkers* set the bars in the forms that hold concrete, following blueprints that show the location, size, and number of reinforcing bars. They fasten the bars together by tying wire around them with pliers. When reinforcing floors, workers place blocks under the reinforcing bars to hold them off the deck. Although these materials usually arrive ready to use, ironworkers occasionally have to cut the bars with metal shears or acetylene torches, bend them by hand or machine, or weld them with arc-welding equipment. Some concrete is reinforced with welded wire fabric. Workers cut and fit the fabric and, while a concrete crew places the concrete, ironworkers use hooked rods to position it properly in the concrete.

Ornamental ironwork and related pieces are installed after the exterior of the building has been completed. As the pieces are hoisted into position, ironworkers bring them into position, make sure they fit correctly, and bolt, braze, or weld them for a secure fit. They also erect metal tanks used to store petroleum, water, or other fluids and assemble prefabricated metal buildings according to plans or specifications.

## Working Conditions

Structural and reinforcing ironworkers usually work outside in all kinds of weather. However, those who work at great heights do not work when it is wet, icy, or extremely windy. Because the danger of injuries due to falls is so great, ironworkers use safety devices such as safety belts, scaffolding, and nets to reduce the risk.

## Employment

Structural and reinforcing ironworkers held about 61,000 jobs in 1994. Almost all of these workers were employed in the construction industry. Nearly 6 of every 10 worked for structural steel erection contractors; most of the remainder worked for a variety of contractors specializing in the construction of homes, factories, commercial buildings, churches, schools, bridges and tunnels, and water, sewer, communications, and power lines. Very few were self-employed.

Ironworkers are employed in all parts of the country, but most work in metropolitan areas, where most commercial and industrial construction takes place.

## Training, Other Qualifications, and Advancement

Most employers recommend apprenticeship as the best way to learn this trade. The apprenticeship consists of three years of on-the-job training and a minimum of 144 hours a year of classroom instruction. Apprenticeship programs are usually administered by joint union-management committees made up of representatives of local unions of the International Association of Bridge, Structural and Ornamental Ironworkers and local chapters of contractors' associations.

Ironworkers generally must be at least 18 years old. A high school diploma may be preferred by employers and may be required by some local apprenticeship committees. High School courses in general mathematics, mechanical drawing, and shop are helpful. Because materials used in ironworking are heavy and bulky, ironworkers must be in good physical condition. They also need good agility, balance, eyesight, and spatial perception in order to work at great heights on narrow beams and girders. Ironworkers should not be afraid of heights or suffer from dizziness.

In the classroom, apprentices study blueprint reading, mathematics for layout work, the basics of structural erecting, rigging, reinforcing, welding and burning, ornamental erection and assembling, and the care and safe use of tools and materials. On the job, apprentices work in all aspects of the trade, such as unloading and storing materials at the job site, rigging materials for movement by crane or derrick, connecting structural steel, and welding.

Some ironworkers learn the trade informally on the job without completing an apprenticeship. These workers generally do not receive classroom training, although some large contractors have extensive training programs. On-the-job trainees usually begin by assisting experienced ironworkers by doing simple jobs, like carrying various materials. With experience, they perform more difficult tasks like cutting and fitting different parts. Learning through work experience alone may not provide training as complete as an apprenticeship program, however, and usually takes longer.

Some experienced workers become supervisors. Others may go into the contracting business for themselves.

## Job Outlook

Employment of structural and reinforcing ironworkers is expected to increase more slowly than the average for all occupations through the year 2005. The rehabilitation and maintenance of an increasing number of older buildings, factories, power plants, and highways and bridges is expected to increase, but employment growth will be slowed by the continued slow growth in industrial and commercial construction. In addition, more ironworkers will be needed to build incinerators and other structures to contain hazardous materials as part of ongoing toxic waste cleanup. Although employment growth will create many new jobs for structural and reinforcing ironworkers, most openings will result from the need to replace experienced ironworkers who transfer to other occupations or leave the labor force.

The number of job openings fluctuates from year to year as economic conditions and the level of construction activity change. During economic downturns, ironworkers can experience high rates of unemployment. Similarly, job opportunities for ironworkers may vary widely by geographic area. Job openings for ironworkers usually are more abundant during the spring and summer months, when the level of construction activity increases.

## Earnings

Median weekly earnings of structural and reinforcing ironworkers employed full-time were about $611 a week in 1994. The middle 50 percent earned between $494 and $813 a week. The top 10 percent earned more than $1,040 and the lowest 10 percent less than $414 a week.

According to the *Engineering News Record*, prevailing union wage rates—including benefits—for ironworkers averaged about $28.95 an hour in 1994. Their wages ranged from a low of about $18.50 in New Orleans, to a high of between $42.26 and $52.85 in New York City.

Apprentices generally start at about 40 percent of the rate paid to experienced workers. They receive periodic increases throughout the course of the apprenticeship program as they acquire the skills of the trade until their pay approaches that of experienced workers.

Earnings for ironworkers may be reduced on occasion because work can be limited by bad weather and the short-term nature of construction jobs.

Many workers in this trade are members of the International Association of Bridge, Structural and Ornamental Ironworkers.

### Related Occupations

Structural and reinforcing ironworkers play an essential role in erecting buildings, bridges, highways, power lines, and other structures. Others who also work on these construction jobs are operating engineers, concrete masons, and welders.

### Related *D.O.T.* Jobs

These job titles are related to or more specific than the more general description above. They will help you identify job options you may not otherwise discover. These descriptions are in the current edition of the *Dictionary of Occupational Titles* and classified by numerical order.

801.361-014 STRUCTURAL-STEEL WORKER; 801.361-018 STRUCTURAL-STEEL-WORKER APPRENTICE; 801.361-022 TANK SETTER; 801.381-010 ASSEMBLER, METAL BUILDING; 801.684-026 REINFORCING-METAL WORKER; 809.381-022 ORNAMENTAL-IRON WORKER; 809.381-026 ORNAMENTAL-IRON-WORKER APPRENTICE

### Sources of Additional Information

For more information on apprenticeships or other work opportunities, contact local general contractors; a local of the International Association of Bridge, Structural and Ornamental Ironworkers union; a local joint ironworkers' union-management apprenticeship committee; a local or state chapter of the Associated Builders and Contractors, or the nearest office of the state employment service or apprenticeship agency.

For general information about ironworkers, contact:

❏ Associated General Contractors of America, Inc., 1300 North 17th St., Rosslyn, VA 22209-3883

❏ International Association of Bridge, Structural and Ornamental Ironworkers, 1750 New York Ave. NW, Suite 400, Washington, DC 20006.

❏ National Erectors Association, 1501 Lee Hwy., Suite 202, Arlington, VA 22209.

❏ National Association of Reinforcing Steel Contractors, P.O. Box 280, Fairfax, VA 22030.

# Surgical Technologists

## Nature of the Work

Surgical technologists, also called surgical or operating room technicians, assist in operations under the supervision of surgeons, registered nurses, or other surgical personnel. Before an operation, surgical technologists help set up the operating room with surgical instruments and equipment, sterile linens, and sterile solutions. They assemble, adjust, and check nonsterile equipment to ensure that it is working properly. Technologists also prepare patients for surgery by washing, shaving, and disinfecting incision sites. They transport patients to the operating room, help position them on the operating table, and cover them with sterile surgical "drapes." Technologists also observe patients' vital signs, check charts, and help the surgical team scrub and put on gloves, gowns, and masks.

During surgery, technologists pass instruments and other sterile supplies to surgeons and surgeon assistants. They may hold retractors, cut sutures, and help count sponges, needles, supplies, and instruments. Surgical technologists help prepare, care for, and dispose of specimens taken for laboratory analysis and may help apply dressings. They may operate sterilizers, lights, or suction machines, and help operate diagnostic equipment. Technologists may also maintain supplies of fluids, such as plasma and blood.

After an operation, surgical technologists may help transfer patients to the recovery room and clean and restock the operating room.

## Working Conditions

Surgical technologists work in clean, well-lit, cool environments. They must stand for long periods of time and remain alert during operations. At times they may be exposed to communicable diseases and unpleasant sights, odors, and materials.

Most surgical technologists work a regular 40-hour week, although they may be on call or work nights, weekends and holidays on a rotating basis.

## Employment

Surgical technologists held about 46,000 jobs in 1994. Most surgical technologists are employed by hospitals, mainly in operating and delivery rooms. Others are employed in clinics and surgical centers, and in the offices of physicians and dentists who perform outpatient surgery. A few, known as private scrubs, are employed directly by surgeons who have special surgical teams like those for liver transplants.

## Training, Other Qualifications, and Advancement

Surgical technologists receive their training in formal programs offered by community and junior colleges, vocational schools, universities, hospitals, and the military. In 1995, the Commission on Accreditation of Allied Health Education Programs (CAAHEP) recognized 147 accredited programs. High school graduation normally is required for admission. Programs last 9 to 24 months and lead to a certificate, diploma, or associate degree. Shorter programs are designed for students who are already licensed practical nurses or military personnel.

Programs provide classroom education and supervised clinical experience. Students take courses in anatomy, physiology, microbiology, pharmacology, professional ethics, and medical terminology. Other studies cover the care and safety of patients during surgery, aseptic techniques, and surgical procedures. Students also learn to sterilize instruments; prevent and control infection; and handle special drugs, solutions, supplies, and equipment.

Technologists may obtain voluntary professional certification from the Liaison Council on Certification for the Surgical Technologist by graduating from a formal program and passing a national certification examination. They may then use the designation Certified Surgical Technologist, or CST. Continuing education or reexamination is required to maintain certification, which

must be renewed every six years. Some employers prefer to hire certified technologists.

Surgical technologists need manual dexterity to handle instruments quickly. They also must be conscientious, orderly, and emotionally stable to handle the demands of the operating room environment. Technologists must respond quickly and know procedures well so that they may have instruments ready for surgeons without having to be told. They are expected to keep abreast of new developments in the field. Recommended high school courses include health, biology, chemistry, and mathematics.

Technologists advance by specializing in a particular area of surgery, such as neurosurgery or open heart surgery. They may also work as circulating technologists. A circulating technologist is the "unsterile" member of the surgical team who prepares patients; helps with anesthesia; gets, opens, and holds packages for the "sterile" persons during the procedure; interviews the patient before surgery; keeps a written account of the surgical procedure; and answers the surgeon's questions about the patient during the surgery. With additional training, some technologists advance to first assistants, who help with retracting, sponging, suturing, cauterizing bleeders, and closing and treating wounds. Some surgical technologists manage central supply departments in hospitals, or take positions with insurance companies, sterile supply services, and operating equipment firms.

## Job Outlook

Employment of surgical technologists is expected to grow much faster than the average for all occupations through the year 2005, as the volume of surgery increases and operating room staffing patterns change.

The number of surgical procedures is expected to rise as the population grows and ages. Older people require more surgical procedures. Technological advances, such as fiber optics and laser technology, will also permit new surgical procedures. Some employers may seek to substitute surgical technologists for operating room nurses to reduce costs.

Hospitals will continue to be the primary employer of surgical technologists. Nonetheless, the shift to outpatient or ambulatory surgery will create much faster than average growth for technologists in offices and clinics of physicians, including surgical centers.

## Earnings

According to a University of Texas Medical Branch survey of hospitals and medical centers, the median annual salary of surgical technologists, based on a 40-hour week and excluding shift or area differentials, was $22,285 in October 1994. The average minimum salary was $18,881 and the average maximum was $27,690.

## Related Occupations

Other health occupations requiring approximately one year of training after high school include licensed practical nurses, respiratory therapy technicians, medical laboratory assistants, medical assistants, dental assistants, optometric assistants, and physical therapy aides.

## Related *D.O.T.* Jobs

These job titles are related to or more specific than the more general description above. They will help you identify job options you may not otherwise discover. These descriptions are in the current edition of the *Dictionary of Occupational Titles* and classified by numerical order.

079.374-022 SURGICAL TECHNICIAN

## Sources of Additional Information

For additional information on a career as a surgical technologist and a list of CAAHEP-accredited programs, contact:

❏ Association of Surgical Technologists, 7108-C S. Alton Way, Englewood, CO 80112.

For information on certification, contact:

❏ Liaison Council on Certification for the Surgical Technologist, 7108-C S. Alton Way, Englewood, CO 80112.

# Surveyors

## Nature of the Work

Three groups of workers measure and map the earth's surface. *Land surveyors* establish official land, air space, and water boundaries. They write descriptions of land for deeds, leases, and other legal documents; define air space for airports; and measure construction and mineral sites. *Survey technicians*, assist land surveyors by operating survey instruments and collecting information. *Mapping scientists* and other surveyors collect geographic information and prepare maps of large areas.

Land surveyors manage survey parties that measure distances, directions, and angles between points and elevations of points, lines, and contours on the earth's surface. They plan the fieldwork, select known survey reference points, and determine the precise location of important features in the survey area. Surveyors research legal records and look for evidence of previous boundaries. They record the results of the survey, verify the accuracy of data, and prepare plats, maps, and reports. Surveyors who establish boundaries must be licensed by the state in which they work.

The information needed by the land surveyor is gathered by a survey party. A typical survey party is made up of a party chief and several survey technicians and helpers. The party chief, who may be either a land surveyor or a senior survey technician, leads the day-to-day work activities. The party chief is assisted by survey technicians, who adjust and operate surveying instruments such as the theodolite (used to measure horizontal and vertical angles) and electronic distance-measuring equipment. Survey technicians or assistants position and hold the vertical rods or targets that the theodolite operator sights on to measure angles, distances, or elevations. They may also hold measuring tapes and chains if electronic distance-measuring equipment is not used. Survey technicians compile notes, make sketches, and enter the data obtained from these instruments into computers. Some survey parties include laborers or helpers to clear brush from sight lines, drive stakes, carry equipment, and perform other less skilled duties.

New technology is changing the nature of the work of surveyors and survey technicians. For larger surveying projects, surveyors are increasingly using the Global Positioning System (GPS), a satellite system which precisely locates points on the earth using radio signals transmitted by satellites. To use it, a surveyor places a satellite receiver—about the size of a backpack—on a desired point. The receiver collects information from several differently positioned satellites simultaneously to locate its precise position. Two receivers are generally operated in synchronization, one at a known point and the other at the unknown point. The receiver can also be placed in a vehicle to trace out road systems, or for other uses. The cost of the receivers has fallen and much more surveying work is being done by GPS.

Mapping scientists, like land surveyors, measure, map, and chart the earth's surface but generally cover much larger areas. Unlike land surveyors, however, mapping scientists work mainly in offices and seldom visit the sites they are mapping. Mapping scientists include workers in several occupations. *Cartographers* prepare maps using information provided by geodetic surveys, aerial photographs, and satellite data. *Photogrammetrists* prepare maps and drawings by measuring and interpreting aerial photographs, using analytical processes and mathematical formulas. Photogrammetrists make detailed maps of areas that are inaccessible or difficult to survey by other methods. *Map editors* develop and verify map contents from aerial photographs and other reference sources.

Some surveyors perform specialized functions which are closer to mapping science than traditional surveying. *Geodetic surveyors* use high-accuracy techniques, including satellite observations, to measure large areas of the earth's surface. *Geophysical prospecting surveyors* mark sites for subsurface exploration, usually petroleum related. *Marine surveyors* survey harbors, rivers, and other bodies of water to determine shorelines, topography of the bottom, water depth, and other features.

The work of mapping scientists is changing due to advancements in technology. These advancements include the GPS, Geographic Information Systems (GIS)—which are computerized data banks of spatial data—new earth resources data satellites, and improved aerial photography. From the older specialties of photogrammetrist or cartographer, a new type of mapping scientist is emerging. The *geographic information specialist* combines the functions of mapping science and surveying into a broader field concerned with the collection and analysis of geographic spatial information.

## Working Conditions

Surveyors usually work an eight-hour day, five days a week, and spend a lot of their time outdoors. Sometimes they work longer hours during the summer, when weather and light conditions are most suitable for fieldwork.

Land surveyors and technicians do active and sometimes strenuous work. They often stand for long periods, walk long distances, and climb hills with heavy packs of instruments and equipment. They are also exposed to all types of weather. Occasionally, they may commute long distances, stay overnight, or even temporarily relocate near a survey site.

Surveyors also spend considerable time in offices, planning surveys, analyzing data, and preparing reports and maps. Most computations and map drafting are performed on a computer. Mapping scientists spend virtually all their time in offices.

## Employment

Surveyors held about 96,000 jobs in 1994. Engineering, architectural, and surveying firms employed over three-fifths of all surveyors. Federal, state, and local government agencies employed an additional quarter. Major federal government employers are the U.S. Geological Survey, the Bureau of Land Management, the Army Corps of Engineers, the Forest Service, the National Oceanic and Atmospheric Administration, and the Defense Mapping Agency. Most surveyors in state and local government work for highway departments and urban planning and redevelopment agencies. Construction firms, mining and oil and gas extraction companies, and public utilities also employ surveyors. About 7,000 surveyors were self-employed in 1994.

## Training, Other Qualifications, and Advancement

Most people prepare for a career as a licensed surveyor by combining postsecondary school courses in surveying with extensive on-the-job training. About 25 universities offer four-year programs leading to a B.S. degree in surveying. Junior and community colleges, technical institutes, and vocational schools offer one-, two-, and three-year programs in both surveying and surveying technology.

All 50 states license land surveyors. For licensure, most state licensing boards require that individuals pass two written examinations, one prepared by the state and one given by the National Council of Examiners for Engineering and Surveying. In addition, they must meet varying standards of formal education and work experience in the field. In the past, many surveyors started as members of survey crews and worked their way up to licensed surveyor with little formal training in surveying. However, due to advancing technology and an increase in licensing standards, formal education requirements are increasing. Most states at the present time require some formal post-high school education coursework and 10 to 12 years of surveying experience to gain licensure. However, requirements vary among the states. Generally, the quickest route to licensure is a combination of four years of college, two to four years of experience (a few states do not require any), and passing the licensing examinations. An increasing number of states require a bachelor's degree in surveying or in a closely related field, such as civil engineering or forestry, with courses in surveying.

High school students interested in surveying should take courses in algebra, geometry, trigonometry, drafting, mechanical drawing, and computer science.

High school graduates with no formal training in surveying usually start as an apprentice. Beginners with postsecondary school training in surveying can generally start as technicians or assistants. With on-the-job experience and formal training in surveying—either in an institutional program or from a correspondence school—workers may advance to senior survey technician, then to party chief, and in some cases, to licensed surveyor (depending on state licensing requirements).

The American Congress on Surveying and Mapping has a voluntary certification program for survey technicians. Technicians are certified at four levels that require progressive amounts of experience and passing written examinations. Although not required for state licensure, many employers require certification for promotion to positions with greater responsibilities.

Cartographers and photogrammetrists usually have a bachelor's degree in engineering or a physical science. It also is possible to enter these positions through previous experience as a photogrammetric or cartographic technician. Most cartographic and photogrammetric technicians have had some specialized postsecondary school training. With the development of Geographic Information Systems, cartographers, photogrammetrists, and other mapping scientists need additional education and more experience with computers than in the past.

The American Society for Photogrammetry and Remote Sensing has voluntary certification programs for photogrammetrists and mapping scientists. To qualify for these professional distinctions, individuals must meet work experience standards and pass an oral or written examination.

Surveyors should have the ability to visualize objects, distances, sizes, and other abstract forms. They have to work with precision and accuracy because mistakes can be costly. Surveying is a cooperative process, so good interpersonal skills and the ability to work as part of a team are important. Leadership qualities are important for party chief and other supervisory positions.

Members of a survey party must be in good physical condition to work outdoors and carry equipment over difficult terrain. They need good eyesight, coordination, and hearing to communicate via hand and voice signals.

## Job Outlook

Employment of surveyors is expected to decline slightly through the year 2005. The widespread use of GPS and remote sensing technologies is increasing both the accuracy and productivity of surveyors. Job openings will result from the need to replace workers who transfer to other occupations or leave the labor force.

Growth in construction through the year 2005 should require surveyors to lay out streets, shopping centers, housing developments, factories, office buildings, and recreation areas. Continuing road and highway construction and improvements should also require surveyors. However, employment may fluctuate from year to year along with construction activity.

The employment of mapping scientists and other surveyors by private firms, and the federal government is expected to decline due to budget cutbacks and technological efficiency.

Opportunities will be best for surveyors and mapping scientists who have at least a bachelor's degree as a result of trends toward more complex technology, upgraded licensing requirements, and the increased demand for geographic spatial data (as opposed to traditional surveying services). New technology such as GPS and GIS may increase productivity for larger projects and may enhance employment opportunities for surveyors and survey technicians who have the educational background to use it, but limit opportunities for those with less education.

## Earnings

The median weekly earnings for surveyors and mapping scientists were about $590 a week in 1994. The middle 50 percent earned between $420 and $840 a week; 10 percent earned less than $340 a week; 10 percent earned more than $950 a week.

The median annual earnings for survey technicians were about $520 a week in 1994. The middle 50 percent earned between $390 and $750 a week; 10 percent earned less than $300 a week; 10 percent earned more than $960 a week.

In 1995, the federal government hired high school graduates with little or no training or experience at salaries or about $15,800 annually for entry-level jobs on survey crews. Those with one year of related postsecondary training earned about $18,500 a year. Those with an associate degree that included coursework in surveying generally started as instrument assistants with an annual salary of about $21,300. In 1995, entry-level land surveyors or cartographers with the federal government earned about $24,500 or $29,900 a year, depending on their qualifications. The average annual salary for federal land surveyors in 1995 was about $44,200, for cartographers, about $47,700, and for geodesists, about $50,200. The average annual salary for federal surveying technicians was about $24,400, for cartographic technicians, about $32,100, and for geodetic technicians, about $40,900.

## Related Occupations

Surveying is related to the work of civil engineers and architects, since an accurate survey is the first step in land development and construction projects. Mapping science and geodetic surveying are related to the work of geologists and geophysicists, who study the earth's internal composition, surface, and atmosphere. Mapping science is also related to the work of geographers and urban planners, who study how the earth's surface is used.

## Related *D.O.T.* Jobs

These job titles are related to or more specific than the more general description above. They will help you identify job options you may not otherwise discover. These descriptions are in the current edition of the *Dictionary of Occupational Titles* and classified by numerical order.

018.131-010 SUPERVISOR, CARTOGRAPHY; 018.161-010 SURVEYOR, MINE; 018.167-010 CHIEF OF PARTY; 018.167-014 GEODETIC COMPUTATOR; 018.167-018 LAND SURVEYOR; 018.167-026 PHOTOGRAMMETRIC ENGINEER; 018.167-030 SUPERVISOR, MAPPING; 018.167-034 SURVEYOR ASSISTANT, INSTRUMENTS; 018.167-038 SURVEYOR, GEODETIC; 018.167-042 SURVEYOR, GEOPHYSICAL PROSPECTING; 018.167-046 SURVEYOR, MARINE; 018.261-010 DRAFTER, CARTOGRAPHIC; 018.261-018 EDITOR, MAP; 018.261-022 MOSAICIST; 018.261-026 PHOTOGRAMMETRIST; 018.262-010 FIELD-MAP EDITOR; 018.281-010 STEREO-PLOTTER OPERATOR; 024.061-014 GEODESIST

## Sources of Additional Information

Information about career opportunities, licensure requirements, and the survey technician certification program is available from:

❏ American Congress on Surveying and Mapping, 5410 Grosvenor Lane, Bethesda, MD 20814-2122.

General information on careers in photogrammetry is available from:

❏ American Society for Photogrammetry and Remote Sensing, 5410 Grosvenor Lane, Suite 200, Bethesda, MD 20814.

# Taxi Drivers and Chauffeurs

## Nature of the Work

Taxi drivers and chauffeurs pick up and drive people to their destination in cars, limousines, or vans. Except for a small number of chauffeurs employed in private service, most charge passengers a fee.

*Taxi drivers*, also known as cab drivers, drive taxicabs, which are custom automobiles modified for transporting passengers. Taxi drivers take passengers to such places as airports, convention centers and hotels, or places of entertainment. Drivers collect fees from passengers based on the number of miles that are traveled or the amount of time spent reaching the destination. They record on a log, or trip sheet, the length of each trip, the point of pick-up, and the destination.

At the start of their driving shift, cab drivers usually report to a cab service or garage where they are assigned a cab. They are given a trip sheet, where they record their name, date of work, and cab identification number. They check the cab's fuel and oil levels, and make sure the lights, brakes, and windshield wipers are in good working order. Drivers adjust rear and side mirrors and their seat for comfort. Any equipment or parts not in good working order are reported to the dispatcher or company mechanic.

Taxi drivers pick up their passengers in one of three ways. Customers requesting transportation may call the cab company and give a place and an approximate time they wish to be picked up, and their destination. The cab company dispatcher then relays the information to a driver by two-way radio. In urban areas, drivers may cruise streets and pick up passengers who hail them, or "wave them down." Drivers also may get passengers by waiting at cab stands or in taxi lines at airports, train stations, hotels, and other places where people frequently seek taxis.

Drivers should be familiar with streets in the areas they service so they can use the most efficient route to destinations. They also should know the locations of frequently requested destinations, such as airports, bus and railroad terminals, convention centers, hotels, popular restaurants, sport facilities, museums, art galleries and other points of interest. Locations of the fire and police departments, as well as hospitals, should also be known in case of emergency.

Upon reaching the destination, drivers determine the fare and announce it to the rider. Fares often consist of many parts. One part is called a "drop charge," which is a flat fee just for using the cab. Another part of the fare is based on the length of the trip and the amount of time it took. In many taxicabs this is measured by a taximeter, a machine which drivers turn on as soon as passengers enter the cab and turn off when the destination is reached that displays the fare as it accrues. The fare may also include a surcharge for additional passengers or for handling luggage. In addition to paying the fare, most passengers will give the driver a tip. The amount of the gratuity depends on the passengers' satisfaction with the quality and efficiency of the ride and courtesy of the driver. When passengers request, a driver issues a receipt. Drivers enter onto the trip sheet all information regarding the trip, such as place and time of pick-up and drop-off and total fee. They also must fill out accident reports when necessary.

*Chauffeurs* drive passengers in private automobiles, limousines, or vans owned by limousine companies. Chauffeurs drive many types of passengers. Many transport travelers and other persons between hotels and airports or bus and train terminals in large vans. Others are hired to drive luxury automobiles, such as limousines, to popular entertainment and social events. Still others are employed full-time by wealthy families and private companies to provide personal transportation.

At the start of the work day, chauffeurs make sure their automobile is ready for use. They inspect it for cleanliness and, when needed, vacuum the interior and wash windows, the exterior car body, and mirrors. They check fuel and oil levels and make sure the lights, tires, brakes, and windshield wipers are in good working order. Chauffeurs may perform routine maintenance and make minor repairs, such as changing tires or adding oil and other fluids when needed. If more serious repairs are needed, the chauffeur takes the vehicle to a professional mechanic.

Chauffeurs often strive to pamper their passengers with attentive service. They assist riders into the car, usually holding the door, holding umbrellas when raining, and loading packages and luggage into the trunk of the car. They may perform errands for their employers, such as delivering packages or picking up items. They also may meet persons arriving at airports. Many chauffeurs offer conveniences and luxuries in their limousines to insure a pleasurable ride, such as newspapers, music, drinks, televisions, and telephones.

## Working Conditions

Taxi drivers and chauffeurs occasionally have to load and unload heavy luggage and packages. Driving for long periods of time can be tiring, especially in densely populated urban areas, and driving in bad weather, heavy traffic, or mountainous and hilly areas can be nerve racking. Sitting for long periods of time can be uncomfortable. Drivers must be alert to conditions on the road, especially in heavy and congested traffic or in bad weather, to prevent accidents and to avoid sudden stops, turns, and other driving maneuvers that would jar the passenger.

Work hours of taxi drivers and chauffeurs vary greatly. Some jobs offer full-time or part-time employment; in others hours are very flexible. Hours can change from day to day or be the same every day. Drivers sometimes must report to work on short notice. Chauffeurs who work for a single employer may be on call much of the time. For those who work for a limousine service, evening and weekend work is common.

The work schedule of chauffeurs is usually dictated by the needs of their client or employer. The work of taxi drivers is much less structured. Working free from supervision, they may break for a meal or a rest whenever their vehicle is unoccupied. However, taxi drivers risk robbery because they work alone and often carry a lot of cash.

Full-time taxi drivers usually work one shift a day, which may last from 8 to 12 hours. Part-time drivers may work half a shift each day, or work a full shift once or twice a week. Because most taxi companies offer services 24 hours a day, drivers must be on duty at all times of the day and night. Early morning and late night shifts are not uncommon. Drivers also work long hours during holidays, weekends, and other special events. Independent drivers, however, can often set their own hours and schedules.

Taxi drivers and chauffeurs meet many different types of people. Patience is required when waiting for passengers or when dealing with rude customers. Many municipalities and taxicab and chauffeur companies require dress codes. In many cities, taxicab drivers are required to wear clothes that are clean and neat. Many chauffeurs wear more formal attire, such as a coat and tie or a dress, or sometimes a uniform and cap or a tuxedo.

## Employment

Taxi drivers and chauffeurs held about 129,000 jobs in 1994. About five out of nine were wage and salary workers employed by a company or business. Of these, about 31 percent worked for local and suburban transportation companies and about 21 percent worked for taxicab companies. Others worked for automotive rental dealerships, private households, and funeral homes. About four out of nine were self-employed.

## Training, Other Qualifications, and Advancement

Local governments regulate taxicabs and set standards and tests required to be licensed as a taxi driver or chauffeur. Although requirements vary, most municipalities have minimum qualifications for age and driving experience. Many taxi and limousine companies have higher standards than the ones required by law: They ask to see a driving record and check credit and criminal records. In addition, many companies require a higher minimum age and prefer that drivers be high school graduates.

Persons interested in driving a limousine or taxicab must first have a regular automobile drivers license. They also must acquire a chauffeur or taxi driver's license, commonly called a "hacker's" license. Local authorities generally require applicants for a hacker's license to pass a written exam or complete a training program. To qualify either through an exam or a training program, applicants must know local geography, motor vehicle laws, safe driving practices, regulations governing taxicabs, and display some aptitude for being able to deal courteously with the public. In many municipalities, applicants sponsored by taxicab or limousine companies may be given a temporary permit that allows them to drive, even though they may not yet have finished the training program or taken the test. Many localities are adding a test on English usage, usually in the form of listening comprehension. Applicants who do not pass the English exam must take an English course sponsored by the municipality. Many local authorities require that applicants pass a physical exam and many take applicants' fingerprints to check for a criminal record.

The majority of taxi drivers and chauffeurs are called "lease drivers." Lease drivers pay a monthly or weekly fee to the company that allows them to lease their vehicle and have access to the company dispatch system. The fee may also include a charge for vehicle maintenance and a deposit. Lease drivers may take their cars home with them when they are not on duty.

Some taxi and limousine companies give new drivers on-the-job training. They may show drivers how to operate the taximeter and two-way radio, and how to complete paperwork. Other topics covered may include driver safety and popular sightseeing and entertainment destinations. Many companies have contracts with social service agencies and transportation services to transport elderly and disabled citizens, so new drivers may get special training on how to properly handle wheelchair lifts and other mechanical devices.

Taxi drivers and chauffeurs should be able to get along with many different types of people. They must be patient when waiting for passengers or when dealing with rude customers, and driving in heavy and congested traffic requires tolerance and a mild temperament. Drivers should also be dependable because passengers rely on them to be picked up at prearranged times and taken to the correct destination. Because drivers work with little supervision, they must be responsible and self-motivated if they are to be successful.

Opportunities for advancement are limited for taxi drivers and chauffeurs. Experienced drivers may obtain preferred routes or shifts. Some advance to dispatcher or to manager jobs; others may start their own limousine company. On the other hand, many drivers like the independent, unsupervised work of driving their own automobile.

In many small and medium size communities, drivers are able to purchase their own taxi, limousine, or other type of automobile and go into business for themselves. These independent owner-drivers are usually required to get an additional permit that allows them to operate their vehicle as a company. In some big cities, however, the number of operating permits is limited and may only be obtained by purchasing one from an owner-driver who is leaving the business. Although many independent owner-drivers are successful, some fail to cover expenses and eventually lose their permit and their automobile. Independent owner-drivers should have good business sense and courses in accounting, business, and business arithmetic are helpful. Knowledge of mechanics can enable independent owner-operators to cut expenses and perform their own routine maintenance and minor repairs.

### Job Outlook

Persons seeking jobs as taxi drivers and chauffeurs should encounter good opportunities. Thousands of job openings will occur each year as drivers transfer to other occupations or leave the labor force. However, driving jobs vary greatly in terms of earnings, work hours, and working conditions. Because driving does not require education beyond high school, competition is expected for jobs that offer regular hours and attractive earnings and working conditions. Opportunities should be best for persons with good driving records who are able to be flexible in their work schedules.

Employment of taxi drivers and chauffeurs is expected to grow faster than average for all occupations through the year 2005 as local and intercity travel increases with population growth. Opportunities should be best in metropolitan areas that are growing rapidly.

Job opportunities may fluctuate from season to season and from month to month. Extra drivers may be hired during holiday seasons and peak travel and tourist times. During economic slowdowns, drivers are seldom laid off but they may have to increase their working hours and their earnings may decline somewhat. Independent owner-operators are particularly vulnerable to economic slowdowns.

### Earnings

Earnings of taxi drivers and chauffeurs vary greatly, depending on the number of hours worked, customers' tips, and other factors. Those who usually worked full-time had median weekly earnings of $375 in 1994. The middle 50 percent earned between $262 and $510 a week. The lowest 10 percent earned less than $204, while the highest 10 percent earned more than $759 a week. Earnings were generally higher in more urban areas.

According to limited information available, the majority of independent taxi owner-drivers earned from about $20,000 to $30,000, including tips. However, professional drivers with a regular clientele often earn more. Many chauffeurs who worked full-time earned from about $25,000 to $50,000 including tips.

### Related Occupations

Other workers who drive vehicles on highways and city streets are ambulance drivers, bus drivers, and truck drivers.

### Related *D.O.T.* Jobs

These job titles are related to or more specific than the more general description above. They will help you identify job options you may not otherwise discover. These descriptions are in the current edition of the *Dictionary of Occupational Titles* and classified by numerical order.

359.673-010 CHAUFFEUR; 359.673-014 CHAUFFEUR, FUNERAL CAR; 913.463-018 TAXI DRIVER; 913.663-010 CHAUFFEUR; 919.663-010 DELIVERER, CAR RENTAL; 919.683-014 DRIVER

### Sources of Additional Information

Information on licensing and registration of taxi drivers and chauffeurs is available from offices of local governments that regulate taxicabs. For information about work opportunities as a taxi driver or chauffeur, contact local taxi or limousine services or state employment service offices.

For general information about the work of taxi drivers, contact:

❏ International Taxicab and Livery Association, 3849 Farragut Ave., Kensington, MD 20895.

For general information about the work of limousine drivers, contact:

❏ National Limousine Association, 1300 L Street NW, Suite 1050, Washington, DC. 20005-4107.

# Telephone Installers and Repairers

### Nature of the Work

Telephone installers and repairers install, service, and repair telephones and other communications equipment on customers' property. When customers move or request new types of service, installers relocate telephones or make changes to existing equipment. In buildings under construction, they install wiring and telephone jacks.

Telephone installers, sometimes called station installers or service technicians, assemble equipment and install wiring and switches on the customers' premises. They connect telephones to outside service wires and sometimes climb poles or ladders to make these connections. In apartment and office buildings, they connect wires and cables to terminals and test equipment to make sure it works properly.

Some experienced installers and repairers have multiple skills. They are considered especially valuable by many small companies. Installers and repairers may handle special cases such as complaints to public service commissions, illegal or unauthorized use of equipment, and electric or acoustic shocks.

## Working Conditions

Some telephone installers and repairers work shifts, including weekends and holidays. Shifts are generally assigned on the basis of seniority. Repairers may also be on call at any time to handle equipment failure.

Telephone installers and repairers may work on rooftops, ladders, and telephone poles.

The work of most installers and repairers involves lifting, reaching, stooping, crouching, and crawling. Adherence to safety precautions is essential to guard against work hazards such as minor burns and electrical shock.

## Employment

Telephone installers and repairers held about 37,000 jobs in 1994. More than 9 out of 10 worked full-time for telecommunications companies.

## Training, Other Qualifications, and Advancement

Most employers prefer applicants with formal training in electronics. Electronic training is offered by public postsecondary vocational-technical schools, private vocational schools and technical institutes, junior and community colleges, and some high schools and correspondence schools. Programs take one to two years. The military services also offer formal training and work experience.

Applicants for entry-level jobs may have to pass tests that measure mechanical aptitude, knowledge of electricity or electronics, manual dexterity, and general intelligence. Newly hired repairers, even those with formal training, usually receive some training from their employer. They also get hands-on experience with equipment, doing basic maintenance, and using diagnostic programs to locate malfunctions. Training may be in a classroom or it may be self-instruction, consisting of videotapes, programmed computer software, or workbooks that allow trainees to learn at their own pace.

Experienced technicians attend training sessions and read manuals to keep up with design changes and revised service procedures. Many technicians also take advanced training in a particular system or type of repair.

Good eyesight and color vision are needed to inspect and work on small, delicate parts and good hearing to detect malfunctions revealed by sound. Because field repairers usually handle jobs alone, they must be able to work without close supervision. For those who have frequent contact with customers, a pleasant personality, neat appearance, and good communications skills are important.

Experienced installers and repairers with advanced training may become specialists or troubleshooters who help other repairers diagnose difficult problems, or work with engineers in designing equipment and developing maintenance procedures.

## Job Outlook

Employment of telephone installers and repairers is expected to decline sharply through the year 2005. Employment will continue to fall due to technological improvements. For example, prewired buildings that enable customers to buy telephones and plug them into prewired jacks have effectively eliminated the functions of the installer. The modular assembly of telephones, where components plug in and out, also will reduce the time and skills needed for repair. Also, fewer phones will be worth repairing as prices continue to decline. In addition, the use of portable terminals which hook into a central testing system makes repairers more efficient. Increased competition for customers due to consolidations and mergers of cable and telephone companies will further contribute to the decline of telephone installers and repairers.

With employment projected to decline, job openings will result exclusively from the need to replace persons who transfer to other occupations or leave the labor force. Traditionally, most openings for telephone installers and repairers have been filled by workers in other telephone company jobs. As technology continues to displace installers and repairers, it will remain difficult for telephone workers without additional training and virtually impossible for "outsiders" without the necessary skills to get these jobs.

## Earnings

In 1994, median weekly earnings of full-time telephone installers and repairers were $679. Central office installers, central office technicians, PBX installers, and telephone installers and repairers employed by AT&T and the Bell Operating Companies and represented by the Communications Workers of America and the International Brotherhood of Electrical Workers earned between $469 and $1,063 a week in 1994.

## Related Occupations

Workers in other occupations who repair and maintain the circuits and mechanical parts of electronic equipment include appliance and power tool repairers, automotive electricians, broadcast technicians, electronic organ technicians, and vending machine repairers. Electronics engineering technicians may also repair electronic equipment as part of their duties.

## Related *D.O.T.* Jobs

These job titles are related to or more specific than the more general description above. They will help you identify job options you may not otherwise discover. These descriptions are in the current edition of the *Dictionary of Occupational Titles* and classified by numerical order.

822.261-022 STATION INSTALLER-AND-REPAIRER; 822.281-018 MAINTENANCE MECHANIC, TELEPHONE

## Sources of Additional Information

For career, certification, and FCC licensing information, contact:

❑ The International Society of Certified Electronics Technicians, 2708 West Berry St., Fort Worth, TX 76109.

For certification, career, placement, and FCC licensing information, contact:

❑ Electronics Technicians Association, 604 North Jackson, Greencastle, IN 46135.

For a list of FCC licensing administrators, write to:

❏ Federal Communications Commission, Consumer Assistance Office, 1270 Fairfield Rd., Gettysburg, Pa 17325-7245 or call 1-800-322-1117.

For information on the telephone industry and career opportunities contact:

❏ United States Telephone Association, 1401 H St., Suite 600, Washington, DC 20005-2136.

For information on electronic equipment repairers in the telephone industry, write to:

❏ Communications Workers of America, 501 3rd St. NW, Washington, DC 20001.

# Textile Machinery Operators

## Nature of the Work

Textile machinery operators tend machines that manufacture a wide range of textile products. Hosiery, skirts, and socks are familiar examples of these products, but many people are surprised to learn that textile products are used in such things as roofs, tires, and roads. There are many phases in the textile production process, and operators' duties and responsibilities depend on the product and the type of machinery in use. Machinery operators control equipment that cleans, cards, combs, and draws the fiber; spins the fiber into yarn; and weaves, knits, or tufts the yarn into textile products. They are responsible for numerous machines that they start, stop, clean, and monitor for proper functioning.

The textile production process begins with the preparation of synthetic or natural fibers for spinning. Fibers are cleaned and aligned through carding and combing. To prepare the fiber for the spinning process, very short fibers and any foreign matter are removed and the fibers are drawn into a substance called sliver. During this process, different types of fibers may be combined to give products the desired textures, durability, or other characteristics. This is how "50 percent cotton, 50 percent polyester" blends, for example, are created. Operators constantly monitor their machines during this stage, checking the movement of the fiber, removing and replacing cans of sliver, repairing breaks in the sliver, and making minor repairs to the machinery.

The full cans of sliver are then taken to the spinning area. Spinning draws and twists the sliver to produce yarn which is then wound onto conical structures called bobbins or cones. This is an automated version of the old fashion spinning wheel.

Some workers oversee machinery that makes manufactured fibers. These fibers, used in many textile products, are created from materials that, unlike cotton, wool, and flax, are not fibrous in their natural form. To make this fiber, wood pulp or chemical compounds are dissolved or melted in a liquid which is then extruded, or forced, through holes in a metal plate, called a spinneret. The sizes and shapes of the holes in the spinneret determine the shape and the uses of the fiber. Workers adjust the flow of fiber base through the spinneret, repair breaks in the fiber, and make minor adjustments to the machinery. Because this fiber is created by a chemical process, the majority of these workers are employed by chemical companies, not textile mills.

When the yarn is ready, it is taken to be woven, knitted, tufted, or bonded with heat or chemicals. Each of these processes produces a different type of textile product and requires a different type of machine. For example, woven fabrics are made on looms that interlace the yarn. Knit products, such as socks or women's hosiery, are produced by intermeshing loops of yarn. Carpeting is made through the tufting process, in which the loops of yarn are pushed through a material backing. Although the processes are now highly automated, these concepts have been used for many centuries to produce textile products.

Even though operators work with many different kinds of machines, they share many responsibilities. Each operator oversees numerous machines—repairing breaks in the yarn, monitoring the supply of yarn, and making minor repairs to the machinery. As increasingly automated machinery is used in textile mills, more processes are controlled by computers, making it possible for each operator to monitor a larger area or number of machines. Because of the complexity of many machines, operators often specialize in a particular type of machine. In addition, operators prepare the machinery prior to a production run and help maintain the equipment. For example, they adjust the timing on a machine, thread the harnesses that create patterns in textile goods, and repair machinery.

Once the yarn has been woven, knitted, or tufted, the resulting fabric is ready to be dyed and finished either at the textile mill or at a plant specializing in textile finishing. Because of the variety of consumer preferences, manufacturers print and dye textiles in thousands of different designs and colors. Depending upon the end use of the yarn, it may be dyed before or after it is woven, knitted, or tufted. Some fabric is treated before it is dyed to remove other chemical additives that could affect the quality of the finished product.

In addition to dyeing and printing, products are often finished by treating them to prevent excessive shrinkage, to provide strength, to make them stain-resistant, or to give a silky luster. In the production of hosiery and socks, for example, the stocking or sock is placed on a form and then exposed to steam and heat to give it shape.

## Working Conditions

Most textile machine operators work in textile mills or chemical plants. Working conditions depend upon the age of the facility or equipment and its degree of modernization. Newer facilities usually offer better ventilation and climate control that reduce potential problems caused by airborne fibers and fumes. Workers in areas with high levels of these airborne materials often use protective glasses and masks that cover their nose and mouth.

Although some of the newer machinery has reduced the level of noise, workers in some areas still must wear ear protection. Because many machines operate at high speeds, workers must be careful not to wear clothing or jewelry that could get caught in moving parts. In addition, extruding and forming machine operators wear protective shoes and clothing when working with some types of chemical compounds.

Most textile machinery operators worked a standard 40-hour week. Because many textile and fiber mills operate 24 hours a day, night and weekend shifts are common. However, many employers use a rotating schedule of shifts so operators don't consistently work nights or weekends. Operators are on their feet moving between machines during most of their shift.

Although workers have traditionally worked under close supervision, new management philosophies are placing an increasing emphasis on teamwork, which will allow operators greater interpersonal contact and more initiative.

## Employment

Textile machinery operators held about 281,000 jobs in 1994. Most of these workers were employed in weaving, finishing, yarn, and thread mills. Knitting mills and manufactured fiber producers also employed a substantial number of these workers. Most extruding and forming machine operators were employed in chemical plants.

North Carolina was the leading state in the employment of textile workers, accounting for about 30 percent of the total. Georgia and South Carolina combined accounted for another 30 percent. Most of the remaining workers were employed in other Southern states and in the Northeast.

## Training, Other Qualifications, and Advancement

Education and training are becoming increasingly important for working with complex machinery and advanced manufacturing methods. A high school diploma in addition to extensive technical training is becoming a prerequisite for entry to many jobs. This training may be obtained, in part, at a formal training institution such as a technical school. Extensive on-the-job training by more experienced workers or representatives of machinery manufacturers is also common.

As the textile industry becomes more highly automated, operators will need to understand complex machinery and be able to diagnose problems. Because textile machinery is increasingly controlled electronically, many operators will need good computer skills.

Physical stamina and manual dexterity are important attributes for these jobs. In addition, self-direction and interpersonal skills are becoming more important for textile machinery operators. Organizational changes that promote teamwork and encourage fewer levels of management are leading operators to assume greater responsibility and to take more initiative.

Textile machinery operatives can advance in several ways. Some workers become instructors and train new employees. Others advance by taking positions requiring higher skills and greater responsibility. First-line supervisory positions usually are filled from the ranks of skilled operators.

## Job Outlook

Employment of textile machinery operators is expected to decline over the 1994-2005 period. Changing trade regulations and greater productivity through the introduction of labor-saving machinery are the major factors influencing employment in this occupation. In spite of the projected decline, thousands of openings will be created annually as workers change occupations or leave the labor force.

The greatest uncertainty facing textile machinery operators is the future of trade. Recent trade agreements, like the North American Free Trade Agreement and the Uruguay Round of the General Agreement on Tariffs and Trade, will help to open export markets for textiles produced in the United States. At the same time, they will dismantle much of the protection that has been provided to the industry for decades. While the textile industry is highly efficient and will be able to compete in many product lines, the more labor-intensive U.S. apparel industry will be more adversely affected. Because the apparel industry is the largest consumer of American-made textiles, this will negatively affect the demand for textile machinery operators.

Textile firms will respond to this growing competition by investing in new equipment, reorganizing their work practices, and developing new uses for textiles. New machinery, such as faster shuttleless and air jet looms and computer-integrated manufacturing processes, increase productivity by producing goods at a faster rate. They also allow each operator to monitor a larger number of machines. Many factories are also reorganizing production floors to further increase productivity and to give workers more responsibility. In addition, textile firms are developing new uses for textiles that replace non-textiles, such as wall coverings, medical products, and dome covers.

Because the textile industry is highly automated, persons with technical skills and some computer training will have the best opportunities. In particular, bleaching and dyeing machine operator employment is expected to grow in coming years. Also, extruding machine operators who produce synthetic fibers will encounter growing employment opportunities as the demand for synthetic fiber grows.

## Earnings

Average weekly earnings for production workers in the textile and manufactured fiber industries were $380 in 1994, compared to about $510 for production workers throughout all manufacturing industries. Earnings vary significantly, depending upon the type of mill, job specialty, shift, and seniority. Average weekly earnings for production workers in the chemical industry, where most extruding machine operators are found, were around $660 in 1994.

Benefits usually include paid holidays and vacations, health and life insurance, a retirement plan, and sick leave. Some firms provide on-site daycare facilities. Employees may also receive discounts in company-owned outlet stores.

## Related Occupations

Metalworking and plastics-working machine operators perform similar duties and have many of the same entry and training requirements as extruding and forming machine operators and tenders, textile machine operators and tenders, and textile bleaching and dyeing machine operators. Setters and set-up operators in other industries—metal fabrication and plastics manufacturing, for example—perform duties comparable to those of textile machine setters and set-up operators.

## Related *D.O.T.* Jobs

These job titles are related to or more specific than the more general description above. They will help you identify job options you may not otherwise discover. These descriptions are in the current edition of the *Dictionary of Occupational Titles* and classified by numerical order.

There are too many *D.O.T.* titles to list here. Most are variations related to a specific industry, and we have included a small number of representative *D.O.T.* titles as examples. Complete lists are available in various career software published by JIST or directly from the U.S. Department of Labor.

551.585-022 ROTARY-CUTTER OPERATOR; 585.685-086 ROUNDING-MACHINE OPERATOR; 585.685-118 STRIPPING CUTTER AND WINDER; 681.685-046 DOUBLING-MACHINE OPERATOR; 683.682-010 CARPET WEAVER; 685.665-014 KNITTING-MACHINE OPERATOR; 686.685-022 CUTTER; 686.685-042 PINKING-MACHINE OPERATOR; 686.685-066 STRIP-CUTTING-MACHINE OPERATOR; 689.260-010 MACHINE FIXER; 689.260-018 SECTION LEADER AND MACHINE SETTER; 689.260-026 KNITTING-MACHINE FIXER; 689.280-010 BOX TENDER; 689.360-010 NEEDLE-LOOM SETTER; 689.662-010 NEEDLE-LOOM OPERATOR; 689.685-042 CLOTH REELER; 689.685-046 CLOTH WINDER; 689.685-166 UTILITY TENDER, CARDING; 690.682-026 CUTTER, BARREL DRUM

### Sources of Additional Information

Information about job opportunities in textile and synthetic fiber production is available from local employers or local offices of the state employment service.

For general information on careers, technology, or trade regulations in the textile industry, write to:

❏ American Textile Manufacturers Institute, Inc., 1801 K St. NW, Suite 900, Washington, DC 20006.

❏ Institute of Textile Technology, P.O. Box 391, Charlottesville, VA 22901.

# Tilesetters

### Nature of the Work

In ancient Egypt and Rome, tile was used for mosaics—an art form using small, decorative ceramic squares. Over the years, tile has been a popular building material because it is durable, impervious to water, and easy to clean. It is used today, for instance, in shopping centers, hospitals, tunnels, lobbies of buildings, bathrooms, and kitchens.

Tilesetters, like the ancient artists, apply tile to floors, walls, and ceilings. To set tile, which generally ranges in size from one to twelve inches square, they use cement or "mastic," a very sticky paste. When using cement, tilesetters nail a support of metal mesh to the wall or ceiling to be tiled. They use a trowel to apply a cement mortar—called a "scratch coat"—onto the metal screen and scratch the surface of the soft mortar with a small tool, similar to a rake. After the scratch coat has dried, tilesetters apply another coat of mortar to level the surface and then apply mortar to the back of the tile and place it onto the surface.

To set tile in mastic or a cement adhesive, called "thin set," tilesetters need a flat, solid surface such as drywall, concrete, plaster, or wood. They use a tooth-edged trowel to spread mastic on the surface or apply cement adhesive to the back of the tile and then properly position it.

Because tile varies in color, shape, and size, workers sometimes prearrange tiles on a dry floor according to a specified design. This allows workers to examine the pattern and make changes. In order to cover all exposed areas, including corners and around pipes, tubs, and wash basins, tilesetters cut tiles to fit with a machine saw or a special cutting tool. Once the tile is placed, they gently tap the surface with their trowel handle or a small block of wood to seat the tiles evenly.

When the cement or mastic has set, tilesetters fill the joints with "grout," a very fine cement. They then scrape the surface with a rubber-edged device called a "squeegee" to dress the joints and remove excess grout. Before the grout sets, they finish the joints with a damp sponge for a uniform appearance.

### Working Conditions

Tilesetters generally work indoors. Because most of the structure has been completed, the work area is relatively clean and uncluttered. Much of the workday is spent bending, kneeling, and reaching, activities that require endurance but not exceptional strength. To protect their knees, most workers wear kneepads.

Although workers are subject to cuts from tools or materials, falls from ladders, and strained muscles, the occupation is not as hazardous as some other construction occupations.

### Employment

Tilesetters held about 27,000 jobs in 1994. Most wage and salary tilesetters were employed by tilesetting contractors who work mainly on nonresidential construction projects, such as schools, hospitals, and office buildings. Nearly one of every two tilesetters is self-employed, compared to one of every four construction workers. Most self-employed tilesetters work on residential projects.

Tilesetters are employed throughout the country but are found largely in urban areas.

### Training, Other Qualifications, and Advancement

Most tilesetters acquire their skills on the job by working as helpers to experienced workers. They begin by learning about the tools of the trade, and then they learn to mix and apply cement and to apply mastic. As they progress, they learn to cut and install tile, apply grout, and do finishing work.

Employers recommend completion of a three-year apprenticeship program, which consists of on-the-job training and related classroom instruction in subjects such as blueprint reading, layout, and basic mathematics.

When hiring apprentices or helpers, employers usually prefer high school graduates who have had courses in general mathematics, mechanical drawing, and shop. Good physical condition, manual dexterity, and a good sense of color harmony also are important assets.

Skilled tilesetters may start their own contracting businesses or may become supervisors or estimators for other contractors.

### Job Outlook

Employment of tilesetters is expected to increase more slowly than the average for all occupations through the year 2005. Increased demand for tilesetters will stem from population and business growth, which should result in more construction of shopping malls, hospitals, schools, restaurants, and other structures where tile is used extensively. Tile is expected to continue to increase in popularity as a building material and be used more extensively, particularly in more expensive homes, whose construction is expected to increase. In more modestly priced homes, however, the use of tile substitutes, such as plastic or fiberglass tub and shower enclosures, is expected to increase, slowing the growth in demand for tilesetters.

Despite the increased demand for tilesetting, most job openings will result from the need to replace tilesetters who retire or leave the occupation for other reasons. Job opportunities will not be as plentiful as in other construction occupations because the occupation is small and turnover is relatively low.

### Earnings

The median weekly earnings for tilesetters were about $450 a week in 1994. The middle 50 percent earned between $340 and $710 a week; 10 percent earned less than $280 a week; 10 percent earned more than $960 a week.

Apprentices usually start earning 50 percent of experienced workers' wages. Earnings vary greatly by geographic location. They tend to be highest in the North and lowest in the South.

Some tilesetters belong to the International Union of Bricklayers and Allied Craftsmen or the United Brotherhood of Carpenters and Joiners of America.

### Related Occupations

Tilesetters use their knowledge of tools and masonry materials along with skill and dexterity to produce attractive, durable surfaces. Other workers with similar abilities include bricklayers, concrete masons, marble setters, plasterers, stonemasons, and terrazzo workers.

### Related D.O.T. Jobs

These job titles are related to or more specific than the more general description above. They will help you identify job options you may not otherwise discover. These descriptions are in the current edition of the *Dictionary of Occupational Titles* and classified by numerical order.

861.381-054 TILE SETTER; 861.381-058 TILE SETTER APPRENTICE; 861.684-018 TILE SETTER

### Sources of Additional Information

For details about apprenticeship or other work opportunities in this trade, contact local tilesetting contractors; locals of the unions previously mentioned; or the nearest office of the state employment service or state apprenticeship agency.

# Tool and Die Makers

### Nature of the Work

Tool and die makers are highly skilled workers who produce tools, dies, and special guiding and holding devices that are used in machines that produce a variety of products—from clothing and furniture to heavy equipment and parts for aircraft.

Toolmakers craft precision tools which are used to cut, shape, and form metal and other materials. They also produce jigs and fixtures (devices that hold metal while it is bored, stamped, or drilled) and gauges and other measuring devices. Diemakers construct metal forms (dies) that are used to shape metal in stamping and forging operations. They also make metal molds for diecasting and for molding plastics, ceramics, and composite materials. In addition, tool and die makers may repair worn or damaged tools, dies, gauges, jigs, and fixtures, and design tools and dies.

Tool and die makers must have a much broader knowledge of machining operations, mathematics, and blueprint reading than most other machining workers. They use many types of machine tools and precision measuring instruments and must be familiar with the machining properties, such as hardness and heat tolerance, of a wide variety of common metals and alloys.

Working from blueprints or instructions, tool and die makers plan the sequence of operations necessary to manufacture the tool or die. They measure and mark the pieces of metal that will be cut to form parts of the final product. They then cut, bore, or drill the part as required. They also check the accuracy of what they have done to ensure that the final product will meet specifications. Then they assemble the parts and perform finishing jobs such as filing, grinding, and smoothing surfaces.

Modern technology is helping to change tool and die makers' jobs. Firms commonly use computer aided design (CAD) to develop products. Specifications from the computer program can then be used to develop designs electronically for the required tools and dies. The designs can then be sent to computer numerically controlled (CNC) machines to produce the die. Programs can also be electronically stored and adapted for future use. This saves time and increases productivity of the workers.

In shops that use numerically controlled (NC) machine tools, tool and die makers' duties may be slightly different. For example, although they still manually check and assemble the tool or die, each of its components may be produced on an NC machine. In addition, they often assist in the planning and writing of NC programs.

### Working Conditions

Tool and die makers usually work in tool rooms. These areas are quieter than the production floor because there are fewer machines in use at one time. Machines have guards and shields that minimize the exposure of workers to moving parts. Tool and die makers, however, must follow safety rules and wear protective equipment, such as safety glasses to shield against bits of flying metal and earplugs to protect against noise. They also may be exposed to hazardous lubricants and cleaners. In addition, they spend much of the day on their feet and may do moderately heavy lifting.

Companies employing tool and die makers traditionally operate one shift per day. However, as the cost of new machinery and technology has increased, many employers now have more than one shift. Overtime and Saturday work are common, especially during peak production periods.

### Employment

Tool and die makers held about 142,000 jobs in 1994. Most worked in industries that manufacture metalworking machinery and equipment, motor vehicles, aircraft, and plastics products. Although they are found throughout the country, jobs are most plentiful in the Midwest and Northeast, where many of the metalworking industries are located.

### Training, Other Qualifications, and Advancement

Tool and die makers learn their trade through formal apprenticeship and postsecondary programs or informal on-the-job training. The best way to learn all aspects of tool and die making, according to most employers, is a formal apprenticeship program that combines classroom instruction and job experience. A growing number of tool and die makers, however, receive most of their formal training from community colleges.

Courses in math, blueprint reading, metalworking, and drafting, as well as machine shop experience, provide a helpful background.

During the four or five years of a tool and die apprenticeship, apprentices learn to operate milling machines, lathes, grinders, and other machine tools. They also learn to use handtools in fitting and assembling tools, gauges, and other mechanical and metal forming equipment, and they study metalworking processes such as heat treating and plating. Classroom training usually consists of mathematics, mechanical drawing, tool designing, tool programming, and blueprint reading.

Workers who become tool and die makers without completing formal apprenticeships generally acquire their skills through a combination of informal on-the-job training and classroom instruction at a vocational school or community college. They often begin as machine operators and gradually take on more difficult assignments. Many machinists become tool and die makers. In fact, tool and die makers are often considered highly specialized machinists.

Because tools and dies must meet strict specifications—precision to one ten-thousandth of an inch is not uncommon—the work of tool and die makers requires a high degree of patience and attention to detail. Good eyesight is essential. Persons entering this occupation should also be mechanically inclined, able to work independently, and capable of doing work that requires concentration and physical effort.

There are several ways for skilled workers to advance. Some move into supervisory and administrative positions in their firms; others become tool designers or tool programmers; and a few may open their own shops.

## Job Outlook

Employment of tool and die makers is expected to decline through the year 2005. Nevertheless, jobseekers with the appropriate skills and background should find excellent opportunities, as employers across the nation report difficulties in finding skilled workers to hire as tool and die makers. Many openings will be created each year by tool and die makers who retire. Three out of 10 tool and die makers are 50 years or older. As older workers begin to leave the occupation in larger numbers, employers in certain parts of the country may face more pronounced shortages.

The projected decline in employment reflects advancements in automation, including computer numerically controlled machine tools and computer aided design. CNC machine tools have made tool and die makers more productive, while CAD has allowed some functions of these workers to be carried out by a computer and tool programmer. In addition, because precision metal products are a primary component of manufacturing machinery, increased imports of finished goods and precision metal products may lessen the demand for tool and die makers. These workers, however, are highly skilled and play a key role in the operation of many firms. This fact, coupled with a growing demand for motor vehicles, aircraft, machinery, and other products that use machined metal parts, should help to moderate the decline in employment.

## Earnings

Median weekly earnings for tool and die makers who worked full-time were $660 in 1994. Most earned between $490 and $860 a week. Ten percent earned less than $380 a week, and the 10 percent with the highest weekly earnings made more than $1,130. In addition to their hourly wage, most workers receive health and life insurance, a pension plan, paid vacations, and sick leave.

## Related Occupations

The occupations most closely related to the work of tool and die makers are the other machining occupations. These include machinist, mold maker, instrument maker, metalworking and plastics-working machine operator, and tool programmer.

Other occupations that require precision and skill in working with metal include blacksmith, gunsmith, locksmith, metal patternmaker, and welder.

## Related *D.O.T.* Jobs

These job titles are related to or more specific than the more general description above. They will help you identify job options you may not otherwise discover. These descriptions are in the current edition of the *Dictionary of Occupational Titles* and classified by numerical order.

601.260-010 TOOL-AND-DIE MAKER; 601.260-014 TOOL-AND-DIE-MAKER APPRENTICE; 601.280-010 DIE MAKER, STAMPING; 601.280-014 DIE MAKER, TRIM; 601.280-018 DIE MAKER, WIRE DRAWING; 601.280-022 DIE SINKER; 601.280-030 MOLD MAKER, DIE-CASTING AND PLASTIC MOLDING; 601.280-034 TAP-AND-DIE-MAKER TECHNICIAN; 601.280-042 TOOL MAKER; 601.280-058 TOOL-MAKER APPRENTICE; 601.281-010 DIE MAKER, BENCH, STAMPING; 601.281-014 DIE-TRY-OUT WORKER, STAMPING; 601.281-026 TOOL MAKER, BENCH; 601.380-010 CARBIDE OPERATOR; 601.381-010 DIE FINISHER; 601.381-014 DIE MAKER; 601.381-022 DIE-MAKER APPRENTICE; 601.381-026 PLASTIC TOOL MAKER; 601.381-030 PLASTIC-FIXTURE BUILDER; 601.381-034 SAW MAKER; 601.381-042 DIE MAKER, ELECTRONIC; 739.381-018 DIE MAKER; 739.381-022 DIE-MAKER APPRENTICE

## Sources of Additional Information

For general information about tool and die makers, contact:

❑ The Association for Manufacturing Technology, 7901 Westpark Dr., McLean, VA 22102.

❑ The National Tooling and Machining Association, 9300 Livingston Rd., Ft. Washington, MD 20744.

❑ The Tooling and Manufacturing Association, ATTN: Education Department, 1177 South Dee Rd., Park Ridge IL 60068.

❑ Precision Metalforming Association, 27027 Chardon Rd., Richmond Heights, OH 44143.

# Truck Drivers

## Nature of the Work

Nearly all goods are transported by truck during some of their journey from producers to consumers. Goods may also be shipped between terminals or warehouses in different cities by train, ship, or plane. But truck drivers usually make the initial pickup from factories, consolidate cargo at terminals for inter-city shipment, and deliver goods from terminals to stores and homes.

Before leaving the terminal or warehouse, truck drivers check their trucks for fuel and oil. They also inspect the trucks to make sure the brakes, windshield wipers, and lights are working and that a fire extinguisher, flares, and other safety equipment are aboard and in working order. Drivers adjust mirrors so that both sides of the truck are visible from the driver's seat, and make sure cargo has been loaded properly so it will not shift during the trip. Drivers report to the dispatcher any equipment that does not work or is missing, or cargo that is not loaded properly.

Once underway, drivers must be alert to prevent accidents. Because drivers of large tractor-trailers sit higher than cars, pick-ups, and vans, they can see farther down the road. They seek traffic lanes that allow them to move at a steady speed, and, when going downhill, they may increase speed slightly to gain momentum for a hill ahead.

Long-distance runs vary widely. On short "turnarounds," truck drivers deliver a load to a nearby city, pick up another loaded trailer, and drive it back to their home base the same day. Other runs take an entire day, and drivers remain away from home overnight. On longer runs, drivers may haul loads from city to city for a week or more before returning home. Some companies use two drivers on very long runs. One drives while the other sleeps in a berth behind the cab. "Sleeper" runs may last for days, or even weeks, usually with the truck stopping only for fuel, food, loading, and unloading.

Some long-distance drivers who have regular runs transport freight to the same city on a regular basis. Because shippers request varying amounts of service to different cities every day, many drivers have unscheduled runs. Dispatchers tell these drivers when to report for work and where to haul the freight.

After long-distance truck drivers reach their destination or complete their operating shift, they are required by the U.S. Department of Transportation to complete reports about the trip and the condition of the truck and to give a detailed report of any accident. In addition, drivers are subject to random alcohol and drug tests while on duty.

Long-distance truck drivers spend most of their working time behind the wheel but may be required to unload their cargo. Drivers hauling specialty cargo often load or unload their trucks, since they may be the only one at the destination familiar with this procedure. Auto-transport drivers, for example, drive and position the cars on the trailers and head ramps and remove them at the final destination. When picking up or delivering furniture, drivers of long-distance moving vans hire local workers to help them load or unload.

When local truck drivers receive assignments from the dispatcher to make deliveries, pickups, or both, they also get delivery forms. Before the drivers arrive for work, material handlers generally have loaded the trucks and arranged the items in order of delivery to minimize handling of the merchandise.

At the customer's place of business, local truck drivers generally load or unload the merchandise. If there are heavy loads or many deliveries to make during the day, drivers may have helpers. Customers must sign receipts for goods and drivers may receive money for material delivered. At the end of the day, they turn in receipts, money, and records of deliveries made and report any mechanical problems their trucks may have.

The work of local truck drivers varies, depending on the product they transport. Produce truckers usually pick up a loaded truck in the early morning and spend the rest of the day delivering produce to many different grocery stores. Lumber truck drivers, on the other hand, make several trips from the lumber yard to one or more construction sites. Gasoline tank truck drivers attach the hoses and operate the pumps on their trucks to transfer the gasoline to gas stations' storage tanks.

Some local truck drivers have sales and customer relations responsibilities. These drivers—called "driver-sales workers" or "route drivers"—are primarily responsible for delivering their firm's products, but they also represent the company. Their reaction to customer complaints and requests for special services can make the difference between a large order and losing a customer. Route drivers also may use their selling ability to increase sales and to gain additional customers.

The duties of driver-sales workers vary according to the industry in which they are employed, the policies of their particular company, and how strongly their sales responsibilities are emphasized. Most have wholesale routes—that is, they deliver to businesses and stores rather than homes. A few distribute various foods, or pick up and deliver dry-cleaning to households, but these retail routes are now rare.

Wholesale bakery driver-sales workers, for example, deliver and arrange bread, cakes, rolls, and other baked goods on display racks in grocery stores. Paying close attention to the items that are selling well and those just sitting on the shelves, they estimate the amount and variety of baked goods that will be sold. They may recommend changes in a store's order or may encourage the manager to stock new bakery products. From time to time, they try to get the business of new stores along their route.

Driver-sales workers employed by laundries that rent linens, towels, work clothes, and other items visit businesses regularly to replace soiled laundry.

Vending machine driver-sales workers service machines in factories, schools, and other buildings. They check items remaining in the machines, replace stock, and remove money deposited in the cash boxes. They also examine each vending machine to see that merchandise and change are dispensed properly, make minor repairs, and clean machines.

After completing their route, driver-sales workers order items for the next day which they think customers are likely to buy, based primarily on what products have been selling well, the weather, time of year, and any customer feedback.

## Working Conditions

Truckdriving has become less physically demanding because most trucks now have more comfortable seats, better ventilation, and improved cab designs. However, driving for many hours at a stretch, unloading cargo, and making many deliveries can be tiring, and driving in bad weather, heavy traffic, or mountains can be nerve racking. Local truck drivers, unlike long-distance drivers, usually can return home in the evening. Some self-employed long distance truck drivers who own as well as operate their trucks spend over 240 days a year away from home.

Local truck drivers frequently work 48 hours or more a week. Many who handle food for chain grocery stores, produce markets, or bakeries drive at night or early in the morning. Although most drivers have a regular route, some have different routes each day. Many local truck drivers—particularly driversales workers—load and unload their own trucks, which requires considerable lifting, carrying, and walking.

The U.S. Department of Transportation governs work hours and other matters of trucking companies engaged in interstate commerce. For example, a long-distance driver cannot be on duty for more than 60 hours in any seven-day period and cannot drive more than 10 hours following at least 8 consecutive hours off duty. Many drivers, particularly on long runs, work close to the maximum time permitted. Drivers on long runs may face boredom, loneliness, and fatigue. Although many drivers work during the day, travel at night and on holidays and weekends is frequently necessary in order to avoid traffic delays and deliver cargo on time.

## Employment

Truck drivers held 2,900,000 jobs in 1994. Jobs are concentrated in and around large cities. Some drivers are employed in almost all communities, however.

Trucking companies employed nearly one-third of all truck drivers, and another one-third worked for companies engaged in wholesale or retail trade, such as auto parts stores, oil companies, lumber yards, or distributors of food and grocery products. The rest were scattered throughout the economy, including government agencies.

Fewer than 1 out of 10 truck drivers are self-employed; of these, a significant number are owner-operators, who either operate independently, serving a variety of businesses, or lease their services and their trucks to a trucking company.

## Training, Other Qualifications, and Advancement

Qualifications and standards for truck drivers are established by state and federal regulations. States must meet federal standards, and some states have more stringent regulations. All truck drivers must have a driver's license issued by the state in which they live, and most employers require a good driving record. All drivers of trucks designed to carry at least 26,000 pounds—which includes most tractor-trailers as well as bigger straight trucks—are required to obtain a special commercial driver's license (CDL) from the state in which they live; in many states a regular driver's license is sufficient for driving light trucks and vans. All truck drivers who operate trucks that carry hazardous materials also must obtain a CDL.

To qualify for a commercial driver's license, applicants must pass a knowledge test and demonstrate that they can operate a commercial truck safely. A national data bank permanently records all driving violations incurred by persons who hold commercial licenses, so drivers whose commercial license is suspended or revoked in one state may not be issued a new one in another state. Trainees must be accompanied by a driver with a CDL until they get their own CDL. Information on how to apply for a commercial driver's license may be obtained from state motor vehicle administrations.

The U.S. Department of Transportation establishes minimum qualifications for truck drivers who are engaged in interstate commerce. A driver must be at least 21 years old and pass a physical examination, which the employer usually pays for. Good

hearing, 20/40 vision with or without glasses or corrective lenses, normal use of arms and legs (unless a waiver is obtained), and normal blood pressure are the main physical requirements. Persons with epilepsy or diabetes controlled by insulin are not permitted to be interstate truck drivers, and drivers may not use any controlled substances unless prescribed by a licensed physician. In addition, drivers must take a written examination on the Motor Carrier Safety Regulations of the U.S. Department of Transportation.

Many trucking operations have higher standards than those described. Many firms require that drivers be at least 25 years old, be able to lift heavy objects, and have driven trucks for three to five years. Many prefer to hire high school graduates and require annual physical examinations. federal regulations require employers to test their drivers for alcohol and drug use as a condition of employment, and require periodic random tests while on duty.

Since drivers often deal directly with the company's customers, they must get along well with people. For jobs as driversales workers, an ability to speak well and a neat appearance are particularly important, as are self-confidence, initiative, and tact. For all truck driver jobs, employers also look for responsible, selfmotivated individuals, since drivers work with little supervision.

Driver-training courses are a desirable method of preparing for truckdriving jobs and for obtaining a commercial driver's license. High school driver-training courses are an asset, and courses in automotive mechanics may help drivers make minor roadside repairs. Many private and public technical-vocational schools offer tractor-trailer driver training programs. Students learn to inspect the trucks and freight, to maneuver large vehicles on crowded streets and in highway traffic, and to comply with federal, state, and local regulations. Some programs provide only a limited amount of actual driving experience, and completion of a program does not assure a job. Persons interested in attending one of these schools should check with local trucking companies to make sure the school's training is acceptable or should seek a school certified by the Professional Truck Driver Institute of America as providing training that meets Federal Highway Administration guidelines for training tractor-trailer drivers.

Training given to new drivers by employers usually is informal and may consist only of a few hours of instruction from an experienced driver, sometimes on the new employee's own time. New drivers also may ride with and observe experienced drivers before being assigned their own runs. Additional training may be given if they are to drive a special type of truck or if they are handling hazardous materials. Some companies give one to two days of classroom instruction which covers general duties, the operation and loading of a truck, company policies, and the preparation of delivery forms and company records. Driver-sales workers also receive training on the various types of products they carry so they will be more effective sales workers and better able to handle customer requests.

Very few people enter truckdriving directly from school; most truck drivers previously held jobs in other occupations. Driving experience in the Armed Forces can be an asset. In some instances, a person also may start as a truck driver's helper, driving part of the day and helping to unload and load freight. When driving vacancies occur, senior helpers usually are promoted.

New drivers sometimes start on panel or other small "straight" trucks. As they gain experience and show good driving skills, they may advance to larger and heavier trucks, and finally to tractor-trailers.

Although most new truck drivers are assigned immediately to regular driving jobs, some start as extra drivers, who substitute for regular drivers who are ill or on vacation. They receive a regular assignment when an opening occurs.

Advancement of truck drivers is generally limited to driving runs that provide increased earnings or preferred schedules and working conditions. For the most part, a local truck driver may advance to driving heavy or special types of trucks, or transfer to long-distance truckdriving. Working for companies that also employ long-distance drivers is the best way to advance to these positions. A few truck drivers may advance to dispatcher, manager, or traffic work—for example, planning delivery schedules.

Some long-distance truckers purchase a truck and go into business for themselves. Although many of these owner-operators are successful, others fail to cover expenses and eventually lose their trucks. Owner-operators should have good business sense as well as truckdriving experience. Courses in accounting, business, and business arithmetic are helpful, and knowledge of truck mechanics can enable owner-operators to perform their own routine maintenance and minor repairs.

## Job Outlook

Opportunities should be favorable for persons who are interested in truckdriving. This occupation has among the largest number of job openings each year. Although thousands of openings will be created by growth in demand for drivers, the majority will occur as experienced drivers transfer to other fields of work or retire or leave the labor force for other reasons. Truck driver jobs vary greatly in terms of earnings, weekly work hours, number of nights that must be spent "on the road," and in the quality of equipment operated. Because truckdriving does not require education beyond high school, competition is expected for jobs with the most attractive earnings and working conditions.

Employment of truck drivers is expected to increase about as fast as the average for all occupations through the year 2005 as the economy grows and the amount of freight carried by trucks increases. However, increased integration of truck and railroad long-distance freight transportation should continue to slow somewhat the growth of truck driver jobs. Trailers are expected increasingly to be carried between distant regions on trains, thus requiring truck drivers only to deliver and pick them up at rail depots. Perishable goods should continue to be shipped long distance by truck.

Average growth of local and long-distance truck driver employment should outweigh the slow growth in driver-sales worker jobs. The number of truck drivers with sales responsibilities is expected to increase slowly because companies are increasingly splitting their responsibilities among other workers, shifting sales, ordering, and customer service tasks to sales and office staffs, and using regular truck drivers to make deliveries to customers.

Job opportunities may vary from year to year because the amount of freight moved by trucks fluctuates with the economy. Many new truck drivers are hired when the economy and the volume of freight are expanding, but fewer when these decline. During economic slowdowns, some truck drivers are laid off and others have decreased earnings because of reduced hours or miles driven. Independent owner-operators are particularly vulnerable to slowdowns. Truck drivers employed in industries such as wholesale food distribution, which is usually not affected much by recessions, are less likely to be laid off.

## Earnings

As a rule, local truck drivers are paid by the hour and receive extra pay for working overtime, usually after 40 hours. Long-distance drivers are generally paid primarily by the mile, and their rate per mile can vary greatly from employer to employer; their earnings increase with mileage driven, seniority, and the size and type of truck. Most driver-sales workers receive a commission based on their sales in addition to an hourly wage.

In 1993, truck drivers had average straight-time hourly earnings of $12.73. Depending on the size of the truck, average hourly earnings were as follows:

| | |
|---|---|
| Medium trucks | $14.87 |
| Tractor-trailers | 13.29 |
| Heavy straight trucks | 11.80 |
| Light trucks | 8.06 |

Drivers employed by trucking companies had the highest earnings, averaging about $15.97 an hour in 1993. Truck drivers in the Northeast and West had the highest earnings; those in the South had the lowest.

Most long-distance truck drivers operate tractor-trailers, and their earnings vary widely, from as little as $20,000 to over $40,000 annually. Most self-employed truck drivers are primarily engaged in long-distance hauling. After deducting their living expenses and the costs associated with operating their trucks, earnings of $20,000 to $25,000 a year are common.

Many truck drivers are members of the International Brotherhood of Teamsters. Some truck drivers employed by companies outside the trucking industry are members of unions that represent the plant workers of the companies for which they work.

## Related Occupations

Other driving occupations include ambulance driver, bus driver, chauffeur, and taxi driver.

## Related *D.O.T.* Jobs

These job titles are related to or more specific than the more general description above. They will help you identify job options you may not otherwise discover. These descriptions are in the current edition of the *Dictionary of Occupational Titles* and classified by numerical order.

292.353-010 DRIVER, SALES ROUTE; 292.363-010 NEWSPAPER-DELIVERY DRIVER; 292.463-010 LUNCH-TRUCK DRIVER; 292.483-010 COIN COLLECTOR; 292.667-010 DRIVER HELPER, SALES ROUTE; 900.683-010 CONCRETE-MIXING-TRUCK DRIVER; 902.683-010 DUMP-TRUCK DRIVER; 903.683-010 EXPLOSIVES-TRUCK DRIVER; 903.683-014 POWDER-TRUCK DRIVER; 903.683-018 TANK-TRUCK DRIVER; 904.383-010 TRACTOR-TRAILER-TRUCK DRIVER; 904.683-010 LOG-TRUCK DRIVER; 905.483-010 MILK DRIVER; 905.663-010 GARBAGE COLLECTOR DRIVER; 905.663-014 TRUCK DRIVER, HEAVY; 905.663-018 VAN DRIVER; 905.683-010 WATER TRUCK

DRIVER II; 906.683-010 FOOD-SERVICE DRIVER; 906.683-014 LIQUID-FERTILIZER SERVICER; 906.683-018 TELEPHONE-DIRECTORY-DISTRIBUTOR DRIVER; 906.683-022 TRUCK DRIVER, LIGHT; 909.663-010 HOSTLER; 919.663-018 DRIVER-UTILITY WORKER; 919.663-022 ESCORT-VEHICLE DRIVER; 919.663-026 TOW-TRUCK OPERATOR; 953.583-010 DRIP PUMPER

### Sources of Additional Information

Information on truck driver employment opportunities is available from local trucking companies and local offices of the state employment service.

Information on career opportunities in truckdriving may be obtained from:

❑ American Trucking Associations, Inc., 2200 Mill Rd., Alexandria, VA 22314.

The Professional Truck Driver Institute of America, a nonprofit organization established by the trucking industry, manufacturers, and others, certifies truck driver training programs that meet industry standards. A free list of certified tractor-trailer driver training programs may be obtained from:

❑ Professional Truck Driver Institute of America, 8788 Elk Grove Blvd., Suite 20, Elk Grove, CA 95624.

# Upholsterers

### Nature of the Work

Whether making a new piece of furniture, restoring a treasured antique, or simply giving an ordinary living room couch a facelift, upholsterers combine knowledge of fabrics and other materials with artistic flair and manual skill. Some repair and replace automobile upholstery and convertible and vinyl tops.

Upholsterers who make new furniture start with a bare wooden frame. Those who recondition old furniture first remove the old cover, padding, and springs, using hammers and tack pullers. They remove the material and padding that cover the arms, back, sides, and seat. They examine the springs and replace broken or bent ones. The springs sit on a cloth mat, called "webbing," that is attached to the frame. If the webbing is worn, upholsterers remove all the springs and webbing. They reglue loose sections of the frame and refinish exposed wood.

The first step in upholstering new furniture or reupholstering old pieces is to install webbing of nylon, jute, or cotton in the frame to hold the springs. Upholsterers tack webbing to one side of the frame, stretch it tight, and tack it to the opposite side. Additional webbing is woven across the first row of webbing and attached to the frame to form a new mat. After putting springs on the mat so they compress evenly, upholsterers sew or staple each spring to the webbing or frame and tie each spring to the ones next to it. Burlap then is stretched over the springs, cut, smoothed, and tacked to the frame. To form a smooth rounded surface over the springs and other parts of the frame, upholsterers cover the furniture with filling material. They then cover this with a layer of felt and heavy cloth, and tack the cloth to the frame. Upholsterers measure and cut fabric for arms, backs, and other sections with as little waste as possible. They temporarily stitch pieces together for fitting and after assuring tight and smooth fit of the cover—or noting where adjustments are necessary—they remove

the cover, sew it together, and tack, staple, or glue it to the frame. To complete the job, upholsterers sew, tack, or glue on fringes, buttons, or other ornaments.

Upholsterers use common handtools, including tack hammers, staple guns, tack and staple removers, pliers, and shears, and special tools such as webbing stretchers and upholstery needles. They also use sewing machines.

Upholsterers who work in upholstery shops pick up and deliver furniture or help customers select new furniture coverings. Those who manage shops also order supplies and equipment and keep business records.

### Working Conditions

Most upholsterers work inside a shop or factory. Working conditions in these facilities vary—many are spacious, adequately lighted, well-ventilated, and well-heated; others are small and dusty.

The work is not dangerous, but upholsterers must be careful to avoid cuts and bruises when they use sharp tools and when they lift and handle furniture or springs. Upholsterers stand most of the workday, and they do a lot of bending and heavy lifting. They also have to work in awkward positions for short periods of time.

### Employment

Furniture upholsterers held about 63,000 jobs in 1994. About one in three were self-employed. Of the remaining upholsterers, companies that manufacture household and office furniture employed 65 percent and shops that reupholster and repair furniture employed nearly another 17 percent. Over 10 percent worked in shops that specialize in reupholstering the seats of automobiles and other motor vehicles, and a few worked in furniture stores.

### Training, Other Qualifications, and Advancement

Most upholsterers are trained on the job as a helper to an experienced worker. Usually about three years of on-the-job training are required to become a fully skilled upholsterer. On-the-job training in a furniture factory usually is much shorter because the range of skills required is more limited. Others learn upholstery through apprenticeship or formal training.

When hiring helpers, employers generally prefer people with some knowledge of the trade. Inexperienced persons may get basic training in upholstery in high school, vocational and technical schools, and some community colleges. Programs include sewing machine operation, measuring, cutting, springing, frame repair, tufting, and channeling; as well as business and interior design courses. However, additional training and experience usually are required before graduates can perform as quickly and efficiently as experienced upholsterers.

Upholsterers should have manual dexterity, good coordination, and strength to lift heavy furniture. An eye for detail and flair for color and creative use of fabrics are helpful.

The major form of advancement for upholsterers is opening their own shop. It is relatively easy to open a shop because a small investment in handtools and a sewing machine are all that is needed. The upholstery business is extremely competitive, however, so operating a shop successfully is difficult. In large shops and factories, experienced or highly skilled upholsterers may become supervisors.

## Job Outlook

Employment of upholsterers is expected to grow more slowly than the average for all occupations through the year 2005. Most of the growth will be in furniture manufacturing. Employment in reupholstery shops is expected to remain steady. Each upholstery job is unique, so upholstery work does not lend itself to automation; consequently, technology is not expected to affect employment of upholsterers. Most job openings will arise because of the need to replace experienced workers who transfer to other occupations or leave the labor force.

Opportunities for experienced upholsterers should be very good. The number of upholsterers with experience is limited because few young people want to enter the occupation and because few shops are willing to train people.

## Earnings

Median weekly earnings of upholsterers were $359 in 1994; the middle 50 percent earned between $283 and $490 per week. The lowest 10 percent earned less than $198, and the top 10 percent earned more than $617.

Earnings of self-employed upholsterers depend not only on the size and location of the shop but also on the number of hours worked.

## Related Occupations

Other workers who combine manual skills and knowledge of materials such as fabrics and wood are fur cutters, furniture finishers, pattern and model makers, and casket coverers.

## Related *D.O.T.* Jobs

These job titles are related to or more specific than the more general description above. They will help you identify job options you may not otherwise discover. These descriptions are in the current edition of the *Dictionary of Occupational Titles* and classified by numerical order.

780.381-010 AUTOMOBILE UPHOLSTERER; 780.381-014 AUTOMO-BILE-UPHOLSTERER APPRENTICE; 780.381-018 FURNITURE UPHOLSTERER; 780.381-022 FURNITURE-UPHOLSTERER APPRENTICE; 780.381-026 UPHOLSTERER, LIMOUSINE AND HEARSE; 780.381-038 UPHOLSTERER, INSIDE; 780.384.010 AUTOMOBILE SEAT COVER AND CONVERTIBLE TOP INSTALLER; 780.384-014 UPHOLSTERER; 780.684-034 CHAIR UPHOLSTERER; 780.684-118 UPHOLSTERER, OUTSIDE; 780.684-122 UPHOLSTERY REPAIRER

## Sources of Additional Information

For details about work opportunities for upholsterers in your area, contact local upholstery shops or the local office of the state employment service.

To receive a list of technical schools accredited by the Accrediting Commission of Career Schools and Colleges of Technology that have programs in upholstery, contact:

❏ Accrediting Commission of Career Schools and Colleges of Technology, 2101 Wilson Blvd., Suite 302, Arlington, VA 22201.

# Vending Machine Servicers and Repairers

## Nature of the Work

Coin-operated vending machines are a familiar sight. These machines dispense many types of refreshments, from cold soft drinks to hot meals. Vending machine servicers and repairers install, service, and stock these machines and keep them in good working order.

*Vending machine servicers* periodically visit coin-operated machines that dispense soft drinks, candy and snacks, and food items. They collect coins from the machines, restock merchandise, change labels to indicate new selections, and adjust temperature gauges so that items are kept at the right temperature. They are also responsible for keeping the machines clean. Because many vending machines dispense food, these workers must comply with state and local public health and sanitation standards.

Servicers make sure machines operate correctly. When checking complicated electrical and electronic machines, such as beverage dispensers, they make sure that the machines mix drinks properly and that refrigeration and heating units work correctly. On the relatively simple gravity-operated machines, servicers check handles, springs, plungers, and merchandise chutes. They also test coin and change-making mechanisms. When installing the machines, they make the necessary water and electrical connections and recheck the machines for proper operation. They also make sure installations comply with local plumbing and electrical codes.

Preventive maintenance—avoiding trouble before it starts—is a major job of these workers. For example, they periodically clean refrigeration condensers, lubricate mechanical parts, and adjust machines to perform properly.

If a machine breaks down, *vending machine repairers* inspect it for obvious problems, such as loose electrical wires, malfunctions of the coin mechanism, and leaks. If the problem cannot be readily located, they refer to technical manuals and wiring diagrams and use testing devices such as electrical circuit testers to find defective parts. Repairers sometimes fix faulty parts at the site, but they often install replacements and take broken parts to the company shop for repair. When servicing electronic machines, repairers may only have to replace a circuit board or other component. They also repair microwave ovens used to heat food dispensed from machines.

In repair and maintenance work, repairers use hammers, pliers, pipe cutters, soldering guns, wrenches, screwdrivers, and electronic testing devices. In the repair shop, they use power tools, such as grinding wheels, saws, and drills as well as voltmeters, ohmmeters, oscilloscopes, and other testing equipment.

Vending machine servicers and repairers employed by small companies may both fill and fix machines on a regular basis. These combination servicers-repairers stock machines, collect money, fill coin and currency changers, and repair machines when necessary.

Servicers and repairers also do some clerical work, such as filing reports, preparing repair cost estimates, ordering parts, and keeping daily records of merchandise distributed. However, many of the new computerized machines reduce the paperwork that a servicer performs.

## Working Conditions

Some vending machine repairers work primarily in company repair shops, but many servicers and repairers spend much of their time on the road visiting machines wherever they have been placed. Vending machines operate around the clock, so repairers often work at night and on weekends and holidays.

Vending machine repair shops generally are quiet, well lighted, and have adequate work space. However, when servicing machines on location, the work may be done where pedestrian traffic is heavy, such as in busy supermarkets, industrial complexes, offices, or schools. Repair work is relatively safe, although servicers and repairers must take care to avoid hazards such as electrical shocks and cuts from sharp tools and metal objects. They also must follow safe work procedures, especially when moving heavy vending machines or working with electricity and radiation from microwave ovens.

## Employment

Vending machine servicers and repairers held about 19,000 jobs in 1994. Most repairers work for vending companies that sell food and other items through machines. Others work for soft drink bottling companies that have their own coin-operated machines. Some work for companies that own video games, pin-ball machines, juke boxes, and similar types of amusement equipment. Although vending machine servicers and repairers are employed throughout the country, most are located in areas with large populations and many coin and vending machines.

## Training, Other Qualifications, and Advancement

Employers generally prefer to hire high school graduates and to train them to fill and fix machines informally on the job by observing, working with, and receiving instruction from experienced repairers. High school or vocational school courses in electricity, refrigeration, and machine repair are an advantage in qualifying for entry jobs. Employers usually require applicants to demonstrate mechanical ability, either through their work experience or by scoring well on mechanical aptitude tests. Because vending machine servicers and repairers sometimes handle thousands of dollars in merchandise and cash, employers hire persons who have a record of honesty and respect for the law. The ability to deal tactfully with people also is important. A commercial driver's license and a good driving record are essential for most vending machine repairer jobs.

Electronics are becoming more prevalent in vending machines, so employers increasingly prefer applicants to have some training in electronics. Technologically advanced machines with features such as multilevel pricing, inventory control, and scrolling messages extensively use electronics and microchip computers. Some vocational high schools and junior colleges offer one- to two-year training programs in basic electronics for vending machine servicers and repairers.

Beginners may start their training with simple jobs such as cleaning or painting machines. They then may learn to rebuild machines—removing defective parts, repairing, adjusting, and testing the machines. Next, they accompany an experienced repairer on service calls, and finally make visits on their own. This learning process may take from six months to three years, depending on the individual's abilities, previous education, types of machines, and the quality of instruction.

The National Automatic Merchandising Association has established an apprenticeship program for vending machine repairers. Apprentices receive 144 hours of home-study instruction in subjects such as basic electricity and electronics, blueprint reading, customer relations, and safety. Upon completion of the program, performance and written tests must be passed to become certified.

To learn about new machines, repairers and servicers sometimes attend training sessions sponsored by manufacturers, which may last from a few days to several weeks. Both trainees and experienced workers sometimes take evening courses in basic electricity, electronics, microwave ovens, refrigeration, and other related subjects. Skilled servicers and repairers may be promoted to supervisory jobs.

## Job Outlook

Employment of vending machine servicers and repairers is expected to decline through the year 2005. More vending machines are likely to be installed in industrial plants, hospitals, stores, and other business establishments to meet the public demand for vending machine items. In addition, the range of products dispensed by machine can be expected to increase as vending machines continue to become more automated and more are built with microwave ovens, mini-refrigerators, and freezers. However, improvements in technology should require servicers and repairers to check on machines less frequently, reducing their employment. New machines will need to be repaired and restocked less often, and contain computers that record sales and inventory data, reducing time-consuming paperwork now done by servicers. Some new machines will even be able to signal the vending machine company when they need to be restocked or repaired, allowing servicers and repairers to be dispatched only when needed, instead of their having to check each machine on a regular schedule.

Although employment is expected to decline, job openings will nevertheless arise as experienced workers transfer to other occupations or leave the labor force. Persons with some background in electronics should have the best job prospects because electronic circuitry is an increasingly important component of vending machines. If firms cannot find trained or experienced workers for these jobs, they are likely to train qualified route drivers or hire inexperienced people who have acquired some mechanical, electrical, or electronic training by taking high school or vocational courses.

## Earnings

According to a survey conducted by the National Automatic Merchandising Association, the average hourly wage rate for non-union vending machine servicers was $8.30 in 1994, with rates ranging from just under $4.25 to nearly $16.00 an hour, depending on the size of the firm and the region of the country. Non-union repairers averaged $10.21 an hour in 1994, but rates ranged from $5.00 to $22.00. Servicers and repairers who were members of unions generally earned slightly more.

Most vending machine repairers work eight hours a day, five days a week, and receive premium pay for overtime. Some union contracts stipulate higher pay for night work and for emergency repair jobs on weekends and holidays.

Some vending machine repairers and servicers are members of the International Brotherhood of Teamsters.

## Related Occupations

Other workers who repair equipment with electrical and electronic components include home appliance and power tool repairers, electronic equipment repairers, and general maintenance mechanics.

## Related *D.O.T.* Jobs

These job titles are related to or more specific than the more general description above. They will help you identify job options you may not otherwise discover. These descriptions are in the current edition of the *Dictionary of Occupational Titles* and classified by numerical order.

319.464-014 VENDING-MACHINE ATTENDANT; 639.281-014 COIN-MACHINE-SERVICE REPAIRER

## Sources of Additional Information

Further information on job opportunities in this field can be obtained from local vending machine firms and local offices of the state employment service. For general information and a list of schools offering courses in vending machine repair, write to:

❏ National Automatic Merchandising Association, 20 N. Wacker Dr., Suite 3500, Chicago, IL 60606-3102.

# Water and Wastewater Treatment Plant Operators

## Nature of the Work

Clean water is essential for many things: Health, recreation, fish and wildlife, and industry. Water treatment plant operators treat water so that it is safe to drink. Wastewater treatment plant operators remove harmful pollutants from domestic and industrial wastewater so that it is safe to return to the environment.

Water is pumped from wells, rivers, and streams to water treatment plants where it is treated and distributed to customers. Waste is collected from customers, carried by water through sewer pipes to wastewater treatment plants where it is treated and returned to streams, rivers, and oceans. Operators in both types of plants control processes and equipment to remove solid materials, chemical compounds, and micro-organisms from the water or to render them harmless. They also control pumps, valves, and other processing equipment to move the water or wastewater through the various treatment processes, and dispose of the waste materials removed from the water.

Operators read and interpret meters and gauges to make sure plant equipment and processes are working properly and adjust controls as needed. They operate chemical-feeding devices; take samples of the water or wastewater; perform chemical and biological laboratory analyses; and test and adjust the amount of chemicals such as chlorine in the water. Operators also make minor repairs to valves, pumps, and other equipment. They use gauges, wrenches, pliers, and other common handtools, as well as special tools.

Water and wastewater treatment plant operators increasingly rely on computers to help them monitor equipment, store sampling results, make process control decisions, and produce reports. When problems occur, operators may use their computers to determine the cause of and solution to the malfunction.

Occasionally operators must work under emergency conditions. A heavy rainstorm, for example, may cause large amounts of wastewater to flow into sewers, exceeding a plant's treatment capacity. Emergencies also can be caused by conditions inside a plant, such as chlorine gas leaks or oxygen deficiencies. To handle these conditions, operators are trained in emergency management response using special safety equipment and procedures to protect public health and the facility. During these periods, operators may work under extreme pressure to correct problems as quickly as possible. These periods may create dangerous working conditions and operators must be extremely cautious.

The specific duties of plant operators depend on the type and size of plant. In smaller plants, one operator may control all machinery, perform tests, keep records, handle complaints, and do repairs and maintenance. Some operators may handle both a water treatment and a wastewater treatment plant. In larger plants with many employees, operators may be more specialized and only monitor one process. The staff may also include chemists, engineers, laboratory technicians, mechanics, helpers, supervisors, and a superintendent.

Water pollution standards have become increasingly stringent since adoption of the Federal Water Pollution Control Act of 1972, which implemented a national system of regulation on the discharge of pollutants. Under the 1972 law and subsequent reauthorizations in 1977 and 1987, it is illegal to discharge any pollutant without a permit. Industrial facilities that send their wastes to municipal treatment plants must meet certain minimum standards and ensure that these wastes have been adequately pretreated so that they do not damage municipal treatment facilities. Municipal treatment plants also must meet stringent discharge standards set forth in the Clean Water Act of 1972 and the Safe Drinking Water Act of 1974. Operators must be familiar with the guidelines established by the Clean Water Act and how they affect their plant. In addition to federal regulations, operators also must be aware of any guidelines imposed by the state or locality in which the plant operates.

## Working Conditions

Water and wastewater treatment plant operators work both indoors and outdoors and may be exposed to noise from machinery and some unpleasant odors, although chemicals may be used to minimize these. Operators have to stoop, reach, and climb and sometimes get their clothes dirty. They must pay close attention to safety procedures for they may be confronted with hazardous conditions, such as slippery walkways, dangerous gases, and malfunctioning equipment. Because plants operate 24 hours a day, seven days a week, operators work one of three 8-hour shifts and on a rotational basis, weekends and holidays. Whenever emergencies arise, operators may be required to work overtime.

## Employment

Water and wastewater treatment plant operators held about 95,000 jobs in 1994. The vast majority worked for local governments; some worked for private water supply and sanitary services companies, some of which provide operation and management services to local governments on a contract basis. About half worked as water treatment plant operators and half worked as wastewater treatment plant operators.

Water and wastewater treatment plant operators are employed throughout the country, with most jobs in larger towns and cities. Although nearly all work full-time, those who work in small towns may only work part-time at the water or wastewater treatment plant—the remainder of their time may be spent handling other municipal duties.

## Training, Other Qualifications, and Advancement

Trainees usually start as attendants or operators-in-training and learn their skills on the job under the direction of an experienced operator. They learn by observing the processes and equipment in operation and by doing routine tasks such as recording meter readings; taking samples of wastewater and sludge; and doing simple maintenance and repair work on pumps, electric motors, and valves. They also clean and maintain plant equipment. Larger treatment plants generally combine this on-the-job training with formal classroom or self-paced study programs.

Operators need mechanical aptitude and should be competent in basic mathematics, as they need to apply data to formulas of treatment requirements, flow levels, and concentration levels. Because of the introduction of computer-controlled equipment and more sophisticated instrumentation, a high school diploma generally is required. In addition, employers prefer those who have had high school courses in chemistry, biology, and mathematics.

Some positions, particularly in larger cities and towns, are covered by civil service regulations, and applicants may be required to pass written examinations testing elementary mathematics skills, mechanical aptitude, and general intelligence.

Some two-year programs leading to an associate degree in waste-water technology and one-year programs leading to a certificate are available; these provide a good general knowledge of water treatment processes as well as basic preparation for becoming an operator. Because plants are becoming more complex, completion of such courses increases an applicant's chances for employment and promotion.

Most state water pollution control agencies offer training courses to improve operators' skills and knowledge. These courses cover principles of treatment processes and process control, laboratory procedures, maintenance, management skills, collection systems, safety, chlorination, sedimentation, biological treatment, sludge treatment and disposal, and flow measurements. Some operators take correspondence courses on subjects related to wastewater treatment, and some employers pay part of the tuition for related college courses in science or engineering.

As operators are promoted, they become responsible for more complex treatment processes. Some operators are promoted to plant supervisor or superintendent, while others advance by transferring to a larger facility. Some postsecondary training in water and wastewater treatment coupled with increasingly responsible experience as an operator may be sufficient to qualify for superintendent of a small plant, since at many small plants the superintendent also serves as an operator. However, educational requirements are rising as larger, more complex treatment plants are built to meet new water pollution control standards. With each promotion, the operator must have greater knowledge of federal, state, and local regulations. Superintendents of large plants generally need an engineering or science degree. A few operators get jobs with state water pollution control agencies as technicians, who monitor and provide technical assistance to plants throughout the state. Vocational-technical school or community college training generally is preferred for technician jobs. Experienced operators may transfer to related jobs with industrial wastewater treatment plants, companies selling wastewater treatment equipment and chemicals, engineering consulting firms, or vocational-technical schools.

In 49 states, operators must pass an examination to certify that they are capable of overseeing wastewater treatment plant operations. A voluntary certification program is in effect in the remaining state. Water plant operators must also be certified in most states. Typically, there are different levels of certification depending on the operator's experience and training. Higher certification levels qualify the operator for a wider variety of treatment processes. Certification requirements vary by state, and by size of treatment plants.

There is no nationally mandated certification program for operators, and relocation may mean having to become certified in a new location. However, many states have begun accepting other states' certifications.

## Job Outlook

Those who wish to become water and wastewater treatment plant operators should have good opportunities through the year 2005. Despite low turnover and job growth that is expected to be slower than average, the number of applicants in this field is normally low, making for good job prospects for qualified applicants.

The increasing population and growth of the economy are expected to increase demand for water and wastewater treatment services. As new plants are constructed to meet this demand, employment of water and wastewater treatment plant operators should increase. In addition, some job openings will occur as experienced operators transfer to other occupations or leave the labor force.

Although local government is the largest employer of water and wastewater treatment plant operators, increased reliance on private firms specializing in the operation and management of water and wastewater treatment facilities should shift some employment demand to these companies. Increased pre-treatment activity by manufacturing firms should also create new job opportunities.

Water and wastewater treatment plant operators generally have steady employment because the services they provide are essential even during economic downturns.

## Earnings

Annual salaries of water and wastewater treatment plant operators averaged $27,100 in 1994; the lowest paid 10 percent of the occupation earned about $16,600, the middle 50 percent of the occupation earned between $22,300 and $35,200, and the top 10 percent earned about $42,100. Salaries depend, among other things, on the size and location of the plant, the complexity of the operator's job, and the operator's level of certification.

In addition to their annual salaries, water and wastewater treatment plant operators generally receive benefits that include health and life insurance, a retirement plan, and educational reimbursement for job-related courses.

## Related Occupations

Other workers whose main activity consists of operating a system of machinery to process or produce materials include boiler operators, gas-compressor operators, power plant operators, power reactor operators, stationary engineers, turbine operators, chemical plant operators, and petroleum refinery operators.

## Related *D.O.T.* Jobs

These job titles are related to or more specific than the more general description above. They will help you identify job options you may not otherwise discover. These descriptions are in the current edition of the *Dictionary of Occupational Titles* and classified by numerical order.

954.382-010 PUMP-STATION OPERATOR, WATERWORKS; 954.382-014 WATER-TREATMENT-PLANT OPERATOR; 955.362-010 WASTEWATER-TREATMENT-PLANT OPERATOR; 955.382-010 CLARIFYING-PLANT OPERATOR; 955.382-014 WASTE-TREATMENT OPERATOR; 955.585-010 WASTEWATER-TREATMENT-PLANT ATTENDANT

## Sources of Additional Information

For information on certification, contact:

❏ Association of Boards of Certification, 208 Fifth St., Suite 1A, Ames, IA 50010-6259.

For educational information on careers as a water treatment plant operator, contact:

❏ American Waterworks Association, 6666 West Quincy Ave., Denver, CO 80235.

❏ Water Environment Federation, 601 Wythe St., Alexandria, VA 22314.

For information on jobs, contact state or local water pollution control agencies, state water and waste water operator associations, state environmental training centers, or local offices of the state employment service.

# Water Transportation Occupations

## Nature of the Work

Workers in water transportation occupations operate and maintain deep sea merchant ships, tugboats, towboats, ferries, dredges, research vessels, and other waterborne craft on the oceans and the Great Lakes, in harbors, on rivers and canals, and on other waterways.

*Captains* or *masters* are in overall command of the operation of a vessel and they supervise the work of the other officers and the crew. They set course and speed, maneuver the vessel to avoid hazards and other ships, and periodically determine position using navigation aids, celestial observations, and charts. They direct crew members who steer the vessel, operate engines, signal to other vessels, perform maintenance and handle lines, or operate towing or dredging gear. Captains insure that proper procedures and safety practices are followed, check that machinery and equipment are in good working order, and oversee the loading and unloading of cargo or passengers. They also maintain logs and other records of ships' movements and cargo carried.

Captains on large vessels are assisted by *deck officers* or *mates*. Merchant marine vessels—those carrying cargo overseas—have a chief or first mate, a second mate, and a third mate. Mates oversee the operation of the vessel, or "stand watch" for specified periods, usually four hours on and eight off. On smaller vessels, there may be only one mate (called a pilot on some inland vessels) who alternates watches with the captain.

*Engineers* or *marine engineers* operate, maintain, and repair propulsion engines, boilers, generators, pumps, and other machinery. Merchant marine vessels usually have four engineering officers: A chief engineer and a first, second, and third assistant engineer. Assistant engineers stand periodic watches, overseeing the operation of engines and machinery.

*Seamen*, also called *deckhands*, particularly on inland waters, operate the vessel and its deck equipment under the direction of the ship's officers, and keep the nonengineering areas in good condition. They stand watch, looking out for other vessels, obstructions in the ship's path, and aids to navigation. They also steer the ship, measure water depth in shallow water, and maintain and operate deck equipment such as life boats, anchors, and cargo-handling gear. When docking or departing, they handle lines. They also perform maintenance chores such as repairing lines, chipping rust, and painting and cleaning decks and other areas. Seamen may also load and unload cargo. On vessels handling liquid cargo, they hook up hoses, operate pumps, and clean tanks. Deckhands on tugboats or tow vessels tie barges together into tow units, inspect them periodically, and disconnect them when the destination is reached. Larger vessels have a *boatswain* or head seaman.

*Marine oilers* work below decks under the direction of the ship's engineers. They lubricate gears, shafts, bearings, and other moving parts of engines and motors, read pressure and temperature gauges and record data, and may repair and adjust machinery.

A typical deep sea merchant ship has a captain, three deck officers or mates, a chief engineer and three assistant engineers, plus six or more seamen and oilers. Depending on their size, vessels operating in harbors, rivers, or along the coast may have a crew comprising only of a captain and one deckhand, or as many as a captain, a mate or pilot, an engineer, and seven or eight seamen. Large vessels also have a full-time cook and helper, while on small ones, a seaman does the cooking. Merchant ships also have an electrician, machinery mechanics, and a radio officer.

*Pilots* guide ships in and out of harbors, through straits, and on rivers and other confined waterways where a familiarity with local water depths, winds, tides, currents, and hazards such as reefs and shoals is of prime importance. Pilots on river and canal vessels usually are regular crew members, like mates. Harbor pilots are generally independent contractors, who accompany vessels while they enter or leave port. They may pilot many ships in a single day.

## Working Conditions

Merchant mariners are away from home for extended periods, but earn long leaves. Most are hired for one voyage, with no job security after that. At sea, they usually stand watch for 4 hours and are off for 8 hours, 7 days a week. Those employed on Great Lakes ships work 60 days and have 30 days off, but do not work in the winter when the lakes are frozen over. Workers on rivers and canals and in harbors are more likely to have year-round work. Some work 8- or 12-hour shifts and go home every day. Others work steadily for a week or month and then have an extended period off. When working, they are usually on duty for 6 or 12 hours and are off for 6 or 12 hours.

People in water transportation occupations work in all weather conditions and although merchant mariners try to avoid severe storms while at sea, working in damp and cold conditions is unpleasant. It is uncommon for vessels to sink, but workers nevertheless face the possibility that they may have to abandon their craft on short notice if it collides with other vessels or runs aground. They also risk injury or death from falling overboard and hazards associated with working with machinery, heavy loads, and dangerous cargo.

Some newer vessels are air-conditioned, soundproofed from noisy machinery, and have comfortable living quarters. Nevertheless, some workers do not like the long periods away from home and the confinement aboard ship.

## Employment

Water transportation workers held about 48,000 jobs in 1994. Many merchant marine officers and seamen worked only part of the year, so the total number who worked some time during the year was somewhat greater. The following tabulation shows employment in the occupations that make up this group:

| | |
|---|---|
| Seamen and marine oilers | 20,000 |
| Captains and pilots | 13,000 |
| Engineers | 7,600 |
| Mates | 7,300 |

A few of the captains and pilots were self-employed, operating their own vessel, or were pilots who were independent contractors.

About 45 percent of all water transportation workers were employed on board merchant marine ships or U.S. Navy Military Sealift ships operating on the oceans or Great Lakes. Another 42 percent were employed in transportation services, working on tugs, towboats, ferries, dredges, and other watercraft in harbors, on rivers and canals, and other waterways. Others worked in water transportation services such as piloting vessels in and out of harbors, operating lighters and chartered boats, and in marine construction, salvaging, and surveying. The remaining water transportation workers were employed on vessels that carry passengers, such as cruise ships, sightseeing and excursion boats, and ferries.

## Training and Other Qualifications

Entry, training, and educational requirements for most water transportation occupations are established and regulated by the U.S. Coast Guard. All officers and operators of watercraft must be licensed by the U.S. Coast Guard, which offers nearly 60 different licenses, depending on the position and type of craft. Licensing differs somewhat between the merchant marine and others.

Deck and engineering officers in the merchant marine must be licensed. To qualify for a license, applicants must have graduated from the U.S. Merchant Marine Academy, or one of the six state academies, and pass a written examination. A physical examination and a drug test are also required. Persons with at least three years of appropriate sea experience also can be licensed if they pass the written exam, but it is difficult to pass without substantial formal schooling or independent study. Also, because seamen may work six months a year or less, it can take five to eight years to accumulate the necessary experience. The academies offer four-year bachelor's degree programs (one offers a three-year associate program) in nautical science or marine engineering to prepare students to be third mates or third assistant engineers. With experience and passing of additional exams, third officers may qualify for higher rank. Because of keen competition, however, officers may have to take jobs below the grade for which they are qualified.

For employment in the merchant marine as an unlicensed seaman, a merchant mariner's document is needed. Applicants for merchant marine documents do not need to be U.S. citizens. A medical certificate of excellent health, and a certificate attesting to vision, color perception, and general physical condition may be required for higher-level deckhands. While no experience or formal schooling is required, training at a union-operated school is helpful. Beginners are classified as ordinary seaman and may be assigned to the deck or engineering department. With experience at sea, and perhaps union-sponsored training, an ordinary seaman can pass the able seaman exam.

Merchant marine officers and seamen, both experienced and beginners, are hired for voyages through union hiring halls or directly by shipping companies.

Harbor pilot training is usually an apprenticeship with a shipping company or a pilot employees' association. Entrants may be able seamen or licensed officers.

No training or experience is needed to become a seaman or deckhand on vessels operating in harbors or on rivers or other waterways. Newly hired workers generally learn skills on the job. With experience, they are eligible to take a Coast Guard exam to qualify as a mate, pilot, or captain. Substantial knowledge gained through experience, courses in seamanship schools, and independent study are needed to pass the exam.

## Job Outlook

Keen competition is expected to continue for jobs in water transportation occupations. Overall, employment in these jobs is projected to change little through the year 2005, but opportunities will vary by sector.

Employment in deep sea shipping is expected to continue its long-term sharp decline as U.S.-staffed ships carry an even smaller proportion of international cargo. (In 1992, only 4 percent of our imports and exports were carried on U.S.-staffed ships.) Stringent federal regulations require larger crews on U.S.-staffed ships, which allow vessels that fly foreign flags—and have smaller crew sizes—to operate at lower cost and charge lower shipping rates. A fleet of deep sea U.S.-staffed ships is considered to be vital to the nation's defense, so they receive federal support through operating subsidies and provisions in laws that limit certain federal cargoes to ships that fly the U.S. flag.

Newer ships are designed to be operated safely by much smaller crews. Innovations include automated controls and computerized monitoring systems in navigation, engine control, watchkeeping, ship management, and cargo handling. As older vessels are replaced, crew sizes will shrink, and employed seamen will need greater skills.

Vessels on rivers and canals and on the Great Lakes mostly carry bulk products such as coal, iron ore, petroleum, sand and gravel, grain, and chemicals. Shipments of these products are expected to grow through the year 2005, but productivity increases should cause employment to decline. Employment in water transportation services is likely to show little or no change.

The decline in jobs has created competition for jobs, with many experienced merchant mariners going for long periods without work. As a result, unions generally accept few new members. Also, many merchant marine academy graduates have not found licensed shipboard jobs in the U.S. merchant marine, although most do find related jobs. All are commissioned as ensigns in the U.S. Naval Reserve, and many go on active duty in the Navy. Some find jobs on tugboats or other watercraft or on foreign-flag vessels, or take jobs as seamen on U.S. flag ships. Some take land-based jobs with shipping companies, marine insurance companies, manufacturers of boilers or related machinery, civilian jobs with the U.S. Navy, or other related jobs. Unless the number of people seeking merchant marine jobs declines sharply, the present keen competition is likely to continue.

### Earnings

Water transportation workers who usually worked full-time had median weekly earnings of $595 in 1994. The middle 50 percent earned between $403 and $856 a week. The lowest 10 percent earned less than $284, while the highest 10 percent earned more than $1,092 a week.

Captains and mates had median weekly earnings of $684 a week in 1994. The middle 50 percent earned between $522 and $908 a week. The lowest paid 10 percent earned less than $423, while the highest more than $1,112 a week.

Seamen had median weekly earnings of $533 a week in 1994. The middle 50 percent earned between $336 and $764 a week. The lowest 10 percent earned less than $264 a week, while the highest 10 percent earned more than $970 a week.

### Related Occupations

Workers in occupations having duties and responsibilities similar to these occupations include fishing vessel captains, ferryboat operators, and hatch tenders.

### Related *D.O.T.* Jobs

These job titles are related to or more specific than the more general description above. They will help you identify job options you may not otherwise discover. These descriptions are in the current edition of the *Dictionary of Occupational Titles* and classified by numerical order.

197.130-010 ENGINEER; 197.133-014 MASTER, YACHT; 197.133-022 MATE, SHIP; 197.133-026 PILOT, SHIP; 197.133-030 TUGBOAT CAPTAIN; 197.133-034 TUGBOAT MATE; 197.137-010 DREDGE MATE;

197.161-010 DREDGE CAPTAIN; 197.163-010 FERRYBOAT CAPTAIN; 197.163-014 MASTER, PASSENGER BARGE; 197.163-018 MASTER, RIVERBOAT; 197.167-010 MASTER, SHIP; 911.131-010 BOATSWAIN; 911.133-010 CADET, DECK; 911.137-010 BARGE CAPTAIN; 911.137-014 DERRICK-BOAT CAPTAIN; 911.263-010 DEEP SUBMERGENCE VEHICLE OPERATOR; 911.363.010 FERRYBOAT OPERATOR; 911.363-014 QUARTERMASTER; 911.364-010 ABLE SEAMAN; 911.584-010 MARINE OILER; 911.664-010 FERRYBOAT OPERATOR, CABLE; 911.664-014 SAILOR, PLEASURE CRAFT; 911.687-022 DECKHAND; 911.687-030 ORDINARY SEAMAN; 951.685-018 FIRER, MARINE

### Sources of Additional Information

Information on merchant marine careers, training, and licensing requirements is available from:

❑ Maritime Administration, U.S. Department of Transportation, 400 7th St. SW, Washington, DC 20590.

❑ Coast Guard, Licensing and Evaluation Branch, Merchant Vessel and Personnel Division, 2100 2nd St. SW, Washington, DC 20593.

Individuals interested in attending a merchant marine academy should contact:

❑ Admissions Office, U.S. Merchant Marine Academy, Steamboat Rd., Kings Point, NY 11024.

❑ Admissions Office, California Maritime Academy, P.O. Box 1392, Vallejo, CA 94590.

# Welders, Cutters, and Welding Machine Operators

### Nature of the Work

Welding is the most common way of permanently joining metal parts. Heat is applied to the pieces to be joined, melting and fusing them to form a permanent bond. Because of its strength, welding is used to construct and repair parts of ships, automobiles, spacecraft, and thousands of other manufactured products. Welding is used to join beams when constructing buildings, bridges, and other structures, and pipes in nuclear power plants and refineries.

Welders use all types of welding equipment in a variety of positions, such as flat, vertical, horizontal, and overhead. They may perform manual welding, in which the work is entirely controlled by the welder, or semi-automatic welding, in which the welder uses machinery, such as a wire feeder, to perform welding tasks. They generally plan work from drawings or specifications or by analyzing damaged metal, using their knowledge of welding and metals. They select and set up welding equipment and may also examine welds to insure they meet standards or specifications. Some welders have more limited duties. They perform routine production work that has already been planned and laid out. These jobs do not require knowledge of all welding techniques.

In many production processes—where the work is repetitive and the items to be welded are relatively uniform—automated welding is used. In this process, a machine performs the welding tasks while monitored by a welding machine operator. Welding machine operators set up and operate welding machines as specified by layouts, work orders, or blueprints. Operators must constantly monitor the machine to ensure that it produces the desired weld.

The work of arc, plasma, and flame cutters is closely related to that of welders. However, instead of joining metals, cutters use the heat from burning gases or an electric arc to cut and trim metal objects to specific dimensions. Cutters also dismantle large objects, such as ships, railroad cars, automobiles or aircraft. Some operate and monitor cutting machines similar to those used by welding machine operators.

## Working Conditions

Welders and cutters frequently are exposed to potential hazards. They use protective clothing, safety shoes, goggles, helmets with protective lenses, and other devices to prevent burns and eye injuries and to protect them from falling objects. Automated welding machine operators are not exposed to as many hazards. A face shield or goggles generally provide adequate protection. Because some metals may give off toxic gases and fumes as they melt, federal regulations require ventilation to meet strict guidelines to minimize these hazards. Occasionally, some workers are in contact with rust, grease, and dirt on metal surfaces. Some welders are isolated for short intervals while they work in booths constructed to contain sparks and glare. Welders often work in a variety of awkward positions, having to make welds while bending, stooping, or working overhead. In some settings, however, working conditions are much better and few hazards or discomforts are encountered.

## Employment

Welders, cutters, and welding machine operators held about 416,000 jobs in 1994. About 9 out of 10 welders and cutters were employed in manufacturing, services, construction, or wholesale trade. The majority of those in manufacturing were employed in transportation equipment, industrial machinery and equipment, or fabricated metal products. All welding machine operators were employed in manufacturing industries, primarily fabricated metal products, machinery, and motor vehicles. Almost 2 of 5 welders are employed in six states: Texas, California, Ohio, Pennsylvania, Michigan, and Illinois—states heavily dominated by automobile and fabricated metal products manufacturing, and by the petroleum and chemical industry.

## Training, Other Qualifications, and Advancement

Training for welders can range from a few weeks of school or on-the-job training for low skilled positions to several years of combined school and on-the-job training for highly skilled jobs. Formal training is available in high schools, vocational schools, and postsecondary institutions such as vocational-technical institutes, community colleges, and private welding schools. The Armed Forces operate welding schools as well. Some employers provide training to help welders improve their skills. Courses in blueprint reading, shop mathematics, mechanical drawing, physics, chemistry, and metallurgy are helpful.

Some welders become certified, a process whereby the employer sends a worker to an institution, such as an independent testing lab or technical school to weld a test specimen to specific codes and standards required by the employer. The testing procedures are usually based on the standards and codes set by one of several industry associations the employer may be affiliated with. If the welding inspector at the examining institution determines that the worker has performed according to the employer's guidelines, he or she then certifies that the welder being tested is able to work with a particular welding procedure.

Welders and cutters need manual dexterity, good eyesight, and good hand-eye coordination. They should be able to concentrate on detailed work for long periods and be able to bend, stoop, and work in awkward positions.

Welders can advance to more skilled jobs with additional training and experience. They may be promoted to welding technicians, supervisors, inspectors, or instructors. Some experienced welders open their own repair shops.

## Job Outlook

Opportunities for those who wish to become welders, cutters, and welding machine operators should be good through the year 2005 as the number of qualified (certified) welders graduating from technical schools is expected to be in balance with the number of job openings resulting from the need to replace experienced workers who transfer to other occupations or leave the labor force. Employment of welders, cutters, and welding machine operators is expected to decline through the year 2005.

In certain industries—construction, wholesale trade, and repair services, for example—employment of welders and cutters will increase (see accompanying chart). The level of construction is expected to expand, as is the number of metal products needing repair, increasing the need for welding and cutting. This work is generally less routine and more difficult to automate than other welding jobs. Greater use of welding automation in manufacturing using simple repetitive welds could cause manual welders to be replaced by or retrained to become welding machine operators. Automated welding systems are expected to cause a decline in the employment of welding machine operators. Despite the welding jobs eliminated by automated welding systems, manual welders, especially those with a wide variety of skills, will still be needed for the maintenance, repair, and other work in manufacturing that cannot be automated. Certified welders, especially those certified in more than one process, will have much better employment opportunities than non-certified welders.

Welders, cutters, and welding machine operators in construction and manufacturing are vulnerable to periodic layoffs due to economic downturns.

## Earnings

Median earnings for welders and welding machine operators were about $460 a week in 1994. The middle 50 percent earned between $345 and $597. The top 10 percent earned more than $786, and the lowest 10 percent earned less than $281.

More than one-fourth of welders belong to unions. Among these are the International Association of Machinists and Aerospace Workers; the International Brotherhood of Boilermakers, Iron Ship Builders, Blacksmiths, Forgers and Helpers; the International Union, United Automobile, Aerospace and Agricultural Implement Workers of America; the United Association of Journeymen and Apprentices of the Plumbing and Pipe Fitting Industry of the United States and Canada; and the United Electrical, Radio, and Machine Workers of America.

## Related Occupations

Welders and cutters are skilled metal workers. Other metal workers include blacksmiths, forge shop workers, all-round machinists, machine-tool operators, tool and die makers, millwrights, sheetmetal workers, boilermakers, and metal sculptors.

Welding machine operators run machines that weld metal parts. Others who run metalworking machines include lathe and turning, milling and planing, punching and stamping press, and rolling machine operators.

## Related *D.O.T.* Jobs

These job titles are related to or more specific than the more general description above. They will help you identify job options you may not otherwise discover. These descriptions are in the current edition of the *Dictionary of Occupational Titles* and classified by numerical order.

There are too many *D.O.T.* titles to list here. Most are variations related to a specific industry, and we have included a small number of representative *D.O.T.* titles as examples. Complete lists are available in various career software published by JIST or directly from the U.S. Department of Labor.

613.667-010 LINER ASSEMBLER; 727.684-022 LEAD BURNER; 810.382-010 WELDING-MACHINE OPERATOR, ARC; 810.384-014 WELDER, ARC; 810.664-010 WELDER, GUN; 810.684-010 WELDER, TACK; 811.482-010 WELDING-MACHINE OPERATOR, GAS; 811.684-014 WELDER, GAS; 812.360-010 WELDER SETTER, RESISTANCE MACHINE; 812.682-010 WELDING-MACHINE OPERATOR, RESISTANCE; 814.684-010 WELDER, EXPLOSION; 815.682-010 LASER-BEAM-MACHINE OPERATOR; 815.682-014 WELDING-MACHINE OPERATOR, THERMIT; 816.364-010 ARC CUTTER; 816.464-010 THERMAL CUTTER, HAND I; 819.281-022 WELDER, EXPERIMENTAL; 819.361-010 WELDER-FITTER; 819.381-010 WELDER-ASSEMBLER; 819.384-010 WELDER, COMBINATION; 819.684-010 WELDER, PRODUCTION LINE; 819.685-010 WELDING-MACHINE TENDER

## Sources of Additional Information

For information on training opportunities and jobs for welders, cutters, and welding machine operators, contact local employers, the local office of the state employment service, or schools providing welding training.

Information on careers in welding is available from:

❑ American Welding Society, 550 NW LeJeune Rd., Miami, FL 33126-5699.

For a list of accredited schools that offer training in welding, contact:

❑ Career College Association, 750 1st Street NE, Suite 900, Washington, DC 20002.

# Woodworking Occupations

## Nature of the Work

Wood is one of the oldest, most basic building materials. Yet, even in our age of sophisticated composites and alloys, the demand for wood products continues unabated. Helping to meet this demand are production and precision woodworkers. Production woodworkers can be found in primary industries, such as sawmills and plywood mills, as well as in secondary industries that manufacture furniture, kitchen cabinets, musical instruments, and other fabricated wood products. Precision woodworkers, on the other hand, usually work in small shops that make architectural woodwork, furniture, and many other specialty items.

Woodworkers are employed at some stage of the process through which logs of wood are transformed into finished products. Some of these workers produce the structural elements of buildings; others mill hardwood and softwood lumber; still others assemble finished wood products. They operate machines that cut, shape, assemble, and finish raw wood to make the doors, windows, cabinets, trusses, plywood, flooring, paneling, molding, and trim that are components of most homes. Others may fashion home accessories such as beds, sofas, tables, dressers, and chairs. In addition to these household goods, they also make sporting goods, including baseball bats, racquets, and oars, as well as musical instruments, toys, caskets, tool handles, and thousands of other wooden items.

Production workers usually set up, operate, and tend woodworking machines—such as power saws, planers, sanders, lathes, jointers, and routers—to cut and shape components from lumber, plywood, and other wood panel products. Working from blueprints, instructions from supervisors, or shop drawings that they produce, woodworkers determine the method of shaping and sequence of assembling parts. Before cutting, they must often measure and mark the materials to be cut. They verify dimensions to adhere to specifications and may trim parts to insure a tight fit, using handtools such as planes, chisels, wood files, or sandpaper.

Most production woodworkers operate a specific woodworking machine, but others are responsible for a variety of machines. Lower skilled operators may merely press a switch on a woodworking machine and monitor the automatic operation, while more highly skilled operators set up their equipment, cut and shape wooden parts, and verify dimensions using a template, caliper, or rule. In sawmills, machine operators cut logs into planks, timbers, or boards. In veneer mills, they cut veneer sheets from logs for making plywood. While in furniture plants, they make furniture components such as table legs, drawers, rails, and spindles.

Many companies have installed computer-controlled machinery, which raises worker productivity and reduces wasted resources. With computerized numerical controls, an operator can program a machine to perform a sequence of operations automatically, resulting in greater precision and reliability. The integration of computers with equipment has improved production speeds and capabilities, simplified set-up and maintenance requirements, and increased the demand for workers with some computer skills.

Whether computer-controlled or manual equipment is used to machine the parts, the next step in the manufacturing process is the production of subassemblies using fasteners and adhesives. These pieces are then brought together to form a complete unit. The product is then finish sanded, stained, and if necessary, coated with a sealer such as lacquer or varnish. Woodworkers may perform this work in teams or be assisted by a helper.

Precision or custom woodworkers, such as cabinetmakers, model makers, wood machinists, and furniture and wood finishers, work on a customized basis, often building one-of-a-kind items. For this reason, they normally need substantial training and an ability to work from detailed instructions and specifications. They often are required to exercise independent judgment when undertaking an assignment. Precision woodworkers generally perform a complete cycle of cutting, shaping, surface preparation, and assembling prepared parts of complex wood components into a finished wood product.

## Working Conditions

Working conditions vary from industry to industry, and job to job. In primary industries, such as logging and sawmilling, working conditions are physically demanding due to the handling of heavy, bulky material. Workers in this area may also encounter excessive noise and dust and other air quality pollutants. However, these factors can be controlled by using earplugs and respirators. Rigid adherence to safety precautions minimizes risk of injury from contact with rough woodstock, sharp tools, and power equipment. The risk of injury is also lowered by the installation of computer-controlled equipment that reduces the physical labor and the hands-on contact with the machine.

In secondary industries, such as furniture and kitchen cabinet manufacturing, working conditions also depend on the industry and the particular job. Those employees who operate machinery must wear ear and eye protection, follow operating safety instructions, and use safety shields or guards when appropriate. Those who work in the finishing area must either be provided with an appropriate dust or vapor mask, a complete protective safety suit, or they must be in a finishing environment that removes all vapors and particle matter from the atmosphere. Prolonged standing, lifting, and fitting heavy objects are also common characteristics of the job.

## Employment

Workers in woodworking occupations held about 367,000 jobs in 1994. Self-employed woodworkers, mostly cabinetmakers and furniture finishers, accounted for 50,000 of these jobs. Employment was distributed as follows:

| | |
|---|---|
| Woodworkers, precision | 241,000 |
| Woodworking machine setters and operators | 126,000 |
| Head sawyers | 62,000 |
| Woodworking machine operators | 64,000 |

Eighty percent of salaried woodworkers worked in manufacturing industries. Among these woodworkers, 31 percent were employed in establishments fabricating household and office furniture and fixtures; 24 percent were in establishments making millwork, plywood, and structural wood members, used primarily in construction; and 12 percent worked in sawmills and planing mills manufacturing a variety of raw, intermediate, and finished woodstock. Woodworkers also were employed by wholesale and retail lumber dealers, furniture stores, reupholstery and furniture repair shops, and construction firms.

Woodworking jobs are found throughout the country. However, production jobs are concentrated in the South and Northwest, close to the supply of wood, while furniture makers are more prevalent in the East. Custom shops can be found everywhere, but are generally concentrated in or near highly populated areas.

## Training, Other Qualifications, and Advancement

Most woodworkers are trained on the job, picking up skills informally from experienced workers. Some acquire skills through vocational education or by working as carpenters on construction jobs. Others may attend colleges or universities that offer training in many areas including wood technology, furniture manufacturing, wood engineering, and production management. These programs prepare students for positions in production, supervision, engineering, or management.

Beginners usually observe and help experienced machine operators. They may supply material or remove fabricated products from the machine. Trainees do simple machine operating jobs and are at first closely supervised by experienced workers. As they gain experience, they perform more complex jobs with less supervision. Some may learn to read blueprints, set up machines, and plan the sequence of their work. Most woodworkers learn the basic machine operations or job tasks in a few months, but becoming a skilled woodworker often requires two years or more.

In the past, a high school education was seldom required. However, persons seeking woodworking jobs can enhance their employment and advancement prospects by completing high school. Training in mathematics, science, and computer applications will be beneficial in the future as woodworking technology becomes more sophisticated, and as more companies install computerized equipment. Employers often look for individuals with mechanical ability, manual dexterity, and the ability to pay attention to detail.

Advancement opportunities are often limited and depend upon availability, seniority, and a worker's skills and initiative. Experienced woodworkers may become inspectors or supervisors responsible for the work of a group of woodworkers. Production workers can advance into these positions by assuming additional responsibilities and by attending workshops, seminars, or college programs. Those who are highly skilled may set up their own woodworking shops.

## Job Outlook

Little change is expected in the employment of woodworkers through the year 2005, as growth among precision woodworkers will be offset by the declining employment of woodworking machine operators. As the nation's population, personal income, and business expenditures grow, the demand for wood products will increase. In addition, the continuing need for repair and renovation of residential and commercial properties is expected to stimulate demand. Opportunities for woodworkers who specialize in such items as moldings, cabinets, stairs, and windows should, therefore, be particularly good.

Several factors may limit the growth of woodworking occupations in coming years. Environmental measures designed to control various pollutants used in or generated by woodworking processes are likely to have a significant impact on employment, especially in secondary industries. Primary industries will be more affected by a shortage of timber as the harvesting of old growth forests on federal lands becomes more restricted. Technological advances like computerized numerical control machinery and robots will prevent employment from rising as fast as the demand for wood products, particularly in the mills and manufacturing plants where many of the processes can be automated. In addition, some jobs will be lost in the United States as imports continue to grow and as U.S. firms move production to other countries. Finally, materials such as metal, plastic, and fiberglass will continue to be used as alternatives to wood in many products, primarily because they are cheaper, stronger, or easier to shape.

As a result of these trends, employment opportunities in the primary wood industries may be more limited than those in the secondary industries. Also, as firms automate production, the demand for highly skilled workers will increase. Employment in all of the woodworking occupations is highly sensitive to economic cycles, so the growth in these occupations will be primarily affected by the overall state of the economy. Although this growth will be modest, thousands of openings will arise each year because of the need to replace experienced workers who transfer to other occupations or leave the labor force.

## Earnings

Median weekly earnings for salaried full-time precision woodworkers were about $390 in 1994. The middle 50 percent earned between $280 and $510. The lowest 10 percent earned less than $230, while the highest 10 percent earned over $650. Median weekly earnings for full-time woodworking machine operators were around $310 in 1994. The middle 50 percent earned between $250 and $420. The lowest 10 percent earned less than $200, while the highest 10 percent earned over $525. Earnings vary by industry, geographic region, skill, educational level, and complexity of the machinery operated. Woodworkers usually receive a basic benefit package including medical and dental benefits and a pension plan.

Some woodworkers, such as those in logging or sawmills, who are engaged in processing primary wood and building materials, are members of the International Association of Machinists. Others may belong to the United Furniture Workers of America or the United Brotherhood of Carpenters and Joiners of America.

## Related Occupations

Many woodworkers follow blueprints and drawings and use machines to shape and form raw wood into a final product. Workers who perform similar functions working with other materials include precision metalworkers, metalworking and plastics-working machine operators, metal fabricators, molders and shapers, and leather workers.

## Related *D.O.T.* Jobs

These job titles are related to or more specific than the more general description above. They will help you identify job options you may not otherwise discover. These descriptions are in the current edition of the *Dictionary of Occupational Titles* and classified by numerical order.

There are too many *D.O.T.* titles to list here. Most are variations related to a specific industry, and we have included a small number of representative *D.O.T.* titles as examples. Complete lists are available in various career software published by JIST or directly from the U.S. Department of Labor.

564.682-010 CHIPPING-MACHINE OPERATOR; 660.280-010 CABINET-MAKER; 661.280-010 PATTERNMAKER; 661.281-010 LOFT WORKER; 661.380-010 MODEL MAKER, WOOD; 662.685-026 SANDING-MA-CHINE TENDER; 663.685-022 PUNCHER; 664.382-010 SWING-TYPE-LATHE OPERATOR; 664.382-014 WOOD-TURNING-LATHE OPERATOR; 664.685-022 FRAZER; 664.685-034 TURNING LATHE TENDER; 665.682-010 DOWEL-MACHINE OPERATOR; 665.682-014 HEADER; 665.685-030 STAVE JOINTER; 685-042 ROUTER TENDER; 666.684-010 FRAMER; 667.662-010 HEAD SAWYER; 667.682-042 JIGSAW OPERATOR; 667.685-010 BAND-SAW OPERATOR; 667.687-018 SAWMILL WORKER; 669.682-070 UTILITY OPERATOR; 692.380-010 SET-UP MECHANIC; 761.281-010 CARVER, HAND; 763.380-010 FURNITURE RESTORER; 763.381-010 FURNITURE FINISHER

## Sources of Additional Information

For information about woodworking occupations, contact local furniture manufacturers, sawmills and planing mills, cabinet making or millwork firms, lumber dealers, a local of one of the unions mentioned above, or the nearest office of the state employment service.

For general information about furniture woodworking occupations, contact:

❑ American Furniture Manufacturers Association, Manufacturing Services Division, P.O. Box HP-7, High Point, NC 27261.

### *I know you don't want to read this section.*

"Why," you ask, "should I spend my time reading dull labor market information?" Perhaps I am not being fair to you, but that would be the question I would be asking myself about now.

My response to you is that reading this section will be good for your career health. I say this because it will encourage you to think about your long-term place in the workforce—and how to take advantage of the trends that are beyond your control. You *will* be affected by these trends, and you ignore them only at great risk to your future earning power and satisfaction.

For example, the information in this section will tell you that many of the fastest growing jobs require training or education beyond high school—but not necessarily a four-year college degree. It will inform you of the enormous increase in earnings for those with more education and training. It will encourage you to consider that some industries offer more growth potential than others—and that your career planning and job seeking should consider the industry you select just as carefully as the occupation. And this section presents many other thought-provoking things to consider, things that can make a big difference to you in the future.

So consider curling up with this section and reading it like a good novel. Well, perhaps that's asking too much, but I do encourage you to read it carefully—and consider how you can use this information to make better long-term career and life plans.

## An Overview of Major Trends

The information in this section is based on content from the 1996-97 edition of the *Occupational Outlook Handbook,* published by the U.S. Department of Labor. Because there is a one to two year delay in collecting and analyzing employment data, 1994 data is the most recent available.

### *Employment Will Continue to Grow, But Not as Quickly as in the Recent Past*

- Over the 1994-2005 period, employment is projected to increase by 17.7 million or 14 percent. This is slower than the 24 percent increase attained during the 11-year period from 1983 to 1994, when the economy added 24.6 million jobs.

- Wage and salary worker employment will account for 95 percent of this increase. In addition, the number of self-employed workers is expected to increase by 950,000, to 11.6 million in 2005, while the number of unpaid family workers will decline.

### *Service-Producing Industries Will Account for Most New Jobs (See chart 1.)*

- Employment growth is projected to be highly concentrated by industry. The services and retail trade industries will account for 16.2 million out of a total projected growth of 16.8 million wage and salary jobs.

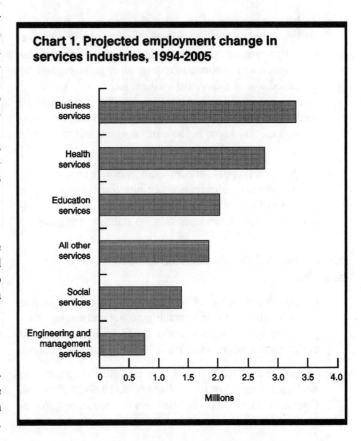

**Chart 1. Projected employment change in services industries, 1994-2005**

- Business, health, and education services will account for 70 percent of the growth—9.2 million out of 13.6 million jobs—within services.

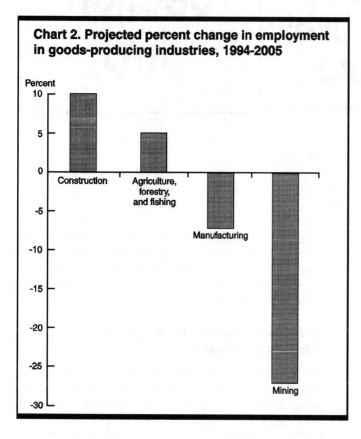

**Chart 2. Projected percent change in employment in goods-producing industries, 1994-2005**

- Health care services will account for almost one-fifth of all job growth from 1994 to 2005. Factors contributing to continued growth in this industry include the aging population, which will continue to require more services, and the increased use of innovative medical technology for intensive diagnosis and treatment. Patients will increasingly be shifted out of hospitals and into outpatient facilities, nursing homes, and home health care in an attempt to contain costs.

- The personnel supply services industry, which provides temporary help to employers in other industries, is projected to add 1.3 million jobs from 1994 to 2005. Temporary workers tend to have low wages, low job stability, and poor job benefits.

### Manufacturing Jobs Will Continue to Decline (See chart 2.)

- The goods-producing sector faces declining employment in two of its four industries: manufacturing and mining. Employment in the other two industries—construction, and agriculture, forestry, and fishing—is expected to increase.

- Employment in manufacturing is expected to continue to decline, losing 1.3 million jobs over the 1994-2005 period. Operators, fabricators, and laborers and precision produc-

tion, craft, and repair occupations are expected to account for more than 1 million of these lost jobs. Systems analysts and other computer-related occupations in manufacturing are expected to increase.

### Opportunities Will Come from Replacement as Well as Growth (See chart 3.)

- Job growth can be measured by percentage change and numerical change. The fastest growing occupations do not necessarily provide the largest numbers of jobs. Even though an occupation is expected to grow rapidly, it may provide fewer openings than a slower growing, larger occupation.

- Opportunities in large occupations are enhanced by the additional job openings resulting from the need to replace workers who leave the occupation. Some workers leave occupations as they are promoted or change careers; others stop working to return to school, assume household responsibilities, or retire.

- Replacement needs are greater in occupations with low pay and status, low training requirements, and a high proportion of young and part-time workers.

- Replacement needs will account for 29.4 million job openings from 1994 to 2005, far more than the 17.7 million openings projected to arise from employment growth.

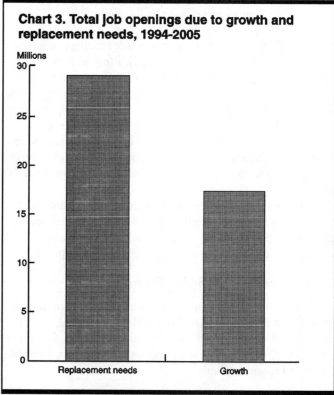

**Chart 3. Total job openings due to growth and replacement needs, 1994-2005**

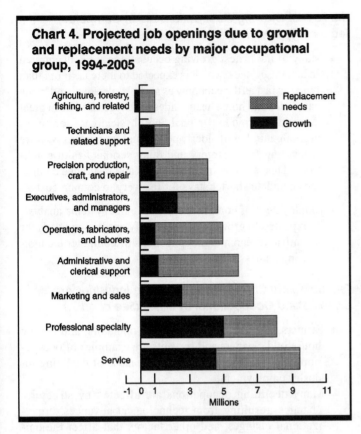

**Chart 4. Projected job openings due to growth and replacement needs by major occupational group, 1994-2005**

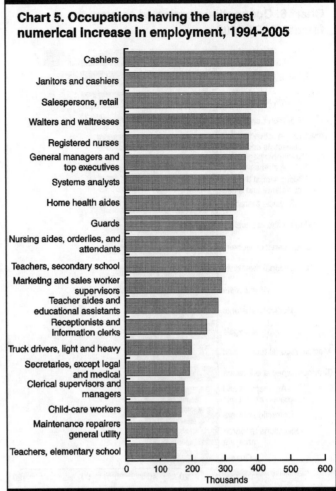

**Chart 5. Occupations having the largest numerical increase in employment, 1994-2005**

## Some Occupations Will Grow More Rapidly Than Others (See chart 4.)

- Employment in professional specialty occupations is projected to increase at a faster rate than any other major occupational group.

- Among the major occupational groups, employment in professional specialty occupations is also projected to account for the most job growth from 1994 to 2005.

- Professional specialty occupations—which require high educational attainment and offer high earnings—and service occupations—which require lower educational attainment and offer lower earnings—are expected to account for more than half of all job growth between 1994 and 2005.

- Agriculture, forestry, fishing, and related occupations is the only major occupational group projected to decline. All job openings in this group will stem from replacement needs.

- Office automation is expected to have a significant effect on many individual administrative and clerical support occupations.

- Precision production, craft, and repair occupations and operators, fabricators, and laborers are projected to grow much more slowly than average due to continuing advances in technology, changes in production methods, and the overall decline in manufacturing employment.

## Twenty Occupations Will Account for Half of All Job Growth (See chart 5.)

- The 20 occupations accounting for half of all job growth over the 1994-2005 period tend to be large in size rather than fast-growing. Three health care occupations are in the top 10, and three education-related occupations are in the second 10.

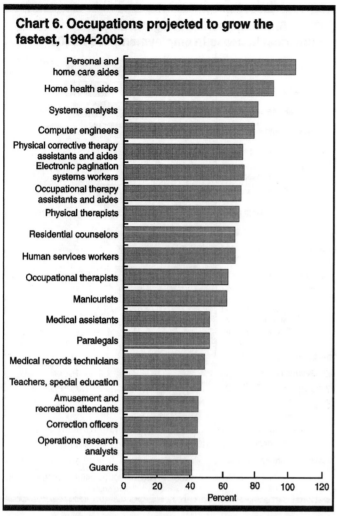

**Chart 6. Occupations projected to grow the fastest, 1994-2005**

(bar chart, x-axis: Percent, 0 to 120)

- Personal and home care aides
- Home health aides
- Systems analysts
- Computer engineers
- Physical corrective therapy assistants and aides
- Electronic pagination systems workers
- Occupational therapy assistants and aides
- Physical therapists
- Residential counselors
- Human services workers
- Occupational therapists
- Manicurists
- Medical assistants
- Paralegals
- Medical records technicians
- Teachers, special education
- Amusement and recreation attendants
- Correction officers
- Operations research analysts
- Guards

### The Fastest Growing Occupations Are in Computer Technology and Health Services (See chart 6.)

- Many of the fastest growing occupations are concentrated in health services, which is expected to increase more than twice as fast as the economy as a whole. Personal and home care aides and home health aides are expected to be in great demand to provide personal and physical care for an increasing number of elderly people and for persons who are recovering from surgery and other serious health conditions. This is occurring as hospitals and insurance companies mandate shorter stays for recovery to contain costs.

- Employment of computer engineers and systems analysts is expected to grow rapidly to satisfy expanding needs for scientific research and applications of computer technology in business and industry.

### Technological Changes and Declining Industries Are Often Behind Occupational Declines (See chart 7.)

- Farmers, garment sewing machine operators, and private household cleaners and servants are examples of occupations that will lose employment because of declining industry employment.
- Many declining occupations are affected by structural changes, resulting from technological advances, organizational changes, and other factors that affect the employment of workers. For example, the use of typists and word processors is expected to decline substantially because of productivity improvements resulting from office automation and the increased use of word processing equipment by professional and managerial employees.

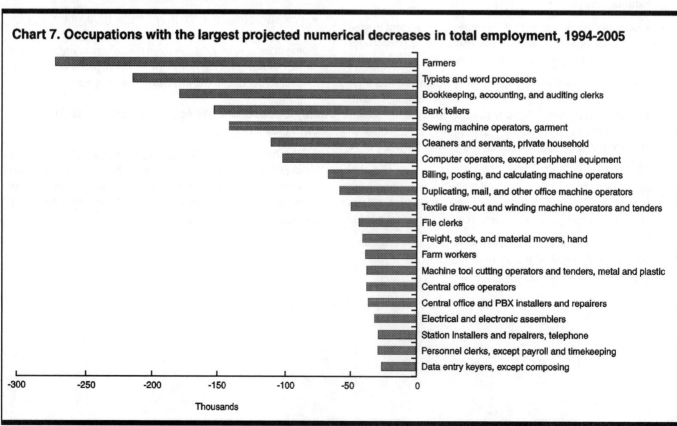

**Chart 7. Occupations with the largest projected numerical decreases in total employment, 1994-2005**

(bar chart, x-axis: Thousands, -300 to 0)

- Farmers
- Typists and word processors
- Bookkeeping, accounting, and auditing clerks
- Bank tellers
- Sewing machine operators, garment
- Cleaners and servants, private household
- Computer operators, except peripheral equipment
- Billing, posting, and calculating machine operators
- Duplicating, mail, and other office machine operators
- Textile draw-out and winding machine operators and tenders
- File clerks
- Freight, stock, and material movers, hand
- Farm workers
- Machine tool cutting operators and tenders, metal and plastic
- Central office operators
- Central office and PBX installers and repairers
- Electrical and electronic assemblers
- Station installers and repairers, telephone
- Personnel clerks, except payroll and timekeeping
- Data entry keyers, except composing

### Education and Training Affect Job Opportunities (See chart 8.)

- Workers in jobs with low education and training requirements tend to have greater occupational mobility. Consequently, these jobs will provide a larger than proportional share of all job openings stemming from replacement needs.

- Jobs requiring the most education and training will grow faster than jobs with lower education and training requirements.

Table 1 presents the fastest growing occupations and those having the largest numerical increase in employment over the 1994-2005 period, categorized by level of education and training.

### Jobs Requiring the Most Education and Training Will Be the Fastest Growing and Highest Paying

- Occupations that require a bachelor's degree or above will average 23 percent growth, almost double the 12 percent growth projected for occupations that require less education and training.

- Occupations that pay above-average wages are projected to grow faster than occupations with below-average wages. Jobs with above-average wages are expected to account for 60 percent of employment growth over the 1994-2005 period. Jobs with higher earnings often require higher levels of education and training.

- Education is important in getting a high-paying job. However, many occupations—for example, registered nurses, blue-collar worker supervisors, electrical and electronic technicians/technologists, carpenters, and police and detectives—do not require a college degree, yet offer higher than average earnings.

- Groups in the labor force with lower than average educational attainment in 1994, including Hispanics and blacks, will continue to have difficulty obtaining a share of the high-paying jobs that is consistent with their share of the labor force, unless their educational attainment rises. Although high-paying jobs will be available without college training, most jobs that pay above-average wages will require a college degree.

- Educational services are projected to increase by 2.2 million jobs and account for one out of every eight jobs that will be added to the economy between 1994 and 2005. Most jobs will be for teachers, who are projected to account for about 20 percent of all jobs available for college graduates.

- Projected employment growth of the occupations whose earnings rank in the top quartile in the nation was highly concentrated. Eight of the 146 occupations will account for about half of the new jobs: registered nurses, systems analysts, blue-collar worker supervisors, general managers and top executives, and four teaching occupations—elementary school teachers, secondary school teachers, college faculty, and special education teachers.

### Jobs Requiring the Least Education and Training Will Provide the Most Openings, but Offer the Lowest Pay (See chart 9)

- The distribution of jobs by education and training and earnings will change little over the 1994-2005 period, with jobs requiring the least amount of education and training, and generally offering low pay, continuing to account for about 4 of every 10 jobs.

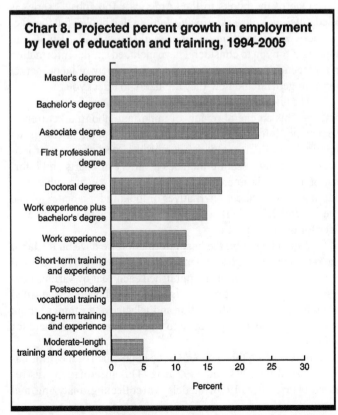

**Chart 8. Projected percent growth in employment by level of education and training, 1994-2005**

**Chart 9. Projected total job openings by level of education and training, 1994-2005**

- Jobs that require moderate-length and short-term training and experience (the two categories requiring the least amount of education and training) will provide over half of total job openings over the 1994-2005 period.

### The Labor Force Will Continue to Grow Faster Than the Population

- Spurred by the growing proportion of women who work, the labor force will grow slightly faster than the population over the 1994-2005 period.

### Women Will Continue to Comprise an Increasing Share of the Labor Force (See chart 10.)

- Women, as a result of a faster rate of growth than men, are projected to represent a slightly greater portion of the labor force in 2005 than in 1994—increasing from 46 to 48 percent.
- The number of men in the labor force is projected to grow, but at a slower rate than in the past, in part reflecting declining employment in good-paying production jobs in manufacturing and a continued shift in demand for workers from the goods-producing sector to the service-producing sector. Men with less education and training may find it increasingly difficult to obtain jobs consistent with their experience.

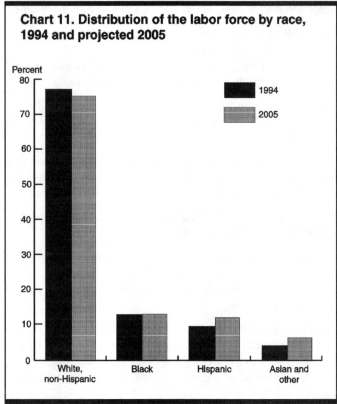

**Chart 11. Distribution of the labor force by race, 1994 and projected 2005**

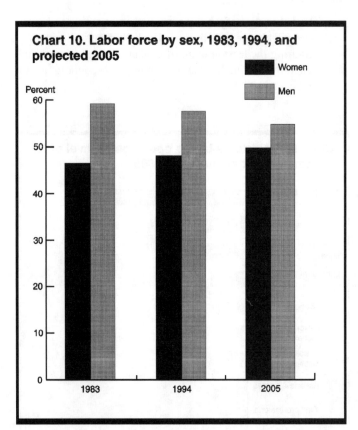

**Chart 10. Labor force by sex, 1983, 1994, and projected 2005**

### The Labor Force Will Become Increasingly Diverse (See chart 11.)

- The number of Hispanics, Asians, and other races will increase much faster than blacks and white non-Hispanics. Blacks will increase faster than white non-Hispanics.

- Despite relatively slow growth, resulting in a declining share of the labor force, white non-Hispanics will still make up the vast majority of workers in 2005.

### More Information on Important Labor Market Trends—and What They Mean to Your Career Planning

One of the books in the "America's Top Jobs™" series is titled *America's Fastest Growing Jobs*. In that book, I put together a variety of information on labor market trends that I think are important for you to consider. I have included similar information in this section, since it provides a good overview of labor market trends in general and how they are likely to effect you.

The information is divided into three major subsections. The first presents a general review of important labor market trends. Next comes information on jobs that are among the fastest growing in terms of percentage growth or in largest numbers of jobs created. The third section includes a variety of charts and information that might interest you. I assume that you are either considering various career alternatives or looking for a better job, so I've selected labor market details most important for you to consider for these purposes.

Without a doubt, the best information we have on the labor market comes from governmental sources. Thousands of pages of labor market information are published each year by various government agencies—entirely too much for most people. I've sifted through much of this information and selected a few things I think will be of particular importance to you and present them here for you to ponder.

In reviewing this, you will notice that much of the information is based on 1994 and 1992 data. This information was released as recently as 1996, but delays in collecting, analyzing, and

## Table 1. Jobs growing the fastest and having the largest numerical increase in employment from 1994-2005, by level of education and training

| Fastest growing occupations | Occupations having the largest numerical increase in employment |
|---|---|
| **First-professional degree** | |
| Chiropractors | Lawyers |
| Lawyers | Physicians |
| Physicians | Clergy |
| Clergy | Chiropractors |
| Podiatrists | Dentists |
| **Doctoral degree** | |
| Medical scientists | College and university faculty |
| Biological scientists | Biological scientists |
| College and university faculty | Medical scientists |
| Mathematicians and all other mathematical scientists | Mathematicians and all other mathematical scientists |
| **Master's degree** | |
| Operations research analysts | Management analysts |
| Speech-language pathologists and audiologists | Counselors |
| Management analysts | Speech-language pathologists and audiologists |
| Counselors | Psychologists |
| Urban and regional planners | Operations research analysts |
| **Work experience plus bachelor's degree** | |
| Engineering, mathematics, and natural science managers | General managers and top executives |
| Marketing, advertising, and public relations managers | Financial managers |
| Artists and commercial artists | Marketing, advertising, and public relations managers |
| Financial managers | Engineering, mathematics, and natural science managers |
| Education administrators | Education administrators |
| **Bachelor's degree** | |
| Systems analysts | Systems analysts |
| Computer engineers | Teachers, secondary school |
| Occupational therapists | Teachers, elementary school |
| Physical therapists | Teachers, special education |
| Special education teachers | Social workers |
| **Associate degree** | |
| Paralegals | Registered nurses |
| Medical records technicians | Paralegals |
| Dental hygienists | Radiologic technologists and technicians |
| Respiratory therapists | Dental hygienists |
| Radiologic technologists and technicians | Medical records technicians |
| **Postsecondary vocational training** | |
| Manicurists | Secretaries, except legal and medical |
| Surgical technologists | Licensed practical nurses |
| Data processing equipment repairers | Hairdressers, hairstylists, and cosmetologists |
| Dancers and choreographers | Legal secretaries |
| Emergency medical technicians | Medical secretaries |
| **Work experience** | |
| Nursery and greenhouse managers | Marketing and sales worker supervisors |
| Lawn service managers | Clerical supervisors and managers |
| Food service and lodging managers | Food service and lodging managers |
| Clerical supervisors and managers | Instructors, adult education |
| Teachers and instructors, vocational and nonvocational training | Teachers and instructors, vocational education and training |
| **Long-term training and experience (more than 12 months of on-the-job training)** | |
| Electronic pagination systems workers | Maintenance repairers, general utility |
| Correction officers | Correction officers |
| Securities and financial services sales workers | Automotive mechanics |
| Patternmakers and layout workers, fabric and apparel | Cooks, restaurant |
| Producers, directors, actors, and entertainers | Police patrol officers |
| **Moderate-length training and experience (1 to 12 months of combined on-the-job experience and informal training)** | |
| Physical and corrective therapy assistants and aides | Human services workers |
| Occupational therapy assistants and aides | Medical assistants |
| Human services workers | Instructors and coaches, sports and physical training |
| Medical assistants | Dental assistants |
| Detectives, except public | Painters and paper hangers, construction and maintenance |
| **Short-term training and experience (up to 1 month of on-the-job experience)** | |
| Personal and home care aides | Cashiers |
| Home health aides | Janitors and cleaners, including maids and housekeepers |
| Amusement and recreation attendants | Salespersons, retail |
| Guards | Waiters and waitresses |
| Adjustment clerks | Home health aides |

publishing the data make it the most recent available. Even so, this is useful information since it clearly points out long-term trends that have already affected you, whether or not you are fully aware of them. Basic labor market trends are typically ones that do not shift quickly, and they are often accurately predicted by our friends at the U.S. Department of Labor.

## Important Labor Market Trends to Consider in Your Career Planning

The labor market is changing rapidly. Total employment in the U.S. economy is projected to increase by 17.7 million jobs, rising from 127.0 million to 144.7 million jobs by the year 2005. The projected 14 percent rate of employment growth is considerably slower than the 24 percent increase attained during the previous 11-year period, 1983-94, during which the economy added 24.6 million jobs. The faster rate of growth in the recent past reflects the entry of baby boomers to the labor force well into the 1980s.

The economy is expected to continue generating jobs for workers at all levels of education and training, although average growth will be greater for occupations requiring a bachelor's degree or more education than for those requiring less training.

While many new jobs will be created, many more existing jobs will also be affected by changing technologies, new products and techniques, foreign trade, changing consumer preferences, and other factors. Almost everyone will be affected by these changes, and it is clear that some occupations will do better than others. Few jobs will remain the same, and many people will need to upgrade their skills, change jobs, or even change careers.

No one can be sure of what will happen in the future, but some trends in the labor market do give clues about what is likely to happen. When making decisions about your education or career, it is important to understand these trends and to make good choices based on this information. While a lot of labor market information is available, I have selected those issues I believe are most important for you to consider. Spend a little time going over each one.

### Growth Rates Vary Among Occupational Groups

Growth rates are projected to be very different among the major occupational groups, resulting in a change in the structure of employment through 2005. In general, occupations that require a bachelor's degree or other postsecondary education or training are projected to have faster than average rates of employment growth. However, many occupations requiring less formal education or training also are projected to have above-average growth.

In addition to the growth rate, employment size is an important factor in determining the numerical change in an occupation. Many slower-growing occupations, some requiring little education and training and others having considerable educational requirements, are expected to add significant numbers of jobs primarily because of their large employment bases. As a result, the economy is projected to continue generating jobs for workers at all levels of education and training.

This section compares 1994-2005 projected changes in the structure of employment at the major occupational group level with the changes that occurred over the previous 11-year period,

1983-1994. It also discusses the detailed occupations that are projected to grow the most rapidly in percentage terms, those with the largest numerical increases, and those with the largest employment declines. Finally, it presents the total number of job openings expected to occur during the projection period because of growth in the economy and the net loss resulting from workers who leave the labor force or transfer to other occupations.

### The Labor Market Will Continue to Grow

From 1950 through 1980, the labor market doubled from 45 million to 90 million nonfarm wage and hourly workers. More than half of this growth occurred in the 1970s, when 24 million new workers were absorbed by the labor market—a 29 percent increase. These were the years when baby boomers were entering the job market in large numbers. The 1980s saw rapid but more modest growth rates, adding about 20 million workers from 1980 through 1992.

Women also entered the labor force in much greater numbers during these years and stayed there longer. In 1950, only 39.1 percent of all women aged 35 to 44 were in the labor market; this had increased to 76.8 percent by 1992. Immigration during these years also increased the number of workers.

While it is not possible to know with certainty what the future holds, projections by the U.S. Department of Labor anticipate continuing increases in the size of our labor market.

### Some Jobs Will Grow More Rapidly Than Others

While there will be growth in most occupations, some will grow much more rapidly than others, and some will even decline. Obviously, occupations that are expected to grow quickly will offer many opportunities. Jobs with the fastest growth rates tend to require education and training beyond the high school level. This "upgrading" of skills is an important trend in our labor force because even entry-level jobs now typically require good academic skills as well as training beyond high school.

### Most People Will Change Jobs and Careers

Young people tend to change jobs more frequently, but even workers older than 25 will change jobs an average of eight or more times during their working lives. Most people will also change their careers—going from truck driver to teacher, for example—four or more times during their working lives. And the trend for changing jobs and careers more often is increasing. Sometimes, these changes will not be anticipated or will occur in unpredictable ways. For these reasons, preparing now for your next job or career change makes more sense than ever.

### Most Jobs Require More Education

Back when factory jobs were plentiful, many people could get a good-paying factory job right out of high school. Today, intense competition exists for the few of these jobs that come open.

While the labor market is projected to continue to grow rapidly, many of the new jobs it creates will differ from those in the past. You can clearly see this by reviewing the lists of rapidly growing jobs I included earlier. Those lists demonstrate that most of the rapidly growing jobs require more education and training than those created in years past.

This trend is likely to accelerate in the years ahead, with more and more jobs requiring technical training or advanced education. A big part of the reason for this is the increasing use of advanced technologies in many jobs, including the widespread use of computers, automation, and other technologies. Even entry-level jobs typically held by high school graduates now often require some computer experience.

This upgrading of required skills to obtain the better jobs will continue. This means that those employed now will need to continue their education to keep up with the changing technology that affects their jobs, and entry-level workers will need more education to be considered for many jobs.

The projected demand for college graduates will remain strong, though some fields will do better than others. College graduates, on the average, earn much more than workers with only a high school degree, and this earnings gap has widened over the past 10 years. But a four-year college degree is not essential to do well in the labor market. Many of the rapidly growing jobs, for example, will require technical training that can be obtained in one or two years at a private vocational school or community college.

Recent studies have shown that the additional cost of education or training is often paid back quickly in higher earnings. And the increased earnings often last a lifetime, making a major difference in lifestyle. So consider investing in yourself, and don't eliminate jobs that interest you if they require additional education. Instead, consider getting it.

### Education and Earnings Are Related

While many of the fastest growing jobs require training beyond high school, the chart that follows indicates there will be opportunities for people at all levels of education. The chart shows the projected growth rates for various major occupational clusters and includes details related to the education and earnings for these jobs. As you can see, while there is job growth projected in all major occupational groups, job growth will be fastest in groups requiring the highest levels of education—and these same groups have the highest earnings. Growth projections are for the 1992-2005 period and earnings are based on 1992 figures.

As the chart shows, occupations that require more education will generally grow faster than occupations with lower educational requirements. Look over the lists of the fastest growing jobs found earlier in this chapter and you will notice that almost all of them require special training beyond high school. Only two occupational groups—health services and personal services—have approximately one-half of workers with a high school education or less.

Three of the fastest growing occupational groups are executive, administrative, and managerial; professional specialty; and technicians and related support occupations. Not surprisingly, these occupations usually require the highest levels of education and skill. These three major occupational groups, which represent a little more than one-fourth of total employment, are expected to account for about 40 percent of the increase in employment through 2005.

In recent years, the educational attainment of the labor force has risen dramatically. Between 1975 and today, the proportion of the labor force aged 25 to 64 with at least one year of college increased from 33 percent to about 50 percent, while the proportion with four years of college or more increased from 18 percent to 26 percent. Even when workers with varying education levels are employed within the same occupation, those with higher education levels often earn considerably more than their less-educated colleagues.

### Many Openings Result from Turnover

While I have emphasized the increase in the size of the labor market and the many new jobs this will create, it is important to note that the majority of job openings result from the need to replace workers. Replacement openings occur as people leave occupations. Some change careers, while others are promoted to other positions. Still others stop working to return to school, assume household responsibilities, or retire.

Through 2005 most jobs will become available due to replacement needs. In some occupational groups, more openings

## Projected Growth by Major Occupational Group and Educational Attainment

| Occupational group | Projected growth 1992-2005 (percent) | Educational attainment (percent) | | | $ Median weekly earnings, 1992 |
| --- | --- | --- | --- | --- | --- |
| | | High school or less | 1 to 3 years of college | 4 or more years of college | |
| Executives, administrators, and managers | 26 | 25 | 27 | 48 | 652 |
| Professional specialty workers | 37 | 9 | 19 | 72 | 596 |
| Technicians and related support workers | 32 | 26 | 45 | 29 | 489 |
| Marketing and sales workers | 21 | 46 | 32 | 22 | 346 |
| Administrative support workers, including clerical | 14 | 50 | 37 | 13 | 341 |
| Service workers | 33 | 68 | 26 | 6 | 232 |
| Agriculture, forestry, fishing, and related workers | 4 | 75 | 17 | 8 | 258 |
| Precision, production, craft, and repair workers | 13 | 68 | 26 | 6 | 470 |
| Operators, fabricators, and laborers | 10 | 80 | 17 | 3 | 331 |
| **Totals** | **22** | **50** | **27** | **23** | **$406** |

are anticipated for replacement workers than from the creation of new positions. For example, marketing and sales positions will require an estimated 4.2 million replacement workers and another 2.3 million additional positions. This means that even in slow- or no-growth occupations, new people will still be hired to replace workers who leave.

Occupations with the most replacement openings tend to be large fields with low pay and status, low training requirements, and a high proportion of young and part-time workers. Cashiers, waiters and waitresses, and child-care workers are examples of jobs with high turnover rates.

Occupations with relatively few replacement openings usually have lengthy training requirements, a high proportion of prime working age, full-time workers, and provide high pay and status. Physical therapists, lawyers, and aircraft pilots are examples of workers who have generally spent several years acquiring training that may not be applicable to other occupations.

## The Importance of Jobs in Small Business

In past years, most people worked for large employers, and many people conduct their career planning and job seeking as if this were still true. But according to government data, about 70 percent of private sector employment is now in businesses with fewer than 500 workers. The largest employers employ fewer workers than they did 10 years ago, and most of the new jobs are being created by small employers. This means that you are now far more likely to work for a small employer than a large one.

Jobs with small employers tend to require more flexibility and more rapid adaptation to change. While large employers remain an important part of our economy, small employers have become increasingly important.

## Additional Information on Labor Market Trends

### Population and Regional Trends

Population trends affect employment opportunities in several ways. In the years to come, changes in the size and composition of the population will influence the demand for goods and services. For example, the population group aged 85 and over will grow about four times as fast as the total population, greatly increasing the demand for health services. Population changes also produce corresponding changes in the size and characteristics of the labor force.

The U.S. civilian noninstitutional population, aged 16 and over, is expected to increase from about 192 to 219 million through 2005, growing more slowly than it did in the previous decade. However, even slower population growth rates will increase the demand for goods and services, as well as the demand for workers in many occupations and industries.

The age distribution will shift toward relatively fewer children and teenagers and a growing proportion of middle-aged and older people into the 21st Century. The decline in the proportion of teenagers reflects the lower birth rates during the 1980s; the impending large increase in the middle-aged population reflects the aging of baby boomers born between 1946 and 1964; and the very rapid growth in the number of elderly people is attributable to high birth rates prior to the 1930s combined with improvements in medical technology that have allowed many Americans to live longer.

Minorities and immigrants will constitute a larger share of the U.S. population in 2005 than they do today. Substantial increases in the number of Hispanics, Asians, and African Americans are anticipated, reflecting immigration and higher birth rates among African Americans and Hispanics. Substantial inflows of immigrants will continue to have significant implications for the labor force. Immigrants tend to be of working age but with different educational and occupational backgrounds than the U.S. population as a whole.

Population growth varies greatly among geographic regions, affecting the demand for goods and services and, in turn, workers in various occupations and industries. During the 1980s and the early 1990s, the population of the Midwest and the Northeast grew by only 3 percent and 4 percent, respectively, compared with 19 percent in the South and 30 percent in the West. These differences reflect the movement of people seeking new jobs or retiring, as well as higher birth rates in some areas.

Projections by the Bureau of the Census indicate that the West and South will continue to be the fastest growing regions, increasing 24 percent and 16 percent, respectively, between now and 2005. The Midwest population is expected to grow by 7 percent, while the number of people in the Northeast is projected to increase by only 3 percent.

Geographic shifts in the population alter the demand for and the supply of workers in local job markets. Moreover, in areas dominated by one or two industries, local job markets may be extremely sensitive to the economic conditions of those industries. For these and other reasons, local employment opportunities may differ substantially from the projections for the nation as a whole presented in this book.

## The Labor Force Will Continue to Grow

Population is the single most important factor governing the size and composition of the labor force, which includes people who are working or looking for work. The civilian labor force, 127 million in 1992, is expected to reach 151 million by 2005.

| The West and South will continue to be the fastest growing regions of the country | | |
|---|---|---|
| | **Percentage growth** | |
| | **1979-1992** | **1992-2005** |
| West | 30 | 24 |
| South | 19 | 16 |
| Midwest | 3 | 7 |
| Northeast | 4 | 3 |

This projected 19 percent increase represents a slight slowdown in the rate of labor force growth, which is largely due to lower population growth.

### An Increasingly Diverse Workforce

America's workers will be an increasingly diverse group as we move toward 2005. White non-Hispanic men will make up a slightly smaller proportion of the workforce, while women and minorities will comprise a larger share than in the past. White non-Hispanics have historically been the largest component of the labor force, but their share has been dropping, and is expected to fall from 78 percent in 1992 to 73 percent by 2005. White workers are projected to grow more slowly than African Americans, Asians, and others, but because of their size, whites will experience the largest numerical increase. Hispanics will add about 6.5 million workers to the labor force through 2005, an increase of 64 percent. Despite this dramatic growth, however, Hispanics' share of the labor force will increase from only 8 percent to 11 percent, as shown in chart 3. African Americans, Hispanics, Asians, and other racial groups will account for roughly 35 percent of all labor force entrants between now and 2005.

### Women Will Continue to Increase Their Participation in the Workforce

Women will continue to join the labor force in growing numbers. The percentage increase of women in the labor force between 1992 and 2005 will be larger than the percentage increase in the total labor force, but smaller than the percentage increase for women in the previous 13 years. In the late 1980s, the labor force participation of women under age 40 began to increase more slowly than in the past. Women accounted for 42 percent of the labor force in 1979; by 2005, they are expected to constitute 48 percent.

### The Workforce Will Continue to Age

The changing age structure of the population will directly affect tomorrow's labor force. Compared to young, inexperienced workers, the pool of older, experienced workers will increase. In 1992, the median age of the labor force was 37.2 years; by 2005, it will be 40.5 years.

Between 1979 and 1992, the youth labor force (16- to 24-year-olds) dropped by 5 million, a 20 percent decline. In contrast, the number of youths in the labor force will increase by 3.7 million over the 1992-2005 period, reflecting an increase of 18 percent, compared to 19 percent growth for the total labor force. As a result, young people are expected to comprise roughly the same percentage of the labor force in 2005 as in 1992.

Among youths, the teenage labor force (16- to 19-year-olds) will increase by 31 percent over the 1992-2005 period, an increase of 2.1 million. The labor force of 20- to 24-year-olds is projected to increase by 12 percent, an increase of 1.6 million workers. The total youth labor force accounted for 24 percent of the entire labor force in 1979, fell to 16 percent in 1992, and should stay about the same through 2005.

The scenario should be somewhat different for prime-age workers (25- to 54-year-olds). The baby-boom generation will continue to add members to the labor force, but their share of the labor force peaked in 1985. These workers accounted for 62 percent of the labor force in 1979, and rose significantly to 72 percent in 1992, but should decline slightly to 70 percent by 2005.

The proportion of workers in the 25-to-34 age range will decline dramatically, from 28 percent to 21 percent in 2005. On the other hand, the growing proportion of workers between the ages of 45 and 54 is equally striking. These workers should account for 24 percent of the labor force by the year 2005, up from 18 percent in 1992. Because workers in their mid-40s to mid-50s usually have substantial work experience and tend to be more stable than younger workers, this could result in improved productivity and a larger pool of experienced applicants from which employers

can choose.

The number of older workers (aged 55 and above) is projected to grow about twice as fast as the total labor force between 1992 and 2005, and about 15 times faster than they grew between 1979 and 1992. As the baby boomers grow older, the number of workers aged 55 to 64 will increase; they exhibit higher labor force participation than their older counterparts. By 2005, workers aged 55 and over will comprise 14 percent of the labor force, up from 12 percent in 1992.

### More Workers Have (and Will Need) More Education

In recent years, the level of educational attainment of the labor force has risen dramatically. In 1992, 27 percent of all workers age 25 and over had a bachelor's degree or higher, while only 12 percent did not possess a high school diploma. The trend toward higher educational attainment is expected to continue. Projected rates of employment growth are faster for occupations requiring higher levels of education or training than for those requiring less.

| The labor force will grow more slowly due to slower population growth | | |
|---|---|---|
| | Numerical change | Percent change |
| 1979-1992 | 22 million | 21 |
| 1992-2005 | 23.5 million | 19 |

Three of the four fastest growing occupational groups will be executive, administrative, and managerial; professional specialty; and technicians and related support occupations. These occupations generally require the highest levels of education and skill, and will comprise an increasing proportion of new jobs. Office and factory automation, changes in consumer demand, and movement of production facilities to offshore locations are expected to cause employment to stagnate or decline in many oc-

| The age distribution in the labor force will continue to shift | | | |
|---|---|---|---|
| | Percentage distribution | | |
| Age | 1979 | 1992 | 2005 |
| 55 and older | 14 | 12 | 14 |
| 45 to 54 | 16 | 18 | 24 |
| 35 to 44 | 19 | 27 | 25 |
| 25 to 34 | 27 | 28 | 21 |
| 16 to 24 | 24 | 16 | 16 |

cupations that require little formal education—apparel workers and textile machinery operators, for example. Opportunities for those who do not finish high school will be increasingly limited, and workers who are not literate may not even be considered for most jobs.

Those who do not complete high school and are employed are more likely to have low-paying jobs with little advancement potential, while workers in occupations requiring higher levels of education have higher incomes. In addition, many of the occupations projected to grow most rapidly between 1992 and 2005 are among those with higher earnings.

Nevertheless, even slower-growing occupations that have large numbers of workers will provide many job openings because the need to replace workers who leave the labor force or transfer to other occupations account for most job openings. Consequently, workers with all levels of education and training will continue to be in demand, although advancement opportunities will generally be best for those with the most education and training.

# Growth Projections Within Major Occupational Groups

The U.S. Department of Labor organizes occupations into groups that have similar characteristics. This is a useful structure, and it is used in a variety of reference sources. While jobs within these groups grow at different rates, it is helpful to know the general trends for the group as a whole. The following information is based on an article by George T. Silvestri, an economist in the office of Employment Projections, Bureau of Labor Statistics and published in the *Monthly Labor Review*, November 1995. It provides a brief review of trends among major job groups.

## Overview

Total employment is expected to increase by millions of jobs by 2005, but they will not be evenly distributed across major industrial and occupational groups, causing some restructuring of employment. Continued faster-than-average employment growth among occupations that require relatively high levels of education or training is expected.

Among the major occupational groups, employment in professional specialty occupations is projected to increase the fastest, and by the greatest number, between 1994 and 2005. This is the only group that is expected to add more jobs over the projections

period than were added from 1983 to 1994. Professional specialty workers is expected to be the third largest occupational group, as it was in 1994.

The group with the second fastest growth rate and the second largest number of jobs added is service occupations. Professional specialty occupations and service occupations, which are on opposite ends of the educational attainment and earnings spectrum, are expected to provide more than half of total job growth between 1994 and 2005. Executive, administrative, and managerial occupations; technicians and related support occupations; and marketing and salesworkers also are expected to have faster-than-average employment growth. Employment in precision production, craft, and repair occupations; the operators, fabricators, and laborers group; and administrative support occupations, including clerical, is expected to increase, but at a slower rate than total employment. The number of agriculture, forestry, fishing, and related occupations is projected to decline slightly.

It is especially noteworthy that employment in administrative support occupations, including clerical, which expanded by 4.3 million workers from 1983 to 1994, is projected to grow by only 994,000 workers through 2005, and to fall from first to second place in size behind employment of service workers. Office automation is expected to have a large impact on many of the individual occupations in this group. The projected 1994-2005 increase of 1.6 million jobs for blue-collar workers—precision production, craft, and repair occupations and operators, fabricators, and laborers—is substantially less than the 3.1 million gain over the 1983-94 period. The smaller projected increase reflects the expected impact of technological change on these occupations and the continuing decline in manufacturing employment through 2005.

As a result of the different growth rates among the major occupational groups, the structure of total employment is projected to change by the year 2005. Executive, administrative, and managerial occupations; professional specialty occupations; technicians and related support occupations; marketing and sales occupations;

| Table 1. | Employment by major occupational group, 1983, 1994, and projected 2005, moderate alternative |

[Numbers in thousands]

| Occupation | 1983 | | 1994 | | 2005 | | Employment change | | | |
|---|---|---|---|---|---|---|---|---|---|---|
| | | | | | | | 1983-94 | | 1994-2005 | |
| | Number | Percent | Number | Percent | Number | Percent | Number | Percent | Number | Percent |
| Total, all occupations | 102,404 | 100.0 | 127,014 | 100.0 | 144,708 | 100.0 | 24,610 | 24.0 | 17,694 | 13.9 |
| Executive, administrative, and managerial occupations | 9,591 | 9.4 | 12,903 | 10.2 | 15,071 | 10.4 | 3,312 | 34.5 | 2,168 | 16.8 |
| Professional specialty occupations | 12,639 | 12.3 | 17,314 | 13.6 | 22,387 | 15.5 | 4,675 | 37.0 | 5,073 | 29.3 |
| Technicians and related support occupations | 3,409 | 3.3 | 4,439 | 3.5 | 5,316 | 3.7 | 1,030 | 30.2 | 876 | 19.7 |
| Marketing and sales occupations | 10,497 | 10.3 | 13,990 | 11.0 | 16,502 | 11.4 | 3,493 | 33.3 | 2,512 | 18.0 |
| Administrative support occupations, including clerical | 18,874 | 18.4 | 23,178 | 18.2 | 24,172 | 16.7 | 4,304 | 22.8 | 994 | 4.3 |
| Service occupations | 15,577 | 15.2 | 20,239 | 15.9 | 24,832 | 17.2 | 4,662 | 29.9 | 4,593 | 22.7 |
| Agriculture, forestry, fishing, and related occupations | 3,712 | 3.6 | 3,762 | 3.0 | 3,650 | 2.5 | 50 | 1.3 | −112 | −3.0 |
| Precision production, craft, and repair occupations | 12,731 | 12.4 | 14,047 | 11.1 | 14,880 | 10.3 | 1,316 | 10.3 | 833 | 5.9 |
| Operators, fabricators, and laborers | 15,374 | 15.0 | 17,142 | 13.5 | 17,898 | 12.4 | 1,768 | 11.5 | 757 | 4.4 |

and service occupations are all projected to increase their shares of total employment. All of these groups had increased their employment shares from 1983 to 1194, as well.

Professional specialty occupations, which registered the largest increase in share in the recent past, is expected to do so again over the projection period. On the other hand, administrative support occupations, including clerical; agriculture, forestry, fishing, and related occupations; precision production, craft, and repair occupations; and operators, fabricators, and laborers are expected to decline as a proportion of total employment. This represents a continuation of the 1983-94 trends for these groups, with the exception of administrative support occupations, including clerical, which had maintained a virtually constant share of total employment over the earlier period.

### Executive, Administrative, and Managerial Occupations

The number of *executive, administrative, and managerial workers* is projected to increase by 17 percent, or 2.2 million, from 1994 to 2005. This rate of growth is half that achieved over the 1983-94 period, during which the occupational group added more than 3.3 million jobs. Further, while managers had the second fastest growth rate among the major occupational groups in the earlier period, they are expected to have only the fifth fastest 1994-2005 growth rate. The result will be only a slight increase in the share of total employment represented by these workers.

Part of the reason for the expected slowdown in job growth for this group is the trend toward job restructuring. Although employment in many different fields may be affected by restructuring, the use of middle managers in the future is expected to be reduced to a greater extent than that of many other occupations. This is especially true in manufacturing, where employment in this group is projected to decline by 67,000 jobs through 2005, after having increased by 171,000 jobs between 1983 and 1994, a period during which total manufacturing employment declined.

In industries other than manufacturing, the overall occupational category of executive, administrative, and managerial workers is expected to grow substantially. The services industry division is expected to account for more than 6 out of 10 of the additional jobs for managers, with large gains registered in engineering and management services and in business services. Other industries with significant projected employment increases for managers are wholesale and retail trade and finance, insurance and real estate.

### Professional Specialty Occupations

Employment in *professional specialty occupations* is projected to grow the fastest and to increase more, by 5 million workers, than any other group. This group also posted the fastest rate of increase and largest job growth from 1983 to 1994. Professional specialty occupations are expected to experience the largest increase in share of total employment, rising from 13.5 percent in 1994 to 15.4 percent by 2005. The largest 1994-2005 numerical increases are expected among teachers, librarians, and counselors (1.6 million jobs); health assessment and training occupations (731,000 jobs); and computer engineers, scientists, and systems analysts (755,000 jobs). These professional specialty occupational groups also registered the largest job gains during the 1980s.

Employment in professional specialty occupations is expected to increase in all major industrial sectors in the economy. Even in manufacturing, which is projected to decline by 1.3 million workers by 2005, employment of professional workers is expected to increase by 100,000 jobs, mainly for computer engineers, scientists, and systems analysts. Despite the widespread growth of the professional specialty occupations, nearly 90 percent of the projected increase in employment for these workers is in the services industry division, led by educational services and health services.

Other service industries that are expected to contribute significantly to the growth of professional jobs are social services, business services, and engineering management services. Federal, state, and local government jobs for professional specialty workers are projected to grow by nearly 150,000, but this is less than half the increase that occurred from 1983 to 1994.

### Technicians and Related Support Occupations

Employment of *technicians and related support workers* is projected to grow by 876,000 jobs by 2005, about 150,000 fewer jobs than during the 1983-94 period. The 20 percent rate of increase is considerably slower than the 30 percent attained in the earlier period. The proportion of total employment in this group was just 3.5 percent in 1994, and is expected to be about the same in 2005. The occupational subgroup health technicians and technologists is expected to increase by 618,000 jobs during 1994-2005 and to account for 70 percent of the growth in the total number of technicians.

Virtually all of the job growth in this group is expected to be in the services industries. During the 1983-94 period, by contrast, much of the job increase was in transportation, communications, and public utilities; wholesale and retail trade; finance, insurance, and real estate; and government. Within services, about half of the jobs for technicians are expected to be in the large and rapidly growing health services industry. Other industries that also are expected to provide large numbers of new jobs for technicians by 2005 are engineering and management services and business services.

### Marketing and Sales Occupations

Employment in the *marketing and sales* occupational group is projected to increase by 2.5 million workers from 1994 to 2005, or by 18 percent. By contrast, this group grew by 3.5 million workers, or 33 percent, from 1983 to 1994. The group's share of total employment will increase slightly through 2005.

In part, this group's reduced pace of job growth is attributable to the smaller employment increase in wholesale and retail trade, which employs the majority of marketing and salesworkers. This slowing of employment growth in wholesale trade is based partly on the expectation that manufacturers will increasingly use new warehouse management systems and distribute their products directly to retailers as they take advantage of reductions in the cost of shipping goods. Both wholesale trade and the much larger retail sector are expected to experience increased productivity as the result of computerized inventory control, which will lessen the overall demand for labor.

Employment growth of marketing and salesworkers also is expected in the services industry division and in finance, insurance, and real estate.

### Administrative Support Occupations, Including Clerical

The number of workers in *administrative support occupations, including clerical*—the largest occupational group in 1983 and 1994—is projected to increase by only 994,000 jobs through 2005, and to grow by 4 percent. This is in marked contrast to the previous 11-year period, during which this group grew as fast as the average for all occupations and added 4.3 million jobs. Consequently, the share of total employment represented by administrative support workers, which held steady during the 1983-94 period, is projected to decline significantly from 18.2 percent in 1994 to 16.7 percent in the target year.

Many detailed occupations in this group also are expected to decline through 2005 instead of expanding as they did over the historical period. Among them are computer and peripheral equipment operators; mail clerks and messengers; file clerks; and bookkeeping, accounting, and auditing clerks, all of which are expected to be affected by continued technological change and further developments in office automation.

Occupations that involve a great deal of contact with people, and therefore are not affected significantly by changes in technology, are projected to have average or higher than average rates of growth. Among these occupations are hotel desk clerks, receptionists and information clerks, and teacher aids and educational assistants. The substantial job growth for administrative support operations, including clerical, of 1.8 million workers in the services industry division is expected to be partially offset by projected declines in every other major industry division, the largest of which are in government and manufacturing.

### Service Occupations

Employment in *service occupations* is projected to increase by 4.6 million and to grow by 23 percent, the second largest numerical gain among the major occupational groups. Employment in this group increased by about the same amount from 1983 to 1994. The proportion of total employment represented by these workers is expected to continue increasing significantly, as it has been since 1983, and to account for the largest share of total employment in 2005—17.2 percent. Nearly 7 in 10 of the additional jobs projected in 2005 are in the rapidly growing services industry division, led by health services, social services, and business services.

Health service occupations, which grew by 270,000 workers between 1983 and 1994, are projected to increase by a substantial 759,000 by 2005. In addition, retail trade, with large numbers of food preparation and service workers, is projected to add more than a million jobs for service workers, and state and local governments, with substantial numbers of law enforcement and fire-fighting occupations, are projected to contribute a combined total of more than 370,000 additional service jobs.

### Agriculture, Forestry, Fishing, and Related Occupations

*Agriculture, forestry, fishing, and related occupations* are projected to decline by 112,000 jobs, after having increased by 50,000 between 1983 and 1994. Within this major group, job losses for farm managers, farm workers, and forestry and logging occupations are expected to be partially offset by job gains for gardening, nursery, greenhouse, and lawn service occupations, which are largely found in the rapidly growing segment of agricultural services that provides nursery products and gardening and lawn services. The share of total employment represented by agriculture, forestry, fishing, and related occupations is expected to continue to decline and to account for only 2.5 percent of all jobs by 2005.

### Other Groups

Employment in *precision production, craft, and repair occupations* is projected to increase by 833,000 jobs and to grow at a rate of 6 percent from 1994 to 2005. This much slower than average growth rate is a continuation of the trend over the 1983-94 period, during which this group expanded by 10 percent and added 1.3 million jobs. These workers are expected to account for 10.3 percent of total employment in 2005—down from 11.1 percent on 1994.

Most of the job growth within the major occupational group is projected to occur among blue-collar worker supervisors; construction trades workers, and mechanics, installers, and repairers. These job categories also registered large increases during the 1980s. The *precision production occupations*, which are highly concentrated in manufacturing, are expected to decline by about 150,000 jobs due to continuing advances in technology, changes in production methods, and the overall decline in manufacturing employment. The large overall projected job losses for precision production, craft, and repair occupations in manufacturing are expected to be offset primarily by the significant gain in services.

The number of *operators, fabricators, and laborers* is expected to increase by 757,000 workers, or by just 4 percent, from 1994 to 2005. During the previous 11-year period, this group grew by 1.8 million workers. Over the longer period 1983-2005, the proportion of total employment represented by these workers is projected to decline substantially from 15.0 percent to 12.4 percent—the largest drop for a major occupational group.

The manufacturing sector is expected to lose more than 700,000 jobs for operators, fabricators, and laborers as a result of the continuing automation of their duties and the overall projected decline in manufacturing employment. However, the decline in this sector is expected to be more than offset by gains in services, transportation, and construction. It is also noteworthy that jobs for these workers in wholesale and retail trade, which increased by 452,000 from 1983 to 1994, are projected to decline slightly between 1994 and 2005, largely as a result of the increased use of automated material moving equipment that will curtail employment of freight, stock, and material movers, hand.

### The Fastest Growing Occupations

In this section you will find information on jobs that are growing the fastest—or that are creating the most openings. High growth rates can be misleading, since jobs with high percentages of growth may offer limited job opportunities if they employ few people. For example, occupational therapy assistants and aides are projected to grow very rapidly—by 82 percent by 2005—but will increase by just 13,000 jobs. In contrast, the employment of secretaries, which is expected to grow by only 12 percent, will increase by 390,000 jobs. Both offer opportunities, but you need to consider other things other than high growth percentages.

Note that Appendix C provides growth projections for many more jobs than I could cover in this section, and I suggest you refer to it—and the job descriptions in Section One—for information on jobs that interest you.

### Fast-Growing Occupations Tend to Cluster in Certain Industries

Most of the occupations with the fastest projected employment growth are concentrated in one or more of the rapidly growing industries. Many of the 30 occupations with the fastest projected growth rates are concentrated in the health services sector, which is expected to expand more than twice as fast as the economy as a whole (see Table 2). Health service occupations also dominated this list in the 1983-94 period.

Employment in the two occupations projected to grow most rapidly from 1994 to 2005—personal and home care aides and home health aides—is concentrated in home health care services and individual and miscellaneous social services industries. These occupations also grew the fastest during 1983-94. Home health aides provide personal and physical care for an increasing number of elderly people and for patients who are recovering from surgery and other serious health conditions. Personal and home care aides perform a variety of light housekeeping tasks for those in need of home care.

The number of physical therapists and physical and corrective therapy assistants and aids is expected to grow rapidly as a result of new treatments for life-threatening and disabling conditions that involve therapy. Another factor is the growing elderly population, whose members are particularly vulnerable to chronic and debilitating conditions that will require more therapeutic services. The number of occupational therapists and occupational therapy assistants and aides also is expected to increase due to medical advances that make it possible for more patients with critical problems to survive. These workers help individuals with mentally, physically, developmentally, or emotionally disabling conditions to develop, recover, or maintain daily living and work skills.

Employment of medical records technicians is projected to expand rapidly, despite considerably slower than average growth for the hospital industry, which employs the majority of these workers. These jobs will be added in response to the need to maintain records for an increasing number of medical tests, treatments, and procedures that will undergo increasing scrutiny by third-party payers, courts, and consumers.

Employment of medical assistants is expected to be driven by an increase in the number of group and other health care practices that use support personnel. These workers are employed primarily in outpatient settings, which are projected to grow rapidly.

The demand for dental hygienists and dental assistants is expected to be spurred by growth in the population and greater awareness of the need for preventive dental care. The number of dental hygienists is projected to grow somewhat more slowly than during the previous 11-year period, 1983-94. The number of dental assistants, on the other hand, is expected to grow significantly faster than in the past.

Other occupations in the health field that are projected to grow rapidly include human services workers (large numbers of whom also are found in social services and in state and local governments), surgical technologists, and speech-language pathologists and audiologists.

Robust growth is projected in some computer-related occupations, because of the continuing spread of computer technology. Employment of computer engineers and systems analysts is expected to increase rapidly to satisfy expanding needs for scientific research and applications of computer technology in business and industry. These occupations also are included in Table 3, which shows the list of occupations with the largest projected job

growth through 2005. They experienced very fast rates of growth and large numerical increases in employment from 1983 to 1994, as well.

Expanding use of operations research to improve productivity and reduce costs is expected to increase the demand for operations research analysts. The number of electronic pagination systems workers is projected to grow very rapidly in the printing and publishing industry, as more page layout and design is performed electronically by computer. More data processing equipment repairers will be needed to install, maintain, and repair the growing number of computers in use.

One computer occupation that one may expect to find on the list of fastest growing occupations is conspicuous by its absence. The computer programmers group, which grew much faster than the average for all occupations during the 1980s, is projected to increase more slowly than average through 2005 due to improved software and programming techniques that simplify or eliminate some programming tasks.

Paralegals are expected to be in great demand in legal and related fields, reflecting efforts to provide more cost-effective legal services to the public. This occupation was among the top 10 fastest growing occupations over the 1983-94 period. The number of special education teachers is expected to grow due to legislation requiring training and employment for individuals with disabilities and growing public interest in people with special needs.

Jobs for correction officers are projected to increase in response to the need to supervise and counsel a rapidly expanding inmate population. Increased concern about crime, vandalism, and terrorism is expected to result in larger numbers of guards and detectives, except public. The majority of residential counselors are employed in the rapidly growing residential care industry, which provides social and personal care for children, the aged, and others with limited ability for self-care. Finally, the expanding agricultural services (except animal services) industry is projected to provide numerous jobs for nursery and greenhouse managers.

## Should I Consider Only the Fastest-Growing Jobs?

With all the labor market change that is projected in the coming years, it would seem wise to consider those jobs that are growing most rapidly. Rapidly growing jobs are projected to increase the numbers of people they employ and offer better-than-average opportunities for employment and job security. For this reason, you should certainly pay attention to jobs that are projected to grow rapidly. But you should also consider jobs that simply interest you, even if they are not among the fastest-growing ones.

There will always be some openings for new people, even in slower-growing or declining jobs. Some of these jobs are numerous and will create many openings due to retirement, people leaving the field, and other reasons. My point is that you should consider a slower-growing field if that is really what you want to do.

## Occupations with the Largest Number of Openings

Most of the occupations with the largest increases in numbers of jobs are concentrated in three industries that are expected to provide nearly half of the total growth in wage and salary jobs from 1994 to 2005: retail trade, health services, and educational services (see Table 3). Within retail trade, employment of sales-persons, retail; cashiers; waiters and waitresses; food preparation workers; marketing and salesworker supervisors; and food service and lodging managers is expected to grow substantially. All of these occupations also had large employment increases from 1983 to 1994.

The health services sector is expected to provide many opportunities for registered nurses, licensed practical nurses, nursing aides, orderlies, and attendants, home health aides, and personal and home care aides. (The last two also are on the list of the fastest-growing occupations.) Of the occupations in this group, only registered nurses and home health aides were also on the list of the 30 occupations with the largest job growth between 1983 and 1994.

The public and private education industry is projected to provide large employment increases for elementary school teachers, secondary school teachers, teacher aides and educational assistants, and special education teachers.

The remaining occupations listed in Table 3 are found in a wide variety of industries throughout the economy, and their growth, as a consequence, is dependent upon many factors. More than 6 in 10 new jobs for general managers and top executives in 2005 will be in the services sector. As mentioned in the previous section, employment for systems analysts is expected to grow with the continued spread of computer technology. Jobs for receptionists and information clerks are projected to increase significantly because such workers interact a great deal with people and their duties are difficult to automate.

The number of child-care workers, who experienced a large employment increase during the 1980s, is expected to continue to expand significantly though 2005 as a result of anticipated growth in the number of young children and a change in the type of child-care arrangements parents choose. The switch from informal arrangements with family or friends to formal child care is projected to continue. Other large and slower-growing occupations that are expected to provide numerous additional jobs are truck drivers, light and heavy; janitors and cleaners; maintenance repairers, general utility; and secretaries, except legal and medical.

An interesting contrast exists between the total increase in employment from those occupations that are projected as the fastest-growing (Table 2) and the increase from those projected to account for the largest numerical increases (Table 3). The first group accounts for 18 percent of the projected overall growth in employment, while the second accounts for almost 55 percent (several occupations are included in both groups).

## Educational Requirements and Earnings of High-Growth Jobs

Educational requirements and median weekly earnings of workers vary widely among the 30 occupations that are projected to grow the most rapidly and the 30 occupations with the largest numerical increases. About one-half of the occupations on both lists require education or training beyond high school. Occupations that generally require a bachelor's degree or more education are concentrated in the professional specialty group, and all had median weekly earnings in 1994 that were higher than the average for all full-time wage and salary wage workers. Examples of occupations in this category include computer engineers, systems analysts, operations research analysts, physical therapists, occupational therapists, and elementary and secondary school teachers.

Several occupations require specific formal training obtained in public and private institutions, including community and junior colleges, which offer occupational-oriented training programs. About half of these occupations had higher than average earnings, including registered nurses, paralegals, medical records technicians, surgical technicians, and dental hygienists. A few occupations—such as maintenance repairers, general utility—require skills obtained through employer training programs.

| Table 2. | Fastest growing occupations, 1994-2005, moderate alternative projection | | | |
|---|---|---|---|---|
| [Numbers in thousands] | | | | |
| Occupation | Employment | | Numerical change | Percent change |
| | 1994 | 2005 | | |
| Personal and home care aides | 179 | 391 | 212 | 119 |
| Home health aides | 420 | 848 | 428 | 102 |
| Systems analysts | 483 | 928 | 445 | 92 |
| Computer engineers | 195 | 372 | 177 | 90 |
| Physical and corrective therapy assistants and aides | 78 | 142 | 64 | 83 |
| Electronic pagination systems workers | 18 | 33 | 15 | 83 |
| Occupational therapy assistants and aides | 16 | 29 | 13 | 82 |
| Physical therapists | 102 | 183 | 81 | 80 |
| Residential counselors | 165 | 290 | 126 | 76 |
| Human services workers | 168 | 293 | 125 | 75 |
| Occupational therapists | 54 | 93 | 39 | 72 |
| Manicurists | 38 | 64 | 26 | 69 |
| Medical assistants | 206 | 327 | 121 | 59 |
| Paralegals | 110 | 175 | 64 | 58 |
| Medical records technicians | 81 | 126 | 45 | 56 |
| Teachers, special education | 388 | 593 | 206 | 53 |
| Amusement and recreation attendants | 267 | 406 | 139 | 52 |
| Correction officers | 310 | 468 | 158 | 51 |
| Operations research analysts | 44 | 67 | 22 | 50 |
| Guards | 867 | 1,282 | 415 | 48 |
| Speech-language pathologists and audiologists | 85 | 125 | 39 | 46 |
| Detectives, except public | 55 | 79 | 24 | 44 |
| Surgical technologists | 46 | 65 | 19 | 43 |
| Dental hygienists | 127 | 180 | 53 | 42 |
| Dental assistants | 190 | 269 | 79 | 42 |
| Adjustment clerks | 373 | 521 | 148 | 40 |
| Teacher aides and educational assistants | 932 | 1,296 | 364 | 39 |
| Data processing equipment repairers | 75 | 104 | 29 | 38 |
| Nursery and greenhouse managers | 19 | 26 | 7 | 37 |
| Securities and financial services sales workers | 246 | 335 | 90 | 37 |

| Table 3. | Occupations with the largest job growth, 1994-2005 moderate alternative projection |
|---|---|

[Numbers in thousands]

| Occupation | Employment | | Numerical change | Percent change |
|---|---|---|---|---|
| | 1994 | 2005 | | |
| Cashiers | 3,005 | 3,567 | 562 | 19 |
| Janitors and cleaners, including maids and housekeeping cleaners | 3,043 | 3,602 | 559 | 18 |
| Salespersons, retail | 3,842 | 4,374 | 532 | 14 |
| Waiters and waitresses | 1,847 | 2,326 | 479 | 26 |
| Registered nurses | 1,906 | 2,379 | 473 | 25 |
| General managers and top executives | 3,046 | 3,512 | 466 | 15 |
| Systems analysts | 483 | 928 | 445 | 92 |
| Home health aides | 420 | 848 | 428 | 102 |
| Guards | 867 | 1,282 | 415 | 48 |
| Nursing aides, orderlies, and attendants | 1,265 | 1,652 | 387 | 31 |
| Teachers, secondary school | 1,340 | 1,726 | 386 | 29 |
| Marketing and sales worker supervisors | 2,293 | 2,673 | 380 | 17 |
| Teacher aides and educational assistants | 932 | 1,296 | 364 | 39 |
| Receptionists and information clerks | 1,019 | 1,337 | 318 | 31 |
| Truckdrivers light and heavy | 2,565 | 2,837 | 271 | 11 |
| Secretaries, except legal and medical | 2,842 | 3,109 | 267 | 9 |
| Clerical supervisors and managers | 1,340 | 1,600 | 261 | 19 |
| Child care workers | 757 | 1,005 | 248 | 33 |
| Maintenance repairers, general utility | 1,273 | 1,505 | 231 | 18 |
| Teachers, elementary | 1,419 | 1,639 | 220 | 16 |
| Personal and home care aides | 179 | 391 | 212 | 119 |
| Teachers, special education | 388 | 593 | 206 | 53 |
| Licensed practical nurses | 702 | 899 | 197 | 28 |
| Food service and lodging managers | 579 | 771 | 192 | 33 |
| Food preparation workers | 1,190 | 1,378 | 187 | 16 |
| Social workers | 557 | 744 | 187 | 34 |
| Lawyers | 656 | 839 | 183 | 28 |
| Financial managers | 768 | 950 | 182 | 24 |
| Computer engineers | 195 | 372 | 177 | 90 |
| Hand packers and packagers | 942 | 1,102 | 160 | 17 |

The remainder of the occupations require high school graduation or less education. Examples include home health aides, human services workers, personal and home care aides, salespersons, cashiers, truck drivers, correction officers, and clerical supervisors and managers. Very few of the occupations in this group had average or higher than average earnings in 1994. Some occupations—such as secretaries, except legal and medical—may require high school vocational training, but many others have no specific formal training requirements, and job skills in these occupations generally are learned on the job in a relatively short time.

The two lists of growth occupations show that employers will continue to require workers at all levels of education and training. Nevertheless, the fact remains that workers with higher levels of education or training usually will have more options in the job market and better prospects for obtaining the higher-paying jobs.

## Declining Occupations

Decreases in industry employment and changes in occupational staffing patterns are expected to reduce the demand for workers in several occupations over the 1994-2005 period (see Table 4). This section focuses on those occupations with the largest job declines rather than on those with the fastest rates of decline. Many detailed occupations in the latter category are very small and, consequently, the resulting employment losses are not very significant.

Industry employment change is the major cause of projected employment decreases for farmers; sewing machine operators, garment; textile draw-out and winding machine operators and tenders; electrical and electronic assemblers; and cleaners and servants, private households. Declining occupations that are expected to be affected almost equally by industry employment changes and by occupational structure changes include farm workers, central office and PBX installers and repairers, central office operators, station installers and repairers, and directory assistance operators.

Most of the other declining occupations are affected more by occupational structure changes—which are the result of technological advances, organizational changes, and other factors that affect the use of workers—than by industry employment changes. The large drop in employment for bartenders in the eating and drinking places industry is attributable to the projected decline in the consumption of alcoholic beverages outside of the home.

Employment of typists and word processors is expected to decrease substantially, by 212,000 jobs across all industries, because of productivity improvements resulting from office automation and the increased use of word processing equipment by professional and managerial employees. Jobs for these workers declined by 173,000 during 1983-94. Data entry keyers, except composing, and personnel clerks, except payroll and timekeeping, also are expected to continue their long-run employment losses through 2005.

Several other occupations—all of which registered employment increases during the 1980s—are projected to decline through 2005 due to that much greater impact of office automation. Among these are bookkeeping, accounting, and auditing clerks; duplicating, mail, and other office machine operators; billing, posting, and calculating machine operators; and file clerks. The demand for computer operators (except peripheral equipment, which increased modestly from 1983 to 1994) is expected to fall, because these employees work mainly with large computer systems—the part of the overall computer market that is projected to slow down. Employment for bank tellers is expected to decline because of increased use of automated teller machines, terminals, and other electronic equipment for customer fund transactions.

Several blue-collar occupations in manufacturing are expected to decline because of changes in the occupational structure of many of the detailed industries in that sector. For example, the installation of computer-controlled technology, including advanced systems that combine production tasks and link machines, will reduce the demand for machine forming operators and tenders, metal and plastic, and for machine tool cutting operators and tenders, metal and plastic.

Laser inspection devices and other automated inspection equipment are expected to reduce the demand for inspectors, testers, and graders, precision, an occupation for which employment also decreased during the 1980s. Automated material moving equipment will reduce employment for freight, stock, and

| Table 4. | Occupations with the largest job growth, 1994-2005 moderate alternative projection |
|---|---|

[Numbers in thousands]

| Occupation | Employment | | Numerical change | Percent change |
|---|---|---|---|---|
| | 1994 | 2005 | | |
| Farmers ................................................. | 1,276 | 1,003 | −273 | −21 |
| Typists and word processors ............................ | 646 | 434 | −212 | −33 |
| Bookkeeping, accounting, and auditing clerks ................................................ | 2,181 | 2,003 | −178 | −8 |
| Bank tellers ............................................ | 559 | 407 | −152 | −27 |
| Sewing machine operators, garment .............. | 531 | 391 | −140 | −26 |
| Cleaners and servants, private household ....... | 496 | 387 | −108 | −22 |
| Computer operators, except peripheral equipment ............................................ | 259 | 162 | −98 | −38 |
| Billing, posting, and calculating machine operators ............................................ | 96 | 32 | −64 | −67 |
| Duplicating, mail, and other office machine operators ............................................ | 222 | 166 | −56 | −25 |
| Textile draw-out and winding machine operators and tenders ........................... | 190 | 143 | −47 | −25 |
| File clerks ............................................ | 278 | 236 | −42 | −15 |
| Freight, stock, and material movers, hand ....... | 765 | 728 | −36 | −5 |
| Farm workers ......................................... | 906 | 870 | −36 | −4 |
| Machine tool cutting operators and tenders, metal and plastic .................................... | 119 | 85 | −34 | −29 |
| Central office operators ............................... | 48 | 14 | −34 | −70 |
| Central office and PBX installers and repairers ............................................ | 84 | 51 | −33 | −39 |
| Electrical and electronic assemblers .............. | 212 | 182 | −30 | −14 |
| Station installers and repairers, telephone ....... | 37 | 11 | −26 | −70 |
| Personnel clerks, except payroll and timekeeping ......................................... | 123 | 98 | −26 | −21 |
| Data entry keyers, except composing .............. | 395 | 370 | −25 | −6 |
| Bartenders ............................................ | 373 | 347 | −25 | −7 |
| Inspectors, testers, and graders, precision ....... | 654 | 629 | −25 | −4 |
| Directory assistance operators ...................... | 33 | 10 | −24 | −70 |
| Lathe and turning machine tool setters and set-up operators, metal and plastic ........ | 71 | 50 | −22 | −31 |
| Custom tailors and sewers ........................... | 84 | 63 | −21 | −25 |
| Machine feeders and offbearers ..................... | 262 | 242 | −20 | −8 |
| Machinists ............................................ | 369 | 349 | −20 | −5 |
| Service station attendants ............................ | 167 | 148 | −20 | −12 |
| Machine forming operators and tenders, metal and plastic .................................... | 171 | 151 | −19 | −11 |
| Communication, transportation, and utilities operations managers .............................. | 154 | 135 | −19 | −12 |

exceed those resulting from employment growth. Even occupations that are projected to decline provide some job openings.

The measurement of replacement needs is very complex because there is a continuous movement of workers into and out of occupations. The measure used in this discussion is based on the net change in employment (entrants minus separations) in each age cohort over the projection period. Consequently, net replacements do not measure all workers who leave an occupation; nor do they represent the total number of jobs that will be filled due to the need to replace workers. These net replacements understate the total number of job openings in an occupation because they relate only to the difference between the number of experienced workers who enter and the number who leave that occupation. However, net replacements are used in this discussion because the measure best represents the job openings for new labor force entrants over the projection period.

Over the 1994-2005 period, more job openings are expected to result from replacement needs (31.9 million) than from employment growth in the economy (17.7 million). However, this pattern differs for professional specialty occupations, which has the fastest rate of growth among the major occupational groups, and for many detailed occupations that are projected to grow faster than the average. In contrast, for the major occupational groups that are projected to grow more slowly than average—administrative support operations, including clerical; precision production, craft, and repair occupations; operators, fabricators, and laborers; and farming, forestry, and fishing occupations—the numbers of job openings attributable to net replacements are expected to greatly exceed those due to growth.

material movers, hand. Similarly, the number of machine feeders and offbearers is projected to decline as a result of the introduction of more computer-controlled equipment and machinery that loads and unloads products automatically. Greater use of numerical-controlled machine tools and changes in production methods is expected to lessen demand for lathe and turning machine tool setters and set-up operators, metal and plastic.

A few occupations are expected to be adversely affected by changes in business practices and other factors. For example, the number of service station attendants will continue to decline because most gas stations no longer provide automobile maintenance services. Also, the demand for station installers and repairers, telephone, will fall due to a continuation of a trend toward customer installation of telephones.

### Even More Jobs Opportunities Come from Replacements

In addition to occupational employment growth, another aspect of the demand for workers is the need to replace workers who leave their jobs to enter other occupations, retire, or leave the labor force for other reasons. Job openings resulting from replacement needs are very important because, in most occupations, they

| Occupation | Percentage decline |
|---|---|
| Frame wirers, central office (telephone) | -75 |
| Peripheral electronic data processing equipment operators | -60 |
| Directory assistance operators | -51 |
| Central office operators | -50 |
| Station installers and repairers, telephone | -50 |
| Portable machine cutters | -40 |
| Computer operators, except peripheral equipment | -39 |
| Shoe sewing machine operators and tenders | -38 |
| Central office and PBX installers and repairers (telephone) | -36 |
| Childcare workers, private household | -35 |
| Job printers | -35 |
| Roustabouts | -33 |
| Separating and still machine operators and tenders | -33 |

| Occupation | Percentage decline |
|---|---|
| Cleaners and servants, private household | -32 |
| Coil winders, tapers, and finishers | -32 |
| Billing, posting, and calculation machine operators | -29 |
| Sewing machine operators, garment | -29 |
| Signal or track switch maintenance | -28 |
| Compositors and typesetters, precision | -27 |
| Data entry keyers, composing | -26 |
| Drilling machine tool setters and set-up operators, metal and plastic | -26 |
| Motion picture projectionists | -26 |
| Boiler operators and tenders, low pressure | -25 |
| Statement clerks | -24 |
| Telephone and cable TV line installers and repairers | -24 |
| Watchmakers | -23 |
| Head sawyers and sawing machine operators and tenders | -22 |
| Packaging and filling machine operators and tenders | -22 |
| Tire building machine operators | -22 |
| Farmers | -21 |

The number of job openings for service occupations from 1994 to 2005 is projected to be 9.8 million, and to exceed the number for professional occupations, the next largest group, by 1.4 million. Accounting for 21 percent of total job openings, numerous openings for service workers are expected to result from both net replacements and employment growth. Large numbers of replacements are expected to result from the movement of young workers in food preparation and service occupations to other occupations.

# Industry Trends

While much of this book focuses on occupations, another way of looking at the labor market is from the perspective of various industries. I've selected information on trends in various industry sectors, with an emphasis on those growing most rapidly.

The long-term shift from goods-producing to service-producing employment is expected to continue. For example, service-producing industries—including transportation, communications, and utilities; retail and wholesale trade; services; government; and finance, insurance, and real estate—are expected to account for approximately 24.5 million of the 26.4 million jobs projected for the 1992-2005 period. In addition, the services division within this sector, which includes health, business, and educational services, contains 15 of the 20 fastest-growing industries. Expansion of service sector employment is linked to a number of factors, including changes in consumer tastes and preferences, legal and regulatory changes, advances in science and technology, and changes in the way businesses are organized and managed. Specific factors responsible for varying growth prospects in major industry divisions are discussed in the following table.

| Service-Producing Industries Will Continue to Account for Most Job Growth | | | |
|---|---|---|---|
| (Nonfarm wage and salary employment, in millions) | | | |
| **Industry sector** | **1979** | **1992** | **2005** |
| Goods-producing | 26.5 | 23.1 | 23.7 |
| Service-producing | 63 | 84.7 | 109.2 |
| Total | 89.5 | 107.9 | 133 |

## Service-Producing Industries Are Increasingly Important

It is not true that we are becoming a service economy: We already are one, and have been for some time. By the year 2005, projections indicate that nearly four out of five jobs will be in industries that provide services rather than in manufacturing. Expansion of service-sector employment is linked to a number of factors, including changes in consumer tastes and preferences, legal and regulatory changes, advances in science and technology, and changes in the organization and management of businesses. Contrary to popular belief, many of these jobs pay well.

Many people think of a service economy as one in which the workforce is dominated by retail sales workers, restaurant workers, and cashiers. In reality the fastest-growing occupations will be those that require the most education. The two largest industries in this sector are health services and business services. Together, they account for 6.1 million of the projected jobs, or about one-fourth of the total increase.

### The Difference Between the Service Industry and Service Workers

Many people get confused about this difference and it is easy to understand why, because the terminology is so similar. Data is collected by type of establishment (or industry) as well as by type of occupation. For example, an accountant could work in auto manufacturing (a goods-producing industry) or a hospital (which does not produce goods and is, therefore, part of the service industry). Same occupation, different industries.

The government uses 12 clusters of related occupations, and accountant falls under one called "Executive, Administrative, and Managerial." One of those occupational clusters just happens to be called "Service Occupations," and it includes jobs such as kitchen workers, flight attendants, dental assistants, and preschool workers. So, if you worked in the cafeteria of a hospital, you would be a service worker in a service industry. Well, yes, this is a bit confusing . . .

## Trends Within the Services Industry

Services is both the largest and fastest-growing division within the service-producing sector. This division provided 38.6 million jobs in 1992. Employment is expected to rise 40 percent, to 54.2 million by 2005, accounting for almost two-thirds of all new jobs. Jobs will be found in small firms and large corporations and in industries as diverse as hospitals, data processing, and management consulting. Health services and business services are projected to continue to grow very rapidly. In addition, social, legal, and engineering and management services industries further illustrate this sector's strong growth.

| Services Will Remain the Fastest-Growing Major Industry Division | |
| --- | --- |
| **Percentage change in employment, 1992-2005** | |
| **Goods** | **Services** |
| Services ................................................................ 40 | |
| Construction .......................................................... 26 | |
| Retail trade ........................................................... 23 | |
| Finance, insurance and real estate ........................... 21 | |
| Wholesale trade ..................................................... 19 | |
| Transportation and public utilities .......................... 14 | |
| Agriculture, forestry, and fishing ............................ 14 | |
| Government ........................................................... 10 | |
| Manufacturing ....................................................... -3 | |
| Mining .................................................................. -11 | |
| Total, all industries ............................................... 23 | |

## Health Services

Health services will continue to be one of the fastest-growing industries in the economy, with employment increasing from 9.6 to 13.8 million. Improvements in medical technology and a growing and aging population will increase the demand for health services. Employment in home health care services—the second fastest-growing industry in the economy—nursing homes, and offices and clinics of physicians and other health practitioners is projected to increase rapidly.

However, not all health industries will grow at the same rate. Despite being the largest health services industry, hospitals will grow more slowly than most other health services industries. Because of the rapid expansion, 6 of the 10 fastest growing occupations between now and 2005 will be health-related.

## Business Services

Demand for jobs that provide services to businesses are expected to increase rapidly. These jobs include many that require advanced training, such as computer technicians and systems analysts, as well as those requiring minimal training, such as janitors. Jobs in accounting, marketing, engineering, finance, truck driving, and many others providing services to businesses are expected to increase.

Business services industries also will generate many jobs. Employment is expected to grow from 5.3 million in 1992 to 8.3 million in 2005. Personnel supply services, composed primarily of temporary help agencies, is the largest sector in this group and will increase by 57 percent, from 1.6 to 2.6 million jobs. However, due to a slowdown in labor force participation by young women and the proliferation of personnel supply firms in recent years, this industry will grow more slowly than during the 1979-92 period.

Business services also includes one of the fastest-growing industries in the economy: computer, and data processing. This industry's rapid growth stems from advances in technology, worldwide trends toward office and factory automation, and increases in demand from business firms, government agencies, and individuals.

## Education

Education is expected to add 2.8 million more jobs to the 9.7 million held in 1992. This increase reflects population growth and, in turn, rising enrollments projected for elementary, secondary, and postsecondary schools. The elementary school-age population (ages 5 to 13) will rise by 2.8 million between 1992 and 2005, the secondary school-age (14 to 17) by 3.4 million, and the traditional postsecondary school-age (18 to 24) by 2.2 million. In addition, continued rising enrollment of older, foreign, and part-time students is expected to enhance employment in postsecondary education.

Not all of the increase in employment in education, however, will be for teachers: Jobs for teacher aides, counselors, and administrative staff are also projected to increase.

## Social Services

Employment in social services is expected to increase by 1.7 million, bringing the total to 3.7 million by 2005, reflecting the growing elderly population. For example, residential care institutions, which provide around-the-clock assistance to older persons and others who have limited ability for self-care, is projected to be the fastest-growing industry in the U.S. economy. Other social services industries that are projected to grow rapidly include child daycare services and individual and miscellaneous social services, which include elderly daycare and family social services.

## Wholesale and Retail Trade

Employment in wholesale and retail trade is expected to rise by 19 and 23 percent, respectively, from 6 to 7.2 million in wholesale trade and from 19.3 to 23.8 million in retail trade. Spurred by higher levels of personal income, the fastest projected job growth in retail trade is in apparel and accessory stores, and appliance, radio, television, and music stores.

Substantial increases in retail employment are anticipated in large industries, including eating and drinking establishments, grocery stores, automotive dealers and service stations, and general merchandise stores.

## Finance, Insurance, and Real Estate

Employment is expected to increase by 21 percent in these industries, adding 1.4 million jobs to the 1992 level of 6.6 million. The strong demand for financial services is expected to continue. Bank mergers, consolidations, and closings resulting from overexpansion and competition from nonbank corporations which offer bank-like services are expected to limit job growth among commercial banks and savings and loan associations. The fastest-growing industries within this sector are expected to be holding and investment offices and mortgage bankers and brokers. Insurance agents, brokers, and services are expected to register the largest increases in jobs.

## Transportation, Communications, and Public Utilities

Overall employment in these sectors will increase by 14 percent. Employment in the transportation sector is expected to increase by 24 percent, from 3.5 to 4.3 million. Truck transportation will account for 50 percent of all new jobs; air transportation will account for 29 percent. The projected gains in transportation jobs reflect the continued shift from rail to road freight transportation, rising personal incomes, and growth in foreign trade. In addition, deregulation in the transportation industry has increased personal and business travel options, spurring strong job growth in the passenger transportation arrangement industry, which includes travel agencies.

Employment in communications is projected to decline by 12 percent due to labor-saving technology and industry competition. Employment in utilities, however, is expected to grow by 117,000 new jobs, driven by strong growth in water supply and sanitary services.

### Government

By 2005, government employment, excluding public education and public hospitals, is expected to increase 10 percent, from 9.5 to 10.5 million jobs. The growth will occur at state and local government levels only. Employment in the federal government and U.S. Postal Service is expected to decline by 113,000 and 41,000 jobs, respectively.

## Goods-Producing Industries

While there are more jobs in the services industries, the goods-producing industries remain an important part of our labor market. Many service-industry jobs, for example, provide support to or benefit from employment and income produced by the goods-producing sector of our economy.

Employment in this sector has not recovered from the recessionary period of the early 1980s and the trade imbalances that began in the mid-1980s. Although overall employment in goods-producing industries is expected to show little change, growth prospects within the sector vary considerably.

### Construction

Construction is expected to increase by 26 percent, from 4.5 to 5.6 million jobs. The need to improve the nation's infrastructure will result in increases in road, bridge, and tunnel construction. This will offset the decrease in demand for new housing, which reflects the slowdown in population growth and the overexpansion of office building construction in recent years.

### Agriculture, Forestry, and Fishing

After declining for many decades, overall employment in agriculture, forestry, and fishing is projected to grow by 14 percent, from 1.7 to 2 million jobs. Strong growth in agricultural services will more than offset an expected continued decline in crops, livestock, and livestock products.

### Manufacturing

Manufacturing jobs are expected to decline by 3 percent from the 1992 level of 18 million. The projected loss of manufacturing jobs reflects productivity gains achieved from increased investment in manufacturing technologies. The composition of manufacturing employment is expected to shift because most of the jobs that will disappear are production jobs. On the other hand, the number of professional positions in manufacturing firms will increase.

### Mining

Mining employment is expected to decline 11 percent, from 631,000 to 562,000 jobs. Underlying this projection is the assumption that domestic oil production will drop and oil imports will rise, reducing employment in the crude petroleum industry. In addition, employment in coal mining should continue to decline sharply due to the expanded use of labor-saving machinery.

## Career Planning and Job Seeking Skills Are More Important Than Ever

If you bought this book and have waded through all the information in this section, I have to figure that you are motivated to improve your lot in life. Assuming this is so, you need to keep one thing in your mind at all times: To succeed in today's labor market, you will need to spend more time on career planning and preparation.

Those who spend this extra time are more likely to do better in the labor market—and are more likely to find satisfying careers. Good career planning includes more than just picking a job. It includes knowing what you want to accomplish, knowing which skills you enjoy using most, seeking a work environment that is satisfying to you, and finding work that is meaningful to you.

## A Few Words on Selecting a Career

A job is something you might take simply because it is available when you need one. A career is a longer-term decision to work within a certain area of expertise that may require special training or experience. When considering a long-term career choice, it is important to understand that it is often better to prepare for or select a job you will really enjoy. This increases your chances for long-term career satisfaction.

Most people will change jobs many times and change careers several times during their working lives. When you are doing this, consider factors other than simply how fast an occupational group is growing. Even in careers that are projected to have slow or no growth, opportunities will remain. But if you are interested in a career within an occupation that is growing quickly, that can certainly work to your long-term advantage.

Because you are more likely to change jobs now than in the past, it is wise to learn how to conduct a more effective job search. Depending on unemployment rates, the average length of unemployment ranges from 12 to 16 weeks and can be much longer for some people. For example, older workers and those with higher earnings tend to take longer than average to find new jobs. Because of the major changes in the labor market, many people find that they are forced to look for work and don't know how to go about it effectively. The traditional job-seeking techniques simply don't work very well and can lead to a lot of frustration.

I've spent the past 20 years researching ways to find jobs, and I have found that some job search methods work better than others. I have identified those that reduce the time it takes to find a job and increase your chances of getting more desirable ones. If you know more about looking for a job, it can make a big difference in your earnings and long-term career satisfaction.

I've included career planning and job search information in Section 3. It is enough to get you started, but I encourage you to learn more about this than what is presented in one section. It makes sense to learn as much as you can about career planning and job seeking. In today's economy, knowledge of these techniques is an essential economic survival skill. Those who do a thorough job planning their careers will clearly do better than those who do not.

# Additional Details and Charts of Interest

## Education and Earnings

If you have been paying attention so far, it should come as no surprise to you that higher pay is related to higher educational attainment. Not always, of course, but on average. The table below provides a variety of information for major occupational groups. You can see the percentage of people working in each cluster at various levels of education. Clusters that have higher average educational requirements tend to pay higher too.

## Growth of Jobs with Above Average Earnings Projected at All Education Levels

The information that follows is based on 1992 data released by the U.S. Department of Labor in BLS Summary 94-2. It includes several lists I thought you would find interesting, since they combine jobs with high earnings and high rates of projected growth.

The Bureau of Labor Statistics (BLS) projects the nation's employment to grow by almost 26.4 million over the 1992-2005 period. The majority of these new jobs will be in higher-paying occupations. Entry requirements of the new jobs in occupations having above-average earnings will range from no more then a high school education to a college bachelor's degree or even higher.

Occupations for which the most common entry requirement is a bachelor's degree or higher are projected to have the greatest increase of jobs with above-average earnings. Jobs for college graduates with above-average earnings will comprise over 30 percent—nearly 8.1 million—of the new jobs. Nearly one-quarter of the new jobs that require at least a four-year college degree will be in just five occupations: accountants and auditors, systems analysts, and elementary, secondary, and special education teachers.

Occupations that most commonly require postsecondary training less than a bachelor's degree are also expected to have significant growth of jobs with above-average earnings. Jobs in this group are projected to increase by nearly 2.8 million, constituting over 10 percent of the new jobs. Nearly half of the new jobs with higher earnings that will require postsecondary training less than a bachelor's degree will be in only four occupations: food and service lodging managers, licensed practical nurses, registered nurses, and radiologic technologists and technicians.

The majority of all jobs do not require education beyond high school. Although the share of jobs that require this level of education is projected to decline in the years ahead, more then half of the total job growth over the 1992-2005 period will, nevertheless, occur in these occupations. Job growth among occupations that most commonly require a high school education or employer training is expected to be greatest in occupations with below-average earnings. Jobs in occupations with above-average earnings in this education group are also projected to increase by almost 4.3 million, comprising over 28 percent of the economy's total job growth.

Across the three education groups, over 57 percent of the nation's total job growth is expected to be in occupations that had above-average earnings in 1992. The table below lists for the three groups the occupations with above-average earnings projected to have the greatest net employment change over the 1992-2005 period.

**Table 5.   Occupations with Above-Average Earnings Projected to Have the Greatest Net Employment Change, 1992-2005, by Level of Education or Training Most Often Required (employment in thousands)**

| High school education or employer training | | |
|---|---|---|
| Occupation | 1992 | Net change 1992-2005 |
| Truck drivers, light and heavy | 2,391 | 648 |
| Marketing and sales worker supervisors | 2,036 | 407 |
| Maintenance repairers, general utility | 1,145 | 319 |
| Clerical supervisors and managers | 1,267 | 301 |
| Human services workers | 189 | 256 |
| Blue-collar worker supervisors | 1,757 | 217 |
| Carpenters | 978 | 198 |
| Correction officers | 282 | 197 |
| Automotive mechanics | 739 | 168 |
| Painters and paperhangers, construction and maintenance | 440 | 128 |
| Electricians | 518 | 100 |
| Police and detectives | 700 | 92 |
| Bus and truck mechanics and diesel engine specialists | 263 | 64 |
| Heat, air conditioning, and refrigeration mechanics and installers | 212 | 62 |
| Driver/sales workers | 329 | 60 |
| Fire-fighting occupations | 305 | 50 |
| Welders and cutters | 306 | 46 |
| Dispatchers | 221 | 46 |
| Drywall installers and finishers | 121 | 44 |
| Insurance claims clerks | 116 | 43 |

| Postsecondary education or formal training, less than a bachelor's degree | | |
|---|---|---|
| Occupation | 1992 | Net change 1992-2005 |
| Registered Nurses | 1,835 | 765 |
| Licensed practical nurses | 659 | 261 |
| Food service and lodging managers | 532 | 232 |
| Radiologic technologists and technicians | 162 | 102 |
| Paralegals | 95 | 81 |
| Electrical and electronic technicians and technologists | 323 | 74 |
| Science and mathematics technicians | 244 | 61 |
| Musicians | 236 | 59 |
| Cost estimators | 163 | 49 |
| Medical records technicians | 76 | 47 |
| Dental hygienists | 108 | 46 |

| Occupation | 1992 | Net change 1992-2005 |
|---|---|---|
| Inspectors and compliance officers, except construction | 155 | 42 |
| Respiratory therapists | 74 | 36 |
| Drafters | 314 | 35 |
| Sales agent, real estate | 283 | 32 |
| Construction and building inspectors | 66 | 20 |
| Physician assistants | 58 | 20 |

**Bachelor's or higher degree**

| Occupation | 1992 | Net change 1992-2005 |
|---|---|---|
| Systems analysts | 455 | 501 |
| Teachers secondary | 1,263 | 462 |
| General managers and top executives | 2,871 | 380 |
| Teachers, elementary | 1,456 | 311 |
| Accountants and auditors | 939 | 304 |
| Teachers, special education | 358 | 267 |
| Lawyers | 626 | 195 |
| Physicians | 556 | 195 |
| Social workers | 484 | 191 |
| Financial managers | 701 | 174 |
| Computer programmers | 555 | 169 |
| Marketing, advertising, and public relations managers | 432 | 156 |
| Teachers and instructors, vocational education and training | 305 | 111 |
| Engineering, mathematical and natural science managers | 337 | 106 |
| Personnel, training, and labor relations specialists | 281 | 102 |
| Instructors and coaches, sports and physical training | 260 | 94 |
| Electrical and electronics engineers | 370 | 90 |
| Management analysts | 208 | 89 |
| Property and real estate managers | 243 | 85 |
| Construction managers | 180 | 85 |

# Fastest-Growing Jobs Requiring a College Degree

Here is a list of the fastest growing jobs typically requiring a four-year college degree.

| Occupation | Percentage Growth |
|---|---|
| Computer engineers and scientists | 112 |
| Systems analysts | 110 |
| Physical therapists | 88 |
| Teachers, special education | 74 |
| Operations research analysts | 61 |
| Occupational therapists | 60 |
| Teachers, preschool and kindergarten | 54 |
| Psychologists | 48 |
| Speech-language pathologists and audiologists | 48 |
| Construction managers | 47 |
| Management analysts | 43 |
| Recreational therapists | 40 |
| Social workers | 40 |
| Recreation workers | 38 |
| Podiatrists | 37 |
| Teachers, secondary schools | 37 |
| Instructors and coaches, sports and physical training | 36 |
| Marketing, advertising, and public relations managers | 36 |
| Personnel training and labor relations specialists | 36 |
| Teachers and instructors, vocational education and training | 36 |

# Fastest-Growing Jobs Requiring Some Postsecondary Training

Here is a list of jobs that don't require a four-year college degree but do require either formal training or education after high school or, in some cases, substantial on-the-job experience. Some of these jobs can pay pretty well, so it is not entirely true that a four-year college degree is required to do well.

| Percentage Employment Growth of Occupations Requiring Some Postsecondary or Extensive Employer Training, Projected 1992-2005 | |
|---|---|
| **Occupation** | **Percentage growth** |
| Physical and corrective therapy assistants and aides | 93 |
| Paralegals | 86 |
| Occupation therapy assistants and aides | 78 |
| Medical assistants | 71 |
| Radiologic technologists and technicians | 63 |
| Medical records technicians | 61 |
| Legal secretaries | 57 |
| EEG technologists | 54 |
| Producers, directors, actors, and entertainers | 54 |
| Nuclear medicine technologists | 50 |
| Insurance adjusters, examiners, and investigators | 49 |

| Occupation | Percentage growth |
|---|---|
| Respiratory therapists | 48 |
| Cooks, restaurant | 46 |
| Data processing equipment repairers | 45 |
| Medical secretaries | 45 |
| Food service and lodging managers | 44 |
| Dental hygienists | 43 |
| Surgical technologists | 42 |
| Pharmacy assistants | 42 |
| Licensed practical nurses | 40 |

## Fastest-Growing Jobs Requiring High School Education or Less

Here is a list of the fastest-growing jobs that don't require education beyond the high school level. As you can see, some have very high growth rates projected through 2005. A few of these jobs pay pretty well, although many of these, like detectives, require substantial on-the-job experience. You should also realize (should you be pondering this list for good jobs you can get without going to school) that high school graduates often have to compete with those who have more education. For example, many detectives have college degrees, and they will often be given a preference in hiring or promotion. I'm not saying you can't get ahead without an education, just that it is highly competitive for some jobs if you don't have the best credentials.

| Fastest-Growing Jobs Requiring a High School Education or Less ||
|---|---|
| Occupation | Percentage growth |
| Home health aides | 138 |
| Human services workers | 136 |
| Personal and home health care aides | 130 |
| Electronic pagination systems workers | 78 |
| Corrections officers | 70 |
| Detectives, except public | 70 |
| Child-care workers | 66 |
| Travel agents | 66 |
| Nursery workers | 62 |
| Subway and streetcar operators | 57 |
| Manicurists | 54 |
| Flight attendants | 51 |
| Guards | 51 |
| Paving, surfacing, and tamping equipment operators | 48 |
| Bakers, bread and pastry | 47 |
| Amusement and recreation attendants | 46 |
| Baggage porters and bellhops | 46 |
| Laundry and drycleaning machine operators and tenders, except pressing | 46 |
| Bicycle repairers | 45 |
| Nursing aides, orderlies, and attendants | 45 |

## Fastest-Growing Jobs in Manufacturing

Here are the fastest growing manufacturing jobs, arranged in projected percentage of growth through 2005.

| Occupation | Percentage employment growth |
|---|---|
| All other printing workers, precision | 92.3 |
| Electronic pagination system workers | 77.9 |
| Systems analysts | 65.1 |
| All other printing press setters and set-up operators | 51.1 |
| Medical scientists | 47.5 |
| Computer engineers and scientists | 41.8 |
| Offset lithographic press operators | 40.3 |
| Cabinet makers and bench carpenters | 37 |
| Screen printing machine setters and set-up operators | 36.7 |
| Advertising clerks | 34.3 |
| Meat, poultry and fish cutters and trimmers | 32.9 |
| Biological scientists | 31 |
| All other printing, binding and related workers | 30.3 |
| Wood machinists | 29.4 |
| All other professional workers | 29.2 |
| Operations research analysts | 28.4 |
| Reporters and correspondents | 26.9 |
| All other precision woodworkers | 26.7 |
| Paper goods machine setters and set-up operators | 26.3 |
| Personnel, training, and labor relations specialists | 26.3 |

## New and Replacement Openings by Occupational Group

The emphasis in this book is on jobs that are growing rapidly, but I have pointed out that some slower-growing jobs will also have many openings. The following chart will give you some details by occupational group on where the openings will come from. This table is based on openings from 1992 through 2005

| Projected Job Openings Due to Growth and Replacement Needs (in millions) ||||
|---|---|---|---|
| Occupation group | Replacement needs | Growth | Total |
| Service workers | 5.9 | 6.8 | 12.7 |
| Professional specialty workers | 3.6 | 6.2 | 9.8 |
| Administrative support workers, including clerical | 5.5 | 3.5 | 9.0 |
| Operators, fabricators, and laborers | 4.3 | 2.7 | 7.0 |
| Marketing and sales workers | 4.2 | 2.3 | 6.5 |
| Precision production, craft, and repair workers | 4.0 | 2.1 | 6.1 |
| Executives, administrators, and managers | 2.5 | 3.1 | 5.7 |
| Technicians and related support workers | 1.0 | 1.4 | 2.4 |
| Agriculture, forestry, fishing, and related workers | .7 | .5 | 1.2 |

# More Than 300 Additional Jobs Listed in Order of Projected Growth

I've already provided a list of 50 fastest-growing jobs in order of their projected percentage of growth. Here's a list that picks up from there, providing more than 300 additional jobs in order of their projected growth percentage. Because these jobs are the largest ones in our economy, they cover about 85 percent of the labor force. Occupations beginning with "All other" refer to miscellaneous occupations within a category. You can obtain additional information on many of these jobs in Appendix C.

Because the labor market is expected to grow about 20 percent between now and the year 2005, occupations that are projected to grow at or below 20 percent or so are actually growing more slowly than average. That doesn't mean they are "bad," it's just something to consider when making your career plans.

| Occupation | Percentage growth projected |
|---|---|
| Hotel desk clerks | 41.3 |
| All other service workers | 40.2 |
| Bill and account collectors | 40.0 |
| Loan officers and counselors | 40.0 |
| Animal caretakers, except farm | 39.8 |
| Insulation workers | 39.8 |
| Recreational therapists | 39.8 |
| Licensed practical nurses | 39.7 |
| Social workers | 39.5 |
| Dental assistants | 39.3 |
| All other management support workers | 39.0 |
| Recreation workers | 38.1 |
| Real estate appraisers | 38.1 |
| All other teachers and instructors | 37.9 |
| Paving, surfacing, and tamping equipment operators | 37.7 |
| Advertising clerks | 37.5 |
| Podiatrists | 37.4 |
| Offset lithographic press operators | 37.2 |
| Insurance claims clerks | 37.0 |
| Drywall installers and finishers | 36.9 |
| Electromedical and biomedical equipment repairers | 36.8 |
| Screen printing machine setters and set-up operators | 36.7 |
| Teachers, secondary school | 36.6 |
| Teachers and instructors, vocational education and training | 36.5 |
| Counter and rental clerks | 36.3 |
| Waiters and waitresses | 36.3 |
| All other food preparation and service workers | 36.2 |
| Instructors and coaches, sports and physical training | 36.2 |
| Marketing, advertising, and public relations managers | 36.1 |
| Personnel, training, and labor relations specialists | 36.1 |
| Cooks, short order and fast food | 36.0 |
| Emergency medical technicians | 35.9 |
| Chiropractors | 35.8 |
| Opticians, dispensing and measuring | 35.7 |
| All other hand workers | 35.7 |

| Occupation | Percentage growth projected |
|---|---|
| Hosts and hostesses, restaurant, lounge, or coffee shop | 35.6 |
| Parking lot attendants | 35.3 |
| Aircraft pilots and flight engineers | 35.2 |
| Gardeners and groundskeepers, except farm | 35.2 |
| Cardiology technologists | 35.0 |
| Physicians | 35.0 |
| Property and real estate managers | 35.0 |
| All other managers and administrators | 34.7 |
| Hairdressers, hairstylists, and cosmetologists | 34.7 |
| Interviewing clerks, except personnel and social welfare | 34.4 |
| Physician assistants | 33.8 |
| Receptionists and information clerks | 33.8 |
| Institutional cleaning supervisors | 33.7 |
| Technicians, except health, engineering, and science | 33.3 |
| Meat, poultry, and fish cutters and trimmers, hand | 32.9 |
| Securities and financial services sales workers | 32.8 |
| Veterinarians and veterinary inspectors | 32.7 |
| Accountants and auditors | 32.3 |
| Counselors | 32.2 |
| Engineering, mathematical, and natural science managers | 31.5 |
| Lawyers | 31.1 |
| Medical scientists | 30.8 |
| Computer programmers | 30.4 |
| All other printing, binding, and related workers | 30.3 |
| Automotive body and related repairers | 30.2 |
| Reservation and transportation ticket agents and travel clerks | 30.1 |
| All other legal assistants, including law clerks | 30.0 |
| Directors, religious activities and education | 29.9 |
| Clergy | 29.8 |
| Construction and building inspectors | 29.8 |
| Cost estimators | 29.8 |
| Dining room and cafeteria attendants and bar helpers | 29.8 |
| All other protective service workers | 29.7 |
| Heat, air conditioning, and refrigeration mechanics and installers | 29.4 |
| Ushers, lobby attendants, and ticket takers | 29.3 |
| All other agricultural, forestry, fishing, and related workers | 29.2 |
| Painters and paperhangers, construction and maintenance | 29.2 |
| Highway maintenance workers | 29.0 |
| Pharmacists | 29.0 |
| Wood machinists | 28.7 |
| Metallurgists and metallurgical, ceramic, and materials engineers | 28.3 |
| Painting, coating, and decorating workers, hand | 28.0 |
| Railroad conductors and yardmasters | 27.9 |
| Maintenance repairers, general utility | 27.8 |
| Bus drivers, school | 27.6 |
| Psychiatric aides | 27.5 |
| Truck drivers, light and heavy | 27.1 |
| Inspectors and compliance officers, except construction | 27.0 |
| Adjustment clerks | 26.5 |
| All other motor vehicle operators | 26.5 |

| Occupation | Percentage growth projected |
|---|---|
| Clinical lab technologists and technicians | 26.5 |
| College and university faculty | 26.4 |
| Paper goods, machine setters and set-up operators | 26.4 |
| Pipelayers and pipelaying fitters | 26.4 |
| All other construction trades workers | 26.3 |
| Architects, except landscape and marine | 26.3 |
| Dietitians and nutritionists | 26.3 |
| Landscape architects | 26.3 |
| Loan interviewers | 26.3 |
| Public relations specialists and publicity writers | 26.3 |
| All other helpers, laborers, and material movers, hand | 26.1 |
| Loan and credit clerks | 26.1 |
| Photographic process workers, precision | 26.1 |
| Reporters and correspondents | 26.1 |
| Psychiatric technicians | 26.0 |
| Bricklayers and stone masons | 25.7 |
| Instructors, adult (nonvocational) education | 25.7 |
| Economists | 25.3 |
| Strippers, printing | 25.3 |
| Hard tile setters | 25.2 |
| Personnel clerks, except payroll and timekeeping | 25.2 |
| Personnel, training, and labor relations managers | 25.2 |
| Radio and TV announcers and newscasters | 25.1 |
| Biological scientists | 25.0 |
| Science and mathematics technicians | 25.0 |
| Technical assistants, library | 25.0 |
| Musicians | 24.9 |
| Photographers | 24.9 |
| Dancers and choreographers | 24.8 |
| Financial managers | 24.8 |
| Cabinet makers and bench carpenters | 24.5 |
| Bus and truck mechanics and diesel engine specialists | 24.4 |
| Cashiers | 24.4 |
| Meteorologists | 24.4 |
| General office clerks | 24.3 |
| Electrical and electronics engineers | 24.2 |
| Shampooers | 24.2 |
| Credit authorizers | 24.1 |
| Underwriters | 24.1 |
| Combination machine tool setters, set-up operators, operators, and tenders | 24.0 |
| Court clerks | 23.9 |
| Clerical supervisors and managers | 23.8 |
| Vehicle washers and equipment cleaners | 23.7 |
| Civil engineers including traffic engineers | 23.6 |
| Dispatchers, except police, fire, and ambulance | 23.3 |
| All other material recording, schedule, and distribution workers | 23.2 |
| Urban and regional planners | 23.2 |
| Writers and editors, including technical writers | 23.2 |
| Camera operators, television, motion picture, video | 23.0 |

| Occupation | Percentage growth projected |
|---|---|
| Artists and commercial artists | 22.9 |
| Electrical and electronic technicians/technologists | 22.8 |
| Automotive mechanics | 22.7 |
| Forest and conservation workers | 22.4 |
| Structural and reinforcing metal workers | 22.4 |
| Geologists, geophysicists, and oceanographers | 22.2 |
| All other mechanics, installers, and repairers | 22.1 |
| Employment interviewers, private or public employment service | 21.8 |
| Optical goods workers, precision | 21.7 |
| Roofers | 21.7 |
| Carpet installers | 21.6 |
| Salespersons, retail | 21.5 |
| Vehicle and mobile equipment mechanics and repairers | 21.4 |
| Farm managers | 21.1 |
| Teachers, elementary | 21.3 |
| Chemists | 21.2 |
| Brokerage clerks | 20.9 |
| Designers, except interior designers | 20.6 |
| Photoengravers | 20.6 |
| Grader, dozer, and scraper operators | 20.5 |
| Small engine specialists | 20.5 |
| Brokers, real estate | 20.4 |
| Crossing guards | 20.4 |
| All other social scientists | 20.3 |
| Mechanical engineers | 20.3 |
| Budget analysts | 20.1 |
| Excavation and loading machine operators | 20.1 |
| Marketing and sales worker supervisors | 20.0 |
| Numerical control machine tool operators and tenders, metal and plastic | 19.9 |
| Insurance policy processing clerks | 19.8 |
| Food counter, fountain, and related workers | 19.7 |
| Chemical engineers | 19.4 |
| Electricians | 19.3 |
| Cleaning and building service occupations, except private household | 19.2 |
| Data entry keyers, except composing | 19.2 |
| All other printing press setters and set-up operators | 19.1 |
| Customer service representatives, utilities | 19.1 |
| Janitors and cleaners, including maids and housekeeping cleaners | 19.1 |
| Jewelers and silversmiths | 19.1 |
| Tile examiners and searchers | 19.1 |
| File clerks | 18.9 |
| Photographics processing machine operators and tenders | 18.8 |
| Locksmiths and safe repairers | 18.5 |
| Water and liquid waste treatment plant and system operators | 18.4 |
| Taxi drivers and chauffeurs | 18.3 |
| Tire repairers and changers | 18.3 |
| Curators, archivists, museum technicians, and restorers | 18.2 |
| All other precision woodworkers | 18.1 |
| Driver/sales workers | 18.1 |

| Occupation | Percentage growth projected |
|---|---|
| Elevator installers and repairers | 18.1 |
| Furniture finishers | 18.0 |
| Mail clerks, except mail machine operators and postal service | 17.9 |
| Library assistants and bookmobile drivers | 17.8 |
| Traffic, shipping, and receiving clerks | 17.8 |
| Funeral directors and morticians | 17.6 |
| Credit checkers | 17.5 |
| Sheet metal workers and duct installers | 17.5 |
| Helpers, construction trades | 17.4 |
| All other adjusters and investigators | 17.2 |
| Operating engineers | 17.2 |
| Industrial engineers, except safety engineers | 16.8 |
| Welfare eligibility workers and interviewers | 16.8 |
| Ambulance drivers and attendants except EMTs | 16.7 |
| Municipal clerks | 16.7 |
| Fire fighters | 16.6 |
| Supervisors, farming, forestry, and agricultural related occupations | 16.6 |
| All other transportation and material moving equipment operators | 16.4 |
| Bindery machine operators and set-up operators | 16.3 |
| Dispatchers, police, fire, and ambulance | 16.3 |
| Plasterers | 16.3 |
| Tax examiners, collectors, and revenue agents | 16.2 |
| All other transportation and related workers | 16.1 |
| Fire-fighting and prevention supervisors | 16.1 |
| Power generating and reactor plant operators | 16.1 |
| Crane and tower operators | 16.0 |
| All other engineering technicians and technologists | 15.8 |
| Order fillers, wholesale and retail sales | 15.8 |
| Cooks, institution or cafeteria | 15.7 |
| Optometrists | 15.7 |
| Camera and photographic equipment repairers | 15.5 |
| Welders and cutters | 15.2 |
| All other technicians | 15.1 |
| All other plant and system operators | 15.0 |
| Insurance sales workers | 15.0 |
| Agricultural and food scientists | 14.4 |
| All other law enforcement occupations | 14.4 |
| All other sales and related workers | 14.2 |
| Aeronautical and astronautical engineers | 14.1 |
| Bookbinders | 14.1 |
| All other precision assemblers | 14.0 |
| Police patrol officers | 13.9 |
| Sheriffs and deputy sheriffs | 13.9 |
| Aircraft mechanics | 13.8 |
| Fire inspection occupations | 13.2 |
| Concrete and terrazzo finishers | 13.4 |
| Cooking and roasting machine operators and tenders, food and tobacco | 13.4 |
| Production, planning, and expediting clerks | 13.4 |
| Wholesale and retail buyers, except for products | 13.3 |

| Occupation | Percentage growth projected |
|---|---|
| General managers and top executives | 13.2 |
| Surveyors | 13.2 |
| All other extraction and related workers | 13.1 |
| Athletes, coaches, umpires, and related workers | 13.1 |
| Cannery workers | 13.1 |
| Duplicating, mail, and other office machine operators | 13.1 |
| Freight, stock, and material movers, hand | 13.1 |
| Farm equipment mechanics | 12.8 |
| Material recording, scheduling, dispatching, and distributing occupations | 12.7 |
| Police and detective supervisors | 12.6 |
| Billing, cost, and rate clerks | 12.4 |
| Blue-collar worker supervisors | 12.4 |
| Hand packers and packagers | 12.4 |
| All other cleaning and building service workers | 12.3 |
| Librarians, professional | 12.3 |
| Foresters and conservation scientists | 12.2 |
| Interior designers | 12.2 |
| Drafters | 11.3 |
| Sales agents, real estate | 11.3 |
| Upholsterers | 11.2 |
| Photoengraving and lithographic machine operators and tenders | 10.7 |
| Refuse collectors | 10.5 |
| Pressing machine operators and tenders, textile, garment, and related materials | 10.3 |
| Communication, transportation, and utilities operations managers | 10.0 |
| Construction managers | 10.0 |
| Air traffic controllers | 9.9 |
| Electric power generating plant operators, distributors and dispatchers | 9.9 |
| All other precision workers | 9.8 |
| New accounts clerks banking | 9.3 |
| Statisticians | 9.3 |
| Musical instrument repairers and tuners | 9.0 |
| Dairy processing equipment operators, including setters | 8.9 |
| Stock clerks | 8.8 |
| Electrical power line installers and repairers | 8.5 |
| Aircraft engine specialists | 8.4 |
| Locomotive engineers | 8.3 |
| Office machine and cash register servicers | 8.1 |
| Programmers, numerical, tool, and process control | 8.1 |
| Solderers and brazers | 8.1 |
| Police detectives and investigators | 8.0 |
| Plumbers, pipefitters, and steamfitters | 7.8 |
| Railroad brake, signal, and switch operators | 7.7 |
| Mathematicians and all other mathematical scientists | 7.6 |
| Captains and other officers, fishing vessels | 7.4 |
| Electronics repairers, commercial and industrial equipment | 7.4 |
| Printing press machine setters operators and tenders | 7.3 |
| Camera operators | 7.2 |

| Occupation | Percentage growth projected |
|---|---|
| Plastic molding machine operators and tenders setters and set-up operators | 7.1 |
| Correspondence clerks | 7.0 |
| Industrial truck and tractor operators | 7.0 |
| Platemakers | 7.0 |
| Precision instrument repairers | 6.9 |
| Railyard engineers, dinkey operators, and hostlers | 6.3 |
| Hoist and winch operators | 6.2 |
| Proofreaders and copy markers | 6.2 |
| All other precision food and tobacco workers | 6.0 |
| Bus drivers | 5.9 |
| Bakers, manufacturing | 5.8 |
| Dentists | 5.2 |
| Stationary engineers | 5.1 |
| Fishers, hunters, and trappers | 4.7 |
| Pest controllers and assistants | 4.6 |
| Order clerks, materials, merchandise, and service | 4.4 |
| Electronic semiconductor processors | 4.3 |
| Secretaries, except legal and medical | 4.3 |
| Broadcast technicians | 4.0 |
| Logging tractor operators | 4.0 |
| Machine builders and other precision machine assemblers | 4.0 |
| Mobile heavy equipment mechanics | 4.0 |
| Credit analysts | 3.7 |
| Bookkeeping, accounting, and auditing clerks | 3.5 |

| Occupation | Percentage growth projected |
|---|---|
| Foundry mold assembly and shakeout workers | 3.4 |
| Dental lab technicians, precision | 3.1 |
| Government chief executives and legislators | 3.1 |
| Painters, transportation equipment | 2.9 |
| All other electrical and electronic equipment mechanics, installers, and repairers | 2.5 |
| All other clerical and administrative support workers | 2.4 |
| All other metal and plastic machine setters, operators, and related workers | 2.4 |
| Industrial production managers | 2.4 |
| Judges, magistrates, and other judicial workers | 2.3 |
| Mining engineers, including mine safety engineers | 2.1 |
| Extruding and forming machine setters, operators, and tenders | 1.7 |
| Messengers | 1.7 |
| Grinders and polishers, hand | 1.6 |
| All other precision metal workers | 1.3 |
| Riggers | 1.1 |
| Chemical plant and system operators | 1.0 |
| Postal mail carriers | 0.9 |
| Machine feeders and offbearers | 0.7 |
| Nuclear engineers | 0.5 |
| Coating, painting, and spraying machine operators, tenders, setters and set-up operators | 0.4 |
| Metal fabricators, structural metal products | 0.4 |
| Power distributors and dispatchers | 0.2 |
| Meter readers, utilities | 0.3 |

## Find Better Jobs in Less Time

I've spent much of the past 20 years of my professional life learning more about career planning and job search methods. My original interest was in helping people find jobs in less time, and in helping them find better jobs. In a broad sense, that is—or should be—the real task of career counseling and job seeking. While there is some complexity to these tasks, I have also found some elements of simplicity:

1. If you are going to work, you might as well define what it is you really want to do and what you are good at.

2. If you are looking for a job, you might as well use techniques that will reduce the time it takes to find one—and that will help you get a *better* job.

This section covers these topics, along with a few others. While I have written much more detailed works on career planning and job seeking, I present the basics in this section. I think there is enough information here to make a difference for most people, and I hope that it gives you some things to think about as well as some techniques you have not considered.

## The Two Subsections

This section is divided into two distinct subsections. Here are some details on each:

### The Job Matching Chart

I included this chart in a book titled *Getting the Job You Really Want,* and I think it's worth including here. It lists more than 200 jobs within clusters of related jobs, including many whose descriptions are included in this book. It also provides an interesting way to explore various job possibilities you might otherwise overlook.

If you are already certain about the type of job you want, you might not need to spend time with this chart.

### The Quick Job Search

About 10 years ago, I decided to write something very short that would cover the most important elements of effective career planning and job seeking. Writing short things is harder for me than writing longer things, since every word has to count. I began by asking myself, "If I had only 30 or so pages, what are the most important things to tell someone?"

*The Quick Job Search* was the result. I've revised it several times over the years, and this is the newest revision. It is published as a separate book and has sold about 200,000 copies in its various forms. It is included here pretty much in its entirety, and I hope you can make good use of it.

### Avoid the Temptation, Do the Activities

I already know that you will resist doing the activities in this section. But trust me, doing them is worthwhile. Those who do them will have a better sense of what they are good at, what they want to do, and how to go about doing it. They are more likely to get more interviews and to present themselves better in those interviews. Is this worth giving up a night of TV? Yes, I think so.

Interestingly enough, you will—after reading this section and doing its activities—have spent more time on planning your career than most people. And you will know far more than the average job seeker about how to go about finding a job. You may find when you are finished that you want to know even more, but I hope this is enough to get you started.

# The Job Matching Chart

The chart on the following pages provides information on about 200 jobs, covering about 80 percent of the labor force.

The jobs are arranged into groups of related jobs. While some clusters will interest you more than others, I suggest that you review all the clusters so you can consider jobs you may have previously overlooked. If a job interests you, put a checkmark by it. After you have reviewed the entire chart, go back over the checked jobs and circle those that interest you most. These are the jobs worth learning more about.

Note that the information in the chart includes estimates, averages, and projections that may or may not be true in your area.

## Codes Used in the Job Matching Chart

Most of the information provided in the chart is easy to understand, but following are the keys for several codes used:

### Education Code Keys

**H** = **High school diploma**

**P** = **Postsecondary training** (training or education beyond a high school degree)

**C** = **College degree (four year) and above**, including master's degree, doctorate, and professional degrees

**—** = **No formal training required** or typically learned on the job

### Skills and Working Conditions Columns

These columns list the characteristics found in many jobs. Columns that are marked indicate that the conditions are typical in those jobs.

### Employment Columns

There are four columns under the "Employment" heading that provide you with information you should consider in making a career decision. Following is a key for understanding the codes used in these columns, and some tips for how to use this information.

## Employment Columns Keys

**VL** = **Very Low:** Within the lowest 20 percent of all occupations

**L** = **Low:** Within the next 20 percent of all occupations

**A** = **Average:** Within the middle or average 20 percent of all occupations

**H** = **High:** Within the next 20 percent of all occupations

**VH** = **Very High:** Within the highest 20 percent of all occupations

- **Average Earnings:** Better paying jobs usually require higher levels of education, training, or responsibility. Most occupations have a wide range of earnings and some lower paying jobs might be more enjoyable to you. People who are just entering the labor market, those who have limited education or training, and those in smaller cities often earn much less than average.

- **Projected Growth:** Our economy is projected to create many new jobs in the years to come. Some jobs will grow rapidly while others will decline. It is helpful to know if the demand for a job will increase, but you should not select one job over another simply because it is projected to grow more rapidly. Even in jobs where little growth is projected, new jobs will open as people retire or move to other jobs.

- **Number of Openings:** Some occupations employ large numbers of people and others don't. Occupations employing large numbers of people often have many openings even though they are not growing rapidly. These jobs may also be easier to get, though they sometimes do not pay well.

- **Unemployment Rate:** Those seeking jobs in occupations with lower unemployment rates will often have fewer problems in finding a job.

# Job Matching Chart

Skill / condition column key:
**Working with Data/Information Skills:** 1. Researching and Compiling · 2. Analyzing and Evaluating · 3. Troubleshooting · 4. Artistic Expression
**Working with People Skills:** 5. Instructing · 6. Treating and Advising · 7. Supervising · 8. Persuading · 9. Public Contact
**Working with Things Skills:** 10. Mechanical Ability · 11. Operating a Vehicle
**Working Conditions:** 12. Repetitious · 13. Geographically Concentrated · 14. Mobile · 15. Physical Stamina · 16. Part-time · 17. Irregular Hours
**Employment:** 18. Average Earnings · 19. Projected Growth · 20. Number of Openings · 21. Unemployment Rate

| Occupation | ED | 1 | 2 | 3 | 4 | 5 | 6 | 7 | 8 | 9 | 10 | 11 | 12 | 13 | 14 | 15 | 16 | 17 | 18 | 19 | 20 | 21 |
|---|---|---|---|---|---|---|---|---|---|---|---|---|---|---|---|---|---|---|---|---|---|---|
| **Management and Financial Occupations** | | | | | | | | | | | | | | | | | | | | | | |
| *General Management Occupations* | | | | | | | | | | | | | | | | | | | | | | |
| Administrative services managers | HPC | | ■ | ■ | | | | ■ | | | | | | | | | | | H | L | VL | H |
| Employment interviewers/personnel specialists | P | | ■ | | | | | | ■ | ■ | | | | | | | | | VH | H | VH | L |
| Hotel managers and assistants | C | | ■ | ■ | | | | ■ | | ■ | | | | | | | | ■ | VL | VH | H | VH |
| Inspectors and compliance officers, except construction | C | ■ | ■ | ■ | | | | | | ■ | | | | | ■ | | | | H | H | H | L |
| General managers and top executives | C | | ■ | ■ | | | | ■ | ■ | | | | | | | | | | VH | A | L | H |
| Government chief executives and legislators | C | | ■ | ■ | | | | ■ | ■ | ■ | | | | | ■ | | ■ | ■ | H | VL | A | VL |
| Personnel, training, and labor relations managers | C | | ■ | ■ | | | | ■ | ■ | | | | | | | | | | VH | VH | H | L |
| Purchasing agents and managers | PC | ■ | ■ | ■ | | | | ■ | ■ | | | | | | | | | | VH | A | H | VL |
| *Financial Occupations* | | | | | | | | | | | | | | | | | | | | | | |
| Accountants and auditors | C | ■ | ■ | ■ | | | | | | | | | | | | | | | H | VH | VH | L |
| Budget analysts | C | ■ | ■ | ■ | | | | | | | | | | | | | | | A | A | A | H |
| Cost estimators | C | ■ | ■ | | | | | | | | | | | | | | | | A | L | L | H |
| Financial managers | C | ■ | ■ | ■ | | | | ■ | | | | | | | | | | | VH | H | VH | L |
| **Mathematical, Scientific, and Related Occupations** | | | | | | | | | | | | | | | | | | | | | | |
| *Mathematical Occupations* | | | | | | | | | | | | | | | | | | | | | | |
| Actuaries | C | ■ | ■ | | | | | | | | | | | | | | | | A | H | L | L |
| Computer systems analysts | C | ■ | ■ | ■ | | | | | | | | | | | | | | | VH | VH | H | L |
| Computer programmers | C | | ■ | ■ | | | | | | | | | | | | | | | H | H | H | L |
| Mathematicians | C | ■ | ■ | | | | | | | | | | | | | | | | H | L | L | A |
| Operations research analysts | C | ■ | ■ | ■ | | | | | | | | | | | | | | | VH | VH | H | L |
| Statistician clerks | C | ■ | ■ | | | | | | | | | | | | | | | | A | VL | VL | L |
| *Engineering Occupations* | | | | | | | | | | | | | | | | | | | | | | |
| Drafters | P | | ■ | ■ | | | | | | | | | | | | | | | H | A | H | L |
| Engineers (aerospace, chemical, civil, electrical and electronic industrial, mechanical, metallurgical, mining, nuclear, petroleum) | C | ■ | ■ | ■ | | | | | | | | | | | | | | | VH | A | H | L |
| Engineering, science, and data processing managers | C | ■ | ■ | ■ | | | ■ | | | | | | | | | | | | VH | H | H | L |
| All other engineering technicians and technologists | P | ■ | ■ | ■ | | | | | | | ■ | | | | | | | | H | A | H | A |
| *Scientists and Related Occupations* | | | | | | | | | | | | | | | | | | | | | | |
| Agricultural scientists | C | ■ | ■ | | | | | | | | | | | | | | | | A | A | A | L |
| Biological scientists | C | ■ | ■ | | | | | | | | | | | | | | | | H | VH | A | L |
| Foresters | C | ■ | ■ | | | | | | | | | | | ■ | ■ | ■ | | | L | L | A | A |
| Physical scientists (chemists, geologists and geophysicists, meteorologists, physicists, astronomers) | C | ■ | ■ | | | | | | | | | | | | | | | | H | A | A | L |
| Cartographers and geographers | C | ■ | ■ | | | | | | | | | | | | | | | | | | | |
| Science and mathematics technicians | P | ■ | | | | | | | | | | | | | | | | | L | H | H | A |
| *Architects and Surveyors* | | | | | | | | | | | | | | | | | | | | | | |
| Architects | C | ■ | ■ | | ■ | | | | | | | | | | | | | | VH | H | H | VL |
| Landscape architects | C | ■ | ■ | | ■ | | | | | | | | | | ■ | | | | H | A | A | L |
| Surveyors | PC | ■ | ■ | ■ | | | | | | | | | | | ■ | | | | A | A | A | A |

# Job Matching Chart

| | EDUCATION AND TRAINING | SKILLS — WORKING WITH DATA/INFORMATION SKILLS | | | | SKILLS — WORKING WITH PEOPLE SKILLS | | | | | SKILLS — WORKING WITH THINGS SKILLS | | WORKING CONDITIONS | | | | | | EMPLOYMENT | | | |
|---|---|---|---|---|---|---|---|---|---|---|---|---|---|---|---|---|---|---|---|---|---|---|
| | | 1. Researching and Compiling | 2. Analyzing and Evaluating | 3. Troubleshooting | 4. Artistic Expression | 5. Instructing | 6. Treating and Advising | 7. Supervising | 8. Persuading | 9. Public Contact | 10. Mechanical Ability | 11. Operating a Vehicle | 12. Repetitious | 13. Geographically Concentrated | 14. Mobile | 15. Physical Stamina | 16. Part-time | 17. Irregular Hours | 18. Average Earnings | 19. Projected Growth | 20. Number of Openings | 21. Unemployment Rate |
| **Legal, Social Science, and Human Service Occupations** | | | | | | | | | | | | | | | | | | | | | | |
| **Legal Occupations** (also see stenographers and court reporters under administrative support occupations) | | | | | | | | | | | | | | | | | | | | | | |
| Lawyers | C | ■ | ■ | ■ | | | ■ | | ■ | ■ | | | | | | | | | VH | VH | VH | VL |
| Paralegals | P | ■ | ■ | | | | | | | ■ | | | | | | | | | L | H | H | L |
| **Social Scientists and Urban Planners** | | | | | | | | | | | | | | | | | | | | | | |
| Anthropologists and archaeologists | C | ■ | ■ | | | | | | | | | | | ■ | ■ | | | | H | A | L | A |
| Archivists, curators, and historians | C | ■ | ■ | | | | | | | | | | | | | | | | H | A | L | A |
| Economists | C | ■ | ■ | | | | | | | | | | | | | | | | VH | A | A | A |
| Marketing research analysts | C | ■ | ■ | | | | | | | ■ | | | | | | | | | H | A | A | H |
| Psychologists | C | ■ | ■ | ■ | | | ■ | | ■ | ■ | | | | | | | | | H | A | VH | VL |
| Urban and regional planners | C | ■ | ■ | ■ | | | | | ■ | ■ | | | | | | | | | H | A | A | L |
| Sociologists | C | ■ | ■ | | | | | | | ■ | | | | | | | | | H | L | L | H |
| **Social and Recreation Workers** | | | | | | | | | | | | | | | | | | | | | | |
| Human services workers | PC | ■ | ■ | | | | ■ | | | ■ | | | | | ■ | | | ■ | H | VH | VH | L |
| Recreation workers | HPC | | | ■ | | | | | | ■ | | | | | ■ | ■ | ■ | ■ | VL | H | H | H |
| Social workers | C | ■ | ■ | ■ | | | ■ | | ■ | ■ | | | | | ■ | | | | H | VH | VH | L |
| Clergy | PC | | | | | ■ | ■ | ■ | ■ | ■ | | | | | ■ | | | ■ | A | L | A | VL |
| **Education and Related Occupations** | | | | | | | | | | | | | | | | | | | | | | |
| **Education Occupations** | | | | | | | | | | | | | | | | | | | | | | |
| Adult education teachers | C | ■ | ■ | ■ | | ■ | ■ | | | | | | | | | | ■ | ■ | A | H | H | L |
| Counselors | C | | ■ | ■ | | ■ | ■ | | ■ | ■ | | | | | | | | | H | VH | H | VL |
| Education administrators | C | | ■ | ■ | | ■ | | ■ | ■ | ■ | | | | | | | | | VH | H | H | VL |
| Kindergarten, elementary, and secondary school teachers | C | | | | | | | | | | | | | | | | ■ | | H | VH | VH | VL |
| Preschool workers | HPC | | ■ | | | ■ | ■ | | | ■ | | | | | | | | | L | H | H | L |
| Teacher aides and education assistants | HP | | | | | ■ | | | | | | | | | | | ■ | | VL | VH | VH | A |
| **Library Occupations** | | | | | | | | | | | | | | | | | | | | | | |
| Librarians | C | ■ | | ■ | | | | | | ■ | | | | | | | ■ | ■ | H | L | A | VL |
| Library assistants and bookmobile drivers | H | | | | | | | | | ■ | | ■ | | | ■ | | ■ | ■ | VL | L | A | A |
| Library technicians | H | ■ | | | | | | | | ■ | | | | | | | ■ | ■ | L | A | L | H |
| **Health Care Occupations** | | | | | | | | | | | | | | | | | | | | | | |
| Health diagnosing practitioners, chiropractors, dentists, optometrists, physicians, podiatrists, veterinarians | C | ■ | ■ | ■ | | ■ | ■ | | | ■ | | | | | | | ■ | ■ | VH | H | A | VL |
| Health services managers | C | ■ | ■ | ■ | | | | ■ | ■ | | | | | | | | | | VH | VH | H | L |
| **Health Assessment and Treating Occupations** | | | | | | | | | | | | | | | | | | | | | | |
| Dietitians and nutritionists | C | | ■ | ■ | | ■ | ■ | | | ■ | | | | | | | ■ | | L | A | A | A |
| Occupational therapists | C | | ■ | ■ | | ■ | ■ | | | ■ | | | | | | | | | A | VH | H | L |
| Pharmacists | C | | ■ | ■ | | ■ | ■ | | | ■ | | | | | | | | | H | A | H | VL |
| Physical therapists | C | | ■ | ■ | | ■ | ■ | | | ■ | | | | | | ■ | ■ | | H | VH | H | VL |
| Physician assistants | C | | ■ | ■ | | ■ | ■ | | | ■ | | | | | | | | ■ | H | H | H | L |
| Recreational therapists | C | | ■ | ■ | | ■ | ■ | | | ■ | | | | | ■ | ■ | ■ | | L | H | H | L |
| Registered nurses | PC | | ■ | ■ | | ■ | ■ | | | ■ | | | | | | ■ | ■ | ■ | H | H | VH | VL |
| Respiratory therapists | PC | | ■ | ■ | | ■ | ■ | | | ■ | | | | | | | | A | VH | H | VL | |
| Speech-language pathologists and audiologists | C | | ■ | ■ | | ■ | ■ | | | ■ | | | | | | | | | H | VH | A | VL |

# Job Matching Chart

Legend — EDUCATION AND TRAINING column abbreviations (H, P, C, etc.). Employment columns use: VH = Very High, H = High, A = Average, L = Low, VL = Very Low, V = varies.

| Occupation | Education and Training | 1. Researching and Compiling | 2. Analyzing and Evaluating | 3. Troubleshooting | 4. Artistic Expression | 5. Instructing | 6. Treating and Advising | 7. Supervising | 8. Persuading | 9. Public Contact | 10. Mechanical Ability | 11. Operating a Vehicle | 12. Repetitious | 13. Geographically Concentrated | 14. Mobile | 15. Physical Stamina | 16. Part-time | 17. Irregular Hours | 18. Average Earnings | 19. Projected Growth | 20. Number of Openings | 21. Unemployment Rate |
|---|---|---|---|---|---|---|---|---|---|---|---|---|---|---|---|---|---|---|---|---|---|---|
| **Health Technologists and Technicians** | | | | | | | | | | | | | | | | | | | | | | |
| Clinical laboratory technologists and technicians | PC | | ■ | | | | | | | | | | ■ | | | | | | A | H | H | L |
| Dental hygienists | P | | | | | ■ | ■ | | | ■ | | | | | | | ■ | | A | VH | H | VL |
| Opticians, dispensing and measuring | HP | | | | | | | | | ■ | | | | | | | | | A | VH | A | A |
| EEG technologists | P | ■ | | | | | | | | ■ | | | ■ | | | | | | L | VH | H | L |
| EKG technicians | H | ■ | | | | | | | | ■ | | | ■ | | | | | | L | VH | H | L |
| Emergency medical technicians | P | | ■ | ■ | | | ■ | | | ■ | | | | | ■ | | ■ | ■ | L | VH | H | L |
| Licensed practical nurses | P | | | | | | ■ | | | ■ | | | | | ■ | ■ | ■ | ■ | L | VH | VH | L |
| Medical record technicians | P | ■ | ■ | | | | | | | | | | | | | | | ■ | L | VH | V | L |
| Nuclear medicine, radiologic technicians and technologists | P | ■ | | | | | | | | ■ | | | | | | | | | H | VH | VH | VL |
| Radiological technologists | P | ■ | | | | | | | | ■ | | | ■ | | | | | | L | VH | H | L |
| Surgical technicians | P | | | | | | ■ | | | ■ | | | | | | | | | L | VH | H | L |
| **Health Service Occupations** | | | | | | | | | | | | | | | | | | | | | | |
| Dental assistants | H | | | | | | ■ | | | ■ | | | | | | | ■ | | VL | VH | H | A |
| Nursing aides, orderlies, and attendants | HP | | | | | | ■ | | | ■ | | | | | | | ■ | ■ | VL | VH | VH | H |
| Homemaker-home health aides | HP | | | | | | ■ | | | ■ | | | | | ■ | | ■ | | L | VH | VH | L |

## Communication, Visual Arts, and Performing Arts Occupations

| Occupation | Education and Training | 1 | 2 | 3 | 4 | 5 | 6 | 7 | 8 | 9 | 10 | 11 | 12 | 13 | 14 | 15 | 16 | 17 | 18 | 19 | 20 | 21 |
|---|---|---|---|---|---|---|---|---|---|---|---|---|---|---|---|---|---|---|---|---|---|---|
| **Communications Occupations** | | | | | | | | | | | | | | | | | | | | | | |
| Broadcast technicians | P | | | ■ | | | | | | | ■ | | | | | | | ■ | L | L | L | H |
| Marketing, advertising, and public relations managers | C | | ■ | ■ | ■ | | | ■ | ■ | ■ | | | | ■ | | | | | VH | VH | VH | L |
| Public relations specialists and publicity writers | C | ■ | ■ | ■ | ■ | | | | ■ | ■ | | | | ■ | | | | | VH | A | A | L |
| Radio and television announcers and newscasters | HPC | ■ | ■ | | ■ | | | | ■ | ■ | | | | | | | | ■ | L | A | A | A |
| Reporters and correspondents | C | ■ | ■ | | ■ | | | | ■ | ■ | | | | | ■ | | | ■ | L | A | L | A |
| Writers | PC | ■ | ■ | | ■ | | | | ■ | ■ | | | | | | | | | L | H | H | L |
| **Visual Arts Occupations** | | | | | | | | | | | | | | | | | | | | | | |
| Designers | HPC | | | | ■ | | | | | ■ | | | | | | | | | A | A | L | H |
| Photographers and camera operators | P | | | | ■ | | | | ■ | ■ | ■ | | | | ■ | | | | A | H | H | L |
| Visual artists | HPC | | | | ■ | | | | | | | | | | | | | | L | A | L | H |
| **Performing Artists** | | | | | | | | | | | | | | | | | | | | | | |
| Musicians | HC | | | | ■ | | | | | ■ | | | | | ■ | ■ | ■ | ■ | L | L | A | A |
| Producers, directors, actors, and entertainers | PC | ■ | ■ | ■ | ■ | ■ | | ■ | ■ | ■ | | | | | ■ | | | ■ | — | VH | H | VH |

## Sales and Related Occupations

| Occupation | Education and Training | 1 | 2 | 3 | 4 | 5 | 6 | 7 | 8 | 9 | 10 | 11 | 12 | 13 | 14 | 15 | 16 | 17 | 18 | 19 | 20 | 21 |
|---|---|---|---|---|---|---|---|---|---|---|---|---|---|---|---|---|---|---|---|---|---|---|
| **Marketing, Retail and Sales Occupations** | | | | | | | | | | | | | | | | | | | | | | |
| Cashiers | H | | | | | | | | | ■ | | | ■ | | | | ■ | ■ | VL | H | VH | VH |
| Counter and rental clerks | H | | | | | | | | | ■ | | | ■ | | | | ■ | ■ | VL | VH | H | H |
| Manufacturers' and wholesale sales representatives | C | ■ | ■ | ■ | | ■ | | | ■ | ■ | | | | | ■ | | | | L | L | L | H |
| Retail salesworkers | H | | | | | | | | ■ | ■ | | | | | | | ■ | ■ | VL | H | VH | H |
| Securities and financial services sales workers | C | ■ | ■ | | | | ■ | | ■ | ■ | | | | | | | | | VH | VH | H | L |
| Services sales representatives | H | | | | | ■ | | | ■ | ■ | | | | | | | | | L | H | H | L |
| Travel agents | H | ■ | | ■ | | | | | ■ | ■ | | | | | | | ■ | ■ | VL | VH | H | L |
| Wholesale and retail buyers | PC | ■ | ■ | ■ | | | | ■ | | ■ | | | | | | | | | H | A | H | L |

# Job Matching Chart

Column key — SKILLS: Working with Data/Information Skills: 1. Researching and Compiling, 2. Analyzing and Evaluating, 3. Troubleshooting; 4. Artistic Expression; Working with People Skills: 5. Instructing, 6. Treating and Advising, 7. Supervising, 8. Persuading, 9. Public Contact; Working with Things Skills: 10. Mechanical Ability, 11. Operating a Vehicle. WORKING CONDITIONS: 12. Repetitious, 13. Geographically Concentrated, 14. Mobile, 15. Physical Stamina, 16. Part-time, 17. Irregular Hours. EMPLOYMENT: 18. Average Earnings, 19. Projected Growth, 20. Number of Openings, 21. Unemployment Rate.

| Occupation | Educ. & Training | 1 | 2 | 3 | 4 | 5 | 6 | 7 | 8 | 9 | 10 | 11 | 12 | 13 | 14 | 15 | 16 | 17 | 18 | 19 | 20 | 21 |
|---|---|---|---|---|---|---|---|---|---|---|---|---|---|---|---|---|---|---|---|---|---|---|
| **Insurance Occupations** (also see adjusters, investigators, and collectors under administrative support occupations; and actuaries under mathematical occupations) | | | | | | | | | | | | | | | | | | | | | | |
| Insurance sales workers | PC | ■ | ■ | | | | ■ | | ■ | ■ | | | | | | | | | H | A | H | VL |
| Underwriters | PC | ■ | ■ | | | | | | | | | | | | | | | | A | H | A | VL |
| **Real Estate Occupations** | | | | | | | | | | | | | | | | | | | | | | |
| Property and real estate managers | C | ■ | ■ | ■ | | | | ■ | ■ | ■ | | | | | ■ | | | | A | VH | H | L |
| Real estate agents, brokers, and appraisers | HP | ■ | ■ | ■ | | | ■ | | ■ | ■ | | | | | ■ | | ■ | ■ | H | A | H | VL |
| **Administrative Support Occupations** | | | | | | | | | | | | | | | | | | | | | | |
| Adjusters, investigators, and collectors | HPC | ■ | ■ | | | | | | | ■ | | | | | | | | | L | A | H | L |
| Bank tellers | HP | | | | | | | | | ■ | | | ■ | | | | ■ | | VL | VL | VL | A |
| Clerical supervisors and managers | HPC | | ■ | ■ | | | | ■ | | | | | | | | | | | H | A | VH | VL |
| Computer operators | P | | | ■ | | | | | | | | | | | | | | ■ | A | A | H | A |
| Credit clerks and authorizers | H | ■ | | | | | | | | | | | ■ | | | | | | A | H | VH | A |
| Dispatchers | H | | | ■ | | | | | | ■ | | | ■ | | | | | ■ | A | H | H | A |
| General office clerks | H | | | | | | | | | | | | | | | | ■ | | L | H | VH | A |
| Postal mail carriers | H | | | | | | | | | ■ | | ■ | ■ | | ■ | ■ | ■ | | H | H | H | VL |
| Mail clerks | H | | | | | | | | | | | | ■ | | | | | | L | L | A | H |
| Material, recording, scheduling, and distributing occupations (stock clerks, shipping and receiving clerks) | H | | | | | | | | | | | | ■ | | | | | | L | A | H | H |
| Messengers | H | | | | | | | | | ■ | | ■ | ■ | ■ | ■ | ■ | ■ | | L | L | A | H |
| Postal service clerks | H | | | | | | | | | ■ | | | ■ | | | | ■ | | H | L | L | A |
| Receptionists and other information clerks | H | | | | | | | | | ■ | | | ■ | | | | | | VL | VH | VH | H |
| Records clerks (billing, bookkeeping, accounting, brokerage, file, order, payroll, and personnel clerks) | H | ■ | | | | | | | | | | | ■ | | | | | | VL | L | H | L |
| Secretaries | H | | | ■ | | | | | | ■ | | | | | | | | | L | A | VH | A |
| Stenographers | P | | | | | | | | | | | | ■ | | | | ■ | | L | VL | VL | VL |
| Telephone operators | H | | | | | | | | | ■ | | | ■ | | | | | ■ | L | VL | VL | H |
| Typists and word processors | H | | | | | | | | | | | | ■ | | | | | | L | VL | VL | VL |
| **Service Occupations** | | | | | | | | | | | | | | | | | | | | | | |
| **Protective Service Occupations** | | | | | | | | | | | | | | | | | | | | | | |
| Correction officers | H | | | | | | ■ | | | | | | | | | | | ■ | A | VH | H | VL |
| Firefighters | H | | ■ | | | | ■ | | ■ | | | ■ | | | ■ | ■ | | ■ | A | H | H | L |
| Guards | H | | | | | | | | | ■ | | | | ■ | | | ■ | | VL | VH | VH | H |
| Police detectives and patrol officers | H | ■ | ■ | ■ | | | ■ | | | ■ | | | | | ■ | ■ | | ■ | A | H | VH | VL |
| **Food and Beverage Preparation and Service Occupations** | | | | | | | | | | | | | | | | | | | | | | |
| Chefs | P | | | | ■ | | ■ | | | | | | | | | | | ■ | A | VH | VH | L |
| Cooks and other kitchen workers | H | | | | | | | | | | | | ■ | | | | ■ | ■ | VL | VH | VH | L |
| Food and beverage service occupations | H | | | | | | | | | ■ | | | ■ | | | | ■ | ■ | VL | VH | VH | L |
| Restaurant and food service managers | C | | ■ | ■ | | | | ■ | | ■ | | | | | | | | ■ | L | VH | H | L |
| **Personal Service and Facility Maintenance Occupations** | | | | | | | | | | | | | | | | | | | | | | |
| Animal caretakers, except farm | H | | | | | | | | | | | | | ■ | ■ | | | ■ | L | VH | H | A |
| Barbers | P | | | | | | | | ■ | | | | | ■ | | | ■ | ■ | L | VL | VL | VL |
| Gardeners and groundskeepers (except farm) | — | | | | | | | | | | ■ | ■ | | ■ | ■ | ■ | ■ | ■ | VL | VH | VH | VH |
| Janitors and cleaners | — | | | | | | | | | | | | ■ | | | ■ | ■ | ■ | VL | A | VH | VH |
| Private household workers | — | | | | | | | | | | | | | ■ | ■ | | ■ | ■ | VL | VL | VL | H |

# Job Matching Chart

| | EDUCATION AND TRAINING | 1. Researching and Compiling | 2. Analyzing and Evaluating | 3. Troubleshooting | 4. Artistic Expression | 5. Instructing | 6. Treating and Advising | 7. Supervising | 8. Persuading | 9. Public Contact | 10. Mechanical Ability | 11. Operating a Vehicle | 12. Repetitious | 13. Geographically Concentrated | 14. Mobile | 15. Physical Stamina | 16. Part-time | 17. Irregular Hours | 18. Average Earnings | 19. Projected Growth | 20. Number of Openings | 21. Unemployment Rate |
|---|---|---|---|---|---|---|---|---|---|---|---|---|---|---|---|---|---|---|---|---|---|---|
| **Agricultural, Forestry, Fishing, and Related Occupations** | | | | | | | | | | | | | | | | | | | | | | |
| Farm operators and managers | PC | ■ | ■ | | | | | ■ | | | | ■ | ■ | ■ | ■ | | | ■ | L | A | A | A |
| Fishers, hunters, and trappers | — | | | | | | | | | | | | | ■ | ■ | ■ | ■ | ■ | A | L | L | VH |
| Timber cutting and logging workers | — | | | | | | | | | | | | | ■ | ■ | ■ | | ■ | VL | VL | VL | VH |
| **Mechanics, Installers, and Repairers** (also see aircraft mechanics under air transportation occupations) | | | | | | | | | | | | | | | | | | | | | | |
| Automotive body repairers | P | | | ■ | | | | | | | ■ | | | | | ■ | | | A | H | H | A |
| Electronic equipment repairers (commercial and industrial electronic equipment, communications equipment, home entertainment, and telephone repairers) | P | | | ■ | | | | | | ■ | ■ | | | | ■ | ■ | | | A | VL | L | L |
| Home appliance and power tool repairers | HP | | | ■ | | | | | | ■ | ■ | | | | ■ | ■ | | | A | L | VL | L |
| Mechanics (automotive diesel, farm equipment, mobile heavy equipment, motorcycle, boat, small engine, and general maintenance mechanics) | P | | | ■ | | | | | | ■ | ■ | | | | | ■ | | | L | A | H | L |
| Musical instrument repairers and tuners | — | | | ■ | | | | | | ■ | ■ | | | ■ | ■ | | | | L | L | A | H |
| Vending machine servicers and repairers | H | | | ■ | | | | | | ■ | ■ | | | ■ | ■ | | | | VL | L | A | A |
| **Construction and Related Occupations** | | | | | | | | | | | | | | | | | | | | | | |
| Bricklayers and stonemasons | HP | | | | | | | | | | | | ■ | | ■ | ■ | | | A | A | H | VH |
| Carpenters | HP | | | | | | | | | | | | | | ■ | ■ | | | A | A | VH | VH |
| Carpet installers | HP | | | | | | | | | | | | ■ | | ■ | ■ | | | L | A | A | H |
| Concrete masons and terazzo workers | HP | | | | | | | | | | | | | | ■ | ■ | | | A | A | A | VH |
| Construction and building inspectors | HP | | ■ | ■ | | | | | | ■ | | | | | ■ | ■ | | | A | A | A | L |
| Construction contractors and managers | PC | ■ | ■ | ■ | | | | ■ | ■ | ■ | | | | | ■ | | | | H | L | VH | L |
| Drywall workers and lathers | HP | | | | | | | | | | | | | | ■ | ■ | | | A | H | H | VH |
| Electricians | HP | | | ■ | | | | | | | ■ | | | | ■ | ■ | | | H | H | VH | H |
| Elevator installers and repairers | H | | | ■ | | | | | | | ■ | | | | ■ | ■ | | | A | A | A | L |
| Glaziers | HP | | | | | | | | | | | | | | ■ | ■ | | | A | H | A | H |
| Heating, air-conditioning, and refrigeration technicians | HP | | | ■ | | | | | | | ■ | | | | ■ | ■ | | | A | A | H | A |
| Insulation workers | HP | | | | | | | | | | | | ■ | | ■ | ■ | | | L | H | A | VH |
| Line installers and cable splicers | — | | | ■ | | | | | | | ■ | | | | ■ | ■ | | | H | VL | VL | L |
| Painters and paperhangers | HP | | | | | | | | | | | | ■ | | ■ | ■ | ■ | | L | H | VH | L |
| Plasterers | HP | | | | | | | | | | | | ■ | | ■ | ■ | | | H | A | L | H |
| Plumbers, pipefitters, and steamfitters | P | | | ■ | | | | | | | ■ | | | | ■ | ■ | | | A | H | H | A |
| Roofers | HP | | | | | | | | | | | | ■ | | ■ | ■ | | | L | H | H | H |
| Roustabouts | — | | | | | | | | | | ■ | | | ■ | ■ | ■ | | ■ | L | VL | VL | VH |
| Sheet-metal workers | P | | | | | | | | | | | | | | ■ | ■ | | | L | A | H | H |
| Structural and reinforcing ironworkers | HP | | | | | | | | | | ■ | | | ■ | ■ | ■ | | | H | A | A | VH |
| Hand tilesetters | HP | | | | | | | | | | | | ■ | | ■ | ■ | | | A | H | L | VH |
| **Production Occupations** | | | | | | | | | | | | | | | | | | | | | | |
| **Plant and Systems Operations** | | | | | | | | | | | | | | | | | | | | | | |
| Electric power generating plant operators and power dispatchers | H | | ■ | ■ | | | | | | | ■ | | | | | | | ■ | A | L | L | H |
| Stationary engineers | H | | | ■ | | | | | | | ■ | | | | | | | ■ | A | L | L | VL |
| Water and wastewater treatment plant operators | H | ■ | ■ | ■ | | | | | | | ■ | | | | | | | ■ | A | H | A | VL |
| **Printing Occupations** | | | | | | | | | | | | | | | | | | | | | | |
| Prepress workers | H | | | ■ | | | | | | | ■ | | | | | | | ■ | A | VL | VL | H |

# Job Matching Chart

| | EDUCATION AND TRAINING | 1. Researching and Compiling | 2. Analyzing and Evaluating | 3. Troubleshooting | 4. Artistic Expression | 5. Instructing | 6. Treating and Advising | 7. Supervising | 8. Persuading | 9. Public Contact | 10. Mechanical Ability | 11. Operating a Vehicle | 12. Repetitious | 13. Geographically Concentrated | 14. Mobile | 15. Physical Stamina | 16. Part-time | 17. Irregular Hours | 18. Average Earnings | 19. Projected Growth | 20. Number of Openings | 21. Unemployment Rate |
|---|---|---|---|---|---|---|---|---|---|---|---|---|---|---|---|---|---|---|---|---|---|---|
| Printing press operators | H | | | ■ | | | | | | | ■ | | ■ | | | | | ■ | A | A | H | A |
| Bindery workers | H | | | ■ | | | | | | | ■ | | ■ | | | | | | VL | A | L | A |
| **Textile, Apparel, and Furnishing Occupations** | | | | | | | | | | | | | | | | | | | | | | |
| Apparel workers | — | | | | | | | | | | ■ | | | | | | | | VL | L | H | L |
| Shoe and leather workers and repairers | — | | | | | | | | | ■ | ■ | | | | | | | ■ | VL | L | L | H |
| Textile machinery operators | H | | | ■ | | | | | | | ■ | | ■ | ■ | | | | ■ | L | L | A | A |
| Upholsterers | H | | | | | | | | | | ■ | | | | | | | | L | L | L | A |
| **Miscellaneous Production Occupations** | | | | | | | | | | | | | | | | | | | | | | |
| Blue-collar worker supervisors | H | | ■ | | | | | ■ | | | | | | | | | | ■ | H | L | VH | L |
| Boilermakers | H | ■ | ■ | | | | | | | | ■ | | | | ■ | ■ | | | A | VL | VL | H |
| Butcher, meat, and poultry cutters | H | | | | | | | ■ | | | ■ | | | | | | | | L | VL | VL | H |
| Handlers, equipment cleaners, helpers, and laborers | — | | | | | | | | | | ■ | | | | | ■ | | | VL | A | H | L |
| Industrial machinery repairers | P | ■ | ■ | | | | | | | | ■ | | | | ■ | ■ | | ■ | H | L | H | A |
| Millwrights | P | ■ | ■ | | | | | | | | ■ | | | | ■ | ■ | | ■ | H | A | A | H |
| Industrial production managers | C | ■ | ■ | | | | | ■ | | | | | | | | | | | VH | VL | A | L |
| Inspectors, testers, and graders | H | ■ | ■ | | | | | | | | ■ | | | | | | | ■ | L | VL | L | H |
| Jewelers | P | | ■ | | | | | | | ■ | ■ | | | | | | | | L | A | H | A |
| Machinists | P | | ■ | | | | | | | | ■ | | | | | | | ■ | A | L | H | A |
| Tool and die makers | P | | ■ | | | | | | | | ■ | | | | | | | ■ | H | L | L | L |
| Metal and plastics working machine operators | H | | ■ | | | | | | | | ■ | | ■ | | | | | ■ | L | VL | VL | VH |
| Numerical control machine tool operators | H | | ■ | | | | | | | | ■ | | ■ | | | | | ■ | H | A | L | L |
| Painting and coating machine operators | — | | | | | | | | | | ■ | | | | | | | | L | L | VL | VH |
| Photographic process workers | H | | | | | | | | | | ■ | | | | | | ■ | ■ | VL | A | L | A |
| Precision assemblers | H | | | ■ | | | | | | | ■ | | | | | | | | VL | L | L | A |
| Tool programmers, numerical control | PC | ■ | ■ | | | | | | | | ■ | | | | | | | | H | H | L | L |
| Welders, cutters, and welding machine operators | P | | | | | | | | | | ■ | | ■ | | | ■ | | ■ | A | L | A | VH |
| Woodworking occupations | H | | | | | | | | | | ■ | | ■ | | | | | | L | A | A | VH |
| **Transportation Occupations** | | | | | | | | | | | | | | | | | | | | | | |
| *Air Transportation Occupations* | | | | | | | | | | | | | | | | | | | | | | |
| Aircraft pilots | C | | | ■ | | | | | | | | ■ | | | ■ | | | ■ | VH | H | A | H |
| Air traffic controllers | HPC | ■ | ■ | | | | | | | | | | | | | | | ■ | H | L | L | L |
| Aircraft mechanics and engine specialists | P | | | ■ | | | ■ | | | | | | | | | ■ | | ■ | VH | H | L | L |
| Flight attendants | HP | | | ■ | | | | | | ■ | | | | | ■ | | | ■ | VL | L | H | H |
| **Ground Transportation Occupations** | | | | | | | | | | | | | | | | | | | | | | |
| Busdrivers | H | | | ■ | | | | | | ■ | ■ | ■ | | | ■ | | ■ | ■ | A | VH | VH | A |
| Material moving equipment operators | HP | | | | | | | | | | ■ | ■ | | | ■ | | | ■ | A | L | A | VH |
| Rail transportation occupations | H | | | ■ | | | | | | | ■ | | | | ■ | | | ■ | A | VL | VL | A |
| Truck drivers | H | | | ■ | | | | | | | ■ | ■ | | | ■ | ■ | | ■ | A | H | VH | H |
| **Water Transportation Occupations** | | | | | | | | | | | | | | | | | | | | | | |
| Marine engineers and captains | C | | | ■ | | | | ■ | | | ■ | ■ | | | ■ | | | ■ | H | L | VL | VH |
| Mates and seamen | H | | | ■ | | | | | | | ■ | | | | ■ | ■ | | ■ | L | L | VL | VH |

# THE QUICK JOB SEARCH—TIPS TO MAKE GOOD CAREER DECISIONS AND GET A JOB IN LESS TIME

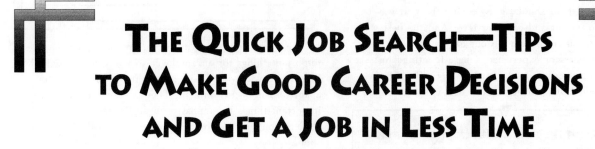

## ▼ INTRODUCTION

*While this book will teach you techniques to find a better job in less time, job seeking requires you to act, not just learn. So, in going through this book, consider what you can do to put the techniques to work for you. Do the activities. Create a daily plan. Get more interviews. Today, not tomorrow. You see, the sooner and harder you get to work on your job search, the shorter it is likely to be.*

## Changing Jobs and Careers Is Often Healthy

Most of us were told from an early age that each career move must be up—involving more money, responsibility, and prestige. Yet research indicates people change careers for many other reasons as well.

In a survey conducted by the Gallup Organization for the National Occupational Information Coordinating Committee, 44 percent of the working adults surveyed expected to be in a different job within three years. This is a very high turnover rate, yet only 41 percent had a definite plan to follow in mapping out their careers.

Logical, ordered careers are found more often with increasing levels of education. For example, while 25 percent of the high school dropouts took the only job available, this was true for only 8 percent of those with at least some college. But you should not assume this means that such occupational stability is healthy. Many adult developmental psychologists believe occupational change is not only normal but may even be necessary for sound adult growth and development. It is common, even normal, to reconsider occupational roles during your twenties, thirties,

and forties—even in the absence of economic pressure to do so.

One viewpoint is that a healthy occupational change is one that allows some previously undeveloped aspect of yourself to emerge. The change may be as natural as from clerk to supervisor; or as drastic as from professional musician to airline pilot. Although risk is always a factor when change is involved, reasonable risks are healthy and can raise self-esteem.

## But Not Just Any Job Should Do—Nor Any Job Search

Whether you are seeking similar work in another setting or changing careers, you need a workable plan to find the right job. This small book will give you the information you need to help you find a good job quickly.

While the techniques are presented here briefly, they are based on my years of experience in helping people find good jobs (not just any job) and to find jobs in less time. The career decision-making section will help you consider the major issues you need to make a good decision about the job you want. The job-seeking skills are ones that have been proven to reduce the amount of time required to find a good job.

Of course, more thorough books have been written on job-seeking techniques and you may want to look into buying one or more of the better ones to obtain additional information. (A list of such books is included in the last few pages of this book.) But, short as this book is, it DOES present the basic skills to find a good job in less time. The techniques work.

# THE SIX STEPS FOR A QUICK AND SUCCESSFUL JOB SEARCH

You can't just read about getting a job. The best way to get a job is to go out and get interviews! And the best way to get interviews is to make a job out of getting a job.

After many years of experience, I have identified just six basic things you need to do that make a big difference in your job search. Each will be covered in this book.

▼

### THE SIX STEPS FOR A QUICK JOB SEARCH

1. *Know your skills.*
2. *Have a clear job objective.*
3. *Know where and how to look for job leads.*
4. *Spend at least 25 hours a week looking.*
5. *Get two interviews a day.*
6. *Follow up on all contacts.*

# Identify Your Key Skills

One survey of employers found that 90 percent of the people they interviewed did not present the skills they had to do the job they sought. They could not answer the basic question, "Why should I hire you?"

Knowing your skills is essential to do well in an interview. This same knowledge is important in deciding what type of job you will enjoy and do well. For these reasons, I consider identifying your skills an essential part of a successful career plan or job search.

## THE THREE TYPES OF SKILLS

Most people think of "skills" as job-related skills such as using a computer. But we all have other types of skills that are also important for success on a job—and that are very important to employers. The triangle below presents skills in three groups, and I think that this is a very useful way to consider skills for our purposes.

### THE SKILLS TRIAD

Let's review these three types of skills and identify those that are most important to you.

## SELF-MANAGEMENT SKILLS

Write down three things about yourself that you think make you a good worker.

> ✔
> **YOUR "GOOD WORKER" TRAITS**
> 1. _____
> 2. _____
> 3. _____

The things you just wrote down are among the most important things for an employer to know about you! They have to do with your basic personality—your ability to adapt to a new environment. They are some of the most important things to emphasize in an interview, yet most job seekers don't realize their importance—and don't mention them.

Review the Self-Management Skills Checklist and put a checkmark beside any skills you have. The Key Self-Management Skills are skills that employers find particularly important. If one or more of the Key Self-Management Skills apply to you, mentioning them in an interview can help you greatly.

> ✔
> **SELF-MANAGEMENT SKILLS CHECKLIST**
>
> ## KEY SELF-MANAGEMENT SKILLS
>
> ___accept supervision ___hard worker
> ___get along with coworkers ___honest
> ___get things done on time ___productive
> ___good attendance ___punctual
>
> ## OTHER SELF-MANAGEMENT SKILLS
>
> ___able to coordinate ___friendly
> ___ambitious ___good-natured
> ___assertive ___helpful
> ___capable ___humble
> ___cheerful ___imaginative
> ___competent ___independent
> ___complete assignments ___industrious
> ___conscientious ___informal
> ___creative ___intelligent
> ___dependable ___intuitive
> ___discreet ___learn quickly
> ___eager ___loyal
> ___efficient ___mature
> ___energetic ___methodical
> ___enthusiastic ___modest
> ___expressive ___motivated
> ___flexible ___natural

___formal
___open-minded
___optimistic
___original
___patient
___persistent
___physically strong
___practice new skills
___reliable
___resourceful
___responsible
___self-confident

___sense of humor
___sincere
___solve problems
___spontaneous
___steady
___tactful
___take pride in work
___tenacious
___thrifty
___trustworthy
___versatile
___well-organized

## OTHER SELF-MANAGEMENT SKILLS YOU HAVE:

_____
_____
_____

After you are done with the list, circle the five skills you feel are most important and list them in the box below.

**Note:** *Some people find it helpful to now complete the "Essential Job Search Data Worksheet" provided later in this book. It organizes skills and accomplishments from previous jobs and other life experiences.*

### YOUR TOP 5 SELF-MANAGEMENT SKILLS

1. _____
2. _____
3. _____
4. _____
5. _____

## TRANSFERABLE SKILLS

We all have skills that can transfer from one job or career to another. For example, the ability to organize events could be used in a variety of jobs and may be essential for success in certain occupations. Your mission should be to find a job that requires the skills you have and enjoy using.

In the following list, put a checkmark beside the skills you have. You may have used them in a previous job or in some nonwork setting.

### TRANSFERABLE SKILLS CHECKLIST

#### KEY TRANSFERABLE SKILLS

___instruct others
___manage money, budget
___manage people
___meet deadlines
___meet the public

___negotiate
___organize/manage projects
___public speaking
___written communication skills

#### SKILLS WORKING WITH THINGS

___assemble things
___build things
___construct/repair
___drive, operate vehicles
___good with hands

___observe/inspect
___operate tools, machines
___repair things
___use complex equipment

#### SKILLS WORKING WITH DATA

___analyze data
___audit records
___budget
___calculate/compute
___check for accuracy
___classify things
___compare
___compile
___count
___detail-oriented

___evaluate
___investigate
___keep financial records
___locate information
___manage money
___observe/inspect
___record facts
___research
___synthesize
___take inventory

#### SKILLS WORKING WITH PEOPLE

___administer
___advise
___care for
___coach
___confront others
___counsel people
___demonstrate
___diplomatic
___help others
___instruct
___interview people
___kind
___listen
___negotiate

___outgoing
___patient
___perceptive
___persuade
___pleasant
___sensitive
___sociable
___supervise
___tactful
___tolerant
___tough
___trusting
___understanding

#### SKILLS WORKING WITH WORDS, IDEAS

___articulate
___communicate verbally
___correspond with others
___create new ideas
___design
___edit
___ingenious

___inventive
___library research
___logical
___public speaking
___remember information
___write clearly

## LEADERSHIP SKILLS

____arrange social functions
____competitive
____decisive
____delegate
____direct others
____explain things to others
____influence others
____initiate new tasks
____make decisions
____manage or direct others

____mediate problems
____motivate people
____negotiate agreements
____plan events
____results-oriented
____risk-taker
____run meetings
____self-confident
____self-motivate
____solve problems

## CREATIVE/ARTISTIC SKILLS

____artistic
____dance, body movement
____drawing, art

____expressive
____perform, act
____present artistic ideas

## OTHER SIMILAR SKILLS YOU HAVE:

_____
_____
_____
_____
_____
_____

When you are finished, identify the five transferable skills you feel are most important for you to use in your next job and list them in the box below.

### YOUR TOP 5 TRANSFERABLE SKILLS

1. _____
2. _____
3. _____
4. _____
5. _____

## JOB-RELATED SKILLS

Job content or job-related skills are those you need to do a particular job. A carpenter, for example, needs to know how to use various tools and be familiar with a variety of tasks related to that job.

You may already have a good idea of the type of job that you want. If so, it may be fairly simple for you to identify your job-related skills to emphasize in an interview. But I recommend that you complete at least two other things in this book first:

1. Complete the material that helps you define your job objective more clearly. Doing so will help you clarify just what sort of a job you want and allow you to better select those skills that best support it.

2. Complete the Essential Job Search Data Worksheet that appears later in this book (page 22). It will give you lots of specific skills and accomplishments to consider.

Once you have done these two things, come back and complete the box below. Include the job-related skills you have that you would most like to use in your next job.

### YOUR TOP 5 JOB-RELATED SKILLS

1. _____
2. _____
3. _____
4. _____
5. _____

# BEGIN BY DEFINING YOUR IDEAL JOB (YOU CAN COMPROMISE LATER . . . )

Too many people look for a job without having a good idea of exactly what they are looking for. Before you go out looking for "a" job, I suggest that you first define exactly what it is you really want—"the" job. Most people think a job objective is the same as a job title, but it isn't. You need to consider other elements of what makes a job satisfying for you. Then, later, you can decide what that job is called and what industry it might be in.

### THE EIGHT FACTORS TO CONSIDER IN DEFINING THE IDEAL JOB FOR YOU

Following are eight factors to consider when defining your ideal job. Once you know what you want, your task then becomes finding a job that is as close to your ideal job as you can find.

#### 1. WHAT SKILLS DO YOU WANT TO USE?

From the previous skills lists, select the top five skills that you enjoy using and most want to use in your next job.

1. _____
2. _____
3. _____
4. _____
5. _____

## 2. WHAT TYPE OF SPECIAL KNOWLEDGE DO YOU HAVE?

Perhaps you know how to fix radios, keep accounting records, or cook food. Write down the things you know about from schooling, training, hobbies, family experiences, and other sources. One or more of them could make you a very special applicant in the right setting.

_____

_____

_____

_____

_____

## 3. WITH WHAT TYPE OF PEOPLE DO YOU PREFER TO WORK?

Do you like to work with aggressive hardworking folks, creative types, or what?

_____

_____

_____

_____

## 4. WHAT TYPE OF WORK ENVIRONMENT DO YOU PREFER?

Do you want to work inside, outside, in a quiet place, a busy place, a clean place, have a window with a nice view, or what? List those things that are important to you.

_____

_____

_____

_____

_____

## 5. WHERE DO YOU WANT YOUR NEXT JOB TO BE LOCATED—IN WHAT CITY OR REGION?

Near a bus line? Close to a child care center? If you are open to live or work anywhere, what would your ideal community be like?

_____

_____

_____

_____

## 6. HOW MUCH MONEY DO YOU HOPE TO MAKE IN YOUR NEXT JOB?

Many people will take less money if the job is great in other ways—or to survive. Think about the minimum you would take as well as what you would eventually like to earn. Your next job will probably be somewhere between.

_____

_____

_____

_____

_____

## 7. HOW MUCH RESPONSIBILITY ARE YOU WILLING TO ACCEPT?

Usually, the more money you want to make, the more responsibility you must accept. Do you want to work by yourself, be part of a group, or be in charge? If so, at what level?

_____

_____

_____

_____

_____

## 8. WHAT THINGS ARE IMPORTANT OR HAVE MEANING TO YOU?

Do you have values that you would prefer to include as a basis of the work you do? For example, some people want to work to help others, clean up our environment, build things, make machines work, gain power or prestige, or care for animals or plants. Think about what is important to you and how you might include this in your next job.

_____

_____

_____

_____

## YOUR IDEAL JOB

Use the points above and on previous pages to help you define your ideal job. Think about each one and select the points that are most important to you. Don't worry about a job title yet, just focus on the most important things to include from the previous questions to define your ideal job.

### MY IDEAL JOB OBJECTIVE: ✔

_____

_____

_____

_____

_____

_____

_____

_____

_____

_____

## SETTING A SPECIFIC JOB OBJECTIVE

Whether or not you have a good idea of the type of job you want, it is important to know more about various job options. About 85 percent of all workers work in one of the 250 jobs in the list that follows.

A very simple but effective way for exploring job alternatives is to simply go through this list and check those about which you want to learn more. Descriptions for all of them can be found in books titled the *Occupational Outlook Handbook* and *America's Top 300 Jobs*. I encourage you to learn more about the jobs that interest you.

If you need help figuring out what type of job to look for, remember that most areas have free or low-cost career counseling and testing services. Contact local government agencies and schools for referrals.

# THE TOP 250 JOBS IN OUR WORKFORCE

## EXECUTIVE, ADMINISTRATIVE, AND MANAGERIAL OCCUPATIONS

- Accountants and auditors
- Administrative services managers
- Budget analysts
- Construction and building inspectors
- Construction contractors and managers
- Cost estimators
- Education administrators
- Employment interviewers
- Engineering, science, and data processing managers
- Financial managers
- Funeral directors
- General managers and top executives
- Government chief executives and legislators
- Health services managers
- Hotel managers and assistants
- Industrial production managers
- Inspectors and compliance officers, except construction
- Loan officers and counselors
- Management analysts and consultants
- Marketing, advertising, and public relations managers
- Personnel, training, and labor relations specialists and managers
- Property and real estate managers
- Purchasers and buyers
- Restaurant and food service managers
- Retail managers
- Underwriters

## PROFESSIONAL SPECIALTY OCCUPATIONS

### ENGINEERS

- Aerospace engineers
- Chemical engineers
- Civil engineers
- Electrical and electronics engineers
- Industrial engineers
- Mechanical engineers
- Metallurgical, ceramic, and materials engineers
- Mining engineers
- Nuclear engineers
- Petroleum engineers

### ARCHITECTS AND SURVEYORS

- Architects
- Landscape architects
- Surveyors

### COMPUTER, MATHEMATICAL, AND OPERATIONS RESEARCH OCCUPATIONS

- Actuaries
- Computer scientists and systems analysts
- Mathematicians
- Operations research analysts
- Statisticians

### LIFE SCIENTISTS

- Agricultural scientists
- Biological scientists
- Foresters and conservation scientists

### PHYSICAL SCIENTISTS

- Chemists
- Geologists and geophysicists
- Meteorologists
- Physicists and astronomers

### LAWYERS AND JUDGES

### SOCIAL SCIENTISTS AND URBAN PLANNERS

- Economists and marketing research analysts
- Psychologists
- Sociologists
- Urban and regional planners

### SOCIAL AND RECREATION WORKERS

- Human services workers
- Recreation workers
- Social workers

### RELIGIOUS WORKERS

- Protestant ministers
- Rabbis
- Roman Catholic priests

### TEACHERS, LIBRARIANS, AND COUNSELORS

- Adult education teachers
- Archivists and curators
- College and university faculty
- Counselors
- Librarians
- School teachers - kindergarten, elementary, and secondary

### HEALTH DIAGNOSING PRACTITIONERS

- Chiropractors
- Dentists
- Optometrists
- Physicians
- Podiatrists
- Veterinarians

### HEALTH ASSESSMENT AND TREATING OCCUPATIONS

- Dietitians and nutritionists
- Occupational therapists

Pharmacists

Physical therapists

Physician assistants

Recreational therapists

Registered nurses

Respiratory therapists

Speech-language pathologists and audiologists

## COMMUNICATIONS OCCUPATIONS

Public relations specialists

Radio and television announcers and newscasters

Reporters and correspondents

Writers and editors

## VISUAL ARTS OCCUPATIONS

Designers

Photographers and camera operators

Visual artists

## PERFORMING ARTS OCCUPATIONS

Actors, directors, and producers

Dancers and choreographers

Musicians

# TECHNICIANS AND RELATED SUPPORT OCCUPATIONS

## HEALTH TECHNOLOGISTS AND TECHNICIANS

Cardiovascular technologists and technicians

Clinical laboratory technologists and technicians

Dental hygienists

Dispensing opticians

EEG technologists

Emergency medical technicians

Licensed practical nurses

Medical record technicians

Nuclear medicine technologists

Radiologic technologists

Surgical technicians

## TECHNOLOGISTS, EXCEPT HEALTH

Aircraft pilots

Air traffic controllers

Broadcast technicians

Computer programmers

Drafters

Engineering technicians

Library technicians

Paralegals

Science technicians

# MARKETING AND SALES OCCUPATIONS

Cashiers

Counter and rental clerks

Insurance agents and brokers

Manufacturers' and wholesale sales representatives

Real estate agents, brokers, and appraisers

Retail sales workers

Securities and financial services sales representatives

Services sales representatives

Travel agents

# ADMINISTRATIVE SUPPORT OCCUPATIONS, INCLUDING CLERICAL

Adjusters, investigators, and collectors

Bank tellers

Billing clerks

Bookkeeping, accounting, and auditing clerks

Brokerage clerks and statement clerks

Clerical supervisors and managers

Computer and peripheral equipment operators

Credit clerks and authorizers

Dispatchers

File clerks

General office clerks

Hotel and motel clerks

Information clerks

Interviewing and new accounts clerks

Library assistants and bookmobile drivers

Mail clerks and messengers

Material recording, scheduling, dispatching, and distributing workers

Order clerks

Payroll and timekeeping clerks

Personnel clerks

Postal clerks and mail carriers

Receptionists

Record clerks

Reservation and transportation ticket agents and travel clerks

Secretaries

Stenographers and court reporters

Stock clerks

Teacher aides

Telephone operators

Traffic, shipping, and receiving clerks

Typists, word processors, and data entry keyers

# SERVICE OCCUPATIONS

## PROTECTIVE SERVICE OCCUPATIONS

Correction officers

Firefighters

Guards

Police, detectives, and special agents

## FOOD AND BEVERAGE PREPARATION AND SERVICE OCCUPATIONS

Chefs, cooks, and other kitchen workers

Food and beverage service workers

## HEALTH SERVICE OCCUPATIONS

Dental assistants

Medical assistants

Nursing aides and psychiatric aides

## PERSONAL SERVICE AND BUILDING AND GROUNDS SERVICE OCCUPATIONS

Animal caretakers, except farm

Barbers and cosmetologists

Flight attendants

Gardeners and groundskeepers

Homemaker-home health aides

Janitors and cleaners

Preschool workers

Private household workers

## Agriculture, Forestry, Fishing, and Related Occupations

Farm operators and managers

Fishers, hunters, and trappers

Forestry and logging workers

## Mechanics, Installers, and Repairers

Aircraft mechanics and engine specialists

Automotive body repairers

Automotive mechanics

Commercial and industrial electronic equipment repairers

Communications equipment mechanics

Computer and office machine repairers

Diesel mechanics

Electronic equipment repairers

Electronic home entertainment equipment repairers

Elevator installers and repairers

Farm equipment mechanics

General maintenance mechanics

Heating, air-conditioning, and refrigeration mechanics

Home appliance and power tool repairers

Industrial machinery repairers

Line installers and cable splicers

Millwrights

Mobile heavy equipment mechanics

Motorcycle, boat, and small-engine mechanics

Musical instrument repairers and tuners

Telephone installers and repairers

Vending machine servicers and repairers

## Construction Trades and Extractive Occupations

Bricklayers and stonemasons

Carpenters

Carpet installers

Concrete masons and terrazzo workers

Drywall workers and lathers

Electricians

Glaziers

Insulation workers

Painters and paperhangers

Plasterers

Plumbers and pipefitters

Roofers

Roustabouts

Sheetmetal workers

Structural and reinforcing ironworkers

Tilesetters

## Production Occupations

### Assemblers

Precision assemblers

### Blue-Collar Worker Supervisors

### Food Processing Occupations

Butchers and meat, poultry, and fish cutters

### Inspectors, Testers, and Graders

## Metalworking and Plastics-Working Occupations

Boilermakers

Jewelers

Machinists and tool programmers

Metalworking and plastics-working machine operators

Tool and die makers

Welders, cutters, and welding machine operators

## Plant and Systems Operators

Electric power generating plant operators and power distributors and dispatchers

Stationary engineers

Water and wastewater treatment plant operators

## Printing Occupations

Bindery workers

Prepress workers

Printing press operators

## Textile, Apparel, and Furnishings Occupations

Apparel workers

Shoe and leather workers and repairers

Textile machinery operators

Upholsterers

## Woodworking Occupations

## Miscellaneous Production Occupations

Dental laboratory technicians

Ophthalmic laboratory technicians

Painting and coating machine operators

Photographic process workers

## Transportation and Material Moving Occupations

Bus drivers

Material moving equipment operators

Rail transportation workers

Taxi drivers and chauffeurs

Truck drivers

Water transportation workers

## Handlers, Equipment Cleaners, Helpers, and Laborers

## Job Opportunities in the Armed Forces

# Job Search Methods That Help You Get a Better Job in Less Time

One survey found that 85 percent of all employers don't advertise at all. They hire people they already know, people who find out about the jobs through word of mouth, or people who simply happen to be in the right place at the right time. This is sometimes just luck, but this book will teach you ways to increase your "luck" in finding job openings.

# TRADITIONAL JOB SEARCH METHODS ARE NOT VERY EFFECTIVE

Most job seekers don't know how ineffective some traditional job hunting techniques tend to be.

## HOW PEOPLE FIND JOBS

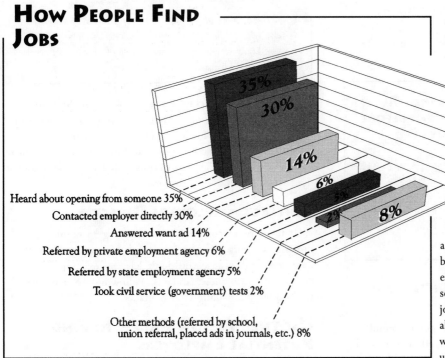

Heard about opening from someone 35%
Contacted employer directly 30%
Answered want ad 14%
Referred by private employment agency 6%
Referred by state employment agency 5%
Took civil service (government) tests 2%

Other methods (referred by school, union referral, placed ads in journals, etc.) 8%

The chart above shows that fewer than 15 percent of all job seekers get jobs from reading the want ads. Let's take a quick look at want ads and other traditional job search methods.

**Help Wanted Ads:** As you should remember, only about 15 percent of all people get their jobs through the want ads. Everyone who reads the paper knows about these job openings so competition for advertised jobs is fierce. Still, some people do get jobs this way, so go ahead and apply. Just be sure to spend most of your time using more effective methods.

**The State Employment Service:** Each state has a network of local offices to administer unemployment compensation and provide job leads and other services. These services are provided without charge to you or employers. Names vary by state, so it may be called "Job Service," "Department of Labor," "Unemployment Office," or another name.

Nationally, only about 5 percent of all job seekers get their jobs here and these organizations typically know of only one-tenth (or fewer) of the actual job openings in a region. Still, it is worth a weekly visit. If you ask for the same counselor, you might impress the person enough to remember you and refer you for the better openings.

You should also realize that some of the state employment services provide substantial help in the form of job search workshops and other resources. Look into it, the price is right.

**Private Employment Agencies:** Recent studies have found that private agencies work reasonably well for those who use them. But there are cautions to consider. For one thing, these agencies work best for entry-level positions or for those with specialized skills that are in demand. Most people who use a private agency usually find their jobs using some other source and their success record is quite modest.

Private agencies also charge a fee either to you (as high as 20 percent of your annual salary!) or to the employer. Most of them call employers asking if they have any openings, something you could do yourself.

Unless you have skills that are in high demand, you may do better on your own—and save money. At the least, you should rely on a private agency as only one of the techniques you use and not depend on them too heavily.

**Temporary Agencies:** These can be a source of quick but temporary jobs to bring in some income as well as give you experience in a variety of settings— something that can help you land full-time jobs later. More and more employers are also using them as a way to evaluate workers for permanent jobs. So consider using these agencies if it makes sense to do so but make certain that you continue an active search for a full-time job as you do.

**Sending Out Resumes:** *One survey found that you would have to mail more than 500 unsolicited resumes to get one interview!* A much better approach is to contact the person who might hire you by phone to set up an interview directly, then send a resume. If you insist on sending out unsolicited resumes, do this on weekends—save your "prime time" for more effective job search techniques.

**Filling Out Applications:** Most applications are used to screen you out. Larger organizations may require them, but remember that your task is to get an interview, not fill out an application. If you do complete them, make them neat, error-free, and do not include anything that could get you screened out. If necessary, leave a problematic section blank. It can always be explained after you get an interview.

**Personnel Departments:** Hardly anyone gets hired by interviewers in a personnel department. Their job is to screen you and refer the "best" applicants to the person who would actually supervise you. You may need to cooperate with them, but it is often better to go directly to the person who is most likely to supervise you—even if no job opening exists at the moment. And remember that most organizations don't even have a personnel office, only the larger ones!

# THE TWO JOB SEARCH METHODS THAT WORK BEST

Two-thirds of all people get their jobs using informal methods. These jobs are often not advertised and are part of the "hidden" job market. How do **you** find them?

There are two basic informal job search methods: networking with people you know (which I call warm contacts), and making direct contacts with an employer (which I call cold contacts). They are both based on the most important job search rule of all.

▼

## THE MOST IMPORTANT JOB SEARCH RULE: DON'T WAIT UNTIL THE JOB IS OPEN BEFORE CONTACTING THE EMPLOYER!

*Most jobs are filled by someone the employer meets before the job is formally "open." So the trick is to meet people who can hire you before a job is available! Instead of saying, "Do you have any jobs open?" say, "I realize you may not have any openings now, but I would still like to talk to you about the possibility of future openings."*

## DEVELOP A NETWORK OF CONTACTS IN FIVE EASY STEPS

One study found that 40 percent of all people found their jobs through a lead provided by a friend, a relative, or an acquaintance. Developing new contacts is called "networking" and here's how it works:

**1. Make lists of people you know.** Develop a list of anyone with whom you are friendly, then make a separate list of all your relatives. These two lists alone often add up to 25-100 people or more. Next, think of other groups of people with whom you have something in common, such as former coworkers or classmates; members of your social or sports groups; members of your professional association; former employers; and members of your religious group. You may not know many of these people personally, but most will help you if you ask them.

**2. Contact them in a systematic way.** Each of these people is a contact for you. Obviously, some lists and some people on those lists will be more helpful than others, but almost any one of them could help you find a job lead.

**3. Present yourself well.** Begin with your friends and relatives. Call them and tell them you are looking for a job and need their help. Be as clear as possible about what you are looking for and what skills and qualifications you have. Look at the sample JIST Card and phone script later in this book for presentation ideas.

**4. Ask them for leads.** It is possible that they will know of a job opening just right for you. If so, get the details and get right on it! More likely, however, they will not, so here are three questions you should ask.

▼

## THE THREE MAGIC NETWORKING QUESTIONS

1. *Do you know of any openings for a person with my skills?* If the answer is no (which it usually is), then ask:

2. *Do you know of someone else who might know of such an opening?* If your contact does, get that name and ask for another one. If he or she doesn't, ask:

3. *Do you know of anyone who might know of someone else who might?* Another good way to ask this is, "Do you know someone who knows lots of people?" If all else fails, this will usually get you a name.

**5. Contact these referrals and ask them the same questions.** For each original contact, you can extend your network of acquaintances by hundreds of people. Eventually, one of these people will hire you or refer you to someone who will! This process is called networking and it does work if you are persistent.

## CONTACT EMPLOYERS DIRECTLY

It takes more courage, but contacting an employer directly is a very effective job search technique. I call these cold contacts because you don't have an existing connection with these contacts. Following are two basic techniques for making cold contacts.

## USE THE "YELLOW PAGES" TO FIND POTENTIAL EMPLOYERS

One effective cold contact technique uses the *Yellow Pages*. You can begin by looking at the index and asking for each entry, "Would an organization of this kind need a person with my skills?" If the answer is "yes" then that type of organization or business is a possible target. You can also rate "yes" entries based on your interest, giving an A to those that seem very interesting, a B to those you are not sure of, and a C to those that don't seem interesting at all.

Next, select a type of organization that got a "yes" response (such as "hotels") and turn to the section of the *Yellow Pages* where they are listed. Then call the organizations listed and ask to speak to the person who is most likely to hire or supervise you. A sample telephone script is included later in this book to give you ideas about what to say.

## DROP IN WITHOUT AN APPOINTMENT

You can also simply walk in to many potential employers' organizations and ask to speak to the person in charge. This is particularly effective in small businesses, but it works surprisingly well in larger ones, too. Remember, you want an interview even if there are no openings now. If your timing is inconvenient, ask for a better time to come back for an interview.

## Most Jobs Are with Small Employers

About 70 percent of all people now work in small businesses—those with 250 or fewer employees. While the largest corporations have reduced the number of employees, small businesses have been creating as many as 80 percent of the new jobs. There are many opportunities to obtain training and promotions in smaller organizations, too. Many do not even have a personnel department, so nontraditional job search techniques are particularly effective with them.

## JIST Cards—an Effective "Mini Resume"

JIST Cards are a job search tool that get results. Typed, printed, or even neatly written on a 3-by-5-inch card, a JIST Card contains the essential information most employers want to know. Look at the sample cards that follow:

JIST Cards are an effective job search tool! Give them to friends and to each of your network contacts. Attach one to your resume. Enclose one in your thank-you notes before or after an interview. Leave one with employers as a "business card." Use them in many creative ways. Even though they can be typed or even handwritten, it is best to have 100 or more printed so you can put lots of them in circulation. Thousands of job seekers have used them, and they get results!

## Use the Phone to Get Job Leads

Once you have created your JIST Card, it is easy to create a telephone contact "script" based on it. Adapt the basic script to call people you know or your *Yellow Pages* leads. Select *Yellow Pages* index categories that might use a person with your skills and get the numbers of specific organizations in that category. Then ask for the person who is most likely to supervise you and present your phone script.

While it doesn't work every time, most people, with practice, can get one or more interviews in an hour by making these "cold" calls. Here is a phone script based on a JIST card:

*"Hello, my name is Pam Nykanen. I am interested in a position in hotel management. I have four years experience in sales, catering, and accounting with a 300-room hotel. I also have an associate degree in Hotel Management plus one year of experience with the Bradey Culinary Institute. During my employment, I helped double revenues from meetings and conferences and increased bar revenues by 46 percent. I have good problem-solving skills and am good with people. I am also well-organized, hardworking, and detail-oriented. When can I come in for an interview?"*

While this example assumes you are calling someone you don't know, the script can be easily modified for presentation to warm contacts, including referrals. Using the script for making cold calls takes courage, but it does work for most people.

---

### Sandy Zaremba

**Home:** (219) 232-7608          **Message:** (219) 234-7465
**Position:** General Office/Clerical

Over two years work experience plus one year of training in office practices. Type 55 wpm, trained in word processing operations, post general ledger, handle payables, receivables, and most accounting tasks. Responsible for daily deposits averaging $5,000. Good interpersonal skills. Can meet strict deadlines and handle pressure well.

Willing to work any hours

Organized, honest, reliable, and hardworking

---

### Chris Vorhees

**Home:** (602) 253-9678
**Leave Message:** (602) 257-6643

**OBJECTIVE:** Electronics—installation, maintenance, and sales

**SKILLS:** Four years work experience plus two years advanced training in electronics. A.S. degree in Electronics Engineering Technology. Managed a $300,000/yr. business while going to school full time, with grades in the top 25%. Familiar with all major electronic diagnostic and repair equipment. Hands-on experience with medical, consumer, communications, and industrial electronics equipment and applications. Good problem-solving and communication skills. Customer service oriented.

Willing to do what it takes to get the job done.

---

# Make Your Job Search a Full-Time Job

On the average, job seekers spend fewer than 15 hours a week actually looking for work. The average length of unemployment varies from three or more months, with some being out of work far longer (older workers and higher earners are two groups who take longer). I believe there is a connection.

Based on many years of experience, I can say that the more time you spend on your job search each week, the less time you are likely to remain unemployed. Of course, using more effective job search methods also helps. Those who follow my advice have proven, over and over, that they get jobs in less than half the average time and they often get better jobs too. Time management is the key.

## SPEND AT LEAST 25 HOURS A WEEK LOOKING FOR A JOB

If you are unemployed and looking for a full-time job, you should look for a job on a full-time basis. It just makes sense to do so, although many do not due to discouragement, lack of good techniques, and lack of structure. Most job seekers have no idea what they are going to do next Thursday—they don't have a plan. The most important thing is to decide how many hours you can commit to your job search and stay with it. You should spend a minimum of 25 hours a week on hard-core job search activities with no goofing around. Let me walk you through a simple but effective process to help you organize your job search schedule.

Write here how many hours you are willing to spend each week looking for a job: _____

## DECIDE ON WHICH DAYS YOU WILL LOOK FOR WORK

Answering the questions below requires you to have a schedule and a plan, just like you had when you were working, right?

Which days of the week will you spend looking for a job? _____

How many hours will you look each day? _____

At what time will you begin and end your job search on each of these days? _____

_____

## CREATE A SPECIFIC DAILY SCHEDULE

Having a specific daily job search schedule is very important because most job seekers find it hard to stay productive each day. You already know which job search methods are most effective and you should plan on spending most of your time using those methods. The sample daily schedule that follows has been very effective for people who have used it and it will give you ideas for your own. Although you are welcome to create your own daily schedule, I urge you to consider one similar to this one. Why? Because it works.

### A DAILY SCHEDULE THAT WORKS

| | |
|---|---|
| 7:00 - 8:00 a.m. | Get up, shower, dress, eat breakfast. |
| 8:00 - 8:15 a.m. | Organize work space; review schedule for interviews or follow-ups; update schedule. |
| 8:15 - 9:00 a.m. | Review old leads for follow-up; develop new leads (want ads, *Yellow Pages*, networking lists, etc.). |
| 9:00 - 10:00 a.m. | Make phone calls, set up interviews. |
| 10:00 - 10:15 a.m. | Take a break! |
| 10:15 - 11:00 a.m. | Make more calls. |
| 11:00 - 12:00 p.m. | Make follow-up calls as needed. |
| 12:00 - 1:00 p.m. | Lunch break. |
| 1:00 - 5:00 p.m. | Go on interviews; call cold contacts in the field; research for upcoming interviews at the library. |

## DO IT NOW: GET A SCHEDULE BOOK AND WRITE DOWN YOUR JOB SEARCH SCHEDULE

*A good daily planner is a cheap investment because cutting your unemployment time by just a few hours will pay for it. I like and use the "Two Page Per Day Original" provided by Day-Timers, Inc. (215-266-9000) because it provides lots of room for notes. It costs about $25 but most stationery stores have others at various prices, although getting an inferior system is unwise.*

This is important: If you are not accustomed to using a daily schedule book or planner, promise yourself that you will get a good one tomorrow. Choose one that allows plenty of space for each day's plan on an hourly basis plus room for daily "to do" listings. Write in your daily schedule in advance, then add interviews as they come. Get used to carrying it with you and use it!

# Redefine What "Counts" as an Interview, Then Get Two a Day

The average job seeker gets about five interviews a month—fewer than two interviews a week. Yet many job seekers using the techniques I suggest routinely get two interviews a day. But to accomplish this, you must redefine what an interview is.

> **THE NEW DEFINITION OF AN INTERVIEW:** *An interview is any face-to-face contact with someone who has the authority to hire or supervise a person with your skills—even if they don't have an opening at the time you interview.*

With this definition, it is *much* easier to get interviews. You can now interview with all kinds of potential employers, not only those who have a job opening. Many job seekers use the *Yellow Pages* to get two interviews with just one hour of calls by using the telephone contact script discussed earlier. Others simply drop in on potential employers and ask for an unscheduled interview—and they get them. And getting names of others to contact from those you know—networking—is quite effective if you persist.

Getting two interviews a day equals 10 a week and 40 a month. That's 800 percent more interviews than the average job seeker gets. Who do you think will get a job offer quicker? So set out each day to get at least two interviews. It's quite possible to do now that you know how.

# How to Answer Tough Interview Questions

Interviews are where the job search action happens. You have to get them, then you have to do well in them. If you have done your homework, you are getting interviews for jobs that will maximize your skills. That is a good start, but your ability to communicate your skills in the interview makes an enormous difference. This is where, according to employer surveys, most job seekers have problems. They don't effectively communicate the skills they have to do the job and they answer one or more problem questions poorly.

While thousands of problem interview questions are possible, I have listed just 10 that, if you can answer them well, will prepare you for most interviews.

> ## THE TOP 10 PROBLEM QUESTIONS
>
> 1. Why don't you tell me about yourself?
> 2. Why should I hire you?
> 3. What are your major strengths?
> 4. What are your major weaknesses?
> 5. What sort of pay do you expect to receive?
> 6. How does your previous experience relate to the jobs we have here?
> 7. What are your plans for the future?
> 8. What will your former employer (or references) say about you?
> 9. Why are you looking for this type of position and why here?
> 10. Why don't you tell me about your personal situation?

I don't have the space here to give thorough answers to all of these questions and there are potentially hundreds more. Instead, let me suggest several techniques that I have developed which you can use to answer almost any interview question.

## A TRADITIONAL INTERVIEW IS NOT A FRIENDLY EXCHANGE

Before I present the techniques for answering interview questions, it is important to understand what is going on. In a traditional interview situation, there is a job opening and you are one of several (or one of a hundred) applicants. In this setting, the employer's task is to eliminate all but one applicant.

Assuming that you got as far as an interview, the interviewer's questions are designed to elicit information that can be used to screen you out. If you are wise, you know that your task is to avoid getting screened out. It's not an open and honest interaction, is it?

This illustrates yet another advantage of nontraditional job search techniques: the ability to talk to an employer before an opening exists. This eliminates the stress of a traditional interview. Employers are not trying to screen you out and you are not trying to keep them from finding out stuff about you.

Having said that, knowing a technique for answering questions that might be asked in a traditional interview is good preparation for whatever you might run into during your job search . . .

## THE THREE-STEP PROCESS FOR ANSWERING INTERVIEW QUESTIONS

I know this might seem too simple, but the Three-Step Process is easy to remember. Its simplicity allows you to evaluate a question and create a good answer. The technique is based on sound principles send has worked for thousands of people, so consider trying it.

## STEP 1. UNDERSTAND WHAT IS REALLY BEING ASKED.

Most questions are really designed to find out about your self-management skills and personality. While they are rarely this blunt, the employer's *real* question is often:

- ✓ Can I depend on you?
- ✓ Are you easy to get along with?
- ✓ Are you a good worker?
- ✓ Do you have the experience and training to do the job if we hire you?
- ✓ Are you likely to stay on the job for a reasonable period of time and be productive?

Ultimately, if the employer is not convinced that you will stay and be a good worker, it won't matter if you have the best credentials—her or she won't hire you.

## STEP 2. ANSWER THE QUESTION BRIEFLY.

Acknowledge the facts, but . . .

- ✓ Present them as an advantage, not a disadvantage.

There are lots of examples in which a specific interview question will encourage you to provide negative information. The classic is the "What are your major weaknesses?" question that I included in my top 10 problem questions list. Obviously, this is a trick question and many people are just not prepared for it. A good response might be to mention something that is not all that damaging such as "I have been told that I am a perfectionist, sometimes not delegating as effectively as I might." But your answer is not complete until you continue.

## STEP 3. ANSWER THE REAL CONCERN BY PRESENTING YOUR RELATED SKILLS.

- ✓ Base your answer on the key skills that you have identified and that are needed in this job.
- ✓ Give examples to support your skills statements.

For example, an employer might say to a recent graduate, "We were looking for someone with more experience in this field. Why should we consider you?" Here is one possible answer: "I'm sure there are people who have more experience, but I *do* have more than six years of work experience including three years of advanced training and hands-on experience using the latest methods and techniques. Because my training is recent, I am open to new ideas and am used to working hard and learning quickly."

In the example I presented in Step 2 (about your need to delegate), a good skills statement might be, "I have been working on this problem and have learned to be more willing to let my staff do things, making sure that they have good training and supervision. I've found that their performance improves and it frees me up to do other things."

Whatever your situation, learn to use it to your advantage. It is essential to communicate your skills during

an interview and The Three-Step Process gives you a technique that can dramatically improve your responses. It works!

## INTERVIEW DRESS AND GROOMING RULE

If you make a negative first impression, you won't get a second chance to make a good one. So do everything possible to make a good impression.

▼

> **A GOOD RULE FOR DRESSING FOR AN INTERVIEW IS:**
> Dress like you think
> the boss will dress—*only neater.*

Dress for success! If necessary, get help selecting an interview outfit from someone who dresses well. Pay close attention to your grooming, too. Written things like correspondence and resumes must be neat and errorless because they create an impression as well.

# Follow Up on All Contacts

People who follow up with potential employers and with others in their network get jobs faster than those who do not.

▼

> **FOUR RULES FOR EFFECTIVE FOLLOW-UP**
>
> 1. Send a thank-you note to every person who helps you in your job search.
> 2. Send the thank-you note within 24 hours after you speak with the person.
> 3. Enclose JIST Cards with thank-you notes and all other correspondence.
> 4. Develop a system to keep following up with "good" contacts.

## THANK-YOU NOTES MAKE A DIFFERENCE

Thank-you notes can be handwritten or typed on quality paper and matching envelopes. Keep them simple, neat, and errorless. Following is a sample:

April 16, 19XX

2234 Riverwood Ave.
Philadelphia, PA 17963

Ms. Sandra Kijek
Henderson & Associates, Inc.
1801 Washington Blvd., Suite 1201
Philadelphia, PA 17963

Dear Ms. Kijek:

Thank you for sharing your time with me so generously today. I really appreciated seeing your state-of-the-art computer equipment.

Your advice has already proved helpful. I have an appointment to meet with Mr. Robert Hopper on Friday as you anticipated.

Please consider referring me to others if you think of someone else who might need a person with my skills.

Sincerely,

*William Richardson*

William Richardson

## USE JOB LEAD CARDS TO ORGANIZE YOUR CONTACTS

Use a simple 3-by-5-inch card to keep essential information on each person in your network. Buy a 3-by-5-inch card file box and tabs for each day of the month. File the cards under the date you want to contact the person, and the rest is easy. I've found that staying in touch with a good contact every other week can pay off big. Here's a sample card to give you ideas to create your own:

ORGANIZATION: *Mutual Health Insurance*

CONTACT PERSON: *Anna Tomey*     PHONE: *317-355-0216*

SOURCE OF LEAD: *Aunt Ruth*

NOTES: *4/10 Called. Anna on vacation. Call back 4/15. 4/15 Interview set 4/20 at 1:30. 4/20 Anna showed me around. They use the same computers we used in school! (Friendly people) Sent thank-you note and JIST Card. Call back 5/1. 5/1 Second interview 5/8 at 9 a.m.!*

# Resumes: Write a Simple One Now, and a "Better" One Later

You have already learned that sending out resumes and waiting for responses is not an effective job seeking technique. However, many employers *will* ask you for them, and they are a useful tool in your job search. If you feel that you need a resume, I suggest that you begin with a simple one that you can complete quickly. I've seen too many people spend weeks working on their resume while they could have been out getting interviews instead. If you want a "better" resume, you can work on it on weekends and evenings. So let's begin with the basics.

## BASIC TIPS TO CREATE A SUPERIOR RESUME

The following tips make sense for any resume format.

**Write it yourself.** It's OK to look at other resumes for ideas, but write yours yourself. It will force you to organize your thoughts and background.

**Make it errorless.** One spelling or grammar error will create a negative impressionist (see what I mean?). Get someone else to review your final draft for any errors. Then review it again because these rascals have a way of slipping in.

**Make it look good.** Poor copy quality, cheap paper, bad type quality, or anything else that creates a poor physical appearance will turn off employers to even the best resume content. Get professional help with design and printing if necessary. Many resume writers and print shops have desktop publishing services and can do it all for you.

**Be brief, be relevant.** Many good resumes fit on one page and few justify more than two. Include only the most important points. Use short sentences and action words. If it doesn't relate to and support the job objective, cut it!

**Be honest.** Don't overstate your qualifications. If you end up getting a job you can't handle, it will not be to your advantage. Most employers will see right through it and not hire you.

**Be positive.** Emphasize your accomplishments and results. This is no place to be too humble or to display your faults.

**Be specific.** Rather than saying "I am good with people," say "I supervised four people in the warehouse and increased productivity by 30 percent." Use numbers whenever possible, such as the number of people served, percent of sales increase, or dollars saved.

You should also know that everyone feels he or she is a resume expert. Whatever you do, someone will tell you it is wrong. For this reason, it is important to understand that a resume is a job search tool. You should never delay or slow down your job search because your resume is not "good enough." The best approach is to create a simple and acceptable resume as soon as possible, then use it. As time permits, create a better one if you feel you must.

## CHRONOLOGICAL RESUMES

Most resumes use the chronological format. It is a simple format where the most recent experience is listed first, followed by each previous job. This arrangement works fine for someone with work experience in several similar jobs, but not as well for those with limited experience or for career changers.

Look at the two Judith Jones' resumes. Both use the chronological approach, but notice that the second one includes some improvements over her first. The improved resume is clearly better, but either would be acceptable to most employers.

### TIPS FOR WRITING A SIMPLE CHRONOLOGICAL RESUME

Here are some tips for writing a basic chronological resume.

**Name.** Use your formal name rather than a nickname if it sounds more professional.

**Address.** Be complete. Include your zip code and avoid abbreviations. If moving is a possibility, use the address of a friend or relative or be certain to include a forwarding address.

**Telephone Number.** Employers are most likely to try to reach you by phone, so having a reliable way to be reached is very important. Always include your area code because you never know where your resume might travel. If you don't have an answering machine get one, and make sure you leave it on whenever you are not home. Listen to your message to be sure it presents you in a professional way. Also available are a

variety of communication systems: voice mail, professional answering services, beepers, mobile phones, online e-mail programs, etc. If you do provide an alternative phone number or other way to reach you, just make it clear to the caller what to expect.

**Job Objective.** This is optional for a very basic resume but is still important to include. Notice that Judy is keeping her options open with her objective. Writing "Secretary" or "Clerical" might limit her to lower paying jobs or even prevent her from being considered for jobs she might take.

**Education and Training.** Include any formal training you've had plus any training that supports the job you seek. If you did not finish a formal degree or program, list what you did complete. Include any special accomplishments.

---

*[Sample of a simple chronological resume.]*

# Judith J. Jones

115 South Hawthorne Avenue
Chicago, Illinois 46204
(312) 653-9217 (home)
(312) 272-7608 (message)

### JOB OBJECTIVE

Desire a position in the office management, secretarial, or clerical area. Prefer a position requiring responsibility and a variety of tasks.

### EDUCATION AND TRAINING

Acme Business College, Chicago, Illinois
Graduate of a one-year business/secretarial program, 1996

John Adams High School, South Bend, Indiana
Diploma: Business Education

### U.S. Army

Financial procedures, accounting functions. Other: Continuing education classes and workshops in Business Communication, Scheduling Systems, and Customer Relations.

### EXPERIENCE

1995-1996 — Returned to school to complete and update my business skills. Learned word processing and other new office techniques.

1992-1995 — Claims Processor, Blue Spear Insurance Co., Chicago, Illinois. Handled customer medical claims, filed, miscellaneous clerical duties.

1990-1992 — Sales Clerk, Judy's Boutique, Chicago, Illinois. Responsible for counter sales, display design, and selected tasks.

1988-1990 — Specialist, U.S. Army. Assigned to various stations as a specialist in finance operations. Promoted prior to honorable discharge.

Previous Jobs — Held part-time and summer jobs throughout high school.

### PERSONAL

I am reliable, hardworking, and good with people.

---

**Previous Experience.** The standard approach is to list employer, job title, dates employed, and responsibilities. But there are better ways of presenting your experience. Look over the "Improved Chronological Resume" for ideas. The improved version emphasizes results, accomplishments, and performance.

**Personal Data.** Neither of the sample resumes have the standard height, weight, or marital status included on so many resumes. That information is simply not relevant! If you do include some personal information, put it at the bottom and keep it related to the job you want.

**References.** There is no need to list references. If employers want them, they will ask. If your references are particularly good, it's okay to say so.

Include those things that relate to doing well in the job you seek now. Even "small" things count. Maybe your attendance was perfect, you met a tight deadline, did the work of others during vacations, etc. Be specific and include numbers—even if you have to estimate them.

**Job Titles.** Many job titles don't accurately reflect the job you did. For example, your job title may have been "Cashier" but you also opened the store, trained new staff, and covered for the boss on vacations. Perhaps "Head Cashier and Assistant Manager" would be more accurate. Check with your previous employer if you are not sure.

**Promotions.** If you were promoted or got good evaluations, say so. A promotion to a more responsible job can be handled as a separate job if this makes sense.

## TIPS FOR AN IMPROVED CHRONOLOGICAL RESUME

Once you have a simple, errorless, and eye-pleasing resume, get on with your job search. There is no reason to delay! But you may want to create a better one in your spare time (evenings or weekends). If you do, here are some additional tips.

**Job Objective.** Job objectives often limit the type of jobs for which you will be considered. Instead, think of the type of work you want to do and can do well and describe it in more general terms. Instead of writing "Restaurant Manager," write "Managing a small to mid-sized business" if that is what you are qualified to do.

**Education and Training.** New graduates should emphasize their recent training and education more than those with five years or so of recent and related work experience. Think about any special accomplishments while in school and include these if they relate to the job. Did you work full time while in school? Did you do particularly well in work-related classes, get an award, or participate in sports?

**Skills and Accomplishments.** Employers are interested in what you accomplished and did well.

---

*[Sample of an improved chronological resume.]*

# Judith J. Jones

115 South Hawthorne Avenue
Chicago, Illinois 46204
(312) 653-9217 (home)
(312) 272-7608 (message)

### JOB OBJECTIVE

Seeking position requiring excellent management and secretarial skills in an office environment. Position should require a variety of tasks including typing, word processing, accounting/bookkeeping functions, and customer contact.

### EDUCATION AND TRAINING

Acme Business College, Chicago, Illinois.
Completed one-year program in Professional Secretarial and Office Management. Grades in top 30 percent of my class. Courses: word processing, accounting theory and systems, time management, basic supervision, and others.

John Adams High School, South Bend, Indiana.
Graduated with emphasis on business and secretarial courses. Won shorthand contest.

Other: Continuing education at my own expense (Business Communications, Customer Relations, Computer Applications, other courses).

### EXPERIENCE

1995-1996 — Returned to business school to update skills. Advanced course work in accounting and office management. Learned to operate word processing and PC-based accounting and spreadsheet software. Gained operating knowledge of computers.

1992-1995 — Claims Processor, Blue Spear Insurance Company, Chicago, Illinois. Handled 50 complex medical insurance claims per day — 18 percent above department average. Received two merit raises for performance.

1990-1992 — Assistant Manager, Judy's Boutique, Chicago, Illinois. Managed sales, financial records, inventory, purchasing, correspondence, and related tasks during owner's absence. Supervised four employees. Sales increased 15 percent during my tenure.

1988-1990 — Finance Specialist (E4), U.S. Army. Responsible for the systematic processing of 500 invoices per day from commercial vendors. Trained and supervised eight employees. Devised internal system allowing 15 percent increase in invoices processed with a decrease in personnel.

1984-1988 — Various part-time and summer jobs through high school. Learned to deal with customers, meet deadlines, work hard, and other skills.

### SPECIAL SKILLS AND ABILITIES

Type 80 words per minute and can operate most office equipment. Good communication and math skills. Accept supervision, able to supervise others. Excellent attendance record.

---

**Problem Areas.** Employers look for any sign of instability or lack of reliability. It is very expensive to hire and train someone who won't stay or who won't work out. Gaps in employment, jobs held for short periods of time, or a lack of direction in the jobs you've held are all things that employers are concerned about. If you have any legitimate explanation, use it. For example:

"1994—Continued my education at . . ."

"1995—Traveled extensively throughout the United States."

"1995 to present—Self-employed barn painter and widget maker."

"1995—Had first child, took year off before returning to work."

Use entire years or even seasons of years to avoid displaying a shorter gap you can't explain easily: "Spring 1994—Fall 1995" will not show you as unemployed from October to November, 1995, for example.

Remember that a resume can get you screened out, but it is up to you to get the interview and the job. So, cut out *anything* that is negative in your resume!

## SKILLS AND COMBINATION RESUMES

The functional or "skills" resume emphasizes your most important *skills,* supported by specific examples of how you have used them. This approach allows you to use any part of your life history to support your ability to do the job you seek.

While the skills resume can be very effective, it does require more work to create. And some employers don't like them because they can hide a job seeker's faults (such as job gaps, lack of formal education, or no related work experience) better than a chronological resume.

Still, a skills resume may make sense for you. Look over the sample resumes for ideas. Notice that one resume includes elements of a skills *and* a chronological resume. This is called a "combination" resume—an approach that makes sense if your previous job history or education and training is positive.

---

*[Sample of a simple skills resume.]*

## ALAN ATWOOD

3231 East Harbor Road
Woodland Hills, California 91367
Home: (818) 447-2111          Message (818) 547-8201

**Objective:** A responsible position in retail sales

**Areas of Accomplishment:**

Customer Service
- Communicate well with all age groups.
- Able to interpret customer concerns to help them find the items they want.
- Received 6 Employee of the Month awards in 3 years.

Merchandise Display
- Developed display skills via in-house training and experience.
- Received Outstanding Trainee Award for Christmas toy display.
- Dress mannequins, arrange table displays, and organize sale merchandise.

Stock Control and Marketing
- Maintained and marked stock during department manager's 6-week illness.
- Developed more efficient record-keeping procedures.

Additional Skills
- Operate cash register, IBM compatible hardware, calculators, and electronic typewriters.
- Punctual, honest, reliable, and a hard-working self-starter.

**Experience:** Harper's Department Store
Woodland Hills, California
1995 to Present

**Education:** Central High School
Woodland Hills, California
3.6/4.0 Grade Point Average
Honor Graduate in Distributive Education

Two years retail sales training in Distributive Education. Also courses in Business Writing, Accounting, Typing, and Word Processing.

---

*[Sample skills resume for someone with substantial experience—but using only one page. Note that no dates are included.]*

## Ann McLaughlin

| | |
|---|---|
| **Career Objective** | Challenging position in programming or related areas which would best utilize expertise in the business environment. This position should have many opportunities for an aggressive, dedicated individual with leadership abilities to advance. |
| **Programming Skills** | Include functional program design relating to business issues including payroll, inventory and database management, sales, marketing, accounting, and loan amortization reports. In conjunction with design would be coding, implementation, debugging, and file maintenance. Familiar with distributed network systems including PC's and Mac's and working knowledge of DOS, UNIX, COBOL, BASIC, RPG, and FORTRAN. Also familiar with mainframe environments including DEC, Prime, and IBM, including tape and disk file access, organization, and maintenance. |
| **Areas of Expertise** | Interpersonal communication strengths, public relations capabilities, innovative problem-solving and analytical talents. |
| Sales | A total of nine years experience in sales and sales management. Sold security products to distributors and burglar alarm dealers. Increased company's sales from $16,000 to over $70,000 per month. Creatively organized sales programs and marketing concepts. Trained sales personnel in prospecting techniques while also training service personnel in proper installation of burglar alarms. Result: 90% of all new business was generated through referrals from existing customers. |
| Management | Managed burglar alarm company for four years while increasing profits yearly. Supervised office, sales, and installation personnel. Supervised and delegated work to assistants in accounting functions and inventory control. Worked as assistant credit manager, responsible for over $2 million per month in sales. Handled semiannual inventory of five branch stores totaling millions of dollars and supervised 120 people. |
| Accounting | Balanced all books and prepared tax forms for burglar alarm company. Eight years experience in credit and collections, with emphasis on collections. Collection rates were over 98% each year, and was able to collect a bad debt in excess of $250,000 deemed "uncollectible" by company. |
| **Education** | School of Computer Technology, Pittsburgh, PA<br>Business Applications Programming/TECH EXEC- 3.97 GPA<br><br>Robert Morris College, Pittsburgh, PA<br>Associate degree in Accounting, Minor in Management |

**2306 Cincinnati Street, Kingsford, PA 15171 (412) 437-6217**
**Message: (412) 464-1273**

*[Sample combination resume emphasizing skills and accomplishments within jobs. Note that each position within a company is listed.]*

## THOMAS P. MARRIN
80 Harrison Avenue
Baldwin L.I., New York 11563
Answering Service: (716) 223-4705

**OBJECTIVE:**

A middle/upper-level management position with responsibilities including problem solving, planning, organizing, and budget management.

**EDUCATION:**

University of Notre Dame, B.S. in Business Administration. Course emphasis on accounting, supervision, and marketing. Upper 25% of class. Additional training: Advanced training in time management, organization behavior, and cost control.

**MILITARY:**

U.S. Army — 2nd Infantry Division, 1985 to 1989, 1st Lieutenant and platoon leader — stationed in Korea and Ft. Knox, Kentucky. Supervised an annual budget of nearly $4 million and equipment valued at over $40 million. Responsible for training, scheduling, and activities of as many as 40 people. Received several commendations. Honorable discharge.

**BUSINESS EXPERIENCE:**

**Wills Express Transit Co., Inc.** — Mineola, New York

*Promoted to Vice President, Corporate Equipment* — 1994 to Present
Controlled purchase, maintenance, and disposal of 1100 trailers and 65 company cars with $6.7 million operating and $8.0 million capital expense responsibilities.

- Scheduled trailer purchases, six divisions.
- Operated 2.3% under planned maintenance budget in company's second best profit year while operating revenues declined 2.5%.
- Originated schedule to correlate drivers' needs with available trailers.
- Developed systematic Purchase and Disposal Plan for company car fleet.
- Restructured Company Car Policy, saving 15% on per car cost.

*Promoted to Asst. Vice President, Corporate Operations* — 1993 to 1994
Coordinated activities of six sections of Corporate Operations with an operating budget over $10 million.

- Directed implementation of zero-base budgeting.
- Developed and prepared Executive Officer Analyses detailing achievable cost reduction measures. Resulted in cost reduction of over $600,000 in first two years.
- Designed policy and procedure for special equipment leasing program during peak seasons. Cut capital purchases by over $1 million.

*Manager of Communications* — 1991 to 1993
Directed and managed $1.4 million communication network involving 650 phones, 150 WATS lines, 3 switchboards, 1 teletype machine, 5 employees.

- Installed computerized WATS Control System. Optimized utilization of WATS lines and pinpointed personal abuse. Achieved payback earlier than originally projected.
- Devised procedures that allowed simultaneous 20% increase in WATS calls and a $75,000/year savings.

**Hayfield Publishing Company, Hempstead, New York**

*Communications Administrator* — 1989 to 1991

Managed daily operations of a large Communications Center. Reduced costs and improved services.

# THE QUICK JOB SEARCH REVIEW

There are a few thoughts I want to emphasize in closing my brief review of job seeking skills:

1. Approach your job search as if it were a job itself.

2. Get organized and spend at least 25 hours per week actively looking.

3. Follow up on all the leads you generate and send out lots of thank-you notes and JIST Cards.

4. If you want to get a good job quickly, you must get lots of interviews!

5. Pay attention to all the details, then be yourself in the interview. Remember that employers are people, too. They will hire someone who they feel will do the job well, be reliable, and fit easily into the work environment.

6. When you want the job, tell the employer that you want the job and why. You need to have a good answer to the question "Why should I hire you?" It's that simple.

# ESSENTIAL JOB SEARCH DATA WORKSHEET

Completing this worksheet will help you create your resume, fill out applications, and answer interview questions. Take it with you as a reference as you look for a job. Use an erasable pen or pencil so you can make changes. In all sections, emphasize skills and accomplishments that best support your ability to do the job you want. Use extra sheets as needed.

## KEY ACCOMPLISHMENTS

List three accomplishments that best prove your ability to do well in the kind of job you want.

1. _____
   _____

2. _____
   _____

3. _____
   _____

### EDUCATION/TRAINING

**Name of high school(s)/years attended:** _____
_____
_____
_____

Subjects related to job objective: _____
_____
_____
_____

Extracurricular activities/Hobbies/Leisure activities:
_____
_____
_____

Accomplishments/Things you did well: _____
_____
_____
_____
_____

**Schools you attended after high school, years attended, degrees/certificates earned:** _____
_____
_____
_____
_____

Courses related to job objective: _____
_____
_____
_____

Extracurricular activities/Hobbies/Leisure activities:
_____
_____
_____
_____

Accomplishments/Things you did well: _____
_____
_____
_____

**Military training, on-the-job, or informal training, such as from a hobby; dates of training; type of certificate earned:** _____
_____
_____
_____

Specific things you can do as a result: _____
_____
_____
_____

# WORK AND VOLUNTEER HISTORY

List your most recent job first, followed by each previous job. Include military experience and unpaid work here too, if it makes sense to do so. Use additional sheets to cover *all* your significant jobs or unpaid experiences.

Whenever possible, provide numbers to support what you did: number of people served over one or more years, number of transactions processed, percentage of sales increase, total inventory value you were responsible for, payroll of the staff you supervised, total budget you were responsible for, etc. As much as possible, mention results using numbers because they can be impressive when mentioned in an interview or resume.

**Job #1** _____

Name of Organization: _____
_____
_____

Address: _____
_____
_____

Phone Number: _____
_____

Dates Employed: _____

Job Title(s): _____
_____
_____

Supervisor's Name: _____
_____

Details of any raises or promotions: _____
_____
_____
_____

Machinery or equipment you handled: _____
_____
_____
_____

Special skills this job required: _____
_____
_____
_____

List what you accomplished or did well: _____
_____
_____
_____

**Job #2** _____
Name of Organization: _____
_____
_____

Address: _____
_____
_____

Phone Number: _____
_____

Dates Employed: _____

Job Title(s): _____
_____
_____

Supervisor's Name: _____
_____

Details of any raises or promotions: _____
_____
_____
_____

Machinery or equipment you handled: _____
_____
_____
_____

Special skills this job required: _____
_____
_____
_____

List what you accomplished or did well: _____
_____
_____
_____

**Job #3** _____
Name of Organization: _____
_____
_____

Address: _____
_____
_____

Phone Number: _____
_____

Dates Employed: _____

Job Title(s): _____
_____
_____

Supervisor's Name: _____
_____

Details of any raises or promotions: _____
_____
_____
_____

Machinery or equipment you handled: _____
_____

Special skills this job required: _____

_____

_____

List what you accomplished or did well: _____

_____

_____

_____

## REFERENCES

Contact your references and let them know what type of job you want and why you are qualified. Be sure to review what they will say about you. Because some employers will not give out references by phone or in person, have previous employers write a letter of reference for you in advance. If you worry about a bad reference from a previous employer, negotiate what they will say about you or get written references from other people you worked with there. When creating your list of references, be sure to include your reference's name and job title, where he or she works, a business address and phone number, how that person knows you, and what your reference will say about you.

---

*The following material is based on content from a book titled* Job Strategies for Professionals *written by a team of authors from the U.S. Employment Service for use by the unemployed. (published by JIST)*

# Some Tips for Coping with Job Loss

Being out of work is not fun for most people and is devastating to some. It may help you to know that you are not alone in this experience and I've included some information here on what to expect and some suggestions for getting through it.

## SOME PROBLEMS YOU MAY EXPERIENCE

Here are some feelings and experiences that you may have after losing your job.

**Loss of professional identity:** Most of us identify strongly with our careers and unemployment can often lead to a loss of self-esteem. Being employed garners respect in the community and in the family. When a job is lost, part of your sense of self may be lost as well.

**Loss of a network:** The loss may be worse when your social life has been strongly linked to the job. Many ongoing "work friendships" are suddenly halted. Old friends and colleagues often don't call because they feel awkward or don't know what to say. Many don't want to be reminded of what could happen to them.

**Emotional unpreparedness:** If you have never before been unemployed you may not be emotionally prepared for it and devastated when it happens. It is natural and appropriate to feel this way. You might notice that some people you know don't take their job loss as hard as you have taken it. Studies show that those who change jobs frequently, or who are in occupations prone to cyclic unemployment, suffer far less emotional impact after job loss than those who have been steadily employed and who are unprepared for cutbacks.

## ADJUSTING

You can often adjust to job loss by understanding its psychology. There have been a lot of studies done on how to deal with loss. Psychologists have found that people often have an easier time dealing with loss if they know what feelings they might experience during the "grieving process." Grief doesn't usually overwhelm us all at once; it usually is experienced in stages. The stages of loss or grief may include:

*Shock* - you may not be fully aware of what has happened.

*Denial* - usually comes next; you cannot believe that the loss is true.

*Relief* - you may feel a burden has lifted and opportunity awaits.

*Anger* - often follows; you blame (often without cause) those you think might be responsible, including yourself.

*Depression* - may set in some time later, when you realize the reality of the loss.

*Acceptance* - the final stage of the process; you come to terms with the loss and get the energy and desire to move beyond it. The "acceptance" stage is the best place to be when starting a job search, but you might not have the luxury of waiting until this point to begin your search.

Knowing that a normal person will experience some predictable "grieving" reactions can help you deal with your loss in a constructive way. The faster you can begin an active search for a new job, the better off you will be.

## KEEP HEALTHY

Unemployment is a stressful time for most people and it is important to keep healthy and fit. Try to:

✓ **Eat properly.** How you look and your sense of self-esteem can be affected by your eating habits. It is very easy to snack on junk food when you're home all day. Take time to plan your meals and snacks so they are well-balanced and nutritious. Eating properly will help you maintain the good attitude you need during your job search.

✓ **Exercise.** Include some form of exercise as part of your daily activities. Regular exercise reduces stress and depression and can help you get through those tough days.

✓ **Allow time for fun.** When you're planning your time, be sure to build fun and relaxation into your plans. You are allowed to enjoy life even if you are unemployed. Keep a list of activities or tasks that you want to accomplish such as volunteer work, repairs around the house, or hobbies. When free time occurs, you can refer to the list and have lots of things to do.

## Family Issues

Unemployment is a stressful time for the entire family. For them, your unemployment means the loss of income and the fear of an uncertain future, and they are also worried about your happiness. Here are some ways you can interact with your family to get through this tough time.

✓ **Do not attempt to "shoulder" your problems alone.** Be open with family members even though it may be hard. Discussions about your job search and the feelings you have allow your family to work as a group and support one another.

✓ **Talk to your family.** Let them know your plans and activities. Share with them how you will be spending your time.

✓ **Listen to your family.** Find out their concerns and suggestions. Maybe there are ways they can assist you.

✓ **Build family spirit.** You will need a great deal of support from your family in the months ahead, but they will also need yours.

✓ **Seek outside help.** Join a family support group. Many community centers, mental health agencies, and colleges have support groups for the unemployed and their families. These groups can provide a place to let off steam and share frustrations. They can also be a place to get ideas on how to survive this difficult period. More information about support groups is presented later in this chapter.

### Helping Children

If you have children, realize that they can be deeply affected by a parent's unemployment. It is important for them to know what has happened and how it will affect the family. However, try not to overburden them with the responsibility of too many emotional or financial details.

✓ **Keep an open dialogue with your children.** Letting them know what is really going on is vital. Children have a way of imagining the worst so the facts can actually be far less devastating than what they envision.

✓ **Make sure your children know it's not anyone's fault.** Children may not understand about job loss and may think that *you* did something wrong to cause it. Or they may feel that somehow *they* are responsible or financially burdensome. They need reassurance in these matters, regardless of their age.

✓ **Children need to feel they are helping.** They want to help and having them do something like taking a cut in allowance, deferring expensive purchases, or getting an after-school job can make them feel as if they are part of the team.

Some experts suggest that it can be useful to alert the school counselor to your unemployment so that they can watch the children for problems at school before the problems become serious.

## Coping with Stress

Here are some coping mechanisms that can help you deal with the stress of being unemployed.

✓ **Write down what seems to be causing the stress.** Identify the "stressors," then think of possible ways to handle each one. Can some demands be altered, lessened, or postponed? Can you live with any of them just as they are? Are there some that you might be able to deal with more effectively?

✓ **Set priorities.** Deal with the most pressing needs or changes first. You cannot handle everything at once.

✓ **Establish a workable schedule.** When you set a schedule for yourself, make sure it is one that can be achieved. As you perform your tasks, you will feel a sense of control and accomplishment.

✓ **Reduce stress.** Learn relaxation techniques or other stress-reduction techniques. This can be as simple as sitting in a chair, closing your eyes, taking a deep breath and breathing out slowly while imagining all the tension going out with your breath. There are a number of other methods, including listening to relaxation tapes, which may help you cope with stress more effectively. Check the additional source material books that offer instruction on these techniques—many of these are available at your public library.

✓ **Avoid isolation.** Keep in touch with your friends, even former coworkers, if you can do that comfortably. Unemployed people often feel a sense of isolation and loneliness. See your friends, talk with them, socialize with them. You are the same person you were before unemployment. The same goes for the activities that you have enjoyed in the past. Evaluate them. Which can you afford to continue? If you find that your old hobbies or activities can't be part of your new budget, maybe you can substitute new activities that are less costly.

✓ **Join a support group.** No matter how understanding or caring your family or friends might be, they may not be able to understand all that you're going through, and you might be able to find help and understanding at a job seeking support group.

These groups consist of people who are going through the same experiences and emotions as you. Many groups also share tips on job opportunities, as well as feedback on ways to deal more effectively in the job search process. *The National Business Employment Weekly,* available at major newsstands, lists support groups throughout the country. Local churches, YMCAs, YWCAs, and libraries often list or facilitate support groups. A list of self-help organizations—some of which cover the unemployed—is available from the National Self-Help Clearinghouse, 25 West 43rd St., Room 620, New York, NY 10036. The cost is $3, plus a self-addressed, stamped envelope.

Forty Plus is a national nonprofit organization and an excellent source of information about clubs around the country and on issues concerning older employees and the job search process. The address is 15 Park Row, New York, NY 10038. Their telephone number is (212) 233-6086.

# KEEPING YOUR SPIRITS UP

Here are some ways you can build your self-esteem and avoid depression.

✓ **List your positives.** Make a list of your positive qualities and your successes. This list is always easier to make when you are feeling good about yourself. Perhaps you can enlist the assistance of a close friend or caring relative, or wait for a sunnier moment.

✓ **Replay your positives.** Once you have made this list, replay the positives in your mind frequently. Associate the replay with an activity you do often; for example, you might review the list in your mind every time you go to the refrigerator!

✓ **Use the list before performing difficult tasks.** Review the list when you are feeling down or to give you energy before you attempt some difficult task.

✓ **Recall successes.** Take time every day to recall a success.

✓ **Use realistic standards.** Avoid the trap of evaluating yourself using impossible standards that come from others. You are in a particular phase of your life; don't dwell on what you think society regards as success. Remind yourself that success will again be yours.

✓ **Know your strengths and weaknesses.** What things do you do well? What skills do you have? Do you need to learn new skills? Everyone has limitations. What are yours? Are there certain job duties that are just not right for you and that you might want to avoid? Balance your limitations against your strong skills so that you don't let the negatives eat at your self-esteem. Incorporate this knowledge into your planning.

✓ **Picture success.** Practice visualizing positive results or outcomes and view them in your mind before the event. Play out the scene in your imagination and picture yourself as successful in whatever you're about to attempt.

✓ **Build success.** Make a "to do" list. Include small, achievable tasks. Divide the tasks on your list and make a list for every day so you will have some "successes" daily.

✓ **Surround yourself with positive people.** Socialize with family and friends who are supportive. You want to be around people who will "pick you up," not "knock you down." You know who your fans are. Try to find time to be around them. It can really make you feel good.

✓ **Volunteer.** Give something of yourself to others through volunteer work. Volunteering will help you feel more worthwhile and may actually give you new skills.

## OVERCOMING DEPRESSION

Are you depressed? As hard as it is to be out of work, it also can be a new beginning. A new direction may emerge that will change your life in positive ways. This may be a good time to reevaluate your attitudes and outlook.

✓ **Live in the present.** The past is over and you cannot change it. Learn from your mistakes and use that knowledge to plan for the future; then let the past go. Don't dwell on it or relive it over and over. Don't be overpowered by guilt.

✓ **Take responsibility for yourself.** Try not to complain or blame others. Save your energy for activities that result in positive experiences.

✓ **Learn to accept what you cannot change.** However, realize that in most situations, you do have some control. Your reactions and your behavior are in your control and will often influence the outcome of events.

✓ **Keep the job search under your own command.** This will give you a sense of control and prevent you from giving up and waiting for something to happen. Enlist everyone's aid in your job search, but make sure you do most of the work.

✓ **Talk things out with people you trust.** Admit how you feel. For example, if you realize you're angry, find a positive way to vent it, perhaps through exercise.

✓ **Face your fears.** Try to pinpoint them. "Naming the enemy" is the best strategy for relieving the vague feeling of anxiety. By facing what you actually fear you can see if your fears are realistic or not.

✓ **Think creatively.** Stay flexible, take risks, and don't be afraid of failure. Try not to take rejection personally. Think of it as information that will help you later in your search. Take criticism as a way to learn more about yourself. Keep plugging away at the job search despite those inevitable setbacks. Most importantly, forget magic. What lies ahead is hard work!

## SOURCES OF PROFESSIONAL HELP

If your depression won't go away, or leads you to self-destructive behaviors such as abuse of alcohol or drugs, you may consider asking a professional for help. Many people who have never sought professional assistance before find that in a time of crisis it really helps to have someone listen and give needed aid. Consult your local mental health clinics, social services agencies, religious organizations, or professional counselors for help for yourself and family members who are affected by your unemployment. Your health insurance may cover some assistance or, if you do not have insurance, counseling is often available on a "sliding scale" fee based on income.

# MANAGING YOUR FINANCES WHILE OUT OF WORK

As you already know, being unemployed has financial consequences. While the best solution to this is to get a good job in as short a time as possible, you do need to manage your money differently during the time between jobs. Following are some things to think about.

## APPLY FOR BENEFITS WITHOUT DELAY

Don't be embarrassed to apply for unemployment benefits as soon as possible, even if you're not sure you are eligible. This program is to help you make a transition between jobs and you helped pay for it by your previous employment. Depending on how long you have worked, you can collect benefits for up to 26 weeks and sometimes even longer. Contact your state labor department or employment security agency for further information. Their addresses and telephone numbers are listed in your phone book.

## PREPARE NOW TO STRETCH YOUR MONEY

Being out of work means lower income and the need to control your expenses. Don't avoid doing this because the more you plan, the better you can control your finances.

## EXAMINE YOUR INCOME AND EXPENSES

Create a budget and look for ways to cut expenses. The Monthly Income and Expense Worksheet can help you isolate income and expense categories, but your own budget may be considerably more detailed. I've included two columns for each expense category. Enter in the "Normal" column what you have been spending in that category during the time you were employed. Enter in the "Could Reduce To" column a lower number that you will spend by cutting expenses in that category.

## TIPS ON CONSERVING YOUR CASH

While unemployed, it is likely that your expenses will exceed your income and it is essential that you be aggressive in managing your money. Your objective here is very clear: you want to conserve as much cash as possible early on so you can have some for essentials later. Here are some suggestions.

✓ **Begin cutting all nonessential expenses right away.** Don't put this off! There is no way to know how long you will be out of work and the faster you deal with the financial issues, the better.

✓ **Discuss the situation with other family members.** Ask them to get involved by helping you identify expenses they can cut.

✓ **Look for sources of additional income.** Can you paint houses on weekends? Pick up a temporary job or consulting assignment? Deliver newspapers in the early morning? Can a family member get a job to help out? Any new income will help and the sooner the better.

✓ **Contact your creditors.** Even if you can make full payments for awhile, work out interest-only or reduced amount payments as soon as possible. When I was unemployed, I went to my creditors right away and asked them to help. They were very cooperative and most are, if you are reasonable with them.

✓ **Register with your local consumer credit counseling organization.** Many areas have free consumer credit counseling organizations that can help you get a handle on your finances and encourage your creditors to cooperate.

✓ **Review your assets.** Make a list of all your assets and their current value. Money in checking, savings, and other

## MONTHLY INCOME AND EXPENSE WORKSHEET

### INCOME

| | | | |
|---|---|---|---|
| Unemployment benefits | _____ | Interest/Dividends | _____ |
| Spouse's income | _____ | Other income | _____ |
| Severance pay | _____ | **TOTALS** | _____ |

### EXPENSES

| | NORMAL | COULD REDUCE TO | | NORMAL | COULD REDUCE TO |
|---|---|---|---|---|---|
| **Mortgage/rent:** | _____ | _____ | | _____ | _____ |
| maintenance/ repairs | _____ | _____ | **Health insurance:** | _____ | _____ |
| **Utilities:** | | | Other medical/ dental expenses | _____ | _____ |
| electric | _____ | _____ | **Tuition:** | _____ | _____ |
| gas/oil heat | _____ | _____ | other school costs | _____ | _____ |
| water/sewer | _____ | _____ | **Clothing:** | _____ | _____ |
| telephone | _____ | _____ | **Entertainment:** | _____ | _____ |
| **Food:** | _____ | _____ | **Taxes:** | _____ | _____ |
| restaurants | _____ | _____ | **Job hunting costs:** | _____ | _____ |
| **Car payment:** | _____ | _____ | **Other expenses:** | _____ | _____ |
| fuel | _____ | _____ | | _____ | _____ |
| maintenance/ repairs | _____ | _____ | | _____ | _____ |
| insurance | _____ | _____ | | _____ | _____ |
| **Other loan payments:** | | | | _____ | _____ |
| _____ | _____ | _____ | **TOTALS** | _____ | _____ |

accounts is the most available, but you may have additional assets in pension programs, life insurance, and stocks that could be converted to cash if needed. You may also have an extra car that could be sold, equity in your home that could be borrowed against, and other assets that could be sold or used if needed.

✓ **Reduce credit card purchases.** Try to pay for things in cash to save on interest charges and prevent overspending. Be disciplined, you can always use your credit cards later if you are getting desperate for food and other basics.

✓ **Consider cashing in some "luxury" assets.** For example, sell a car or boat you rarely use to generate cash and to save on insurance and maintenance costs.

✓ **Comparison shop** for home/auto/life insurance and other expenses to lower costs.

✓ **Deduct job hunting expenses from your taxes.** Some job hunting expenses may be tax deductible as a "miscellaneous deduction" on your federal income tax return. Keep receipts for employment agency fees, resume expenses, and transportation expenses. If you find work in another city and you must relocate, some moving expenses are tax deductible. Contact an accountant or the IRS for more information.

## REVIEW YOUR HEALTH COVERAGE

You already know that it is dangerous to go without health insurance, so there is no need to lecture you on this, but here are some tips.

✓ **You can probably maintain coverage at your own expense.** Under the COBRA law, if you worked for an employer that provided medical coverage and had 20 or more employees you may continue your health coverage. However, you must tell your former employer within 60 days of leaving the job.

✓ **Contact professional organizations to which you belong.** They may provide group coverage for their members at low rates.

✓ **Speak to an insurance broker.** If necessary, arrange for health coverage on your own or join a local health maintenance organization (HMO).

✓ **Practice preventive medicine.** The best way to save money on medical bills is to stay healthy. Try not to ignore minor ills. If they persist, phone or visit your doctor.

✓ **Investigate local clinics.** Many local clinics provide services based on a sliding scale. These clinics often provide quality health care at affordable prices. In an emergency, most hospitals will provide you with services on a sliding scale and most areas usually have one or more hospitals funded locally to provide services to those who can't afford them.

# Researching Sources of Job Leads and Other Information

If you have been to a large bookstore lately, you may have noticed that there are many, many books in the "career" section. Each year, there are more and more books published on this topic and, unfortunately, most of them are not very good. From among all the books and other sources of information available, I have selected resources that I believe are of particular importance to you in your job search. Of course, I have included many of the books I have written and/or that are published by JIST—it seemed only fair. Most are available through a bookstore or good library.

## INFORMATION ON OCCUPATIONS AND INDUSTRIES

*Occupational Outlook Handbook (OOH)*. Published every two years by the U.S. Department of Labor's Bureau of Labor Statistics. Provides excellent descriptions of 250 of the most popular jobs, covering about 85 percent of the workforce. Well-written descriptions provide information on skills required, working conditions, duties, qualifications, pay, and advancement potential. Very helpful for preparing for interviews by identifying key skills to emphasize. (U.S. Department of Labor, JIST publishes a reprint)

*America's Top 300 Jobs*. This is a version of the *OOH* that is available from bookstores or in the circulation department of your library. Because the *OOH* itself is typically in the reference section of a library, this version, which can often be checked out, can allow you to access the same information at your leisure. (JIST)

*Career Guide to America's Top Industries*. Provides trends and other information on more than 40 major industries and summary data on many others. Excellent for getting information on an industry prior to an interview. Includes details on employment projections, advancement opportunities, major trends, and a complete narrative description of each industry. (JIST)

*The Complete Guide for Occupational Exploration (CGOE)*. This book lists more than 12,000 job titles in a format that makes it easy to use as a tool for exploring career alternatives or other jobs you may seek based on current skills. Jobs with similar characteristics are grouped together. Each group's description includes details on skills required, nature of work, and other information. The *CGOE* also cross-references to other standard reference sources for additional information on the jobs it lists. (JIST)

*The Enhanced Guide for Occupational Exploration (EGOE)*. Uses the same organizational structure as the *CGOE* but includes brief descriptions of about 2,800 jobs. Useful for career exploration, identifying skills used in previous jobs, researching new job targets, and preparing for interviews. (JIST)

*Dictionary of Occupational Titles (DOT).* Provides descriptions for more than 12,000 jobs, covering virtually all jobs in our economy. This is the only book of its kind and can be used to identify jobs in different fields that use skills similar to those you have acquired in your past jobs, identify key skills to emphasize in interviews, and much more. It provides brief descriptions for each job and additional coded information. (U.S. Department of Labor, JIST publishes a reprint)

*The Top Job™ Series.* Each book in the *America's Top Jobs™* series, has a specific emphasis. Each provides thorough descriptions for the top jobs in a specific area, career planning and job search tips, plus details on growth projections, education required, and other data on 500 additional jobs. (JIST)

> *America's Fastest Growing Jobs*
> *America's Federal Jobs*
> *America's Top Office, Management, Sales & Professional Jobs*
> *America's Top Medical, Education & Human Services Jobs*
> *America's Top Military Careers*
> *America's Top Jobs™ for People Without College Degrees*
> *America's Top Jobs for College Graduates*
> *America's Top Jobs Book Plus CD-Rom*

*Dictionary of Occupational Terms—A Guide to the Special Language and Jargon of Hundreds of Careers* by Nancy Shields. An interesting reference book that will answer most of your questions on more than 3,000 terms. (JIST)

## SOURCES OF INFORMATION ON SPECIFIC ORGANIZATIONS

After you have a good idea of the industries, fields of work, and geographical areas in which you want to concentrate your job search, the next step is to locate companies that might employ people in your field. A large number of publications are available that contain lists of companies by industry, location, size, and other defining characteristics. A few of them are discussed below.

*The Job Hunter's Guide to 100 Great American Cities* (Brattle Communications). Rather than concentrating on a particular locale, this guide gives the principal-area employers for 100 of America's largest cities.

*Macrae's State Industrial Directories.* Published for 15 Northeastern states. Similar volumes are produced for other parts of the country by other publishers. Each book lists thousands of companies, concentrating almost exclusively on those that produce products, rather than services.

*National Business Telephone Directory* (Gale Research). An alphabetical listing of companies across the United States with their addresses and phone numbers. It includes many smaller firms (20 employees minimum).

*Thomas Register.* Lists more than 100,000 companies across the country. Contains listings by company name,

type of product made, and brand name of product produced. Catalogs provided by many of the companies also are included.

*America's Fastest Growing Employers* (Bob Adams Inc., Holbrook, MA). Lists more than 700 of the fastest growing companies in the country.

*The Hidden Job Market: A Guide to America's 2000 Little-Known Fastest Growing High-Tech Companies* (Peterson's Guides). Concentrates on high-tech companies with good growth potential.

*Dun & Bradstreet Million Dollar Directory.* Provides information on 180,000 of the largest companies in the country. Gives the type of business, number of employees, and sales volume for each. It also lists the company's top executives.

*Standard & Poor's Register of Corporations, Directors and Executives.* Information similar to that in Dun & Bradstreet's directory. Also contains a listing of the parent companies of subsidiaries and the interlocking affiliations of directors.

*The Career Guide—Dun's Employment Opportunities Directory.* Aimed specifically at the professional job seeker. Lists more than 5,000 major U.S. companies which plan to recruit in the coming year. Lists personnel directors and gives information about firms' career opportunities and benefits packages.

There are many directories that give information about firms in a particular industry. A few samples are listed below:

> *The Blue Book of Building and Construction*
> *Directory of Advertising Agencies*
> *Directory of Computer Dealers*
> *McFadden American Bank Directory*

The Chamber of Commerce and local business associations may also publish directories listing companies within a specific geographic area. These are available in libraries or by writing to the individual associations. And, of course, the *Yellow Pages* provide local listings of governmental and business organizations for every section of the country.

## PROFESSIONAL AND TRADE ASSOCIATIONS

These associations offer another excellent avenue for getting information about where the type of work you want to do might be found. These associations:

✓ Help you identify areas where growth is occurring.

✓ Provide the names of firms that might employ people in a specific type of work.

✓ Can identify the best information sources for developments within the field.

✓ Can provide more information on leads in small firms than directories.

✓ Publish newsletters or journals that provide information on companies needing increased staff in the near future.

Some publications that list trade and professional associations are:

*Encyclopedia of Associations* (Gale Research). A listing of more than 22,000 professional, trade, and other nonprofit organizations in the United States.

*Career Guide to Professional Associations* (Garrett Park Press). Describes more than 2,500 professional associations. The information is more specifically oriented to the job seeker than is the *Encyclopedia of Associations*. A word of caution, this guide has not been updated since 1980 and some of the information may not be current.

## NEWSPAPERS

Newspapers not only contain want ads but lots of other useful employment information. Articles about new or expanding companies can be valuable leads for new job possibilities.

If relocating is a possibility, look at newspapers from other areas. They can serve as a source of job leads as well as indicate some idea of the job market. The major out-of-town newspapers are sold in most large cities and are also available in many public libraries.

Some newspapers such as *The New York Times, The Chicago Tribune,* and *The Financial Times* are national in scope. *The National Business Employment Weekly,* published by *The Wall Street Journal,* contains much information of interest to professional job seekers.

## NETWORKING

Networking is another excellent way of gathering information about a particular field. It is one of the best ways of discovering the existence of smaller companies which often are not listed in directories.

# SOURCES OF ADDITIONAL INFORMATION ON CAREER PLANNING, JOB SEEKING, RESUMES, AND CAREER SUCCESS

## JOB SEEKING AND INTERVIEW TECHNIQUES

*The Very Quick Job Search: Get a Good Job in Less Time* by J. Michael Farr (Revised 1996). This is my most thorough job search book and it includes lots of information on career planning and, of course, job seeking. This is the book I would recommend to a friend who was out of work if I had to recommend just one book. (JIST)

*The Quick Interview & Salary Negotiation Book— Dramatically Improve Your Interviewing Skills and Pay in a Matter of Hours* by J. Michael Farr. While this is a substantial book with lots of information, I've arranged it so that you can read the first section and go out and do better in interviews later that day. (JIST)

*Getting the Job You Really Want* by J. Michael Farr. This one provides career planning and job search methods in a workbook format that includes lots of worksheets as well as the needed narrative. It has sold more than 150,000 copies and counting. (JIST)

*Career Satisfaction and Success—A Guide to Job and Personal Freedom* by Bernard Haldane. This is a complete revision of a "classic" by an author many consider to be one of the founders of the modern career planning movement. It's not a job search book as much as a job success book. Contains solid information. (JIST)

*Using the Internet and the World Wide Web in Your Job Search* by Fred E. Jandt and Mary B. Nemnich. For new or more experienced users of online computer services, this book gives you lots of good information on finding job opportunities on the "net." (JIST)

*The PIE Method for Career Success—A Unique Way to Find Your Ideal Job* by Daniel Porot. The author is one of Europe's major career consultants and this book presents his powerful career planning and job seeking concepts in a visual and memorable way. (JIST)

*Job Strategies for Professionals* by U.S. Employment Service. Job search advice for the millions of professionals and managers who have lost their jobs. (JIST)

*What Color Is Your Parachute?* by Richard N. Bolles. It is the bestselling career planning book of all time and the author continues to improve it. (Ten Speed Press)

*The Complete Job Search Handbook: All the Skills You Need to Get Any Job, and Have a Good Time Doing It* by Howard Figler. A very good book. (Henry Holt)

*Who's Hiring Who?* by Richard Lathrop. Another good book. (Ten Speed Press)

*Job Hunters Sourcebook: Where to Find Employment Leads and Other Job Search Sources* by Michelle LeCompte. (Gale Research)

*Sweaty Palms Revised: The Neglected Art of Being Interviewed* by Anthony Medley. (Ten Speed Press)

*Dare to Change Your Job and Your Life* by Carole Kanchier. Practical and motivating guidance on achieving career and personal growth and satisfaction. (JIST)

## RESUMES AND COVER LETTERS

*The Quick Resume & Cover Letter Book—Write and Use an Effective Resume in Only One Day* by J. Michael Farr. Starting with an "instant" resume worksheet and basic formats that you can complete in an hour or so, this book then takes you on a tour of everything you ever wanted to know about resumes and, more importantly, how to use them in your job search. (JIST)

*The Resume Solution—How to Write (and Use) a Resume That Gets Results* by David Swanson. Lots of good advice and examples for creating superior resumes. Very strong on resume design and layout and provides a step-by-step approach that is very easy to follow. (JIST)

*Gallery of Best Resumes* by David F. Noble. Advice and over 200 examples from professional resume writers. Lots of variety in content and design, an excellent resource. I consider it to be the best resume "library" since all the resumes are organized into useful categories. (JIST)

*Gallery of Best Resumes for Two-Year Degree Graduates* by David F. Noble. Written especially for anyone with special education, training, or experience beyond high school. This gallery showcases professionally written resumes that have helped two-year degree graduates compete successfully for jobs held traditionally by workers with four-year and higher degrees. (JIST)

*The Working Parents' Handbook* by Katherine Murray. This book is a must for every working parent! This upbeat, encouraging, easy-to-read guide is for anyone juggling home, family, and job. The author shows how to set priorities between worker and parent to construct more balanced and satisfying lives. (Park Avenue Productions)

*Using WordPerfect in Your Job Search* by David F. Noble. A unique and thorough book that reviews how to use WordPerfect to create effective resumes, correspondence, and other job search documents. (JIST)

*The Perfect Resume* by Tom Jackson. (Doubleday)

*Dynamite Cover Letters* by Ron and Caryl Krannich. (Impact Publications)

*Dynamite Resumes* by Ron and Caryl Krannich. A good book. (Impact Publications)

*The Damn Good Resume Guide* by Yana Parker. Lots of good examples and advice. (Ten Speed Press)

## EDUCATION, SELF-EMPLOYMENT, AND STARTING A BUSINESS

*Mind Your Own Business—Getting Started as an Entrepreneur* by LaVerne Ludden and Bonnie Maitlen. A good book for those considering their own business, with lots of good advice. (JIST)

*Directory of Franchise Opportunities* by U.S. Department of Commerce and LaVerne Ludden. Lists 1,500 franchise opportunities and information on selecting and financing a start-up. (JIST)

*The Career Connection for College Education—A Guide to College Education and Related Career Opportunities* by Fred Rowe. Covers about 100 college majors and their related careers. (JIST)

*The Career Connection for Technical Education—A Guide to Technical Training and Related Career Opportunities* by Fred Rowe. Describes more than 60 technical education majors and the careers to which they lead. (JIST)

*Back to School: A College Guide for Adults* by LaVerne L. Ludden. A former Dean of Graduate and Adult Studies has written the definitive guidebook on adults returning to college. This inside advice and invaluable information will help millions select the college and program that's right for

them and reduce the time required to get that college degree! (JIST)

*Luddens' Adult Guide to Colleges and Universities* by LaVerne L. Ludden and Marsha Ludden. This companion book to *Back to School* is a comprehensive resource for adults going back to school and contains the latest information on more than 1,500 degree programs geared for working adults. (JIST)

## COMPUTER SOFTWARE

Any good software store will carry programs to help you write a resume, organize your job leads and contacts, and create your correspondence. Some packages are also designed to provide "career counseling," occupational information, or advice on your job search. Some of these programs are good and some are not.

Here are some of the good ones that I know of first hand.

*JIST's Multimedia Occupational Outlook Handbook* (CD-ROM and disk versions)

*JIST's Electronic Occupational Outlook Handbook* (CD-ROM and disk—no multimedia features)

*JIST's Electronic Enhanced Dictionary of Occupational Titles* (CD-ROM)

*JIST's Electronic Dictionary of Occupational Titles* (Disk-based Windows and DOS versions)

*America's Top Jobs™ on CD-ROM* (JIST)

# IN CLOSING

Few people will get a job offer because someone knocks on their door and offers one. The craft of job seeking does involve some luck, but you are far more likely to get lucky if you are out getting interviews. Structure your job search as if it were a full-time job and try not to get discouraged. There are lots of jobs out there and someone needs what you can do—your job is to find them.

I hope this little book helps, though you should consider learning more. Career planning and job seeking skills are, I believe, adult survival skills for our new economy. Good luck!

*Mike Farr*

## Good Articles

I've selected articles for this section that provide insights you may find interesting. All were written by staff of the U.S. Department of Labor and were published in various D.O.L. publications. They provide good, well-researched information.

Keep in mind that, while some of the information is old, it is among the most recent available and is quite relevant to the present labor market.

# What Is a Technician?

## By Douglas Braddock

Technician and related terms—such as technologist or service technician—are the source of a great deal of confusion and misinterpretation. In various publications from the Department of Labor, including the *Occupational Outlook Handbook* and other federal government publications such as the *Standard Occupational Classification Manual* and the *Dictionary of Occupational Titles,* relatively few occupations or occupational groups have the title technician. In general, government definitions of technicians restrict the term to those who assist scientists, engineers, or health professionals. Adding to the confusion are occupations officially classified as technicians, such as aircraft pilot and computer programmer, that many would not think of as technicians. Yet it seems that technicians are on the job wherever you look.

- When your car or air conditioner or office copier or personal computer needs repair, increasingly the person who does the repairs will be called a service technician rather than a *mechanic* or *repairer.*

- It is becoming common for factory workers—such as machine operators—to hold a title such as *production technician,* especially if the job has been redefined and expanded to include multiple skills and duties.

- If you visit a library, you may request help from a *library technician* instead of a librarian.

## Who Is a Technician?

The term technician—and, to a lesser extent, technologist—seems to be popping up everywhere. Secretary of Labor Robert B. Reich alluded to the expanding number and kinds of occupations called technicians when he recently said, "There's the truck driver who has a computer and modem in his cab, so that he can time deliveries to exactly when the customer needs them, and can help assemble complex machinery. He's not a trucker in the old sense of the term. He's a technician, and he's making good money." Have truck drivers become technicians? What's going on here?

Technique, according to the *American Heritage Dictionary,* is "the systematic procedure by which a complex or scientific task is accomplished." Technicians are workers who use such procedures. They have become more common for many reasons, including the increased complexity of jobs, the need to raise productivity, and, not least of all, the prestige of the term.

As products and services become more sophisticated, it is only natural that the people who produce, operate, and repair these products become increasingly knowledgeable as well. As Secretary Reich implies, a person who only drives a truck is a truck driver, but someone who drives a truck and operates a computer and assembles complex machinery is something more. Walt Edling, Vice President of Programs at the Center for Occupational Research and Development in Waco, Texas, observes that many occupations now require more education than in the past, which often justifies the use of the term technician in their names.

Further, as the economy becomes more competitive, the drive for increased productivity makes it ever more important that each worker's time is spent as efficiently as possible. It doesn't make sense for a physician or lawyer to perform functions that can be performed by technicians. For example, paralegals can prepare and file court document, sparing lawyers time to consult with clients or appear in court.

Another reason for the increased use of the term is that it sounds good to customers, employers, and employees. Most customers presumably prefer that their cars be repaired by a "service technician" rather than a mechanic. This term implies to the customer a highly skilled worker—maybe one wearing a white lab coat—who diagnoses and repairs the car using sophisticated electronic equipment. A mechanic, to some customers, is a less skilled worker—probably covered with grease—who crawls under the car and bangs on the oil pan with a wrench. Employers and employees like the prestige the term conveys, just as customers do. According to John Antrim, General Manager of the National Institute for Certification in Engineering Technology, "Flattery is great." Employers also use the term to encourage workers to think of themselves as technical specialists with a broad range of skills rather than, for example, simply machine operators.

Does this trend of using technician more widely disturb those in well-established technician occupations? Not according to Antrim. He thinks the spread of the term beyond the traditional areas simply means that skilled workers are getting more and long overdue recognition.

## Technologists—Another Step Up in Training and Skill Level

Technologist is related to technician. Sometimes the terms are used almost interchangeably; but, in general, the term technologist implies a worker who is more highly skilled than a technician. Often, a technologist has more autonomy and theoretical knowledge than a technician. For example, many *engineering technologists* have a bachelor's degree and are considered engineers by their employers. Technicians rarely have bachelor's degrees.

In the area of health care, there are many kinds of technologists with strict training and licensing standards. In general, a *medical technologist* has more training and autonomy than a medical technician. Sometimes the title technologist implies a supervisory role: many *clinical laboratory technologists* supervise *clinical laboratory technicians,* for example.

## The Traditional Technician Occupations

Workers in the following occupations are traditionally considered technicians. Most of them work with sophisticated machinery.

- *Engineering and science technicians* use the principles and theories of science, engineering, and mathematics to solve problems in research and development, manufacturing, sales, construction, and customer service. Many engineering and science technicians assist engineers and scientists, especially in research and development. Others work in production or inspection jobs.

- *Drafters* prepare technical drawings used by production workers to build a wide variety of products and structures. Their drawings show the technical details of the products and structures from all sides, with exact dimensions, the specific materials to be used, procedures to be followed, and other information needed to carry out the job. Drafters produce the drawings either manually or with computer-aided design (CAD) equipment using rough sketches, specifications, and calculations made by engineers, surveyors, architects, and scientists.

- *Broadcast technicians* install, test, repair, set up, and operate the electronic equipment used to record and transmit radio and television programs. They work with television cameras, microphones, tape recorders, light and sound effects, transmitters, antennas, and other equipment.

- *Clinical laboratory technicians* examine and analyze body fluids, tissues, and cells. They look for bacteria, parasites, or other micro-organisms, analyze the chemical content of fluids, match fluid for transfusions, and test for drug levels in the blood. They also prepare specimens for examination, count cells, and look for abnormal cells. They use automated equipment and instruments that perform a number of tests simultaneously, as well as microscopes, cell counters, and other kinds of sophisticated laboratory equipment to perform tests. Then they interpret the results and relay them to physicians.

- *Dental hygienists* provide preventive dental care and teach patients how to practice good dental hygiene.

- *Dispensing opticians* fit eyeglasses and contact lenses.

- *EEG technologists* operate machines that record electrical activity in the brain.

- *Emergency medical technicians* give immediate emergency medical care and transport the sick or injured to medical facilities.

- *Licensed practical nurses* care for the sick, injured, convalescing, and disabled under the direction of physicians and registered nurses.

- *Nuclear medicine technologists* administer radiopharmaceuticals—drugs that emit radiation—to patients so the characteristics or functioning of the tissues or organs in which they localize can be assessed.

- *Radiologic technologists* make x-rays of patients. Some radiologic technologists administer radiation therapy to cancer patients, and others operate ultrasound equipment.

- *Surgical technologists* assist in operations under the supervision of physicians or registered nurses.

## The New Technicians

Besides operators of complex machinery, such as workers in the occupations described above, many people are now called technicians who service or repair equipment, produce precision tools or medical devices, or work in paraprofessional fields.

## Service Technicians

*Automotive mechanics, aircraft mechanics and engine specialists, diesel mechanics, farm equipment mechanics, mobile heavy equipment mechanics,* and *motorcycle, boat, and small-engine mechanics* have been called service technicians in popular usage for some time. For the most part, they are classified as *repairers* in the *Occupational Outlook Handbook* and other occupational literature.

*Electronic equipment repairers and installers* are often called electronics technicians, service technicians, or field service representatives. They install, maintain, and repair electronic equipment used in offices, factories, homes, hospitals, and other places. Some of the specific kinds of repairers include *commercial and industrial electronic equipment repairers, communications equipment mechanics, computer and office machine repairers, electronic home entertainment equipment repairers,* and *telephone installers and repairers.* The use of "electronics technician" for these workers is especially confusing because the similar term *electronics engineering technician* refers to workers who—rather than simply make repairs—help develop, manufacture, and service electronic equipment.

Workers in other repair or installation occupations referred to as technicians or service technicians include heating, air conditioning, and refrigeration technicians, home appliance and power tool repairers, and vending machine servicers and repairers.

## Production Technicians

Workers in these occupations make or assemble precision tools and medical devices. Machinists, tool and die makers, and other precision metalworkers are highly skilled workers who produce metal parts in numbers too small to warrant automation. Because of the high skill and technical knowledge needed to do these jobs, these workers are often referred to collectively as technicians, especially in discussions of jobs for which technical skills are important, although workers in the individual occupations are rarely called technicians.

The term technician has long been applied to *dental laboratory technicians,* who fill prescriptions for dental crowns, bridges, and dentures. Although classified as a production occupation, these workers are highly skilled, work in a laboratory setting, and produce individualized items. Similarly, *ophthalmic laboratory technicians* are highly skilled and work in a laboratory setting and may be called technicians. They produce prescription eyeglass lenses and lenses for other optical instruments.

The term technician is increasingly applied to a variety of production workers, especially those who have been trained to do several jobs rather than perform one specific operation. For example, *precision assemblers,* especially those who make electronic products, are often referred to as technicians.

## Administrative, Clerical, and Paraprofessional Technicians

Usually, the term *technician* implies expertise in an area of scientific, engineering, mechanical, or medical technology and the manipulation of objects and tools. However, it is creeping into areas previously considered administrative, clerical, or professional. These workers are technicians in the sense that they specialize, but their specialty doesn't involve physical objects.

For example, *medical record technicians* are expert in the "mechanics" of maintaining and storing medical records. *Library technicians* are experts in certain technical library procedures and assist librarians. There are emerging occupations for which technical knowledge of administrative procedures is increasingly important. For example, eligibility technicians in local government social services departments are experts in the procedures and rules of this specialized area. Undoubtedly other workers who become experts in other administrative procedures or who assist professionals will take the title technician.

## Training and Licenses

Most technicians have some formal training beyond high school. In fact, the need for some specialized training after high school but less than four years of college is almost part of the definition of technician. Few workers enter technician jobs with only a high school education, and these jobs almost always require formal company training, specific experience, or both. Workers whose jobs require a bachelor's degree, on the other hand, are more usually called technologists or professionals.

For many technician occupations, there is a wide variety of ways to obtain training, including on-the-job training, apprenticeships, and Armed Forces training. Training in technical institutes, vocational-technical schools, junior or community colleges, and other postsecondary schools is also common for these occupations. For some, prior experience in another occupation is helpful or required; for example, many numerical control tool programmers have experience as *machinists* or *tool and die makers.* Many health technician occupations are entered by people with health-related experience—frequently *licensed practical nurse*—even though these occupations may have very specific training and licensing requirements.

In a few technician occupations a bachelor's degree is common, although this isn't a formal requirement of the job. For example, many *science technicians* have bachelor of science degrees but enter the occupation because they can't find jobs as scientists. Employers of *science technicians* prefer to hire workers with laboratory skills gained in an appropriate technical school or junior or community college, but they hire those with bachelor's degrees because they often can't find someone with the appropriate training.

In addition to training, states require technicians in some occupations to be licensed. Most of these occupations are in health care. Usually, formal training at an accredited institution is required before the licensing examination can be administered. These requirements vary greatly by occupation and state.

## Sources of Training

As indicated above, the sources of training available for technicians range from employers to formal programs in colleges and other schools.

### On-the-Job and Employer-Provided Training

It is possible to enter many technician occupations with on-the-job or formal employer-provided training. This sort of training is much more common in some occupations than others. For the emerging production technician occupations, it is the predominate or only possible training. In some repairer occupations, on-the-job and employer training is sufficient for entry, but workers without formal training may be limited to lower level, lower paid jobs. In technical health occupations, many workers have received their training from employers, such as hospitals. Sometimes the training is for those with no previous training or experience beyond a high school diploma, as is the case with training for licensed practical nurse.

The Armed Forces provide training and work experience in many technical occupations. Armed Forces training can be a big advantage in getting a job, and may be all that is needed to qualify for some technician jobs, although in many cases additional training may be required to qualify.

Apprenticeships also offer people the opportunity to learn a job while they are employed. The training usually combines work with formal training. For skilled metalworking occupations, such as machinist or tool and die maker, formal apprenticeship training is preferred. Apprenticeships are also a common way to learn the skills needed in many repairer occupations.

## Formal Schooling

Programs in schools that prepare students for technician occupations can last a few months or several years. Technical institutes, junior and community colleges, and area vocational-technical schools all have courses for some technical occupations, usually for the kinds of jobs found in their locality. The nature of the training sometimes depends on the type of school giving it, although often there is little or no difference between technical institute and community college programs. One difference is that courses taken at junior or community colleges are more likely to be accepted for credit at four-year colleges than those at technical institutes. Junior and community colleges may also offer more theory and general education than technical institutes. Another distinction is that technical institutes may be run by private, often for-profit organizations. These are sometimes called proprietary schools. Junior and community colleges are more likely to be part of a state university system. However, the distinction is not ironclad. Some technical institutes are part of state systems, and some junior colleges are private.

## The Outlook for Most Technicians Is Bright

The employment of technicians, both those in traditional fields and in emerging ones, is projected to grow slightly less than the average for all occupations (see the accompanying table). This overall growth rate, however, is held down by the many assembler, mechanic, installer, and repairer occupations that are expected to grow only slowly or not at all. In general, traditional technician occupations are expected to grow faster than average.

No matter their growth rate, most occupations in both categories have good or even excellent employment opportunities. An important reason for the good outlook is that students have been told for generations that a college degree is essential for a good job. Therefore, a large proportion of students with good math and science skills who do well in high school go to four-year colleges. Unfortunately, students who don't intend to go to college may not try very hard in high school and don't have the solid backgrounds in math and science needed to enter technician occupations. This leaves a gap: Many high school graduates don't have the math and science background necessary, while those who do go on to four-year colleges aren't interested in these jobs. Therefore, these occupations generally offer excellent opportunities for good, relatively high-paying jobs to students who make an extra effort in high school, even though they represent less than 10 percent of all the jobs in the country.

Not all technician occupations, however, have good outlooks. Employment of *broadcast technicians* is expected to show little or no change through the year 2005 because of advances such as computer-controlled programming and remote-controlled transmitters. *Library technicians* will be affected by budgetary constraints in school, public, and college and university libraries. Keen competition for jobs as *paralegals* is expected because, despite projected rapid growth, the number of graduates of paralegal programs is expected to continue to increase.

Technological change is lessening the demand for some kinds of technicians. Improvements in reliability, ease of service, and lower prices of products will restrict opportunities for *electronic equipment repairers* and *communication equipment mechanics*. Employment of *telephone installers and repairers* is expected to decline dramatically as prewired homes and telephones bought by customers greatly reduce the need to install telephones.

**Table 1. Employment in technician occupations, 1992 and projected 2005**

| Occupation | 1992 employment (thousands) | Projected 2005 employment (thousands) | Projected growth, 1992-2005 (percent) |
|---|---|---|---|
| **Total** | 10,493 | 12,665 | 21 |
| **Technician occupations according to current standard classification guidelines** | 4,282 | 5,664 | 32 |
| EKG technicians | 16 | 14 | −14 |
| Broadcast technicians | 35 | 37 | 4 |
| Programmers, numerical, tool, and process control | 7 | 8 | 8 |
| Air traffic controllers | 23 | 25 | 10 |
| Drafters | 314 | 350 | 11 |
| All other technicians | 33 | 37 | 15 |

| Occupation | 1992 employment (thousands) | Projected 2005 employment (thousands) | Projected growth, 1992-2005 (percent) |
|---|---|---|---|
| All other engineering technicians and technologists | 372 | 431 | 16 |
| Title examiners and searchers | 29 | 35 | 19 |
| Electrical and electronic technicians and technologists | 323 | 396 | 23 |
| Science and mathematics technicians | 244 | 305 | 25 |
| Technical assistants, library | 71 | 89 | 25 |
| Clinical laboratory technologists and technicians | 268 | 339 | 26 |
| Psychiatric technicians | 72 | 90 | 26 |
| Computer programmers | 555 | 723 | 30 |
| All other legal assistants, including law clerks | 68 | 88 | 30 |
| Cardiology technicians | 14 | 19 | 35 |
| Aircraft pilots and flight engineers | 85 | 115 | 35 |
| Emergency medical technicians | 114 | 155 | 36 |
| Opticians, dispensing and measuring | 63 | 86 | 36 |
| Licensed practical nurses | 659 | 920 | 40 |
| Surgical technologists | 44 | 62 | 42 |
| Dental hygienists | 108 | 154 | 43 |
| All other health professionals and paraprofessionals | 413 | 595 | 44 |
| Nuclear medicine technologists | 12 | 18 | 50 |
| EEG technologists | 6 | 10 | 54 |
| Medical records technicians | 76 | 123 | 61 |
| Radiologic technologists and technicians | 162 | 264 | 63 |
| Paralegals | 95 | 176 | 86 |
| **Occupations increasingly referred to as technicians** | 6,211 | 7,001 | 13 |
| Frame wirers, central office | 11 | 3 | −75 |
| Signal or track switch maintainers | 3 | 1 | −75 |
| Station installers and repairers, telephone | 40 | 20 | −50 |
| Central office and PBX installers and repairers | 70 | 45 | −36 |
| All other communications equipment mechanics, installers, and repairers | 15 | 11 | −30 |
| Telephone and cable TV line installers and repairers | 165 | 125 | −24 |
| Watchmakers | 9 | 7 | −23 |
| Shipfitters | 13 | 11 | −18 |
| Electrical and electronic equipment assemblers, precision | 150 | 129 | −14 |
| Electromechanical equipment assemblers, precision | 48 | 42 | −13 |
| Radio mechanics | 9 | 8 | −11 |
| Tool and die makers | 138 | 128 | −7 |
| Electric meter installers and repairers | 13 | 13 | −6 |
| Electronic home entertainment equipment repairers | 39 | 37 | −5 |
| Motorcycle repairers | 11 | 10 | −4 |
| Boilermakers | 26 | 25 | −4 |
| Industrial machinery mechanics | 477 | 462 | −3 |
| Coin and vending machine servicers and repairers | 20 | 20 | ([1]) |
| Home appliance and power tool repairers | 74 | 74 | ([1]) |

| Occupation | 1992 employment (thousands) | Projected 2005 employment (thousands) | Projected growth, 1992-2005 (percent) |
|---|---|---|---|
| Fitters, structural metal, precision | 15 | 14 | -1 |
| Machinists | 352 | 348 | |
| Riggers | 12 | 12 | 1 |
| All other precision metal workers | 88 | 89 | 1 |
| All other electrical and electronic equipment mechanics, installers, and repairers | 42 | 43 | 3 |
| Dental laboratory technicians, precision | 48 | 50 | 3 |
| Mobile heavy equipment mechanics | 96 | 100 | 4 |
| Aircraft assemblers, precision | 26 | 27 | 4 |
| Machine builders and other precision machine assemblers | 57 | 59 | 4 |
| Electronics repairers, commercial and industrial equipment | 68 | 73 | 7 |
| Precision instrument repairers | 45 | 48 | 7 |
| Aircraft engine specialists | 26 | 28 | 8 |
| Office machine and cash register servicers | 60 | 65 | 8 |
| Electrical power line installers and repairers | 108 | 117 | 9 |
| Millwrights | 73 | 79 | 9 |
| Musical instrument repairers and tuners | 12 | 13 | 9 |
| All other precision workers | 120 | 132 | 10 |
| Farm equipment mechanics | 47 | 53 | 13 |
| Aircraft mechanics | 105 | 120 | 14 |
| All other precision assemblers | 40 | 45 | 14 |
| Camera and photographic equipment repairers | 8 | 9 | 16 |
| Sheetmetal workers and duct installers | 208 | 244 | 1 |
| Elevator installers and repairers | 22 | 25 | 18 |
| Tire repairers and changers | 80 | 95 | 18 |
| Locksmiths and safe repairers | 18 | 22 | 19 |
| Jewelers and silversmiths | 30 | 35 | 19 |
| Small engine specialists | 35 | 43 | 21 |
| All other mechanics, installers, and repairers | 338 | 413 | 22 |
| Optical goods workers, precision | 19 | 23 | 22 |
| Automotive mechanics | 739 | 907 | 23 |
| Bus and truck mechanics and diesel engine specialists | 263 | 327 | 24 |
| Photographic process workers, precision | 14 | 18 | 26 |
| Maintenance repairers, general utility | 1,145 | 1,464 | 28 |
| Heating, air conditioning, and refrigeration mechanics and installers | 212 | 274 | 29 |
| Automotive body and related workers | 202 | 263 | 30 |
| Electromechanical and biomedical equipment repairers | 10 | 13 | 37 |
| Data processing equipment repairers | 83 | 120 | 45 |
| Bicycle repairers | 14 | 20 | 45 |

(¹) A decline of fewer than 1,000 workers.

# High-Earning Workers Who Don't Have a Bachelor's Degree

## By Theresa Cosca

What makes a job good? To many people, it's earnings. For them, the good news is that over 9 million, or one in every six, full-time salaried workers age 25 and older who didn't have a bachelor's degree in 1993 earned $700 or more a week. That's close to the median for college graduates. However, it is necessary to go beyond wages in determining whether a position is the right one for you. Job characteristics, such as the nature of the work and working conditions, are also important.

Still, everyone agrees that high earnings are better than low earnings. Furthermore, earnings can be measured, but many other factors cannot. The following pages discuss occupations in which many highly paid workers do not have a college degree and point out other factors that make for a good job.

Many people are concerned that high-paid jobs are no longer available for those without a bachelor's degree. Employment has declined in manufacturing, telephone communications, and some other industries that traditionally provided high-paying jobs. For men without a four-year degree, earnings adjusted for inflation have fallen over the past 15 years, due at least in part to these declines. Rising entry requirements for some professional, managerial, and other jobs have made entry without a degree more difficult. Despite these trends, many people without college degrees, including many people under 35, still have high earnings. In fact, 1 of these workers in 20 earns $1,000 or more a week.

## What the Numbers Say

There is no accepted definition of high earnings. Among the more objective measures available is the median earnings of all workers, the median being the point at which half the workers earned more and half earned less. The median earnings of workers with a bachelor's degree is another possible yardstick.

In 1993, the median for all workers was about $500 a week. More precisely, median weekly earnings for all full-time, year-round workers age 25 and older were $493, or about $25,600 annually. The median for those with at least a bachelor's degree was $716, or about $37,200 annually. The low figure is almost three times higher than the minimum wage ($4.25 an hour) and the high figure is more than four times higher.

| Number of Workers, by Usual Weekly Earnings and Education, 1993 (numbers in millions) | | |
|---|---|---|
| | Less than a bachelor's degree | Bachelor's degree or higher |
| Less than $500 | 32.7 | 4.7 |
| $500-699 | 12.1 | 5.2 |
| $700-999 | 6.6 | 5.5 |
| $1000 or more | 2.7 | 5.8 |

In 1993, 21.4 million workers without four-year degrees earned $500 or more a week, and 9.3 million earned $700 or more. In other words, two out of five workers without a college degree earned more than the median for all workers.

| Percentage of Workers, by Usual Weekly Earnings and Education, 1993 (numbers in millions) | | |
|---|---|---|
| | Less than a bachelor's degree | Bachelor's degree or higher |
| Less than $500 | 61% | 23% |
| $500-699 | 22 | 25 |
| $700-999 | 12 | 26 |
| $1000 or more | 5 | 27 |

As these charts show, earnings were even higher, at $1,000 or more a week, for many workers. In a few occupations, more than 10 percent of the workers without college degrees earned over $1,000 a week. Consider the top earners—the most motivated, best prepared, or most fortunate workers—in these occupations:

| Occupation | Minimum weekly earnings of the top 10%, 1993 |
|---|---|
| Mining, manufacturing, and wholesale sales representatives | $1,051 |
| Production occupation supervisors | 1,000 |
| Registered nurses | 961 |
| Police and detectives | 889 |
| Administrative support occupations, supervisors | 888 |
| Engineering and related technologists and technicians | 856 |
| Carpenters | 801 |
| Truck drivers | 800 |

To some extent, earnings reflect the innate skill and talent of the worker. Other factors, such as geographic region, urban or rural environment, industry, size of the facility, and unionization also affect earnings. And men, on average, earn more than women. Three other factors significantly affect the proportion of workers who have high earnings:

- Occupation
- Age
- Education and training

## Occupation

Tables 1 and 2 list all occupations that have more than 50,000 full-time wage and salary workers age 25 and older who usually earn $700 a week or more. Some small occupations in which workers have high earnings are not listed; among these are elevator installer and air traffic controller. Table 1 lists the occupations and the number and percentage of workers who do not have a bachelor's degree. Table 2 lists the occupations by the percentage who usually earn $700 a week or more. Tables for all workers would show somewhat lower earnings, because part-timers and workers under 25 typically make less. Also, in seasonal occupations, annual earnings may be lower than implied by weekly earnings.

## Age

Generally speaking, earnings increase with age, as workers gain experience and seniority. This progression usually peaks between the ages of 45 to 54. For the same reasons, the number of high-wage earners is concentrated in the 35-to-44 and 45-to-54 age groups. Some may argue from this that highly paid workers without bachelors' degrees entered the job market years ago, when entry standards were lower and more high-wage manufacturing jobs were available. However, some workers without a bachelor's degree achieve high earnings at a relatively young age, and obviously did so since "the good old days." For example, 2.2 million workers without a degree, age 25 to 29, earned $500 or more a week; and 725,000, $700 or more.

| Percentage of Workers Without College Degrees Earning $500 or More a Week, by Age, 1993 | | |
|---|---|---|
| Age group | $500 or more a week | $700 or more a week |
| 25-29 | 25.7% | 8.4% |
| 30-34 | 36.1 | 14.7 |
| 35-44 | 43.6 | 19.3 |
| 45-54 | 46.5 | 22.4 |
| 55 and over | 39.3 | 17.2 |

## Education

Lack of a four-year degree doesn't mean one has no postsecondary education or training. In fact, research done for the *Occupational Outlook Handbook* indicates that training other than a bachelor's degree is the most appropriate preparation for some high-paying jobs. In general, workers with more training are more likely to have high earnings. Some high-wage occupations are difficult to enter without training, and within occupations, workers with the most training tend to have the highest paid and supervisory jobs. A 1991 study of job training also found that workers who said they needed some kind of training for their jobs earned substantially more than those who said they didn't.

High-wage earners develop the skills they need in many ways: associate degree programs, college courses, postsecondary vocational schools and technical institutes, apprenticeships or other formal employer training, informal on-the-job training, and Armed Forces experience. Earnings data are not available for all these types of training, but the chart below shows that earnings increase steadily with education.

| Percentage of Workers Without College Degrees Earning $500 or More a Week, by Education, 1993 | | |
|---|---|---|
| Education level | $500 or more | $700 or more |
| Less than high school | 19.4% | 6.8% |
| High school | 37 | 14.5 |
| Some college, no degree | 48.4 | 23.1 |
| Associate degree | 55.6 | 27.8 |

## What's Good Besides Earnings?

As I said above, many people equate high earnings with good jobs. But jobs with relatively low wages in certain areas of the country may be better than the salary indicates because living costs are also likely to be lower. And there is more to work than wages. Other important concerns when evaluating an occupation include the following:

- Benefits
- Projected growth and openings
- Unemployment rate
- Advancement potential
- Nature of the work and working conditions.

Depending on the importance you give each of these factors, a good job might be one with lower than average earnings.

## Benefits

Employee benefits, once a minor addition to wages and salaries, are an increasingly important factor in defining a good job. In 1993, benefits averaged about 29 percent of total compensation costs. Some benefits, such as health and life insurance or subsidized child care, are virtually the same as cash, because they would otherwise have to be paid for out of earnings. Paid holidays and vacation leave improve the recipients' quality of life. Most employers also provide other benefits that add to the quality of a job, such as sick leave. Some employers, like airlines, provide free or subsidized travel, while retailers may provide discounts on merchandise.

## Projected Growth and Openings

The projected growth rate and number of job openings serve to gauge how easy or difficult it will be to find a job in an occupation and, perhaps, also to be promoted. Section 1 of this book provides projections for the jobs described there, and the appendices provide additional growth projections for many other jobs. In some cases, information on competition for jobs is also given. Some high-wage occupations available without a college degree, such as the precision production occupations, are not expected to grow. Others are expected to grow about as fast as the average for all workers, including engineering and science technicians; construction workers; and mechanics, installers, and repairers. Registered nurse and most health technician and technologist occupations are projected to grow much faster than average.

More job openings result from the need to replace workers who transfer to different occupations, retire, or stop working for some other reason than from growth. For example, employment of secretaries is projected to increase by 386,000 jobs by 2005, but net replacement needs are expected to provide more than twice as many openings. Even occupations with little or no projected job growth have some openings. For example, precision production occupations are expected to have 68,000 job openings annually due to net replacement needs.

## Unemployment Rate

Some occupations have high unemployment rates. This does not necessarily disqualify them as high-paying jobs. Those that provide high hourly earnings and unemployment compensation can still yield a high annual income. Furthermore, many workers in these occupations do have steady year-round jobs. High unemployment rates are common in many construction occupations, such as carpenter and electrician, as well as manufacturing jobs, such as assembler and machine operator.

Unemployment rates actually reflect two kinds of unemployment: cyclical and long-term. Recessions and seasonal changes in production create cyclical unemployment in many occupations. During slack periods, workers may face temporary layoffs but can expect to be reemployed when conditions improve. On the other hand, long-term unemployment or even permanent job loss may be caused by restructuring or plant closings. Jobs in organizations or industries with good long-term prospects are obviously more desirable. Even if you lose your job, you are more likely to find another one in such an industry.

## Advancement Potential

Some occupations offer a natural progression of career advancement, such as from electrician apprentice to journey-level electrician to electrician supervisor or contractor. Workers in other occupations may need to carve their own paths to success, following less orthodox routes. Still other occupations or jobs offer few if any chances for advancement.

Often, promotion potential varies from employer to employer. In general, fast-growing occupations and organizations offer better promotion prospects. Large employers offer better prospects, at least without the need to change employers, but small organizations may offer broader responsibilities and opportunities to learn a wider range of skills. In any job, it is important to be ready to act on opportunities as they arise.

## Nature of the Work

For most people, a good job is one that they find interesting, that fully uses their skills, or that satisfies their needs in other ways. Almost everybody appreciates a job in which they can see the results of their work and feel a sense of accomplishment. Others seek a job related to an interest, such as cars, music, or children. Helping others is often the central satisfaction for those in health, teaching, or social work occupations. Satisfying aspects of a job may include analyzing data or information, coordinating events and activities, teaching or mentoring, selling to or persuading others, operating or fixing machinery, or designing or creating new ideas, concepts, or works of art.

Other characteristics that define a good job include the level of physical exertion necessary, cleanliness and safety of the workplace, level of contact with people, ability to decide how work is to be done, and the level of stress. For some, no amount of money is worth the grueling hours and stress that many physicians live with, or the physical exertion, danger, or dirt faced by coal miners and some construction workers, or the boredom of assembly line work. Others find job pressures exciting, don't mind the danger or dirt, or welcome the stress.

For many, working with people they like and respect and having a good supervisor are essential elements of a good job. They may also want an employer whose goals and policies they agree with. Likewise, some workers seek the security of a salaried job with a well-established, stable organization, but others find stimulation in risk taking—running their own business, working for a fledgling organization, or selling on commission.

Where a job is located may also be important. Some people do not want a long commute or a geographic relocation. For them, a good job is one that is available where they live.

Finally, the steady hours that high pay demands may be just the opposite of what a worker wants. Some only want part-time work, due to family responsibilities, school, or other pursuits.

## Will You Be Ready?

Despite the public's perception that the economy is creating mostly lower-skill, low-wage jobs, examination of the data reveals that there are many good jobs for those who do not have a bachelor's degree—not only jobs with high wages but also jobs that are good for other, less tangible reasons.

Any job is a complicated medley of positives and negatives. One factor seldom makes a job good or bad. Get to know all you can about occupations you are considering. It is extremely important to research the entry requirements and other characteristics, so that you will know what to expect out of the job. Above all, remember that it is important to make a career choice that is good for you. The demand for skilled workers will remain strong. Will you be ready?

## Table 1. Occupations of workers with less than a bachelor's degree, 1993

| Occupation[1] | Number (thousands)[2] | Percentage |
|---|---|---|
| Total all workers | 54,095 | 71 |
| Accountants and auditors | 313 | 28 |
| Administrators and officials, public administration | 215 | 42 |
| Assemblers | 845 | 96 |
| Automobile mechanics | 480 | 96 |
| Bus, truck, and stationary engine mechanics | 274 | 98 |
| Carpenters | 606 | 93 |
| Computer operators | 367 | 82 |
| Computer programmers | 197 | 40 |
| Computer system analysts and scientists | 190 | 31 |
| Correctional institution officers | 261 | 91 |
| Designers | 154 | 53 |
| Electrical and electronic engineers | 121 | 26 |
| Electrical and electronic equipment repairers, except telephone | 271 | 87 |
| Electrical and electronic technicians | 212 | 83 |
| Electrical power installers and repairers | 101 | 96 |
| Electricians | 475 | 95 |
| Financial managers | 203 | 42 |
| Fire-fighting occupations | 155 | 90 |
| Health technologists and technicians | 808 | 79 |
| Industrial, mechanical, and all other engineers | 274 | 27 |
| Industrial machinery repairers | 487 | 96 |
| Insurance sales occupations | 200 | 55 |
| Investigators and adjusters, insurance and other | 673 | 75 |
| Machine operators and tenders, except precision | 3,667 | 96 |
| Machinists and precision metalworking occupations | 669 | 96 |
| Mail carriers and postal clerks | 513 | 89 |
| Managers, marketing, advertising, and public relations | 181 | 41 |
| Managers, properties and real estate | 201 | 65 |
| Managers, food service and lodging establishments | 469 | 78 |
| Managers and administrators not elsewhere classified | 2,065 | 57 |
| Other financial officers | 249 | 43 |
| Personnel, training, and labor relations specialists | 164 | 47 |
| Plumbers, pipefitters, and steamfitters | 287 | 96 |
| Police and detectives | 353 | 75 |
| Purchasing agents and buyers | 260 | 66 |
| Rail transportation occupations | 95 | 94 |
| Real estate sales occupations | 168 | 54 |
| Registered nurses | 656 | 51 |
| Sales occupations, other business services | 190 | 53 |
| Sales representatives, mining and manufacturing and wholesale | 635 | 56 |
| Science and engineering technicians | 287 | 75 |
| Secretaries | 2,326 | 90 |
| Stationary engineers and other plant and system operators | 230 | 91 |
| Supervisors, police and fire fighting | 92 | 71 |
| Supervisors, mechanics and repairers | 181 | 89 |
| Supervisors, construction occupations | 419 | 88 |
| Supervisors, production occupations | 1,010 | 87 |
| Supervisors, administrative support occupations | 519 | 73 |
| Supervisors and proprietors, sales occupations | 1,658 | 72 |
| Telephone and telephone line installers and repairers | 211 | 95 |
| Truck drivers | 2,000 | 96 |
| Welders and cutters | 438 | 98 |
| All other occupations | 26,021 | 70 |

[1]Includes only occupations with at least 50,000 workers with less than a bachelor's degree whose usual weekly earnings are $700 or more.
[2]Employed wage and salary workers.
**Source:** Current Population Survey.

## Table 2. Workers with less than a bachelor's degree and usual weekly earnings of $700 or more, by occupation, 1993

| Occupation[1] | Number (thousands)[3] | Percentage |
|---|---|---|
| Total | 9,269 | 17 |
| Electrical and electronic engineers[2] | 81 | 67 |
| Industrial, mechanical, and all other engineers[2] | 165 | 60 |
| Rail transportation occupations | 56 | 59 |
| Computer system analysts and scientists[2] | 108 | 56 |
| Supervisors, police and fire fighting | 50 | 54 |
| Electrical power installers and repairers | 55 | 54 |
| Computer programmers | 107 | 54 |
| Managers, marketing, advertising, and public relations[2] | 91 | 50 |
| Supervisors, mechanics and repairers | 81 | 45 |
| Fire-fighting occupations | 69 | 44 |
| Telephone and telephone line installers and repairers | 92 | 44 |
| Financial managers[2] | 87 | 43 |
| Managers and administrators not elsewhere classified | 874 | 42 |
| Supervisors, construction occupations | 177 | 42 |
| Registered nurses | 269 | 41 |
| Real estate sales occupations | 65 | 39 |
| Police and detectives | 135 | 38 |
| Electrical and electronic technicians | 75 | 35 |
| Designers | 52 | 34 |
| Sales representatives, mining and manufacturing and wholesale | 212 | 33 |
| Stationary engineers and other plant and system operators | 75 | 33 |
| Supervisors, production occupations | 326 | 32 |
| Sales occupations, other business services | 61 | 32 |
| Personnel, training, and labor relations specialists[2] | 52 | 32 |
| Other financial officers | 79 | 32 |
| Electricians | 149 | 31 |
| Administrators and officials, public administration | 66 | 30 |
| Electrical and electronic equipment repairers, except telephone | 82 | 30 |
| Plumbers, pipefitters, and steamfitters | 78 | 27 |
| Insurance sales occupations | 52 | 26 |
| Supervisors, administrative support occupations | 134 | 26 |
| Managers, properties and real estate[2] | 51 | 25 |
| Machinists and precision metalworking occupations | 165 | 25 |
| Science and engineering technicians | 69 | 24 |
| Industrial machinery repairers | 116 | 24 |
| Supervisors and proprietors, sales occupations | 378 | 23 |
| Accountants and auditors[2] | 68 | 22 |
| Mail carriers and postal clerks | 109 | 21 |
| Purchasing agents and buyers | 51 | 20 |
| Bus, truck, and stationary engine mechanics | 53 | 19 |
| Truck drivers | 382 | 19 |
| Correctional institution officers | 50 | 19 |
| Managers, food service and lodging establishments | 83 | 18 |
| Carpenters | 107 | 18 |
| Automobile mechanics | 81 | 17 |
| Welders and cutters | 64 | 15 |
| Computer operators | 50 | 14 |
| Health technologists and technicians | 106 | 13 |
| Assemblers | 96 | 11 |
| Investigators and adjusters, insurance and other | 73 | 11 |
| Machine operators and tenders, except precision | 255 | 7 |
| Secretaries | 117 | 5 |
| All other occupations | 2,687 | 10 |

[1]Includes only occupations with at least 50,000 workers with less than a bachelor's degree.

[2]A bachelor's degree is usually required for entry. Those without a degree may have entered the occupation when requirements were lower or may be in the limited number of positions that do not require a degree.

[3]Employed wage and salary workers.

**Source:** Current Population Survey.

# Manufacturing: It's Still the Industrial Age

## By Mark Mittelhauser

You may find this hard to believe, but manufacturing in the United States is not dead. True, the images of decline come readily to mind. Dilapidated steel mills in Pennsylvania, closed auto plants in Michigan, abandoned apparel factories in North Carolina. These powerful images represent a harsh reality for many workers, but they give an inaccurate picture of U.S. manufacturing. In terms of production, efficiency, and competitiveness, U.S. manufacturing is holding its own. It currently accounts for 30 percent of the nation's total output of goods and services, only slightly less than its share three decades ago (see chart 1). And in coming years, it will remain one of the most dynamic sectors in the economy.

Why do so many people think manufacturing is in such bad shape? Undoubtedly, because manufacturing employment has declined. It lost 3 million jobs (14 percent) between 1979 and 1992. Another 400,000 jobs are projected to disappear by 2005. But it still provides employment for more than 18 million workers, one of every seven workers in the economy. Furthermore, some parts of the manufacturing sector are thriving.

The size and complexity of the manufacturing sector may obscure the good health of some of its industries. It is difficult to take into account the many different trends affecting manufacturing because it encompasses such a wide variety of industries and jobs. For example, newspapers are part of the manufacturing sector and so, therefore, are most reporters. So are more than 280,000 secretaries.

The different industries and occupations in manufacturing are often affected by economic change in contradictory ways. Expanding trade is a boon for some manufacturing industries while it threatens the very existence of others. Similarly, technology is fostering the growth of certain occupations while ushering in the demise of others.

## Major Factors Affecting Manufacturing Employment

Manufacturing employment in coming years will be affected by three major forces:

- Changes in domestic demand
- Increased international trade
- Improved productivity

### The Domestic Market

The health and direction of American manufacturing is still largely determined by consumer demand for goods in the United States. Personal consumption expenditures—what people pay for the goods and services they buy—account for more than 60 percent of the gross domestic product (GDP) and are expected to grow between 1992 and 2005. As the population ages, this consumption will increasingly be directed toward medical supplies and health care products. Demand for housing and household fixtures will also be strong. Purchases by businesses of durable capital equipment, like machine tools, will also be an abiding source of manufacturing jobs in coming years.

In contrast to recent years, however, American manufacturers will not be able to count on strong demand generated by government spending for national defense. The end of the Cold War

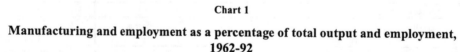

**Chart 1**

**Manufacturing and employment as a percentage of total output and employment, 1962-92**

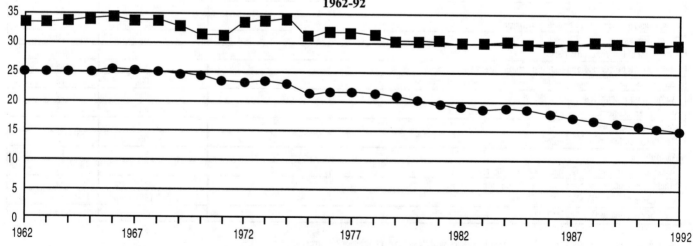

**Chart 2**

**The relationship between output and employment in manufacturing,
1979-92 and projected 1993-2005**

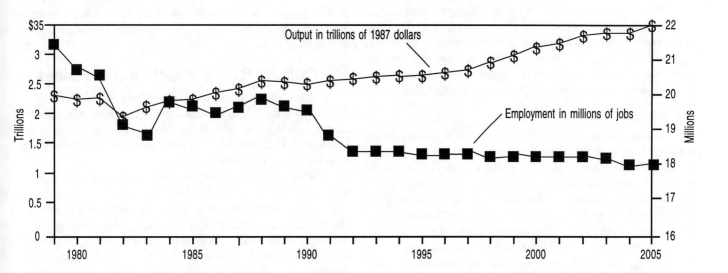

and corresponding reductions in defense outlays have meant lost jobs for many workers in the manufacturing sector. Although defense spending was a relatively small part of GDP, reductions have had effects throughout the economy, especially in manufacturing industries like shipbuilding, aircraft, ammunition and ordnance, and guided missiles and space vehicles.

## International Trade

Increasing international trade has been a growing source of demand, as well as anxiety, for U.S. producers in recent years. Manufactured goods accounted for about 80 percent of U.S. merchandise trade in 1990, and this share is projected to grow as more nations develop their manufacturing sectors. Major U.S. trading partners include Canada, Mexico, Japan, the United Kingdom, and Germany. In recent years, trade has grown rapidly with Asian nations, especially the newly industrializing economies of Singapore, Hong Kong, South Korea, and Taiwan.

Growing international trade has been made possible by technological advances in transportation, communications, and production. Moreover, the increasing international mobility of capital, technology, and labor has been promoted by a more open trading environment fashioned by agreements like the General Agreement on Tariffs and Trade (GATT) and the North American Free Trade Agreement (NAFTA). Although passage of these agreements has often been accompanied by heated debate, they have been ratified largely because most nations see growing, open trade as serving their interests. For example, tennis shoes can be produced at lower cost in nations with relatively low-skilled, low-wage workers. On the other hand, devices like semiconductors require more highly skilled workers to fabricate, and so are more efficiently produced in nations with an educated workforce. When nations trade tennis shoes and semiconductors, each has access to lower-priced products than if the same products were produced at home. In this way, consumers are able to purchase lower-priced products, and resources are used more efficiently.

Consumers are not the only people affected by growing trade, though. Trade obviously has an important impact on producers as well. When U.S. consumers buy more television sets from abroad, workers in the United States may lose their jobs due to the increased competition. On the other hand, when European countries buy more U.S. computers, chances are that more American workers will be employed to produce them. This is why foreign economic conditions increasingly influence employment in this country. The recent recessions in Japan and Europe have hampered U.S. export growth in spite of the stronger competitiveness of American-made products.

Purchasing and investment decisions by firms also play a large part in determining manufacturing employment in the United States. Just like consumers, firms have a variety of suppliers to choose from. Firms that make plastic products such as mugs or Frisbees, for example, can buy their machine tools at home or abroad. U.S. manufacturing jobs increasingly rely on these decisions.

Another important question is site location. When U.S. firms locate production centers in other countries, it detracts from U.S. manufacturing employment. Likewise, when foreign companies manufacture goods in the United States, it adds to manufacturing employment.

In these ways, the international economy is becoming more interconnected at every level and, with it, trade is becoming a more powerful influence. Growth in trade, however, has not been without its problems. It does not make everyone better off. Prices are lowered on some products and overall employment may even rise, but some workers lose their jobs. They may remain unemployed for long periods, be hired at a lower wage in their next position, or face retirement with a smaller pension than expected. The fear of a continuing decline in manufacturing employment was highlighted during the fierce debate over NAFTA. The intensity of this debate was a telling indicator of the major role trade has come to play in the U.S. economy and the lives of American workers.

Clearly, international trade means different things to different workers. To an auto worker or a sewing machine operator, it has mostly posed a threat. To some machine tool and computer fabricators, however, it has presented an opportunity. Between 1992 and 2005, exports of American-made goods are projected to grow more rapidly than imports. In this environment, manufacturing firms may be able to take advantage of an increasing number of export opportunities to create jobs, but they must still compete with imports in the U.S. market. The future of American manufacturing depends on the ability of its firms to do both simultaneously.

## Productivity

A major factor in determining whether U.S. manufacturers will grow is their ability to increase productivity. Simply defined, labor productivity is a worker's output in a given period. For example, say bagel bakers each produce 320 bagels during an eight-hour day. Their productivity is 40 bagels per hour. Now suppose that a new oven can bake more bagels at a time. This new oven could raise productivity to 50 bagels per hour. Part of this increase in revenue may go to increase wages, another part to pay for the new oven, and the rest to increase the company's profits. In this way, productivity gains can be the basis for a higher standard of living in a community.

Purchasing capital equipment like the new oven is the most common way of improving worker productivity in manufacturing. The increasing use of computer-controlled machine tools and office machines has paid off in productivity gains. Worker productivity can also be augmented through training and education. A well-trained worker is more flexible and capable of fulfilling a number of roles for a company as it adapts to changing market conditions. Reorganizing workplaces can also save time and prevent wasted effort.

Productivity increases are vital to economic growth, but they frequently have another effect. Suppose that our bagel baker is 1 of 10 bakers in the company. Using the new oven, the bakers produce many more bagels in the same amount of time. But what if the townspeople do not want to buy more bagels? Or worse still, what if they have given up on their diets and are now eating doughnuts instead of bagels? Fewer bakers will be needed. One baker is then laid off, and 9 bakers do the work that used to require 10. The company then pays less in total wages and can lower the price of a dozen bagels in order to keep its customers. Everyone is better off, except the laid-off bagel baker, who must now find a new job, and the other bagel maker in town, who might now have to take a smaller profit to meet the new competition or be put out of business. So productivity gains are a mixed blessing for workers and companies, improving wages or profits for some while displacing others.

Because productivity has risen faster in manufacturing than in the economy as a whole, its effects in this sector have been especially significant. Chart 2 shows the relationship between rising output and declining employment in the sector. Over the 1992-2005 period, manufacturing output is projected to increase 2.4 percent annually, while total manufacturing jobs decline an average of 0.2 percent every year. This trend is especially dramatic in the computer equipment industry, which is expected to increase output 8.1 percent annually and see a 3 percent decline in employment.

Some economists interpret declining employment and increasing output as a sign of a sector's strength and growing competitiveness. Although productivity growth by itself is often associated with job loss, the increasing role of international competition may be one reason that recent evidence finds industries with higher productivity growth to have among the highest rates of net job growth.

## The Outlook for Manufacturing Industries

To understand the future of manufacturing employment in the United States, all of the above factors are important. Fundamentally, though, jobs follow the demand for goods made in the United States because increased demand stimulates output, which may require increased employment.

While there will be a wide variety of industries experiencing rapid growth (as shown in Table 1), many of the major ones tend to be driven by the same trends in consumption. For example, demand for information technology will drive growth in the output of computer equipment, semiconductors, broadcasting and communications equipment, and miscellaneous electronic equipment. The increasing demand for health care products and medical testing equipment associated with the needs of an aging population will generate growth in industries that produce medical instruments and supplies, x-ray and other electromedical apparatus, and measuring and controlling devices. Also notable is increasing demand for commercial and leisure vehicles. Industries affected by the increasing demand are boat building and repairing; truck and bus bodies, trailers, and motor homes; aircraft and missile parts and equipment; and railroad equipment.

| Table 1. Manufacturing Industries Projected to Have the Fastest Annual Output Growth, 1992-2005 | |
|---|---|
| **Industry** | **Annual percentage change** |
| Railroad equipment | 3.4% |
| Miscellaneous electronic components | 3.5 |
| Measuring and controlling devices, watches | 3.7 |
| X-ray and other electromedical apparatus | 3.7 |
| Miscellaneous chemical products | 3.9 |
| Miscellaneous publishing | 3.9 |
| Metal services n.e.c. | 4.1 |
| Miscellaneous plastic products n.e.c. | 4.2 |
| Aircraft and missile parts and equipment n.e.c. | 4.2 |
| Broadcasting and communications equipment | 4.4 |
| Truck and bus bodies, trailers, and motor homes | 4.8 |
| Semiconductors and related devices | 5.6 |
| Boat building and repairing | 5.9 |
| Medical instruments and supplies | 6.1 |
| Computer equipment | 8.1 |

n.e.c. = not elsewhere classified

Several of the growing industries supply intermediate goods to other firms rather than to individual consumers. This helps explain the rapid growth in miscellaneous plastics products, not elsewhere classified (n.e.c.). Over 95 percent of this industry's output is purchased by hospitals, construction firms, and manufacturers of electronics, computer and telephone equipment, and motor vehicles. Metal services, n.e.c., also sells nearly all of its output to other firms. Workers in this industry are responsible for coloring, finishing, enameling, varnishing, and performing similar services on metal products like motor vehicle parts, electronic components, and communication equipment.

As you saw with productivity, however, output growth does not always translate into employment growth. Table 2, which lists the manufacturing industries whose employment is projected to grow the fastest, clearly shows this. Interestingly, some of the leading industries in output growth are not included. The most noticeable absences are the computer equipment and semiconductor and related devices industries. Output gains in these industries are expected to be realized with significantly fewer workers. Some of the fast-growing industries, like railroad equipment and boat building and repairing, are rather small, so their rapid growth may produce relatively few jobs.

### Table 2. Manufacturing Industries with the Fastest Growing Projected Annual Employment Growth, 1992-2005

| Industry | Annual percentage change |
|---|---|
| Periodicals | 1.3 |
| Partitions and fixtures | 1.4 |
| Industrial machinery n.e.c. | 1.5 |
| X-ray and other electromedical apparatus | 1.5 |
| Miscellaneous chemical products | 1.5 |
| Metal services n.e.c. | 1.7 |
| Books | 1.7 |
| Boat building and repairing | 2 |
| Millwork and structural wood members n.e.c. | 2.2 |
| Miscellaneous plastic products n.e.c. | 2.4 |
| Truck and bus bodies, trailers, and motor homes | 2.4 |
| Medical equipment and supplies | 2.4 |
| Railroad equipment | 2.5 |
| Miscellaneous publishing | 3 |
| Aircraft missile parts and equipment n.e.c. | 3.2 |

n.e.c. = nmot elsewhere classified

Actual job growth is concentrated in a small number of industries. In fact, the 15 industries listed in Table 3 account for over three-quarters of all manufacturing jobs that are expected to be created during the 1992-2005 period. Some of these industries are large, though relatively slow-growing, such as metalworking machinery. Others are smaller but fast-growing, such as truck and bus bodies, trailers, and motor homes. The list primarily includes heavy industries—which require many workers to operate machines and move materials—and printing and publishing industries. These latter industries employ not only workers to print materials but also a substantial number of writers, sales people, and delivery workers.

### Table 3. Manufacturing Industries Projected to Generate the Most Job Growth, 1992-2005

| Industry | Number of jobs (in thousands) |
|---|---|
| Metal services n.e.c. | 27 |
| Books | 28 |
| Truck and bus bodies, trailers, and motor homes | 28 |
| Metalworking machinery | 29 |
| Converted paper products, except containers | 37 |
| Miscellaneous publishing | 37 |
| Drugs | 41 |
| Millwork and structural wood members n.e.c. | 60 |
| Industrial machinery | 61 |
| Newspapers | 61 |
| Meat products | 62 |
| Commercial printing and business forms | 78 |
| Medical instruments and supplies | 79 |
| Aircraft and missile parts and equipment n.e.c. | 85 |
| Miscellaneous plastic products n.e.c. | 224 |

n.e.c. = not elsewhere classified

The largest job producer in manufacturing is projected to be miscellaneous plastics products n.e.c. Growing demand for plastic products coupled with a projected slowdown in productivity growth will mean about 225,000 new jobs over the 1992-2005 period. The four printing and publishing industries taken together will generate roughly the same number as miscellaneous plastics in these years, but these jobs will differ markedly. Production workers will be the main beneficiaries of growth in plastics, as it produces a number of machine operator, assembly, packing, and blue-collar supervisory positions. In contrast, new jobs in printing and publishing will be distributed more widely among occupations requiring different levels of education, as jobs will be created in professional service occupations—such as reporter and writer—as well as in production positions, like press operator. As these examples show, manufacturing will generate jobs for a variety of different workers, indicating the dynamism and diversity of the sector.

## The Outlook for Occupations in Manufacturing

In each growing manufacturing industry, there are numerous occupations with a bright outlook. In fact, some occupations are even projected to grow in declining industries. Table 4 presents many of the occupations in manufacturing that are projected to grow most rapidly over the 1992-2005 period.

| Table 4. Fast-Growing Occupations in Manufacturing, 1992-2005, Projected | |
|---|---|
| Occupation | Percentage employment growth |
| Personnel, training, and labor relations specialists | 26.3 |
| Paper goods machine setters and set-up operators | 26.3 |
| All other precision workers | 26.7 |
| Reporters and correspondents | 26.9 |
| Operations research analysts | 28.4 |
| All other professional workers | 29.2 |
| Wood machinists | 29.4 |
| All other printing, binding, and related workers | 30.3 |
| Biological scientists | 31 |
| Meat, poultry, and fish cutters and trimmers, hand | 32.9 |
| Advertising clerks | 34.3 |
| Screen printing machine setters and set-up operators | 36.7 |
| Cabinetmakers and bench carpenters | 37 |
| Offset lithographic press operators | 40.3 |
| Computer engineers and scientists | 41.8 |
| Medical scientists | 47.5 |
| All other printing press setters and set-up operators | 51.1 |
| Systems analysts | 65.1 |
| Electronic pagination system workers | 77.9 |
| All other printing workers, precision | 92.3 |

Not surprisingly, Table 4 closely reflects growth in manufacturing industries. Five of the 10 fastest-growing occupations are concentrated in printing and publishing. Other occupations that are being propelled by their concentration in a certain industry are cabinetmaker and bench carpenter, wood machinist, and all other precision woodworker occupations, which are concentrated in woodworking industries, as well as meat, poultry, and fish cutters and trimmers, which are growing along with the meat products industry.

Some occupations, however, are widely distributed throughout the manufacturing sector or the economy as a whole. These occupations are projected to grow because they are closely connected to new technologies or organizational trends. For example, systems analysts and computer engineers and scientists are growing in nearly every sector because of the increasing importance and sophistication of computers in today's workplaces. Also, increasing international competition is leading many American firms to rethink their production techniques and management practices. Assisting these firms are operations research specialists and management analysts. This rethinking has led, in turn, to an emphasis on flexible production techniques, which require workers who are more broadly skilled. The expected strong growth for combination machine tool setters and operators is in many ways a result of the demand for greater flexibility.

As with the growth of industries, both the rate of growth and the absolute growth are important. Chart 3 lists the occupations expected to generate the most jobs in manufacturing between 1992 and 2005. Some occupations listed in both charts are particularly promising. These include systems analysts, computer engineers and scientists, offset lithographic press operators, cabinetmakers and bench carpenters, and meat, poultry, and fish cutters and trimmers.

The occupations providing the most new jobs include possibilities for job seekers at every level of educational attainment. Those right out of high school can be employed as meat cutters, hand workers, helpers and laborers, and truck drivers. Occupations that generally require an apprenticeship or some postsecondary education include offset lithographic press operator, combination machine tool setter and operator, numerical control machine tool operator, and cabinetmaker and bench carpenter. Still others require at least a four-year degree. At this education level, there will be especially strong demand for job seekers with

**Chart 3**

**Occupations in manufacturing adding the most jobs, 1992-2005 projected**

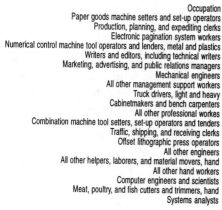
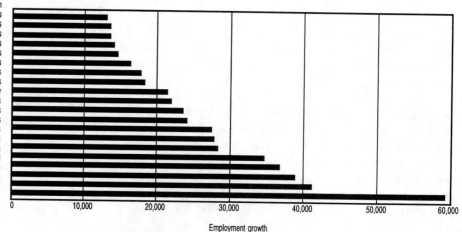

Employment growth

backgrounds in mathematics, science, computer science, and engineering. These workers will be needed to help organize production and conduct research for tomorrow's manufacturing firms.

There is clearly something for everyone in the manufacturing sector, but all jobs are not created equal. In manufacturing, as in other sectors, earnings and job security tend to mirror educational attainment levels. As you receive more education and training, you will, on average, have a higher income and a smaller risk of unemployment. Sometimes these differences can be substantial. But remember that these figures represent averages. There are many good, financially rewarding jobs in the manufacturing sector for workers without college degrees. Moreover, a variety of job qualities not linked to pay attracts people to certain occupations and determines their job satisfaction. Still, now more than ever, your job security and earnings will be affected by the skills you possess and your ability to acquire new ones.

## The Trend Toward Using Temporary Workers

Recently, the employment of substitute and temporary workers has risen sharply. Driving this trend is an increasing need for firms to become more flexible and cut costs to remain competitive. Firms have found it less expensive in many cases to hire contractors to perform tasks that were formerly carried out by their employees. The trend has affected every industry, including manufacturing. For example, custodians who used to work for a manufacturing firm are now employed by a cleaning service company. They work in the same building performing the same tasks, but because they now receive their paychecks from a service company, they are counted as part of the service sector rather than as workers in manufacturing. Other examples of this phenomenon can be found in cafeteria services, data processing, engineering, accounting, maintenance, and administrative support.

It is not clear to what degree this trend is affecting manufacturing employment, but it appears, on the whole, to be reducing the number of workers classified in this sector. These shifts affect job hunters because hiring practices, employment, and earnings in manufacturing are all changed by them. You may need to look for a "manufacturing" job at the temporary employment service rather than at the factory. And you may have to accept a lower wage, fewer benefits, and less job security than manufacturing employment once offered.

So although overall employment in manufacturing is projected to decline, the vital role this sector plays in the economy will not. It will contribute to rising productivity, lead in high-tech research and development, and provide the basis for many jobs in other sectors. Manufacturing is facing unprecedented levels of competition from abroad, and to meet these challenges it will need to be even more dynamic. As this article has demonstrated, some industries are doing just that. If they continue to thrive, the vivid images of job destruction in the steel mills of Pennsylvania and auto plants of Michigan will be replaced by the quieter job creation in the plastics firms, medical instrument plants, and publishing houses of tomorrow.

# College, No; Training, Yes: A Guide for High School Graduates

## By Rachel Moskowitz

High school diploma in hand, you want a good-paying job without going to college. What are your choices? You could go fight to work in an occupation that does not require any training. Or you could take some additional training either from an employer or at a school. What's the difference? More than $150 a week, on average. That's how much more money high school graduates make when they have jobs that require training compared to when they have jobs that don't (see Table 1). Training that takes less time and costs less than four years of college can prepare you for a better paying, more highly skilled job with advancement opportunities.

Most jobs require some form of qualifying training, which provides the skills and knowledge people need to begin working. In 1991, more than 21 million employed high school graduates, or 46 percent of the total, said they needed specific training to obtain their current job, according to the Current Population Survey for January of that year. They got this training in many different ways, such as the following:

- Postsecondary school courses
- Formal and informal on-the-job training, including the Armed Forces
- Other sources of training, such as informal training from a friend or relative

Often, the different kinds of training are associated with specific occupations.

## Postsecondary School Courses

Several different kinds of schools offer training to prepare high school graduates for specific occupations. These include postsecondary vocational programs, junior or community colleges, and technical institutes. See the accompanying box, "What to Look For in a Vocational or Technical Program," for some pointers on choosing a program that's right for you.

### Postsecondary Vocational Programs

These programs are designed to teach a specialized skill or trade in a relatively short period of time. They stress hands-on training. Programs are flexible, offering both day and evening classes, and range from several months to a couple of years. Good programs use modern, state-of-the-art equipment, employ qualified instructors who have related work experience, and provide job placement assistance. Postsecondary vocational programs do not award degrees or college credit upon completion.

The cost of attending a postsecondary vocational program varies widely, depending on the occupation, length of the program, and type of institution. Private, for-profit institutions generally are more expensive than public institutions, which receive government assistance. Students at accredited private or public

postsecondary vocational programs may qualify for federal or state financial aid.

In 1991, hairdresser and cosmetologist, registered nurse, nursing aide, orderly, licensed practical nurse, bookkeeper, accounting clerk, and barber were among the occupations in which many workers said they needed post-high school vocational training in order to qualify for their jobs.

| Table 1. Median Weekly Earnings of Full-Time Workers Who are High School Graduates and Need Qualifying Training for Their Jobs Compared with Those Who Did Not, 1991 | Training needed | No training needed |
|---|---|---|
| All workers | $491 | $322 |
| Professional specialty | 581 | 390 |
| Precision production, craft, and repair | 551 | 428 |
| Transportation and material moving | 540 | 365 |
| Executive, administrative, and managerial | 533 | 437 |
| Technicians and related support | 511 | 495 |
| Machine operators, assemblers, and inspectors | 502 | 311 |
| Sales | 497 | 280 |
| Farming, forestry, and fishing | 470 | 251 |
| Service, except private household | 465 | 250 |
| Handlers, equipment cleaners, helpers, and laborers | 398 | 311 |
| Administrative support, including clerical | 375 | 340 |

## Junior and Community Colleges and Technical Institutes

In addition to awarding associate degrees and offering courses that transfer with credit to other colleges and universities, junior and community colleges also offer a wide variety of technical and vocational training programs. Technical institutes award an associate degree or a certificate of completion to graduates of their programs, which range from one to three years in length. Similar to technical programs in junior and community colleges, technical institute programs are designed to teach students marketable skills.

Junior and community colleges offer a wide variety of technical programs, such as accounting, advertising, tourism, and zoology. Graduates are awarded a general degree, such as associate in applied science (AAS) or associate in occupational studies (AOS), or an occupation-specific degree, such as associate of science in business (ASB).

Technical institutes teach many of the same subjects as postsecondary vocational programs, but training is more intense and advanced mathematics and science courses may be included in the curriculum. Graduates of technical institutes may be qualified for more responsible jobs than graduates of postsecondary vocational programs.

Technical institutes often have contacts in various fields that may lead to job opportunities for their graduates. Many businesses donate equipment and supplies and take a personal interest in students, who are prospective employees. Like some four-year colleges, technical institutes may offer co-op programs that give students an opportunity for additional hands-on training and provide exposure to on-the-job situations that may not occur in a classroom setting. Co-op students alternate periods of work and study. Some students who successfully complete these programs are hired by the company upon graduation.

Junior and community colleges and technical institutes offer many advantages for some students. The schools generally practice a liberal admissions policy and offer day and evening classes. Convenient locations mean an easy commute to classes, which keeps living expenses down. Tuition is relatively inexpensive but can vary, depending on the length of the program and the type of equipment used. For example, programs in aircraft mechanics and maintenance and computer-aided drafting are likely to cost more than programs in accounting, and two-year programs cost more than those that last only one year.

Among the occupations in which many workers said that junior college or technical institutes were important sources of training were registered nurse, licensed practical nurse, hairdresser and cosmetologist, real estate sales, computer programmer, drafter, and designer.

## Correspondence Courses

All types of schools offer correspondence courses. They allow people to study independently in their own homes. Subjects range from English and basic mathematics to electronics and automotive engine repair. Students take the courses through the mail or by means of specially designed computer software that links students to instructors. Using a computer, a telephone, and a modem, students "attend" lectures, take tests, and submit homework. Some schools offer such courses at off-campus sites, where students have use of the necessary computers, videotapes, and two-way television broadcasts. Correspondence courses often use television to broadcast lectures. Students taking such courses also study print material and may communicate with instructors and other students by telephone.

Correspondence courses were an important source of training for insurance sales workers, electronic equipment repairers, industrial machinery repairers, electrical and electronic technicians, securities and financial services sales workers, and aircraft engine mechanics, according to the 1991 survey.

## On-the-Job Training

Almost all employers provide new workers with some kind of training, even if it is just a quick introduction to the office's equipment and procedures. In many cases, however, the training is more extensive, especially in the Armed Forces. Training that is given from time to time as the worker needs to learn a new task is called informal on-the-job training. Janitors and cleaners, fast-food cooks, stock clerks, and waiters and waitresses, to name a few, generally learn their jobs this way. Formal company training is much more structured.

## Formal Company Training

Any structured classroom or on-the-job training held during the workday is formal company training. It is always paid for by the employer. It is often taught by a supervisor or a trainer the firm employs for just this purpose; in other cases, companies pay for courses held outside of work. Electricians, insurance sales workers, police officers and detectives, insurance adjusters, and securities and financial services sales workers were among those who said that formal company training was an important source of qualifying training for their positions in 1991.

One of the best-known and most beneficial forms of formal company training is the apprenticeship. An apprentice is paid by the company and follows a specified course of on-the-job and classroom training. Often, the apprenticeship is managed by a union. By the end of the apprenticeship, which often lasts about four years, the worker reaches journey worker status. Apprenticeships are most common in the construction trades, such as carpenter, plumber, and electrician; but they are also offered to laboratory technicians, horse trainers, and a wide range of other occupations.

Competition for apprenticeships is often fierce. The availability of apprenticeships in any area depends on economic conditions, the willingness of employers to train employees as skilled craft workers, and new technology.

At least one employer provides formal training for everyone it hires: the Armed Forces. The first responsibility of military personnel is to defend the United States. But since the defense of our nation is so encompassing, there are a wide variety of jobs available. All branches of the uniformed services—Army, Navy, Air Force, and Coast Guard—offer education and career training.

All new members of the Armed Forces receive basic training to prepare them for military life. Most then go on to advanced training for specific occupations. Although many of these occupations, such as infantryman, exist only in the military, most have a civilian counterpart, such as electronics specialist or pilot. The job training may also count toward academic credit in a civilian college. Occupations for which Armed Forces training is important, according to the 1991 survey, include electrician, police officer and detective, aircraft engine mechanic, electrical and electronic engineer, airplane pilot and navigator, electronic repairer, telephone installer and repairer, and data processing equipment repairer.

## Other Sources of Training

Besides receiving training from schools and employers, people learn job skills in many other ways, such as from friends and relatives. Private lessons can also be important, as is the case with musicians. Other sources of training include conventions, seminars, conferences, trade shows, and workshops —often sponsored by various associations, societies, or unions.

One or another of these sources of training is important in a great variety of occupations, such as actor, athlete, barber, bookkeeper and accounting clerk, camera instrument repairer, computer science teacher, farmer, hairdresser and cosmetologist, heavy truck driver, pattern maker, real estate sales worker, and secretary.

## What to Look for in a Vocational or Technical Program

When investigating postsecondary technical programs and schools, there are several things you'll want to look into:

- Accreditation
- State license
- Certification
- Tuition policy
- Job placement
- The campus and faculty

Accreditation may be very important. Accreditation certifies that the school and its programs offer high-quality training. Some employers, especially those in technical fields such as computers or electronics, will only hire graduates of accredited institutions. And only students enrolled in an accredited institution or program usually qualify for government financial aid.

Schools and programs are accredited by agencies recognized by the U.S. Department of Education. Accreditation may be awarded through a regional accrediting commission or through a national association such as the Commission on Recognition of Postsecondary Accreditation. Specialized programs, such as dietetics, interior design, and auto repair, are accredited by their professional trade organizations. A list of recognized accrediting agencies is available from the U.S. Department of Education, Accreditation and State Liaison Division, Room 3036, 400 Maryland Ave. SW, Washington, DC 20202.

In order to operate, many states require that schools be licensed; to verify if a school is licensed, contact the Department of Education in your state.

If you are interested in a career that requires a state certificate to practice, such as real estate or cosmetology, verify that you will be prepared for the state examination upon graduation. Find out the proportion of students who pass the examination. You should also inquire about the student dropout rate and instructor turnover. A high dropout rate may mean student dissatisfaction and inadequate education, and high instructor turnover may signify problems within the school's programs and administration.

Make sure the school's tuition and refund policy are in writing. Find out if tuition is refundable, in full or in part, if an unexpected emergency occurs or if your career plans change.

Find out about the job placement services provided. Quality schools generally offer these services, which can be helpful in finding your first job. A competent and successful job placement service will help you write your resume, strengthen your interview skills, and host employer visits and interviews. Ask what proportion of students find jobs upon graduation—a high placement rate is a good sign. Before applying to a school, you should also tour the school and attend some classes. Talk to students already enrolled and meet the teachers and instructors.

## Introduction

As you know, most jobs have requirements for certain levels of education, training, previous experience, or some combination of these. If you do not have a college degree, for example, many jobs are not available to you—or at least are more difficult to obtain.

The chart that follows organizes 513 occupations into groups based on the level of education, training, or experience typically needed to qualify for them. If you are looking for a job or want to change careers based on your current level of experience and education or training, this chart can help you identify other potential options. It is also helpful if you are considering getting additional training or education.

This system of organizing jobs at various levels is a new one developed after considerable research by the U.S. Department of Labor. It organizes jobs into these 11 groupings:

- **First professional degree:** Requires at least two years of full-time academic study beyond the bachelor's degree.

- **Doctoral degree:** Requires two to three years of full-time academic study beyond the bachelor's degree.

- **Master's degree:** Requires one or two years of full-time study beyond the bachelor's degree.

- **Work experience plus a bachelor's degree or higher degree:** Requires at least a bachelor's degree and some work experience.

- **Bachelor's degree:** Requires four but not more than five years of full-time academic study beyond high school.

- **Associate degree:** Requires at least two years of full-time study beyond high school.

- **Postsecondary vocational training:** Work-related vocational training programs or job-related college courses that do not result in a degree.

- **Work experience in a related occupation:** Requires work experience in another occupation in order to become qualified.

- **Long-term on-the-job training:** Requires more than 12 months of on-the-job training or combined work experiences and classroom instruction before achieving average performance.

- **Moderate-length on-the-job training:** Requires 1 to 12 months of combined on-the-job experience and informal training.

- **Short-term on-the-job training:** Requires from a few days to several weeks of working with and observing experienced employees and asking questions.

In reviewing the chart, keep in mind that there is more than one way to qualify for most occupations. For example, registered nurses may obtain their training in a bachelor's degree program or in a hospital diploma program, although most are trained in associate degree programs. The chart reflects the typical conditions in that occupation and the preferences of most employers.

## Occupational employment by education or training category

| Occupation | 1994 employment (thousands) | Occupation | 1994 employment (thousands) |
|---|---|---|---|
| **Total, all occupations** | **127,017** | Government chief executives and legislators | 91 |
| | | Judges, magistrates, and other judicial workers | 79 |
| **First professional degree** | **1,702** | Farm managers | 51 |
| Lawyers | 656 | | |
| Physicians | 539 | **Bachelor's degree** | **14,011** |
| Clergy | 195 | Teachers, elementary school | 1,419 |
| Dentists | 164 | Teachers, secondary school | 1,340 |
| Veterinarians and veterinary inspectors | 56 | Accountants and auditors | 962 |
| Chiropractors | 42 | All other management support workers | 940 |
| Optometrists | 37 | All other professional workers | 822 |
| Podiatrists | 13 | Social workers | 557 |
| | | Computer programmers | 537 |
| **Doctoral degree** | **976** | Systems analysts | 483 |
| College and university faculty | 823 | Teachers, preschool and kindergarten | 462 |
| Biological scientists | 82 | Teachers, special education | 388 |
| Medical scientists | 36 | Electrical and electronics engineers | 349 |
| Physicists and astronomers | 20 | Personnel, training, and labor relations specialists | 307 |
| Mathematicians and all other mathematical scientists | 14 | All other engineers | 292 |
| All other life scientists | 1 | Clinical laboratory technologists and technicians | 274 |
| | | Writers and editors, including technical writers | 272 |
| **Master's degree** | **1,499** | Property and real estate managers | 261 |
| All other teachers and instructors | 596 | Designers, except interior | 238 |
| Management analysts | 231 | Mechanical engineers | 231 |
| Counselors | 165 | Recreation workers | 222 |
| Librarians, professional | 148 | Purchasing agents, except wholesale, retail, and farm products | 215 |
| Psychologists | 144 | Loan officers and counselors | 214 |
| Speech-language pathologists and audiologists | 85 | Industrial production managers | 206 |
| Operations research analysts | 44 | Construction managers | 197 |
| All other social scientists | 38 | Computer engineers | 195 |
| Urban and regional planners | 29 | Civil engineers, including traffic engineers | 184 |
| Curators, archivists, museum technicians, and restorers | 19 | Wholesale and retail buyers, except farm products | 180 |
| | | Pharmacists | 168 |
| **Work experience plus bachelor's or higher degree** | **8,193** | Residential counselors | 165 |
| General managers and top executives | 3,046 | All other computer scientists | 149 |
| All other managers and administrators | 1,829 | Industrial engineers, except safety engineers | 115 |
| Financial managers | 768 | Public relations specialists and publicity writers | 107 |
| Marketing, advertising, and public relations managers | 461 | Physical therapists | 102 |
| Education administrators | 393 | Chemists | 97 |
| Engineering, mathematics, and natural science managers | 337 | Underwriters | 96 |
| Administrative services managers | 279 | Architects, except landscape and marine | 91 |
| Artists and commercial artists | 273 | Directors, religious activities and education | 81 |
| Purchasing managers | 226 | | |
| Personnel, training, and labor relations managers | 206 | | |
| Communications, transportation, and utilities operations managers | 154 | | |

## Occupational employment by education or training category—Continued

| Occupation | 1994 employment (thousands) | Occupation | 1994 employment (thousands) |
|---|---|---|---|
| Employment interviewers, private or public employment service | 77 | Psychiatric technicians | 72 |
| Budget analysts | 66 | Veterinary technicians and technologists | 22 |
| Tax examiners, collectors, and revenue agents | 63 | Cardiology technologists | 14 |
| Interior designers | 63 | Nuclear medicine technologists | 13 |
| Reporters and correspondents | 59 | | |
| Claims examiners, property and casualty insurance | 56 | **Postsecondary vocational training** | **7,101** |
| Physician assistants | 56 | Secretaries, except legal and medical | 2,842 |
| Aeronautical and astronautical engineers | 56 | Licensed practical nurses | 702 |
| Occupational therapists | 54 | Hairdressers, hairstylists, and cosmetologists | 595 |
| Dietitians and nutritionists | 53 | Data entry keyers, except composing | 395 |
| Chemical engineers | 50 | Welders and cutters | 314 |
| Economists | 48 | Drafters | 304 |
| Geologists, geophysicists, and oceanographers | 46 | Legal secretaries | 281 |
| Foresters and conservation scientists | 41 | Sales agents, real estate | 260 |
| All other physical scientists | 40 | Medical secretaries | 226 |
| Credit analysts | 39 | Emergency medical technicians | 138 |
| All other therapists | 36 | Travel agents | 122 |
| Recreational therapists | 31 | Stenographers | 105 |
| Agricultural and food scientists | 26 | Aircraft mechanics | 96 |
| Metallurgists and metallurgical, ceramic, and materials engineers | 19 | Surveyors | 96 |
| Actuaries | 17 | Central office and PBX installers and repairers | 84 |
| Animal breeders and trainers | 16 | Data processing equipment repairers | 75 |
| Nuclear engineers | 15 | Electronics repairers, commercial and industrial equipment | 66 |
| Statisticians | 14 | Barbers | 64 |
| Farm and home management advisors | 14 | Surgical technologists | 46 |
| Landscape architects | 14 | Broadcast technicians | 42 |
| Petroleum engineers | 14 | All other electrical and electronic equipment mechanics, installers, and repairers | 39 |
| Meteorologists | 7 | Manicurists | 38 |
| Mining engineers, including mine safety engineers | 3 | Station installers and repairers, telephone | 37 |
| | | Electronic home entertainment equipment repairers | 34 |
| **Associate degree** | **3,955** | All other communications equipment mechanics, installers, and repairers | 27 |
| Registered nurses | 1,906 | Dancers and choreographers | 24 |
| All other health professionals and paraprofessionals | 374 | Aircraft engine specialists | 23 |
| All other engineering technicians and technologists | 371 | Data entry keyers, composing | 19 |
| Electrical and electronic technicians and technologists | 314 | Radio mechanics | 7 |
| Science and mathematics technicians | 231 | | |
| Radiologic technologists and technicians | 167 | **Work experience** | **9,992** |
| Dental hygienists | 127 | Marketing and sales worker supervisors | 2,293 |
| Paralegals | 110 | Blue-collar worker supervisors | 1,884 |
| Medical records technicians | 81 | Clerical supervisors and managers | 1,340 |
| All other legal assistants, including law clerks | 80 | All other service workers | 1,020 |
| Respiratory therapists | 73 | Inspectors, testers, and graders, precision | 654 |
| | | Food service and lodging managers | 579 |
| | | Teachers and instructors, vocational education and training | 299 |
| | | Instructors, adult (nonvocational) education | 290 |

**Occupational employment by education or training category—Continued**

| Occupation | 1994 employment (thousands) | Occupation | 1994 employment (thousands) |
|---|---|---|---|
| Cost estimators ............................... | 179 | All other mechanics, installers, and repairers ................................ | 371 |
| Inspectors and compliance officers, except construction .................... | 157 | Machinists ...................................... | 369 |
| Electrical and electronic equipment assemblers, precision .................... | 144 | Correction officers ......................... | 310 |
| | | Musicians ....................................... | 256 |
| Institutional cleaning supervisors .............. | 125 | Bus and truck mechanics and diesel engine specialists .......................... | 250 |
| New accounts clerks, banks ............... | 114 | Securities and financial services sales workers ................................ | 246 |
| Police and detective supervisors ................ | 87 | |
| Supervisors, farm, forestry, and agriculture related occupations ........... | 85 | Heating, air-conditioning, and refrigeration mechanics and installers ...... | 233 |
| Custom tailors and sewers ................ | 84 | Butchers and meatcutters ................ | 219 |
| Brokers, real estate ........................ | 67 | Firefighters ..................................... | 219 |
| Police detectives and investigators ............. | 66 | Automotive body and related repairers ........ | 209 |
| Construction and building inspectors ......... | 64 | Telephone and cable TV line installers and repairers ............................ | 191 |
| Machine builders and other precision machine assemblers ..................... | 58 | Insurance adjusters, examiners, and investigators ......................... | 162 |
| Fire fighting and prevention supervisors ..... | 52 | |
| Real estate appraisers ..................... | 47 | Bricklayers and stone masons ............ | 147 |
| Electromechanical equipment assemblers, precision .................... | 47 | Tool and die makers ....................... | 142 |
| | | Cabinetmakers and bench carpenters .......... | 131 |
| All other precision assemblers ............ | 40 | Concrete and terrazzo finishers ............... | 126 |
| Lawn service managers .................... | 36 | All other precision workers ............... | 117 |
| Railroad conductors and yardmasters ......... | 26 | Electric power line installers and repairers .. | 112 |
| Locomotive engineers ..................... | 22 | Flight attendants ............................. | 105 |
| Aircraft assemblers, precision ............ | 20 | Mobile heavy equipment mechanics ........... | 101 |
| Nursery and greenhouse managers .............. | 19 | Water and liquid waste treatment plant and system operators ...................... | 95 |
| Railroad brake, signal, and switch operators ................................. | 19 | Producers, directors, actors, and entertainers ............................. | 93 |
| Fitters, structural metal, precision ............... | 14 | All other plant and system operators ........... | 93 |
| Fire inspection occupations ................ | 13 | Aircraft pilots and flight engineers .............. | 91 |
| Captains and pilots, ship ................. | 13 | All other precision metal workers ............... | 90 |
| Ship engineers ............................... | 8 | Sheriffs and deputy sheriffs ......................... | 86 |
| Mates, ship, boat, and barge ............ | 7 | Millwrights ..................................... | 77 |
| Programmers, numerical, tool, and process control .......................... | 7 | Home appliance and power tool repairers .... | 70 |
| Captains and other officers, fishing vessels .................................. | 7 | Upholsterers ................................... | 63 |
| | | Opticians, dispensing and measuring .......... | 63 |
| Rail yard engineers, dinkey operators, and hostlers ............................. | 6 | Structural and reinforcing metal workers ..... | 61 |
| | | Office machine and cash register servicers .. | 59 |
| **Long-term on-the-job training ................** | **13,676** | All other precision textile, apparel, and furnishings workers ..................... | 51 |
| Farmers ......................................... | 1,276 | Radio and TV announcers and newscasters ............................. | 50 |
| Maintenance repairers, general utility ......... | 1,273 | |
| Carpenters...................................... | 992 | Wood machinists ............................. | 50 |
| Automotive mechanics .................... | 736 | Dental laboratory technicians, precision ...... | 49 |
| Cooks, restaurant ........................... | 704 | Farm equipment mechanics .................. | 41 |
| Electricians ................................... | 528 | Precision instrument repairers ................... | 40 |
| Industrial machine mechanics .................. | 464 | Athletes, coaches, umpires, and related workers.............................. | 38 |
| Insurance sales workers .................. | 418 | |
| Cooks, institution or cafeteria ................. | 412 | All other precision food and tobacco workers.............................. | 38 |
| Police patrol officers ...................... | 400 | |
| Plumbers, pipefitters, and steamfitters ........ | 375 | |

## Occupational employment by education or training category—Continued

| Occupation | 1994 employment (thousands) | Occupation | 1994 employment (thousands) |
|---|---|---|---|
| Furniture finishers | 38 | Typists and word processors | 646 |
| Chemical plant and system operators | 37 | Sewing machine operators, garment | 531 |
| Small engine specialists | 35 | Painters and paperhangers, construction and maintenance | 439 |
| Glaziers | 34 | All other machine operators, tenders, setters, and set-up operators | 407 |
| Gas and petroleum plant and system occupations | 31 | Packaging and filling machine operators and tenders | 329 |
| Strippers, printing | 31 | Instructors and coaches, sports and physical training | 283 |
| Jewelers and silversmiths | 30 | Computer operators, except peripheral equipment | 259 |
| Stationary engineers | 30 | Sheet metal workers and duct installers | 222 |
| Plasterers | 30 | Medical assistants | 206 |
| Air traffic controllers and airplane dispatchers | 29 | All other material moving equipment operators | 201 |
| Hard tile setters | 27 | All other machine tool cutting and forming setters and set-up operators | 191 |
| Funeral directors and morticians | 26 | Textile draw-out and winding machine operators and tenders | 190 |
| Power generating and reactor plant operators | 26 | Dental assistants | 190 |
| Elevator installers and repairers | 24 | Insurance policy processing clerks | 179 |
| Shoe and leather workers and repairers, precision | 24 | Laundry and drycleaning machine operators and tenders, except pressing | 175 |
| Paste-up workers | 22 | Machine forming operators and tenders, metal and plastic | 171 |
| All other precision woodworkers | 22 | Bakers, bread and pastry | 170 |
| Boilermakers | 20 | Human services workers | 168 |
| Coin and vending machine servicers and repairers | 19 | Plastic mold machine operators and tenders, setters, and set-up operators | 165 |
| Optical goods workers, precision | 19 | Bus drivers, except school | 165 |
| Mining, quarrying, and tunneling occupations | 18 | All other construction trades workers | 155 |
| Electronic pagination systems workers | 18 | Operating engineers | 146 |
| Power distributors and dispatchers | 18 | All other transportation and material moving equipment operators | 145 |
| Patternmakers and layout workers, fabric and apparel | 17 | Dispatchers, except police, fire, and ambulance | 141 |
| Camera operators | 15 | Crushing and mixing machine operators and tenders | 137 |
| Job printers | 14 | All other extraction and related workers | 136 |
| Photographic process workers, precision | 14 | Drywall installers and finishers | 133 |
| Platemakers | 13 | Sewing machine operators, nongarment | 129 |
| All other printing workers, precision | 13 | All other metal and plastic machine setters, operators, and related workers | 127 |
| Electric meter installers and repairers | 12 | Roofers | 126 |
| Shipfitters | 12 | Photographers | 121 |
| Riggers | 11 | Machine tool cutters, operators, and tenders, metal and plastic | 119 |
| Motorcycle repairers | 11 | Insurance claims clerks | 119 |
| Compositors and typesetters, precision | 11 | Printing press machine setters, operators, and tenders | 113 |
| Musical instrument repairers and tuners | 10 | | |
| Electromedical and biomedical equipment repairers | 10 | | |
| Photoengravers | 7 | | |
| Watchmakers | 6 | | |
| **Moderate length on-the-job training** | **16,222** | | |
| All other sales and related workers | 3,349 | | |
| Bookkeeping, accounting, and auditing clerks | 2,181 | | |

**Occupational employment by education or training category—Continued**

| Occupation | 1994 employment (thousands) | Occupation | 1994 employment (thousands) |
|---|---|---|---|
| Coating, painting, and spraying machine operators, tenders, and setters .................. | 111 | Painters, transportation equipment ............... | 45 |
| Grader, dozer, and scraper operators ............ | 108 | Metal fabricators, structural metal products ....................................... | 44 |
| Combination machine tool setters, set-up operators, and operators ........................... | 106 | All other printing, binding, and related workers ..................................... | 43 |
| Welfare eligibility workers and interviewers ...................................... | 104 | Other law enforcement occupations ............ | 43 |
| Welding machine setters, operators, and tenders ...................................... | 103 | Electrolytic plating machine operators and tenders, setters, and set-up operators ....... | 42 |
| Extruding and forming machine setters, operators, and tenders ...................... | 102 | All other adjusters and investigators ............ | 41 |
| Cutting and slicing machine setters, operators, and tenders ...................... | 92 | Metal mold machine operators and tenders, setters, and set-up operators .................... | 40 |
| Excavation and loading machine operators ....................................... | 88 | Bicycle repairers ............................................. | 40 |
| Dispatchers, police, fire, and ambulance ..... | 83 | Textile machine setters and set-up operators ....................................... | 39 |
| Pharmacy technicians ............................... | 81 | All other oil and gas extraction occupations ....................................... | 38 |
| Offset lithographic press operators ............. | 79 | Cement and gluing machine operators and tenders ....................................... | 36 |
| Physical and corrective therapy assistants and aides ...................................... | 78 | Bakers, manufacturing.................................. | 36 |
| Pressing machine operators and tenders, textile, garment, and related materials ..... | 77 | Directory assistance operators..................... | 33 |
| Statistical clerks ....................................... | 75 | Electronic semiconductor processors .......... | 33 |
| Numerical control machine tool operators and tenders, metal and plastic .................. | 75 | Textile bleaching and dyeing machine operators and tenders ............................. | 30 |
| Chemical equipment controllers, operators, and tenders ....................................... | 75 | Peripheral EDP equipment operators .......... | 30 |
| Paving, surfacing, and tamping equipment operators ....................................... | 73 | Cooking and roasting machine operators and tenders, food and tobacco .................. | 28 |
| Bindery machine operators and set-up operators ....................................... | 72 | Title examiners and searchers ...................... | 28 |
| Lathe and turning machine tool setters and set-up operators, metal and plastic .... | 71 | Furnace, kiln, or kettle operators and tenders ....................................... | 28 |
| Carpet installers ....................................... | 66 | Screen printing machine setters and set-up operators ....................................... | 26 |
| Woodworking machine operators and tenders, setters and set-up operators ........ | 64 | All other technicians.................................... | 24 |
| Insulation workers ....................................... | 64 | Extruding and forming machine operators and tenders, synthetic fiber .................. | 22 |
| Grinding machine setters and set-up operators, metal and plastic ...................... | 64 | Furnace operators and tenders ..................... | 20 |
| Head sawyers and sawing machine operators and tenders ............................. | 62 | Logging tractor operators ............................ | 20 |
| Pipelayers and pipelaying fitters .................. | 57 | Separating and still machine operators and tenders ....................................... | 20 |
| Pest controllers and assistants ..................... | 56 | Typesetting and composing machine operators and tenders ............................. | 20 |
| Detectives, except public ............................ | 55 | Housekeepers and butlers............................. | 20 |
| Paper goods machine setters and set-up operators ....................................... | 51 | Heat treating machine operators and tenders, metal and plastic ........................ | 20 |
| Central office operators ............................ | 48 | Locksmiths and safe repairers ...................... | 20 |
| Punching machine setters and set-up operators, metal and plastic ...................... | 48 | Camera operators, television, motion picture, and video ............................. | 18 |
| Drilling machine tool setters and set-up operators, metal and plastic .................. | 45 | Boiler operators and tenders, low pressure ....................................... | 18 |
| Crane and tower operators ........................... | 45 | EKG technicians ............................................ | 16 |
| | | Log handling equipment operators.............. | 16 |
| | | Ceiling tile installers and acoustical carpenters.................................. | 16 |

## Occupational employment by education or training category—Continued

| Occupation | 1994 employment (thousands) | Occupation | 1994 employment (thousands) |
|---|---|---|---|
| Occupational therapy assistants and aides ... | 16 | All other clerical and administrative support workers ..................................... | 721 |
| Sprayers and applicators ............................. | 15 | Gardeners and groundskeepers, except farm .................................................. | 569 |
| Shoe sewing machine operators and tenders .................................................. | 14 | Bank tellers ............................................... | 559 |
| Dairy processing equipment operators, including setters ..................................... | 14 | Helpers, construction trades ....................... | 513 |
| Tire building machine operators .................. | 14 | Cleaners and servants, private household .... | 496 |
| Letterpress operators ................................. | 14 | Industrial truck and tractor operators ........... | 464 |
| All other printing press setters and set-up operators ................................................ | 13 | Home health aides .................................... | 420 |
| Subway and streetcar operators ................. | 12 | Dining room and cafeteria attendants and bartender helpers ...................... | 416 |
| Camera and photographic equipment repairers ............................................... | 11 | Bus drivers, school .................................... | 404 |
| Foundry mold assembly and shakeout workers ................................................. | 10 | Adjustment clerks ...................................... | 373 |
| Soldering and brazing machine operators and setters ........................................... | 10 | Bartenders ............................................... | 373 |
| All other communications equipment operators .............................................. | 9 | Counter and rental clerks........................... | 341 |
| Hoist and winch operators .......................... | 9 | Driver/sales workers .................................. | 331 |
| Cooks, private household ........................... | 9 | Billing, cost, and rate clerks ...................... | 323 |
| Electroneurodiagnostic technologists........... | 6 | Postal mail carriers ................................... | 320 |
| Bookbinders.............................................. | 6 | Order clerks, material, merchandise, and service ..................................... | 310 |
| Photoengraving and lithographic machine operators and tenders ............................. | 5 | Childcare workers, private household ......... | 283 |
| | | File clerks ................................................. | 278 |
| **Short-term on-the-job training** ................. | **49,694** | Amusement and recreation attendants ......... | 267 |
| Salespersons, retail .................................. | 3,842 | Machine feeders and offbearers .................. | 262 |
| Janitors and cleaners, including maids and housekeepers .................................. | 3,043 | All other agriculture, forestry, fishing, and related workers ............................. | 255 |
| Cashiers ................................................... | 3,005 | Bill and account collectors ........................... | 250 |
| General office clerks .................................. | 2,946 | Vehicle washers and equipment cleaners ..... | 249 |
| Truckdrivers, light and heavy ...................... | 2,565 | Hosts and hostesses, restaurant, lounge, and coffee shop .................................. | 248 |
| Waiters and waitresses ............................... | 1,847 | Production, planning, and expediting clerks | 239 |
| Stock clerks .............................................. | 1,759 | Switchboard operators ............................... | 228 |
| All other helpers, laborers, and material movers, hand ......................................... | 1,727 | All other cleaners and building service workers................................................ | 226 |
| Food counter, fountain, and related workers ................................................. | 1,630 | Duplication, mail, and other office machine operators ............................... | 222 |
| All other assemblers, fabricators, and hand workers ........................................ | 1,583 | Order fillers, wholesale and retail sales ....... | 215 |
| Nursing aides, orderlies, and attendants ....... | 1,265 | All other food preparation and service workers ............................................... | 213 |
| Food preparation workers .......................... | 1,190 | Electrical and electronic assemblers ............ | 212 |
| Receptionists and information clerks .......... | 1,019 | Loan and credit clerks ................................ | 187 |
| Hand packers and packagers ....................... | 942 | Personal and home care aides ..................... | 179 |
| Teacher aides and educational assistants ...... | 932 | Service station attendants ........................... | 167 |
| Farm workers ............................................ | 906 | Highway maintenance workers...................... | 167 |
| Guards...................................................... | 867 | All other material recording, scheduling, and distribution workers ........................ | 161 |
| Traffic, shipping, and receiving clerks......... | 798 | Payroll and timekeeping clerks ................... | 157 |
| Freight, stock, and material movers, hand.... | 765 | All other health service workers.................... | 157 |
| Cooks, short order and fast food ................. | 760 | Postal Service clerks .................................. | 154 |
| Childcare workers...................................... | 757 | Customer service representatives, utilities ... | 150 |
| | | Reservation and transportation ticket agents and travel clerks ......................... | 139 |

**Occupational employment by education or training category—Continued**

| Occupation | 1994 employment (thousands) | Occupation | 1994 employment (thousands) |
|---|---|---|---|
| Hotel desk clerks | 136 | Cutters and trimmers, hand | 51 |
| Messengers | 133 | Weighers, measurers, checkers, and samplers | 45 |
| Meat, poultry, and fish cutters and trimmers, hand | 132 | Photographic processing machine operators and tenders | 43 |
| Taxi drivers and chauffeurs | 129 | Fishers, hunters, and trappers | 42 |
| Mail clerks, except mail machine operators and Postal Service | 127 | Forest and conservation workers | 42 |
| All other protective service workers | 126 | Credit checkers | 40 |
| Animal caretakers, except farm | 125 | Baggage porters and bellhops | 35 |
| Personnel clerks, except payroll and timekeeping | 123 | Painting, coating, and decorating workers, hand | 33 |
| Library assistants and bookmobile drivers | 121 | Veterinary assistants | 31 |
| Refuse collectors | 111 | Fallers and buckers | 29 |
| Psychiatric aides | 105 | Correspondence clerks | 29 |
| Lawn maintenance workers | 96 | Roustabouts | 28 |
| Billing, posting, and calculating machine operators | 96 | Solderers and brazers | 27 |
| Tire repairers and changers | 89 | Pruners | 26 |
| Nursery workers | 83 | Proofreaders and copy markers | 26 |
| Technical assistants, library | 75 | All other motor vehicle operators | 26 |
| Grinders and polishers, hand | 74 | Statement clerks | 25 |
| Cannery workers | 73 | Real estate clerks | 24 |
| Brokerage clerks | 73 | Municipal clerks | 22 |
| Interviewing clerks, except personnel and social welfare | 69 | Coil winders, tapers, and finishers | 21 |
| Parking lot attendants | 64 | Able seamen, ordinary seamen, and marine oilers | 20 |
| Ushers, lobby attendants, and ticket takers | 59 | Sewers, hand | 19 |
| Crossing guards | 58 | Ambulance drivers and attendants, except emergency medical technicians | 18 |
| Meter readers, utilities | 57 | Advertising clerks | 17 |
| Procurement clerks | 57 | All other timber cutting and related logging workers | 17 |
| Pharmacy assistants | 52 | Pressers, hand | 16 |
| Court clerks | 51 | Loan interviewers | 16 |
| Machine assemblers | 51 | Credit authorizers | 15 |
| | | Shampooers | 12 |
| | | Motion picture projectionists | 8 |

# Employment Trends Within Major Industries

# Appendix B

## Introduction

This appendix is divided into two parts. The first provides general information on industry trends and the second provides specific data on all major industries.

While industry information may not seem important to you, it should be. When planning their careers, most people think in terms of the type of job they want. But they should also think in terms of the industry or industries they prefer. This combination of occupation and industry is the basis for good career planning, and one should not be separated from the other.

For example, if you were interested in becoming a registered nurse, that is a decision about an **occupation**. Nurses mostly work in the health care **industry**, but they also work in other industries. And even within the health care industry, there are enormous variations in where a nurse might work and in what a nurse might do.

If you combine nursing with various industries that interest you, you will begin to see a variety of new possibilities. The question you should ask is this: *"What sorts of jobs could a person with nursing skills do within this industry?"*

If you select a variety of industries that interest you—or that you have some experience in—the creative job possibilities can seem endless. Here are just a few examples:

| Nursing Skills in This Industry/Employer Type | Possible Jobs |
| --- | --- |
| Hospital | Admissions, pediatrics, intensive care, administration, and many others |
| Education/School | school nurse, teacher of nursing education, health teacher, college infirmary |
| Airline | Airport nursing station, employee health administrator, industrial medical clinic, pre-employment screening |
| Temporary Employment | Own, operate, or work for a medically oriented placement service |
| Pharmaceutical | Drug sales, customer relations, consumer education coordinator, clinical research |
| Child Care | Manage a childcare facility; |

For jobs that are more general, such as accountant or secretary, the possibilities are boundless. The point is to identify an industry that appeals to you, then look for a way to use your occupation-specific skills in that industry. In this way, you just may find job opportunities to fit your preferences that others have overlooked. And, if you select carefully, you are more likely to be satisfied with your work.

Section 2 provides more career planning and job search advice. If you have not already read that section, consider this: The time spent can be repaid many times over.

# A Review of Growth and Other Trends in Major Industries

The material that follows is from the first section of a book titled *Career Guide to America's Top Industries* (published by JIST). This book is based on information obtained from the U.S. Department of Labor and was designed to help people in their career planning.

The material provides a general overview of important trends within major industries. If you want to learn more about a specific industry, I suggest you begin by reading more about that industry in the *Career Guide to America's Top Industries*, which covers 40 major industries and provides information that helpful in career planning—including types of jobs available, working conditions, training and advancement, earnings and benefits, and other details.

As noted earlier, there are delays in collecting and interpreting national employment data, and the information in this appendix was the latest available at the time of this writing. Unless otherwise indicated, the source of information is the Bureau of Labor Statistics. A chart provided later in this appendix provides additional information on a large number of industries that you may find of interest.

## Major Trends in Major Industries

Many career-minded people think in terms of industries rather than occupations. Your personal circumstances or choice of lifestyle may compel you to remain in your area, limiting prospective jobs to those offered by the distinctive mix of industries in your state or community. Or you may be attracted to a particular industry for other reasons—the glamour and travel associated with airlines, the high potential earnings in the securities and commodities industry, the high technology in aerospace manufacturing, the opportunity to work with children offered by the educational services industry, or the stability of jobs in the federal government, to name just a few.

Focusing on industries gives you a point of view that is different than simply thinking about occupations. For example, some occupations are unique to a particular industry, and they are not described in major occupational reference sources such as the *Occupational Outlook Handbook*. Additionally, some industries offer specific paths of career advancement that are not addressed in the *OOH* or other major career references.

## Things to Consider When Reviewing Various Industries

### Nature of the Industry

Workers produce many products for and provide many services to domestic and foreign consumers, to businesses, and to government. Places of work, called *establishments*, range from large factories and office complexes employing thousands of workers to small businesses employing only a few. Establishments that produce similar goods or services are grouped together into *in-dustries*. Industries that produce related types of goods or services are, in turn, grouped together into *major industry divisions*, which are further categorized as *goods-producing* (agriculture, forestry, and fishing; mining; construction; and manufacturing) or *service-producing* (transportation, communications, and public utilities; wholesale and retail trade; finance, insurance, and real estate; services; and government).

The types of occupations found in each industry depend on the types of services or goods produced. For example, manufacturing companies use machinery and other industrial equipment to make goods and need workers to operate that equipment. Typical manufacturing occupations include assemblers, inspectors, machine setters, and material movers. Retail trade, on the other hand, displays manufactured goods for purchase by consumers and hires workers for a variety of different jobs, such as sales clerks, cashiers, and stock clerks.

In 1991, there were more than 6 million business establishments with employees in the United States. Some industries characteristically have small establishments employing few workers, and others have predominantly large establishments employing many workers. The size of an establishment is important to workers for many reasons. Large establishments generally offer workers greater occupational mobility and advancement potential, whereas small establishments may offer employees broader experience by requiring them to assume a wider range of responsibilities. Also, small establishments are distributed throughout the nation; every community has at least a few small businesses.

Large establishments, by contrast, are less common, yet hire more workers. Establishments in the United States are predominantly small; 54 percent of all establishments employed fewer than five workers in 1991. The medium to large establishments, however, employ a greater proportion of all workers. For example, establishments that employed 50 or more workers accounted for only 5 percent of all establishments, yet employed 57 percent of all workers. The large establishments—those with more than 500 workers—accounted for only 0.3 percent of all establishments, but employed 20 percent of all workers. Table 1 presents the percentage distribution of employment according to establishment size.

Among industry divisions, manufacturing included many industries having among the highest employment per establishment in 1991. For example, industries manufacturing tobacco, transportation equipment, and primary metals each averaged 100 or more employees per establishment. Nonmanufacturing industries with relatively high employment per establishment included general merchandise stores and metal mining, each with 50 or more workers per establishment.

Most small establishments are in the retail trade and services industries. Other industries that tended to have relatively few employees per establishment included auto repair and parking services, agricultural services, insurance agents and brokers, and real estate—each averaged 6 or fewer workers per establishment in 1991. On the other hand, educational services had nearly 50 employees per establishment.

| Table 1. Percentage distribution of establishments in all industries by establishment size, 1991 | | |
|---|---|---|
| Establishment size | Percentage of establishments | Percentage of workers |
| Total | 100.0 | 100.0 |
| 1-4 workers | 54.5 | 6.4 |
| 5-9 | 20.0 | 8.9 |
| 10-19 | 12.4 | 11.2 |
| 20-49 | 8.1 | 16.5 |
| 50-99 | 2.8 | 12.7 |
| 100-249 | 1.5 | 15.5 |
| 250-499 | 0.4 | 8.8 |
| 500-999 | 0.2 | 6.8 |
| 1,000 or more | 0.1 | 13.2 |

## Employment Trends and Opportunities

The number of wage and salary worker jobs in the United States totaled nearly 111 million in 1992, and by 2005 it is projected to reach almost 136 million. There were also more than 10 million self-employed workers and more than 340,000 unpaid family workers in 1992, but the information here concentrates on wage and salary worker employment.

Employment is not evenly divided among the various industries. Wage and salary employment ranged from just 171,000 in motion picture production and distribution to 9.7 million in educational services. Three industries—educational services, health services, and eating and drinking places—together accounted for about 26 million jobs, or 23 percent of the nation's employment.

**Table 2. Wage and salary employment in selected industries, 1992 and projected change, 1992 to 2005 (Employment in thousands)**

| Industry | 1992 | | 2005 | 1992-2005 | |
|---|---|---|---|---|---|
| | Employment | Percentage | Employment | Employment change | Percentage change |
| **All Industries** | 110,746 | 100.0 | 135,735 | 24,989 | 22.6 |
| **Goods-Producing industries** | 24,883 | 22.5 | 25,691 | 808 | 3.2 |
| **Agriculture, forestry, and fishing** | 1,740 | 1.6 | 1,974 | 234 | 13.5 |
| Agricultural Services | 653 | 0.6 | 918 | 265 | 40.5 |
| **Mining** | 631 | 0.6 | 562 | −69 | −11.0 |
| Oil and gas extraction | 350 | 0.3 | 300 | −50 | −14.3 |
| Mining and quarrying | 280 | 0.3 | 261 | −19 | −6.8 |
| **Construction** | 4,471 | 4.0 | 5,632 | 1,161 | 26.0 |
| **Manufacturing** | 18,041 | 16.3 | 17,523 | −518 | −2.9 |
| Food processing | 1,655 | 1.5 | 1,646 | −7 | −0.4 |
| Printing and publishing | 1,504 | 1.4 | 1,751 | 247 | 16.4 |
| Electronics manufacturing | 1,463 | 1.3 | 1,224 | −239 | −16.3 |
| Apparel and other textile products manufacturing | 1,005 | 0.9 | 760 | −245 | −24.4 |
| Chemicals manufacturing, except drugs | 827 | 0.7 | 794 | −33 | −4.0 |
| Motor vehicle and equipment manufacturing | 809 | 0.7 | 759 | −50 | −6.1 |
| Aerospace manufacturing | 756 | 0.7 | 776 | 19 | 2.5 |
| Textile mill products manufacturing | 671 | 0.6 | 571 | −101 | −15.0 |
| Drug manufacturing | 256 | 0.2 | 297 | 41 | 15.9 |
| Steel manufacturing | 250 | 0.2 | 224 | −26 | −10.5 |
| **Service-Producing industries** | 85,864 | 77.5 | 110,045 | 24,181 | 28.2 |

**Table 2. Wage and salary employment in selected Industries, 1992 and projected change, 1992 to 2005 (Employment in thousands)** *(continued)*

| Industry | 1992 | | 2005 | 1992-2005 | |
|---|---|---|---|---|---|
| | Employment | Percentage | Employment | Employment change | Percentage change |
| **Transportation, communications, and public utilities** | 5,709 | 5.1 | 6,497 | 789 | 13.8 |
| Trucking and warehousing | 1,606 | 1.4 | 2,019 | 413 | 25.7 |
| Public Utilities | 955 | 0.9 | 1,071 | 117 | 12.2 |
| Telephone communications | 912 | 0.8 | 724 | −188 | −20.6 |
| Air Transportation | 729 | 0.7 | 967 | 238 | 32.7 |
| Radio and television broadcasting | 355 | 0.3 | 392 | 37 | 10.5 |
| **Wholesale and retail trade** | 25,391 | 22.9 | 30,968 | 5,576 | 22.0 |
| Eating and drinking places | 6,602 | 6.0 | 8,778 | 2,176 | 33.0 |
| Wholesale trade | 6,045 | 5.5 | 7,191 | 1,146 | 19.0 |
| Department, clothing, and variety stores | 3,553 | 3.2 | 3,987 | 434 | 12.2 |
| Grocery stores | 2,842 | 2.6 | 3,475 | 633 | 22.3 |
| Motor vehicle dealers | 940 | 0.9 | 1,093 | 153 | 16.3 |
| **Finance, insurance, and real estate** | 6,571 | 5.9 | 7,969 | 1,398 | 21.3 |
| Insurance | 2,132 | 1.9 | 2,631 | 499 | 23.4 |
| Banking | 2,103 | 1.9 | 2,195 | 91 | 4.3 |
| Securities and commodities | 439 | 0.4 | 570 | 131 | 29.9 |
| **Services** | 38,647 | 34.9 | 54,153 | 15,506 | 40.1 |
| Educational services | 9,718 | 8.8 | 12,476 | 2,757 | 28.4 |
| Health services | 9,613 | 8.7 | 13,789 | 4,176 | 43.4 |
| Personnel supply services | 1,649 | 1.5 | 2,581 | 933 | 56.6 |
| Hotels and other lodging services | 1,572 | 1.4 | 2,209 | 637 | 40.5 |
| Social services | 1,509 | 1.4 | 2,914 | 1,405 | 93.1 |
| Amusement and recreation services | 1,169 | 1.1 | 1,626 | 457 | 39.1 |
| Computer and data processing services | 831 | 0.8 | 1,626 | 795 | 95.7 |
| Management and public relations services | 655 | 0.6 | 1,110 | 455 | 69.5 |
| Child-care services | 449 | 0.4 | 777 | 328 | 73.0 |
| Advertising | 226 | 0.2 | 287 | 62 | 27.5 |
| Motion picture production and distribution | 171 | 0.2 | 274 | 104 | 60.8 |
| **Government** | 9,545 | 8.6 | 10,458 | 913 | 9.6 |
| State and local government | 6,576 | 5.9 | 7,642 | 1,067 | 16.2 |
| Federal government | 2,177 | 2.0 | 2,064 | −113 | −5.2 |

The number of job openings provided by any industry depends on its current employment level, its growth rate, and its need to replace workers who leave their jobs. Replacement needs are determined, in part, by an industry's worker age distribution—young workers tend to be less settled into jobs and careers, and are more likely to change jobs. For example, retail trade provides entry-level jobs to many young workers, reflected by a median age well below the average for all industries. In addition, employment in retail trade is projected to grow 23 percent over the 1992-2005 period—matching the projected growth rate for all industries combined.

Employment growth, coupled with high turnover among the many young, entry-level workers in retail trade, will produce an unusually large number of job openings in this field. By contrast, manufacturing provided nearly as many jobs as retail trade in 1992—roughly 18 million in manufacturing compared to more than 19 million in retail trade—but a projected decline in manufacturing employment, coupled with more older workers than in retail trade (reflected by a median age slightly above the average for all industries), will result in fewer job openings. Almost one-third of the workers in retail trade were 24 years of age or younger, whereas only 10 percent of workers in manufacturing were 24 or younger. Table 3 contrasts the age distribution of workers in all industries with the distributions in retail trade and manufacturing.

### Table 3. Percentage distribution of industry sector employment by age group and median age, 1992

| Age group | All industries | Retail trade | Manu-facturing |
|---|---|---|---|
| Total | 100.0 | 100.0 | 100.0 |
| 16-19 | 4.6 | 14.3 | 1.9 |
| 20-24 | 10.3 | 17.7 | 8.3 |
| 25-29 | 12.9 | 13.5 | 13.3 |
| 30-34 | 14.7 | 12.6 | 15.8 |
| 35-44 | 26.9 | 19.1 | 29.0 |
| 45-54 | 18.0 | 12.3 | 19.9 |
| 55-64 | 9.6 | 7.5 | 10.3 |
| 65 and older | 3.0 | 3.0 | 1.6 |
| Median Age | 37.6 | 31.7 | 38.4 |

Some industries are concentrated in one region of the country, and the job opportunities in these industries should be best in the states in which the establishments are concentrated. Such industries usually are located near a source of raw materials upon which they rely. For example, oil and gas extraction jobs are concentrated in Texas, Louisiana, and Oklahoma; many textile mill product manufacturing jobs are found in North Carolina, Georgia, and South Carolina; and a significant proportion of motor vehicle and equipment manufacturing jobs are located in Michigan. On the other hand, in some industries—such as grocery stores and educational services—jobs are distributed throughout the nation, reflecting the population density in different areas.

### Working Conditions

Working conditions vary greatly among industries. In some industries, the work setting is quiet, temperature-controlled, and virtually hazard-free. Other industries are characterized by a noisy, uncomfortably hot or cold, and sometimes dangerous environment. Some industries require long workweeks and shift work; in many industries, standard 35- to 40-hour workweeks are common. Still other industries are seasonal, requiring long hours during busy periods and abbreviated schedules during slower months.

Similar to the median age of workers, the contrast in an average workweek was most notable between retail and trade and manufacturing—28.8 hours and 41.4 hours, respectively, in 1993. One-third of workers in retail trade worked part-time (1 to 34 hours per week), compared to 5 percent in manufacturing. Table 4 presents industries having relatively high and low percentages of part-time workers.

### Table 4. Percentage of part-time workers in selected industries, 1992

| Industry | Percentage part-time |
|---|---|
| **All industries** | 17.5 |
| **Many part-time workers** | |
| Eating and drinking places | 42.1 |
| Apparel and accessory stores | 38.6 |
| Department stores | 36.0 |
| Child daycare services | 32.2 |
| Personnel supply services | 25.1 |
| **Few part-time workers** | |
| Construction | 10.1 |
| Computer and data processing services | 6.4 |
| Chemicals and allied products manufacturing | 3.4 |
| Telephone communications | 2.9 |
| Motor vehicle manufacturing | 1.4 |

The low proportion of part-time workers in some manufacturing industries reflects the continuity of the production process. Once begun, these processes cannot be stopped; machinery and materials must be tended and moved continuously. For example, the chemical manufacturing industry produces many different chemical products through controlled chemical reactions. These processes require chemical operators to monitor and adjust the flow of materials into and out of the line of operation. Processes sometimes continue 24 hours a day, seven days a week, under the watchful eyes of chemical operators who work in shifts. Interruptions in the process can be costly and sometimes dangerous.

Retail trade and service industries have seasonal cycles marked by various events, such as school openings or important holidays, that affect the hours worked. During busy times of the year, longer hours are common, whereas lulls lead to cutbacks and shorter workweeks. Jobs in these industries are generally appealing to students and others who desire flexible, part-time schedules.

Almost 6.8 million nonfatal injuries and illnesses were reported throughout private industry in 1992. Analyzing the injury and illness rate of an industry is one method of determining which industries are potentially hazardous and which are not. Among major industry divisions, construction had the highest rate of injury and illness—13.1 cases for every 100 full-time workers—while finance, insurance, and real estate had the lowest rate—2.9.

Overexertion, contact with objects and equipment, falls, repetitive motion trauma, and fires were among the causes of injury and illness. About 6,000 work-related fatalities were reported in 1992; transportation accidents, violent acts, contact with objects and equipment, falls, and exposure to harmful substances or environments were among the causes. Table 5 presents selected industries with relatively high and low rates of injury and illness.

### Table 5. Injury and illness rates of selected industries, 1992

| Industry | Cases per 100 full-time employees |
|---|---|
| **All industries** | **8.9** |
| Iron and steel foundries | 27.7 |
| Motor vehicle manufacturing | 24.5 |
| Food processing | 18.8 |
| Lumber and building materials stores | 14.0 |
| Trucking and warehousing | 13.4 |
| **Low rates** | |
| Apparel and accessory stores | 4.3 |
| Computer and office equipment manufacturing | 3.9 |
| Radio and television broadcasting | 2.6 |
| Legal services | 1.2 |
| Security and commodity brokers | 0.7 |

## Occupations Typically Found in the Industry

Some occupations are concentrated in one or a few industries. For example, nearly 5 out of 6 cashiers work in retail trade. Other occupations, such as general manager or secretary, are found in all industries. Table 6 presents 1992 employment in major occupational groups and expected growth through the year 2005. Detailed occupations within these major groups range from machinist (precision production, craft, and repair) to secretary (administrative support, including clerical), and from cashier (marketing and sales) to top executive (executive, administrative, and managerial).

Reflecting differences among occupations, staffing patterns vary widely among industries. As indicated by Table 7, construction employs primarily production workers, while administrative support workers dominate finance, insurance, and real estate. Some industries, such as government, have workers evenly distributed throughout the occupational groups. Other industries, such as agriculture, have many workers concentrated in a few occupations. Projected employment growth of an occupation depends largely on growth of the industries in which it is concentrated.

### Table 6. Employment in broad occupational groups, 1992 and projected change, 1992-2005 (employment in thousands)

| Occupational Group | 1992 Employment | 1992-2005 Percentage change |
|---|---|---|
| Total, all occupations | 121,099 | 21.8 |
| Executive, administrative, and managerial | 12,066 | 25.9 |
| Professional specialty | 16,592 | 37.4 |
| Technicians and related support | 4,282 | 32.3 |
| Marketing and sales | 12,993 | 20.6 |
| Administrative support, including clerical | 22,349 | 13.7 |
| Services | 19,358 | 33.4 |
| Agriculture, forestry and fishing | 3,530 | 3.4 |
| Precision production, craft, and repair | 13,580 | 13.3 |
| Operators, fabricators, and laborers | 16,349 | 9.5 |

### Table 7. Industry divisions and largest occupational concentration, 1992

| Industry division | Largest occupational group | Percentage of jobs |
|---|---|---|
| Agriculture, forestry, and fishing | Agriculture and related | 76.1 |
| Mining | Precision production | 36.8 |
| Construction | Precision production | 53.1 |
| Manufacturing | Operators, fabricators, and laborers | 44.1 |
| Transportation, communications, and public utilities | Operators, fabricators and laborers | 30.5 |
| Wholesale and retail trade | Marketing and sales | 32.4 |
| Finance, insurance, and real estate | Administrative support | 51.1 |
| Services | Professional specialty | 28.8 |
| Government | Administrative support | 27.1 |

## Training and Advancement Needed

In 1992, about 14 percent of all workers had less than a high school diploma; 35 percent were high school graduates or the equivalent; 27 percent had some college or an associate degree; and almost 25 percent had a bachelor's degree or higher. However, the occupational composition of an industry greatly affects the education or training needed by its workers.

For example, machine operators in manufacturing generally need little formal education after high school, but sometimes complete considerable on-the-job training. Almost 70 percent of workers in agriculture, forestry, and fishing, 66 percent in construction, and nearly 60 percent in manufacturing and retail trade had a high school diploma or less. On the other hand, 66 percent of workers in government, 64 percent in finance, insurance, and real estate, and 63 percent in services had at least some college. Table 8 shows overall education attainment by industry division, while Tables 9 and 10 show industries with the highest percentages of college graduates and workers who have less than 12 years of schooling or no high school diploma.

| Table 8. Percentage of highest grade completed or degree received by industry division, 1992 | | | | |
| --- | --- | --- | --- | --- |
| Industry division | Bachelor's degree or higher | Some college or associate degree | High school graduate or equivalent | Less than 12 years or no diploma |
| Agriculture, forestry, and fishing | 11.5 | 19.5 | 36.7 | 32.3 |
| Mining | 22.0 | 23.2 | 39.7 | 15.2 |
| Construction | 10.1 | 23.9 | 45.6 | 20.5 |
| Manufacturing | 18.1 | 22.8 | 42.1 | 17.0 |
| Transportation, communications, and public utilities | 17.6 | 32.2 | 40.8 | 9.4 |
| Wholesale and retail trade | 14.0 | 28.7 | 39.4 | 17.9 |
| Finance, insurance, and real estate | 32.3 | 32.0 | 31.2 | 4.5 |
| Services | 36.5 | 26.3 | 26.9 | 10.3 |
| Government | 32.6 | 33.9 | 30.5 | 3.1 |

| Table 9. Industries with the highest percentage of workers who are college graduates, 1992 | |
| --- | --- |
| Industry | Percentage |
| Miscellaneous professional and related services | 68.9 |
| Offices and clinics of health practitioners, not elsewhere classified | 66.7 |
| Management and public relations services | 65.3 |
| Elementary and secondary schools | 62.2 |
| Accounting, auditing, and bookkeeping services | 58.7 |

| Table 10. Industries with the highest percentage of workers who have less than 12 years of schooling or no diploma, 1992 | |
| --- | --- |
| Industry | Percentage |
| Shoe repair shops | 48.1 |
| Private households | 42.5 |
| Agricultural production, crops | 41.4 |
| Meat products manufacturing | 36.7 |
| Dairy products stores | 36.6 |

Besides formal education, other sources of qualifying training include formal company training, informal on-the-job training, correspondence courses, the Armed Forces, and friends, relatives, and other nonwork-related training. In 1991, 57 percent of workers throughout industry said they needed training to qualify for their jobs: 33 percent needed formal schooling, 27 percent completed informal on-the-job training, and 12 percent qualified for their jobs through formal company training. However, sources of qualifying training varied widely by industry (see Table 11).

For example, the highest proportion of workers—75 percent—who indicated they need formal schooling were in professional and related services, including accounting, legal, and engineering services, among other industries. Similarly, 23 percent of workers in finance, insurance, and real estate, 21 percent in public administration, and 20 percent in transportation, communications, and public utilities said they qualified for their jobs through formal company training programs.

Table 11. Sources of qualifying training by industry group, 1991

| Industry group | Percentage of all workers who needed training | Source of training (percentage of all workers) | | | |
| --- | --- | --- | --- | --- | --- |
| | | School | Formal company training | Informal on-the-job training | Other |
| Total, all industries | 57 | 33 | 12 | 27 | 10 |
| Agriculture, forestry, and fishing | 33 | 13 | 3 | 20 | 14 |
| Mining | 63 | 31 | 17 | 38 | 11 |
| Construction | 59 | 18 | 14 | 37 | 17 |
| Manufacturing, durable goods | 56 | 29 | 15 | 32 | 10 |
| Manufacturing, nondurable goods | 48 | 22 | 10 | 29 | 7 |
| Transportation, communications, and public utilities | 58 | 23 | 20 | 30 | 13 |
| Wholesale trade | 47 | 23 | 11 | 27 | 9 |
| Retail trade | 33 | 11 | 7 | 21 | 7 |
| Finance, insurance, and real estate | 67 | 38 | 23 | 34 | 11 |
| Business and repair services | 61 | 34 | 13 | 31 | 15 |
| Personal services | 42 | 20 | 6 | 16 | 12 |
| Entertainment and recreation services | 57 | 24 | 10 | 32 | 19 |
| Professional and related services | 75 | 61 | 8 | 24 | 9 |
| Public Administration | 74 | 46 | 21 | 34 | 18 |

## Earnings and Benefits Vary Widely Within Industries

Like training requirements, working conditions, and other characteristics, earnings vary widely by industry. For example, production and nonsupervisory workers in petroleum refining averaged $902 a week in 1993, compared to only $134 in eating and drinking places—reflecting the types of jobs in the industry, average hours worked, the region of the country in which the industry is concentrated, whether the establishments are located in predominantly urban or rural locations, union affiliation, and educational requirements.

Wages generally are highest in metropolitan areas to compensate for the higher cost of living. Also, industries that employ few minimum-wage or part-time workers tend to have higher earnings. In the example above, the petroleum refining industry employs a relatively highly skilled, highly unionized workforce. On the other hand, eating and drinking places employ many relatively low-skilled, part-time workers who rely largely on tips, which are not included in the industry earnings data. Table 12 presents the average weekly wages in a selection of industries. The data understate the average earnings for all workers in any given industry because supervisors are excluded.

Table 12. Average weekly earnings of production or nonsupervisory workers in selected industries, 1993

| Industry | Average weekly earnings |
| --- | --- |
| **All industries** | **$374** |
| **Industries with high earnings** | |
| Petroleum refining | 902 |
| Flat glass manufacturing | 805 |
| Coal mining | 766 |
| Motion picture production and services | 731 |
| Aircraft and parts | 720 |
| Electric, gas, and sanitary services | 708 |
| Engineering services | 660 |
| Telephone communications | 646 |
| Electrical work contractors | 618 |
| Security and commodity brokers | 569 |

| Industry | Average weekly earnings |
|---|---|
| **Industries with low earnings** | |
| Commercial banks | 304 |
| Agricultural services | 288 |
| Apparel and other textile products manufacturing | 264 |
| Personal supply services | 259 |
| Social services | 244 |
| Grocery stores | 236 |
| Hotels and other lodging places | 234 |
| Child daycare services | 196 |
| Apparel and accessory stores | 184 |
| Eating and drinking places | 134 |

Employee benefits, once a minor addition to wages and salaries, are growing in diversity and cost, amounting to 29 percent of total compensation costs in 1993. In addition to traditional benefits—including paid vacations, life and health insurance, and pensions—employers are beginning to offer various benefits to accommodate the needs of a changing labor force—for example, child care, employee assistance, programs that provide counseling for personal problems, and wellness programs that provide exercise, stress management, and other classes. Benefits vary among occupational groups, full- and part-time workers, public- and private-sector workers, regions, unionized and nonunionized workers, and small and large establishments. Data indicate that full-time workers and those in medium-sized and large establishments—those with 100 or more workers—invariably receive better benefits than part-time workers and those in small establishments—those with fewer than 100 employees. Table 13 compares benefits for workers in private industry and state and local government.

### Table 13. Percentage of employees participating in selected benefit plans in private industry and state and local government, 1991-92

| Benefit | All employees | Private sector | State and local government |
|---|---|---|---|
| Paid holidays | 76 | 77 | 71 |
| Paid vacations | 79 | 82 | 63 |
| Medical care | 68 | 65 | 85 |
| Life insurance | 69 | 67 | 84 |
| Retirement plan | 59 | 54 | 89 |
| Employee assistance plan | 36 | 31 | 62 |
| Wellness programs | 19 | 18 | 29 |
| Child care | 5 | 4 | 7 |

State and local government workers had a higher incidence of most benefits than workers in the private sector. Retirement plan participation differed noticeably between the two sectors—nearly 90 percent of state and local government workers were covered, compared to only 54 percent of private-sector employees. It should be noted, however, that all private-sector workers are covered by Social Security while not all public-sector workers are, and public-sector plans frequently require an employee contribution while private-sector plans are almost always fully employer-paid. Private-sector workers had a much higher incidence of paid vacations, primarily because of the large number of teachers in local government who do not receive paid vacations.

About 18 percent of workers throughout the industry are union members or are covered by union contracts. Unionization of workers varies by industry—nearly 40 percent of workers in transportation, communications, and public utilities are union members or are covered by union contracts, compared to less than 4 percent in finance, insurance, and real estate (see Table 14).

### Table 14. Percentage of workers who are union members or covered by union contracts by industry division, 1992

| Industry division | Percentage union members or covered by union contracts |
|---|---|
| Total, all industries | 17.9 |
| Agriculture, forestry, and fishing | 3.3 |
| Mining | 16.1 |
| Construction | 23.0 |
| Manufacturing | 21.2 |
| Transportation, communications, and public utilities | 39.4 |
| Wholesale and retail trade | 7.3 |
| Finance, insurance, and real estate | 3.6 |
| Services | 17.4 |
| Government | 37.8 |

## Outlook for Growth Within Major Industry Groupings

As indicated in the discussion of employment, the number of job openings available in any industry stems from growth and the need to replace workers who transfer to another industry, retire, die, or stop working for other reasons. Throughout the economy, replacement needs will create more job openings than employment growth.

Employment size is a major determinant of job openings—larger industries generally provide more openings. The occupational composition of an industry is another factor. Industries with a high concentration of professional, technical, and other jobs that require more formal education generally have fewer openings resulting from replacement needs, because these workers are more attached to their occupations. On the other hand, industries with a high concentration of service, laborer, and other jobs that require little formal education generally have more replacement openings, because these workers are more likely to leave their occupations.

Employment growth depends on changes in demand for the goods and services produced by an industry and on changes in productivity in that industry. Each industry is affected by a different set of variables that determine how many and what types of jobs will be available. Even within an industry, employment in different occupations may grow at different rates. For example, changes in technology, production methods, and business practices in an industry may eliminate some jobs while creating others. Some industries may be growing rapidly overall, yet opportunities for workers in occupations that are adversely affected by technological change could be stagnant. The rate of growth of some occupations may be declining in the economy as a whole, yet may be increasing in a particular, rapidly growing industry, even though they comprise a shrinking share of jobs in that industry.

Total employment in the United States is projected to increase about 22 percent over the 1992-2005 period. Growth rates will vary widely among industry sectors.

Despite rising demand, employment in **mining** is expected to decline, due to the spread of labor-saving technology and increased reliance on foreign sources of energy. Consequently, employment opportunities in mining are expected to be limited. On the other hand, **construction industry employment** is expected to increase about as fast as the average for the economy in general. Although projections indicate a slowdown in single- and multi-family housing construction, construction job growth will be spurred by new factory construction as existing facilities are modernized; by new school construction, reflecting growth in the school-aged population; and by infrastructure improvements, such as road and bridge construction.

Overall employment in **agriculture, forestry, and fishing** will grow more slowly than average, with almost all new jobs occurring in the rapidly growing agricultural services industry—which includes landscaping, farm management, veterinary, soil preparation, and crop services.

Employment in **manufacturing industries** will decline as improvements in production technology eliminate many production occupations. **Apparel manufacturing** is projected to lose about 250,000 jobs over the 1992-2005 period—more than any other manufacturing industry. Some manufacturing industries with strong domestic markets and export potential, however, are expected to experience increases in employment. For example, miscellaneous **plastics** products manufacturing will benefit from the substitution of plastics for glass and metal, and its almost exclusive use as inputs by a wide range of industries. Projected growth in **drug manufacturing** is based on strong domestic demand—reflecting an expanding elderly population—and strong export growth.

**Trucking and air transportation** are expected to add more than 600,000 jobs over the projection period. Trucking industry growth will be fueled by growth in the volume of goods that need to be shipped as the economy expands; air transportation will expand as consumer demand increases, reflecting rising personal incomes and relatively cheap fares resulting from airline deregulation.

Despite strong growth in demand for telephone services, employment in the **telephone communications industry** will decline due to labor-saving technology and increased competition. More than 175,000 jobs are expected to be lost in this industry from 1992 to 2005. Broadcasting industry employment will not sustain the rapid growth of the past, as the cable television market approaches saturation.

**Wholesale trade** is expected to add 1.1 million jobs, in part due to increases in exports. **Retail trade** is expected to add 4.4 million jobs over the 1992-2005 period, resulting largely from increased personal income levels. **Eating and drinking places** will account for half of the employment growth in retail trade.

Overall growth in **finance, insurance, and real estate** is expected to be about as fast as average, adding 1.4 million jobs by 2005. Services traditionally offered by commercial banks are increasingly offered by a range of institutions. Nondepository institutions—including personal and business credit institutions, as well as mortgage banks—are expected to grow at a rapid rate, at the expense of commercial banks. Real estate is expected to add the most jobs—over 340,000—within this major industry sector.

As the largest and fastest growing major industry sector, **services** is projected to provide 15.5 million new wage and salary jobs—more than 3 out of 5 new jobs—throughout the economy.

**Health, education, and business services** will account for almost 10 million of these new jobs. Overall population growth, the rise in the elderly and school aged population, and the trend toward contracting out for computer, personnel, and other business services will stimulate job growth in the services sector.

All 900,000 new **government jobs** will occur in state and local government, reflecting growth in the population and its demand for public services. The federal government is expected to lose more than 100,000 jobs.

# Employment Growth Projections for All Major Industries

The table that follows provides information on the numbers of people employed and the growth in employment projected in all major industries. While this is a lot of small print to scan, it can be useful to you in a variety of ways.

The large number of industries listed in the chart will give you an idea of the many opportunities available in areas you may not have considered. Look through the major industry groupings and check those that interest you or those in which you have related experience or training. Major industry groupings are those not indented in the "Industry title" column. For each industry grouping you check, ask yourself, "How interested am I in working in this industry?" Write a 1 if you are very interested, a 2 if you are somewhat interested, and a 3 if you are not very interested.

In this way, you can identify those industries that are of particular interest to you—and those where your skills might be in particular demand.

## Employment by industry, 1983, 1994, and projected 2005

| Standard Industrial Classification | Industry title | Employment (in thousands) | | | | | Annual rate of growth[1] | |
|---|---|---|---|---|---|---|---|---|
| | | 1983 | 1994 | 2005 | | | Employ-ment 1994-2005 | Output 1994-2005 |
| | | | | Low | Moderate | High | | |
| | Nonfarm wage and salary[2] ........................ | 89,734 | 113,340 | 125,631 | 130,185 | 135,729 | 1.3 | — |
| 10 - 14 | Mining .................................................... | 952 | 601 | 450 | 439 | 509 | −2.8 | −.4 |
| 10 | Metal mining ................................................ | 56 | 49 | 38 | 42 | 44 | −1.5 | 1.4 |
| 12 | Coal mining ................................................ | 194 | 112 | 63 | 70 | 77 | −4.3 | .2 |
| 131, 132 | Crude petroleum, natural gas, and gas liquids ................................................ | 265 | 168 | 138 | 105 | 124 | −4.2 | −1.9 |
| 138 | Oil and gas field service ......................... | 333 | 168 | 127 | 136 | 173 | −1.9 | 3.2 |
| 14 | Nonmetallic minerals, except fuels ......... | 104 | 104 | 85 | 88 | 91 | −1.5 | .9 |
| 15, 16, 17 | Construction .................................................... | 3,946 | 5,010 | 5,193 | 5,500 | 5,966 | .9 | 1.5 |
| 20-39 | Manufacturing ............................................ | 18,430 | 18,304 | 16,218 | 16,991 | 18,000 | −.7 | 2.0 |
| 24, 25, 32-39 | Durable manufacturing ............................. | 10,707 | 10,431 | 8,803 | 9,290 | 10,045 | −1.0 | 2.2 |
| 24 | Lumber and wood products .................... | 670 | 752 | 649 | 685 | 729 | −.9 | .9 |
| 241 | Logging .................................................... | 83 | 82 | 73 | 74 | 75 | −.9 | .6 |
| 242 | Sawmills and planing mills .................... | 193 | 189 | 140 | 150 | 161 | −2.1 | .1 |
| 243 | Millwork, plywood, and structural members ................................................ | 207 | 271 | 236 | 250 | 269 | −.7 | 1.3 |
| 244, 9 | Wood containers and miscellaneous wood products ..................................... | 119 | 138 | 133 | 139 | 147 | .0 | 2.2 |
| 245 | Wood buildings and mobile homes ....... | 69 | 73 | 67 | 72 | 78 | −.1 | .0 |
| 25 | Furniture and fixtures ............................. | 448 | 502 | 486 | 515 | 581 | −.2 | 1.3 |
| 251 | Household furniture ................................. | 279 | 284 | 264 | 280 | 327 | −.1 | 1.0 |
| 254 | Partitions and fixtures ............................. | 59 | 80 | 83 | 88 | 95 | .9 | 1.2 |
| 252, 3, 9 | Office and miscellaneous furniture and fixtures ............................................ | 110 | 138 | 138 | 146 | 159 | .5 | 1.6 |
| 32 | Stone, clay, and glass products ............. | 541 | 533 | 413 | 434 | 463 | −1.8 | .5 |
| 102403.5 | Glass and glass products ..................... | 165 | 153 | 118 | 125 | 24,611 | −1.8 | .4 |
| 324 | Hydraulic cement .................................... | 25 | 18 | 14 | 14 | 14 | −2.2 | .2 |
| 325, 6, 8, 9 | Stone, clay, and miscellaneous mineral products ..................................... | 167 | 164 | 115 | 124 | 136 | −2.5 | .2 |
| 327 | Concrete, gypsum, and plaster products ................................................ | 184 | 198 | 166 | 172 | 180 | −1.3 | .9 |
| 33 | Primary metal industries ......................... | 832 | 699 | 508 | 532 | 565 | −2.5 | .1 |
| 331 | Blast furnaces and basic steel products ................................................ | 341 | 239 | 150 | 155 | 163 | −3.9 | −.5 |
| 332 | Iron and steel foundries ......................... | 139 | 125 | 88 | 92 | 99 | −2.7 | −1.2 |
| 333 | Primary nonferrous smelting and refining ................................................ | 50 | 41 | 32 | 36 | 39 | −1.2 | 2.3 |
| 334, 9 | All other primary metals ......................... | 41 | 44 | 40 | 40 | 40 | −.8 | 1.8 |
| 335 | Nonferrous rolling and drawing ............. | 184 | 167 | 130 | 135 | 141 | −1.9 | .0 |
| 336 | Nonferrous foundries ............................. | 78 | 84 | 68 | 74 | 82 | −1.2 | −.2 |
| 34 | Fabricated metal products ..................... | 1,368 | 1,387 | 1,114 | 1,181 | 1,271 | −1.5 | .5 |
| 341 | Metal cans and shipping containers .... | 60 | 42 | 27 | 27 | 27 | −3.9 | .9 |
| 342 | Cutlery, hand tools, and hardware ....... | 138 | 129 | 85 | 90 | 97 | −3.2 | −.2 |
| 343 | Plumbing and nonelectric heating equipment ............................................ | 62 | 60 | 46 | 48 | 52 | −1.9 | −.3 |
| 344 | Fabricated steel metal products ........... | 416 | 409 | 299 | 315 | 339 | −2.3 | .4 |
| 345 | Screw machine products, bolts, rivets, etc. ............................................ | 86 | 96 | 73 | 78 | 84 | −1.8 | .5 |
| 346 | Metal forgings and stampings ............... | 224 | 234 | 183 | 194 | 211 | −1.7 | .2 |
| 347 | Metal coating, engraving, and allied services ................................................ | 96 | 124 | 134 | 140 | 150 | 1.1 | 2.5 |
| 348 | Ordnance and ammunition ..................... | 67 | 54 | 49 | 51 | 51 | −.5 | −.8 |
| 349 | Miscellaneous fabricated metal products ................................................ | 219 | 241 | 218 | 238 | 260 | −.1 | .9 |
| 35 | Industrial machinery and equipment .... | 2,052 | 1,985 | 1,687 | 1,769 | 1,904 | −1.0 | 3.9 |
| 351 | Engines and turbines ............................. | 104 | 90 | 69 | 70 | 73 | −2.2 | .2 |
| 352 | Farm and garden machinery and equipment ............................................ | 107 | 105 | 84 | 87 | 91 | −1.7 | 1.6 |
| 353 | Construction and related machinery ... | 245 | 210 | 182 | 188 | 204 | −1.0 | 1.6 |
| 354 | Metalworking machinery and equipment ............................................ | 298 | 322 | 283 | 291 | 304 | −.9 | −.4 |
| 355 | Special industry machinery ................... | 151 | 155 | 149 | 150 | 151 | −.3 | 1.8 |
| 356 | General industrial machinery and equipment ............................................ | 234 | 243 | 228 | 235 | 250 | −.3 | −.4 |
| 357 | Computer and office equipment ......... | 474 | 351 | 240 | 263 | 293 | −2.6 | 7.3 |
| 358 | Refrigeration and service industry machinery ............................................ | 158 | 190 | 181 | 192 | 210 | .1 | 1.1 |
| 359 | Industrial machinery, n.e.c. ................. | 282 | 319 | 273 | 292 | 329 | −.8 | 1.7 |
| 36 | Electronic and electric equipment ........ | 1,704 | 1,571 | 1,347 | 1,408 | 1,524 | −1.0 | 3.5 |
| 361 | Electric distribution equipment ............. | 103 | 82 | 69 | 70 | 71 | −1.5 | .1 |
| 362 | Electrical industrial apparatus ............. | 190 | 156 | 115 | 116 | 118 | −2.7 | .3 |

## Employment by industry, 1983, 1994, and projected 2005

| Standard Industrial Classification | Industry title | Employment (in thousands) | | | | | Annual rate of growth¹ | |
|---|---|---|---|---|---|---|---|---|
| | | 1983 | 1994 | 2005 | | | Employ-ment 1994-2005 | Output 1994-2005 |
| | | | | Low | Moderate | High | | |
| 363 | Household appliances ........................... | 138 | 123 | 92 | 98 | 109 | −2.1 | 1.5 |
| 364 | Electric lighting and wiring equipment .. | 187 | 176 | 148 | 155 | 167 | −1.2 | 1.3 |
| 365 | Household audio and video equipment ... | 87 | 89 | 55 | 55 | 54 | −4.2 | 1.2 |
| 366 | Communications equipment ................. | 279 | 244 | 200 | 210 | 225 | −1.3 | 3.8 |
| 367 | Electronic components and accessories ...................................... | 563 | 544 | 522 | 553 | 620 | .1 | 5.5 |
| 369 | Miscellaneous electrical equipment ...... | 157 | 156 | 146 | 151 | 159 | −.3 | 1.9 |
| 37 | Transportation equipment ..................... | 1,731 | 1,749 | 1,455 | 1,567 | 1,744 | −1.0 | 1.8 |
| 371 | Motor vehicles and equipment ............. | 754 | 899 | 715 | 775 | 883 | −1.3 | 1.6 |
| 372, 6 | Aerospace ............................................ | 702 | 587 | 517 | 552 | 605 | −.6 | 2.2 |
| 373 | Ship and boat building and repairing .... | 183 | 159 | 120 | 131 | 140 | −1.8 | −1.0 |
| 374 | Railroad equipment ............................... | 30 | 35 | 34 | 35 | 36 | −.1 | 3.6 |
| 375, 9 | Miscellaneous transportation equipment .......................................... | 62 | 69 | 69 | 75 | 81 | .8 | 3.5 |
| 38 | Instruments and related products .......... | 990 | 863 | 771 | 798 | 836 | −.7 | 2.9 |
| 381 | Search and navigation equipment ........ | 311 | 180 | 126 | 132 | 141 | −2.8 | .5 |
| 382 | Measuring and controlling devices ....... | 300 | 284 | 234 | 248 | 273 | −1.2 | 1.9 |
| 384 | Measuring equipment, instruments, and supplies .................................... | 198 | 265 | 305 | 306 | 307 | 1.3 | 5.7 |
| 385 | Ophthalmic goods ................................. | 38 | 37 | 36 | 37 | 38 | −.1 | 3.9 |
| 386 | Photographic equipment and supplies . | 128 | 89 | 66 | 70 | 72 | −2.2 | 2.1 |
| 387 | Watches, clocks, and parts .................. | 16 | 8 | 4 | 5 | 5 | −5.3 | −.5 |
| 39 | Miscellaneous manufacturing industries | 370 | 391 | 374 | 404 | 428 | .3 | 1.8 |
| 391 | Jewelry, silverware, and plated ware .... | 54 | 51 | 43 | 44 | 44 | −1.5 | −0.0 |
| 394 | Toys and sporting goods ...................... | 106 | 115 | 120 | 135 | 143 | 1.4 | 2.8 |
| 393, 5, 6, 9 | Manufactured products, n.e.c. ............. | 211 | 224 | 211 | 225 | 240 | .0 | 1.9 |
| 2023, 2631 | Nondurable manufacturing .................... | 7,723 | 7,873 | 7,415 | 7,700 | 7,955 | −.2 | 1.8 |
| 20 | Food and kindred products ................... | 1,612 | 1,680 | 1,693 | 1,696 | 1,696 | .1 | 1.3 |
| 201 | Meat products ....................................... | 346 | 451 | 514 | 515 | 513 | 1.2 | 1.2 |
| 202 | Dairy products ...................................... | 164 | 149 | 132 | 133 | 133 | −1.0 | 1.9 |
| 203 | Preserved fruits and vegetables .......... | 220 | 245 | 252 | 260 | 264 | .5 | 1.4 |
| 204, 7 | Grain mill products and fats and oils .... | 170 | 160 | 166 | 161 | 158 | .0 | 1.4 |
| 205 | Bakery products .................................... | 220 | 213 | 196 | 195 | 194 | −.8 | .4 |
| 206 | Sugar and confectionery products ........ | 103 | 99 | 89 | 90 | 90 | −.9 | .4 |
| 208 | Beverages ............................................ | 222 | 178 | 130 | 132 | 134 | −2.7 | .8 |
| 209 | Miscellaneous food and kindred products .......................................... | 165 | 185 | 213 | 211 | 210 | 1.2 | 2.3 |
| 210 | Tobacco products ................................. | 68 | 42 | 28 | 26 | 26 | −4.2 | −.4 |
| 22 | Textile mill products ............................. | 742 | 673 | 521 | 568 | 608 | −1.5 | .2 |
| 2214, 6, 8 | Weaving, finishing, yarn, and thread mills .............................................. | 432 | 358 | 253 | 281 | 303 | −2.2 | −.2 |
| 225 | Knitting mills ........................................ | 207 | 199 | 157 | 173 | 187 | −1.2 | .0 |
| 227 | Carpets and rugs .................................. | 49 | 64 | 64 | 65 | 68 | .1 | 1.0 |
| 229 | Miscellaneous textile goods ................. | 55 | 52 | 47 | 49 | 51 | −.6 | 1.3 |
| 23 | Apparel and other textile products ........ | 1,163 | 969 | 723 | 772 | 815 | −2.1 | .5 |
| 2318 | Apparel ................................................ | 990 | 755 | 512 | 547 | 577 | −2.9 | −.4 |
| 239 | Miscellaneous fabricated textile products .......................................... | 173 | 215 | 211 | 225 | 238 | .4 | 2.6 |
| 26 | Paper and allied products ..................... | 654 | 691 | 674 | 708 | 730 | .2 | 2.5 |
| 261-3 | Pulp, paper, and paperboard mills ....... | 249 | 232 | 211 | 218 | 222 | .6 | 2.7 |
| 265 | Paperboard containers and boxes ....... | 191 | 213 | 216 | 230 | 240 | .7 | 1.8 |
| 267 | Converted paper products except containers ...................................... | 214 | 246 | 247 | 260 | 267 | .5 | 2.9 |
| 27 | Printing and publishing ......................... | 1,298 | 1,542 | 1,576 | 1,627 | 1,676 | .5 | 2.5 |
| 271 | Newspapers ......................................... | 426 | 450 | 400 | 413 | 424 | .8 | −.4 |
| 272 | Periodicals ........................................... | 100 | 135 | 156 | 163 | 169 | 1.7 | 2.1 |
| 273 | Books ................................................... | 98 | 120 | 125 | 130 | 134 | .8 | 2.7 |
| 274 | Miscellaneous publishing .................... | 56 | 84 | 84 | 85 | 86 | .1 | 3.6 |
| 275, 6 | Commercial printing and business forms ............................................. | 480 | 597 | 653 | 675 | 699 | 1.1 | 3.3 |
| 277 | Greeting cards ...................................... | 23 | 29 | 33 | 32 | 32 | 1.0 | 4.7 |
| 278 | Blankbooks and bookbinding ............... | 65 | 70 | 75 | 77 | 80 | .8 | 2.6 |
| 279 | Service industries for the printing trade | 49 | 57 | 51 | 53 | 54 | −.7 | 2.6 |
| 28 | Chemicals and allied products .............. | 1,043 | 1,061 | 1,032 | 1,067 | 1,089 | .1 | 2.0 |
| 281, 6 | Industrial chemicals ............................. | 314 | 277 | 253 | 259 | 260 | −.6 | .9 |
| 282 | Plastics materials and synthetics ......... | 177 | 162 | 138 | 143 | 145 | −1.1 | 1.4 |
| 283 | Drugs ................................................... | 201 | 263 | 309 | 325 | 337 | 1.9 | 4.0 |
| 284 | Soap, cleaners, and toilet goods ......... | 142 | 153 | 164 | 165 | 166 | .7 | 2.5 |
| 285 | Paints and allied products .................... | 60 | 58 | 46 | 48 | 51 | −1.6 | 1.4 |
| 287 | Agricultural chemicals .......................... | 61 | 55 | 39 | 43 | 44 | −2.3 | 1.2 |
| 289 | Miscellaneous chemical products ........ | 89 | 93 | 83 | 85 | 87 | −.9 | .9 |

## Employment by industry, 1983, 1994, and projected 2005

| Standard Industrial Classification | Industry title | Employment (in thousands) | | | | | Annual rate of growth[1] | |
|---|---|---|---|---|---|---|---|---|
| | | 1983 | 1994 | 2005 | | | Employ-ment 1994-2005 | Output 1994-2005 |
| | | | | Low | Moderate | High | | |
| 29 | Petroleum and coal products ................. | 196 | 149 | 142 | 140 | 137 | −.5 | 2.1 |
| 291 | Petroleum refining ............................. | 158 | 109 | 105 | 103 | 98 | −.5 | 2.2 |
| 295, 9 | Miscellaneous petroleum and coal products ........................................ | 37 | 40 | 37 | 38 | 39 | −.5 | .9 |
| 30 | Rubber and miscellaneous plastics products ........................................ | 743 | 952 | 972 | 1.030 | 1,100 | .7 | 2.9 |
| 301 | Tires and inner tubes ........................... | 94 | 80 | 59 | 60 | 63 | −2.5 | .2 |
| 302, 5, 6 | Rubber products and plastic hose and footwear ..................................... | 171 | 182 | 158 | 170 | 185 | −.6 | 1.9 |
| 308 | Miscellaneous plastics products, n.e.c. | 478 | 690 | 755 | 800 | 853 | 1.4 | 3.4 |
| 31 | Leather and leather products ................ | 205 | 114 | 54 | 65 | 79 | −4.9 | −1.9 |
| 313, 4 | Footwear, except rubber and plastic .... | 136 | 61 | 20 | 29 | 40 | −6.7 | −5.0 |
| 311, 57, 9 | Luggage, handbags, and leather products, n.e.c. ................................ | 69 | 53 | 34 | 37 | 39 | −3.3 | −.3 |
| 4042, 4449 | Transportation, communications, utilities ........................................ | 4,958 | 6,006 | 6,431 | 6,723 | .6 | 3.2 | |
| 4042, 4447 | Transportation ................................... | 2,748 | 3,775 | 4,060 | 4,251 | 4,438 | 1.1 | 4.0 |
| 40 | Railroad transportation ........................ | 376 | 241 | 172 | 186 | 199 | −2.3 | 1.3 |
| 41 | Local and inter-urban passenger transit | 257 | 410 | 474 | 490 | 499 | 1.6 | .0 |
| 42 | Trucking and warehousing .................... | 1,222 | 1,797 | 1,903 | 2,000 | 2,099 | 1.0 | 5.0 |
| 44 | Water transportation ............................ | 189 | 169 | 158 | 165 | 175 | −.2 | 2.0 |
| 45 | Air transportation ................................ | 455 | 748 | 830 | 870 | 910 | 1.4 | 3.7 |
| 46 | Pipelines, except natural gas ............... | 20 | 18 | 14 | 15 | 16 | −1.6 | −.2 |
| 47 | Transportation services ........................ | 229 | 393 | 509 | 525 | 541 | 2.7 | 6.5 |
| 472 | Passenger, transportation arrangement ................................ | 120 | 197 | 237 | 255 | 272 | 2.4 | 6.2 |
| 473, 4, 8 | Miscellaneous transportation services | 109 | 195 | 272 | 270 | 269 | 3.0 | 6.7 |
| 48 | Communications .................................. | 1,324 | 1,305 | 1,190 | 1,235 | 1,279 | −.5 | 3.1 |
| 49 | Electric, gas, and sanitary services ....... | 887 | 927 | 895 | 945 | 1,007 | .2 | 2.0 |
| 491, pt. 493 | Electric utilities ................................ | 560 | 516 | 465 | 485 | 517 | −.6 | 2.2 |
| 492, pt. 493 | Gas utilities ...................................... | 224 | 197 | 159 | 160 | 164 | −1.9 | 1.5 |
| 4947, pt. 493 | Water and sanitation .......................... | 102 | 213 | 272 | 300 | 327 | 3.2 | 2.7 |
| 50, 51 | Wholesale trade ................................. | 5,283 | 6,140 | 6,389 | 6,559 | 6,765 | .6 | 2.2 |
| 5259 | Retail trade ........................................ | 15,587 | 20,438 | 22,781 | 23,094 | 23,417 | 1.1 | 2.4 |
| 5257, 59 | Retail trade, except eating and drinking places ............................. | 10,549 | 13,369 | 14,523 | 15,005 | 15,495 | 1.1 | 2.7 |
| 58 | Eating and drinking places ................... | 5,038 | 7,069 | 8,258 | 8,089 | 7,922 | 1.2 | 1.1 |
| 6067 | Finance, insurance, and real estate ......... | 5,466 | 6,933 | 7,076 | 7,373 | 7,721 | .6 | 2.3 |
| 60 | Depository institutions ......................... | 2,048 | 2,076 | 1,812 | 1,886 | 1,961 | −.9 | 2.0 |
| 61, 67 | Nondepository, holding, and investment offices ......................... | 385 | 730 | 968 | 970 | 973 | 2.6 | 3.0 |
| 62 | Security and commodity brokers ............ | 308 | 518 | 679 | 700 | 719 | 2.8 | 7.0 |
| 63 | Insurance carriers ............................... | 1,229 | 1,551 | 1,597 | 1,633 | 1,668 | .5 | 1.9 |
| 64 | Insurance agents, brokers, and services | 499 | 686 | 696 | 702 | 709 | .2 | 2.6 |
| 65 | Real estate ........................................ | 997 | 1,373 | 1,324 | 1,482 | 1,691 | .7 | 2.2 |
| NA | Royalties .......................................... | — | — | — | — | — | .0 | 2.6 |
| NA | Owner-occupied dwellings .................... | — | — | — | — | — | .0 | .7 |
| 70-87, 89 | Services[3] ........................................ | 19,242 | 30,792 | 42,072 | 42,810 | 43,678 | 3.0 | 3.0 |
| 70 | Hotels and other lodging places ............ | 1,172 | 1,618 | 1,875 | 1,899 | 1,926 | 1.5 | 1.5 |
| 72 | Personal services ............................... | 869 | 1,139 | 1,372 | 1,374 | 1,373 | 1.7 | 1.0 |
| 721, 5 | Laundry, cleaning, and shoe repair ...... | 356 | 428 | 487 | 500 | 510 | 1.4 | .5 |
| 722, 9 | Personal services, n.e.c. .................... | 118 | 225 | 331 | 314 | 299 | 3.1 | 2.3 |
| 723, 4 | Beauty and barber shops ..................... | 323 | 397 | 455 | 460 | 462 | 1.3 | .6 |
| 726 | Funeral service and crematories .......... | 72 | 89 | 98 | 100 | 102 | 1.1 | −1.0 |
| 73 | Business services ............................... | 2,948 | 6,239 | 9,796 | 10,032 | 10,313 | 4.4 | 4.5 |
| 731 | Advertising ...................................... | 171 | 224 | 250 | 250 | 250 | 1.0 | 1.4 |
| 734 | Services to buildings ........................... | 559 | 855 | 1,325 | 1,350 | 1,379 | 4.2 | 3.6 |
| 735 | Miscellaneous equipment rental and leasing ................................ | 111 | 216 | 319 | 325 | 332 | 3.8 | .3 |
| 736 | Personnel supply services ................... | 619 | 2,254 | 3,507 | 3,564 | 3,635 | 4.3 | 6.0 |
| 737 | Computer and data processing services ................................ | 416 | 950 | 1,516 | 1,611 | 1,725 | 4.9 | 4.9 |
| 732, 3, 8 | Miscellaneous business services ......... | 1,074 | 1,741 | 2,880 | 2,932 | 4.9 | 4.7 | |
| 75 | Auto repair, services, and garages ........ | 619 | 971 | 1,304 | 1,345 | 1,368 | 3.0 | 2.3 |
| 751 | Automotive rentals, without drivers ...... | 126 | 174 | 222 | 227 | 231 | 2.4 | 2.6 |
| 752-4 | Automobile parking, repair, and services ................................ | 493 | 796 | 1,082 | 1,119 | 1,137 | 3.1 | 2.0 |
| 76 | Miscellaneous repair shops .................. | 287 | 334 | 393 | 400 | 407 | 1.7 | 2.2 |
| 762 | Electrical repair shops ........................ | 91 | 105 | 123 | 125 | 127 | 1.6 | 1.8 |
| 763, 4 | Watch, jewelry, and furniture repair ...... | 28 | 26 | 25 | 25 | 25 | −.5 | 3.2 |
| 769 | Miscellaneous repair services ............. | 169 | 202 | 245 | 250 | 255 | 1.9 | 2.2 |

## Employment by industry, 1983, 1994, and projected 2005

| Standard Industrial Classification | Industry title | Employment (in thousands) | | | | | Annual rate of growth[1] | |
|---|---|---|---|---|---|---|---|---|
| | | 1983 | 1994 | 2005 | | | Employment 1994-2005 | Output 1994-2005 |
| | | | | Low | Moderate | High | | |
| 78 | Motion pictures | 268 | 471 | 588 | 591 | 596 | 2.1 | 3.1 |
| 781-3 | Motion pictures | 214 | 333 | 433 | 426 | 419 | 2.2 | 3.0 |
| 784 | Video tape rental | 54 | 138 | 155 | 165 | 177 | 1.7 | 3.2 |
| 79 | Amusement and recreation services | 853 | 1,344 | 1,846 | 1,844 | 1,848 | 2.9 | 2.4 |
| 792 | Producers, orchestras, and entertainers | 94 | 148 | 197 | 200 | 204 | 2.8 | 3.0 |
| 793 | Bowling centers | 97 | 85 | 73 | 73 | 73 | −1.5 | −1.8 |
| 794 | Commercial sports | 76 | 106 | 147 | 137 | 131 | 2.4 | 1.1 |
| 791, 9 | Amusement and recreation services, n.e.c. | 586 | 1,005 | 1,431 | 1,434 | 1,441 | 3.3 | 2.6 |
| 80 | Health services | 5,986 | 9,001 | 11,985 | 12,075 | 12,321 | 2.7 | 2.9 |
| 801-4 | Offices of health practitioner | 1,503 | 2,546 | 3,560 | 3,525 | 3,472 | 3.0 | 3.4 |
| 805 | Nursing and personal care facilities | 1,106 | 1,649 | 2,377 | 2,400 | 2,474 | 3.5 | 3.1 |
| 806 | Hospitals, private | 3,037 | 3,774 | 4,175 | 4,250 | 4,451 | 1.1 | 1.6 |
| 807-9 | Health services, n.e.c. | 341 | 1,032 | 1,873 | 1,900 | 1,925 | 5.7 | 6.2 |
| 81 | Legal services | 602 | 927 | 1,240 | 1,270 | 1,300 | 2.9 | 2.9 |
| 82 | Educational services | 1,225 | 1,822 | 2,336 | 2,400 | 2,437 | 2.5 | 2.8 |
| 83 | Social services | 1,118 | 2,181 | 3,637 | 3,639 | 3,623 | 4.8 | 3.3 |
| 832, 9 | Individual and miscellaneous social services | 464 | 779 | 1,273 | 1,314 | 1,335 | 4.9 | 3.8 |
| 833 | Job training and related services | 190 | 298 | 443 | 425 | 411 | 3.3 | .7 |
| 835 | Child daycare services | 284 | 502 | 840 | 800 | 766 | 4.3 | 1.0 |
| 836 | Residential care | 251 | 602 | 1,082 | 1,100 | 1,111 | 5.6 | 5.4 |
| 84 | Museums, botanical, zoological gardens | 43 | 79 | 112 | 112 | 112 | 3.2 | 4.7 |
| 86 | Membership organizations | 1,510 | 2,059 | 2,156 | 2,336 | 2,488 | 1.2 | 2.6 |
| 87, 89 | Engineering, management, and related services | 1,673 | 2,607 | 3,431 | 3,494 | 3,565 | 2.7 | 2.5 |
| 871 | Engineering and architectural services | 576 | 775 | 1,008 | 1,044 | 1,086 | 2.7 | 2.2 |
| 873 | Research and testing services | 384 | 563 | 743 | 745 | 747 | 2.6 | 5.0 |
| 874 | Management and public relations | 327 | 716 | 1,037 | 1,049 | 1,062 | 3.5 | 1.7 |
| 872, 89 | Accounting, auditing, and other services | 387 | 553 | 642 | 656 | 670 | 1.6 | 1.4 |
| | Government | 15,870 | 19,117 | 19,307 | 20,990 | 22,951 | .9 | 1.0 |
| | Federal government | 2,774 | 2,870 | 2,607 | 2,635 | 2,667 | −.8 | .2 |
| | Federal enterprises | 890 | 1,017 | 898 | 935 | 976 | −.8 | 2.3 |
| | U.S. Postal Service | 685 | 818 | 726 | 760 | 797 | −.7 | 2.8 |
| | Federal electric utilities | 43 | 27 | 24 | 25 | 27 | −.9 | .5 |
| | Federal government enterprises, n.e.c. | 162 | 172 | 18 | 150 | 152 | −1.2 | 2.2 |
| | Federal general government | 1,884 | 1,853 | 1,709 | 1,700 | 1,691 | −.8 | −.7 |
| | State and local government | 13,096 | 16,247 | 16,701 | 18,355 | 20,284 | 1.1 | 1.4 |
| | State and local enterprises | 782 | 941 | 1,073 | 1,113 | 1,146 | 1.5 | 2.2 |
| | Local government passenger transit | 180 | 214 | 249 | 260 | 266 | 1.8 | −.1 |
| | State and local electric utilities | 73 | 86 | 102 | 100 | 98 | 1.3 | 1.6 |
| | State and local government enterprises, n.e.c. | 529 | 641 | 722 | 753 | 782 | 1.5 | 2.7 |
| | State and local general government | 12,314 | 15,306 | 15,628 | 17,242 | 19,138 | 1.1 | 1.2 |
| | State and local government hospitals | 1,115 | 1,081 | 994 | 1,090 | 1,202 | .1 | −.2 |
| | State and local government education | 6,589 | 8,365 | 9,058 | 10,000 | 11,108 | 1.6 | 1.8 |
| | State and local general government, n.e.c. | 4,610 | 5,860 | 5,576 | 6,152 | 6,829 | .4 | .4 |
| 01,02,07,08,09 | Agriculture[4] | 3,508 | 3,623 | 3,431 | 3,399 | 3,361 | −.6 | 1.0 |
| 01, 02 | Agricultural production | 2,727 | 2,326 | 1,813 | 1,799 | 1,783 | −2.3 | .9 |
| 07 | Agricultural services | 699 | 1,197 | 1,528 | 1,514 | 1,494 | 2.2 | 2.2 |
| 08, 09 | Forestry, fishing, and trapping | 82 | 100 | 90 | 87 | 84 | −1.3 | −2.3 |
| 88 | Private households wage and salary | 1,247 | 966 | 818 | 800 | 779 | −1.7 | .4 |
| | Nonagricultural self-employed and unpaid family[5] | 7,914 | 9,085 | 10,382 | 10,324 | 10,343 | 1.2 | — |
| | Total[6] | 102,404 | 127,014 | 140,261 | 144,708 | 150,212 | 1.2 | 2.2 |

[1]Rates are based on moderate scenario.

[2]Comparable estimate of output growth is not available.

[3]Excludes SIC 074,5,8 (agricultural service) and 99 (nonclassifiable establishments). The data, therefore, are not exactly comparable with data published in *Employment and Earnings.*

[4]Excludes government wage and salary workers, and includes private SIC 08, 09 (forestry and fisheries).

[5]Excludes SIC 08, 09 (forestry and fisheries).

[6]Employment for wage and salary workers are from the Current Employment Statistics (payroll) survey, which counts jobs, whereas self-employed, unpaid family worker, agricultural, and private household data are from the Current Population Survey (household survey), which counts workers. These totals for 1983 and 1994, therefore, differ from the official estimates of the Bureau of Labor Statistics.

NOTE: Dash indicates data not available. n.e.c. = not elsewhere classified.

SOURCE: Historical output data are from the Bureau of Economic Analysis, U.S. Department of Commerce.

# Employment Projections, Earnings, and Education Required for the 500 Largest Occupations

# Appendix C

## Introduction

Just as I was finishing up this book, I received new information from the Department of Labor providing projections for all major jobs through the year 2005. While the descriptions in Section 1 provide information that is far more detailed, the tables in this appendix provide information on many more jobs.

There are some useful things you can do with the information in this appendix. For example, let's say you are good with math and like to figure out how things work. There are many jobs in Section 1 that will interest you, but even more are included in this appendix. Some of these jobs may require a college degree and provide a path of upward mobility and higher earnings that you can consider as a long-term goal. Others in this appendix are more specialized or in other areas that also interest you.

The occupations listed in this appendix cover about 90 percent of the labor market. Table 1 organizes jobs into groups and includes information on growth, earnings, and typical education requirements. Table 2 provides brief comments related to major trends affecting each occupation.

When considering various career or job options, most people have some basic questions, such as, "How much will this job pay?" or, "What are the future opportunities in this career?" While there is more to consider in making a career choice than the answers to these questions, much of the basic information people ask about when making career decisions has been assembled in this appendix.

This is a very long appendix, and I really don't expect you to "read" it. The information it presents on each job spreads across two pages and includes details many people want to know when considering career alternatives. One way to use it is to locate clusters of jobs that interest you and look at the jobs within those categories. You may find jobs you had not previously considered and you want to learn more about. Make note of those jobs and, if descriptions of them are not included in this book, find descriptions of similar jobs in the current edition of the *Occupational Outlook Handbook* or in *America's Top 300 Jobs,* available at most libraries or bookstores.

Note that one of the columns indicates the source of training most often required for each job. Another appendix in this book organizes jobs into groupings based on education or training needed. This allows you to quickly identify jobs within occupational groupings and education or training requirements.

The information in this appendix comes from the U.S. Department of Labor's bulletin 2472. It provides data on the numbers of people working in each job in 1994 and projected to work in that job by 2005. Information on earnings is by "quartile," with each quartile equal to the earnings of about 25 percent of the labor force. Those in the first quartile had the highest earnings. Information on source of training indicates the training or education typically required for entry into that job.

**Table C-1. Employment by occupation, 1994 and projected 2005, moderate alternative**
(Employment and job openings numbers in thousands)

| Occupation | Employment | | Employment change, 1994-2005 | | Total openings due to growth and net replacements, 1994-2005[1] | Earnings quartile[2] | Most significant source of training |
|---|---|---|---|---|---|---|---|
| | 1994 | Projected, 2005 | Percent | Number | | | |
| Total, all occupations .................... | 127,014 | 144,708 | 14 | 17,694 | 49,631 | | |
| **Executive, administrative, and managerial occupations** .................... | 12,903 | 15,071 | 17 | 2,168 | 4,844 | | |
| Managerial and administrative occupations ........... | 9,058 | 10,575 | 17 | 1,517 | 3,467 | | |
| Administrative services managers ...................... | 279 | 307 | 10 | 28 | 87 | 1 | Work experience, plus degree |
| Communication, transportation, and utilities operations managers .................... | 154 | 135 | −12 | −19 | 32 | 1 | Work experience, plus degree |
| Construction managers .................... | 197 | 253 | 28 | 56 | 97 | 1 | Bachelor's degree |
| Education administrators .................... | 393 | 459 | 17 | 66 | 176 | 1 | Work experience, plus degree |
| Engineering, mathematical, and natural science managers .................... | 337 | 432 | 28 | 95 | 165 | 1 | Work experience, plus degree |
| Financial managers .................... | 768 | 950 | 24 | 182 | 324 | 1 | Work experience, plus degree |
| Food service and lodging managers .................... | 579 | 771 | 33 | 192 | 313 | 3 | Work experience |
| Funeral directors and morticians .................... | 26 | 29 | 11 | 3 | 8 | 1 | Long-term O-J-T |
| General managers and top executives .................... | 3,046 | 3,512 | 15 | 466 | 1,104 | 1 | Work experience, plus degree |
| Government chief executives and legislators ...... | 91 | 94 | 4 | 4 | 26 | 1 | Work experience, plus degree |
| Industrial production managers .................... | 206 | 191 | −7 | −15 | 43 | 1 | Bachelor's degree |
| Marketing, advertising, and public relations managers .................... | 461 | 575 | 25 | 114 | 211 | 1 | Work experience, plus degree |
| Personnel, training, and labor relations managers .................... | 206 | 252 | 22 | 46 | 104 | 1 | Work experience, plus degree |
| Property and real estate managers .................... | 261 | 298 | 14 | 37 | 81 | 2 | Bachelor's degree |
| Purchasing managers .................... | 226 | 235 | 4 | 9 | 55 | 1 | Work experience, plus degree |
| All other managers and administrators .................... | 1,829 | 2,081 | 14 | 252 | 639 | 1 | Work experience, plus degree |
| Management support occupations .................... | 3,845 | 4,496 | 17 | 651 | 1,377 | | |
| Accountants and auditors .................... | 962 | 1,083 | 13 | 121 | 312 | 1 | Bachelor's degree |
| Budget analysts .................... | 66 | 74 | 12 | 8 | 19 | 1 | Bachelor's degree |
| Claims examiners, property and casualty insurance .................... | 56 | 65 | 15 | 9 | 14 | 2 | Bachelor's degree |
| Construction and building inspectors .................... | 64 | 79 | 22 | 14 | 28 | 1 | Work experience |
| Cost estimators .................... | 179 | 210 | 17 | 31 | 48 | 2 | Work experience |
| Credit analysts .................... | 39 | 48 | 24 | 9 | 16 | 1 | Bachelor's degree |
| Employment interviewers, private or public employment service .................... | 77 | 104 | 36 | 27 | 43 | 1 | Bachelor's degree |
| Inspectors and compliance officers, except construction .................... | 157 | 175 | 12 | 18 | 50 | 1 | Work experience |
| Loan officers and counselors .................... | 214 | 264 | 23 | 50 | 85 | 1 | Bachelor's degree |
| Management analysts .................... | 231 | 312 | 35 | 82 | 109 | 1 | Master's degree |
| Personnel, training, and labor relations specialists .................... | 307 | 374 | 22 | 67 | 129 | 1 | Bachelor's degree |
| Purchasing agents, except wholesale, retail, and farm products .................... | 215 | 226 | 5 | 12 | 64 | 1 | Bachelor's degree |
| Tax examiners, collectors, and revenue agents .................... | 63 | 63 | 0 | 0 | 14 | 1 | Bachelor's degree |
| Underwriters .................... | 96 | 103 | 7 | 7 | 25 | 1 | Bachelor's degree |
| Wholesale and retail buyers, except farm products .................... | 180 | 178 | −2 | −3 | 50 | 2 | Bachelor's degree |
| All other management support workers .................... | 940 | 1,138 | 21 | 198 | 371 | 1 | Bachelor's degree |
| **Professional specialty occupations** .................... | 17,314 | 22,387 | 29 | 5,073 | 8,376 | | |
| Engineers .................... | 1,327 | 1,573 | 19 | 246 | 581 | | |
| Aeronautical and astronautical engineers ........... | 56 | 59 | 6 | 3 | 16 | 1 | Bachelor's degree |
| Chemical engineers .................... | 50 | 57 | 13 | 7 | 21 | 1 | Bachelor's degree |
| Civil engineers, including traffic engineers ........... | 184 | 219 | 19 | 34 | 90 | 1 | Bachelor's degree |
| Electrical and electronics engineers .................... | 349 | 417 | 20 | 69 | 157 | 1 | Bachelor's degree |
| Industrial engineers, except safety engineers .................... | 115 | 131 | 13 | 15 | 47 | 1 | Bachelor's degree |
| Mechanical engineers .................... | 231 | 276 | 19 | 45 | 98 | 1 | Bachelor's degree |
| Metallurgists and metallurgical, ceramic, and materials engineers .................... | 19 | 20 | 5 | 1 | 6 | 1 | Bachelor's degree |
| Mining engineers, including mine safety engineers .................... | 3 | 3 | −18 | −1 | 1 | 1 | Bachelor's degree |
| Nuclear engineers .................... | 15 | 15 | 4 | 1 | 5 | 1 | Bachelor's degree |
| Petroleum engineers .................... | 14 | 11 | −21 | −3 | 4 | 1 | Bachelor's degree |
| All other engineers .................... | 292 | 367 | 26 | 75 | | 1 | Bachelor's degree |
| Architects and surveyors .................... | 200 | 215 | 7 | 14 | 70 | | |

**Table C-1. Employment by occupation, 1994 and projected 2005, moderate alternative—Continued**
(Employment and job openings numbers in thousands)

| Occupation | Employment | | Employment change, 1994-2005 | | Total openings due to growth and net replacements, 1994-2005[1] | Earnings quartile[2] | Most significant source of training |
|---|---|---|---|---|---|---|---|
| | 1994 | Projected, 2005 | Percent | Number | | | |
| Architects, except landscape and marine ........ | 91 | 106 | 17 | 15 | 35 | 1 | Bachelor's degree |
| Landscape architects ................................. | 14 | 16 | 17 | 2 | 5 | 1 | Bachelor's degree |
| Surveyors ................................................. | 96 | 92 | −3 | −3 | 30 | 2 | Postsecondary vocational training |
| Life scientists ............................................ | 186 | 230 | 24 | 44 | 94 | | |
| Agricultural and food scientists ................ | 26 | 31 | 19 | 5 | 12 | 1 | Bachelor's degree |
| Biological scientists ................................. | 82 | 103 | 25 | 21 | 43 | 1 | Doctor's degree |
| Foresters and conservation scientists ............. | 41 | 49 | 18 | 8 | 18 | 1 | Bachelor's degree |
| Medical scientists ................................... | 36 | 47 | 31 | 11 | 21 | 1 | Doctor's degree |
| All other life scientists ............................ | 1 | 1 | 1 | 0 | 0 | 1 | Doctor's degree |
| Computer, mathematical, and operations research occupations ................................. | 917 | 1,696 | 85 | 779 | 863 | | |
| Actuaries ................................................. | 17 | 18 | 4 | 1 | 4 | 1 | Bachelor's degree |
| Computer systems analysts, engineers, and scientists ..................................... | 828 | 1,583 | 91 | 755 | 819 | | |
| Computer engineers and scientists ............. | 345 | 655 | 90 | 310 | 338 | | |
| Computer engineers ........................... | 195 | 372 | 90 | 177 | 191 | 1 | Bachelor's degree |
| All other computer scientists ................. | 149 | 283 | 89 | 134 | 147 | 1 | Bachelor's degree |
| Systems analysts ............................... | 483 | 928 | 92 | 445 | 481 | 1 | Bachelor's degree |
| Statisticians ............................................ | 14 | 15 | 3 | 0 | 3 | 1 | Bachelor's degree |
| Mathematicians and all other mathematical scientists .............................................. | 14 | 15 | 5 | 1 | 3 | 1 | Doctor's degree |
| Operations research analysts ......................... | 44 | 67 | 50 | 22 | 35 | 1 | Master's degree |
| Physical scientists ...................................... | 209 | 250 | 19 | 41 | 104 | | |
| Chemists ................................................. | 97 | 115 | 19 | 18 | 45 | 1 | Bachelor's degree |
| Geologists, geophysicists, and oceanographers ..................................... | 46 | 54 | 17 | 8 | 24 | 1 | Bachelor's degree |
| Meteorologists ........................................ | 7 | 7 | 7 | 0 | 2 | 1 | Bachelor's degree |
| Physicists and astronomers ......................... | 20 | 18 | −9 | −2 | 5 | 1 | Doctor's degree |
| All other physical scientists ......................... | 40 | 56 | 41 | 16 | 27 | 1 | Bachelor's degree |
| Social scientists ......................................... | 259 | 318 | 23 | 59 | 103 | | |
| Economists ............................................. | 48 | 59 | 25 | 12 | 30 | 1 | Bachelor's degree |
| Psychologists .......................................... | 144 | 177 | 23 | 33 | 45 | 1 | Master's degree |
| Urban and regional planners ......................... | 29 | 35 | 24 | 7 | 13 | 1 | Master's degree |
| All other social scientists ......................... | 38 | 45 | 19 | 7 | 15 | 1 | Master's degree |
| Social, recreational, and religious workers .......... | 1,387 | 1,924 | 39 | 536 | 810 | | |
| Clergy ................................................... | 195 | 234 | 20 | 38 | 77 | 2 | First professional degree |
| Directors, religious activities and education ..... | 81 | 96 | 19 | 15 | 31 | 2 | Bachelor's degree |
| Human services workers ............................. | 168 | 293 | 75 | 125 | 170 | 4 | Moderate-term O-J-T |
| Recreation workers ................................... | 222 | 266 | 20 | 45 | 86 | 2 | Bachelor's degree |
| Residential counselors ................................. | 165 | 290 | 76 | 126 | 158 | 1 | Bachelor's degree |
| Social workers ........................................ | 557 | 744 | 34 | 187 | 288 | 2 | Bachelor's degree |
| Lawyers and judicial workers ......................... | 735 | 918 | 25 | 183 | 279 | | |
| Judges, magistrates, and other judicial workers ................................................. | 79 | 79 | 1 | 1 | 11 | 1 | Work experience, plus degree |
| Lawyers ................................................. | 656 | 839 | 28 | 183 | 268 | 1 | First professional degree |
| Teachers, librarians, and counselors ................ | 6,246 | 7,849 | 26 | 1,603 | 2,886 | | |
| Teachers, preschool and kindergarten ........ | 462 | 602 | 30 | 140 | 215 | 3 | Bachelor's degree |
| Teachers, elementary ............................... | 1,419 | 1,639 | 16 | 220 | 511 | 1 | Bachelor's degree |
| Teachers, secondary school ......................... | 1,340 | 1,726 | 29 | 386 | 782 | 1 | Bachelor's degree |
| Teachers, special education ......................... | 388 | 593 | 53 | 206 | 262 | 1 | Bachelor's degree |
| College and university faculty ......................... | 823 | 972 | 18 | 150 | 395 | 1 | Doctor's degree |
| Other teachers and instructors ......................... | 886 | 1,151 | 30 | 265 | 331 | | |
| Farm and home management advisors ........ | 14 | 14 | −1 | 0 | 1 | 2 | Bachelor's degree |
| Instructors and coaches, sports and physical training ................................. | 282 | 381 | 35 | 98 | 119 | 2 | Moderate-term O-J-T |
| Adult and vocational education teachers ...... | 590 | 757 | 28 | 167 | 211 | | |
| Instructors, adult (nonvocational) education ................................. | 290 | 376 | 29 | 85 | 107 | 2 | Work experience |
| Teachers and instructors, vocational education and training ......................... | 299 | 381 | 27 | 81 | 104 | 2 | Work experience |
| All other teachers and instructors .................... | 596 | 769 | 29 | 173 | 251 | 1 | Master's degree |
| Librarians, archivists, curators, and related workers ................................. | 168 | 182 | 8 | 14 | 56 | | |
| Curators, archivists, museum technicians, and restorers ................................. | 19 | 23 | 19 | 4 | 9 | 1 | Master's degree |
| Librarians, professional ............................. | 148 | 159 | 7 | 10 | 47 | 1 | Master's degree |
| Counselors ................................................. | 165 | 215 | 31 | 50 | 83 | 1 | Master's degree |
| Health diagnosing occupations ......................... | 850 | 1,003 | 18 | 153 | 312 | | |

**Table C-1. Employment by occupation, 1994 and projected 2005, moderate alternative—Continued**
(Employment and job openings numbers in thousands)

| Occupation | Employment | | Employment change, 1994-2005 | | Total openings due to growth and net replacements, 1994-2005[1] | Earnings quartile[2] | Most significant source of training |
|---|---|---|---|---|---|---|---|
| | 1994 | Projected, 2005 | Percent | Number | | | |
| Chiropractors ............................... | 42 | 54 | 29 | 12 | 20 | 1 | First professional degree |
| Dentists ........................................ | 164 | 173 | 5 | 9 | 54 | 1 | First professional degree |
| Optometrists ................................ | 37 | 42 | 12 | 4 | 12 | 1 | First professional degree |
| Physicians .................................... | 539 | 659 | 22 | 120 | 205 | 1 | First professional degree |
| Podiatrists .................................... | 13 | 15 | 15 | 2 | 5 | 1 | First professional degree |
| Veterinarians and veterinary inspectors ........... | 56 | 62 | 11 | 6 | 17 | 1 | First professional degree |
| Health assessment and treating occupations ...... | 2,563 | 3,294 | 29 | 731 | 1,101 | | |
| Dietitians and nutritionists ............... | 53 | 63 | 19 | 10 | 24 | 2 | Bachelor's degree |
| Pharmacists ................................. | 168 | 196 | 17 | 28 | 54 | 1 | Bachelor's degree |
| Physician assistants ..................... | 56 | 69 | 23 | 13 | 22 | 1 | Bachelor's degree |
| Registered nurses ........................ | 1,906 | 2,379 | 25 | 473 | 740 | 1 | Associate degree |
| Therapists .................................... | 380 | 586 | 54 | 207 | 262 | | |
| Occupational therapists ............... | 54 | 93 | 72 | 39 | 47 | 1 | Bachelor's degree |
| Physical therapists ...................... | 102 | 183 | 80 | 81 | 96 | 1 | Bachelor's degree |
| Recreational therapists ................ | 31 | 37 | 22 | 7 | 11 | 1 | Bachelor's degree |
| Respiratory therapists ................. | 73 | 99 | 36 | 26 | 37 | 1 | Associate degree |
| Speech-language pathologists and audiologists ................ | 85 | 125 | 46 | 39 | 52 | 1 | Master's degree |
| All other therapists ...................... | 26 | 50 | 39 | 14 | 19 | 1 | Bachelor's degree |
| Writers, artists, and entertainers ...... | 1,612 | 1,975 | 22 | 363 | 680 | | |
| Artists and commercial artists ...... | 273 | 336 | 23 | 64 | 117 | 2 | Work experience, plus degree |
| Athletes, coaches, umpires, and related workers ..................... | 8 | 46 | 20 | 8 | 19 | 2 | Long-term O-J-T |
| Dancers and choreographers ....... | 24 | 30 | 24 | 6 | 11 | 2 | Postsecondary vocational training |
| Designers .................................... | 301 | 384 | 28 | 84 | 130 | | |
| Designers, except interior designers ......... | 238 | 314 | 32 | 76 | 113 | 1 | Bachelor's degree |
| Interior designers ..................... | 63 | 70 | 12 | 8 | 17 | 1 | Bachelor's degree |
| Musicians ................................... | 256 | 317 | 24 | 62 | 105 | 3 | Long-term O-J-T |
| Photographers and camera operators ......... | 139 | 172 | 24 | 34 | 61 | | |
| Camera operators, television, motion picture, video ..................... | 18 | 19 | 6 | 1 | 5 | 2 | Moderate-term O-J-T |
| Photographers ........................... | 121 | 153 | 27 | 32 | 57 | 2 | Moderate-term O-J-T |
| Producers, directors, actors, and entertainers ..................... | 93 | 121 | 30 | 28 | 47 | 2 | Long-term O-J-T |
| Public relations specialists and publicity writers ..................... | 107 | 128 | 20 | 21 | 44 | 2 | Bachelor's degree |
| Radio and TV announcers and newscasters | 50 | 51 | 1 | 0 | 21 | 2 | Long-term O-J-T |
| Reporters and correspondents .................. | 59 | 57 | −4 | −2 | 13 | 1 | Bachelor's degree |
| Writers and editors, including technical writers ..................... | 272 | 332 | 22 | 59 | 111 | 1 | Bachelor's degree |
| All other professional workers .......... | 882 | 1,142 | 39 | 319 | 494 | 2 | Bachelor's degree |
| **Technicians and related support occupations** | **4,439** | **5,316** | **20** | **876** | **1,798** | | |
| Health technicians and technologists ............. | 2,197 | 2,815 | 28 | 618 | 1,024 | | |
| Cardiology technologists ............... | 14 | 17 | 22 | 3 | 6 | 3 | Associate degree |
| Clinical laboratory technologists and technicians ..................... | 274 | 307 | 12 | 33 | 86 | 2 | Bachelor's degree |
| Dental hygienists ........................ | 127 | 180 | 42 | 53 | 74 | 2 | Associate degree |
| Electroneurodiagnostic technologists .......... | 6 | 8 | 28 | 2 | 3 | 3 | Moderate-term O-J-T |
| EKG technicians .......................... | 16 | 11 | −30 | −5 | 3 | 3 | Moderate-term O-J-T |
| Emergency medical technicians ................... | 138 | 187 | 36 | 49 | 72 | 3 | Postsecondary vocational training |
| Licensed practical nurses ............ | 702 | 899 | 28 | 197 | 341 | 2 | Postsecondary vocational training |
| Medical records technicians .......... | 81 | 126 | 56 | 45 | 59 | 2 | Associate degree |
| Nuclear medicine technologists ................. | 13 | 16 | 26 | 3 | 5 | 2 | Associate degree |
| Opticians, dispensing and measuring .......... | 63 | 76 | 21 | 13 | 28 | 3 | Long-term O-J-T |
| Pharmacy technicians .................. | 81 | 101 | 24 | 20 | 33 | 3 | Moderate-term O-J-T |
| Psychiatric technicians ................. | 72 | 80 | 11 | 8 | 18 | 4 | Associate degree |
| Radiologic technologists and technicians ..... | 167 | 226 | 35 | 59 | 82 | 2 | Associate degree |
| Surgical technologists ................... | 46 | 65 | 43 | 19 | 27 | 3 | Postsecondary vocational training |
| Veterinary technicians and tehnologists ....... | 22 | 26 | 18 | 4 | 8 | 2 | Associate degree |
| All other health professionals and paraprofessionals ..................... | 374 | 488 | 30 | 114 | 179 | 2 | Associate degree |
| Engineering and science technicians and technologists ..................... | 1,220 | 1,312 | 8 | 92 | 357 | | |
| Engineering technicians ................ | 685 | 746 | 9 | 61 | 207 | | |
| Electrical and electronic technicians and technologists ..................... | 314 | 349 | 11 | 35 | 108 | 1 | Associate degree |

**Table C-1. Employment by occupation, 1994 and projected 2005, moderate alternative—Continued**
(Employment and job openings numbers in thousands)

| Occupation | Employment | | Employment change, 1994-2005 | | Total openings due to growth and net replacements, 1994-2005[1] | Earnings quartile[2] | Most significant source of training |
|---|---|---|---|---|---|---|---|
| | 1994 | Projected, 2005 | Percent | Number | | | |
| All other engineering technicians and technologists | 371 | 397 | 7 | 26 | 99 | 2 | Associate degree |
| Drafters | 304 | 304 | 0 | 1 | 70 | 2 | Postsecondary vocational training |
| Science and mathematics technicians | 231 | 262 | 13 | 31 | 79 | 2 | Associate degree |
| Technicians, except health and engineering and science | 1,023 | 1,189 | 16 | 167 | 418 | | |
| Aircraft pilots and flight engineers | 91 | 97 | 8 | 7 | 32 | 1 | Long-term O-J-T |
| Air traffic controllers and airplane dispatchers | 29 | 29 | 0 | 0 | 6 | 1 | Long-term O-J-T |
| Broadcast technicians | 42 | 40 | –4 | –2 | 9 | 1 | Postsecondary vocational training |
| Computer programmers | 537 | 601 | 12 | 65 | 228 | 1 | Bachelor's degree |
| Legal assistants and technicians, except clerical | 219 | 301 | 38 | 82 | 103 | | |
| Paralegals | 110 | 175 | 58 | 64 | 74 | 2 | Associate degree |
| Title examiners and searchers | 28 | 28 | 0 | 0 | 3 | 2 | Moderate-term O-J-T |
| All other legal assistants, including law clerks | 80 | 98 | 22 | 18 | 27 | 1 | Associate degree |
| Programmers, numerical, tool, and process control | 7 | 6 | –9 | –1 | 2 | 1 | Work experience |
| Technical assistants, library | 75 | 91 | 21 | 16 | 32 | 2 | Short-term O-J-T |
| All other technicians | 24 | 24 | 0 | 0 | 5 | 2 | Moderate-term O-J-T |
| **Marketing and sales occupations** | 13,990 | 16,502 | 18 | 2,512 | 6,706 | | |
| Cashiers | 3,005 | 3,567 | 19 | 562 | 1,772 | 4 | Short-term O-J-T |
| Counter and rental clerks | 341 | 451 | 32 | 109 | 203 | 4 | Short-term O-J-T |
| Insurance sales workers | 418 | 436 | 4 | 18 | 88 | 1 | Long-term O-J-T |
| Marketing and sales worker supervisors | 2,293 | 2,673 | 17 | 380 | 788 | 2 | Work experience |
| Real estate agents, brokers, and appraisers | 374 | 407 | 9 | 33 | 113 | | |
| Brokers, real estate | 67 | 75 | 12 | 8 | 22 | 1 | Work experience |
| Real estate appraisers | 47 | 53 | 13 | 6 | 16 | 1 | Work experience |
| Sales agents, real estate | 260 | 279 | 7 | 19 | 75 | 1 | Postsecondary vocational training |
| Salespersons, retail | 3,842 | 4,374 | 14 | 532 | 1,821 | 3 | Short-term O-J-T |
| Securities and financial services sales workers | 246 | 335 | 37 | 90 | 126 | 1 | Long-term O-J-T |
| Travel agents | 122 | 150 | 23 | 28 | 55 | 3 | Postsecondary vocational training |
| All other sales and related workers | 3,349 | 4,109 | 23 | 760 | 1,741 | 2 | Moderate-term O-J-T |
| **Administrative support occupations, including clerical** | 23,178 | 24,172 | 4 | 994 | 6,991 | | |
| Adjusters, investigators, and collectors | 1,229 | 1,507 | 23 | 277 | 399 | | |
| Adjustment clerks | 373 | 521 | 40 | 148 | 175 | 3 | Short-term O-J-T |
| Bill and account collectors | 250 | 342 | 36 | –91 | 112 | 3 | Short-term O-J-T |
| Insurance claims and policy processing occupations | 461 | 495 | 8 | 35 | 92 | | |
| Insurance adjusters, examiners, and investigators | 162 | 192 | 19 | 30 | 45 | 2 | Long-term O-J-T |
| Insurance claims clerks | 119 | 135 | 13 | 16 | 27 | 2 | Moderate-term O-J-T |
| Insurance policy processing clerks | 179 | 168 | –6 | –12 | 20 | 3 | Moderate-term O-J-T |
| Welfare eligibility workers and interviewers | 104 | 108 | 4 | 4 | 16 | 2 | Moderate-term O-J-T |
| All other adjusters and investigators | 41 | 40 | –1 | 0 | 4 | 2 | Moderate-term O-J-T |
| Communications equipment operators | 319 | 266 | –17 | –53 | 83 | | |
| Telephone operators | 310 | 260 | –16 | –50 | 81 | | |
| Central office operators | 48 | 14 | –70 | –34 | 12 | 3 | Moderate-term O-J-T |
| Directory assistance operators | 33 | 10 | –70 | –24 | 8 | 3 | Moderate-term O-J-T |
| Switchboard operators | 228 | 236 | 3 | 7 | 62 | 3 | Short-term O-J-T |
| All other communications equipment operators | 9 | 6 | –31 | –3 | 2 | 3 | Moderate-term O-J-T |
| Computer operators and peripheral equipment operators | 289 | 175 | –39 | –114 | 62 | | |
| Computer operators, except peripheral equipment | 259 | 162 | –38 | –98 | 56 | 3 | Moderate-term O-J-T |
| Peripheral EDP equipment operators | 30 | 13 | –55 | –16 | 6 | 3 | Moderate-term O-J-T |
| Information clerks | 1,477 | 1,832 | 24 | 355 | 699 | | |
| Hotel desk clerks | 136 | 163 | 20 | 27 | 84 | 3 | Short-term O-J-T |
| Interviewing clerks, except personnel and social welfare | 69 | 83 | 20 | 14 | 36 | 3 | Short-term O-J-T |
| New accounts clerks, banking | 114 | 116 | 2 | 2 | 40 | 3 | Work experience |
| Receptionists and information clerks | 1,019 | 1,337 | 31 | 318 | 508 | 4 | Short-term O-J-T |
| Reservation and transportation ticket agents and travel clerks | 139 | 133 | –4 | –6 | 31 | 3 | Short-term O-J-T |
| Mail clerks and messengers | 260 | 256 | –1 | –4 | 70 | | |

**Table C-1. Employment by occupation, 1994 and projected 2005, moderate alternative—Continued**
(Employment and job openings numbers in thousands)

| Occupation | Employment | | Employment change, 1994-2005 | | Total openings due to growth and net replacements, 1994-2005[1] | Earnings quartile[2] | Most significant source of training |
|---|---|---|---|---|---|---|---|
| | 1994 | Projected, 2005 | Percent | Number | | | |
| Mail clerks, except mail machine operators and postal service | 127 | 116 | −8 | −10 | 35 | 4 | Short-term O-J-T |
| Messengers | 133 | 140 | 5 | 7 | 35 | 3 | Short-term O-J-T |
| Postal clerks and mail carriers | 474 | 481 | 1 | 7 | 126 | | |
| Postal mail carriers | 320 | 320 | 0 | −1 | 85 | 1 | Short-term O-J-T |
| Postal service clerks | 154 | 161 | 5 | 7 | 41 | 1 | Short-term O-J-T |
| Material recording, scheduling, dispatching, and distributing occupations | 3,556 | 3,688 | 4 | 132 | 863 | | |
| Dispatchers | 224 | 258 | 15 | 34 | 65 | | |
| Dispatchers, except police, fire, and ambulance | 141 | 168 | 19 | 27 | 46 | 3 | Moderate-term O-J-T |
| Dispatchers, police, fire, and ambulance | 83 | 90 | 8 | 7 | 18 | 3 | Moderate-term O-J-T |
| Meter readers, utilities | 57 | 46 | −19 | −11 | 13 | 3 | Short-term O-J-T |
| Order fillers, wholesale and retail sales | 215 | 231 | 8 | 1.6 | 63 | 2 | Short-term O-J-T |
| Procurement clerks | 57 | 52 | −9 | −5 | 13 | 3 | Short-term O-J-T |
| Production, planning, and expediting clerks | 239 | 251 | 5 | 12 | 56 | 2 | Short-term O-J-T |
| Stock clerks | 1,759 | 1,800 | 2 | 41 | 443 | 3 | Short-term O-J-T |
| Traffic, shipping, and receiving clerks | 798 | 827 | 4 | 29 | 150 | 3 | Short-term O-J-T |
| Weighers, measurers, checkers, and samplers, recordkeeping | 45 | 46 | 3 | 1 | 12 | 3 | Short-term O-J-T |
| All other material recording, scheduling, and distribution workers | 161 | 177 | 10 | 16 | 47 | 3 | Short-term O-J-T |
| Records processing occupations | 3,733 | 3,438 | −8 | −294 | 877 | | |
| Advertising clerks | 17 | 18 | 5 | 1 | 5 | 2 | Short-term O-J-T |
| Brokerage clerks | 73 | 73 | 1 | 1 | 9 | 3 | Short-term O-J-T |
| Correspondence clerks | 29 | 27 | −8 | −2 | 6 | 2 | Short-term O-J-T |
| File clerks | 278 | 236 | −15 | −42 | 102 | 4 | Short-term O-J-T |
| Financial records processing occupations | 2,757 | 2,506 | −9 | −250 | 573 | | |
| Billing, cost, and rate clerks | 323 | 328 | 2 | 5 | 98 | 2 | Short-term O-J-T |
| Billing, posting, and calculating machine operators | 96 | 32 | −67 | −64 | 40 | 2 | Short-term O-J-T |
| Bookkeeping, accounting, and auditing clerks | 2,181 | 2,003 | −8 | −178 | 400 | 3 | Moderate-term O-J-T |
| Payroll and timekeeping clerks | 157 | 144 | −9 | −14 | 35 | 3 | Short-term O-J-T |
| Library assistants and bookmobile drivers | 121 | 127 | 5 | 7 | 57 | 3 | Short-term O-J-T |
| Order clerks, materials, merchandise, and service | 310 | 337 | 9 | 27 | 95 | 2 | Short-term O-J-T |
| Personnel clerks, except payroll and timekeeping | 123 | 98 | −21 | −26 | 27 | 2 | Short-term O-J-T |
| Statement clerks | 25 | 16 | −38 | −9 | 3 | 3 | Short-term O-J-T |
| Secretaries, stenographers, and typists | 4,100 | 4,276 | 4 | 175 | 1,230 | | |
| Secretaries | 3,349 | 3,739 | 12 | 390 | 1,102 | | |
| Legal secretaries | 281 | 350 | 24 | 68 | 128 | 3 | Postsecondary vocational training |
| Medical secretaries | 226 | 281 | 24 | 55 | 103 | 3 | Postsecondary vocational training |
| Secretaries, except legal and medical | 2,842 | 3,109 | 9 | 267 | 871 | 3 | Postsecondary vocational training |
| Stenographers | 105 | 102 | −3 | −3 | 22 | 3 | Postsecondary vocational training |
| Typists and word processors | 646 | 434 | −33 | −212 | 106 | 3 | Moderate-term 0-J-T |
| Other clerical and administrative support workers | 7,740 | 8,253 | 7 | 513 | 2,582 | | |
| Bank tellers | 559 | 407 | −27 | −152 | 244 | 4 | Short-term O-J-T |
| Clerical supervisors and managers | 1,340 | 1,600 | 19 | 261 | 613 | 2 | Work experience |
| Court clerks | 51 | 59 | 15 | 8 | 12 | 2 | Short-term O-J-T |
| Credit authorizers, credit checkers, and loan and credit clerks | 258 | 267 | 4 | 9 | 49 | | |
| Credit authorizers | 15 | 19 | 24 | 4 | 5 | 2 | Short-term O-J-T |
| Credit checkers | 40 | 35 | −14 | −6 | 3 | 3 | Short-term O-J-T |
| Loan and credit clerks | 187 | 196 | 5 | 10 | 37 | 3 | Short-term O-J-T |
| Loan interviewers | 16 | 17 | 10 | 2 | 4 | 3 | Short-term O-J-T |
| Customer service representatives, utilities | 150 | 179 | 19 | 29 | 61 | 2 | Short-term O-J-T |
| Data entry keyers, except composing | 395 | 370 | −6 | −25 | 17 | 3 | Postsecondary vocational training |
| Data entry keyers, composing | 19 | 6 | −67 | −13 | 1 | 3 | Postsecondary vocational training |
| Duplicating, mail, and other office machine operators | 222 | 166 | −25 | −56 | 99 | 2 | Short-term O-J-T |
| General office clerks | 2,946 | 3,071 | 4 | 126 | 908 | 3 | Short-term O-J-T |
| Municipal clerks | 22 | 21 | −3 | −1 | 2 | 2 | Short-term O-J-T |
| Proofreaders and copy markers | 26 | 20 | −20 | −5 | 7 | 3 | Short-term O-J-T |
| Real estate clerks | 24 | 25 | 5 | 1 | 8 | 3 | Short-term O-J-T |
| Statistical clerks | 75 | 68 | −10 | −7 | 11 | 3 | Moderate-term O-J-T |
| Teacher aides and educational assistants | 932 | 12 | 39 | 364 | 480 | 4 | Short-term O-J-T |

**Table C-1. Employment by occupation, 1994 and projected 2005, moderate alternative—Continued**
(Employment and job openings numbers in thousands)

| Occupation | Employment | | Employment change, 1994-2005 | | Total openings due to growth and net replacements, 1994-2005[1] | Earnings quartile[2] | Most significant source of training |
|---|---|---|---|---|---|---|---|
| | 1994 | Projected, 2005 | Percent | Number | | | |
| All other clerical and administrative support workers | 721 | 698 | −3 | −23 | 69 | 2 | Short-term O-J-T |
| **Service occupations** | 20,239 | 24,832 | 23 | 4,593 | 9,813 | | |
| Cleaning and building service occupations, except private household | 3,450 | 4,071 | 18 | 621 | 1,293 | | |
| Institutional cleaning supervisors | 125 | 147 | 18 | 22 | 58 | 3 | Work experience |
| Janitors and cleaners, including maids and housekeeping cleaners | 3,043 | 3,602 | 18 | 559 | 1,140 | 4 | Short-term O-J-T |
| Pest controllers and assistants | 56 | 76 | 36 | 20 | 31 | 4 | Moderate-term O-J-T |
| All other cleaning and building service workers | 226 | 245 | 8 | 19 | 63 | 4 | Short-term O-J-T |
| Food preparation and service occupations | 7,964 | 9,057 | 14 | 1,093 | 3,498 | | |
| Chefs, cooks, and other kitchen workers | 3,237 | 3,739 | 16 | 502 | 1,102 | | |
| Cooks, except short order | 1,286 | 1,492 | 16 | 206 | 524 | | |
| Bakers, bread and pastry | 170 | 230 | 35 | 60 | 102 | 4 | Moderate-term O-J-T |
| Cooks, institution or cafeteria | 412 | 435 | 6 | 23 | 125 | 4 | Long-term O-J-T |
| Cooks, restaurant | 704 | 827 | 17 | 123 | 297 | 4 | Long-term O-J-T |
| Cooks, short order and fast food | 760 | 869 | 14 | 109 | 297 | 4 | Short-term O-J-T |
| Food preparation workers | 1,190 | 1,378 | 16 | 187 | 282 | 4 | Short-term O-J-T |
| Food and beverage service occupations | 4,514 | 5,051 | 12 | 537 | 2,263 | | |
| Bartenders | 373 | 347 | −7 | −25 | 138 | 4 | Short-term O-J-T |
| Dining room and cafeteria attendants and bar helpers | 416 | 416 | 0 | 0 | 157 | 4 | Short-term O-J-T |
| Food counter, fountain, and related workers | 1,630 | 1,669 | 2 | 40 | 463 | 4 | Short-term O-J-T |
| Hosts and hostesses, restaurant, lounge, or coffee shop | 248 | 292 | 18 | 44 | 114 | 3 | Short-term O-J-T |
| Waiters and waitresses | 1,847 | 2,326 | 26 | 479 | 1,390 | 4 | Short-term O-J-T |
| All other food preparation and service workers | 213 | 267 | 25 | 54 | 132 | 4 | Short-term O-J-T |
| Health service occupations | 2,086 | 2,846 | 36 | 759 | 1,131 | | |
| Ambulance drivers and attendants, except EMTs | 18 | 21 | 15 | 3 | 8 | 4 | Short-term O-J-T |
| Dental assistants | 190 | 269 | 42 | 79 | 137 | 3 | Moderate-term O-J-T |
| Medical assistants | 206 | 327 | 59 | 121 | 155 | 3 | Moderate-term O-J-T |
| Nursing aides and psychiatric aides | 1,370 | 1,770 | 29 | 400 | 594 | | |
| Nursing aides, orderlies, and attendants | 1,265 | 1,652 | 31 | 387 | 566 | 4 | Short-term O-J-T |
| Psychiatric aides | 105 | 118 | 12 | 13 | 28 | 4 | Short-term O-J-T |
| Occupational therapy assistants and aides | 16 | 29 | 82 | 13 | 16 | 3 | Moderate-term O-J-T |
| Pharmacy assistants | 52 | 64 | 23 | 12 | 22 | 3 | Short-term O-J-T |
| Physical and corrective therapy assistants and aides | 78 | 142 | 83 | 64 | 87 | 4 | Moderate-term O-J-T |
| All other health service workers | 157 | 224 | 43 | 67 | 112 | 4 | Short-term O-J-T |
| Personal service occupations | 2,530 | 3,719 | 47 | 1,189 | 1,670 | | |
| Amusement and recreation attendants | 267 | 406 | 52 | 139 | 211 | 3 | Short-term O-J-T |
| Baggage porters and bellhops | 35 | 44 | 26 | 9 | 16 | 4 | Short-term O-J-T |
| Barbers | 64 | 60 | −6 | −4 | 20 | 4 | Postsecondary vocational training |
| Child-care workers | 757 | 1,005 | 33 | 248 | 321 | 4 | Short-term O-J-T |
| Cosmetologists and related workers | 645 | 754 | 17 | 109 | 273 | | |
| Hairdressers, hairstylists, and cosmetologists | 595 | 677 | 14 | 82 | 233 | 4 | Postsecondary vocational training |
| Manicurists | 38 | 64 | 69 | 26 | 36 | 4 | Postsecondary vocational training |
| Shampooers | 12 | 13 | 8 | 1 | 4 | 4 | Short-term O-J-T |
| Flight attendants | 105 | 135 | 28 | 30 | 49 | 2 | Long-term O-J-T |
| Homemaker-home health aides | 598 | 1,238 | 107 | 640 | 747 | | |
| Home health aides | 420 | 848 | 102 | 428 | 488 | 4 | Short-term O-J-T |
| Personal and home care aides | 179 | 391 | 119 | 212 | 259 | 4 | Short-term O-J-T |
| Ushers, lobby attendants, and ticket takers | 59 | 77 | 29 | 17 | 33 | 3 | Short-term O-J-T |
| Private household workers | 808 | 682 | −16 | −126 | 245 | | |
| Child-care workers, private household | 283 | 278 | −2 | −5 | 139 | 4 | Short-term O-J-T |
| Cleaners and servants, private household | 496 | 387 | −22 | −108 | 100 | 4 | Short-term O-J-T |
| Cooks, private household | 9 | 5 | −49 | −4 | 2 | 4 | Moderate-term O-J-T |
| Housekeepers and butlers | 20 | 12 | −37 | −7 | 4 | 4 | Moderate-term O-J-T |
| Protective service occupations | 2,381 | 3,199 | 34 | 818 | 1,514 | | |
| Fire-fighting occupations | 284 | 328 | 16 | 44 | 169 | | |
| Fire fighters | 219 | 258 | 15 | 40 | 138 | 1 | Long-term O-J-T |
| Fire-fighting and prevention supervisors | 52 | 56 | 7 | 4 | 24 | 1 | Work experience |
| Fire inspection occupations | 13 | 14 | 7 | 1 | 6 | 1 | Work experience |
| Law enforcement occupations | 992 | 1,316 | 33 | 324 | 610 | | |
| Correction officers | 310 | 468 | 51 | 158 | 194 | 2 | Long-term O-J-T |
| Police and detectives | 682 | 848 | 24 | 166 | 416 | | |

**Table C-1. Employment by occupation, 1994 and projected 2005, moderate alternative—Continued**
(Employment and job openings numbers in thousands)

| Occupation | Employment | | Employment change, 1994-2005 | | Total openings due to growth and net replacements, 1994-2005[1] | Earnings quartile[2] | Most significant source of training |
|---|---|---|---|---|---|---|---|
| | 1994 | Projected, 2005 | Percent | Number | | | |
| Police and detective supervisors | 87 | 93 | 7 | 6 | 45 | 1 | Work experience |
| Police detectives and investigators | 66 | 80 | 20 | 13 | 40 | 1 | Work experience |
| Police patrol officers | 400 | 511 | 28 | 112 | 271 | 1 | Long-term O-J-T |
| Sheriffs and deputy sheriffs | 86 | 110 | 29 | 25 | 42 | 2 | Long-term O-J-T |
| Other law enforcement occupations | 43 | 54 | 25 | 11 | 19 | 2 | Moderate-term O-J-T |
| Other protective service workers | 1,106 | 1,554 | 41 | 449 | 735 | | |
| Detectives, except public | 55 | 79 | 44 | 24 | 35 | 3 | Moderate-term O-J-T |
| Guards | 867 | 1,282 | 48 | 415 | 580 | 3 | Short-term O-J-T |
| Crossing guards | 58 | 60 | 3 | 2 | 17 | 3 | Short-term O-J-T |
| All other protective service workers | 126 | 133 | 6 | 8 | 104 | 4 | Short-term O-J-T |
| All other service workers | 1,020 | 1,259 | 23 | 240 | 462 | 3 | Work experience |
| **Agriculture, forestry, fishing, and related occupations** | 3,762 | 3,650 | −3 | −112 | 988 | | |
| Animal breeders and trainers | 15 | 15 | −5 | −1 | 3 | 1 | Bachelor's degree |
| Animal caretakers, except farm | 125 | 158 | 26 | 33 | 62 | 4 | Short-term O-J-T |
| Farm workers | 906 | 870 | −4 | −36 | 263 | 4 | Short-term O-J-T |
| Gardening, nursery, and greenhouse and lawn service occupations | 844 | 986 | 17 | 142 | 271 | | |
| Gardeners and groundskeepers, except farm | 569 | 623 | 9 | 54 | 128 | 4 | Short-term O-J-T |
| Lawn maintenance workers | 96 | 127 | 32 | 31 | 43 | 4 | Short-term O-J-T |
| Lawn service managers | 36 | 47 | 33 | 12 | 18 | 3 | Work experience |
| Nursery and greenhouse managers | 19 | 26 | 37 | 7 | 11 | 3 | Work experience |
| Nursery workers | 83 | 109 | 31 | 26 | 50 | 4 | Short-term O-J-T |
| Pruners | 26 | 34 | 32 | 8 | 14 | 4 | Short-term O-J-T |
| Sprayers/applicators | 15 | 20 | 32 | 5 | 7 | 4 | Moderate-term O-J-T |
| Farm operators and managers | 1,327 | 1,050 | −21 | −277 | 221 | | |
| Farmers | 1,276 | 1,003 | −21 | −273 | 211 | 4 | Long-term O-J-T |
| Farm managers | 51 | 46 | −9 | −5 | 10 | 4 | Work experience, plus degree |
| Fishers, hunters, and trappers | 49 | 47 | −4 | −2 | 11 | | |
| Captains and other officers, fishing vessels | 7 | 6 | −11 | −1 | 2 | 2 | Work experience |
| Fishers, hunters, and trappers | 42 | 41 | −3 | −1 | 9 | 2 | Short-term O-J-T |
| Forestry and logging occupations | 124 | 118 | −5 | −6 | 34 | | |
| Forest and conservation workers | 42 | 42 | 1 | 1 | 12 | 3 | Short-term O-J-T |
| Timber cutting and logging occupations | 82 | 76 | −8 | −7 | 22 | | |
| Fallers and buckers | 29 | 27 | −9 | −3 | 8 | 3 | Short-term O-J-T |
| Logging tractor operators | 20 | 20 | −1 | 0 | 4 | 2 | Short-term O-J-T |
| Log handling equipment operators | 16 | 15 | −9 | −1 | 5 | 3 | Short-term O-J-T |
| All other timber cutting and related logging workers | 17 | 15 | −13 | −2 | 5 | 3 | Short-term O-J-T |
| Supervisors, farming, forestry, and agricultural related occupations | 85 | 91 | 7 | 6 | 22 | 3 | Work experience |
| Veterinary assistants | 31 | 37 | 19 | 6 | 13 | 4 | Short-term O-J-T |
| All other agricultural, forestry, fishing, and related workers | 255 | 278 | 9 | 23 | 87 | 4 | Short-term O-J-T |
| **Precision production, craft, and repair occupations** | 14,047 | 14,880 | 6 | 833 | 4,489 | | |
| Blue-collar worker supervisors | 1,884 | 1,894 | 1 | 11 | 480 | 1 | Work experience |
| Construction trades | 3,616 | 3,956 | 9 | 340 | 1,183 | | |
| Bricklayers and stone masons | 147 | 162 | 10 | 15 | 43 | 2 | Long-term O-J-T |
| Carpenters | 992 | 1,074 | 8 | 82 | 290 | 2 | Long-term O-J-T |
| Carpet installers | 66 | 72 | 9 | 6 | 28 | 3 | Moderate-term O-J-T |
| Ceiling tile installers and acoustical carpenters | 16 | 14 | −10 | −2 | 3 | 2 | Moderate-term O-J-T |
| Concrete and terrazzo finishers | 126 | 141 | 12 | 15 | 41 | 3 | Long-term O-J-T |
| Drywall installers and finishers | 133 | 143 | 7 | 9 | 50 | 2 | Moderate-term O-J-T |
| Electricians | 528 | 554 | 5 | 25 | 152 | 2 | Long-term O-J-T |
| Glaziers | 34 | 34 | 2 | 1 | 9 | 2 | Long-term O-J-T |
| Hard tile setters | 27 | 28 | 1 | 0 | 7 | 2 | Long-term O-J-T |
| Highway maintenance workers | 167 | 182 | 9 | 15 | 62 | 3 | Short-term O-J-T |
| Insulation workers | 64 | 77 | 20 | 13 | 34 | 2 | Moderate-term O-J-T |
| Painters and paperhangers, construction and maintenance | 439 | 509 | 16 | 70 | 174 | 2 | Moderate-term O-J-T |
| Paving, surfacing, and tamping equipment operators | 73 | 93 | 26 | 19 | 37 | 2 | Moderate-term O-J-T |
| Pipelayers and pipelaying fitters | 57 | 63 | 12 | 7 | 23 | 3 | Moderate-term O-J-T |

**Table C-1. Employment by occupation, 1994 and projected 2005, moderate alternative—Continued**
(Employment and job openings numbers in thousands)

| Occupation | Employment | | Employment change, 1994-2005 | | Total openings due to growth and net replacements, 1994-2005[1] | Earnings quartile[2] | Most significant source of training |
|---|---|---|---|---|---|---|---|
| | 1994 | Projected, 2005 | Percent | Number | | | |
| Plasterers | 30 | 33 | 11 | 3 | 11 | 2 | Long-term O-J-T |
| Plumbers, pipefitters, and steamfitters | 375 | 390 | 4 | 15 | 92 | 2 | Long-term O-J-T |
| Roofers | 126 | 143 | 13 | 17 | 42 | 3 | Moderate-term O-J-T |
| Structural and reinforcing metal workers | 61 | 64 | 5 | 3 | 19 | 2 | Long-term O-J-T |
| All other construction trades workers | 155 | 181 | 17 | 26 | 68 | 3 | Moderate-term O-J-T |
| Extractive and related workers, including blasters | 220 | 204 | −7 | −16 | 59 | | |
| Oil and gas extraction occupations | 66 | 39 | −41 | −27 | 12 | | |
| Roustabouts | 28 | 13 | −55 | −16 | 5 | 1 | Short-term O-J-T |
| All other oil and gas extraction occupations | 38 | 26 | −30 | −11 | 7 | 1 | Moderate-term O-J-T |
| Mining, quarrying, and tunneling occupations | 18 | 12 | −34 | −6 | 3 | 1 | Long-term O-J-T |
| All other extraction and related workers | 136 | 153 | 12 | 17 | 43 | 1 | Moderate-term O-J-T |
| Mechanics, installers, and repairers | 5,012 | 5,586 | 11 | 574 | 1,950 | | |
| Communications equipment mechanics, installers, and repairers | 118 | 78 | −34 | −41 | 26 | | |
| Central office and PBX installers and repairers | 84 | 51 | −39 | −33 | 17 | 1 | Postsecondary vocational training |
| Radio mechanics | 7 | 6 | −16 | −1 | 2 | 2 | Postsecondary vocational training |
| All other communications equipment mechanics, installers, and repairers | 27 | 20 | −25 | −7 | 6 | 1 | Postsecondary vocational training |
| Electrical and electronic equipment mechanics, installers, and repairers | 554 | 555 | 0 | 1 | 175 | | |
| Data processing equipment repairers | 75 | 104 | 38 | 29 | 49 | 2 | Postsecondary vocational training |
| Electrical power line installers and repairers | 112 | 123 | 10 | 11 | 37 | 1 | Long-term O-J-T |
| Electronic home entertainment equipment repairers | 34 | 30 | −10 | −3 | 9 | 2 | Postsecondary vocational training |
| Electronics repairers, commercial and industrial equipment | 66 | 68 | 2 | 1 | 20 | 2 | Postsecondary vocational training |
| Station installers and repairers, telephone | 37 | 11 | −70 | −26 | 7 | 1 | Postsecondary vocational training |
| Telephone and cable TV line installers and repairers | 191 | 181 | −5 | −9 | 43 | 1 | Long-term O-J-T |
| All other electrical and electronic equipment mechanics, installers, and repairers | 39 | 38 | −3 | −1 | 10 | 2 | Postsecondary vocational training |
| Machinery and related mechanics, installers, and repairers | 1,815 | 2,072 | 14 | 258 | 700 | | |
| Industrial machinery mechanics | 464 | 502 | 8 | 38 | 173 | 2 | Long-term O-J-T |
| Maintenance repairers, general utility | 1,273 | 1,505 | 18 | 231 | 508 | 2 | Long-term O-J-T |
| Millwrights | 77 | 66 | −15 | −11 | 20 | 1 | Long-term O-J-T |
| Vehicle and mobile equipment mechanics and repairers | 1,502 | 1,736 | 16 | 234 | 655 | | |
| Aircraft mechanics, including engine specialists | 119 | 134 | 13 | 15 | 49 | | |
| Aircraft engine specialists | 23 | 25 | 8 | 2 | 8 | 1 | Postsecondary vocational training |
| Aircraft mechanics | 96 | 109 | 14 | 13 | 40 | 1 | Postsecondary vocational training |
| Automotive body and related repairers | 209 | 243 | 17 | 35 | 92 | 2 | Long-term O-J-T |
| Automotive mechanics | 736 | 862 | 17 | 126 | 347 | 2 | Long-term O-J-T |
| Bus and truck mechanics and diesel engine specialists | 250 | 293 | 17 | 42 | 100 | 2 | Long-term O-J-T |
| Farm equipment mechanics | 41 | 47 | 14 | 6 | 17 | 2 | Long-term O-J-T |
| Mobile heavy equipment mechanics | 101 | 110 | 9 | 9 | 37 | 2 | Long-term O-J-T |
| Motorcycle, boat, and small engine mechanics | 46 | 48 | 4 | 2 | 14 | | |
| Motorcycle repairers | 11 | 12 | 4 | 0 | 4 | 2 | Long-term O-J-T |
| Small engine specialists | 35 | 36 | 4 | 1 | 11 | 2 | Long-term O-J-T |
| Other mechanics, installers, and repairers | 1,023 | 1,145 | 12 | 122 | 394 | | |
| Bicycle repairers | 40 | 44 | 10 | 4 | 13 | 2 | Moderate-term O-J-T |
| Camera and photographic equipment repairers | 11 | 12 | 9 | 1 | 4 | 2 | Moderate-term O-J-T |
| Coin and vending machine servicers and repairers | 19 | 17 | −14 | −3 | 4 | 2 | Long-term O-J-T |
| Electric meter installers and repairers | 12 | 10 | −18 | −2 | 3 | 2 | Long-term O-J-T |
| Electromedical and biomedical equipment repairers | 10 | 11 | 17 | 2 | 4 | 2 | Long-term O-J-T |
| Elevator installers and repairers | 24 | 28 | 15 | 4 | 10 | 2 | Long-term O-J-T |
| Heat, air conditioning, and refrigeration mechanics and installers | 233 | 299 | 29 | 66 | 125 | 2 | Long-term O-J-T |
| Home appliance and power tool repairers | 70 | 66 | −6 | −4 | 19 | 1 | Long-term O-J-T |
| Locksmiths and safe repairers | 20 | 21 | 10 | 2 | 7 | 2 | Moderate-term O-J-T |
| Musical instrument repairers and tuners | 10 | 11 | 15 | 1 | 4 | 2 | Long-term O-J-T |
| Office machine and cash register servicers | 59 | 63 | 6 | 4 | 29 | 2 | Long-term O-J-T |

**Table C-1. Employment by occupation, 1994 and projected 2005, moderate alternative—Continued**
(Employment and job openings numbers in thousands)

| Occupation | Employment | | Employment change, 1994-2005 | | Total openings due to growth and net replacements, 1994-2005[1] | Earnings quartile[2] | Most significant source of training |
|---|---|---|---|---|---|---|---|
| | 1994 | Projected, 2005 | Percent | Number | | | |
| Precision instrument repairers | 40 | 40 | 0 | 0 | 10 | 2 | Long-term O-J-T |
| Riggers | 11 | 11 | −4 | 0 | 2 | 2 | Long-term O-J-T |
| Tire repairers and changers | 89 | 95 | 7 | 6 | 42 | 4 | Short-term O-J-T |
| Watchmakers | 6 | 5 | −15 | −1 | 2 | 2 | Long-term O-J-T |
| All other mechanics, installers, and repairers | 371 | 412 | 11 | 42 | 116 | 2 | Long-term O-J-T |
| Production occupations, precision | 2,986 | 2,906 | −3 | −80 | 730 | | |
| Assemblers, precision | 324 | 315 | −3 | −9 | 91 | | |
| Aircraft assemblers, precision | 20 | 19 | −8 | −2 | 4 | 2 | Work experience |
| Electrical and electronic equipment assemblers, precision | 144 | 127 | −12 | −17 | 36 | 3 | Work experience |
| Electromechanical equipment assemblers, precision | 47 | 44 | −6 | −3 | 12 | 3 | Work experience |
| Fitters, structural metal, precision | 14 | 9 | −35 | −5 | 3 | 2 | Work experience |
| Machine builders and other precision machine assemblers | 58 | 65 | 11 | 6 | 18 | 2 | Work experience |
| All other precision assemblers | 40 | 50 | 26 | 11 | 18 | 2 | Work experience |
| Food workers, precision | 292 | 282 | −4 | −11 | 81 | | |
| Bakers, manufacturing | 36 | 40 | 12 | 4 | 12 | 3 | Moderate-term O-J-T |
| Butchers and meatcutters | 219 | 202 | −8 | −17 | 58 | 3 | Long-term O-J-T |
| All other precision food and tobacco workers | 38 | 39 | 4 | 2 | 11 | 3 | Long-term O-J-T |
| Inspectors, testers, and graders, precision | 654 | 629 | −4 | −25 | 138 | 2 | Work experience |
| Metal workers, precision | 885 | 824 | −7 | −61 | 190 | | |
| Boilermakers | 20 | 19 | −4 | −1 | 4 | 2 | Long-term O-J-T |
| Jewelers and silversmiths | 30 | 32 | 6 | 2 | 8 | 2 | Long-term O-J-T |
| Machinists | 369 | 349 | −5 | −20 | 79 | 2 | Long-term O-J-T |
| Sheet metal workers and duct installers | 222 | 205 | −8 | −17 | 45 | 2 | Moderate-term O-J-T |
| Shipfitters | 12 | 11 | −10 | −1 | 2 | 2 | Long-term O-J-T |
| Tool and die makers | 142 | 127 | −11 | −15 | 34 | 1 | Long-term O-J-T |
| All other precision metal workers | 90 | 82 | −9 | −8 | 18 | 2 | Long-term O-J-T |
| Printing workers, precision | 150 | 157 | 4 | 7 | 53 | | |
| Bookbinders | 6 | 6 | −4 | 0 | 1 | 3 | Moderate-term O-J-T |
| Prepress printing workers, precision | 131 | 132 | 1 | 1 | 43 | | |
| Compositors and typesetters, precision | 11 | 8 | −23 | −2 | 2 | 2 | Long-term O-J-T |
| Job printers | 14 | 11 | −27 | −4 | 3 | 2 | Long-term O-J-T |
| Paste-up workers | 22 | 16 | −28 | −6 | 4 | 2 | Long-term O-J-T |
| Electronic pagination systems workers | 18 | 33 | 83 | 15 | 19 | 2 | Long-term O-J-T |
| Photoengravers | 7 | 5 | −20 | −1 | 1 | 2 | Long-term O-J-T |
| Camera operators | 15 | 14 | −6 | −1 | 3 | 2 | Long-term O-J-T |
| Strippers, printing | 31 | 34 | 9 | 3 | 9 | 2 | Long-term O-J-T |
| Platemakers | 13 | 11 | −15 | −2 | 2 | 2 | Long-term O-J-T |
| All other printing workers, precision | 13 | 19 | 44 | 6 | 8 | 2 | Long-term O-J-T |
| Textile, apparel, and furnishings workers, precision | 240 | 219 | −9 | −21 | 40 | | |
| Custom tailors and sewers | 84 | 63 | −25 | −21 | 10 | 4 | Work experience |
| Patternmakers and layout workers, fabric and apparel | 17 | 23 | 31 | 5 | 7 | 4 | Long-term O-J-T |
| Shoe and leather workers and repairers, precision | 24 | 17 | −28 | −7 | 2 | 4 | Long-term O-J-T |
| Upholsterers | 63 | 64 | 1 | 1 | 9 | 4 | Long-term O-J-T |
| All other precision textile, apparel, and furnishings workers | 51 | 51 | 0 | 0 | 11 | 4 | Long-term O-J-T |
| Woodworkers, precision | 241 | 277 | 15 | 36 | 86 | | |
| Cabinetmakers and bench carpenters | 131 | 151 | 15 | 20 | 45 | 3 | Long-term O-J-T |
| Furniture finishers | 38 | 40 | 6 | 2 | 12 | 3 | Long-term O-J-T |
| Wood machinists | 50 | 59 | 19 | 10 | 19 | 3 | Long-term O-J-T |
| All other precision woodworkers | 22 | 26 | 19 | 4 | 10 | 3 | Long-term O-J-T |
| Other precision workers | 199 | 204 | 2 | 5 | 52 | | |
| Dental laboratory technicians, precision | 49 | 47 | −5 | −2 | 11 | 3 | Long-term O-J-T |
| Optical goods workers, precision | 19 | 22 | 12 | 2 | 7 | 3 | Long-term O-J-T |
| Photographic process workers, precision | 14 | 16 | 15 | 2 | 6 | 4 | Long-term O-J-T |
| All other precision workers | 117 | 119 | 2 | 3 | 28 | 3 | Long-term O-J-T |
| Plant and system occupations | 330 | 334 | 1 | 4 | 87 | | |
| Chemical plant and system operators | 37 | 36 | −3 | −1 | 8 | 1 | Long-term O-J-T |
| Electric power generating plant operators, distributors, and dispatchers | 43 | 42 | −3 | −1 | 10 | | |
| Power distributors and dispatchers | 18 | 15 | −14 | −2 | 4 | 1 | Long-term O-J-T |
| Power generating and reactor plant operators | 26 | 26 | 4 | 1 | 6 | 1 | Long-term O-J-T |
| Gas and petroleum plant and system occupations | 31 | 28 | −10 | −3 | 7 | 1 | Long-term O-J-T |

**Table C-1. Employment by occupation, 1994 and projected 2005, moderate alternative—Continued**
(Employment and job openings numbers in thousands)

| Occupation | Employment | | Employment change, 1994-2005 | | Total openings due to growth and net replacements, 1994-2005[1] | Earnings quartile[2] | Most significant source of training |
|---|---|---|---|---|---|---|---|
| | 1994 | Projected, 2005 | Percent | Number | | | |
| Stationary engineers ............................ | 30 | 27 | −10 | −3 | 7 | 1 | Long-term O-J-T |
| Water and liquid waste treatment plant and system operators ............................. | 95 | 104 | 9 | 9 | 30 | 1 | Long-term O-J-T |
| All other plant and system operators .............. | 93 | 97 | 5 | 4 | 25 | 1 | Long-term O-J-T |
| **Operators, fabricators, and laborers** .................. | 17,142 | 17,898 | 4 | 757 | 5,626 | | |
| Machine setters, set-up operators, operators, and tenders ......................... | 4,779 | 4,505 | −6 | −274 | 1,353 | | |
| Numerical control machine tool operators and tenders, metal and plastic ............................. | 75 | 94 | 26 | 20 | 34 | 3 | Moderate-term O-J-T |
| Combination machine tool setters, set-up operators, operators, and tenders ................. | 106 | 123 | 16 | 17 | 38 | 2 | Moderate-term O-J-T |
| Machine tool cut and form setters, operators, and tenders, metal and plastic ...................... | 709 | 593 | −16 | −116 | 175 | | |
| Drilling and boring machine tool setters and set-up operators, metal and plastic ............. | 45 | 30 | −35 | −16 | 9 | 3 | Moderate-term O-J-T |
| Grinding machine setters and set-up operators, metal and plastic .................. | 64 | 52 | −18 | −12 | 13 | 3 | Moderate-term O-J-T |
| Lathe and turning machine tool setters and set-up operators, metal and plastic ............. | 71 | 50 | −31 | −22 | 14 | 3 | Moderate-term O-J-T |
| Machine forming operators and tenders, metal and plastic ...................................... | 171 | 151 | −11 | −19 | 58 | 3 | Moderate-term O-J-T |
| Machine tool cutting operators and tenders, metal and plastic ...................................... | 119 | 85 | −29 | −34 | 23 | 3 | Moderate-term O-J-T |
| Punching machine setters and set-up operators, metal and plastic ...................... | 48 | 37 | −21 | −10 | 12 | 3 | Moderate-term O-J-T |
| All other machine tool cutting and forming etc. ...................................... | 191 | 188 | −1 | −2 | 46 | 3 | Moderate-term O-J-T |
| Metal fabricating machine setters, operators, and related workers ...................... | 157 | 138 | −12 | −19 | 39 | | |
| Metal fabricators, structural metal products .. | 44 | 43 | −3 | −1 | 9 | 3 | Moderate-term O-J-T |
| Soldering and brazing machine operators and tenders ...................................... | 10 | 8 | −17 | −2 | 3 | 3 | Moderate-term O-J-T |
| Welding machine-setters, operators, and tenders ...................................... | 103 | 87 | −16 | −16 | 28 | 2 | Moderate-term O-J-T |
| Metal and plastic processing machine setters, operators, and related workers ...................... | 425 | 444 | 4 | 19 | 152 | | |
| Electrolytic plating machine operators and tenders, setters and set-up operators, metal and plastic ...................................... | 42 | 45 | 6 | 2 | 14 | 3 | Moderate-term O-J-T |
| Foundry mold assembly and shakeout workers ...................................... | 10 | 8 | −23 | −2 | 4 | 3 | Moderate-term O-J-T |
| Furnace operators and tenders .................... | 20 | 19 | −8 | −2 | 4 | 2 | Moderate-term O-J-T |
| Heat treating machine operators and tenders, metal and plastic ...................... | 20 | 17 | −12 | −2 | 5 | 3 | Moderate-term O-J-T |
| Metal molding machine operators and tenders setters and set-up operators .......... | 40 | 40 | 0 | 0 | 14 | 3 | Moderate-term O-J-T |
| Plastic molding machine operators and tenders, setters and set-up operators ......... | 165 | 177 | 7 | 12 | 68 | 3 | Moderate-term O-J-T |
| All other metal and plastic machine setters, operators, and related workers .................. | 127 | 137 | 8 | 10 | 44 | 3 | Moderate-term O-J-T |
| Printing, binding, and related workers .................. | 384 | 387 | 1 | 3 | 108 | | |
| Bindery machine operators and set-up operators ...................................... | 72 | 77 | 7 | 5 | 18 | 2 | Moderate-term O-J-T |
| Prepress printing workers, production .......... | 25 | 9 | −64 | −16 | 5 | | |
| Photoengraving and lithographic machine operators and tenders ........................... | 5 | 3 | −32 | −2 | 1 | 2 | Moderate-term O-J-T |
| Typesetting and composing machine operators and tenders ........................... | 20 | 6 | −71 | −14 | 4 | 2 | Moderate-term O-J-T |
| Printing press operators ............................ | 218 | 223 | 2 | 5 | 62 | | |
| Letterpress operators ............................ | 14 | 4 | −71 | −10 | 3 | 2 | Moderate-term O-J-T |
| Offset lithographic press operators .......... | 79 | 84 | 7 | 5 | 22 | 2 | Moderate-term O-J-T |
| Printing press machine setters, operators and tenders ...................................... | 113 | 119 | 6 | 6 | 31 | 2 | Moderate-term O-J-T |
| All other printing press setters and set-up operators ...................................... | 13 | 16 | 24 | 3 | 6 | 2 | Moderate-term O-J-T |
| Screen printing machine setters and set-up operators ...................................... | 26 | 30 | 16 | 4 | 10 | 2 | Moderate-term O-J-T |

**Table C-1. Employment by occupation, 1994 and projected 2005, moderate alternative—Continued**
(Employment and job openings numbers in thousands)

| Occupation | Employment | | Employment change, 1994-2005 | | Total openings due to growth and net replacements, 1994-2005[1] | Earnings quartile[2] | Most significant source of training |
|---|---|---|---|---|---|---|---|
| | 1994 | Projected, 2005 | Percent | Number | | | |
| All other printing, binding, and related workers ..................... | 43 | 48 | 10 | 5 | 13 | 2 | Moderate-term O-J-T |
| Textile and related setters, operators, and related workers ...................... | 1,018 | 829 | −19 | −188 | 222 | | |
| Extruding and forming machine operators and tenders, synthetic or glass fibers ......... | 22 | 28 | 28 | 6 | 11 | 4 | Moderate-term O-J-T |
| Pressing machine operators and tenders, textile, garment, and related materials ....... | 77 | 76 | −1 | −1 | 19 | 4 | Moderate-term O-J-T |
| Sewing machine operators, garment ........... | 531 | 391 | −26 | −140 | 106 | 4 | Moderate-term O-J-T |
| Sewing machine operators, non-garment ..... | 129 | 117 | −9 | −12 | 26 | 4 | Moderate-term O-J-T |
| Textile bleaching and dyeing machine operators and tenders ......................... | 30 | 37 | 24 | 7 | 14 | 4 | Moderate-term O-J-T |
| Textile draw-out and winding machine operators and tenders ......................... | 190 | 143 | −25 | −47 | 38 | 4 | Moderate-term O-J-T |
| Textile machine sellers and set-up operators ...................................... | 39 | 36 | −6 | −2 | 8 | 4 | Moderate-term O-J-T |
| Woodworking machine setters, operators, and other related workers ..................... | 126 | 97 | −23 | −29 | 32 | | |
| Head sawyers and sawing machine operators and tenders, sellers and set-up operators ...................................... | 62 | 47 | −24 | −15 | 16 | 4 | Moderate-term O-J-T |
| Woodworking machine operators and tenders, setters and set-up operators ......................... | 64 | so | −22 | −14 | 16 | 4 | Moderate-term O-J-T |
| Other machine setters, set-up operators, operators and tenders ...................... | 1,779 | 1,799 | 1 | 20 | 554 | | |
| Boiler operators and tenders, low pressure ...... | 18 | 12 | −32 | −6 | 4 | 1 | Moderate-term O-J-T |
| Cement and gluing machine operators and tenders ..................................... | 36 | 25 | −30 | −11 | 9 | 3 | Moderate-term O-J-T |
| Chemical equipment controllers, operators and tenders ..................................... | 75 | 67 | −11 | −8 | 28 | 1 | Moderate-term O-J-T |
| Cooking and roasting machine operators and tenders, food and tobacco ................... | 28 | 30 | 8 | 2 | 9 | 3 | Moderate-term O-J-T |
| Crushing and mixing machine operators and tenders ..................................... | 137 | 136 | −1 | −1 | 36 | 3 | Moderate-term O-J-T |
| Cutting and slicing machine sellers, operators and tenders ..................................... | 92 | 103 | 12 | 11 | 29 | 3 | Moderate-term O-J-T |
| Dairy processing equipment operators, including setters ............................. | 14 | 14 | −1 | 0 | 5 | 1 | Moderate-term O-J-T |
| Electronic semiconductor processors ............ | 33 | 34 | 4 | 1 | 10 | 3 | Moderate-term O-J-T |
| Extruding and forming machine sellers, operators and tenders ............................. | 102 | 95 | −8 | −8 | 27 | 3 | Moderate-term O-J-T |
| Furnace, kiln, or kettle operators and tenders .. | 28 | 24 | −13 | −4 | 5 | 2 | Moderate-term O-J-T |
| Laundry and drycleaning machine operators and tenders, except pressing ......................... | 175 | 198 | 13 | 23 | 68 | 4 | Moderate-term O-J-T |
| Motion picture projectionists ............................. | 8 | 4 | −47 | −4 | 2 | 3 | Short-term O-J-T |
| Packaging and filling machine operators and tenders ..................................... | 329 | 359 | 9 | 30 | 119 | 4 | Moderate-term O-J-T |
| Painting and coating machine operators .......... | 155 | 159 | 2 | 3 | 47 | | |
| Coating, painting, and spraying machine operators, tenders, setters, and set-up operators ...................................... | 111 | 110 | −1 | −1 | 31 | 3 | Moderate-term O-J-T |
| Painters, transportation equipment .............. | 45 | 49 | 9 | 4 | 16 | 3 | Moderate-term O-J-T |
| Paper goods machine setters and set-up operators ...................................... | 51 | 42 | −16 | −8 | 13 | 3 | Moderate-term O-J-T |
| Photographic processing machine operators and tenders ..................................... | 43 | 49 | 15 | 6 | 17 | 3 | Short-term O-J-T |
| Separating and still machine operators and tenders ..................................... | 20 | 19 | −6 | −1 | 8 | 1 | Moderate-term O-J-T |
| Shoe sewing machine operators and tenders .. | 14 | 5 | −64 | −9 | 2 | 4 | Moderate-term O-J-T |
| Tire building machine operators ....................... | 14 | 13 | −6 | −1 | 4 | 3 | Moderate-term O-J-T |
| All other machine operators, tenders, sellers, and set-up operators ..................................... | 407 | 409 | 1 | 2 | 111 | 3 | Moderate-term O-J-T |
| Hand workers, including assemblers and fabricators ..................................... | 2,605 | 2,665 | 2 | 60 | 784 | | |
| Cannery workers ......................................... | 73 | 82 | 12 | 9 | 29 | 4 | Short-term O-J-T |
| Coil winders, tapers, and finishers ................. | 21 | 15 | −26 | −5 | 5 | 3 | Short-term O-J-T |
| Cutters and trimmers, hand ........................... | 51 | 47 | −8 | −4 | 14 | 3 | Short-term O-J-T |

**Table C-1. Employment by occupation, 1994 and projected 2005, moderate alternative—Continued**
(Employment and job openings numbers in thousands)

| Occupation | Employment | | Employment change, 1994-2005 | | Total openings due to growth and net replacements, 1994-2005[1] | Earnings quartile[2] | Most significant source of training |
|---|---|---|---|---|---|---|---|
| | 1994 | Projected, 2005 | Percent | Number | | | |
| Electrical and electronic assemblers ............... | 212 | 182 | −14 | −30 | 52 | 3 | Short-term O-J-T |
| Grinders and polishers, hand ........................... | 74 | 70 | −6 | −4 | 21 | 3 | Short-term 0-J-T |
| Machine assemblers ........................................ | 51 | 55 | 8 | 4 | 17 | 3 | Short-term O-J-T |
| Meat, poultry, and fish cutters and trimmers, hand .............................................. | 132 | 168 | 28 | 36 | 74 | 3 | Short-term O-J-T |
| Painting, coating, and decorating workers, hand .............................................................. | 33 | 36 | 10 | 3 | 13 | 3 | Short-term O-J-T |
| Pressers, hand ................................................ | 16 | 15 | −4 | −1 | 5 | 3 | Short-term O-J-T |
| Sewers, hand .................................................. | 19 | 17 | −9 | −2 | 2 | 4 | Short-term O-J-T |
| Solderers and brazers .................................... | 27 | 31 | 17 | 5 | 12 | 3 | Short-term O-J-T |
| Welders and cutters ........................................ | 314 | 316 | 1 | 3 | 88 | 2 | Postsecondary vocational training |
| All other assemblers, fabricators, and hand workers ...................................................... | 1,583 | 1,630 | 3 | 46 | 453 | 3 | Short-term O-J-T |
| Transportation and material moving machine and vehicle operators ..................................... | 4,959 | 5,459 | 10 | 500 | 1,434 | | |
| Motor vehicle operators ..................................... | 3,620 | 4,045 | 12 | 425 | 1,066 | | |
| Bus drivers ..................................................... | 568 | 663 | 17 | 95 | 193 | | |
| Bus drivers, except school ......................... | 165 | 193 | 17 | 29 | 57 | 3 | Moderate-term O-J-T |
| Bus drivers, school ..................................... | 404 | 470 | 16 | 66 | 136 | 3 | Short-term O-J-T |
| Taxi drivers and chauffeurs ......................... | 129 | 157 | 22 | 28 | 43 | 3 | Short-term O-J-T |
| Truck drivers .................................................. | 2,897 | 3,196 | 10 | 299 | 823 | | |
| Driver/sales workers ................................... | 331 | 359 | 8 | 28 | 122 | 2 | Short-term O-J-T |
| Truck drivers light and heavy .................... | 2,565 | 2,837 | 11 | 271 | 701 | 2 | Short-term O-J-T |
| All other motor vehicle operators .................... | 26 | 29 | 11 | 3 | 8 | 2 | Short-term O-J-T |
| Rail transportation workers ............................. | 86 | 75 | −12 | −10 | 15 | | |
| Locomotive engineers ................................... | 22 | 19 | −14 | −3 | 3 | 1 | Work experience |
| Railroad brake, signal, and switch operators ... | 19 | 13 | −31 | −6 | 3 | 1 | Work experience |
| Railroad conductors and yardmasters ............. | 26 | 25 | −6 | −2 | 4 | 1 | Work experience |
| Rail yard engineers, dinkey operators, and hostlers ......................................................... | 6 | 4 | −40 | −2 | 1 | 1 | Work experience |
| Subway and streetcar operators ..................... | 12 | is | 23 | 3 | 5 | 1 | Moderate-term O-J-T |
| Water transportation and related workers ........... | 48 | 48 | 0 | 0 | 10 | | |
| Able seamen, ordinary seamen, and marine oilers .................................................. | 20 | 20 | −3 | −1 | 4 | 1 | Short-term O-J-T |
| Captains and pilots, ship ............................... | 13 | 13 | 0 | 0 | 3 | 1 | Work experience |
| Mates, ship, boat, and barge ......................... | 7 | 8 | 6 | 0 | 2 | 1 | Work experience |
| Ship engineers .............................................. | 8 | 8 | 3 | 0 | 2 | 1 | Work experience |
| Material moving equipment operators ............... | 1,061 | 1,129 | 6 | 69 | 298 | | |
| Crane and tower operators ............................. | 45 | 42 | −6 | −3 | 11 | 2 | Moderate-term O-J-T |
| Excavation and loading machine operators ..... | 88 | 100 | 13 | 11 | 31 | 2 | Moderate-term O-J-T |
| Grader, dozer, and scraper operators .............. | 108 | 113 | 5 | 6 | 27 | 2 | Moderate-term O-J-T |
| Hoist and winch operators ............................. | 9 | -9 | −5 | 0 | 2 | 2 | Short-term O-J-T |
| Industrial truck and tractor operators .............. | 464 | 493 | 6 | 29 | 132 | 2 | Moderate-term O-J-T |
| Operating engineers ....................................... | 146 | 154 | 5 | 7 | 37 | 2 | Moderate-term O-J-T |
| All other material moving equipment operators ........................................................ | 201 | 219 | 9 | 18 | 59 | 2 | Moderate-term O-J-T |
| All other transportation and material moving equipment operators ..................................... | 145 | 1-61 | 11 | 16 | 44 | 2 | Moderate-term O-J-T |
| Helpers, laborers, and material movers, hand ........ | 4,799 | 5,270 | 10 | 471 | 2,056 | | |
| Freight, stock, and material movers, hand .......... | 765 | 728 | −5 | −36 | 306 | 4 | Short-term O-J-T |
| Hand packers and packagers ............................. | 942 | 1,102 | 17 | 160 | 429 | 4 | Short-term O-J-T |
| Helpers, construction trades ............................. | 513 | 581 | 13 | 68 | 240 | 4 | Short-term O-J-T |
| Machine feeders and offbearers ........................ | 262 | 242 | −8 | −20 | 80 | 3 | Short-term O-J-T |
| Parking lot attendants ...................................... | 64 | 76 | 20 | 13 | 25 | 2 | Short-term O-J-T |
| Refuse collectors ............................................. | 111 | 115 | 4 | 4 | 31 | 3 | Short-term O-J-T |
| Service station attendants ................................. | 167 | 148 | −12 | −20 | 67 | 4 | Short-term O-J-T |
| Vehicle washers and equipment cleaners .......... | 249 | 299 | 20 | 50 | 133 | 4 | Short-term O-J-T |
| All other helpers, laborers, and material movers, hand ................................................. | 1,727 | 1,980 | 15 | 253 | 744 | 4 | Short-term O-J-T |

[1]Total job openings represent the sum of employment increases and net replacements. If employment change is negative, job openings due to growth are zero and total job openings equal net replacements.

[2]Codes for describing earnings quartiles are: 1 = Highest quartile; 2 = Second quartile; 3 = Third quartile; 4 = Lowest quartile.

**Table C-2. Factors affecting the utilization of occupations within industries**

| Occupation | Factor |
|---|---|
| Accountants and auditors | Small decreases in accounting services result from increasing use of clerk-operated computers to generate routine reports. |
| Actuaries | Small decreases are expected due to continuing insurance industry downsizing, mergers, and acquisition activity. |
| Adjustment clerks | Increasing emphasis on customer service to resolve customer billing problems will cause a moderate to significant increase in utilization. |
| Administrative services managers | Moderate decreases are expected across all industries as the automating of administrative support duties lessens the need for administrative services managers. Moderate increases in engineering and management firms will occur as they increasingly supply administrative services managers to other firms on a contractual basis. |
| Advertising clerks | Small increases are projected due to the growing popularity of classified advertising. Computer driven productivity enhancements in the newspaper industry is expected to cause a small decrease in utilization. |
| Agricultural and food scientists | Moderate increases are expected in crops, livestock, and livestock products; drugs; and research and testing services to maintain crop and livestock productivity growth. |
| Air traffic controllers | Air traffic control technology is improving to allow control of more aircraft in a given area, causing a small reduction in personnel requirements. |
| Aircraft assemblers, precision | Very significant decreases are expected in guided missiles, space vehicles, and parts industries resulting from declining defense expenditures. |
| Aircraft pilots and flight engineers | Larger capacity planes and the use of two-person instead of three-person crews will lead to small decreases in utilization. |
| Amusement and recreation attendants | Expanding amusement, recreation, and health facilities will spur moderate to significant increases in utilization. |
| Animal caretakers, except farm | Growing animal populations will cause a moderate increase in utilization of this occupation. |
| Artists and commercial artists | Small increases across industries as firms place increasing importance on visual appeal of products. |
| Automotive body and related repairers | New materials in use for car passenger safety damage easily and are usually replaced, resulting in less non-accident body work, and causing small decreases in utilization. |
| Automotive mechanics | Gasoline service stations will show small declines in utilization as repair services are slowly phased out of some operations. |
| Bakers, bread and pastry | Increasing consumer demand for low cost fresh baked goods will cause small increases in bakeries and restaurants and moderate to significant increases elsewhere. |
| Bakers, manufacturing | The growing popularity of baked goods and heat-and-serve pastry products will spur small increases in utilization. |
| Bank tellers | Increasing ATM use and bank consolidation will significantly reduce the need for tellers. |
| Bartenders | Changing societal attitudes and stricter laws dealing with drunk drivers are causing moderate decreases in this occupation. |
| Bill and account collectors | Expanding use of consumer credit will lead to moderate increases in utilization. |
| Billing, cost, and rate clerks | Computer software will greatly improve the productivity of these workers, causing significant declines in utilization. |
| Billing, posting, and calculating machine operators | The outdated machines these workers use likely will continue to be only by small businesses, resulting in significant declines in utilization across all industries. |
| Bindery machine operators and set-up operators | Utilization of these workers in commercial printing businesses and newspapers will moderately decrease as a result of more productive binding machinery. |
| Biological scientists | Moderate increases in the federal government and drug manufacturing reflect steady support of health-related research and increasing use of biotechnological techniques by pharmaceutical firms. |

**Table C-2. Factors affecting the utilization of occupations within industries**

| Occupation | Factor |
|---|---|
| Blue-collar worker supervisors | Restructuring of supervisory positions and using self-managing teams of workers in production settings will cause small declines in utilization. |
| Boiler operators and tenders, low pressure | Automatic boiler systems are expected to cause significant reductions in the utilization of boiler operators in all industries. |
| Boilermakers | Automated welding and prefabricated boilers will cause moderate declines overall, but fabricated structural metal products and miscellaneous repair shops are increasingly being contracted for boilermaking services and their utilization will significantly increase. |
| Bookbinders | New technology that performs finishing operations will moderately decrease demand for this occupation. |
| Bookkeeping, accounting, and auditing clerks | Automated accounting systems, which perform all functions except the initial entries, will moderately reduce utilization. |
| Broadcast technicians | Increased productivity of broadcasting technology will cause moderate declines in radio and TV broadcasting and in film production. |
| Brokerage clerks | The computerization of brokerage house clerical duties will cause moderate declines, with significant declines expected in security and commodity exchanges. As they increasingly offer brokerage services, utilization in banking and closely related functions will increase slightly. |
| Bus and truck mechanics and diesel engine specialists | Trucking companies will show small increases in utilization as increasing competition increases the importance of keeping trucks operational and generating revenue. |
| Bus drivers, except school | As more people commute using public transportation, there will be small increases in local and suburban transportation. |
| Bus drivers, school | Slow increases in the school-age population and contracting out of student transportation will cause small decreases in the utilization of school bus drivers. |
| Butchers and meat cutters | These workers are being replaced by lower earning hand cutters, causing small to moderate decreases in utilization. |
| Camera operators, television, motion picture, and video | Improved camera technology allows lower skilled workers to operate cameras; the effect of this will be a small decrease in utilization. |
| Camera operators | Direct conversion form electronic data to plate will moderately decrease demand for camera operators in all industries. |
| Captains and other officers, fishing vessels | Technological innovations will increase productivity of fishing vessels causing small declines in utilization. |
| Carpenters | More efficient tools are increasing productivity, causing moderate declines in utilization. |
| Carpet installers | Installation work is shifting to self-employed contractors, resulting in significantly decreased utilization. |
| Ceiling tile installers and acoustical carpenters | This work will increasingly be done by other construction workers as well as "do-it-yourselfers," causing moderate declines in utilization. |
| Cement and gluing machine operators and tenders | Increasing automation of gluing machines will result in significantly reduced utilization of these workers. |
| Central office and PBX installers and repairers | Digital electronic switching systems will replace PBXS, significantly reducing utilization of this occupation. |
| Central office operators | Voice recognition call waiting, call switching, and ISDN centrex services are leading to significant declines in utilization. |
| Chemical engineers | Small to moderate increases are expected as chemical firms develop more productive processes amid growing foreign competition. |
| Chemical equipment controllers, operators, and tenders | Increasing use of computers to control chemical reactions will cause small decreases in the utilization of these workers. |
| Chemical plant and system operators | The expanding uses of specialty chemicals will spur significant increases in utilization in miscellaneous chemical products industry. |

**Table C-2. Factors affecting the utilization of occupations within industries**

| Occupation | Factor |
|---|---|
| Child-care workers | The declining population of children under age 5 through 2005 will lead to small declines in utilization, except in child daycare services. |
| Civil engineers, including traffic engineers | Increasing investment in the infrastructure is expected to cause moderate increases in utilization by construction firms. |
| Claims examiners, property and casualty insurance | Small increases are expected in fire, marine, and casualty insurance firms and a moderate increase in insurance agents, brokers, and in service firms as increasing competition focuses on the speed of claims processing. |
| Clinical laboratory technologists and technicians | Contracting out of lab services to medical and dental laboratories will moderately decrease utilization in hospitals and physicians' offices. |
| Coil winders, tapers, and finishers | As coils are replaced by electronic components, the utilization of this occupation will moderately decrease. |
| Coin and vending machine servicers and repairers | Improved technology will reduce breakdowns, decrease service needs, and cause a moderate decrease in utilization. |
| College and university faculty | Shrinking university budgets will lead to cost cutting, increasing reliance on part-time faculty, increasing class sizes, and small decreases in utilization for this occupation. |
| Combination machine tool setters, set-up operators, and tenders | The utilization of workers with skills on a number of machines will increase slightly as cellular manufacturing advances. |
| Communication, transportation, and utilities operations managers | Rapidly advancing communications technology, increasing competition in communications and utilities, and consolidation of management responsibilities in transportation firms will cause moderate to significant decreases in utilization. |
| Compositors and typesetters, precision | Technological improvements are causing significant declines in the utilization of workers that arrange type by hand, replacing them with those that use electronic and word processing methods. |
| Computer engineers | The continuing demand for new applications and rapid advancements in technology will result in significant to very significant increases in utilization of computer engineers across all industries. |
| Computer operators, except peripheral equipment | Client-server environments and the automation of operator tasks are expected to cause significant decreases in utilization. |
| Computer programmers | Computer aided software engineering, wider programming skills of systems analysts, and the outsourcing of low-level programming will improve productivity and cause moderate declines in utilization. |
| Construction and building inspectors | Moderate decreases are expected in the utilization of inspectors in federal and state government agencies, as they contract out their inspection responsibilities to engineering and architectural firms, which in turn are expected to have significant increases. |
| Construction managers | Increasing complexity of construction projects and regulations related to the industry will lead to moderate to significant increases in this occupation's utilization by construction-related firms. |
| Cooks, institution or cafeteria | Contracting out cooking services will cause significant increases in utilization in eating and drinking places, and moderate declines elsewhere. |
| Cooks, restaurant | Growth of mid-priced, casual dining establishments will cause a small increase in utilization. |
| Cooks, short order and fast food | Significant increases in food stores are expected as consumers increasingly demand ready-to-eat foods. |
| Cooks, private household | Lower cost services and more easily prepared foods will significantly reduce utilization of these workers. |
| Corrections officers | Tougher sentencing provisions and an increasing prison population will cause increased construction of correctional facilities, which, in turn, will spur significant increases in state and local governments. |
| Correspondence clerks | Increasing office technology will cause moderate to significant reductions in utilization. |

**Table C-2. Factors affecting the utilization of occupations within industries**

| Occupation | Factor |
|---|---|
| Cost estimators | Small to moderate increases across most construction industries as firms increasingly use these specialists to aid in bidding for projects. |
| Counselors | Small increases in education and job training services will arise from increasing concern with preparing individuals with the skills necessary to pursue higher education or enter the workforce. |
| Counter and rental clerks | Increasing demand for rented items such as cars or movies will cause small to moderate increases in utilization. |
| Court clerks | Increased volume of court cases at the local level is fueling small increases in utilization. |
| Crane and tower operators | Increased use of robotic cranes will moderately reduce the need for operators in all industries. |
| Credit analysts | Moderate decreases expected across all industries as credit reporting services become increasingly concentrated in commercial banks, mortgage bankers and brokers, and credit reporting and collection. |
| Credit authorizers | Automated credit card authorization data centers will cause significant reductions in utilization as businesses increase their use of credit card scanners. |
| Credit checkers | Specialized firms with access to huge databases will be increasingly contracted to check credit histories, causing significant decreases in utilization. |
| Crossing guards | Police will increasingly assume the role of crossing guards, moderately reducing utilization in local government. |
| Curators, archivists, museum technicians, and restorers | Tightening budgets and reliance on increasingly scarce funding should cause small decreases in government-run and funded institutions. |
| Custom tailors and sewers | Decreasing demand for tailoring services will significantly decrease utilization in key industries. |
| Customer service representatives, utilities | The growing number of services offered by telephone utilities will cause a moderate increase in utilization. |
| Dancers and choreographers | Small to moderate increases in related industries are expected as dance grows in popularity as a form of artistic expression. |
| Data entry keyers, except composing | Scanners and bar code readers are automating the data entry process, resulting in significant declines in utilization. |
| Data entry keyers, composing | Desktop publishing will significantly reduce utilization. |
| Data processing equipment repairers | Falling prices will rapidly expand equipment sales, spurring significant increases in repairers employed by retail stores. |
| Dental assistants | Dentists will use small increases in utilization of assistants to help meet increased demand. |
| Dental hygienists | Utilization of this occupation will increase slightly to meet the demand for dental services. |
| Dental laboratory technicians, precision | Healthier consumers and improved dental lab technology will significantly reduce demand for these workers. |
| Dentists | There will be a moderate decrease in dental offices as increasing demand is met through the employment of more hygienists and dental assistants. |
| Designers, except interior designers | Increased emphasis on product quality, safety, design of new high technology products, and growing demand for floral and fashion designers will result in small increases in utilization across industries. |
| Detectives, except public | Department stores and miscellaneous business services are projected to show small increases in their employment of these workers to deter crime, cut losses, and protect customers. Hotels are projected to show significant increases. |
| Dietitians and nutritionists | There will be small decreases in the utilization of these workers in hospitals and personal care facilities as providers are increasingly contracting out dietetic and nutritional services or employing more nonregistered personnel to perform these services. |

**Table C-2. Factors affecting the utilization of occupations within industries**

| Occupation | Factor |
|---|---|
| Dining room and cafeteria attendants and bar helpers | Hotels are minimizing eating facilities, and mid-priced casual dining is replacing cafeterias, causing moderate decreases. |
| Directory assistance operators | Voice recognition, call waiting, call switching, and ISDN centrex services are leading to significant declines in utilization. |
| Drafters | Increasing use of computer assisted design (CAD) by architects and engineers will cause small decreases in the utilization of drafters. |
| Drilling and boring machine tool setters and set-up operators, metal and plastic | Computer controlled machine tools reduce the need for set-up operators and will spur moderate decreases in utilization. |
| Driver/sales workers | Increasing demand for a wider variety of fresher foods will cause small increases in utilization in grocery stores and eating and drinking places. Centralized ordering will cause small decreases in utilization in other industries. |
| Drywall installers and finishers | Very significant declines in the utilization of these workers are expected in most industries as work is increasingly contracted to masonry, stonework, and plastering businesses. |
| Duplicating, mail, and other office machine operators | Computer technology will reduce demand significantly. |
| Economists | There will be significant increases in the utilization of economists and marketing research analysts in research firms due to increased needs for statistical quality control. |
| Education administrators | Cost management by school districts will cause small decreases in utilization, with other school occupations growing faster in response to increases in the school-age population. |
| EEG technologists | There will be small increases in this occupation's utilization in hospitals as technology improves and medical procedures involving the brain become more common. |
| EKG technicians | Significant decreases in utilization are expected as other health technicians are increasingly performing this skill. |
| Electric meter installers and repairers | Increased reliability of electric meters will moderately reduce demand for installers and repairers. |
| Electrical and electronic assemblers | Jobs for this assembly occupation are being shipped overseas or automated, resulting in small declines in utilization. |
| Electrical and electronic technicians and technologists | Computers can simulate components and systems more easily and less expensively than technicians can build the components and systems for testing purposes. This will cause small declines in the utilization of this occupation. |
| Electrical and electronics engineers | Because electronics-intensive manufacturing firms are reinvesting large portions of their revenues on research and development and latest technology production equipment, these workers will have moderate increases in utilization. |
| Electromedical and biomedical equipment repairers | Increasing complexity, cost of equipment, and necessity of proper repairs will spur a moderate increase in demand for repairers. |
| Electronic home entertainment equipment repairers | Microelectronic circuitry has reduced maintenance and repair requirements, and will significantly reduce utilization. |
| Electronic pagination systems workers | Technological improvements are replacing paste-up artists with electronic pagination workers, leading to significant increases in utilization. |
| Electronic semiconductor processors | As chips get more complicated, manufacturing techniques become more automated resulting in small reductions in utilization. |
| Emergency medical technicians | A growing urban and elderly population will increasingly demand the services of these workers, causing small to moderate increases of utilization in key industries. |
| Employment interviewers, private or public employment service | Decreasing federal support of state employment services and increasing use of computer systems in job service offices will cause moderate decreases in state governments. |
| Engineering, mathematical, and natural science managers | Moderate increases across all industries are linked to growth of engineering, science, mathematical, and especially computer-related occupations. |
| Excavation and loading machine operators | Increasing construction of water and sewer services and the growth of surface mining will moderately increase the need for these workers. |

**Table C-2. Factors affecting the utilization of occupations within industries**

| Occupation | Factor |
|---|---|
| Extruding and forming machine operators and tenders, synthetic or glass fibers | Increasing demand for synthetic fibers will cause very significant increases in utilization for this occupation. |
| Fallers and buckers | Increasing use of heavy equipment to fell and delimb trees will cause small decreases for these workers. |
| Farm equipment mechanics | As farming equipment becomes more advanced, repairs become critical but less frequent, and are increasingly performed at the dealership, causing a small increase. |
| Farm workers | Improving productivity of agricultural machinery will cause small declines in the utilization of farm workers. |
| File clerks | Very significant declines in utilization are expected as computer file storage systems grow in use. |
| Fire fighters | Increasing concern for public safety will spur small increases in local governments. |
| Fishers, hunters, and trappers | Technological innovations will increase productivity and cause small decreases in utilization. |
| Filters, structural metal, precision | More structural metal products are being produced that are easier to assemble and will require significantly lower utilization of fitters. |
| Flight attendants | Growth in airline seating capacity, with a ratio of 1 attendant per 50 seats mandated by federal regulations, will cause small increases in utilization. |
| Food counter, fountain, and related workers | Mid-priced, casual dining is replacing cafeterias and diners, causing a moderate decline in eating and drinking places. |
| Food preparation workers | Increasing consumer demand for ready-to-eat foods is driving moderate increases in food stores and eating and drinking places. |
| Food service and lodging managers | A significant decrease in utilization is expected in hotels and other lodging places, which are increasingly contracting out or eliminating food services. |
| Foresters and conservation scientists | Small to moderate increases in utilization across all levels of government reflect more emphasis on wildlife and land management of national forests. |
| Freight, stock, and material movers, hand | Material moving equipment is moderately reducing the need for hand movers. |
| Funeral directors and morticians | Small decreases in utilization are expected as the percentage of cremations increases. |
| Gardeners and groundskeepers, except farm | Landscaping services companies will have significant increases in utilization as other industries reduce utilization by contracting out for these services. |
| General office clerks | Some industries are increasing the utilization of clerks with general skills, but most are moderately reducing it as clerical duties become computerized. |
| Geologists, geophysicists, and oceanographers | Environment-related concerns will moderately increase utilization, while firms engaged in oil and gas extraction are expected to moderately decrease utilization in response to reductions in domestic oil and gas extraction. |
| Glaziers | Glazing work will be done increasingly by contractors, moderately reducing utilization in paint, glass, and wallpaper stores. |
| Grader, dozer, and scraper operators | Emphasis on road repair and widening rather than new road construction will moderately reduce utilization in highway and street construction. |
| Grinding machine sellers and set-up operators, metal and plastic | Computer controlled machine tools reduce the need for set-up operators and will spur moderate decreases in utilization. |
| Guards | Guard services will increasingly be contracted out to security service firms, resulting in small declines across industries. |
| Hairdressers, hair stylists, and cosmetologists | Department stores are expected to significantly increase hairdressing and cosmetology services. |
| Hand packers and packagers | Although sometimes difficult to automate, improved packaging methods will cause small reductions in the utilization of these workers. |

**Table C-2. Factors affecting the utilization of occupations within industries**

| Occupation | Factor |
|---|---|
| Hard tile setters | Greater use of tile substitutes, plastic or fiberglass bathtub and shower enclosures, and the "do-it-yourself" trend will cause small declines for these workers. |
| Head sawyers and sawing machine operators and tenders, setters, and set-up operators | Sawing machine operators will continue to be replaced by automated machinery, resulting in moderate to significant decreases in utilization. |
| Heat, air conditioning, and refrigeration mechanics and installers | New construction and increasing retrofit work driven by energy consciousness will lead to a moderate increase in plumbing, heating, and air-conditioning businesses. |
| Highway maintenance workers | Increased maintenance as a percentage of road work will cause a moderate increase in highway and street construction. |
| Home appliance and power tool repairers | Longer lasting parts, micro-electronics, and the trend to replace rather than repair items will cause moderate declines in utilization. |
| Home health aides | Hospitals and residential care establishments will continue to rapidly open and expand home health care departments, spurring significant increases in utilization. |
| Hosts and hostesses, restaurant, lounge, or coffee shop | Newer hotels increasingly do not have dining establishments as part of operations, leading to moderate declines. |
| Housekeepers and butlers | Increasing use of firms to supply household services will moderately reduce demand for this occupation. |
| Human services workers | Small to moderate increases across government and private social services as cost-conscious organizations replace professionals with these workers. |
| Industrial engineers, except safety engineers | Small to moderate increases across all industries as firms use industrial engineers to streamline production, increase productivity, and minimize costs. Significant increases will occur in manufacturing firms producing expensive per-unit items, such as planes and automobiles. |
| Industrial machinery mechanics | As American factories become more capital intensive, the utilization of these workers will increase in varying degrees to perform needed repairs and maintenance. |
| Inspectors, testers, and graders, precision | Automated inspection machines and increased production worker attention to quality and inspection will moderately reduce utilization in manufacturing firms producing highly complicated products such as cars and electrical components. |
| Inspectors and compliance officers, except construction | Increased activity in law enforcement and regulatory actions at each level of government will cause small increases in utilization. |
| Instructors, adult (nonvocational) education | Expanding adult education programs and community college course offerings should cause small increases in utilization. |
| Instructors and coaches, sports and physical training | Moderate increases in recreation services and small increases in education reflect increased public interest in physical fitness for adults and children. |
| Insulation workers | Moderate increases in the utilization of specialty trade contractors will arise from increasing industrial pipe and boiler insulation to reduce costs. |
| Insurance adjusters, examiners, and investigators | Insurance company efforts to reduce claim fraud and control costs will cause small increases in utilization. |
| Insurance policy processing clerks | Insurance applications are being directly input into computer systems during the interview process, causing small to moderate decreases in utilization. |
| Insurance sales workers | Computer network-based software will allow agents to handle more clients and serve more insurance companies; this will result in a small increase in utilization in insurance agents, brokers, and service firms while utilization in insurance carriers decreases. |
| Janitors and cleaners, including maids and housekeeping cleaners | Janitorial services are being increasingly contracted out to temporary help and cleaning services firms, causing moderate declines in utilization in nonservice industries. |
| Jewelers and silversmiths | There will be small decreases in utilization as workers in this occupation are being replaced by sales clerks in stores. |
| Job printers | Technological improvements in word processing are causing significant decreases by increasing productivity of typesetters and those who make corrections in proofs. |

**Table C-2. Factors affecting the utilization of occupations within industries**

| Occupation | Factor |
|---|---|
| Lathe and turning machine tool setters and set-up operators, metal and plastic | Computer controlled machine tools reduce the need for set-up operators and will spur moderate decreases in utilization. |
| Legal secretaries | Legal secretaries will experience moderate declines in utilization due to growing office automation. |
| Letterpress operators | Demand for letterpress operators will decline significantly as many shops switch to newer, faster printers. |
| Librarians, professional | Small decreases in employment in education and local government are projected as library services are automated and as libraries hire library technicians to contain costs. |
| Library assistants and bookmobile drivers | Library technicians will pick up many of the key duties of these personnel as automation progresses, resulting in small decreases in utilization. |
| Licensed practical nurses | As the length of the average hospital stay decreases, quality of care becomes critical, resulting in small decreases in the utilization of these workers as hospitals and residential care facilities switch to registered nurses (RNs) and other higher-level health professionals to provide primary patient care. |
| Loan and credit clerks | Despite automation, this occupation will experience only moderate declines in utilization because of the need for personal contact in the loan process. |
| Loan officers and counselors | Moderate increases are expected in banking institutions as the industry consolidates. Small increases are expected as the growth of nonbank lenders continues. |
| Logging tractor operators | These versatile workers can perform more tasks than less skilled logging industry employees, and will experience small increases in utilization. |
| Machine assemblers | In large electronics and automobile parts manufacturing firms, automating assembly lines will moderately reduce demand for these workers. |
| Machine feeders and offbearers | Computer controlled loading and unloading machinery will cause small reductions in utilization. |
| Machine forming operators and tenders, metal and plastic | Computer controlled machine tools reduce the need for set-up operators and will spur moderate decreases in utilization. |
| Machine tool cuffing operators and tenders, metal and plastic | Computer controlled machine tools reduce the need for set-up operators and will spur moderate decreases in utilization. |
| Mail clerks, except mail machine operators and postal service | Facsimile transmissions, electronic mail, and automated mail processing will moderately reduce utilization across industries. |
| Management analysts | Expected significant increases in the use of management analysts and consultants, across all but management consulting businesses, will help firms downsize, expand, merge, compete, form alliances, and/or cope with technological change, and will create increased demand for these workers. |
| Manicurists | Increased demand for manicuring services will significantly increase utilization in beauty shops. |
| Marketing, advertising, and public relations managers | Small increases in utilization by firms in all industries will result from increasing importance of well-organized customer relations. |
| Mathematicians and all other mathematical scientists | Cutbacks in basic research expenditures will cause small decreases in utilization. |
| Meat, poultry, and fish cutters and trimmers, hand | Relatively low wages, compared to skilled meat cutters, will cause small utilization increases in the meat products industry. |
| Mechanical engineers | Small to moderate increases in utilization are expected across all industries, with significant increases in motor vehicles, as firms concentrate on the quality of product design. |
| Medical assistants | The growth of group practices requires moderate increases of personnel who can perform both clinical and clerical duties. |
| Medical records technicians | Efforts to control health care costs will cause third-party payers to increasingly scrutinize medical records, causing significant increases in utilization for this occupation. |

**Table C-2. Factors affecting the utilization of occupations within industries**

| Occupation | Factor |
|---|---|
| Medical scientists | Moderate increases are expected in most related industries except hospitals, where there is a movement from teaching and research to for-profit hospitals, and a resulting decrease in utilization. |
| Medical secretaries | Each medical secretary will support an increasing number of professionals as automation ensues, leading to small utilization decreases. |
| Messengers | Private delivery companies will moderately increase utilization in response to demand as other industries moderately decrease it due to expanded use of facsimile transmissions and electronic mail. |
| Metallurgists and metallurgical, ceramic, and materials engineers | There will be small increases in primary metal industries, and moderate increases in stone, clay, and glass products, due to increased applications and demand for specialty materials. However, there will be moderate decreases in aircraft and parts as the percentage of defense-related aircraft manufactured falls. |
| Meter readers, utilities | Remote reading of meters will spread throughout utilities companies, improving productivity and significantly reducing utilization. |
| Millwrights | Machinery designed to last longer and be more dependable will cause moderate decreases in utilization of millwrights. |
| Mining, quarrying, and tunneling occupations | Larger, more productive equipment will cause a moderate decline in metal mining. |
| Motion picture projectionists | The growth of multi-screen theaters will cause significant decreases in utilization of projectionists. |
| Municipal clerks | Computers will increase productivity and reduce utilization in local government offices. |
| Nuclear engineers | Small decreases in utilization will arise from the virtual halt in nuclear plant construction. Moderate increases in research and testing services reflect the contracting of these service firms to develop applications for nuclear technology outside power production. |
| Nuclear medicine technologists | Technological improvements in nuclear diagnostic procedures and expanding use will cause a small increase in hospital utilization. |
| Numerical control machine tool operators and tenders, metal and plastic | The demand for more flexibility and precision in the manufacturing sector will lead to an increasing number of numerically controlled machine tools in American factories, causing moderate to significant increases in utilization. |
| Occupational therapists | Significant increases in utilization are expected as outpatient services expand in response to cost consciousness, an aging population, and advances in medical treatment that allow people to survive severe trauma. |
| Occupational therapy assistants and aides | The health care industry's continued increase in the level of outpatient rehabilitative services will cause significant increases in the utilization of these workers. |
| Operations research analysts | Availability of low-cost, high-powered computing ability will allow organizations to significantly increase utilization of these workers to solve operations management problems and optimize efficiency. |
| Optical goods workers, precision | Jobs will continue to shift to retail establishments with on-site lens crafting, causing a small increase in retail stores. |
| Opticians, dispensing and measuring | Moderate decreases in utilization by health services are offset by small increases in retail trade as employment shifts from offices of health practitioners to retail stores. |
| Order clerks, materials, merchandise, and service | Growing home catalog shopping will cause a significant increase in nonstore retailers. |
| Order fillers, wholesale and retail sales | Warehouse and billing automation should cause small declines in utilization. |
| Other law enforcement occupations | Public concern about crime will cause moderate increases in the utilization of these workers in state and local government. |
| Painters, transportation equipment | Increased use of plastics and automated painting machines will cause significant decreases in motor vehicle manufacturing and moderate declines in aircraft manufacturing. |
| Paper goods machine setters and set-up operators | New automated equipment is expected to moderately reduce the demand for these operators. |

**Table C-2. Factors affecting the utilization of occupations within industries**

| Occupation | Factor |
|---|---|
| Paralegals | Paralegals will experience moderate increases at law firms as the cost of hiring them is significantly below lawyers. |
| Paste-up workers | Electronic pagination is causing significant declines in the utilization of these workers. |
| Paving, surfacing, and tamping equipment operators | Increasing road maintenance will spur moderate increases in the highway and street construction and concrete work industries. |
| Payroll and timekeeping clerks | Computer software developed for payroll processing will cause moderate to significant declines in utilization. |
| Peripheral EDP equipment operators | Automated peripheral equipment will significantly decrease the utilization of these workers. |
| Personal and home care aides | Shift to less costly and more accessible care in the home, whenever possible, for the elderly, convalescent, and disabled will drive significant increases in social services. |
| Personnel, training, and labor relations specialists | Increased training needs to keep pace with technology will cause small to moderate increases in utilization across most industries, despite decreasing labor relations needs. |
| Personnel clerks, except payroll and timekeeping | Computer software will allow personnel specialists to store information during interviews and subsequent personnel actions, leading to significant decreases in utilization. |
| Pharmacists | There will be a small increase in utilization in hospitals as large health care networks will be more likely to own and operate their own pharmacies. |
| Pharmacy assistants | Large health care networks will be more likely to own and operate their own pharmacies, causing small increases in utilization. |
| Photoengravers | Increased use of direct digital printing does not require hand preparation of printers and should moderately decrease the need for photoengravers. |
| Photoengraving and lithographic machine operators and tenders | Increasing use of electronic and computer technology should significantly reduce the demand for these workers. |
| Photographers | Increased use of photography and visual images will cause a moderate increase in use of these workers by miscellaneous business services, which includes photofinishing and photography brokers. |
| Photographic process workers, precision | Increased use of computers to edit and manipulate photos will increase productivity and moderately reduce utilization. |
| Photographic processing machine operators and tenders | Improved processing technology and the growth of digital cameras will cause significant declines in this occupation in photo processing labs. |
| Physical and corrective therapy assistants and aides | Increasing use of physical therapists in group practices and for outpatient therapy will moderately to significantly increase demand. |
| Physical therapists | Expanded use of physical therapy services in hospitals and group medical practices will cause a significant increase in utilization. |
| Physician assistants | There will be a small increase in utilization in hospitals as health care organizations will increasingly rely on physician assistants because they provide care at a lower cost |
| Physicists and astronomers | Shrinking defense expenditures and movement from basic research to product development will cause a moderate decline overall and small declines in the federal government. |
| Platemakers | Technology in which data and images are moved directly from computers to the press will moderately reduce demand for these workers. |
| Plumbers, pipefitters, and steamfitters | The growing use of plastic pipe make plumbers more efficient, causing small decreases in utilization. Contracting out plumbing work will cause significant decreases in heavy construction and the federal government. |
| Police and detective supervisors | Public concern about crime will cause small increases in the utilization of this occupation. |
| Police detectives and investigators | Public concern about crime will cause small increases in employment in local governments and moderate to significant increases at the state and federal levels. |
| Police patrol officers | Public concern about crime will cause moderate increases in state and local government. |

**Table C-2. Factors affecting the utilization of occupations within industries**

| Occupation | Factor |
|---|---|
| Postal mail carriers | A growing population and an expanding volume of mail will require a small increase in utilization despite improved route-sequence sorting technology. |
| Postal service clerks | Expanding mail volume will require a small increase in utilization of clerks to process mail. |
| Power distributors and dispatchers | Legislation to increase competition in utilities will cause firms to automate the functions and moderately reduce utilization of distributors and dispatchers to reduce costs. |
| Power generating and reactor plant operators | Legislation to increase competition in utilities will cause a small reduction in utilization by electric services firms to reduce costs. |
| Printing press machine setters, operators, and tenders | New printing presses with more highly automated controls will cause small reductions in utilization for these workers. |
| Procurement clerks | Inventory control, EDI, and automated ordering should cause small decreases in all industries except hospitals and the federal government, where significant decreases are projected. |
| Producers, directors, actors, and entertainers | Rising domestic and foreign demand for film and television productions, as well as a growing movie rental market, will spur significant increases in the utilization of these workers by radio and television broadcasting and advertising industries. |
| Proofreaders and copy markers | Software that checks spelling and grammar will significantly reduce utilization in all industries. |
| Psychiatric technicians | A small decrease is expected in this occupation in hospitals due to decreasing state hospital employment. |
| Punching machine setters and set-up operators, metal and plastic | Punch-press machines are being replaced by automated equipment that requires less set-up time, handles a greater variety of materials, and operates significantly faster, resulting in moderate reductions in utilization. |
| Purchasing managers | Moderate decreases in utilization are expected in wholesale and retail trade as computer inventory and ordering systems grow in use. Significant increases are expected in manufacturing as firms operating JIT inventory systems rely on purchasing managers to keep proper amounts of raw materials available. |
| Radio mechanics | Increased reliability of radios will cause moderate to significant reductions in the utilization of radio mechanics. |
| Radiologic technologists and technicians | Technological advancements in diagnostic imaging will continue to make radiological procedures a viable way of diagnosing ailments and will cause a small increase in utilization by hospitals and a significant increase in medical and dental laboratories. |
| Rail yard engineers, dinkey operators, and hostlers | Switching, locomotive, and dinkey engine automation will cause moderate declines in this occupation. |
| Railroad brake, signal, and switch operators | Computer-controlled switches will cause small decreases in this occupation. |
| Receptionists and information clerks | Firms using advanced phone systems will show small to moderate utilization decreases; firms perceiving personal contact as important will not. |
| Recreational therapists | Expanding hospital outpatient rehabilitation services cause a moderate increase in utilization; a significant decrease due to contracting out for services is expected in nursing and personal care facilities. |
| Registered nurses | Moderate utilization increases are expected in home health care and nursing facilities as levels of patient care increase, but small decreases in doctor's offices as medical assistants increasingly take over clerical and light clinical duties. |
| Reservation and transportation ticket agents and travel clerks | Improved ticket reservation systems will increase productivity of ticket agents and significantly reduce utilization by air carriers. |
| Respiratory therapists | Growing numbers of cardiopulmonary cases will cause a moderate increase in utilization by hospitals. |
| Roofers | More efficient tools and materials will increase productivity of roofers, leading to small decreases in utilization. |

**Table C-2. Factors affecting the utilization of occupations within industries**

| Occupation | Factor |
|---|---|
| Roustabouts | Computerized equipment, more powerful tools and machinery, electronic testers, and hand-held computers are increasing productivity. This combined with diminished domestic drilling and closing of existing wells is causing significant to very significant declines in utilization. |
| Sales agents, real estate | The growing practice of using sales agents to show rental properties will cause a moderate increase in real estate operators and lessors, whereas the projected small decrease in utilization by real estate agents and managers is due to the increasing use of self-employed agents. |
| Science and mathematics technicians | Biotech firms moving into production phases and government-required air and water sampling should cause small increases in utilization in the pharmaceuticals and research and testing services industries. |
| Screen printing machine setters and set-up operators | The increasing popularity of apparel decorated with screen prints will spur moderate increases in utilization of this occupation. |
| Secretaries, except legal and medical | Traditional secretarial duties are being automated, leading to various levels of decline in all industries. |
| Securities and financial services sales workers | Global expansion of financial markets and growing involvement in these markets by banks will lead to small to moderate increases in utilization. |
| Service station attendants | Self-service and the decrease in auto repairs being done at gas stations will very significantly reduce utilization in this occupation at gasoline service stations. |
| Sewing machine operators, garment | Productivity increases and increasing overseas production will cause a small reduction in demand for these workers in the apparel industry. |
| Sheet metal workers and duct installers | Increasing use of robotics and substitute materials will significantly reduce demand for these workers in fabricated structural metal products, motor vehicles and equipment, and in the federal government. |
| Sheriffs and deputy sheriffs | Public concern about rising crime rates will cause moderate increases in utilization in local government. |
| Shipfitters | Defense cutbacks will moderately reduce utilization in the federal government. |
| Shoe and leather workers and repairers, precision | Inexpensive imports and the rising sales of athletic footwear have made consumers more likely to purchase new shoes than to repair old ones, resulting in small decreases in utilization. |
| Shoe sewing machine operators and tenders | Overseas production of shoes is significantly reducing demand for these workers. |
| Small engine specialists | Longer-lasting, more efficient small engines will reduce demand for repair services and cause small decreases in utilization. |
| Social workers | Efforts to coordinate hospital care and outpatient health services, and projected fast growth of public welfare and health services at the state and local government level, should cause small increases in this occupation's utilization in these industries. |
| Soldering and brazing machine operators and tenders | Continuing increases in the use of computer-controlled soldering and brazing equipment will cause small decreases in demand for these workers. |
| Speech-language pathologists and audiologists | Growing hospital outpatient services will lead to a very significant increase in utilization; expanded group practice services will cause a small increase. |
| Statement clerks | Computers will increasingly perform statement processing in financial institutions, causing very significant decreases in utilization. |
| Station installers and repairers, telephone | Very significant declines will occur as replacement heavily outweighs repair, and modular plugs allow consumers to install their own phones. |
| Stationary engineers | Computer-monitored and -controlled building systems are expected to continue to cause small reductions in the need for these workers. |
| Statistical clerks | Increased computing power and advanced statistical software will significantly reduce demand for these workers. |
| Stenographers | Increasing court case volume and demand for transcriptions of medical records will cause small to moderate increases in employment. |

**Table C-2. Factors affecting the utilization of occupations within industries**

| Occupation | Factor |
| --- | --- |
| Stock clerks | Automation such as prelabeling, hand-held scanners, inventory control systems, guided vehicles, and mechanized stackers will cause moderate declines in utilization across industries and small declines in retail trade. |
| Subway and streetcar operators | Growing mass transit systems will moderately increase the need for these workers. |
| Surgical technologists | Increasing numbers of outpatient surgical procedures and substitution for RNs and surgeons' assistants to control costs should cause a small increase in the utilization of these workers in hospitals and a very significant increase in physicians' offices. |
| Surveyors | Small decreases in this occupation will occur due to increasing use and falling cost of the Global Positioning System and the Geographic Information System. |
| Switchboard operators | Voice recognition, call waiting, call switching, and ISDN centrex services are leading to significant declines in utilization. |
| Systems analysts | Very significant increases in utilization across all industries will result as more emphasis is placed on network applications, and rapidly advancing technology continues to merge computers, telecommunications, and video. |
| Teacher aides and educational assistants | Increasing attention to the quality of education is leading schools to moderately increase utilization of support staff for teachers. |
| Teachers, preschool and kindergarten | Cost-cutting measures by social service organizations will cause small decreases in utilization. |
| Teachers, elementary | There will be a small decrease in utilization as the proportion of elementary school students decreases. |
| Teachers, secondary school | A small increase in utilization will result as the proportion of high school students increases. |
| Teachers, special education | Legislative mandates stipulating that special-needs students are entitled to public education will moderately increase utilization. |
| Technical assistants, library | Schools will contain costs by automating library tasks, enabling them to increase the utilization of library technical assistants in place of more highly paid librarians. |
| Telephone and cable TV line installers and repairers | Television cable lines are almost completely installed and fiber-optic cables have significantly lower maintenance requirements, causing moderate declines in utilization. Electrical contractors will benefit from the increasing contracting out of this work, and will significantly increase utilization of these workers. |
| Tire building machine operators | The highly automated tire industry will show moderate increases in this occupation in response to increased demand for tires. |
| Tire repairers and changers | Moderate declines in utilization are expected in gas service stations and auto repair shops due to a shift in business to discount tire retailers. |
| Title examiners and searchers | This work is being taken over by paralegals and legal assistants, resulting in moderately decreasing utilization. |
| Tool and die makers | CNC equipment and quick-die changing extrusion presses will cause moderate declines in utilization of this occupation. |
| Traffic, shipping, and receiving clerks | Automation and self-guided vehicles in distribution centers and warehouses will cause small decreases in utilization. |
| Truck drivers, light and heavy | The growth of chain stores and centralized ordering will cause moderate declines in utilization in wholesale and retail firms. |
| Typesetting and composing machine operators and tenders | The increasing use of electronic and computer technology should very significantly reduce the demand for these workers. |
| Typists and word processors | The increasing use of computers by professional and managerial staff for their own word processing is very significantly reducing utilization of this occupation. |
| Underwriters | Moderate increases are expected in life insurance businesses as the population grows older and demands more life insurance. However, there will be moderate decreases in the utilization of insurance agents, brokers, and in service firms stemming from growing competition and entrance into insurance markets by various financial institutions. |